GENRES REDISCOVERED:

STUDIES IN LATIN MINIATURE EPIC, LOVE ELEGY, AND EPIGRAM OF THE ROMANO-BARBARIC AGE

ANNA MARIA WASYL

GENRES REDISCOVERED:

STUDIES IN LATIN MINIATURE EPIC, LOVE ELEGY, AND EPIGRAM OF THE ROMANO-BARBARIC AGE

JAGIELLONIAN UNIVERSITY PRESS

This volume was supported by the Jagiellonian University – Faculty of Philology and Institute of Classical Studies

REVIEWERS
Dr. Hab. Przemysław Nehring
Prof. Dr. Hab. Jerzy Styka

COVER DESIGN
Jadwiga Burek

Cover illustration: the Rape of Hylas (*opus sectile* panel from the Basilica of Junius Bassus on the Esquiline Hill, Rome, the Museo Nazionale Romano)

First edition, Kraków 2011

ISBN 978-83-233-3089-9

WYDAWNICTWO UNIWERSYTETU JAGIELLOŃSKIEGO

www.wuj.pl

Jagiellonian University Press
ul. Michałowskiego 9/2, 31-126 Kraków
phone: 12-631-18-81, 12-631-18-82, fax 12-631-18-83
Sales: phone 12-631-01-97, phone/ fax 12-631-01-98
mobile: 0506-006-674, e-mail: sprzedaz@wuj.pl
Bank account: PEKAO SA, nr 80 1240 4722 1111 0000 4856 3325

CONTENTS

Introduction

'Change' and 'continuity': these two words, however antonymic, are used repetitively and often simultaneously in studies describing the cultural phenomenon of late antiquity. Indeed, the culture of Spätantike, in particular the literary one, can hardly be defined other than 'post-classical', which means, on the one hand, a culture (naturally enough) based on the classical tradition, developing in and through a dialogue with that unique heritage, but on the other hand, a culture in many aspects simply different from that of classical antiquity. This difference – as students of late antique aesthetics and poetics emphasize with imitable persistence[1] – cannot be reduced to the mere question of quality.

One of more relevant, if not the most relevant, features of late antique poetics is a tendency to mix various genres and styles,[2] to create works that are hardly interpretable in 'old' generic terms or, at least, to widen the semantics of a certain form by adding new, untypical (ostentatiously untypical at times) elements or characteristics. This tendency actually does not point to anything else but the fact that late antique poetry – not less than Greek Hellenistic or Latin neoteric one, which was similarly experimental and manneristic – is composed by and for connoisseurs for whom writing and reading is, and should be, an intellectual adventure, a subtle play with most varied literary codes and tropes.

At the same time, however, it should not be argued that late antiquity is an epoch already wholly blind or indifferent to the notion of a literary genre, or an epoch in which 'traditional' forms are forgotten or laid aside. A telling example, in Latin writings, may be the epithalamium, a genre practiced by the Roman poets since at least Catullus and the Neoterics but apparently reaching its zenith (only?) in Spätantike.[3] Interestingly enough, in Late Latin poetry, and what is more, especially the one composed already in a period once considered the outset of the 'Dark Ages' and nowadays redefined as a part of the

---

[1] See especially – I quote *exempli gratia* – the (already canonical) book by Roberts 1989a, who himself referred in the first place to Marrou's experience in studying the relationship between classical and late antique aesthetics. Actually, Roberts in each of his studies on late antique literature (therefore, I speak above of "imitable persistence") stresses the unique, different character of its poetics, always adding some inspiring observations.

[2] See especially – again I quote *exempli gratia* – Fontaine 1977, 1980, 1981, 1998 (a useful selection of Fontaine's major works in Italian).

[3] As Roberts (1989b: 321) notices, of seventeen extant Latin verse epithalamia, thirteen are by poets of late antiquity. It is usually acknowledged that Latin late antique epithalamia are modeled on Statius's *Silv.* 1.2 (see, apart from Roberts, Pavlovskis 1965; Stehlíková 1990), but, in point of fact, in comparative studies on late antique Latin epithalamia it is important to emphasize profound differences in form, content, poetic imagery, and even metrics between single texts. The systematizations proposed by Horstmann 2004, the author of a recent monograph on the genre, are valuable here.

'long late antiquity',[4] one can find even more surprising instances of similar 'returns' to genres willingly exploited in the 'classical phase' of the Roman literature (if we label so the late Republican, the Augustan, and the early Imperial era) but later, as it seems, fallen into disuse. The present book is dedicated precisely to such generic re-explorations, or indeed rediscoveries, proposed by authors active in Vandal Africa (Dracontius, presumably the anonymous author of the *Aegritudo Perdicae*, Luxorius, and most probably the poet of the *Sylloge*) and in Ostrogothic Italy (Ennodius and quite certainly Maximianus), the authors for whom the *Imperium Romanum* is no longer a political entity but rather an "Empire of a Sign,"[5] the empire of the language and civilization.

Parts One and Two treat of miniature epic and love elegy, the genres 'normally' associated by classical philology with the neoteric poetry and the golden age of the Roman literature, i.e. the Augustan period. Of course, Latinists are – at least ought to be – well aware how fragmentary our knowledge of a history of a certain form usually is: a study conducted from the diachronic perspective is always based on extant texts only. Nevertheless, it does seem that both the epyllion – practiced in Latin by Catullus (*carm.* 64), arguably by Virgil (Aristaeus's episode in *Georg.* 4.315-588),[6] by some poets whose works can be found in the *Appendix Vergiliana*, finally by Ovid (whose *Metamorphoses* are, after all, an impressive collection of interconnected epyllia) – and the Roman love elegy, not without reason called 'Augustan', are the genres which truly 'lay dormant' in subsequent periods. Therefore, it is not, and should not be seen as, a marginal phenomenon that in Latin poetry composed already in the Romano-Barbaric age one can find *again* texts interpretable as miniature epic (Dracontius's poems and the *AeP* are hexametric pieces shorter than 1,000 lines on mythological or quasi mythological topics) or as erotic elegy (Maximianus's elegy /*corpus elegiarum*/ treats of love, however love as a missed opportunity). This proves the fact frequently emphasized in genology, namely that genres – at least in pre-modern literature which hardly ever denies being genre-oriented[7] – do have an intrinsic ability, quite unusual and indeed somewhat mysterious, to regenerate, often unexpectedly. These 'regenerations' may be only momentary – such appear to be those discussed in the present book – nonetheless, they always are a sign of the continuity and the self-consciousness of the literary culture. Therefore, in reference to some late antique littérateurs, it may indeed seem fair (classical scholarship still finds it quite fair at times) to use the label of mere 'latecomers'. In fact, they frequently do make the impression of being ostentatiously anachronistic. A closer reading, however, of Maximianus's elegy for instance – but also of Dracontius's epyllia and Luxorius's *epigrammaton liber*, on which below – does not confirm this stereotype. The poetry which is 'literary', even dense with

[4] The problem of periodization of late antiquity is still – or rather: is *anew* – a matter of debate, even though, as it is well known, in socio-cultural studies Brown's proposal to read late antiquity as 'a long late antiquity' has turned out highly influential. See recently Marcone 2008.

[5] To evoke the inspiring title of the book by Waquet 2001.

[6] Needless to say, not few scholars would argue that the *Aeneid* Book 4 is an epyllion par excellence.

[7] As noted even in the post-structural theory of literature, not rarely hostile to the very idea of literary genres, see Sendyka 2006 for some valuable observations.

literariness, does not have to be 'empty' or 'unoriginal'. Quite the contrary, it is perfectly able to render tensions and dilemmas of its time.

In Part Three, I concentrate on the epigram, a genre, in the Roman literature, created (de facto) by Martial, and yet a genre which remained rather far from standardized even after the poet from Bilbilis and despite his own generic self-consciousness (Martial is undoubtedly one of the best theoreticians of the kind of poetry he practiced). In the history of the Roman epigram after Martial there is apparently but one author of comparable generic self-awareness, namely Luxorius. As I demonstrate, Luxorius can be seen in this sense as a discoverer, or rather re-discoverer, of the Martialian *epigramma*.

The poets of late antiquity hardly if ever acknowledge that their intention is to emulate the masters of old.[8] Much more typical of them is the attitude described by Curtius as *affektierte Bescheidenheit*.[9] This attitude can be also considered idiosyncratic of some authors discussed here. Naturally, such a pose should not be taken at face value, even though it may reveal not only the poet's hypocrisy and playfulness but also a quite serious and bitter reflection of an 'intellectual' (the term, however certainly somewhat anachronistic, is, in my view, applicable at least to Dracontius, a renowned lawyer, and to Luxorius, a *sophista*, but I would not hesitate to call 'intellectuals' also Maximianus and Ennodius) witnessing culture in the time of transition. That transition may well be labeled by pessimists as 'crisis' or 'chaos' (actually it is Maximianus who speaks of *generale chaos*). Nevertheless, one should admit that thanks to Dracontius, Maximianus, and Luxorius the Roman poetry and the Roman literary audience 'recollect' the miniature epic, the love elegy, and the (Martialian) epigram. This fact can be seen as a sign of a certain 'revival' (the word 'renaissance' might be an exaggeration), even if it is, indeed, momentary and even if it inextricably blends hope with despair. Therefore, I find it justifiable after all to use here terms that have positive connotations, like 'return' or precisely 'rediscovery'. What the poets discussed in the present book propose is, in fact, a sort of 'rediscovery' of the features of a certain genre, as regards its composition, content, even metrics (especially in the case of epigram), but also of its potential. This potential of the genre means its ability to develop, change, and absorb new, 'alien' elements, which undoubtedly blur its homogeneity but, as mentioned above, widen its semantics. Thus, a reader of the epyllion by Dracontius, the elegy by Maximianus, and the epigram by Luxorius should not expect that these works – and these new embodiments of the 'old' genres – will be wholly identical with their 'archetypes'. Were it so, it would mean that we read but second-rate versifiers, indeed (which is not the case, and hopefully not solely in my own view). We may expect rather that thanks to the reading of Dracontius's epyllion, Maximianus's elegy, and Luxorius's epigram our understanding of these very genres may become fuller and deeper than if it was narrowed only to the study of the 'classical phase' of the Roman literature.

---

[8] In point of fact, such lack of emulative pretentions is shown already by the Imperial poets. The conclusion of Statius's *Thebaid* may be exemplary here, in which the poet, apostrophizing his epos, states clearly: *nec tu divinam Aeneida tempta, / sed longe sequere et vestigia semper adora* (*Theb.* 12.816-817).

[9] Or "Affected Modesty," see Curtius 1990: 83-85.

***

This book was largely written during my sojourns at the American Academy in Rome as a Visiting Scholar in 2006/2007 and 2009, both times with the assistance of the Andrew W. Mellon Foundation. I am most grateful to Professor Carmela Vircillo-Franklin, Director of the AAR in 2005-2010, and Professor Thomas A.J. McGinn, Andrew W. Mellon Professor-in-Charge of the School of Classical Studies in 2006-2009. My special thanks are also due to the Librarians of the Academy for their many kindnesses. In particular, I would like to record my heartfelt gratitude to the late Christina Huemer, AAR Drue Heinz Librarian Emerita. Access in Rome to that library as well as those of Biblioteca Apostolica Vaticana, l'École française de Rome, and other Academies, Schools, and Institutes is any classicist's highest good fortune.

I would also like to thank my home institution, the Institute of Classical Studies at the Jagiellonian University in Cracow, Poland, for their understanding, which allowed me to conduct a major part of the necessary research abroad.

PART ONE

The Miniature Epic in Vandal Africa and the Heritage of a 'Non-Genre'[1]

[1] By the title of the present part of my book I intend to evoke the monograph by Bright 1987, the most comprehensive study of Dracontius's epyllia and the *Aegritudo Perdicae* to date. It is also Bright who uses the term 'non-genre', very appropriate indeed, however provocative in this context, in reference to the miniature epic (see below). In fact, in quite a few aspects the whole Part One of my present book can be seen as a discussion with certain statements or interpretive proposals by Bright, which of course does not mean that my major goal is to rewrite Bright's material or to propose a sort of 'anti-Bright'.

I. 1. Defining the (Latin) epyllion: some recapitulations

When in 1866 L. Müller referred to a text published for the first time eight years earlier as an anonymous *Carmen epicum inscriptum Orestis Tragoedia*[2] he labeled it as 'epyllion'.[3] At that time the word, Greek in origin but never used by the Greeks in its 'modern' sense,[4] was already becoming a quasi-technical term, adopted to describe miniature epic poems composed in accordance with the canons of the Alexandrian and neoteric poetics. Apparently, the name was not originally intended to denote a literary genre as such but rather single texts showing some formal affinities.[5] It was within a few decades, however, that the first monographic treatments appeared on the theory and history of the 'epyllion', interpreted precisely as a generic category.[6] These

---

[2] (C.G.) Müller 1858. On the first editions of the *Orestis Tragoedia* and the history of its identification as Dracontius's work, see in general Bouquet – Wolff 1995: 8-9; in brief also Castagna 1997a: 58. For general introduction to Dracontius's *oeuvre profane*, see Bouquet – Wolff 1995: 7-84. The French editors, following Díaz de Bustamante (1978: 99-134), prefer to speak of Dracontius's *carmina profana* rather than use the title *Romulea* (see their explanations on pp. 17-24). For readers less familiar with Dracontius's oeuvre, I should explain that the *Hylas* can be quoted as *Rom.* 2, the *De raptu Helenae* as *Rom.* 8, and the *Medea* as *Rom.* 10.

[3] (L.) Müller 1866: 464. In this article, Müller actually focuses on the second edition of the *Tragoedia*, published in the very same year (1866) by J. Mähly. Müller himself had already used the term 'epyllion' before in his study of the Roman metrics in reference to Catullus and Prudentius's *Psychomachia*, as pointed out by Wolff 1988: 302 n. 23.

[4] As it has been emphasized several times by scholars (see the comments in Wolff 1988), in Greek the word denotes firstly *versiculus*, secondly *breve carmen*, both uses have negative connotations, though. In Latin it is not used, if not marginally by Ausonius. The term, in fact, was 'rediscovered', to use the keyword of the present book, by modern philologists; its first employment in the modern sense can be dated, as Wolff indicates, to 1840. In 1855, M. Haupt used the term epyllion in his study on Catullus's *carm.* 64 to denote precisely short epic poems composed in accord with the Alexandrian literary standards.

[5] See Perutelli 1979: 15. In the first chapter of his monograph, entitled quite significantly "Un genere letterario?," the Italian scholar provides an excellent résumé of the scholarly approach to the phenomenon of the 'epyllion' from the mid-nineteenth to the mid-twentieth century.

[6] For a more detailed review of studies treating the 'epyllion problem', see Perutelli 1979: 13-31. On my part, I will list here only the monographic approaches. Among such, first two early studies should be mentioned: Heumann 1904 and May 1910. Next, a paper by Jackson 1913. Worthy of note is also the article of Perrotta 1923, in which, however, the author tries to persuade that the term epyllion is useful not so much to denote a new genre but rather to distinguish the Alexandrian epos from the classical one (which, in fact, is a kind of *Affektierte Bescheidenheit* on the part of Perrotta who defends his position against the criticism by Rostagni). To date, the most compre-

studies received short shrift from W. Allen,[7] who argued that the term should be banished from our critical vocabulary, especially if applied to define a 'genre'; for the American scholar it would be acceptable only if used in a wider sense, with reference not to a narrow group of texts but to "all poems in the new narrative style as opposed to the Homeric epics."[8]

Allen's objections did serve as some counterbalance to certain statements of the 'theoreticians' of the genre, at times too confident in their claims about its characteristics and subdivisions,[9] yet his main conclusion that the word 'epyllion' has "no proper place"[10] in the critical vocabulary of the classical philology gained in effect little acceptance. In the contemporary scholarship, the kinship (or, at least, *a* certain kinship) of the poems grouped under this category[11] is generally recognized, and so is the need to speak of the

hensive study in English is the one by Crump, published in 1931, republished in 1978 and 1997. In more recent time, Perutelli published in 1979 his very inspiring book on the Latin epyllion and its transformations. In 2004, Bartels published a study on the Latin epyllion focused in particular on the problem of narrative strategies. In his book on the aesthetics of Latin Republican poetry, Styka (1994: 157-167; 1995: 220-229) proposes to redirect the focus of studies on the phenomenon of the epyllion from structural to aesthetic aspects, in particular to such categories as *gratia* and *variatio* combined with *brevitas* and learnedness. Indeed, even if purely aesthetic qualities can serve rather as additional criteria for determining which poems are classifiable as epyllia (and which are not), it is beyond doubt that the principles of *gratia* and *varietas*, together with a tendency to display one's learnedness despite the short form, did shape the literary sensitivity of poets writing miniature epic. For some observations on the aspect as noticeable in Dracontius's epyllia, see especially Chs. I. 3 and I. 4.

[7] Allen 1940. The scholar emphasizes three facts: that the term was not used in such a sense in antiquity, that one cannot demonstrate any connection between this type of literature and the hypothetical quarrel between Callimachus and Apollonius Rhodius, and, which is the most important argument in his opinion, that there has been, in effect, no success in ascribing common characteristics to the works usually classed as epyllia.

[8] Allen 1940: 25.

[9] Allen's criticism is directed mainly at the study by M. Crump (in fact, throughout his paper he, rather maliciously I would say, persists in calling her 'Miss Crump', see e.g. p. 3), where, indeed, certain statements or conclusions may seem somewhat premature, like e.g. the sharp division of the epyllion, in Latin as in Greek poetry, into two definite types: the idyllic and the narrative, the idyllic being the earlier (Crump 1931: 48), or the 'confident' observation that the average length of an epyllion was probably four to five hundred lines (p. 22).

[10] Allen 1940: 1.

[11] The usual perspective in 'comprehensive' studies of the epyllion tradition is the one proposed by Crump, "from Theocritus to Ovid." Jackson (1913: 39) lists "two or three among the idylls of Theocritus [yet, as he states, modern scholars are not unanimous in classifying poems of this sort in Theocritus], two of the poems of Moschus, and in Latin the sixty-fourth poem of Catullus, the *Culex* and the *Ciris* in the *Appendix Vergiliana*, and the Aristaeus episode in the fourth book of the *Georgics*." Richardson (1944: 17; 76-77), who focuses on the Latin epyllion, lists: *Attis* (Catullus's *carm.* 63), *Peleus and Thetis* (Catullus's *carm.* 64), *Ciris*, *Culex*, *Moretum*, and Virgil's *Aristaeus* (*Georg.* 4.315-588). Perutelli studies three specific 'moments' of the Latin epyllion: Catullus's *carm.* 64, the *Ciris*, and Ovid's *Metamorphoses*. Bartels focuses on Catullus's *carm.* 64, *Ciris*, *Culex*, *Moretum*, Virgil's *Aristaeus*, Ovid's *Cephalus* (*Met.* 7.490-8.5). The 'kinship' of the poems classified as

'poetics of the epyllion' or of the 'epyllic features'.[12] Consequently, very few scholars nowadays would hesitate to use the term which is so handy, especially if compared with its would-be substitutes, much too lengthy and less easily applicable to poems varying quite significantly in subject and treatment,[13] and the term which has already been sanctioned by the philological tradition.

In a certain sense, however, the epyllion could be considered a 'non-genre', as David Bright stated somewhat provocatively in his monograph dedicated precisely to miniature epic in Vandal Africa. "The ancients themselves never adopted a distinct term for the form, and there is no ancient discussion of what its rules or limits should be."[14] One can hardly point to one single text that would be recognized by authors practicing the short hexameter poem as their archetypic unquestionable model.[15] Rather, what characterizes our (non)genre is the, Alexandrian par excellence, fondness of experimentation, a kind of innate openness to "fundamental changes of style, emphasis, and outlook."[16] As Alessandro Perutelli notes, one of the most persistent and constant qualities of the epyllion tradition is the fact that the choices made by one or another author are never definite and the changes never seem irreversible.[17]

At the same time, it should be emphasized that the miniature epic, experimental in its nature as it may be, turns out not just an ephemeral or marginal phenomenon in the history of ancient literary forms. Undoubtedly, it is not one of the most regularly exploited means of expression; rather, it has a tendency to appear and re-appear at certain moments of transformation, cultural as well as socio-political. As it has been justly pointed out, the epyllion develops in the Hellenistic world in the period of crisis of the values set and respected in

epyllia does not exclude profound and important differences among them resulting from the 'experimental' character of the genre, on which I write below. On the other hand, as I shall emphasize throughout this opening chapter following especially Perutelli (yet interestingly, the observation is also made by Cameron 1995: 451), one can point to relevant common features of the epyllion genre, which do allow us to call it a *genre*, but in particular (if not only) in *Latin* poetry, hence, the stress placed on the *Latin* epyllion in the title of the present chapter. What is no less important is the fact that in Latin poetry, from Catullus to Ovid (as was shown precisely by Perutelli), one can observe the 'dynamics' of some specific qualities, especially of the approach of the speaking *ego* to the narrated story. This can hardly be detected in Greek epyllia.

[12] As emphasized in the very introduction to his study by Bright 1987: 3-4. On some limitations of Bright's approach, see more below.

[13] As emphasized also by Wolff (1988: 303) who concludes his note quoting W. Keach: "epyllion is simply much handier over an extended stretch of writing than erotic mythological narrative poem or even Ovidian narrative poem."

[14] Bright 1987: 3.

[15] Callimachus's *Hecale* certainly does not possess such a paradigmatic value; in fact, in certain aspects it is notably different from subsequent epyllia, as Cameron (1995: 437-453) justly points out in his study. Callimachean narration, especially the one developed in the *Aetia*, is of course an inspiring point of reference for the epyllion poets, in particular the Latin ones, apart from similarities, there are still also significant differences (on both questions, see more below).

[16] Bright 1987: 6. The experimental character of the epyllion is also emphasized by Perutelli 1979: 28.

[17] Perutelli 1979: 117.

the Archaic Greek culture. Instead of heroism and its stereotypic exaltation, it proposes a sort of 'bourgeois' ethics and a 'bourgeois' concept of existence, much more appropriate and understandable for the society of the 'new' era. Hence the focus on human rather than heroic traits of a mythical protagonist, hence also the marginalization of some 'fixed' motifs of the grand epic. Similarly, in the Roman literature the epyllion is introduced by the Neoterics who notice very well that the Alexandrian forms are excellent to describe precisely the crisis of traditional values, the crisis they themselves witnessed in their own culture.[18]

As it appears, the next period that sees a kind of revival of the epyllion genre is late antiquity. Here, as far as the Latin poetry is concerned, particularly relevant seem the texts written in the late fifth century A.D. in Vandal Africa: Dracontius's *Hylas*, De *raptu Helenae*, *Medea*, *Orestis Tragoedia*, and the pseudo-Dracontian *Aegritudo Perdicae*.[19] The interest in the 'old-fashioned', elaborate form, as the miniature epic must have been perceived in those times, the very interest in the 'ancient' myth as such cannot surprise if we take into consideration the fact that the literary culture of late antiquity, especially the one represented by Dracontius, is elitist par excellence.[20] It is a culture created by intellectuals, school professors, connoisseurs and lovers of the classical tradition for whom composing poetry was a kind of snobbish, refined 'game'. In addition, it seems reasonable to suppose that late antique 'littérateurs', in particular those who happened to live their lives in the age 'after Rome', for example in Carthage, one of the true centers of learning of the Roman world occupied by the Vandals, did feel a certain 'sense of mission', a strong need to defend their common cultural heritage, and maybe also an ambition to transmit it and show its richness to the audience of the new 'barbarian' upper classes.[21]

---

[18] See Perutelli 1979: 29-30.

[19] Undoubtedly, we must take into consideration all the limitations in our knowledge on the factual presence of the epyllion genre in ancient literature of the imperial and the late antique era. We cannot even be sure to what extent the texts we possess, Dracontius's four poems and the *Aegritudo* (on its relationship with Dracontius's works, see Ch. I. 6), should be considered exceptional and to what extent they reveal wider interest in composing miniature epic in Latin literature of Vandal Africa. As regards other examples of late antique epyllia, in Greek poetry one can mention Tryphiodorus's *Taking of Ilios*, Musaeus's *Hero and Leander*, the Orphic *Argonautica*, and Colluthus's *Rape of Helen*. In Latin literature, Reposianus's *De concubitu Martis et Veneris* is a certain example. In fact, this quite charming little poem is *the* only certain example of a later Latin epyllion that we possess. Unfortunately, as Kay (2006: 10) notes rightly, it is "remarkable in attracting dates from the second to sixth centuries." Some scholars argue strongly for the contemporaneousness of Reposianus and Dracontius, see notably Courtney 1984: 309 (actually following Gualandri 1974: 876-882); Shanzer 1986: 19-20. If so (and the arguments are sound), it is even more reasonable to speak of the revival of the epyllion genre in late antique Africa. Generally, however, one must admit that the *De concubitu*, comparable to some extent with the *Aegritudo* (especially if aesthetic features are taken into account), is much less interesting to study from the generic perspective that Dracontius's poems and the *AeP*. I do not agree with Bright's (1987: 251 n. 8) listing Claudian's *De bello Getico* and *De bello Gildonico* among late antique Latin epyllia. Similarly, it would be pointless, in my view, to interpret certain Christian poems as 'epyllic' (like Prudentius's *Psychomachia* or Avitus's *De transitu maris rubri*).

[20] Bright (1987: 6) justly points at the 'new Alexandrianism' of late antique poetry.

[21] See Gualandri 1999: 67; similarly Simons 2005: 369-371. Gualandri follows the conclusions of Gianotti concerning the public of Dares and Dictys Cretensis which could include "i ricchi ma

Furthermore, it must be added here that late antiquity is another time of prolonged crisis, virtually in every sector of public life, economic, religious, military, and political, a crisis comparable to some extent with the one caused by the disintegration of the Roman Republic in the first century B.C.[22] Hence once again the epyllion, telling a mythical story, seems an efficient means of expression in a moment of transition, of a decisive change, and apparently it seems so not just for the poet himself, a learned jurist and a former student of the *grammaticus* Felicianus, but also for his public. This simple fact should be emphasized not to see in the African author merely a 'highbrow' or an 'antiquarian' who strives to reactivate the old, pagan myth, hardly understandable if not completely meaningless in his times.[23] Quite the contrary, as Isabella Gualandri[24] convincingly argues, to Dracontius's readership his mythological poems could appeal not just as 'irreal' or not more than 'past', 'bygone' stories. The contemporaries of the poet witnessed tragedies that "would demand, and, in their greatness, perhaps out-task, the power of the tragic language of an Aeschylus or a Sophocles."[25] Thus, Dracontius's mythical narratives could,

---

indocti personaggi che costituivano i vertici sociali e politici delle diverse regioni (occidentali) dell'impero." As a matter of fact, Bright (1987: 20) argues quite similarly, seeing in Dracontius "an author who was at the confluence of so many cultural factors: Greek and Latin letters, a new Germanic strain, the clash of pagan and Christian." Indeed, Bright is inclined to agree with the hypothesis advanced once by Kuijper (1958: 7 ff.) that the poet may have been of mixed Roman and Vandal lineage having a Roman father and a Vandal mother (pp. 14-15 and 67-68). He even wonders (see pp. 65-68) if certain motifs of Dracontius's poems could not be interpreted as taken from the popular, illiterate culture of the Vandals in Africa (like the folk tale elements in the *Medea*). However, this can hardly be proven. One might only note, not wholly seriously of course, that the somewhat 'romantic' image of Dracontius as the heir to the Roman traditions through his father as well as to the 'outlandish' Vandal heritage through his mother does appeal to our 'modern' sensitivity to the value of 'multiculturality'. On the other hand (being more serious now), the hypothesis that Dracontius's audience was indeed 'multicultural' in the sense that it consisted of people of various cultural (as well as maybe ethnical) backgrounds does find some corroboration in what the poet says in *Rom.* 1 about the school of his teacher Felicianus: *qui fugatas Africanae reddis urbi litteras, / barbaris* qui *Romulidas iungis auditorio* (ll. 13-14), even though I would not argue, as Kuijper once did, that Dracontius here places himself among the *barbari.*

[22] As argued by Malamud (1993: 156) in her paper on the *Aegritudo Perdicae* entitled quite significantly "Vandalising epic:" "Late antique society existed in a state of prolonged crisis – economic, religious, military and political – as far reaching in its effects as the crisis caused by the disintegration of the Roman Republic in the first century B.C., and it is not ... methodologically inadmissible to make broad analogies between these two periods and the literature each produced."

[23] Quartiroli (1947: 25) states that Dracontius, in effect, fails to comprehend the 'full' sense of the ancient myth and treats it as 'dead matter': "nell'animo del poeta il mondo pagano è morto, non se ne ha un superamento artistico: rimangono forme vecchie, non meno morte del loro contenuto."

[24] Gualandri 1999: 67-68.

[25] I quote (mentioned by Gualandri and earlier by P. Courcelle) the opening of the letter to Apellion by Theodoret, describing the capture of Carthage by the Vandals in 439: "The sufferings of the Carthaginians would demand, and, in their greatness, perhaps out-task, the power of the tragic language of an Aeschylus or a Sophocles. Carthage of old was with difficulty taken by the Romans. Again and again she contended with Rome for the mastery of the world, and brought Rome within danger of destruction. Now the ruin has been the mere byplay of barbarians. Now dignified mem-

indeed, seem to reflect the 'real' world and the 'real' calamities.[26] It is quite probable that for many of his readers, even those somewhat less familiar with the classical topoi, the figure of Hesione of the *De raptu Helenae* would have been comparable to the widow and the daughters of Valentinian III, whereas the assassinations in the house of the Atreides were not much different from the dynastic dramas of the Vandal rulers. In other words, as the Italian scholar concludes, the 'myth' was not only a merely rhetorical element; it could still be used to represent people's passions and sufferings.

Naturally, particularly relevant in such a context seems the problem to what extent in the miniature epic composed in Vandal Africa one can still discover features peculiar to earlier examples of this literary form. Hence the question of the epyllion 'heritage' posed in the title of the present part of my book. As a matter of fact, the already quoted monograph by Bright does not bring here a fully satisfactory answer, above all for this very reason that the author has not developed in effect a sufficiently thorough definition of what an epyllion really is.[27] Consequently, his book – offering for the most part a good analysis of single poems (even though I do not always agree with certain points he makes) – does not really show in a more systematic way what aspects of Dracontius's poetics could and should be interpreted as 'epyllic' and what is, and precisely how deep is, the epyllion heritage to be found in his poems and in the *Aegritudo*.

Undoubtedly, as I have mentioned above, the miniature epic with its innate experimentalism resists too easy or too narrow classifications. This does not mean, however, that our somewhat 'wayward' genre (or non-genre) cannot be described in any proper manner. Genial in its simplicity and safely applicable to (probably) all texts ever labeled as epyllia seems the formula provided by Bouquet and Wolff in their preface to the edition of Dracontius's works: "poème fini ..., d'une longueur comprise entre 100 et 1000 vers, écrit en hexamètres dactyliques et empruntant son sujet à la mythologie et aux cycles épiques, avec une prédilection pour les histoires amoureuses et criminelles."[28] As it appears though, we need not be so minimalistic in our statements not to risk too much sche-

---

bers of her far-famed senate wander all over the world, getting means of existence from the bounty of kindly strangers, moving the tears of beholders, and teaching the uncertainty and instability of the lot of man." I quote the opening passage of the letter (translated by Blomfield Jackson) from the edition by Philip Schaff, *Theodoret, Jerome, Gennadius and Rufinus: Historical Writings* accessible online at: http://www.ccel.org/ccel/schaff/npnf203.iv.x.xxix.html [May 13, 2010].

[26] Romano (1985: 379), emphasizing the tragic character of Dracontius's poems and of the *Aegritudo Perdicae*, notes rightly: "in una età di angoscia quale quella dei primi tempi della dominazione vandala ..., in cui l'oppressione del nuovo potere era avvertita dalla classe intellettuale romana, un poeta non poteva non essere portato a privilegiare temi di carattere tragico. ... È, quella di Draconzio e dell'autore della *Aegritudo*, un'età che non può e non sa essere lieta."

[27] In fact, what Bright provides are only rather superficial observations. At the very outset of his book he notes (pp. 3-4): "The study of this nongenre has always been fragmented and plagued by incomplete or contradictory definitions. ... At any rate, there has been no dispute with the proposition that the poems are narrative hexameter compositions on heroic or quasi-heroic topics displaying the highest form of Alexandrian polish."

[28] Bouquet – Wolff 1995: 37. See also their further comments on the following pages (37-43).

matization or simplification of the epyllion problem. A good point of departure should be the observation with which even Allen would have agreed concerning the 'non-Homeric', if not 'anti-Homeric' character of the miniature epic. As Jackson notes a bit bombastically, "the epyllion was born of revolt; it constituted a protest against the methods pursued by the poets of the old-fashioned epic."[29] This implied, first of all, a different selection of the events to be narrated, focus on less popular, minor motifs or 'other' versions of the ostensibly well-known tales. This also implied a different kind of narration, more 'digressive',[30] episodic, with marginalization or elimination of the parts of the story between one episode and another and a quasi-dramatic indeed division of the action into scenes, often hardly coordinated.[31]

The third consequence regards not just topics and style but the very 'ideological dimension' of the genre. As I have already mentioned, it is frequently pointed out that in the epyllion the 'epic' heroes and the 'epic' values are usually reduced, if not even subverted or parodied. The protagonists of the miniature epic reveal a kind of 'bourgeois' character: they are presented in situations of everyday life and behave like 'ordinary' people. At the same time, one should be aware that, as Perutelli convincingly argues, this not always must be the case (which does confirm the observation that in the epyllion tradition certain choices and changes are never definite or irreversible). The Italian scholar shows that Catullus, one of the undoubted '*archegetai*' of the Latin miniature epic, in his *carm.* 64 does not depreciate at all the value of mythical heroes, quite the contrary, he opposes them to his depraved contemporaries.[32]

Last but not least, also this 'predilection for love or criminal stories' is related to the 'non-Homeric' character of the epyllion. It is almost commonplace that the 'little epos' focuses on the psyche of the protagonist to the extent unknown to the grand epic poetry.

---

[29] Jackson 1913: 40.

[30] In this context, it would be fair to mention a feature that is often treated as one of the most characteristic of the epyllion, namely the digression as such. Crump (1931: 22) speaks with certainty that digression is almost a 'must' of the genre. Yet Lyne (1978: 34-35) notes rightly that the digression is, in fact, an optional element in the epyllion: "We must not label the 'insert story' as the (or a) defining characteristic of the epyllion."

[31] See Perutelli 1979: 28. The observation was already made and well explained by Richardson 1944: 85: "In this group of poems, not every detail which is pertinent to the story is presented, nor even every detail pertinent to the sequence of events. The main principle of organization is the dramatic selection of the single important scene." Richardson rightly points out the structural analogies between the epyllion and the tragedy (on which more below).

[32] See Perutelli 1979: 44-68 and my additional comments below. It is worth adding that, as Cameron (1995: 442-444) emphasizes, the 'bourgeois ethics' is not present in Callimachus's *Hecale*, either. *Hecale*, in Cameron's view, is not at all a 'proletarian', middle-class epic: the virtues she represents, in particular her hospitality, are archetypally epic ones. In fact, Cameron rightly points out in how many aspects the poem does not really comply with what we would consider typically epyllic features. As he notes (p. 451): "The Hellenistic poems classified as epyllia do not really have that much in common – a good deal less than their Latin counterparts. The only Hellenistic poem that resembles the Latin epyllia in any significant way ... is the *Europa* of Moschus." To be exact, the observation that characteristics of Latin poems, like *Smyrna* or *Ciris*, should not be 'automatically' attributed to Greek texts was made already by Wilamowitz, see Perutelli 1979: 16-17.

As such, it most naturally develops "a romantic theme,[33] generally the unrequited love of a woman for a man."[34] Needless to say, the figure of Medea created by Apollonius reveals paradigmatic in shaping the female characters. A careful reader is well aware that her traits can be discovered in the Ariadne of Catullus in *carm.* 64, the Scylla of the *Ciris*, but also in the Dido of the *Aeneid*[35] (the so-called epyllion within the Virgilian masterpiece). It would be an exaggeration to say that Medea becomes an epyllic heroine par excellence, still her presence appears quite 'symbolic' among Dracontius's protagonists.

An insight into the composition of the epyllic poems shows another important characteristic. The miniature epic is, as if by nature, open to influences of other genres, in particular lyric and drama. These elements, contradictory among themselves as they may be, choose the epos (the epic 'outer structure', so to speak) as their common denominator.[36] In other words, the *Kreuzung der Gattungen* appears to be one of the fundamental markers of the epyllion. But here some additional comments are necessary. Firstly, as Jackson already justly emphasized, exploiting – and combining – various literary strategies, various genres indeed, is peculiar to 'all' epic as such: "as the epic of all literary forms is the most nearly universal, in that it comprises, besides the epic element, the dramatic, the lyric, the satiric, the pastoral, so the epyllion, a microcosm as it were, tends in its narrower field to treat its theme ... in as manifold and comprehensive a manner."[37] In other words, there is nothing 'strange' in the fact that the epyllion, precisely like its 'elder' brother, makes quite extensive use of other genres. The point is that in the little epos the 'other' elements are more visible as the proportion between the 'epic' and the 'non-epic' can be less balanced. Certainly, this is related to the 'Alexandrian' origin of the form and the tendency to focus on the, supposedly, 'marginal' and the 'ancillary', rather than on the 'significant' and the 'major', which was idiosyncratic of the Alexandrian poetics.

Secondly, one more detail must be stressed. It is not enough to say that what is characteristic of the miniature epic is (simply) the *Kreuzung der Gattungen*. If one made only such a statement, it would be difficult to disagree with the ironic remark by Allen: "it seems hardly just to say that poems should be grouped together under a specific name

---

[33] Cameron (1995: 449) in his study on Callimachus's *Hecale* emphasizes how different it is in this respect: "The later epyllia, notably those by the Latin poets, are full of the exotic and the romantic. Yet there is nothing of the sort in the *Hecale*." It should be maybe added that also Jackson (1913: 40-41) spoke of two 'kinds' of epyllia, as he named them: the (much more popular) romantic and the heroic. As the examples of the latter, he listed "the twenty-fourth and the twenty-fifth idylls of Theocritus, both dealing with the Heracles saga, the former describing the earliest exploit of the hero in slaying the snakes ... the latter narrating the visit of Heracles to Augeas." Jackson's proposal of the division of the epyllion into the two 'kinds' was strongly criticized by Allen 1940: 14-15.

[34] Jackson 1913: 40.

[35] Jackson 1913: 45.

[36] To quote Perutelli (1979: 29): "il rapporto di filiazione dall'epos non basta a definire l'epillio; in esso convergono impulsi di altri generi come il dramma o la lirica, i quali vengono a coagularsi in aggregati fra loro contraddittori che eleggono l'epos a comune denominatore."

[37] Jackson 1913: 41-42.

since they have the point in common that they are each a mixture of different types of poetry in different proportions."[38] What is essential is to indicate that – with the whole variety of means that an epyllion poet may use and does use – certain genres and strategies are exploited more frequently and, so to speak, more 'systematically'. It should be emphasized that these are in particular elements determining the 'sentimental' or pathos-arousing character of a work. Therefore the presence of the lyric 'inclusions'[39] and, on the other hand, the use of the tragic forms and motifs. Here, the influence of elegy has been often pointed out as the factor behind the 'lyricization' of the epos, typical of the epyllion. In fact, presumably for most of the ancients, even for the ancient 'literary theorists', the elegy and the epyllion seemed quite close: worth mentioning is the opinion of Parthenius of Nicaea who, dedicating his *Erotica Pathemata* to Gallus, asserted that similar stories, treating usually of unhappy or unnatural loves, were apt both for epic and elegiac verse.[40]

As regards the tragic elements, it can be argued that their exploitation within the miniature epic, especially the Latin one, is precisely 'systematic' in the sense that they often shape the overall composition of a poem.[41] The observation was made as early as in 1944 by Lawrence Richardson who even proposed to interpret the structure of the epyllia in the light of the Aristotelian *Poetics*, not suggesting though a direct influence but rather the knowledge of "the original standards as they were adapted and revised by Aristotle's successors."[42] Richardson's analyses are probably too accurate, or even too sophisticated at certain points, nonetheless some of his remarks are worth quoting.

First of all, relevant is what he writes about the above-mentioned division of the action into scenes. Richardson justly stresses its tragic origin, but he is also very right noting that an epyllion author usually makes a selection of only a few scenes and focuses his

---

[38] Allen 1940: 16.

[39] The most typical examples of 'lyric inclusions' within the epyllion are the lengthy speeches of the protagonists, especially the female ones (like the song of Carme in the *Ciris*). As Perutelli (1979: 55-64) shows, in Catullus's *carm.* 64, the lyric coloring can even be found in the narratorial voice of the poem.

[40] It was already Heinze who argued for the 'sentimentalization' and 'lyricization' of the epyllion resulting from the influence of the subjective elegy. The problem of the relationships between the two genres was amply discussed by Pinotti 1978. She focuses on the relationship between the elegy and the epyllion in view of the ancient authors and quotes (p. 16) this particularly interesting passage of Parthenius's dedication to Gallus. What she notes is that both elegists and epyllionists willingly define their works as *lusus*, a light play. She concludes, however, (p. 18-19): "In definitiva, nella considerazione degli antichi, i generi dell'epillio e dell'elegia sembrano vicini: … Queste testimonianze, tuttavia, non risolvono il problema dei rapporti fra i due generi in ambiente alessandrino, dove mancano i dati per sostenere, come faceva Heinze, la priorità dell'elegia soggettiva e la sua azione sul formarsi di un *epos* liricizzato; si potrà al massimo ipotizzare un'influenza reciproca fra due forme letterarie ancora in elaborazione, l'elegia narrativo-etiologica in cui la presenza del poeta si fa sentire sempre di più accanto al mito, e l'epillio che liricizza l'epos."

[41] Richardson (1944: 22) gives the example of Catullus's *carm.* 64 treating of the story of Ariadne. As he argues, the story behind this poem "is by nature more epic than dramatic, and with shifting scene and episodic action more a narrative than a tragedy; … Catullus has changed the aspect of the story … and … organized an epic into a tragedy."

[42] Richardson 1944: 76.

attention on them, developing their dramatic potential, whereas other motifs and other sections of a story, even those providing necessary advancement for the plot, are omitted or merely touched upon in passages in between the major scenes. As a result, one can, indeed, have the impression that the poet "states rather than presents dramatically what is eventually to happen."[43] Quite interesting is also the observation concerning the characters and their functioning within the story as treated by the epyllion author. As the American scholar highlights, the number of characters in miniature epic is usually limited, they appear – like in tragedy – not in groups but singly or in twos and, if they are presented together, they speak individually and not in a dialogue.[44] Last but not least, worthwhile are Richardson's comments on the tragic error as the factor determining the action of the epyllic poem. In fact, such error on the part of the protagonist "is not, usually, a deliberate or positive intent toward evil…, but rather consists in a casual negligence of human duties."[45]

So far we have focused on aspects connected with the 'narration', i.e. the narrated story within the epyllion. Nevertheless, the very figure of the narrator is also peculiar of the genre. The character of the epyllion is determined – the observation can hardly be overestimated – by its 'Alexandrian' origin and by the fact that it was born in a period of a profound crisis of the ethos, in particular of the ethos of heroism, created by the culture of the Archaic Greece. Similarly, it was transplanted into the Roman poetry in a moment of a comparable crisis of the traditional values precisely to be used as a new and attractive form of expressing, and judging, these changes and transformations. A careful and competent reader (and this is the reader that an 'Alexandrian' poet requires) will easily notice that what is essential in the genre is not just the 'old' mythical material but much more the new way in which this well-known 'myth' is retold and reinterpreted.

What characterizes the *Latin* miniature epic is a very subjective, even emotional approach of the narrating *ego* to the narrated story. This emotional coloring, the expressions of sympathy of the poet to his own protagonists,[46] often given at the very outset of the poem,[47] determine the structure of the whole text and its reception on the part of the reader. Being an anticipation of the tragic outcome, they destroy all elements of suspense[48] (in this context it might even be said that a well-trained reader expects that the epyllion

[43] Richardson 1944: 85.

[44] Richardson 1944: 87.

[45] Richardson 1944: 88. On the tragic error, see his general observations on pp. 79-90 and in particular on p. 81: "This error which causes tragedy should be evident from the outset in every case and must show the portent of tragedy even before the concatenation of events which accomplishes the revolution in the circumstances of the protagonist."

[46] See as early as in Jackson 1913: 49: "The tragic situation in which these heroines are involved leads the poet to break through the epicist's reserve and give expression to his own sympathy. … *Infelix* says Calvus of his Io, Virgil of his Dido, the poet of the *Ciris* of his Scylla, and Valerius Flaccus of his Medea. So Catullus commiserates his heroine by addressing her as *ah misera*."

[47] See Richardson (1944: 49) who points to the subjectivity of the narrator's introduction as different from the one in the long epic.

[48] As noted already by Richardson 1944: 65.

should be a kind of 'mini-tragedy' in the epic form). These 'intrusions' of the narrator into the narrated story become in fact, as Perutelli emphasizes, a peculiar quality of the Latin epyllion that makes it quite different from its Hellenistic counterpart.[49] Indeed, the Hellenistic miniature epic (if we take into consideration Callimachus's *Hecale*, but also Moschus's *Europa*) seems to lack the intrusive presence of the poet-narrator.[50] On the other hand, the 'injection of the personality of the narrator into the narrative' is characteristic of Callimachus's *Aetia*. As Cameron puts it, Callimachus, "while anxious to increase and enhance the role of the narrator in elegiac narrative, was no less anxious to keep it invisible in epic narrative."[51] Thus, it might be implied that, again, it was the Hellenistic elegy and the Hellenistic elegiac narrative like Callimachus's *Aetia* that shaped the Latin epyllion, offering more opportunities for experimentation and innovation in the area of the role of the narrator.

At the same time, the speaking *ego* of the Latin miniature epic, even if inspired by what could be found in Callimachus's major work, is also substantially different from the narrator of the *Aetia*. If in Callimachus the narrator intervened mainly as *philologus doctus*, stressing that "he sings of nothing unattested," for the Roman epyllionists what matters is the moral judgment; the moral interpretation is implicit in their texts.[52] This particular difference reveals, in Perutelli's view, a very 'Roman' attitude: the authors of the Latin epyllia were well aware of their 'high status' as epic poets,[53] a status that gave them the right, if not an inner obligation, to speak about the 'moral' issues.

---

[49] Perutelli (1979: 64) notes: "l'introduzione del racconto *ex abrupto* propria dell'epillio alessandrino non si riprodurrà più nella letteratura latina, dove si registra la presenza quasi costante di varie formule di mediazione, che innescano il mecchanismo del narrare."

[50] As noted by Cameron 1995: 451 (who actually quotes Hunter). As I have already mentioned, Cameron, emphasizing how different from one another the Hellenistic poems classified as epyllia are, points to the *Europa* of Moschus as "the only Hellenistic poem that resembles the Latin epyllia in any significant way," but not as far as the discussed above lack of the intrusive presence of the poet-narrator is concerned. In fact, in Cameron's view (p. 445, again a quotation from Hunter), it is in Apollonius's epic narrative that we find "a far greater prominence for the poet's person, the narrating *ego*, than is found in Homer."

[51] Cameron 1995: 445. He even argues that the so-called 'mixing of genres', often seen as the main principle of the Hellenistic poetry, was not Callimachus's attitude to epic and elegy. As regards the role of the narratorial interludes in the *Aetia* the scholar observes (p. 439): "this is not (of course) a glimpse of the poet's real world; it is not his purpose to communicate information about sources ... Rather, ... by playing with the traditional disclaimers these lines direct our attention less to the poet's sources than to his own personal and original use of them."

[52] See Perutelli 1979: 110-113. The fact was also emphasized by Richardson 1944: 89: "The poet always places emphasis on the moral aspects of the theme of his poem and the lesson that he proposes." Among the Latin epyllia of the classical phase, it is only in the introduction to the *Ciris* that the speaking *ego* adopts the pose of the Alexandrian *poeta doctus*, presenting and discussing the credibility of various versions of a myth, see Perutelli 1979: 74.

[53] Perutelli 1979: 115: "l'autore dell'epillio è consapevole della sua specifica qualità di poeta epico ed avverte in qualche modo l'impegno impostogli da tale qualifica. Così indulge alle discussioni moralistiche che forniscono uno specifico di serietà e di *decus*, di cui fregiarsi rispetto ad altri generi, evitando, almeno nelle parti principali, ogni vulgarismo espressivo. Il carattere paradig-

As it has been mentioned above, Alessandro Perutelli argues convincingly that the Latin miniature epic is specific precisely for its being the "*narrazione commentata*," a story always accompanied by the narratorial voice, the voice of the commentator, the interpreter, and (above all) the judge of the mythical 'events'. From this perspective, the Italian scholar describes a certain 'evolution' that the genre went through in Latin literature from the late Republican to the late Augustan era (which was probably the period of its longest uninterrupted presence in Roman poetry). Perutelli analyzes three, in his view particularly interesting, examples: Catullus's *carm.* 64, the *Ciris*, and selected Ovid's narrations in the *Metamorphoses* (the Scylla story, 8.6 ff., the Myrrha episode, 10.298 ff., and three minor motifs: Io in 1.588 ff., Ariadne in 8.169 ff., and Europa in 2.846 ff.). As he shows, comparing the three 'cases' one can notice changes in the narrator's approach toward the 'mythical story' he recounts and the role that this mythical story should represent for his contemporary public. Catullus in *carm.* 64 points to the age of the heroes as the ideal era of *virtus* and *fides*, thus the 'lyrical' coloring of his narratorial interventions, emphasizing the nostalgia for this ideal remote past[54] that should have a paradigmatic value for the present times. Hence also the severe judgment, a censure indeed, of the contemporaries who have despised religion and banished justice, cherished in the mythical age of innocence.[55]

In the *Ciris*, the focus of the narratorial criticism shifts from the 'real' world, accused of moral degradation, to the very mythical story itself. The narrator still speaks as a 'judge', as a moralist, however, what he judges now is the tale, the plot he narrates as such, and the behavior of its protagonists. His comments follow every moment of the action: he expresses his compassion for the Megarians watching in vain their king's lock, the whole country of Megara, and, especially, the father betrayed by his own daughter.[56] He also tries to understand the motifs behind Scylla's act, wondering whether she should rather be seen as *infelix* or *demens*.[57] Yet whenever his attention concentrates on Nisos, he emphasizes that the king is an innocent victim of a daughter who violated the familial

matico del mito si manifesta in forme diverse, ma innesta sempre una problematica seria e grave, rispettosa in qualche modo della dignità che a Roma aveva sempre rivestito l'epos."

[54] See *carm.* 64.22-24: *o nimis optato saeclorum tempore nati / heroes, salvete, deum genus! o bona matrum / progenies, salvete iter<um... / vos ego saepe, meo vos carmine compellabo.*

[55] See the strongly emotionally marked final of the *carmen* (382-408), where the poet paints in very dark colors the morality of his contemporaries, opposing their behavior to that of the mythical heroes who duly respected the gods and were visited by them in their homes. For the analysis of the narratorial interventions in *carm.* 64, see Perutelli 1979: 44-68. Certainly, Perutelli's reading could be in some respects juxtaposed with ethical interpretations of Catullus's *carm.* 64, see notably Konstan 1977. Catullus's ethical involvement in *carm.* 64 is also emphasized by Styka (1994: 163-166; 1995: 227-229) who, on the other hand, points out the interdependence of ethical and aesthetic attitude of the poet noticeable in this epyllion.

[56] See *Ciris*, 129-132: *nec vero haec vobis custodia vana fuisset / (nec fuerat), ni Scylla novo correpta furore, / Scylla, patris miseri patriaeque inventa sepulcrum, / o nimium cupidis Minoa inhiasset ocellis*. In l. 129, I read *vobis* as proposed by Perutelli 1979: 80-81.

[57] See ll. 181-194; the following passage seems particularly interesting: *namque haec condicio miserae proponitur una, / sive illa ignorans (quis non bonus omnia malit / credere quam tanti sceleris damnare puellam?); / heu tamen infelix: quid enim imprudentia prodest?* (ll. 187-190).

bonds. In this respect, the poem, where the myth is not idealized as opposed to the reality but judged against the categories of the Roman moralism, can be seen as a product of the Augustan culture, the culture that tried to 'regain balance' after the socio-political and moral crisis of the late Republican era, propagating the return to the Roman tradition and ethics.[58]

Ovid's epyllic narration gives up such moralistic ambitions peculiar to the neoteric miniature epic. The speaking *ego* of the *Metamorphoses* with a clear distance describes the reactions of his protagonists, quite often – especially in the case of the heroines – by means of monologues, modeled on rhetorical *controversiae*. He no longer provides profound ethical judgment of their behavior, except for just a few cases, like the Myrrha episode in the *Metamorphoses* Book 10.[59] He does not try to identify with them, either. Ovid – as Perutelli argues – seems not to notice the crisis of values that absorbed his predecessors exploiting the genre of the epyllion. It might even be said that apparently he does not really intend to cast himself in the role of the one who should speak in defense of the endangered values.[60] Hence, so typical of his narrator, the lack of interest or concern for the moral content of the narrated story. In Perutelli's view, Ovid's epyllion can be probably considered the conclusive phase of the process of appropriation of the Alexandrian literary form by the Latin poets. Paradoxically, the Neoterics, who introduced the Hellenistic miniature epos into the system of the Roman literature, marked the genre with traits quite alien to what was postulated by the Hellenistic poetry, celebrating the human rather than the heroic. It is only in Ovid where the mythological protagonists are again reduced to the 'bourgeois' dimension, dictated by the canons of the Alexandrian poetics, and do not appear as admirable heroes[61] born "in happiest time of ages."[62]

---

[58] See Perutelli 1979: 69-93. Perutelli adds (p. 92 n. 29) that his observations on the myth as presented and commented in the *Ciris* could provide certain arguments as regards the dating of the poem. Similarly, Pinotti (1978: 26) argues for the (late) 'neoteric' nature of the Scylla story, whereas Lyne (1971: 233 ff.; 1978: 54 ff.) postdates the poem to the first or even the second century A.D. Yet for Perutelli himself more important than the question of the dating as such is the fact that – as he is convinced – the epyllion should be considered a falsification, a text pretending to be written by Virgil.

[59] One may agree with Perutelli (1979: 99) that the exclamations made from time to time by Ovid's narrator, like e.g. the one to be found in the Scylla episode: *intrat et (heu facinus!) fatali nata parentem / crine suum spoliat* (*Met.* 8.85-86), cannot be seen as serious ethical judgments on the part of the speaking *ego*; rather, their role is to mark the culminating point of the story. In fact, the Myrrha episode in *Met.* 10 seems to be the only one provided with a substantially longer and more elaborated narratorial introduction, focused indeed on the moral content of the story. This detail may be of some importance if we take into consideration the fact that it constitutes a clear model for the author of the *Aegritudo Perdicae*, on which see more in Ch. I. 6.

[60] To illustrate the completely different approach of Ovid to the moral issues, Perutelli (1979: 112-113) quotes the well-known passage from the *Fasti* 1 (201 ff.), where the poet actually ironizes the moralists praising the austere and poor archaic Rome: *laudamus veteres, sed nostris utimur annis: / mos tamen est aeque dignus uterque coli* (225-226).

[61] See Perutelli 1979: 94-113.

[62] See Catullus's *carm.* 64.22, translation by Francis Warre Cornish in Goold 1995: 99.

The characteristics listed above can be now used as points of reference for the reading of miniature hexametric poems composed in the late fifth century Vandal Africa. I wish to concentrate first on the aspect indicated by Perutelli as particularly relevant for the Latin epyllion, namely the role of the narrator. We have just noted that even in the Latin miniature epos of the 'classical phase' the narrator could look at the mythical story as a moralist or judge. Thus, it seems reasonable to expect that a similar approach should be all the more 'natural' if an ancient, pagan myth is to be presented and commented by an *ego* speaking for a poet steeped in *both* the classical tradition and the Christian faith.[63]

Next, I shall analyze Dracontius's poems as 'non-Homeric' epic. Obviously, Allen's expression evoked here is used only metaphorically as a helpful label under which certain compositional features can be grouped. It is not my intention of course to compare – or rather contrast – Dracontius's epyllia to Homer's oeuvre as such. I shall discuss such aspects as the selection of motifs to be elaborated, their treatment, and the portrayal of the protagonists.

Lastly, I shall focus on the problem of the *Kreuzung der Gattungen*, the exploitation of 'other', extra-epic literary forms and strategies in the texts in question. As I have already stressed, the 'mixing of genres' within an epyllic poem is aimed above all to give it some particular coloring, sentimental or, indeed, tragic. It is from this standpoint that Dracontius's texts will be studied here.

In the final chapter, I shall dedicate a few words to the *Aegritudo Perdicae*, a poem inevitably destined to be juxtaposed with Dracontius's miniature epic. In fact, my own approach will not be much different in this respect. Nevertheless, my goal is not to compare certain stylistic peculiarities or to establish who of the two makes a better poet (and why this must be Dracontius). What I shall concentrate on is exactly the question of their understanding of the epyllion tradition: to what extent what they two propose is convergent, what and how deep the differences are.

---

[63] Throughout my study of Dracontius's epyllia, I cannot avoid posing myself questions concerning Dracontius's religious attitude, even though the problem does not constitute my major point of interest and I fully acknowledge my limitations in providing decisive conclusions in this respect. Nevertheless, my personal view is that what we can speak of in Dracontius's case is not so much a conversion *sensu stricto* (therefore, I have stated above "a poet steeped in ... the Christian faith," and hence also the inverted commas whenever I use the term 'conversion' in reference to Dracontius) but rather maturation of faith, or even maturation of religious consciousness, the result of which are (among others) more and more important moral issues that the poet proposes in his epyllia. In other words, what I believe is the decisive factor in Dracontius's religiousness is some kind of dynamics, rather than (only) steadiness emphasized by Bright, who even goes as far as to name the Carthaginian poet a "Christian apologist" (see below in Ch. I. 2). My position then, being, in this respect, somewhat different also from Simons's (for whose book I generally have much appreciation), is close particularly to Grillone's (and earlier Aricò's, still even to Romano's, in fact). Therefore, my reading of the chronology of Dracontius's epyllia is also 'conservative' (for an 'innovative' approach to the problem, see Bright 1999): I see the *Orestis Tragoedia* as (clearly) posterior – and even complementary in some respect – to the *Medea*. The *De raptu Helenae*, in such a context, should seem somewhat 'anterior', even though it is equally impressive in employing varied literary strategies if poetic quality were to be taken into consideration.

Such method of interpretation should provide a more thorough and systematic insight into the 'poetics' – or simply 'genre', if we do not hesitate to use the term in reference to the epyllion – employed in their works by Dracontius and by the anonymous author of the *Aegritudo*. In fact, it should also help to demonstrate that what makes these poems 'epyllic' may be not merely "the interest in elaborate structure ... the recurring interest in erotic themes, including the more peculiar byways of the subject ... a preference for little-known myths and for obscure or invented versions of famous stories,"[64] which are, in effect, the only 'crucial' features persisting in Dracontius's works recognized by Bright. I would still add that my aim here is not so much to determine 'how epyllic the epyllia written by the Latin poets in Vandal Africa are'. What I intend to focus on is rather the question to what extent these poems gained their specific shape and character precisely due to the employment of strategies typical of the epyllion.

Consequently – this concerns the part of my study devoted to Dracontius's four texts – I shall not analyze them as Bright did, one by one as almost self-contained units. In his concluding observations the Canadian scholar emphasized the poet's eclecticism, one of the results of which is the fact that "the poems are quite different from each other as well as from the traditional treatments of the individual themes. One poem is like a pantomime, the next like a tragedy, and the next like a romance."[65] It is hardly questionable that the texts are different for the simple reason that they treat different subjects and – the fact should not be underrated – that they were composed by a very versatile and a very gifted author (in my view, Dracontius is one of the most interesting to read, indeed, one of the best poets of Latin late antiquity). Nonetheless, it is not wholly fair to say that they are different because one resembles a pantomime, the next a tragedy, and the next a romance. Rather, as it will be demonstrated, such elements can be found in (almost) each of them; what may differ – and does differ – is the proportion. Similarly, it should be taken into consideration that Dracontius's epyllia do reveal a certain development of his *art poetica*, and even of his mental attitude, especially if we juxtapose the – undoubtedly juvenile, albeit quite charming – *Hylas*[66] with any of the other three simply more mature and more accomplished works. However, the versatility of our poet, as well as this 'progress' in his literary (and human) capacities, can be, in my view, most effectively demonstrated not when we read his texts separately but precisely by a comparative analysis of analogous qualities in different poems.

One more comment is needed before I begin the discussion. A glance at the titles of Dracontius's works allows us to notice that the author chooses topics that could be considered typical of the epyllion tradition: the Hylas myth, treated in a kind of epyllic narrative al-

---

[64] Bright 1987: 249.

[65] Bright 1987: 248.

[66] Díaz de Bustamante (1978: 137) goes as far as to state in reference to the *Hylas*: "estamos ante una *declamatio scholastica* que, en manos de un poeta menos hábil y sincero que Draconcio, resultaría illegible." Agudo Cubas (1978: 306-328) is less strict in her statements, but she also emphasizes the differences between the *Hylas* and later Dracontius's epyllia.

ready by Theocritus,[67] Medea, the rape of Helen, exploited also by Colluthus of Lycopolis.[68] A bit surprising may only seem the decision to elaborate the Oresteia theme in such a form, yet even in this case one could argue that we deal with "une prédilection pour les histoires ... criminelles." The pseudo-Dracontian *Aegritudo Perdicae*, with its ostensibly 'historical' protagonists, is really developed basing fully on 'literary' motifs and, in addition, clearly evokes one of the most 'horrible' love stories of Ovid's *Metamorphoses*. These few facts should suffice to convince us that the two poets were quite aware of what they intended to compose, even if they did not know the term 'epyllion', and even if they were not quite certain whether it should be interpreted as a 'genre' or merely as a 'narrative style'.

At the same time, Dracontius's poems, *Hylas*,[69] *De raptu Helenae*,[70] or *Medea*,[71] seem by no means a sort of re-writings of the earlier epyllia (at least, as we should add, of those still extant). Similarly, the *Aegritudo Perdicae* – a work by a versifier, not wholly unskillful

[67] Apart from Theocritus's *Id.* 13 (only 75-verses long poem), certain examples of 'epyllia' treating the Hylas theme, yet inserted into a wider structure, can be found in Apollonius's *Argonautica* 1; as for the Latin literature, in Propertius's elegy 1.20 (a 'tale' inserted in an elegiac address written in warning to Gallus) and in Valerius Flaccus's *Argonautica* 3. An excellent review of ancient texts treating the figure of Hylas is given by Weber (1995) in her edition of the epyllion, see in particular the chapter devoted to the Hylas story as a theme of Hellenistic little forms (pp. 61-71). On the Hylas theme in ancient literature, see also Mauerhofer 2004.

[68] In fact, as regards the chronology we are still far from certain whether Colluthus should be seen as anterior or posterior to Dracontius, see most recently Santini 2006: 13.

[69] A very useful comparative analysis of common motifs in Dracontius and other poets treating the Hylas theme is given by Mauerhofer 2004: 373-379. The problem of Dracontius's sources has of course been treated many times by earlier scholars and different conclusions have been proposed, especially as far as Dracontius's knowledge of Greek is concerned.

[70] Some scholars have emphasized analogies between Dracontius's *De raptu* and Colluthus's *Rape of Helen*. Certain details in common can possibly be found, as argued quite convincingly by De Prisco (1977: 295-298), but as Santini (2006: 13) notes, due to the disputable chronology, it cannot be determined whether it was Dracontius to draw upon Colluthus or the other way around. Nevertheless, the overall structure and the choice of motifs to be elaborated and highlighted are substantially different in the two texts.

[71] Dracontius's *Medea* is quite unique in offering within one poem a combination of two segments of the story normally treated separately: (1) the events in Colchis, the female protagonist of which is the young Medea, a figure, so to speak, almost 'taken from the romance tradition', who having fallen in love with Jason helps him gain the Golden Fleece and, consequently, lets the brave newcomer kidnap her, i.e. the motifs exploited in epic versions built upon the theme of the *argonautikà* (Apollonius Rhodius, Valerius Flaccus); (2) the actions of *Medea furens*, the filicide, portrayed willingly by playwrights, to mention only Euripides and Seneca. This text as such finds one significant parallel within the earlier Roman literature, namely Ovid's Medea episode in the *Metamorphoses* 7 (ll. 7-424). What is particularly interesting, however, is the fact how utterly different these two treatments are. It is more than obvious that Ovid was one of Dracontius's most important *auctores* (and certain details of Dracontius's poem have the Ovidian flavor, especially the setting of the scene showing Medea pray the gods of the Underland, see Schetter 1980: 214 = 1994: 319-320), yet at the same time it is also quite clear that the African poet found his very own way of interpreting this peculiar theme. I supply some further notes below, still I have focused specifically on a comparative analysis of the two treatments in Wasyl 2007a.

though,[72] rather than a 'serious' poet – offers a quite interesting reinterpretation of what can be found in the literary tradition, especially in Ovid. If so, it might be said that once again the miniature epic turns out to be a form inviting authors' creativity. It can hardly be considered a drawback.

I. 2. *La narrazione commentata*: the narrator's presence in Dracontius's epyllia

If the presence of a narrator "jealously possessive of his leading role"[73] is to be considered a specific quality of the epyllion, Dracontius's poems do make a perfect example in this respect. A clear voice of the poet who not merely tells but, above all, judges a certain mythical story and its protagonists is one of the first things noticed by any reader of the *De raptu Helenae*, *Medea*, and *Orestis Tragoedia*. This peculiar involvement or, if one prefers, intrusion of the Dracontian narrator upon the narrative usually is – and indeed should be – explained in the context of the author's religious attitude (which does not necessarily mean that the African writer must be seen only as a Christian apologist 'reducing *ad absurdum* the pagan myths'[74]). Nevertheless, to emphasize once again what has already been said, it turns out not less typical of Dracontius than of earlier Roman epyllionists. As a matter of fact, the narrator of the *Ciris*, whose introductory speech occupies – it is worth noting – about one fifth of the entire poem, seems at least as self-oriented as his Dracontian counterpart. His judgment of Scylla, a heroine of an 'exotic' Greek legend,[75] from the standpoint of the Roman ethics is also clearly and consciously 'anachronistic' (indeed, Dracontius is not more anachronistic in his statements). This anachronism of approach constitutes, in fact, one of the mechanisms thanks to which the

[72] Zurli (1996: 261) himself calls the anonymous author of the *AeP* "facitore di versi," yet adding "più abile di quanto solitamente si ritenga." Similarly Grillo (2010^2: 7 n. 3) in his recent edition of the text labels the anonymous poet "un non disprezzabile letterato." In fact, I find much exaggerated Bright's (1987: 222) statement concerning the quality of the epyllion: "As art, to be sure, it is formidably rough."

[73] I quote always inspiring Conte 2007: 52.

[74] As argued by Bright (1987: 43) in his concluding remarks on the *Hylas*. I must admit that I am quite surprised with the decisiveness with which Bright detects 'Christian' elements in this poem, especially if we take into consideration that most of the details he emphasizes (the 'unheroicness' of Hercules, the vengefulness of Venus, etc.) are fully concordant with what we find in the 'pagan' epyllion tradition. On Dracontius's *Romulea* as written "to demonstrate the futility of mythical and polytheistic teaching," see also Edwards 2004; on the *Medea* as a polemic against the cult of the pagan gods, see Klein 2001.

[75] It is interesting that, as Perutelli (1979: 63) notes acutely, the Latin epyllion, unlike the heroic epos, does not start with time to treat 'Roman' themes but always focuses on Greek motifs: "mentre l'epos di tipo omerico, con la mediazione di quello storico ellenistico, era stato adattato a un contenuto nuovo e prettamente romano, l'epillio si conserva celebratore di storie greche e orientali."

poet maintains his dominant position within the text as his voice and his persona cannot be mistaken for a voice of any of the 'simple' protagonists of a story.[76]

Therefore, the narratorial interventions by Dracontius, especially his most characteristic prologues and epilogues, if compared with the analogous passages in the *Ciris* (the above-mentioned introduction), in Catullus's *carm.* 64 (the final), or even sometimes in Ovid (the opening of the Myrrha episode in *Met.* 10), do not seem extravagant in their length or 'rhetoricism'. On the other hand, they are undoubtedly long enough, elaborate enough, and 'literary' enough to invite, if not demand, a close reading, the reading, so to speak, 'for their own sake', not as a mere 'frame' the position of which in the text hierarchy is indisputably inferior to the one of the narrated story as such, but as a unit 'on its own', not less important than the very narrative itself.[77] A unit 'on its own' does not necessarily mean 'self-contained' or 'unrelated' to the narrative. In fact, what I intend to focus on in my research into the narrator's presence in Dracontius's miniature epic is also the question whether and, if so, to what extent his epyllic speaking *ego* through the content but (even more) through the form of his interventions tends to cross the barriers dividing him from his protagonists to pose as a 'witness' or (maybe even) a 'co-participant' of certain events. Nonetheless, just to recapitulate, a reader of the epyllion should not be surprised that what the poet expects him/her to concentrate on is not merely the plot but also his (most often quite verbose) comments. Indeed, it should be admitted that what the epyllic narrator asks of us, the readers, is a challenge. This is not only due to the fact that we are naturally inclined to pay more attention to the 'action' rather than to all that, as we would put it, 'distracts' us, to all that disturbs our perception of the storyline. Another problem seems much more serious. If truth be told, we rarely if ever presume that what the poet-narrator might say about a certain story – especially if he is supposed to give a kind of 'ethical' comment – could really be of some importance. In our view, an 'ethical' comment must be quite obvious: the bad must be condemned and the good who suffer must be bewailed. And it can hardly be denied that it is so, both in the 'classical' Latin epyllia and in Dracontius or the Anonym's *Aegritudo Perdicae*. However, we should make every effort to listen carefully to the poet's words, not just because of their 'content' but precisely because of their 'form'. It is worthwhile taking a closer look at the literary strategies employed by the epyllic narrator in his speeches and seeing how they make the poem more complete

[76] Therefore, I would generally agree with what Conte (2007: 50-54) notes about the differences between the (only ostensibly similar) narrative styles of the Latin epyllion and of the *Aeneid*. As he puts it (pp. 50-51): "it is usually supposed that the form of Virgilian narration can be explained as an intensification of Alexandrian and neoteric subjective technique. But resemblances in the superficial form of expression should not blind us to the significant differences on the construction of the narrative of the *Aeneid*. The process of 'sentimentalization' set in motion by Virgil cuts deep into the flesh of the text, and is no superficial colouring of the discourse, as in Apollonius and Catullus." In fact, the example he provides is quite convincing (pp. 53-54): a comparison of Apollonius's invective against Eros in the passage dedicated to the suffering Medea and Virgil rendering Dido's emotions.

[77] Therefore, I believe that the length of the narratorial speech in the *Ciris* does not have to be interpreted only as the poet's fault, demonstrating his inability to measure proportions between the 'introduction' and the 'main part' of his poem.

and (simply) different. It may also appear that, if read carefully enough, the poet's comments will not sound as obvious and common as we have expected.

I. 2. 1. *HYLAS*

As I have already mentioned, the *Hylas*, most probably a Dracontius's *juvenilium*, differs in some aspects from his later epyllia. This difference can be noticed also when we analyze the category of the narrator and his role within the text. In the *Hylas*, the speaking *ego* reveals itself only in a very short and apparently quite conventional *prooemium*. It is conventional because it contains the most typical elements: the definition of the main subject, the invocation of the Muse, and the question about the primary cause of the events.[78] The only unusual characteristic may be a certain discrepancy between the, rather elevated, epic vocabulary (*Fata canam*; *si, Musa, mones*[79]) and the very topic, relatively light and unheroic (*Fata ... pueri*, l. 1). Possibly, it is here, in this literary joke, that we should suspect the presence of the *epyllic* poet, always ready to play with the 'grand' tradition:

> *Fata canam pueri Nympharum versa calore*
> *in melius, si, Musa, mones. Quis casus ademit*
> *Alcidi comitem, solamen dulce malorum?* (1-3)

The other three works, *De Raptu Helenae*, *Medea*, and *Orestis Tragoedia*, already show a narrator who intends to demonstrate his domination over the text. Each of these poems contains quite extensive prologues and epilogues. In addition, in the *Orestis Tragoedia* the poet intervenes also after certain, particularly relevant scenes; in fact, it is only in this text that we find the one example of a 'proem in the middle'.[80] In all these passages, the speaking *ego* reveals his self-consciousness, both as a poet defining the character of his work and, precisely, as a commentator judging a certain mythical event or a protagonist.

I. 2. 2. *DE RAPTU HELENAE*

In the lengthy introduction to the *De raptu Helenae*,[81] the narrator in a very particular way defines his attitude to the literary tradition. The poem, treating the theme so naturally associable with Homer and Virgil, instead of a conventional apostrophe to the Muse

---

[78] See Weber 1995: 141.

[79] In l. 2 I read *si, Musa, mones*, as Weber (1995: 141-142) proposes. See also the convincing arguments by Grillo 1988: 122-123 n. 30. Similarly, Mauerhofer 2004: 311-312.

[80] See ll. 350-352: *Dic mihi, Musa, precor: qua spe materna noverca / quaerere neglexit pueros et tradere captos / patris in occasus?* The 'proem' marks, as we can see, one of the most crucial moments of the action, the fact that Orestes is saved. However, since its function is quite clear, I do not focus on it more in the analysis below. There are much more interesting, indeed captivating to read, narratorial parts in the *OT*.

[81] The narratorial introduction to the *De raptu Helenae* ends, in fact, only in l. 60.

like in the *Hylas*, contains an invocation addressed directly to the two *auctores* personifying, so to speak, the story of the Trojan war.[82] It is composed de facto as a prayer, as can be inferred from the employment of the expressions like: *numina vestra vocans* (l. 22), *Attica vox te, sancte, fovet* (l. 28), *vulgate, precor* (l. 29).[83] This particular deification of the two greatest poets constitutes part of an interesting autothematic declaration, a declaration that cannot be understood otherwise than as an, ostentatious indeed, *Affektierte Bescheidenheit*,[84] especially if we take into consideration the fact that the speaking *ego* calls his very self here a *vilis vates*:

> *Ergo nefas Paridis, quod raptor gessit adulter,*
> *ut monitus narrare queam te, grandis Homere:*
> *mollia blandifluo delimas verba palato;*
> *quisquis in Aonio descendit fonte poeta,*
> *te numen vult esse suum; nec dico Camenae*
> *te praesente <<veni>>: sat erit mihi sensus Homeri,*
> *qui post fata viget, qui duxit ad arma Pelasgos*
> *Pergama Dardanidum vindex in bella lacessens;*
> *et qui Troianos invasit nocte poeta,*
> *armatos dum clausit equo, qui moenia Troiae*
> *perculit et Priamum Pyrrho feriente necavit:*
> *numina vestra vocans, quicquid contempsit uterque*
> *scribere Musagenes, hoc vilis colligo vates.*
> *Reliquias praedae vulpes sperare leonum*
> *laudis habent, meruisse cibos quos pasta recusant*
> *viscera, quos rabies iam non ieiuna remisit*
> *exultant praedamque putant nuda ossa ferentes.*
> *Attica vox te, sancte, fovet, te lingua Latina*
> *commendat: vulgate, precor, quae causa nocentem*
> *fecit Alexandrum raptu spoliaret Amyclas.* (11-30)

A similar reversal of the topos of emulation is idiosyncratic of late antique poetry[85] and as such can hardly be read as a 'sincere' statement. At the same time, one might be tempted to wonder whether by using this well-known (but not necessarily banal) figure Dracontius – like so many of the intellectuals of his time – does not point at the condition of his contemporary culture, a culture that still feeds upon the tradition but, in truth, seems only a shadow of the past glory.

---

[82] In fact, as Santini (2006: 12 n. 38) notes, Dracontius names personally only Homer (ll. 12 and 16), Virgil is invoked as *poeta* (l. 19) and he is celebrated here (ll. 19-21) mainly as the author of the *Aeneid* Book 2. On the problem whether the passage can bring us some information as regards Dracontius's knowledge of Homer, see Santini 2006: 12-13 and, generally, Brugnoli 2001.

[83] See in particular Grillo 1988: 122-123. I follow Grillo's convincing argumentation on the punctuation – and understanding – of ll. 11-13 and I punctuate above as he proposed (p. 126). On the deification of Homer and Virgil, see also Díaz de Bustamante 1978: 187.

[84] Nonetheless, Brugnoli (2001: 72) notes justly that the passage is not a simple *locus humilitatis propriae* but rather "eccelsa costruzione retorica," though in fact based, as he argues, on school exercise material.

[85] See e.g. Luxorius's opening epigram 287 Riese^2.

Another aspect appears even more relevant though. The narrator, describing briefly the main subject of his poem, stresses that what he will focus on are motifs different from those typical of the grand epic, the motifs that for the heroic poets were only marginal or even negligible (*quicquid contempsit uterque*, l. 22).[86] It should not be an exaggeration to say that these seem to be the words of a fully self-aware epyllic poet who, in reality, has no intention whatsoever to imitate the masters of old, even though he evokes their names with due respect as the names of the icons of the great culture.

Apart from this, quite interesting as I believe, poetological declaration, the proem to the *De raptu Helenae* gives a very clear, univocal indeed, moral judgment of the story to be narrated and of its protagonist (*nefas Paridis*, l. 11; *pastorale scelerati pectoris ausum*, l. 2). In fact, the focus on Paris in the opening lines of the introduction suggests that the characteristics, fully negative of course, of the Trojan prince will constitute one of the major topics of the whole poem. The terms with which the poet describes Paris are far from unexpected (first of all, *pastor* as early as in l. 2; *adulter*, l. 11; *raptor*, l. 11; finally, the keyword *praedo* in l. 1), yet what is quite original, the emphasis is placed on the two aspects of Paris's guilt: the transgression of the marital rights and the violation of hospitality.[87] As it appears, the narrator intentionally employs elements of the legal vocabulary: *ius mariti*, *foedus*, *coniugium*, *consortium*, *pignus*;[88] in addition, as Bright notes, the distinction he makes in ll. 6-10 between the mother's and the father's contribution to their offspring sounds also legalistic, "although it seems to have no genuine relation to legal texts."[89] Undoubtedly, this peculiar approach to the problem reflects Dracontius's personal as well as professional interests as a lawyer,[90] yet – precisely because of the use of the expert jargon – it can also be seen as a well-planned show of erudition. A poet speaking as a jurist is of course quite different from a poet speaking as a *philologus doctus*. Nonetheless, the pose of an expert is clear in both cases. And as such Dracontius's self-presentation is tinged again with some epyllic color:

Troiani praedonis iter raptumque Lacaenae
et pastorale scelerati pectoris ausum
aggrediar meliore via. Nam prodimus hostem
hospitis et thalami populantem iura mariti,

---

[86] Therefore, I can hardly agree with what Wolff (1996: 117 n. 9) writes in his commentary: "Cette invocation signifie aussi que Dracontius revendique une inspiration classique et n'établit pas d'opposition entre l'épopée et le genre qu'il traite (l'*epyllion*)." Quite the contrary, in my opinion, Brugnoli (2001: 72-73) is right reading the passage as "*recusatio* dell'*Aonius fons* d'Ippocrene."

[87] Santini 2006: 32-33.

[88] Santini (2006: 33-37) provides an excellent interpretation of the passage reconstructing Dracontius's possible allusions to certain juridical nexus.

[89] Bright 1987: 87. See also Santini 2006: 34-35.

[90] Romano (1959: 32) in his classic paper notes acutely: "bisogna tenere presente il rapporto tra l'attività forense e la poetica di D., perché questa da quella fu certo influenzata e in modo forse determinante. Negare questa relazione, in ossequio ad un canone critico che trascura i legami tra l'uomo ed il poeta, che tuttavia possono essere negati solo in sede teorica, significa precludersi la via per comprendere quell'impegno problematico e morale che avranno i suoi epilli, dal *De raptu Helenae* all'*Orestes*."

> *foedera coniugii, consortia blanda pudoris,*
> *materiem generis, sobolis spem, pignora prolis:*
> *nam totum de matre venit, de matre creatur*
> *quod membratur homo; pater est fons auctor origo,*
> *sed nihil est <sine> matre pater: quota portio patris*
> *omnis constat homo? Mater fit tota propago.* (1-10)

In his lengthy introduction, the narrator mentions also an event antecedent to the very action of his poem, namely the judgment of Paris. It is not only the conciseness with which he treats the theme (see ll. 34-36) that is worth noting – the conciseness suggesting that the main story has not started, yet – but also a very particular 'accentuation' that he proposes. The poet completely ignores the motif of the reward promised by Venus to the young man,[91] even though the vast majority of his literary audience would probably consider this detail canonic and irremovable. Instead, what he emphasizes is that *pastor ... litem facit ipse suam* (ll. 35-36). A reader, careful enough not to classify this omission as a compositional error ("how is it possible to speak of the judgment of Paris and forget to mention Helen?"), will realize immediately that the narrator's intention is to present the mythical theme not as a romantic tale about a youngster searching for the woman of his dreams, which could seem much more appropriate for the epyllion genre, but precisely – as it has been declared in the opening words of the text (*nefas, scelus*) – as a history of a crime, or even a concatenation of crimes, that must lead to the tragic final. Paris, as depicted in Dracontius's scene of the judgment, is not a mere mythical character but, above all, a corrupted judge, one of those that could be met in the real world, the judge breaking the divine and the *human* law. In this moment, the poet's view of his protagonist turns, indeed, ostentatiously anachronistic which is emphasized again by the use of the legal vocabulary:[92]

> *Solverat Iliacus caeli vadimonia pastor*
> *et litem facit ipse suam: laudata recedit*
> *contempta Iunone Venus. Tunc virgo decore*
> *victa dolet, nam tristis abit: heu nescia mens est,*
> *quae mala circumstent ausum dare iura Minervae.* (34-38)

One might, and even should ask what is the aim of a similar interpretive strategy. In my opinion, what the poet intends to demonstrate here is the fact that the ancient myth can be read and told not only as "forme vecchie, non meno morte del loro contenuto"[93] but, on the contrary, as a story that can provoke important questions, the questions that can truly absorb the attention of his contemporaries. We should notice that the narrator with a particular emphasis shows that Paris's act will determine not only his own future but also the destiny of others: *heu nescia mens est, / quae mala circumstent ausum dare iura Minervae* (ll. 37-38): the lamentative tone will be soon pervasive in his speech. Dra-

---

[91] The promise of a lady fair as the goddess is mentioned only in ll. 64-65.

[92] See Santini 2006: 94 (who develops the observations made already by Gualandri 1974: 882 ff.), Wolff 1996: 120 n. 23.

[93] To quote Quartiroli (1947: 25) once again.

contius's text – without obtrusiveness yet clearly enough – poses the problem of the responsibility of an individual for the evil that, because of his (her) crime, may befall others.

Undoubtedly, it does not seem less noteworthy that the oncoming catastrophe of Troy is also explained here in the most 'traditional' manner as caused by the wrath of the offended goddess Minerva, which could be seen as perfectly concordant with the epyllic convention. Nevertheless, there is one detail that does not wholly match this epyllic context. What Paris commits is not a mere mistake, an unintentional error, like the one of Scylla for example.[94] His act is voluntary, even if undertaken without full knowledge of the consequences (which is the case: *nescia mens est*, l. 37) and even if performed by someone who is unaware that the law must not be broken (which may be the case since the protagonist is a *pastor*). Ignorance of the law and, all the more, ignorance of the moral rules can hardy be a justification.

Paris's partial judgment brings about the catastrophe of other protagonists. The narrator pronounces it, as if it were indeed a sentence. Therefore, one could say that in this moment the poet speaks as a *porte-parole* of the divine tribunal, whereas the accused are the human corrupted judge as well as all those condemned by his crime:[95]

> *Iudicis Idaei pretio sententia fertur*
> *damnaturque Paris; nec solus pastor habetur*
> *ex hac lite reus: damnantur morte parentes,*
> *damnantur fratres, et quisquis in urbe propinquus*
> *aut cognatus erat, cunctos mors explicat una.*
> *Atque utinam infelix urbs tantum morte periret!*
> *Damnantur gentes, damnatur Graecia sollers*
> *heu magnis viduanda viris; orbatur Eous*
> *Memnone belligero, damnatur Thessalus heros*
> *et Telamone satus, pereunt duo fulmina belli.*
> *Pro matris thalamo poenas dependit Achilles*
> *(unde haec causa fuit), forsan Telamonius Aiax*
> *sternitur invictus, quod mater reddita non est*
> *Hesione Priamo; sic est data causa rapinae,*
> *cur gentes cecidere simul, cum sexus uterque*
> *concidit, infanti nullus post bella pepercit.* (39-54)

At the same time, this whole passage because of its rhetoric: the verb *damnatur/ damnantur* repeated six times, the exclamations *atque utinam*, *heu*, turns into a kind of a lament sung by the poet over the heroes doomed to death. A similarly emotional speech of the *ego* is a model example of a feature noticed already by Jackson and Richardson,[96] namely that the narratorial interventions at the very beginning of a story destroy all elements of suspense, determining its tragic outcome.[97]

---

[94] See the *Ciris* (ll. 138-145): *idem tum tristis acuebat parvulus iras / Iunonis magnae, cuius periura puella / olim (sed meminere diu periuria divae) / non ulli licitam* *v i o l a v e r a t i n s c i a s e d e m*, */ dum sacris operata deae lascivit et extra / procedit longe matrum comitumque catervam, / suspensam gaudens in corpore ludere vestem / et tumidos agitante sinus aquilone relaxans.*

[95] See Santini 2006: 97.

[96] See Jackson 1913: 49; Richardson 1944: 65.

[97] In fact, if Paris is labeled by Dracontius as *pastor*, Priam is similarly constantly called *infelix*.

What the poet emphasizes above all is the cruelty of war which costs lives of individuals, families as well as entire nations: men, women, children. War means extermination of ordinary people and of great heroes, like Achilles and Ajax. The passage devoted to them merits a closer look as the narrator once again seems to point to the *fatum* as the factor determining human life and predestining the death of *heros* Achilles. In reference to Ajax's death, another explanation is given, though: *forsan Telamonius Aiax / sternitur invictus, quod mater reddita non est / Hesione Priamo* (ll. 50-52). The adverb *forsan* used by the poet is a clear indication that he himself does not intend to establish which of the two causes of the war could have been more important,[98] but it is worth noting that already for the second time what Dracontius implies is the fact that also the humans may have been (*forsan*) responsible (coresponsible). If the decisions they make are morally wrong, they must bring them a terrible loss.

The mood of catastrophe, so palpable in the introductory part of the poem, is not less apparent in the final scene showing Paris's return to Troy with Helen. It should be noted that the entire closing segment of the epyllion is wholly 'dominated' by the narrator who never allows any of his protagonists to speak,[99] whereas he himself, using his own omniscience, reveals quite willingly their true intentions and emotions.[100] The poet describes first the symbolic (= fictitious) funeral ceremony performed by the king and his subjects to commemorate the prince presumed dead. Yet, what he emphasizes are especially feelings of the participants in the event. If Priam, as it appears (at least the narrator does not comment on it), is sincere in his grief, the Trojans' regret is empty: Paris is bewailed for his royal origin and not for his actual personal advantages. Besides – this observation of the poet seems particularly interesting – Paris would not be regretted even *were* he a true hero. Hector is the one whom the Trojans love, Hector whose fate – if Paris is saved – they seem to be aware of:[101]

sexus uterque gemit, non pro virtutis honore
aut quod talis erat qui posset bella subire
aut ingesta pati vel summis viribus hostem
frangere et ensiferas acie iugulare cohortes
(quamvis Alexander si viribus Herculis esset
aemulus aut certe Meleagrum aut Thesea fortes
aequaret virtute potens, tamen Hectore magno
sospite nemo Parin lugeret corde dolenti),
sed regis quia natus erat, fit planctus in urbe.
Nam quicunque memor Heleni mox dicta tenebat,
laetatur gaudens et tantum voce dolebat. (599-609)

---

[98] See Wolff 1996: 122 n. 35. Certainly, the passage can also be seen as an indication how Dracontius exploits his sources, among which possibly Dares. On Dracontius's contamination of the two sources, Virgil and Dares, see in particular Schetter 1987. On Dracontius and Dares, and even on Dracontius's misunderstanding of Dares, see also Bright 1987: 104-117.

[99] Which is completely different from the structure of the previous scenes abounding in lengthy speeches by the protagonists, see Bright 1987: 132-133.

[100] The problem of the truth and the falsity is essential in this whole poem, see more below in Ch. I. 3. 2.

[101] On the tragic connotations of the scene, see below, especially in Ch. I. 4. 2.

The narrator in like manner comments on the next scene, i.e. the arrival of Paris and Helen, which is almost a mirror image of the previous one. What follows the grief is a sudden and not less 'incredible' joy. The poet does not judge the fact that, apparently, Priam and Hecuba are quite as much happy to see their son as their new daughter-in-law (*suscipiunt sponsam*, l. 621). What he stresses instead is the reaction of Troilus and Hector who in this very moment seem already to foresee their own future: *Non invitus adest, nec gaudet fortior Hector, / quem Troilus sequitur non invitus tamen aeger, / non membris sed mente gravis* (ll. 624-626).[102]

Now, the narrator again turns into a lamenter prophesying the death of the heroes. The simile he gives is particularly expressive: the Trojans (the simile as such refers to Troilus and Polites) are like shadows. Bright notes acutely that the poet is suggesting a specter rather than an optical shadow.[103] Indeed, what he seems to be implying is the image of the land of shades.[104] The disaster, as the reader must conclude, is inevitable:

Mors ore cruento
inter Troianos discurrit saeva caterva,
heu quantos raptura viros, quae fata datura
aut quantas per bella nurus viduare parata!
Troile, sectatur vestigia vestra Polites.
Sic solet umbra sequax hominem larvalis imago
muta sequi nec membra movet, nisi moverit ille
quem sequitur ... (627-634)

It is the main character and his 'bride' for whom the speaking *ego* saves his last words. Thus, the barrier dividing the narrator from the characters seems broken: the poet turns into a participant of the wedding ceremony, an ill-fated wedding at which the shepherd's pipe music blends with the sound of the trumpet of war (*tympana iam quatiunt, iam rustica fistula carmen / pastorale canit*, ll. 642-643).[105] This unique *adlocutio sponsalis*[106] of his makes a bitter conclusion of the whole story, the story that is to be tragic in its consequences. And what he gives to the newlyweds, instead of the usual best wishes, is the vision of the approaching calamity:

Ite pares sponsi, iam somnia taetra probastis
matris et ornati misero flammastis amore
ostensam sub nocte facem, qua Troia cremetur,
qua Phryges incurrant obitum sine crimine mortis.
Sanguine Troiano dabitur dos, clade Pelasgum
ditetur Ledaea fugax per castra propago,

---

[102] The passage is problematic, see Wolff 1996: 171 n. 368. I follow his lection.

[103] Bright 1987: 132.

[104] On the pantomimic connotations of the scene, see more below, especially in Ch. I. 4. 2.

[105] The passage is of course bitterly ironic: the narrator once again derides his protagonist, the shepherd-prince (see more below). As such, the final of the *De raptu Helenae* hardly makes a good example of the epithalamium understood as pastoral, as Wilson (1948: 39) argues. On the other hand still, the two poetics do overlap at times, especially in medieval poetry, as Wilson's paper shows.

[106] Díaz de Bustamante 1978: 213.

orbentur superi, caelum gemat et mare plangat:
crimen adulterii talis vindicta sequatur. (648-655)

It should not be an exaggeration to say that Dracontius's *De raptu Helenae* is impressively rich in literary strategies employed by the poet in his narratorial interventions. The language is sometimes logical and precise as the legal vocabulary can be, sometimes emotionally marked like in the lamentative passages, and sometimes imitates a certain form like the above-mentioned *adlocutio sponsalis*. Consequently, the narrator's parts are, indeed, not less interesting to read than the very story as such (even though, as I shall demonstrate, the story of the epyllion is also told through strikingly diverse poetic devices). Besides, what the narratorial speeches emphasize is the 'message', or rather the essential moral problem of the poem, i.e. the relationship between crime and punishment. Certainly, Dracontius in his epyllion does not treat the Trojan war itself; in this sense one could argue that the ultimate punishment of the main character and his family is merely announced and not really shown,[107] yet on the other hand, its inevitability is constantly stressed throughout the text and as such can hardly be ignored. In addition, Dracontius's story of Paris is aimed at provoking another moral question, exactly the one concerning the responsibility of a human being for his/her deeds. The poet poses this question in the context of the problem of *fatum* as the factor determining human decisions. The notion of *fatum* is ubiquitous in the *De raptu*,[108] therefore one might, indeed, agree with Rosa María Agudo Cubas that the Carthaginian tries to maintain the 'classical', 'pagan', character of the myth.[109] At the same time though, it does not seem that, as Agudo Cubas states, "en Draconcio, Paris y Helena quedan exculpados por completo de su delito."[110] Undoubtedly, what Paris does is determined by the *fatum*, even by the *impia fata*,[111] but he *also* makes conscious decisions: *Pergama sola placent et moenia quaerere Troiae / m e n s et fata iubent* (ll. 67-68). What is more, he commits a crime, even crimes: he turns out a partial judge, an adulterer, a violator of hospitality. Similarly, as regards the very cause of the war, the narrator points out that it is hard to judge to what extent it was predestined and to what extent it broke out as a result of certain human actions and decisions (to quote once again: *f o r s a n Telamonius Aiax / sternitur invictus, quod mater reddita non est / Hesione Priamo*, ll. 50-52). People – Dracontius seems to imply – may not be wholly free in their choices but, nonetheless, they are *always* responsible, or at least corresponsible, for the evil they do and all the consequences it may bring.

---

[107] Thus Aricò 1978: 72.

[108] Except for the narrator himself, who emphasizes the role of the *fatum* is Helen (whose portrayal in the epyllion cannot be considered a favorable one, in fact) in the scene showing her encounter with Paris: *sis mihi tu coniux et sim tibi dignior uxor. / Hoc nam f a t a i u b e n t vel nos hoc Iuppiter urget* (ll. 534-535), and Apollo: *Pellere pastorem patriis de sedibus unquam / fata vetant, quae magna parant* (ll. 190-191), whose speech is, at least, misleading, see more below in Ch. I. 3. 2.

[109] Agudo Cubas 1978: 266.

[110] Agudo Cubas 1978: 270.

[111] See ll. 57-60: *compellunt audere virum fata, i m p i a f a t a , / quae flecti quandoque negant, quibus obvia nunquam / res quaecunque venit, quis semita nulla tenetur / obvia dum veniunt, quibus omnia clausa patescunt.*

In his Christian writings the Carthaginian poet, already matured in his faith and – what must have had a decisive influence on his 'conversion' – traumatically experienced during his imprisonment, will treat more amply and more profoundly the problem of free will and its limits, as well as the very problem of *unde malum*. What he says in the *De raptu* can be interpreted just as a (first?) trace, a stage maybe of his unique 'spiritual path'.[112] But what seems most important is precisely the fact that it is already in his epyllia (and even as early as in the *De raptu* and not only in the *Orestis Tragoedia*) that Dracontius does not hesitate to pose such fundamental questions.

I. 2. 3. *MEDEA*

The self-consciousness of the poet-narrator, noticeable in the *De raptu*, is all the more characteristic of the *Medea*. In the prologue to the poem, the reader is given some information concerning its nature, its structure, as well as its literary inspirations. There is no reason to disdain it. Quite the contrary, what the poetic *ego* says can turn out to be a very helpful interpretive hint:[113]

Nos illa canemus,
quae solet in lepido Polyhymnia docta theatro
muta loqui, cum nauta venit, cum captus amatur
inter vincla iacens mox regnaturus Iason;
vel quod grande boat[114] *longis sublata cothurnis*
pallida Melpomene, tragicis cum surgit iambis,
quando cruentatam fecit de matre novercam
mixtus amore furor dotata paelice flammis,
squamea viperei subdentes colla dracones
cum rapuere rotis post funera tanta nocentem.
Te modo, Calliope, poscunt optantque sorores:
dulcior ut venias (non[115] *te decet ire rogatam)*
ad sua castra petunt. ... (16-28)

What we learn about the *Medea* is that this *carmen* will treat two different aspects, even two different segments of the story: (1) the arrival and the capture of the Greek sailor, crowned with his unexpected triumph over his would-be killer, and (2) the madness of a betrayed wife who from the mother turns into a cruel 'stepmother' and, eventually, flees in a golden chariot driven by dragons (ll. 17-31). Therefore, the whole epyllion is to be a version, even an epic reinterpretation of themes usually exploited in pantomime

[112] To quote Grillone's (1987: 77) "cammino spirituale."

[113] See below in Chs. I. 3. 3 and I. 4. 3.

[114] I find it worthwhile to accept Bährens's (1883: 193) conjecture here (*boat* instead of *boans*); similarly Kaufmann 2006a: 68 & 123. For the text of the *Medea*, I generally quote the edition by Wolff 1996, but I check also, and sometimes prefer (like here, see besides specific notes below), Kaufmann's lections.

[115] Here I also follow Kaufmann's (2006a: 68) lection, see her notes on p. 129.

and tragedy. Such seems to be the sense of the invocation to Calliope (in ll. 26-28)[116] and the mention of the two Muses, the mute Polyhymnia (l. 17), and the pallid Melpomene (l. 21). In the subsequent chapters, I shall demonstrate that the poet is, indeed, a quite good analyst of his own work.

Metatextual as it is, the prologue to the *Medea* is above all a warning. The story to be told, as well as its very heroine, is appalling. The vocabulary used by the narrator leaves no doubt about it: the word *nefas* is repeated three times (ll. 1, 6, 16), Medea is described as *virgo atra*, a priestess of Diana and *xeinoktonos*, a 'witch-tyrant' exercising her power over gods and the entire nature. The narratorial introduction, indeed, "sets the tone for the whole poem:"[117]

> *Fert animus vulgare nefas et virginis atrae*
> *captivos monstrare deos, elementa clientes,*
> *naturam servire reae, servire puellae,*
> *astra poli et Phoebi cursus et sidera caeli*
> *arbitrio mulieris agi, pendere Tonantem,*
> *quod iubeat Medea nefas ...* (1-6)

> *Licet hospite caeso*
> *serviat et Scythicae currat per templa Dianae,*
> *possidet astrigerum funesto pectore caelum*
> *et superos impune premit prece nixa virago*
> *invitos parere sibi. ...* (9-13)

Still, if the prologue to the *Medea* explains the composition, content, and mood of the epyllion, its epilogue turns into a true *aria di bravura* of the speaking *ego*. The very form of his speech is not casual but fully corresponds with what can be found earlier in the text. The culminating moment of the second part of the poem, the Theban[118] or 'tragic' one as inspired by the pallid Melpomene, are the prayers directed by Medea, betrayed by Jason, to the Gods, especially to Dis and the Furies (ll. 436-460).[119] In fact, Medea prays just like Statius's Oedipus who invokes Tisiphone, asking of her to begin a work of vengeance among his sons (*Theb.* 1.56 ff.). The Forces, summoned by the former priestess of Diana, generate a revenge she herself has not imagined.[120]

---

[116] Similarly Wolff 1996: 189 n. 12, Kaufmann 2006a: 128, and earlier, especially, Aricò 1978: 16-17; in passing Bright 1987: 47-48, see more below in Chs. I. 3. 3 and I. 4. 3.

[117] Bright 1987: 48.

[118] After Schetter's (1980 = 1994: 314-327) brilliant explanation, it is beyond doubt that Dracontius's choice of Thebes as the place of action for the tragic part of the Medea story was not a mistake. In fact, the allusions to Statius's *Thebaid* discovered by Schetter determine the perception of the text.

[119] Medea prays first to Luna (ll. 396-430), next to Dis and the Forces of Evil (ll. 436-460), finally to the Sun (ll. 497-508). As it is clear, prayers are the most important compositional element of this part of the epyllion. As Schetter (1980: 214-216 = 1994: 319-321) emphasizes, these prayers are modeled on those to be found in Seneca's play, the *Medea*, whereas the setting as such is Ovidian.

[120] See especially ll. 527-529: *Stabat sola nocens necdum satiata sacerdos / nec secura tamen: nunquam sic posse venena / credidit aut precibus tantum servire furores*. In this context, see Schet-

Therefore, the narratorial final, which is aimed to be a comment or even a reaction to Medea's horrifying words and deeds must also be composed as a prayer. Indeed, those whom the poet addresses are, among others, the very same Furies invoked earlier by the witch. Consequently, what the reader can observe here is precisely the phenomenon of which I have spoken at the outset of the present chapter: the narrator seems to 'take over' the role of his protagonist in order to respond to, or to 'intervene' in, the situation she has created:

> *Saeve Furor, crudele Nefas, infausta Libido,*
> *Impietas, Furiae, Luctus, Mors, Funera, Livor,*
> *linquite mortales miseroque ignoscite mundo,*
> *parcite iam Thebis, diros cohibete furores.*
> *Inde venit quodcunque nefas* ... (570-574)

The prayer of the poetic *ego* is quite unique, being directed, as we can see, to all the embodiments of evil and starting from an urgent appeal: "leave us, humans, alone!" What follows is a long list of calamities inflicted by the Furies upon the House of Thebes with which the Sisters seem, indeed, to have had a peculiar relationship: Cadmus, Athamas, Palaemon, Jocasta and Oedipus, finally the two fratricides, Eteocles and Polynices (ll. 574-586). This catalogue of the damned of the Theban royal family can be interpreted again as a show of erudition on the part of the epyllic narrator, yet one can hardly ignore its expressiveness.

Only in the second part of his speech, does the poet address some 'positive' divinities, Venus, Amor, and Bacchus. Still, even this invocation does not change the mood of this gloomy song of his. Quite the contrary: these very gods, always cherished by the Thebans, have similarly brought humans only pain and death; in fact – as we shall see – it is they who have played decisive roles in generating the catastrophe of Dracontius's Medea. Thus, the prayer of the narrator eventually turns into a curse, an ultimate rejection and denial of gods:

> *Blanda Venus, lascive puer, Semeleie Bacche,*
> *parcite vos saltem*[121] *Thebis quibus auctor origo*
> *aut soboles praeclara fuit: tibi mater Iacche,*
> *Thebana de stripe †tärtara tibi diones†*[122]
> *Harmoniam nupsisse ferunt: pro munere Thebae*
> *et pro tot meritis sic funera tanta merentur?*
> *Crimen erit genuisse deos! Iam Creta Tonantem*
> *depositum nutrisse neget, iam Delos in undas*

---

ter's (1980: 219 = 1994: 324) positive comments on the conjecture *sorores* for *furores* in l. 529, proposed by Bährens (indeed, the conjecture *sorores* is accepted by Kaufmann 2006a: 96 & 423). The above-mentioned Statian connotation (indicated also by Schetter 1980: 216 = 1994: 321) is particularly relevant as the scene, I argue below, corresponds with a parallel one in the *OT*.

[121] I find Kaufmann's (2006a: 100 & 459) arguments for the lection *saltem* convincing.

[122] In l. 590 Wolff (1996: 75 & 224) accepts Kuijper's (1958: 78) conjecture *et, arator, tibi Diones* (*arator* referring to Cadmus), but it may be found problematic, thus I prefer to follow Kaufmann's (2006a: 100 & 460) prudent conservatism and maintain the *crux*.

fluctuet et paveat partus meruisse deorum,
te Venerem freta vestra negent, abiuret Amores
Cyprus et Idalium pigeat coluisse Dionem,
Vulcanus Lemno, Iuno spernatur ab Argis,
Gorgone terribilis Pallas damnetur Athenis,
sit<que> nefas coluisse deos, quia crimen habetur
religionis honos, cum dat pro laude pericla. (587-601)

This whole passage could be, to some extent, juxtaposed with Catullus's final of *carm.* 64.[123] Nevertheless, what one notices upon a closer look is that the sense of the two closures is completely different, or just the opposite. If Dracontius's allusion was intended (which I would not wholly exclude, in fact), what he gives in his epilogue is a sort of 'anti-Catullan' vision. In Catullus, the immortals, warrants of peace and good, stopped to visit the homes of humans seeing their moral corruption.[124] In Dracontius, it is the human race who, oppressed by the unjust gods, tries to withdraw from any form of contact with the supernatural world.

How should we read this peculiar Dracontius's final? Just as a rumination on the cruelty of gods, not at all untypical of the pagan poets? As an indignation of a Christian, pointing out the failure of the ancient beliefs? Some critics would (and did) certainly argue so.[125] But what it seems to be above all is a cry of a man frightened by the power of evil.

I. 2. 4. *ORESTIS TRAGOEDIA*

A continuation, indeed, a complement of the poet's final cry in the *Medea* can be found only in the epilogue of the *Orestis Tragoedia*, presumably the last and certainly considered the most important among Dracontius's epyllia. Undoubtedly, it is also the poem in which the narrator appears even more active and creative in his speeches than he was in the texts discussed above.

---

[123] As Bright (1987: 79) notes in passing.

[124] See *carm.* 64: *praesentes namque ante domos invisere castas / heroum, et sese mortali ostendere coetu, / caelicolae nondum spreta pietate solebant.* (ll. 384-386); *omnia fanda nefanda malo permixta furore / iustificam nobis mentem avertere deorum. / quare nec talis dignantur visere coetus, / nec se contingi patiuntur lumine claro* (ll. 405-408).

[125] Bright 1987: 80. But compare Schetter's (1980: 220 = 1994: 326) opinion. Recently, the interpretation of Dracontius's *Medea* in Christian terms was proposed by Klein 2001; see also especially the book by Simons 2005 (on the *Medea*, see in particular pp. 155-220). What I find particularly valuable in Simons's study is the emphasis she lays on reading Dracontius's writings, mythological *as well as* Christian, from a proper, literary or even poetological perspective (see her notes on pp. 16-18). This, among others, allows her to avoid reducing the problem of the differences between these two 'areas' of his poetry to the simplifying opposition between '*Dracontius paganus*' and '*Dracontius Christianus*'. Nonetheless, as mentioned above, I am prone to believe that Dracontius's writings reflect also the 'dynamics' of his religious attitude, or – to quote Grillone again – his 'spiritual path'. In this sense, in my view, one could speak of a sort of 'vertical orientation' of his literary output with the *Laudes Dei* in particular defined as the crowning of Dracontius's oeuvre.

Still, before we focus on the conclusion of the *OT*, let us start from its prologue, in which the poetic *ego* speaks, first of all, as a critic of his own work, just like he does in the *Medea*. The metatextual hint he gives merits a closer reading, especially among those modern analysts who would tend to interpret the title of Dracontius's poem as a generic label.[126] What the poet emphasizes is the *epic* character of his text, despite its tragic theme. Melpomene is asked to 'step down' from her tragic cothurns since the iambics are to be replaced by the dactylic meter. Concise as it is, this phrase is also very precise:

---

[126] Kelly (1993: 26) in his very helpful study on tragedy notes: "It is disputed whether Dracontius himself was responsible for the title, but it is beyond question that someone, a copyist at least, considered the work a tragedy. It is a quite natural development, similar to that recorded by Placidus: one of the meanings of <<scene>> is any poem fit to be performed with tragic exclamations in the theater. Presumably Placidus is speaking of reciting rather than acting the poems." What Kelly notes in general, as regards the development of the term 'tragedy' and its usage, is correct, but the problem, especially the problem of Dracontius's use of the word *tragedy*, merits a closer explanation. In fact, it seems more reasonable than not to consider the title authentic, i.e. 'authorial' (thus I myself maintain it). The lengthy scholarly dispute on the question was summarized by Bouquet (1995: 161-162 n. 1) in his commentary. What is emphasized by the French editor is the fact that the authenticity of the title seems to be corroborated by Dracontius's invocation of Melpomene in the very text. Certainly, the meaning of the term 'tragedy' as used here can be explained as 'tragic history' (this understanding of the term will become, obviously enough, common in the Middle Ages). Rapisarda (1964: 37) notes that this sense of the word, i.e. "casi luttuosi, triste storia," was common to the ancient authors from Cicero to Lactantius. He continues: "la scelta di tale vocabolo da parte di Draconzio è dovuta al fatto che egli intendeva cantare <<i casi di Oreste>>, noti attraverso le varie rappresentazioni tragiche. Né è da vedere contraddizione alcuna tra il senso di *tragoedia* e la fine dell'epillio, poiché fin da Omero la storia di Oreste si conclude con lieto fine, ed in Eschilo con l'assoluzione di Oreste e la trasformazione delle Erinni in Eumenidi." Still, already quoted Aricò (1978: 12-13) adds justly, referring also to the very problem of the authenticity of the title: "L'argomento dell'*OT* ci riconduce ... a una tradizione tragica ... Era quindi naturale che la cultura tardoantica, e quindi anche quella, retorica e scolastica, dell'Africa vandala, continuasse a sentire il mito di Oreste come legato al genere drammatico. Questo fatto ci è confermato dal titolo dell'epillio draconziano: *Orestis tragoedia* nella forma attestata da *B* – confermata (se ce ne fosse bisogno), piuttosto che smentita, dall'altra che si legge in *A*: *Horestis fabula* – e ora generalmente accettata. Questo titolo … è stato interpretato … come allusivo al carattere luttuoso della vicenda ... Interpretazione senza dubbio esatta, ma che coglie solo una parte della verità: Draconzio ... ha ancora un chiaro senso delle forme letterarie, e in particolare della tragedia." Further, referring also to the above-quoted passage of the *Medea*, Aricò argues, in my view wholly convincingly, that Dracontius's allusions to the tragic genre must be read as a declaration of *aemulatio*: his goal is, precisely, to compete through his epic poem with tragic versions of the two stories (the *Medea furens* and the Oresteia theme). His epyllion is to emulate, in a sense, the tragedy. In my opinion, this is the very point (see also below in Ch. I. 4. 4). Schetter (1985: 51), whose contribution to Dracontian studies can hardly be overestimated, proposes the title *Orestes* as analogous to the titles *Medea* and *Hylas*. He strongly emphasizes the epyllic character of the poem, hence his later (1991a) vehement (maybe too vehement, in fact) reaction to Bright's proposals. Bright (1987: 202) goes as far as to note: "the poet conceives of the poem as essentially a drama, not as a narrative genre," which, in my view too, is definitely exaggerated, see more below in Ch. I. 4. 4.

Te rogo, Melpomene, tragicis descende cothurnis
et pede dactylico resonante quiescat iambus:
da valeam memorare nefas laudabile nati
et purgare foro quem damna<*vere sorores*> (13-16)[127]

Nevertheless, what attracts the reader's attention in the passage quoted above, apart from (again) the poet's theorico-literary competence, is yet another detail. The speaking *ego* openly declares the aim of his poem and even of his view of the Oresteia theme: *purgare foro quem damnavere sorores*. Apparently, he has no intention whatsoever to be an 'objective' narrator. Quite the contrary, his main goal is to tell, or rather retell, the story in a way that will eventually allow a similar 'happy ending'. Indeed, upon a closer look one notices that this initial premise is realized with so to speak mathematical precision: the narratorial interventions – intrusions, if one wishes – explaining or emphasizing certain aspects (not limited just to prologues and epilogues, like in the previous epyllia), quite a few reinterpretations, or simply changes of some crucial motifs, all this leads to the final *purgatio Orestis* as promised in the introduction. In fact, it is promised by the narrator who – the thing seems worth noting – almost poses as an advocate for the title character's cause. Once again, like before in the *De raptu*, Dracontius's speaking *ego* admits that he does have something in common with Dracontius the lawyer, as if he were joking at the expense of all those critics who would fear to identify the author with his literary 'I'.

The third element to be found in the prologue to the *OT* is the usual – in fact, as also argued above, usual not only in Dracontius's poems but in the Roman epyllion in general – stress on the moral interpretation of the story. As we recall, the very first words of the *Medea* pointed at the crime (*nefas*) and the criminality of the heroine, the *virgo atra*. What we face in the *OT* is only partially similar. As we can see, the poet's main subject will be *nefas laudabile* (l. 15). The sequence of oxymorons given at the very outset of the poem,[128] a bit boring as it may be – not for the late antique reader though – is a clear signal that this time the poet's attention will be focused on a case which, although horrifying, in certain circumstances, can be morally acceptable.

As I have already mentioned, in the *OT* the narrator's voice is heard much more often than in the other two epyllia (*Hylas* does not count here) and his every appearance marks a crucial moment of the action. After the prologue, his next intervention takes place following the scene of the regicide. His speech, first typically 'epic' – the narrator compares the dead king to a wild boar caught in nets by hunters (ll. 265-268) – turns into an emotional lament: *sic Asiae domitor consumptus fine cruenta: / heu, pastoralis populavit membra securis* (ll. 269-270). Indeed, one may have an impression that what we hear now is the song of lamentation of the tragic chorus weeping the catastrophe of the protagonist. What suggests such interpretation is the very first sentence (*Aspera sors hominum* ff.), yet

[127] For the text of the *Orestis Tragoedia*, I follow the recent edition by Grillone 2008.

[128] The very first line of the poem being: *Gaudia maesta canam detestandosque triumphos*. To quote only those describing Orestes: *matris in exitium memorem oblitumque parentis, / impietate pium, reprobae probitatis Orestem, / iniustos, sed iure, deos ratione feroci / insontemque reum* (ll. 7-10). On Dracontius's (excessive) use of oxymorons and paradoxes, see recently Bouquet 1995: 162 n. 2.

the 'moral' given in the second part of the passage (*discite felices* ff.) sounds even more typical of a '*kommós*':[129]

> *Aspera sors hominum vel mens ignara futuri!*
> *credere quis posset, si centum flatibus acta,*
> *Delphica fatidicos quateret cortina recessus,*
> *antra movens tripodasque ciens et plectra fatigans,*
> *eversorem Asiae foderet quod cultor agelli*
> *aut desertor iners, ovium pecorumque magister?*
> *et caret igne rogi, dederat qui Pergama flammis!*
> *discite felices non umquam credere fatis.*
> *sunt faciles dare summa dei, tamen ante relinquunt*
> *et miseros in fine nocent, aut forte repente*
> *destituunt poenasque petunt de sorte secunda.*
> *credere qui non vult, Priameia fata revolvat,*
> *atque Agamemnoniam videat male credulus aulam.* (271-283)

Antonino Grillone notes rightly that this lament is performed by the poet in the name of his *dramatis personae*,[130] the Mycenaeans who have just witnessed so horrible and not justifiable a crime. The desperation of the speaker perfectly matches the context but does not seem to be appropriate of the omniscient narrator who is – and indeed should be – aware of the future events and has – should have – a global view of the entire story. Thus, in this moment (once again, like before in the *adlocutio sponsalis* of the *De raptu* and in the final prayer-curse of the *Medea*, but now even more clearly) the speaking *ego* degrades his very self and turns from a "narrator possessive of his leading role" into a mere *dramatis persona* or dramatic *chorus*. For a while he 'disposes' of his main attribute, precisely the omniscience, to see the world exactly as his characters do, obviously the 'good' characters (i.e. Dorilas and the Mycenaeans).[131]

The longest[132] of all narratorial passages of the *OT*, devoted wholly to the two regicides and their 'rule', is particularly interesting. The literary 'I' re-assumes his original

---

[129] One need not look beyond Sophocles's *Oedipus* and the final song of the choir (ll. 1526-1532; but see also earlier, 1185-1222) to find an excellent comparison. In fact, I am rather doubtful as regards Dracontius's knowledge of Greek, thus I would not suggest a direct allusion, yet reading the *OT* and, even more, the tragic part of the *Medea* makes me always see, and indeed admire, his deep understanding of tragic literary strategies (see more below in Ch. I. 4. 3 as well as in my paper on the *Medea*, Wasyl 2007a: 96-98).

[130] Grillone 2008: 117, com. to ll. 271-283: "Draconzio si limita qui a dar voce ai sentimenti dell'uomo comune, adeguandosi alla più diffusa reazione emotiva. Ma non è questa la sua posizione."

[131] Which in fact seems to be an example of the phenomenon of which Conte (2007: 53) spoke in reference to the grand Virgilian epic: the narrator here truly allows "the sentiments of the characters in the action to invade the text." Rare as it may be in the epyllic tradition as such, it happens here in this passage of the *OT*.

[132] Especially ll. 413-452. The history of its own seems to have the problem of the placement of ll. 427-452, but I find fully convincing the arguments provided by Grillone (2008: 126-127, com. to ll. 427-452) who simply leaves the passage where it originally was, explaining how to understand the most problematic moments of the text. Above, I read the passage in the version given by the

role of the observer and judge of his protagonists. The opinion he gives on Aegisthus is not at all hard to guess, but the portrayal of a shepherd-tyrant who cannot be a (decent) king[133] turns out quite expressive. Truly captivating though is the segment dedicated to the Mycenaeans, the citizens seeing the 'coup d'état', so to speak. The poet seems to be asking – and his voice sounds surprisingly 'modern' – "how did it happen, how was it possible that people so valiant in battle turned into slaves, and turned thus so easily?" In fact, one might even say that the question Dracontius poses, to his own self as well as to his audience, does not seem much different from those posed so many times by the twentieth century intellectuals witnessing the evils of the dictatorships of their era. The narrator's language is precise, though emotionally marked as the rhetorical question: *quis rogo non gemeret*? (l. 422) and the pejoratives: *bubulcus* (l. 423), *verbero plectibilis* (l. 426)[134] clearly indicate:

> *sceptra triumphorum data sub pastore tyranno*
> *pro pretio scelerum, mercedem sanguinis ostrum,*
> *matronale nefas, uxorem dedecus aulae,*
> *quis rogo non gemeret? tamen hos formido iubebat*
> *infami parere novo: timuere bubulcum*
> *acrius, Hectoreos qui non timuere furores.*
> *ius Agamemnonium fuerat; post Pergama capta,*
> *verbero plectibilis, comes armipotentis Achillis*
> *possedit regnum. ...* (419-427)

His attitude turns more personal in the very following passage in which he addresses directly Clytemnestra; in fact, Clytemnestra is the only protagonist of the *OT* to whom the poet speaks. It would be incorrect to argue that here again the narratorial *ego* enters into the world of his characters – more than ever does he act now as a judge – but here also he does not hide his involvement and his 'moral' interest in the story. Needless to say, Dracontius's narrator once more proves to be a model epyllic narrator.

What the poet's voice of condemnation emphasizes is, above all, the scale of Clytemnestra's crime. He gives her examples of other female criminals, whose acts, however, could be justified, at least to some extent, as, indeed, crimes of passion. The speaker here is certainly, again, Dracontius the lawyer (or his textual 'I') but also Dracontius the human being, understanding human cases, complicated as they may be. In addition – the poet continues – those women were Barbarians (or barbarous[135]). Clytemnestra, being

---

Italian scholar. For the summary of the discussion on textual problems, see also Grillone's com. to ll. 425-427; 427-452; 427b-36a (pp. 125-127).

[133] See ll. 413-418: *Sed vilis adulter, / nescius atque rudis regnorum frena tenere, / ipse sibi genium fastu facit. ore minaci / asper erat famulis regalibus, advena servis; / imperium non mite dabat quibus, ipse profecto / si famularetur, crimen sibi turpe putarent.*

[134] For the understanding of the expression and the entire passage, see Grillone 2008: 126, com. to ll. 425-427: "Prima aveva avuto il potere Agamennone; dopo la presa di Troia si impadronì del regno, da compagno dell'armipotente Achille, un mascalzone degno di percosse [sc. Egisto]."

[135] According to Grillone (2008: 127, com. to ll. 427b-36a), *barbara turba* refers to the Lemniades, who are Greek (see also his comments to l. 969 on pp. 160-161). Thus (the Italian scholar does not point it out but it seems quite logical in such a context), the adjective actually implies

a daughter of Greece, the mother of the Laws, should have imitated respectable models. It is worth noting how a typical – schoolish, if one wishes – literary device like the catalogue, if elaborated by the Carthaginian, turns into an efficient means of expression:

> *Tamyris regina Getarum,*
> *sed nil turpe gerens, vindex fuit illa suorum;*
> *si fecit Medea nefas, flammata dolore*
> *dulcis amoris erat, cum regia tecta cremabat,*
> *incolumi viduata viro de paelice Glauce;*
> *impia Lemniades sumpserunt arma puellae*
> *atque maritali foedarunt sanguine lectos:*
> *sed Veneris furor acer erat. facinusque nefandum*
> *quod Scythicae gessere nurus; in crimine tanto*
> *barbara turba fuit. nam tu, regina Pelasgum,*
> *Graecia quam genuit legum fecunda creatrix,*
> *clara Mycenaei coniunx et vindicis uxor,*
> *crimen adulterii geminasti caede mariti!*
> *Alcestis meminisse fuit, quae morte maritum*
> *manibus eripuit, pia coniugis, impia de se.*
> *quid loquar Euadnen* ... (427-442)

Nevertheless, the most important, indeed crucial, narratorial speech can be found as always in the epilogue. The epilogue of the *OT* is strongly interrelated with the one of the *Medea*, as dedicated to the very same fundamental problem of the *measure of evil*. Another point of convergence is the fact that in both these poems the finals correspond with certain, particularly relevant, moments of the action as such. In the *Medea*, as we remember, the poet's prayer, or curse thrown on the (pagan) gods, was an answer to the main protagonist's invocation of the Furies. In the *OT*, a careful reader will notice an analogous scene. The faithful Mycenaeans, led by Dorilas, the tutor and savior of Orestes, demanding justice and punishment of the regicides, try to conjure the spirit of the murdered king and (just in case, one could add) summon also, precisely, the Furies (ll. 488 ff.). The whole passage is a clear allusion to Statius's *Thebaid* 1.56 ff., but as such echoes also the parallel episode of the *Medea*[136] (apparently Dracontius expects from his readership a comparative reading of his works). What is more, and what should not be omitted, it seems Dorilas himself is the one to 'remember' the relevant scene of the *Medea* as he adds somewhat anxiously: *sed dubito quia iusta peto*[137] (l. 490), as if he just thought of the horrible effects of the similar prayer directed to the Sisters by the former priestess of Diana.

Therefore, the narratorial epilogue in the *OT*, like before in the *Medea*, imitates the form of speech employed within the plot by one of the characters, as if once again the poet felt obliged to intervene, eventually taking over the role of his protagonist(s). But

that the Lemniades acted *as if* they were Barbarians, i.e. 'barbarously'. *Scythicae nurus*, in Grillone's view, refers to Tamyris and Medea. Tamyris is mentioned also in the catalogue providing *exempla feminarum* in the *Laudes Dei* 3.501-506.

[136] Bright 1987: 166 notices it in passing.

[137] On the reading of *sed* at the beginning of the verse, see quoted above Grillone 2008: 131, com. to ll. 490 ff.

this parallel between the two poems is aimed only at emphasizing the most significant thing, i.e. the differences. In the *Medea*, those whom the poet addressed were, first, the Furies and other forces of evil. Consequently, his 'prayer' turned into a rejection and a denial of all gods, including those that could (should?) be seen as warrants of human love, joy, and peace: Amor, Venus, Bacchus, Jove, Diana, Apollo, Vulcan, Juno, and Athena. What was indicated as a unique 'heritage' of the presence of the Furies, and the forces of evil in general, in the world were the crimes and the calamities which befall the humanity. In the *Orestis Tragoedia*, the narrator's prayer is directed to all gods of all the four elements, invoked in the name of supreme human values: *pietas miseranda, mitis honestas, bona simplicitas, affectus sanguinis*, even *consortia sancta cruoris, stemmata generis, cognatio iuncta*. Therefore, what is emphasized in the final of this, undoubtedly, most important Dracontius's epyllion, is one particular factor – the goodness of a human being. This whole 'catalogue' conveys a profoundly 'humanistic' message, so to speak, as it presents a human being as a creature who is able to be good and to do good. We should note that in the *Medea* the goodness of humans was also mentioned, but there it seemed miserably weak, indeed ignorable, if assessed against the power of evil (*pro tot meritis sic funera tanta merentur*, l. 592). Now, in the *OT* the poet appears to believe, or to start to believe that good – even the good as embodied by the humans, frail as they are – may prevail over evil, even though it can happen only gods (or rather God) willing (*Di* ... *parcite* ... *arcete*). Thus, what the speaking *ego* prays for is a sort of a divine intervention so that evil, too often generated also by the human beings (hence, again, the horrible examples), would not win out. What is different though in comparison with the epilogue to the *Medea*, it is, as I have suggested above, the proportions. And also the very fact that what is mentioned now as primary are the positive values:

Di quibus imperio est facilis concessa Tonantis
aeris et pelagi, terrae caelique potestas,
vos pietas miseranda rogat, vos mitis honestas,
vos bona simplicitas, affectus sanguinis orat,
vos genus humanum, consortia sancta cruoris,
stemmata vos generis, cognatio iuncta precatur.
crimina Lemniadum sat erant, Danaeia facta,
quae thalamos fecere rogos, et facta Thyestis
innumerumque nefas, quod sit narrare pudoris.
ecce Mycenaea triplex iam scaena profanat
Graiugenum famam: vestro iam parcite mundo
atque usum scelerum miseris arcete Pelasgis! (963-974)

One can have an impression that these are the words of someone who has found (anew?) at least some hope and, maybe in a sense, faith.[138] Therefore, it seems all the more

[138] My 'moderately optimistic' reading of the final of the *OT* (indeed, what I emphasize above all is the fact that the reader should pay attention to the differences between the tenor of the two epilogues, of the *Medea* and the *OT*) does not mean that I am wholly 'Rapisardian' in my general view of the poem. As I have noted above, Dracontius's religious attitude is, in my opinion, interpretable rather as a process dynamic in its nature.

reasonable to interpret Dracontius's epyllia as traces of his unique spiritual path;[139] the next stage of which will be further comments on the origins and measure of evil, on God's presence in the world, as well as in the lives of the individuals, comments to be no longer found in poems treating Paris, Medea, or the House of Atreus, but in the *Laudes Dei*.

Is then Dracontius's miniature epic, especially the two texts: the *Medea* and the *OT*, readable as a polemic against the pagan myth as such? It is certainly probable that some readers would (and did) conclude so, in particular hearing the poet's blasphemous 'prayer' in the final of the *Medea*. It seems though that the interpretation of the aims and the message of Dracontius's 'traditional' poetry does not have to be – and should not be – so unilateral. For what we can discover in it is not only a mere *reductio ad absurdum* of a mythical theme or a censure of the view of the world as given in the ancient myth. What we find there is rather (and above all) an attitude of a man who seeks answers to fundamental questions concerning human responsibility for evil and the very measure of evil.

Dracontius, a person of well-defined literary culture, tried first to approach these problems through a 'fictitious' mythological story and through the epyllion form, the form – as we know and as our poet appears to have realized himself – used by his predecessors, the Latin Neoterics and the Augustans, precisely to diagnose the moral condition of their contemporaries. It is only with time that he decided to express his fears as well as his hopes in prayers addressed to the very God in whom he truly believed and to share these prayers, intimate as they are, with his literary audience. In this perspective, the *Orestis Tragoedia* seems to be, in fact, a 'farewell' bidden to the world of the ancient myth: we should note the pronoun *vestro* (l. 973) already implying a distance. But one should also emphasize that this 'goodbye' does not turn into a 'curse'; on the contrary: the poet seems to be lifting the curse thrown on the pagan gods in the last words of the *Medea*. Parting with the protagonists of the cruel ancient myth, humans as well as immortals, the poet-narrator gives them a unique goodbye gift: his own hope, the hope that the measure of evil is full and that good may prevail.

I. 3. Dracontius and the poetics of 'non-Homeric' epic

In Chapter I. 1, recapitulating the most important features of the epyllion, I have used the expression 'non-Homeric epic'. In fact, the 'minor' epic seems to have developed some of its crucial qualities in opposition, so to speak, to its noble predecessor. These are the very characteristics concerning the choice of the main subject, its elaboration, the way in which the protagonists, gods not less than humans, are portrayed. All these elements are related to the new ideological profile of the genre, indeed much different from the one that was idiosyncratic of the heroic epic. Thus, I have mentioned: selection of less popular, minor motifs or 'other' versions of the ostensibly well-known tales, a different narrative style, more episodic, with marginalization or elimination of some parts of the story between one unit and another, and – quasi-dramatic – division of the action into

[139] I have argued so above in Ch. I. 2. 2 already discussing the *De raptu*.

often not fully coordinated scenes. I have also indicated a certain reduction, sometimes even subversion, of 'epic' values which results in the heroes often revealing a kind of 'bourgeois' character. Finally, I have pointed out an emphasis put on the psychological dimension of a story or a persona.

It is enough just to look through Dracontius's poems to conclude that they show almost all of these features. Consequently, their 'epyllicness' seems to be proven; in fact, as I have already noted, is seems to be proven by the very themes they treat. However, what I have also emphasized above, the main goal of my analyses here is not to demonstrate *that* our poet did write epyllia; what I rather want to stress and determine is *how* he used this unique literary heritage, i.e. the literary strategies typical of the epyllic tradition, when composing his four mythological texts. I shall concentrate on this question in the present as well as in the subsequent chapter in which I shall dedicate more attention to Dracontius's exploitation of various generic devices.

I. 3. 1. *HYLAS*

The merely 163-verses long *Hylas* is most probably a sort of school exercise,[140] an elaboration of a well-known (and, needless to say, well-trodden) motif and as such does differ in certain points from other epyllia by Dracontius. One can hardly say anything specific about its narrator, except for the fact that he does not seem to be the narrator-moralist speaking so willingly and so openly in *De raptu*, *Medea*, and the *OT*. The message of the poem is also rather far from tragic.[141] Nevertheless, this *juvenilium*, charming as it is, shows also certain qualities to be found later in Dracontius's more 'mature' mythological texts. In addition, it is quite unique in its *gratia* and *variatio*, i.e. features idiosyncratic of the epyllion tradition.[142]

The poem is composed of a few subsequent and almost, one might argue, self-contained scenes, a sort of 'pictures' that could be entitled, as Bright proposed: "Venus and Cupid," "Transformation of Cupid," "Capture of Hylas," "Lament of Hercules."[143] What seems even more relevant, the ostensibly main theme, the very capture of Hylas, is treated rather curtly (within 45 lines in sum), although structurally it is well-placed as the pen-

---

[140] As noted at the end of Ch. I. 1, Díaz de Bustamante (1978: 137) labels it as a "*declamatio scholastica*."

[141] On the final lament by Hercules, see more below in Ch. I. 4. 1. On the other hand, Agudo Cubas (1978: 307-308) notes shrewdly that it should not be argued that the very Hylas theme as such is much less tragic than, for example, the theme of the rape of Helen. It was certainly the poet's conscious decision to elaborate the story of Paris and Helen as tragic, not as romantic (see my own comments in Ch. I. 2. 2). In other words, it must have also been his conscious decision to present the Hylas theme the way he did, as a 'charming' story rather than as a 'tragic' one.

[142] As emphasized especially by Styka (1994: 157-166; 1995: 220-229) in his study on the neoteric epyllion, in particular Catullus's *carm.* 64. On *gratia* and *varietas* as categories of late antique literary aesthetics in general, see recently Styka 2008: 91-102. On *variatio* in the *Hylas* as the main factor behind the composition of the poem, see also the concluding remarks in Weber 1995: 248-256.

[143] Bright 1987: 28.

ultimate episode.[144] The opening scene is much longer (66 lines out of 163, which is over one third of the whole text) and shows the conversation, or rather the exchange of speeches, between Venus and her son: the goddess asks her little boy to punish Clymene "who has been rehearsing the story of her dalliance with Mars."[145] An apt punishment for the nymph should be making her fall in love with Hercules's companion.[146] Consequently, the leading actors in the whole epyllion are the two divinities, of whom Cupid turns out even more important. It is Cupid, disguised as a nymph, whom we also see play with the naiads in the following episode. It is Cupid of course to make Clymene and her sisters desperately fall for Hylas. Finally, it is Cupid who informs Hercules what has happened to his beloved.

One can have an impression that our poet finds particular pleasure in describing Amor. He portrays him first as a lovely child on his mother's lap, a bit impatient, if not rude indeed as he interrupts Venus, who is just about to formulate her request,[147] and starts to boast enumerating the victims of his bow.[148] Cupid seems not less charming in the subsequent scene in which we see him, first, approach the spring[149] and throw a little stone into the water to wake up the nymphs and, next, disguise himself as one of them.[150]

The child Hylas is similarly beautiful, yet, if compared with Amor, he turns out a mere pawn,[151] having no influence whatsoever on the action as such. Hylas, like Cupid, is quite amusing in his somewhat vain behavior when he strives to carry the Erymanthian boar's hide (ll. 95-97)[152] as if it were his trophy. Later on, he is not only amusing but also moving when we see him captured by the nymphs and crying helplessly.

---

[144] Agudo Cubas (1978: 309) is right to argue that even the very proem to the *Hylas* shows that the poet is only marginally interested in his main theme as such. I need not add once again that this is an epyllic feature par excellence.

[145] To quote Bright (1987: 23), who also notices that the motif of Venus's revenge as the catalyst of action cannot be found in any other version of the story. On the other hand, as Bright adds, "it is popular in late African poets, and it is reasonable to assume that Dracontius himself introduced it here."

[146] Malamud (1993: 164) notes that "this will be a punishment, not a favour, to the nymphs because they will be frustrated at having to wait so long for Hylas to reach maturity."

[147] On Venus's submissive tone, see more below in Ch. I. 4. 1.

[148] It is in his longish catalogue – quite alarming in its tone in fact as all love stories mentioned here are rather incestuous (Bright 1987: 34) – that we find the mention of Perdica's story, elaborated later by the anonymous poet in the *Aegritudo Perdicae* (on the chronology as well as on the poem itself, see more below in Ch. I. 6).

[149] The whole scene takes place *Penei sub fonte* (l. 54), which, among other details, is a clear signal that Dracontius chose a Virgilian setting for his story, alluding especially to *Georg.* 4.515 ff., the Aristaeus episode. On the analogies between the two texts, see especially Martin Puente 1997.

[150] On the pantomimic connotations of the scene, see more below in Ch. I. 4. 1.

[151] See Bright (1987: 33) who is right to note that in fact the poem is about Cupid rather than Hylas. "As in the classical epyllia, the actual focus of interest is not the nominal topic. And, as often in the Hylas tradition, the beautiful youth is a mere pawn."

[152] Certainly, the very negligence with which Dracontius treats the motif of the Erymanthian boar can be also interpreted in terms of epyllic travesty.

The focus on this pair of lovely, though spoiled, children is certainly inspired by the aesthetic principle of *gratia*, idiosyncratic of the Greek Alexandrian poetics and later imitated by the Latin Neoterics practicing the epyllion form. The epyllic feature is also a peculiar reinterpretation, a travesty in fact, of the figure of heroic Hercules shown as a powerless and rather pathetic lamenter.[153] Finally, what must be treated as epyllic is the image of Venus wishing to take revenge on the nymph and the very motif of the divine wrath as the factor behind the action. It should be added though that in this poem it is not so much the anger of the goddess and her vengefulness that draws the reader's attention; the charm of the boy protagonists is too attractive. If we juxtapose the wrath of Venus in the *Hylas* and its consequences – which are quite positive in sum: the little Hercules's companion turns immortal (hence *Fata canam … versa … in melius* in the prologue, ll. 1-2) – with the anger of Juno in the *Ciris* or the curse thrown by Diana on her priestess in Dracontius's own *Medea*, and what they brought to the two heroines, we can see quite clearly how distant our poet's juvenile epyllion is from texts showing tragedies of human protagonists, punished more or less justly by gods.

I. 3. 2. *DE RAPTU HELENAE*

Analyzing the *Hylas* we have noted that it is composed of a few practically separate scenes which combine into a sort of logical unity, but not so much into a seamless narration.[154] The *De raptu* is more than similar in this respect, the only difference being the fact that it is a poem much richer in its literary and compositional diversity.

The text can be easily divided into five segments.[155] The first scene takes place in Troy and shows Paris's arrival to the city, during a religious festival as it appears, and his 'revelation' (*se velit ostendi regni de stripe creatum*, l. 118) to his parents and siblings. Nevertheless, the culminating point of this unit is not so much the self-presentation of the shepherd-prince, even though it says quite much about the character of the protagonist and turns out fully convincing to his parents, but rather the dramatic[156] contrast between the speeches of the twin seers, Helenus and Cassandra, and their divine patron, Apollo. Helenus and Cassandra demand that the brother be killed as he embodies the future catastrophe of Troy and it is only due to the intervention of Apollo, who appears as a true *deus ex machina*, that the newcomer is ultimately welcomed.

A particularly controversial compositional element seems to be the second scene treating the Salaminian mission of Paris, his goal being of course to ask Telamon to return Hesione. The episode is introduced by a short conversation between Paris and Priam

---

[153] Needless to say, Heracles is often presented as a comic hero and as such he is just a model character for the epyllic rewriting. Thus, I must repeat, I do not wholly understand why Bright (1987: 41-42) argues so vehemently for the Christian anti-pagan treatment by Dracontius.

[154] Which, in fact, fully concords with what Roberts (1989a: 3) observed emphasizing that in late antique poetics "the seams not only show, they are positively advertised."

[155] Which is perfectly emphasized by the employment of different generic strategies in each of these segments, see more below in Ch. I. 4. 2.

[156] On the generic connotations of the scene, see Ch. I. 4. 2.

who willingly sends his son with so responsible a task, wishing him, quite fatally in effect, *dat Venus uxorem, faciet te Iuno maritum* (l. 229). Thus, Paris sets out as a legate together with Antenor, Polydamas, and Aeneas, even though, paradoxically, he is the only one among the Trojan legates not to even open his mouth.[157]

The whole segment, composed of three lengthy speeches by Antenor, Telamon, and Polydamas, closed with a shorter "final statement"[158] by Aeneas, shows the full range of Dracontius's rhetorical abilities. The moderate speech by Antenor (*placida voce*) is a skillful mixture of a request and a threat: Hesione, taken once as a captive, should now be returned, otherwise the new war may turn out inevitable and since Troy is again strong, it would not be advisable to provoke her. Telamon's answer, full of emotions and anger, the just anger as the narrator adds (ll. 285-290),[159] is almost a declaration of war. The king of Salamis points out through a series of rhetorical questions that what he expects from the resurrected Troy is a dowry, as Hesione is his legitimate wife; if not, her son Ajax, as well as an army of heroes (ll. 321-326), will certainly demand it. Finally, the third speech by Polydamas, delivered *submissa voce*, is aimed at easing the tension. Polydamas refers to some arguments emphasized by Telamon, accepting them (at least ostensibly) and trying to use them to his own rhetorical advantage. He praises the justice and the clemency of the Salaminian king who has turned a captive into a legitimate spouse, through which she herself, and in her person the whole Troy in a sense, has gained the status of the queen of the Greeks. Telamon, apparently missing the ironic overtone, is mollified, but the problem itself remains unresolved. Aeneas, in his brief farewell, promises that the legates will repeat to Priam the king's words and wishes Telamon to grow old in peace at the same time extolling Ajax's skill-at-arms (the tragic irony is just too obvious).[160]

The unit is remarkable as a literary exercise, but some readers could find it rather difficult to explain its role within the structure of the whole poem. Especially, if one takes into consideration the fact that the subsequent episodes concentrate only on Paris and his encounter with Helen, whereas in the Salaminian scene Paris is virtually absent. Most probably, it should be concluded that the lengthy passage is but a *purpureus pannus*, in the very late antique understanding of the term though: not as a drawback, a useless purple patch (which was Horace's original sense of course), but on the contrary, as an embellishment, positively advertised by Servius or Sidonius.[161] It is worth noting, however,

[157] As pointed out with similar irony by Bright 1987: 103.

[158] Bright 1987: 106.

[159] What Dracontius emphasizes again are the marital rights, the crucial motif of the whole poem. Bright (1987: 110) is right to suggest that in a sense Telamon, who married the captive legitimately, stands in sharp contrast to Paris, the future violator of marriage.

[160] For a more thorough analysis of the three major speeches, see Bright 1987: 107-113. Compare also Simons 2005: 248-251.

[161] On late antique misunderstanding of the Horatian passage, see Roberts 1989a: 68 n. 8; 116. Significant are especially Servius's comments, *ad Aen.* 10.653, and Sidonius's *carm.* 22.6 (on which, see the recent comments in Styka 2008: 165-166). As regards the whole Salaminian scene, it can also be interpreted as an indication of Dracontius's contamination of the two sources, Virgil and Dares, as Schetter (1987) and (independently) Bright (1987: 104-117) argue. See besides Simons 2005: 251-262.

that the Salaminian episode, a detachable compositional element as it is, brings also some important information about the plot as such, in particular the events to come. A careful reader should remember that in his narratorial introduction the poet has emphasized that the Trojan war, apparently, had two major determinants, one was supernatural, the *Fatum*, the other human: *forsan Telamonius Aiax / sternitur invictus, quod mater reddita non est / Hesione Priamo* (ll. 50-52). The Salaminian scene sheds some light upon exactly the latter of the two causes. Besides, through the employment of variegated rhetorical strategies, it shows with admirable precision the attitudes of the two sides of the future conflict, stressing the already easily noticeable tension. As the narrator adds in his comments, the Trojan legates: *Ramos frondentis olivae / portantes ad tecta ducis sub imagine pacis / non pacem, sed bella gerunt; nam dicta tenebant, / quae possent armare virum* (ll. 254-257).[162] The threats to be implied from Antenor's speech and the arrogance of Telamon are also too obvious. One can even wonder if Priam is to be given credence saying earlier to Paris: *Nusquam bella paro, regnum sub pace guberno* (l. 223).

Michael Roberts notes in his study dedicated to late antique poetics: "late antiquity preferred juxtaposition and contrast to logical interrelationship; contiguity no longer required continuity. The impression of an organic whole, the sense of proportion, is lost, but it is compensated for by the elaboration of the individual episode. Late antique poetry has its own unity, but it is conceptual and transcends the immediate historical content of a narrative."[163] As it seems, Dracontius's Salaminian episode exemplifies this very phenomenon. A competent reader is able to see that this single segment together with others, to which it only appears unrelated, combine into one picture: of the genesis of the Trojan war, the war caused by the divine wrath, yet also by human attitudes and actions.

After the Salaminian episode, the next three scenes focus already on Paris and the circumstances of his encounter with Helen. The immediate factor behind the prince's arrival to Cyprus – where Dracontius sets the action[164] – is a storm at sea,[165] liberating the youngster from the company of his 'tutors' (or officially co-legates). Left alone, Paris arrives to the island during a festival of Venus,[166] to which Helen has also come, similarly unaccompanied by her husband. Thus, it is in Cyprus, the island of Venus, that the ill-fated couple finally meets. An attraction could hardly be more instant and the determination of the two lovers is perfectly rendered by Helen's words: *sis mihi tu coniux et sim tibi dignior uxor* (l. 534). Soon, they decide to elope together: *Dixit et egressi puppes et litora poscunt* (l. 540) and, despite Menelaus's chase (all of the sudden the king of Sparta arrives to Cyprus), they luckily manage to reach the ship and sail away, leaving the lamenting husband on the bank.

---

[162] Worth noting is still the next point made by the poet: *nisi iura vetarent / hospitii, quae nemo parat violare modestus* (ll. 257-258). Apparently, Telamon is indeed portrayed as a sort of anti-Paris.

[163] Roberts 1989a: 56-57.

[164] As Bright (1987: 120-123) emphasizes, Dracontius relocated the scene to Cyprus, but, apparently, he used also a source which placed the abduction in Sparta and did not eliminate some of the Spartan details.

[165] Which is another obvious change of the traditional chronology of events, well-motivated as I shall show below in Ch. I. 4. 2.

[166] On the generic connotations of the scene, see also Ch. I. 4. 2.

Finally, in the last episode, clearly parallel with the first one, we can see Paris and Helen return to Troy, again during a religious ceremony, i.e. the prince's symbolic funeral. As I have emphasized, the scene is written in the epic convention as all the events are recounted by the narrator; its sense, however, is tragic. Formally, it could be classified as 'anti-tragedy' since what we observe is how the sadness of the protagonists weeping Paris's death turns into an unexpected joy after his miraculous reappearance. Still, their true feelings are in fact quite the opposite.

A more accurate reading of the *prooemium* of the *De raptu* has made us observe that one of the main subjects of the poem is not only the story of the rape of Helen as such but also the very personage of Paris. The portrayal of the male protagonist merits a closer look because, negatively connoted as it is, it is also a show of the poet's literary skills.

Paris is presented above all as a man deprived of due self-consciousness, a man whose self-perception is based upon wrong principles.[167] He is proud of himself and willingly emphasizes his being the judge of the immortals (*ego iurgia divum / compressi, nam lite caret me iudice caelum*, ll. 98-99; paradoxically also Priam addresses him later: *bonus arbiter Idae*, l. 221) albeit, as we know, he turns out to be a truly corrupted judge. On the one hand, he is well aware he is a prince (*Monitus Paris omnia norat / blandita nutrice puer, quo sanguine cretus, / qui genus, unde domus*, ll. 68-70), but nonetheless, even after regaining his royal status, he still feels the stigma of being a shepherd. This is perfectly epitomized in the narratorial comment opening the second scene: *Iam regno non impar erat, sed sceptra tiaram / imperium trabeas iam post caeleste tribunal / totum vile putat, solam cupit addere famam / maiorum titulis, vivaces quaerere laudes, / ut celet quod pastor erat* (ll. 213-217). The shepherd's life bores him, but when he is supposed to be brave during the storm at sea, he cannot be so and, lamenting, he praises the charms of a simple *vita pastoris*, contrasting it with the dangers to which the kings are constantly exposed.[168] In fact, this unique ambiguity of Paris is noticed – indeed stressed – by other protagonists, not just by Cassandra, who always calls him a *pastor*, but even by Apollo. The god, intervening precisely to guarantee Paris's acceptance into the bosom of his family, uses quite significant arguments: it is enough to change Paris's clothes and he can *become* a prince. I have already emphasized that the whole poem and its message focuses (among others) on the problem of the relationship between the truth and the falsity. Apollo's words that Paris's status may depend on how he looks like[169] point at this very fact. In addition, the god supports his arguments with an 'autobiographic' sweet memory of the time when he himself has served as Admetus's herdsman.[170] The ironic overtone is blatant.

The portrayal of Paris given in the segment treating his encounter with Helen appears particularly informative. As we can see, the narrator here also does not hesitate to judge his protagonist imposing again his view of the prince upon the reader. Hence the use of the indirect speech in the introductory part: before Paris is allowed to speak for

---

[167] See Bright 1987: 93. All this is in fact a model example of tragic irony in portraying the character, see more below in Ch. I. 4. 2.

[168] The scene is an impressive mixture of various generic strategies, see more below in Ch. I. 4. 2.

[169] We shall see that Paris turns out so unimaginably attractive to Helen also because of his spectacular clothes, see Ch. I. 4. 2.

[170] Bucolic flavor is again more than noticeable in this passage.

himself, it is the poet who not just reports but comments on his words. The young Trojan as depicted here might seem simply too typical, yet it is worth noting that, in fact, he acts a bit differently from what we can find for example in Colluthus (ll. 278 ff.), where the protagonist dwells on his very self, rather than complimenting the lady he talks to.[171] In Dracontius's text, as the narrator himself observes, Paris does not draw attention to his provenance and merits but focuses precisely on what may appeal best to 'feminine sensitivity' (or some would say, to feminine vanity). He is excited, speaks in a subdued voice, praising the queen and blaming Menelaus who has neglected his so beautiful wife. Apparently, the poet wants to make it clear that it is Paris who interests him as a character, or – to be exact – as a 'model' seducer:

> *Sed pastor, perfidus hospes,*
> *ut sensit fragiles mulieris pectore sensus,*
> *incipit Iliacus non quo sit sanguine cretus*
> *nec quibus excussus ventis ad litora Cypri*
> *venerit effari; trepidus iam voce remissa*
> *reginam laudabat amans, culpare maritum*
> *coeperat absentem, quod iam pulcherrima coniux*
> *a tepido deserta viro neglecta vacaret,*
> *sacra Dionaeae matris vel templa petisset* (507-515)

Indeed, in what follows the Trojan prince – who is finally given the word – simply shows off his gallantry. It is not only for the sweetness of compliments that he pays to his lovely hostess. Paris, as a well-trained reader will easily notice, behaves like an elegiac lover, declaring himself as *servus amoris* always ready to obey his mistress.[172] The passage is worth quoting in full:

> *adiungens: <<Si talis erit quam forte merebor*
> *uxorem, sic blanda genis, sic ore modesto,*
> *sic oculis ornata suis, sic pulchra decore,*
> *candida sic roseo perfundens membra rubore,*
> *sic flavis ornata comis, sic longior artus*
> *et procera regens in poplite membra venusto;*
> *tali semper ego dignatus coniuge felix*
> *non desim: famuler supplex et iussus adorem,*
> *conubio servus veniam sub lege mariti*
> *nocte diecte pavens quidnam velit illa iubere*
> *quae specie fulgente micat.>>* ... (516-526)

---

[171] Thus, Bright (1987: 125-126) rightly objects to Morelli's conclusion that Dracontius draws on Colluthus. In fact, also in Ovid's *Heroides* 16, a text by genre determined to be Paris's *speculum animi*, the Trojan prince does not shrink from naming his divine ancestors and praising his land (ll. 173-188). In Dracontius, the motif is almost absent: only in conclusion does Paris add: *Menelaus oberrat / numine contempto non dicam, coniuge pulchra, / quamvis numen adest veniens de stripe Tonantis, / unde genus duco* (526-529).

[172] The very description of Helen is based on a very traditional Roman concept of beauty, in this respect it also resembles the 'elegiac' ideals, to quote Ovid's *Am.* 3.3.5-6: *candida candorem roseo suffusa rubore / ante fuit — niveo lucet in ore rubor*. On elegiac, especially Ovidian, elements in this passage, see also Simons 2005: 270-271.

It would be just too obvious to add that this scene introduces the romantic motif, so typical of the epyllion tradition. As Díaz de Bustamante shrewdly notes,[173] in Paris's words one can already hear some topoi exploited later in love poetry of the Troubadours. What is a pity is only the fact that the true goal of so charming a passage, taking into consideration the whole context, is merely to deride the protagonist. We can at most acknowledge how gifted and moving love poet Dracontius could have been, had he ever wanted to be one.

Finally, Paris's pusillanimity is best exemplified in the scene showing the two lovers escape Menelaus's chase. The youngster (which is precisely how Helen is addressing him now: *Iuvenis, quid nostra retardas / pectora colloquiis?*, ll. 551-552) is paralyzed with fear and he stops lamenting and starts acting only thanks to Helen who turns out to be a true "*mujer de character*."[174] The very escape is compared by the narrator to the escape of Jove the bull with Europe (ll. 557-562). Díaz de Bustamante defines it as "*exemplum totum simile*."[175] It seems though that a similar juxtaposition of Paris and Jove is marked ironically:[176] Paris, in his delicateness, does not look very much like a bull, albeit one should admit that, although tired (even *lassus*[177]) and fragile, he strives to be as brave as possible:

Ergo ubi pervenit raptor turbatus ad aequor
et licet exhaustus cursu vel pondere lassus,
qui gratum portabat onus, tamen ipse Lacaenam
litore non posuit, media sed puppe locavit (563-566)

Consequently, the unheroic, unsure of himself and his position protagonist is a model anti-hero of the epyllion genre. Still, unlike Heracles of the *Hylas*, Paris does not only amuse; too strong is the sense of the oncoming catastrophe. In addition, his sensitivity, idiosyncratic of an epyllic character, is also a mere show, a spectacle, an example of (quite insolent) manipulating or juggling with words.

In fact, Paris is not the only protagonist of the *De raptu* to possess so dangerous a skill, namely of juggling with words. It is worthwhile looking more carefully at Apollo's speech, the speech that will contradict, and thus make untrustworthy the (true, as we know) prophecies of his seers, Helenus and Cassandra. The appearance of the god is preceded by a short but very relevant narratorial explanation: Apollo, cheated once by Laomedon – who had him build walls around the city of Troy and promised to reward him well but later refused to fulfill the promise – wants to take revenge now: *genus ingratum poenas persolvat avari / exoptat* (ll. 186-187). Therefore, Apollo's intervention has

[173] Díaz de Bustamante 1978: 210.

[174] Díaz de Bustamante 1978: 211.

[175] Díaz de Bustamante 1978: 211.

[176] As admitted also by Bright 1987: 127.

[177] Wolff (1996: 167 n. 336) emphasizes that "La précision *pondere* (au sens concret de <<charge>>) *lassus* est maladroite, même si le passage veut insister sur la délicatesse de Pâris." Right, but on the other hand, *lassus* with its elegiac erotic connotation matches quite well the ironic portrayal of the protagonist as an adulterer and disruptor of marriage. As we have seen, Dracontius uses precisely the elegiac vocabulary to picture Paris so.

a very well-defined aim, which, however, cannot be guessed by the human protagonists. Apollo orders the Trojans to accept Paris because the *Fatum* dictates so (*Pellere pastorem ... fata vetant*, ll. 190-191) and because of his unique 'merits' for the immortals as their judge: *Mortali divum periet quo iudice iudex?* (l. 200). A reader who remembers the scene as it is presented at the outset of the poem, where Paris turned out but a corrupted judge, must almost feel the ironic smile of the narrator hearing the words of his divine protagonist.

Above all, Apollo stresses the future deeds of the shepherd-prince. A well-trained literary audience will probably notice quite easily that what Apollo says is not simply untrue (it is not a 'naïve' lie, so to say) but rather misleading,[178] in particular since the god is actually implying 'facts' (if the term is applicable to fiction, of course): the slaying of Achilles by Paris (*magnanimum Aeacidem solus prosternet Achillem*, l. 192) and the Trojan hegemony lasting forever as predicted by Jove (*conscripta semel sunt verba Tonantis, / <<imperium sine fine>> dabit*, ll. 198-199). Still, what the god hides is the price to be paid by the Trojans for their future as Romans.[179] In addition, Dracontius's Apollo quotes Virgil's Jove[180] to, so to speak, authorize his own words; yet for one who recognizes it, the allusion evoking the *Aeneid* calls to mind all that is concealed here: the ruin of Troy and the wandering of her remnants. The quotation is, indeed, one more example of tragic irony, so deliberately employed by the poet throughout the epyllion.

Apollo manipulating the truth only to put the pressure on humans and make them act as he wishes, even if the results turn out catastrophic for them, may seem just a 'usual' epyllic god, vengeful and demoralized, as the gods of Ovid's *Metamorphoses* often are.[181] Undoubtedly, a Christian reader could also see him as an example of an anti-god, the

---

[178] Bright (1987: 100) labels it justly as 'sophistry'.

[179] Díaz de Bustamante (1978: 196) proposes an almost allegorical interpretation of the scene and the sense of Apollo's words. In his view, the god does arrive to announce the better destiny of Troy, which from a city corrupted by e.g. Laomedon's fraud, will turn into a true eternal crown of the world. This reading of the episode is related to Díaz's interpretation of the phrase used by the poet in the prologue: *aggrediar meliore via* (l. 3). As he puts it (p. 128), "el *meliore via*, en suma, hace referencia a cómo los hados están ordenados a un fin grandioso que no habrá que buscar en las consecuencias inmediatas del delito de Paris y Helena, sino en las ulteriores." The ethical interpretation of *meliore via* as an emphasis on the moral message of the story was also proposed by Romano 1959: 34; see besides Bertini 1974: 90 and recently Simons 2005: 286 ff. I believe, however, that – despite Dracontius's moralism (or rather, as I see it, his intellectual and spiritual profoundness) – this very expression can be read as simply as possible, as implying the poet's intention to do his best to provide a 'well-done' version of the myth. See also Wolff's (1996: 115 n. 3) useful notes on the *locus*.

[180] See *Aen.* 1.278-279: *His ego nec metas rerum nec tempora pono; / imperium sine fine dedi.* Bright (1987: 100) also points to Apollo's prophecy to the Trojans in *Aen.* 3.97-98: *hic domus Aeneae cunctis dominabitur oris / et nati natorum et qui nascentur ab illis.* Indeed, both in Virgil and in Dracontius Apollo predicts to the Trojans the hegemony over the whole world.

[181] The examples are legion but one of those that I myself find particularly moving is Athena as portrayed in the episode dedicated to Arachne (*Met.* 6.1-145). The piece is fascinating also because it pictures a truly human, bourgeois so to speak, protagonist (so, in a sense, a model 'epyllic' or 'romance' protagonist) of rather mediocre origin and hard-working, punished, indeed persecuted by the invidious goddess.

god who must not be given credence. I would say that Dracontius does not really impose this interpretation upon his audience, but he does not certainly exclude it, either. In my view, however, what the poet suggests is a more general message. By portraying with all his rhetorical skill of an excellent lawyer Apollo the sophist, he warns against not merely a false pagan divinity but, above all, against the danger and the power of a word. A word can almost, as demonstrated in the Salaminian scene, unleash a war. A word (words), if used properly, can seduce, which Paris talking to Helen seems to be only too aware of. A word finally, like the one (the ones) chosen by Apollo, can determine what the listeners will consider truth.

While the *Hylas* is still a poem by a young poet, already quite versatile in imitating the narrative technique and the aesthetic *gratia* of the epyllion genre, the *De raptu Helenae* is a work by an author who did not merely compose a miniature epic but rather – exploiting a certain literary convention, which he apparently found attractive enough – intended to communicate to his literary audience his views on some fundamental problems and pose some fundamental questions.

I. 3. 3. *MEDEA*

While the *Hylas* and the *De raptu* could be easily divided into a few major scenes, the other two of Dracontius's epyllia, the *Medea* and (above all) the *OT*, are much more complex and variegated in their composition. Both of these poems treat synoptically the story of Medea and Jason and the Oresteia theme. As we already know, in the *Medea* the narrator himself informs his readers about the twofold structure of his text focused, first, on the figure of *Medea amans* and, subsequently, on the one of *Medea furens*. In reality, however, this general scheme does not reflect the compositional richness of the poem[182] characterized, especially in the first part, by quick action, even 'despite' (actually, it can hardly be considered a drawback) the fact that one can find there lengthy speeches-prayers, most varied descriptions, charming as well as frightening, and effective similes.[183] The *Medea* is also a work showing particularly well Dracontius's invention and creativity in reinterpreting certain, canonic and unchangeable as it might seem, motifs of the myth. Nevertheless, it would be very unfair to say that the poet's only aim was just a novelty of treatment, a mere 'change for change's sake'. In this respect, the well-known (at least among the students of Dracontius's poetry) case of the relocation of the second segment of the story is most significant. As we have now learned to think, Dracontius's decision to set the action of his *Medea furens* in Thebes is not a schoolish mistake, as it was once seen, but a deliberate literary strategy thanks to which his text is readable in the context of Statius's *Thebaid*.[184]

---

[182] On the richness of generic literary strategies employed by the poet in the *Medea*, see Ch. I. 4. 3.

[183] For example the visual comparison of Cupid to Phoenix (ll. 102-112) emphasized by Bright 1987: 52-53.

[184] See again Schetter 1980 = 1994: 314-327 and my own notes in Ch. I. 2. 3. Díaz de Bustamante (1978: 242) emphasized Dracontius's mistake.

The very narration as such is linear, like in the previous epyllia: Dracontius, as we have already noticed, never uses digressions, nor does he change the chronology of events. The story opens with Jason's arrival to Colchis, as if he were alone in fact (*solus Iason*, l. 42),[185] and ends with a scene showing Medea the avengeress fly somewhere in her golden chariot, maybe back to where she has come from (?). Consequently, the poem could be interpreted as a sort of *Ringkomposition*, especially since at the beginning we see Medea as a cruel priestess of Diana, a *xeinoktonos*, almost a new embodiment of the Iphigenia in Tauris,[186] whereas at the end the heroine, offering a very particular sacrifice of Jason, Glauce, Creon, as well as her two children, seems to return to that her original role.[187]

Certainly, some motifs are treated with an abruptness idiosyncratic of the epyllion genre:[188] the reader may have an impression that the poet mentions them only because they belong to the canon of the story or because his intention is to point out that *he knows* that they belong to this very canon. This is best exemplified by the *Überleitungepisode* between the two main segments of the poem, the Colchian and the Theban one. Within six (!) verses (ll. 361-366), Dracontius presents the theft of the Golden Fleece, apparently committed by Medea,[189] Jason and Medea's escape from Colchis together with their two sons (sic!), the killing of Absyrtus,[190] and, finally, the arrival to Thebes and the bestowal of the Fleece to the king Creon (we shall never know why, possibly as a nice introduction gift[191]). Jason, who after four years of happy marriage spent in Colchis one night, most

---

[185] The motif of the quest of the Golden Fleece is merely touched upon here as well as later in ll. 357-362 (see below). Similarly, more than marginal is the attention the poet has for Jason's companions. In l. 51, we learn only that they all have escaped seeing Jason captured, in l. 353, we see Jason, already a happy husband, remember all of the sudden his companions who do not even know, as he realizes, that their leader is now a king.

[186] See already Friedrich 1967: 71 ff.; Schetter 1980: 210 = 1994: 315; Bright 1987: 54-58; recently Simons 2005: 185-189.

[187] See below and more in my paper, Wasyl 2007a.

[188] As argued by Schetter 1980: 211 = 1994: 317. I do not agree with Bright's (1987: 64-65) objections to his view. In fact, the interpretation Bright proposes, namely that Dracontius in his *Medea* imitates features characteristic of a folk tale, possibly of extra-Roman, Vandal origins, is just fanciful, I must admit. On the other hand, as I have pointed out above, my overall view of his book is not that much Schetterian.

[189] Should we see here a Senecan inspiration? See Seneca's *Medea*, 912-913: *et arcano patrem / spoliasse sacro.*

[190] Obviously, for the story presented by Dracontius the killing of Absyrtus is completely purposeless. Should one seek for an explanation, more profound than the most obvious one that the poet took the opportunity to demonstrate his erudition, it could possibly be argued that this crime, being one of a series, shows how evil generates evil. A morally sensitive reader could draw such a conclusion. Did Dracontius, a morally sensitive author as he was, imply that?

[191] See the text: *Ventum erat ad Thebas, pellis datur aurea regi. / Miratur rex ipse Creon, laudatur Iason / quod freta quod terras sic felix praedo vagetur* (ll. 366-368). Seriously speaking, Dracontius most probably alludes to the version of the myth in which it is Creon who sends Jason to retrieve the Golden Fleece, see Schol. Stat. *Ach.* 65 (I quote after Zurli in Zurli – Scivoletto – Paolucci 2008: 33 n. 105).

probably in a dream,[192] realizes the (ostensibly) main goal of his expedition, seems to be only a bit more interested in the quest for the Golden Fleece than the narrator himself.[193]

The most important rule behind the composition of the poem is the parallelism of the two segments, as justly stressed by Bright.[194] The first part, dedicated to a priestess of Diana who, falling in love with a newcomer, betrays the goddess and must be punished by her patroness, finds its mirror-image in the second part, where a young princess Glauce, Medea's *alter ego* indeed, similarly desires the very same newcomer, ignoring the fact that she "covets her neighbor's spouse."[195] As such, she must also be duly punished by the betrayed wife who now turns into a 'double' of vengeful Diana. The fact that Medea and Glauce are quite identical is best exemplified by the way in which they both treat Jason: for each of them Jason, miserably passive as a figure, is a mere 'object of desire'.[196]

---

[192] The scene showing Jason sigh in his sleep and Medea, later, ask him the reason of his suffering is, as Schetter (1980: 211 = 1994: 316) demonstrated, modeled on Statius's *Theb.* 2.332-335. It is, in fact, the catalyst of the events to come, also in their intertextual dimension as it determines the Statian flavor of the entire second episode.

[193] The motif of the quest for the Golden Fleece is mentioned by Dracontius first at the very outset of the poem: *Dives apud Colchos Phrixei velleris aurum, / pellis erat, servata diu custode dracone. / Hanc propter pelagi temerator primus Iason / venerat, ut rutilas subduceret arbore lanas* (ll. 32-35). Later, it is mentioned again precisely by Jason who finally realizes that he has had some reasons behind his arrival to Colchis and that his companions do not even know how he is: *Tunc sic Aesonides stimulet quae forma medullas / indicat et pellis causas vel tempore tanto / quod lateat socios, quia iam sic regnat amicus, / consumptum quem morte putant planguntque parentes* (ll. 351-354). Needless to say, this whole elaboration of the theme is more than awkward, yet I do think that it is purposeful. Dracontius, first of all, shows his disinterest in the famous motif as such (which is a model attitude of an epyllion poet) and presents Jason in an unfavorable light.

[194] Bright 1987: 71 ff.

[195] Bright 1987: 71. It is not coincidental that the scholar quotes the Ninth Commandment here, see his further comments on pp. 83-84.

[196] It is worth comparing the two passages dedicated to Medea's and Glauce's behavior toward Jason to see this analogy between the two heroines. Dracontius's women are by nature active as opposed to their passive male counterparts. It is so clear that the observation is made by virtually all students of his mythological poems, see recently Simons (2005: 166) or Kaufmann's (2006a: 56) opening note on Jason: "Jasons Hauptmerkmal in *Romul.* 10 ist seine Passivität."

Medea:

Conversa sacerdos
ad iuvenem: <<Dic, nauta fugax, pirata nefande:
est consors matrona decens an caelibe vita
degis adhuc nullumque domi <tibi> pignus
habetur?>>
<<Solus>>, ait captivus, <<ego, mihi pignora nulla
coniugis aut sobolis.>> Dictis gavisa virago
blanda refert: <<Vis ergo meus nunc esse
maritus?>>
<<Servus>>, Iason ait ... (247-254)

Glauce:

Regis nata decens fuerat pulcherrima Glauce,
iam cui virginitas annis matura tumebat;
haec ubi conspexit iuvenem, flammata nitore
aestuat et laudans alieni membra mariti
optat habere virum. Sonuit genitoris ad aures.
(369-373)

In other words, the whole epyllion constitutes, indeed, a story of broken oaths and of consequences that such unfaithfulness must bring.[197] Hence the marginalization of other motifs, especially of the adventurous theme of the quest for the Golden Fleece. Hence also the fact that, like before the *De raptu*, similarly the *Medea* can hardly be interpreted as a romantic piece about (even fatal) love. This is one of the main differences between Dracontius's poem and the Medea episode in the *Metamorphoses* Book 7 in which, in the scene of the famous monologue, the Colchian princess appears as, arguably, one of Ovid's most appealing and memorable heroines.[198]

One could conclude then that Dracontius ignores one of the most fundamental components of the epyllion genre. In fact, the case is much more complex. Dracontius's Medea the priestess is hit by Amor's arrow in the very moment when she, accompanied by her nurse, is about to kill Jason to offer him as a sacrifice to Diana. The sudden change in her behavior is noticed, precisely, by the nurse; it is also the nurse who shares this information with us, the readers. The old woman, following strictly the dictates of the literary convention, describes all symptoms of love to be seen on Medea's face:

torpescit iners antistita Phoebes
permixto pallore rubens, non lumina vibrat,
non furit aut tremuli strident in murmure dentes. (228-230)

Cur explicat artus
aut tangit cur saepe caput, quid spirat hiatus
oris et ad zonam digiti mittuntur inermes? (232-234)

Thus, the scene as such is exemplarily epyllic: we have a girl in love and her old nurse who tries to discover the cause of her unexpected illness.[199] What is more, one should acknowledge the fact that the nurse behaves exactly like her literary archetypes and she does her best to persuade the girl to remain faithful to her vocation and not to commit the 'crime': *Cur homicida vacas et stas rea? Sed rea non es, / si fueris homicida magis* (ll. 231-232).[200] The only problem is that the whole picture is appalling rather than moving and it is quite hard to determine who seems more frightening: Medea (who eventually will save the youngster) or, precisely, her nurse, 'dark as an owl hooting among ruins'.[201] The term parody is not fully appropriate here, yet beyond doubt the epyllic scene of *innamoramento* as depicted by Dracontius is utterly anti-romantic.

[197] See now especially Santini 2006: 21-31; 40-45.

[198] See my comparative analysis in Wasyl 2007a.

[199] Bright (1987: 56-57) notices this in passing but does not draw further conclusions.

[200] See also ll. 303-304: [anus] *haec anxia crimen / virginis et raptum deflebat maesta pudorem.* For a somewhat parallel scene in the epyllion tradition, see e.g. *Met.* 10.424 ff, the reaction of Myrrha's nurse to the girl's behavior.

[201] The simile is quite expressive: *nutrix tamen atria tantum / templorum servabat anus … /…/ qualis in exhaustis per sordida tecta ruinis / strix nocturna sonat rostro stridente per umbras; / qualis et horrendus funesto carmine bubo / conqueritur deflenda gemens, dum tristia maestus / funerea sub nocte canit, sic anxia nutrix / ingemit et tremulas diffundit maesta querelas* (ll. 302-303 & 305-310).

The atmosphere of horror in the poem dedicated to Medea can be hardly surprising. In fact, the poet has already pointed at it in his narratorial prologue, still, Dracontius's ability to contrast scenes marked with different, sometimes dramatically different, emotional coloring is quite worth noting. After having a glance at Jason being captured by the Colchians (*capiuntque paventem / et manibus post terga ligant*, ll. 48-49), the action is shifted to the home of gods atop Mount Olympus. Now, we can hear the two goddesses, Juno and Venus, converse (ll. 49-84) and we learn that the brave sailor is, indeed, in dire peril, but that he also has a divine protectress, Juno,[202] who plans to save him. To do so, Juno is conspiring with Venus[203] against the powerful witch and against Diana whom Medea obediently serves. Naturally, Jason will be saved if the virgin priestess falls in love with him: Cupid's help is then necessary. The next scene, portraying the conversation between Venus and Amor, is already full of typically epyllic charm,[204] so characteristic of the *Hylas*. The visual description makes us almost see the goddess caress tenderly the boy's head (*venit ecce Cupido / fessulus et gremio matris libratur anhelans, / quo sessurus erat. Quem protinus illa volantem / occupat et crines componit mater Amori / ac puerum complexa fovet, dans oscula nato*, ll. 122-126), even though what she asks of him is far from innocent: for Medea, it will mean a disaster. And later, together with Amor, a lovely god whose appearance brings joy even to the land of suffering (*et magis accessu pueri plaga maesta serenat / adventum testata dei*, ll. 174-175), we fly back to Colchis and again see the horrible Medea *xeinoktonos* and her not less horrible nurse (*ecce trahebatur ceu taurus pulcher Iason, / quem sequitur Medea nocens urgetque ministros / nudato mucrone furens*, ll. 179-181).

Let us still consider one more example, particularly moving as a combination of sweetness and horror: the scene of infanticide. When the whole royal palace is on fire, the children instinctively nestle up to their mother, completely unaware of their destiny:

Mermerus insons
et Pheretes matrem blanda pietate vocabant.
Ut flammas vitare queat, infantia simplex
affectu petit ipsa necem vel sponte pericla
quaerit inops, passura necem mucrone parentis,
ignari, quae mater erat quid saeva pararet. (531-536)

Moreover, it is worthwhile paying attention to the above-mentioned Dracontius's novelty of treatment. When reading the *Medea*, the literary audience, especially the contemporary one for whom most probably many of the sources used by our poet are lost, may come to a conclusion that the Carthaginian ostentatiously introduces motifs different from those widely known and accepted. Choosing Thebes as the setting for the tragic segment of the story, important as it is, is but an example of this general tendency. It seems not less relevant that the whole situation is presented as determined by gods and

[202] The explanation of this attitude of hers is again typically epyllic in its conciseness: *est nimis acceptus iuvenis mihi pulcher Iason, / qui gelidum quondam mecum transnaverat Istrum* (ll. 56-57).

[203] The scene is somewhat similar to the one in the *Aeneid* 4 (ll. 90-128), where Juno is also trying to 'conspire' with Venus to make Dido fall in love with Aeneas.

[204] Charming is already the picture of Amor's flight given in ll. 97-118.

their vengefulness. Besides, the readership must get quite surprised finding out that in Dracontius's version Medea and Jason's wedding takes place in Colchis. What is more, they finally gain Aeëtes's acceptation and stay there for four years, it is even in Colchis that their two sons are born. Aeëtes, at first frightened by what his daughter has done (*Nuntius … / natamque tyranno / indicat ignoto passim nupsisse marito*, ll. 311-313), is quite soon mollified by Liber who, having appeared in Colchis like (another) *deus ex machina*, allures the king with the promise of his grandchildren and even persuades him to 'emancipate himself from vain superstitions' (<<*Sic tibi, rector*>>, *ait*, <<*mentem possedit inanis / religio*?>>, ll. 322-323). The mention of sweet children (*dulces … nepotes*, l. 324), certainly, marks the poem with particular emotion as every reader is well aware of the end of this story. Still, Liber's 'rationalistic' reasoning may seem even more alarming. His sophistry is dangerously similar to the one of Apollo in the *De raptu*. In point of fact, it is more evil: Apollo does not really lie, he only does not say the whole truth, whereas here we face a god (almost) promoting blasphemy or at least arguing that one should not observe (religious) rules too strictly. And, to conclude this paragraph devoted to Dracontius's 'deviations' from the mainstream of the Medea myth, let us at least pose the question: why did our poet allow his protagonists the four years of an ostensible peace and happiness? In my own view, it is precisely to emphasize that the fate, the curse (Medea is cursed by Diana right after the goddess learns about her marriage), and also the punishment are not fulfilled at once.[205] These four years are the 'measure' of Medea's unfaithfulness. They are, by the same token, the measure of Jason's faithfulness. A careful reader has certainly noticed a detail stressed earlier in the text. Amor, promising Jason that he will be safe, tells him clearly enough: *Sed memor esto mei, ne te fortuna superbum / reddat et incipias iterum ceu nauta venire* (ll. 214-215). Jason then 'sins', and he does it several times. To be precise, his first sin is, indeed, *superbia*: he wants to return home (which is his second crime) to show to his family and friends that he is a man of success: *indicat … / quod lateat socios, quia iam sic regnat amicus, / consumptum quem morte putant planguntque parentes* (ll. 352-354). The other 'sins' (and especially the adultery) are just a matter of time. Once again, Dracontius's readership is given a clear message that crime generates another crime and, finally, the ultimate disaster.[206]

Last but not least, let us concentrate on the already mentioned question of gods and the role they play in Dracontius's *Medea*. It is, indeed, their will and their 'revenge' to determine the destiny of human protagonists. What we can even see in this poem is a kind of multiplication of this, epyllic par excellence, motif. What happens to Medea as wife and mother reflects exactly the curse thrown upon her by her offended patroness, Diana (ll. 293-300).[207] But the very fact that she *has fallen* in love[208] with Jason was

---

[205] See below in Ch. I. 3. 4 for the parallel message in the *OT* (l. 455).

[206] Thus, it is also ultimately logical that Dracontius's Medea murders Jason. Jason, the sinner must be punished. Certainly, one can hardly deny that Dracontius in having Medea kill Jason, as well as Creon and his daughter, follows – or at least agrees with – Hyginus's version (*fab.* 25): *Creusa munere accepto cum Iasone et Creonte conflagravit.*

[207] See more below in Ch. I. 4. 3.

[208] The very motif of love – especially if it is a sort of *l'amour malheureux* – as a form of divine punishment is, needless to say, inherent in the epyllion tradition: the *Ciris*, Ovid's *Myrrha*, Ano-

planned earlier by Juno who, subsequently, incited Venus to exercise her power over the priestess of the virgin goddess and, in a sense, over Diana herself. Undoubtedly, Medea is not 'without sin': she is the *virgo atra* frightening in her unnatural, inhuman force. Yet, her world, even: her entire universe, is governed by gods who are not less cruel than she is and who must not be trusted (the example of Bacchus is alarming). The bitterness with which the narrator speaks in his epilogue, addressing Liber among others, can hardly surprise in such a context.

A more accurate reading of the *Medea* shows that, despite the variety of motifs that it combines, this poem is very coherent in its composition, indeed, more than the *De raptu Helenae* with the 'controversial' Salaminian episode, even though the two texts are also simply different and as such should not be really compared. At the same time, in the *Medea*, as before in the *De raptu*, we can see how our poet plays with certain themes or schemes belonging to the epyllion tradition, interpreting or reinterpreting them according to his own literary aims. The most telling example may be here his peculiar paraphrase of the romantic scene of falling in love. As I have emphasized, Dracontius's Medea never behaves like her Ovidian counterpart (in *Met.* 7), an anxious and inexperienced girl who cannot choose between the feeling for the unknown sailor and the duty toward the father and the fatherland, who regrets even the decisions already made and, remorseful, considers the suicide. Some readers might possibly find it quite disappointing,[209] yet on the other hand, one can hardly blame the Carthaginian that he was not, or even did not intend to be, an Ovid. Besides, it is worth remembering that in Ovid the strange metamorphosis of a sensitive girl into a soulless witch is not at all psychologically explained. What he proposes, in fact, is just a juxtaposition of two completely incompatible figures, of a *virgo* and a *maga*, much more incompatible than Dracontius's *Medea (xeinoktonos) amans* and *Medea furens*. In addition, it is Dracontius who gives a truly tragic dimension[210] to his epyllion and to its heroine, whereas in Ovid the story of the fury and crime of the betrayed wife is reduced to a four-line mention.

I. 3. 4. *ORESTIS TRAGOEDIA*

The composition of Dracontius's major epyllion appears also coherent, which is quite remarkable considering the multiplicity of motifs that this story devoted to Agamemnon's murder, the avengement of his death by Orestes, and the 'further adventures' (I use the word deliberately) of the latter comprehends. It is so precisely because, as the narrator has clearly indicated in his prologue, the *Orestis Tragoedia* has one well-defined aim: *purgare foro quem damnavere sorores* (l. 16). This is the perspective the poet has in mind employing most varied literary strategies and introducing or emphasizing details hardly

---

nym's *Aegritudo Perdicae* are the most telling examples. Interestingly, Dracontius himself draws upon it only in the *Hylas*, where it does not look so catastrophic though, and precisely in the *Medea*.

[209] Quartiroli (1947: 21) complained about the "superficialità psicologica" of the scene showing Medea falling in love.

[210] See more below in Ch. I. 4. 3.

known as indispensable elements of the Oresteia theme. It seems worthwhile beginning our analysis with enumerating these most surprising points.

A reader, at least a modern one, must be quite astonished to find a scene showing Agamemnon's unexpected visit in Tauris at the outset of Dracontius's version. This unplanned, indeed caused by a storm at sea, stop on the king's way back home allows him to meet his daughter whom he, obviously enough, has considered dead. Not less intriguing must seem what the poet says about the salvation of Orestes. In the *OT*, it is made possible by Electra who takes the boy as well as their father's treasure and escapes to Athens. Interestingly, Dracontius does not spare us further information about the Athenian education of Agamemnon's son,[211] as well as about his friend and classmate Pylades. Orestes's safe life in Athens is additionally facilitated by his *paidagogus*, Dorylas, who in front of Clytemnestra and Aegisthus performs a, fully convincing as it appears, scene of lament on the prince's alleged death in a sea storm. As I have already noted, this is the very point of action stressed by the narrator's proem in the middle. Another novelty is the focus on the figures of the two regicides. The *OT* describes not only the circumstances of Agamemnon's murder but also the moment of the 'takeover' and defines, with striking precision, the duration of Clytemnestra's and Aegisthus's rule (*annorum septem spatiis et mensibus octo*, l. 455).[212] Finally, the whole closing part of the poem leading to the absolution of the title character may also seem surprising. It does look like a combination of most varied motifs related to the figure of Agamemnon's son, yet not having much in common with the Oresteia cycle as such. Dracontius's Orestes finds out that his fiancée, Hermione, has been carried off by Pyrrhus, so he chases and slays him at the altar. Henceforth persecuted by his mother's ghost and in danger of the revenge of Pyrrhus's son, Molossus, he is sent to Tauris by Pylades. Now, in twenty verses (ll. 865-886), the poet tells us about the capture of Orestes as a would-be sacrificial victim, his recognition by his sister, his curing from madness by Iphigenia, and, last but not least, the brother and sister's escape with the statue of Diana. Finally, the closing scene is the formal trial of Orestes taking place in Athens, at which Molossus acts as the accuser and the young king of Mycenae is the advocate in his own case.

In between these ostensible 'purple patches', which in fact, as we shall see, have significant influence on the overall shape and sense of the poem, the reader can find the basic structure of the Oresteia theme: Agamemnon's return to Mycenae, his murder, the return

[211] On this aspect, see especially Privitera 1996.

[212] On this, quite peculiar indeed, exactness on the part of the poet, see Grillone (2008: 128-129, com. to l. 455) who stresses that thanks to this information the reader is persuaded that Orestes at the moment of the avenge is of age (has already become 18 years), therefore, he is a legitimate successor to his father. There are also interesting comments by Privitera (1996: 136-137) who emphasizes that the line shows that in Dracontius one can discover "il preciso intento di rendere ragione nella maniera più opportuna, e scientifica, della sua ricostruzione storica della vicenda." I would also add that the information, analogous (only much more exact) to the one given in the *Medea*, about the four years spent by Medea and Jason in Colchis, can be quite similarly interpreted as a 'measure' of Clytemnestra's crime; which is fully concordant with what Grillone and Privitera point out: Clytemnestra (and Aegisthus of course) goes unpunished until Orestes is mature: this turns out the ultimate 'measure' of evil in her case.

of Orestes and Pylades to avenge his death, and, at last, the absolution of the young man before the Athenian tribunal with the participation of the goddess Minerva.[213]

Thus, when reading, especially if done not too accurately, Dracontius's poem one can, indeed, come to a conclusion that its poetics is somewhat romance-like, with the typical multiplication of events – or rather adventures (as I have suggested above) – connected with the figure of the title character.[214] The association is not wholly mistaken, but some points must be better explained. Above all, one should analyze more closely the passages when the poet does employ a quasi-romance narration, treating only superficially or even merely enumerating one after another new and new events, and when he fully develops the dramatic potential of a certain scene, allowing his protagonists lengthy, at times too lengthy as some critics would say,[215] speeches. I shall concentrate on this question in the following chapter. Now, I would like to emphasize another aspect, namely that it is thanks to this diversity of motifs that Dracontius can effectively play with contrasting images or scenes of different character and emotional coloring (that, as we have already seen in the *Medea*, is both his own peculiarity and a typical feature of late antique poetics in general). Some of such juxtapositions are, so to speak, quite expectable, even though (still) striking, like the image of the two lovers-conspirers concluded with a deliberately disgusting erotic scene,[216] side by side with the portrayal of returning Agamemnon, in glory entering his town and his palace, as if he were a new Jupiter after the triumph over the Giants. Others are made possible precisely because the poet adds new elements to the very core of the Oresteia theme. A particularly good example is the passage devoted to the two young gentlemen and friends, Orestes and Pylades, built upon topoi common in such a context (they exercise together, they hunt together, they are, finally, like Castor and Pollux), followed by an image of Aegisthus, wearing Tyrian purple and royal diadem and searching for the prince as well as for Agamemnon's Trojan treasure (ll. 291-315). The difference between nobleness and baseness could hardly be better epitomized.

---

[213] Therefore, Bright (1987: 139) and Grillone propose to divide the text into three segments, following the Oresteia scheme: *Agamemnon*, *Orestes*, for the third one Bright suggests the title *Orestes furens*, Grillone (2008: 101-102, com. to ll. 1-24) justly objects since the main subject here is certainly not Orestes's furor but his absolution. There are some further minor differences between Bright and Grillone, related to the above-mentioned problem of the placement of ll. 427-452 and to the question where to see the end of the prologue (Grillone, like Schetter 1985: 56 and Arduini 1987, defines as 'prologue' ll. 1-24; Bright, like Polara 1974, extends it up to l. 40). Bouquet (see Bouquet – Wolff 1995: 42) is prone to distinguish two parts: the first treating of mariticide and the matricide (until l. 802) and the second, in which (in his opinion) there is no central episode. Schetter argues differently (1985: 56) as, in his view, the division of the text strongly imitates what is stated in the prologue in which, as he notes, two main heroes are indicated: Agamemnon and his son. Thus, the poem is dividable into a segment devoted to Agamemnon's part (25-426) and the one dedicated to Orestes (515-962) with a sort of intermediary passage in between (453-514).

[214] See Bouquet – Wolff 1995: 30; 43. But compare my further comments in Ch. I. 4. 4.

[215] See Quartiroli 1947: 30.

[216] *motibus his mulier, melius gavisa, resumpsit / turpiter infames animos. redit illa voluptas, / impete plectibili per rustica colla pependit, dulcia lascivis defigens basia labris; / ille vicem redhibens dabat oscula crebra per artus* (ll. 227-231).

The ultimate 'purging of Orestes' according to human and divine law, being, as it has been stressed, the main goal of the poem, determines above all the way in which its protagonists are portrayed,[217] especially the triad, Agamemnon, Clytemnestra, and Orestes. We shall focus on this aspect now.

Agamemnon is, indeed, a man of spotless integrity:[218] a great, victorious and pious, king as well as a caring husband and father. Giuseppe Aricò noted rightly that the picture of the king of Mycenae given at the very outset of Dracontius's epyllion – we see him returning home with lavish gifts for his entire family (ll. 36-40) – has a somewhat bourgeois flavor.[219] It is, in fact, a preview of other romance-like elements and features to be found in the *OT*.

Agamemnon's characterization is focused specifically on his attitude toward his children and wife. We can learn from the opening scene set in Tauris – from Iphigenia herself – that the only person responsible for taking the girl away from home to kill her in sacrifice to Diana was Ulysses, not Agamemnon (ll. 74-83). It is true that a careful reader will not ignore the fact that what justifies the king is much more the testimony given by his daughter than his own conscience (see a few lines earlier: *vidit Iphigeniam … / obstipuit pietas et mens sibi conscia pravi*, ll. 52 & 54),[220] nonetheless, what Iphigenia says eliminates the major mitigating circumstance that might render Clytemnestra's crime less evil. What is more, in Agamemnon's fervent prayer to Diana, the prayer that is rejected – which eventually will turn out providential (Iphigenia will save and cure Orestes)[221] but for now must seem a frightening portent, not less to the pious king than to us, the readers – we can hear a humble request that the daughter be returned to her weeping mother: *nil actum Troiae est, si non comitante Mycenas / virgine pergo redux plangenti reddere matri, / quam putat extinctam: vestra pietate redemptam / sentiat et vertat proprios in gaudia planctus* (ll. 98-101). We shall soon contrast this compassion and care of the husband and the father with Clytemnestra's attitude. Another detail worth emphasizing concerns Agamemnon's continence. The king of Mycenae, as portrayed by Dracontius, has no relationship whatsoever with Cassandra; the poet states clearly: *sors regis erat Cassandra sacerdos, / inter Dardanias clades Danaumque triumphos / n o n h a b i t a i n d i g n e, licet esset portio praedae* (ll. 133-135).[222]

[217] On the portrayal of the protagonists and the influence it has upon the general message and aim of the *OT*, see now especially Grillone 2008: 13-17 as well as his earlier comments on the question in Grillone 1987; see also the bibliography I quote below in my footnotes.

[218] See already Aricò 1978: 77-78, also Corsaro 1979: 334 ff.; Bright 1987: 205-206.

[219] "Un tono borghese che nulla toglie alla maestà del sovrano," see Aricò 1978: 77 n. 182.

[220] This, quite intriguing in fact, detail is also noticed by Corsaro 1979: 336, in passing by Aricò 1978: 78 n. 184.

[221] Grillone 2008: 110, com. to l. 102 ff.

[222] Considering what the poet emphasizes about the relationship between Agamemnon and Cassandra (or rather lack of any relationship whatsoever), it seems reasonable to read ll. 3-4 of the poem as Grillone (2008: 51; 102, com. to l. 4) proposes: *lamentabile votum / coniugis (Iliacum nam quae iugularet Atridem?)*. Logically, *lamentabile votum* refers to Clytemnestra's gift (therefore *coniugis*), the gown. Cassandra does not play any major role in Dracontius's version of the story. She arrives before Agamemnon, which, as Bright (1987: 147) justly emphasizes, indicates how

Clytemnestra then, undoubtedly the central character of the story, is the reverse of Agamemnon, especially in the two aspects in which the king's nobleness is stressed. She is unfaithful (*adultera*, l. 117) and lascivious (*lasciva … gaudia*, l. 128; the erotic scene quoted above, ll. 227-231). In fact, she decides to commit mariticide only because of the *furor amoris* and the fear[223] that her sin will be revealed (*furor urget amoris / sollicitusque timor grassatur mente paventi*, ll. 155-156). She is also – in sharp contrast to her husband – devoid of any concern for her children. Agamemnon, as we remember, has sympathized with the 'weeping mother', apparently not taking into consideration that a woman might lack maternal affection. Clytemnestra though turns out 'psychopathically' cold, so to speak;[224] in truth, she seems quite glad that, as she thinks, Iphigenia is dead and urges Aegisthus: *non est quem metuas: brevis est et parvus Orestes, / unaque natarum cinis est per templa Dianae, / altera sexus iners, recidens, miseranda quid audet?* (ll. 193-195).

Clytemnestra's character is best demonstrated in the scenes in which she appears together with Aegisthus. Her domination is absolute and easy to see: all one has to do is to compare the very lines of the two personae. For instance, in the scene where they are discussing the regicide Clytemnestra's two lengthy speeches (ll. 163-203; 209-218) are separated by Aegisthus's most banal and simple question: <<*Tramite dic, quo*>> *pastor ait* <<*geminare valebo / hoc tam grande nefas? labor est extinguere regem / atque triumphantem (quod plus) in principis aula*>> (ll. 205-207). Therefore, Aegisthus – another of Dracontius's passive and cowardly male protagonists, although, interestingly enough, it will be he, quite astounding in his momentary activism, to slay Agamemnon – is for Clytemnestra a mere executor, an 'instrument of crime'.[225] This is fully reflected in the language she employs; the queen ostentatiously addresses her lover as *iuvenis* (l. 163)[226] or even *pastor*, emphasizing the class difference between them: *iubeoque rogoque / pastorem regina monens* (183-184). Dracontius then reverses the situation known from Seneca's *Agememnon*, where Clytemnestra, anxious and fearful, is urged by strong Aegisthus and the rational arguments he adduces. What we see in the *OT* is quite the opposite: the rational arguments, namely that there will be no-one to avenge the king's death and the whole plan how to execute the crime, all this is provided by Clytemnestra. What is more, she is also quite skillful in using emotional arguments, more typical of a woman, and this casuistry of hers is in a sense impressive: *formidine mortis / territa sollicitor, miserandi femina sexus* (ll. 184-185).

---

unconnected they are, and becomes 'only' (or as much as) the catalyst of the regicide in a sense that she predicts it on seeing Clytemnestra; she also predicts, less clearly though, the subsequent events and the eventual purging of Orestes (ll. 137-151). Her one and only appearance on stage is thus, indeed, fully theatrical.

[223] Clytemnestra's fear is best described in the scene showing her await Agamemnon's return on the seashore (ll. 108-132). Dracontius once again, like earlier in the *De raptu*, exploits the motif he must have considered particularly worthwhile: the relationship between the truth and the falsity (most probably this fascination of his was related to his experience as a lawyer). Clytemnestra pretends to be glad to see her husband soon, whereas in fact she is frightened. Then, since Agamemnon is not arriving, her fear turns into evil joy.

[224] Though, as we shall see, Orestes remembers Clytemnestra as an affectionate mother.

[225] See Aricò 1978: 34-36; 78.

[226] Like Helen does when addressing Paris, see above in Ch. I. 3. 2.

Presumably, the most intriguing image of depravation of the two regicides is given in the section describing the 'takeover'. Aegisthus is deeply worried about not having found Orestes, yet what frightens him even more than the disappearance of the prince[227] is the fact that he cannot find Agamemnon's treasure, either. Without it, as he reasons, he will not be able to maintain his power (ll. 305-315). Clytemnestra allays his fears by promising that she will bribe Mycenaean women with her jewelry hoping that they, subsequently, will persuade their husbands to accept the new rulers (ll. 316-334): *auro foeda placent, auro decorantur honesta, / emollit Cytherea trucem per proelia Martem. / crede mihi, iuvenis, de sexu femina tracto* (ll. 332-334).

In other words, as Dracontius demonstrates, the power of Clytemnestra and Aegisthus is based on a kind of 'escalation of immorality': depraved rulers, consequently, deprave their subjects. The culminating point of this whole segment is, still, the scene showing Clytemnestra deliver her 'coronation speech'[228] (ll. 384-411). Our poet once again gives us an example of pure sophistry. Clytemnestra describes Agamemnon as a tyrant who, waging war for so many years, condemned to death countless number of husbands, fathers, and sons. What the new 'leaders' promise instead is the blessed peace and even a democratic form of government: *germinis ille sui crudelis et impius hostis / rex Agamemnon erat, patriae dominator amarus: / civis Egistus erit me profitente maritum* (ll. 409-411). Clytemnestra's praise of peace sounds strikingly serious and true, in particular the phrase *curventur falcibus enses* (l. 398), having a clearly biblical flavor. Therefore, Bright is certainly not wrong arguing that in Clytemnestra'a speech one can hear "Dracontius's yearning for peace in a turbulent and violent world of the Vandal overlords."[229] It is quite probable that many of Dracontius's readers could and did interpret the passage exactly this way, ignoring completely who the speaker was. Nonetheless, it also seems that what the Carthaginian author wants to emphasize is, again, the problem of the power of a word. He shows how easily a capable sophist can play, indeed, juggle with words and with the very truth. One can hardly disagree that the argument about the 'exhausting war' depriving sons of their fathers is convincing; in fact, it is Orestes himself to admit that his was the life of a child raised by the only parent (*haec pater, haec mihi mater erat pugnante parente*, l. 571).

Finally, let us consider the last of the triad and the title character of the poem. Orestes, as I have already stressed, is above all a young prince (very Hamlet-like, indeed), schooled in Athens, the center of learning, as a boy of his social and material (his father's treasure is mentioned not without a purpose) status should be. The youngster even turns out a truly well-motivated student ([germanum Electra] *bene sollicitum studiis sapientibus addit*, l. 288;[230] *iunxerat hos* [Orestem et Pyladem] *studium sollers et gloria*

---

[227] I follow the lection of Grillone (2008: 121, com. to l. 310) who argues that there is no lacuna between ll. 309 and 310.

[228] As Grillone (2008: 124, com. to ll. 413b-52) calls it.

[229] Bright 1987: 162.

[230] Grillone (2008: 119, com. to l. 288), following Zurli 2001: 304, argues for the lection *sollicitum* in l. 288, which is fully convincing, indeed logical, considering the parallel to be found in the *AeP* (most probably a text modeled on the *OT*, see more in Ch. I. 6) where Perdica appears a similarly eager student (*Athenas / studiis animos praebebat et aures*, *AeP*, 19-20). Still, Orestes's

linguae, l. 292), which, as we shall see, will quite help him when the time comes. A similar portrayal of the protagonist has a palpable bourgeois overtone,[231] the same that could be noticed earlier in the way in which his generous and loving father is depicted. Orestes's nobleness is also revealed in one peculiar quality of his: he is gentle or even somewhat sentimental[232] (again, like a model prince Hamlet). The young man must certainly astound most readers with his childhood memories, quoted above, and with the affection he still has toward his mother (ll. 558-573). Apparently, he sees Clytemnestra as a feeble woman, a *muliercula*, for whom slaying her lover can be a sufficient punishment: *poena sit haec matri, ut prostrato vivat Egisto, / ante oculos recidente suos; muliercula tristis / aspiciat moechum, quae garrula vidit Atriden* (ll. 577-579).

In such a context nobody would expect from Dracontius's Orestes the resoluteness he shows as his father's avenger. Clytemnestra herself is most surprised; in fact, she first reacts exactly as if she had heard the prince's earlier words: *at genetrix dilata putat sibi parcere natum, / et secura sui iam pro pastore dolebat* (ll. 729-730). Nevertheless, the change in the young man's behavior turns out not solely sudden but decisive: Orestes somehow has become a different person. Dracontius's readership, already quite convinced that the poet would not propose haphazard, unconsidered solutions, must ask about the genesis and the sense of this peculiar transformation of the title character. This aspect is related to the central problem of the whole poem, the interpretation of the very matricide as such.

Antonino Grillone demonstrated[233] the fundamental role played here by Dorylas, the same *paidagogus* whose stunning performance given a few years earlier saved Orestes's (and Electra's) life. It is Dorylas, together with a band of faithful servants of the murdered king, who initiates the revenge, or rather the decent punishment of the regicides, begging Agamemnon's ghost for justice. As we remember, his prayer to the king is immediately followed by another one, addressed directly to the Furies, whom Dorylas summons with some anxiety, as if he really recognized the intertextual dimension of his words.[234] In fact, only after the invocation of the Sisters, Agamemnon's ghost, seeking now peace rather than revenge, responds and, eventually, starts to react as Dorylas has beseeched him to.[235] He appears to Orestes and Pylades in their sleep (the friends are so inseparable that they

---

motivation to study is emphasized also, as I shall repeat below, to explain why he turns out so successful in trial: he simply knows how to speak. Indeed, the more I read the *OT*, the more I am impressed by how coherent this poem is (as Grillone has always stressed, see especially his paper published in 1987), even if such little things as Orestes's results in school are taken into account.

[231] As Zurli (2001: 301-302) puts it: "come non consentire che Draconzio abbia (potuto e) inteso recuperare, con gusto alessandrineggiante, la versione 'preziosa' del mitema dell'esilio ad Atene di ascendenza omerica ed integrarla nella sua rivisitazione complessiva della saga di Oreste?" On Orestes educated as a model young prince, see especially Privitera 1996: 129.

[232] As Bright (1987: 170-171) rightly emphasizes.

[233] Now especially Grillone 2008: 16-17, see also his earlier remarks in Grillone 1987: 88-90.

[234] See above in Ch. I. 2. 4.

[235] Thus, Grillone (2008: 17) emphasizes: "Il ruolo dei servi, dunque, risulta tutt'altro che secondario, perché è solo per la costanza della loro supplica e per la loro ira, che il sovrano argivo reagisce alla sua inerzia, e attesta che agirà sul figlio non per risentimenti personali, ma per rendere giustizia ai servi che confidano in lui."

even have the same dreams) and urges the youngster to avenge his death, defining it as a necessary act of justice, indeed purifying the prince's mother from the sin of adultery, and as an 'old custom' through which Orestes will qualify in the eyes of his people, the Mycenaeans, as Agamemnon's legitimate son and heir:[236]

nullum crimen erit matrem punisse nocentem,
morte maritali sceleratam iure necabis.
natus amore pio, flammatus morte paterna,
vindicet ut patrem qui matrem straverit ictam,
crimina purgabit matris; de tempore prisco
nam patrem docet esse suum quem vindicat armis,
dignus adulterii vindex, pius ultor et heres. (539-545)

It is not coincidental that the king's ghost appears *both* to Orestes and Pylades. As we shall immediately see, the young prince, gentle as he still is (the affectionate image of his mother is precisely his reaction to what he has just heard from his father), and even dubious (l. 580), needs his friend's persuasion to become the *Orestes vindex*. Thus, Pylades in Dracontius's version of the story is not a mere foil for Agamemnon's son. Quite the contrary, it is he – with his natural decisiveness, opposed to Orestes's, indeed somewhat Hamletic, hesitation – to help, even to make the young prince change[237] into his father's true heir. As such, Pylades also fully participates in administering this unique act of justice.[238] He is the one to slay Aegisthus, making him die exactly as Agamemnon did. The killing though is a fully 'legal' execution, non a lynch by a blood-thirsty mob: Pylades, first, pierces the usurper with his sword and, only then, allows the royal servants to cut, to chop indeed, his body into pieces[239] (ll. 718-728).

---

[236] Therefore, Orestes's age, and the fact that he is of age, matters, see above the note to l. 455 *annorum septem spatiis et mensibus octo.*

[237] The difference between the two young men is clearly indicated in ll. 580-583: the narrator first recounts Orestes's sweet words about his mother and later shows how Pylades reacts on hearing them: *dixerat* [Orestes] *haec dubius; sed non cunctator amicus. / dentibus infrendens, suspiria traxit ab imo / pectore longa ferox, et sic aggressus Orestem / increpitat.* Right after Pylades's admonition, Orestes transforms into a totally different person, to the extent that now he looks truly like "rugged Pyrrhus;" it is ironic that later on this 'new Orestes' will indeed slay Pyrrhus: *talibus adloquiis accensus felle doloris, / erigitur iuvenale fremens, mortemque minatus / (dentibus illisis frangebat murmura morsus), / et quasi adulterium caperet pastoris Egisti / matris in amplexus infamia membra ligare, / percutit absentes nullo moriente reorum: / qualiter infremuit post somnia Pyrrhus Achillis, / quae sensus monuere suos cum nocte sopora, / Aeacide stimulante truci, cum posceret heros / virginis inferias, in Pergama saevior umbra* (ll. 616-625).

[238] See already Aricò 1978: 80.

[239] The description is, as one can expect, one of the most expressive and gruesome to be found in the poem: *dixit, et exertum costis immerserat ensem. / saucia membra trahunt famuli pede vincla ligantes, / postque fores portae quibus est prostratus Atrides, / ossibus effractis minuunt per mille secures, / et male partitos per vulnera palpitat artus* (ll. 724-728). As Grillone (2008: 15) stresses: "Pilade ha un ruolo basilare ... è il primo ad apparire, nella veste di giustiziere, nella regia: ordina ai servi di fare a pezzi con la scure, per la legge del taglione, Egisto, ma prima lo trafigge con la sua spada, perché la morte del tiranno appaia frutto di giustizia e non di sfrenata ira servile."

Orestes's sole task is to punish his mother, yet at the same time, as indicated by Agamemnon's ghost, to liberate her from her sin. In fact, Clytemnestra's body is not to be profaned like Aegisthus's. Quite the opposite: after death, or even through death, it will regain in a sense its original innocence. As it is well known (again, at least among experts in Dracontius),[240] the dying woman unexpectedly draws her garment down to cover her feet so as not to lie naked after death. This sudden *pudor* of hers does not have to be interpreted only in Christian terms,[241] but it is an excellent, very clear to read, indication that now Clytemnestra is not *polluta* any more.

What may seem surprising, and indeed theatrical, is the conversation between the mother and son in so peculiar a moment, the conversation in which the two interlocutors discuss … the right spot for Clytemnestra's execution. Clytemnestra, as if she were stamping herself as an adulteress, wants to die exactly where Aegisthus did and to be slain by Pylades. Orestes still 'argues' that she must be killed on her legitimate husband's grave as his sacrificial victim. Artificial as it sounds – which certainly was not a drawback for the ancient readership – the scene is also very informative and rhetorically motivated as it emphasizes and explains the crucial point of the story.

Thus, it could be concluded that the very motif of matricide is presented by Dracontius in a way that should make the final absolution of the title character logical, and indeed fair (in a sense at least). Orestes, the son of a noble, ideal father avenges his death and at the same time purifies his mother from her sin. It is the sin of adultery that, as it appears, triggered her further sins: above all mariticide, but also indifference toward her own children, corruption. Consequently, in compliance with an 'old custom', the same son and avenger legitimates himself as his father's decent heir and a true king, not a usurper.

But how so clear a structure can be juxtaposed and logically connected with what follows in the plot, that is the, as put above, romance-like multiplication of most varied events? If one takes into consideration the entire story, in its global sense so to speak, the meaning and function of particular elements, or single 'episodes', should prove understandable. The most controversial among them, the furious[242] (and barbarous) killing of Pyrrhus, is necessary simply to explain why it is Molossus, Pyrrhus's son, to accuse Orestes. Nevertheless, one may have an impression, most probably not wrong at all, that our poet does strive to complicate the action (even: as much as possible) to demonstrate his literary – and legal – skills.

---

[240] Aricò (1978: 93) finds the scene particularly attractive: "Se è vero che <<il criterio per giudicare se un personaggio è spesso risiede nella sua capacità di sorprenderci in modo convincente>> e che, <<se non ci sorprende mai, è piatto>> basterebbe questa 'sorpresa' d'una Clitennestra così delicatamente pudica nel momento della morte a rivelare la complessità del personaggio della regina."

[241] See especially Rapisarda 1964: 187, com. to ll. 786-788. What Bright (1987: 181-182), differently, sees here is above all an Ovidian inspiration (*Met.* 13.478-479): "Polyxenna acts in precisely the same manner as she dies."

[242] In fact, Orestes avenging his fiancée's abduction acts as furiously as if he were, indeed, a sort of Pyrrhus's *alter ego* (as we remember, to some extent Orestes is indeed transformed into a Pyrrhus by Pylades, see the narratorial comments in ll. 622-625). Interestingly, in Dracontius's version, it is only after the slaying of Pyrrhus that Clytemnestra's ghost starts to persecute Orestes.

It would be quite hard, indeed, not to argue so, taking into account the passion and competence with which Dracontius depicts the final court scene in Athens. As Bright and later Grillone[243] justly stressed, what we are given here is a true clash of two rhetorics, or even an illuminating example of a well-composed and a badly-composed speech. Molossus's speech is aggressive and, in addition, rhetorically weak. When the accuser intends to refer to his father's case, he employs wrong arguments: he tries to oppose but in effect compares Pyrrhus to Aegisthus, the adulterer par excellence, and consequently – unintentionally of course – implies his father's sin (a sort of *adulterium*, as the rape of someone else's fiancée must have been seen).[244] Whenever he focuses on Clytemnestra as murdered by her own son, he actually stresses her guilt all the more. A speech of this sort must inevitably fail to win over the audience if placed side by side with a speech by a brilliantly educated *rhetor* who at the very outset emphasizes his deepest respect for his Athenian public,[245] the jury above all, and presents his very self first as a tender and loving fiancé,[246] whose future wife was abducted, and later as a man already judged and even absolved by the gods who have restored his sanity: *non de lite mea sententia vestra ferenda est, / sed de iure deum, qui me purgasse probantur, / dum medicinalem tribuunt per corda salutem* (ll. 921-923).

It might be argued then that it is Orestes himself in his remarkable speech to suggest that his story is interpretable, indeed should be interpreted, as one carrying a much more profound moral message. What it shows is that human paths, curved as they may be, can be made straight precisely thanks to divine providence. It is symbolized – in Orestes's world – first by Diana, thanks to whom Orestes has been cured from his madness (which finally explains why Iphigenia could not leave Tauris earlier with her father), next by Minerva whose vote yields an absolute majority,[247] ultimately confirming the verdict of the human tribunal. This way, Dracontius's Orestes is absolved from a double perspective, human and divine. Nevertheless, in the human dimension, it happens also – if not above all – because the accuser has turned out unfit (as the brilliant law graduate Orestes stresses: *Pyrrhus erat raptor, vindex post bella rapinae: / arguit unus iners quem comprobat ordo deorum*, ll. 934-935). A keen reader might ask then: "what would happen, if the prosecution was better represented?" It is not improbable at all, as I believe, that Dracontius, an excellent lawyer and intelligent writer, did intend to provoke our anxiety thus. That anxiety can, eventually, make us realize that it is only the divine justice, or actually the *clementia caeli* as shown by Minerva, which is truly indisputable, or rather not open to question (*quis temerator erit caelestia iura movere?*, l. 951).

---

243 Bright (1987: 191-196) provides a very good analysis of the two speeches. Grillone (2008: 17; 1987: 102) emphasizes above all that Molossus eventually turns out an unfit accuser.

244 Grillone 2008: 17.

245 Orestes starts (ll. 911-916) by complimenting Athens and Athenian women in particular for being decent, faithful wives, which is in fact, as Grillone (1987: 78-79) pointed out, a very good rhetoric strategy of his, considering the nature of Clytemnestra's crime.

246 Bright (1987: 194) is right noting that here again Orestes appears as a sentimental young man.

247 Bright (1987: 196-197), who generally argues for Dracontius's use of Aeschylus, is also quite convinced here that our poet follows the *Oresteia* and not Aelius Aristides or a scholiast.

I. 4. 'Mixing of genres' in Dracontius's epyllia

The extensive use of various literary strategies, various features typical of 'other' (= non-epic) genres, appears to be one of the fundamental markers of the epyllion genre. To be precise – as Jackson justly argued[248] – the tendency to comprise many different, sometimes contradictory, elements is similarly common in the miniature epic as in its grand counterpart. In the epyllion case, the presence of the 'non-epic' is only easier to see or maybe even more ostentatious since the Alexandrian (and the neo-Alexandrian late antique) poetics positively advertizes all that seems contrary to such compositional categories as 'stylistic uniformity' or 'proportionality'.

As I have emphasized, the epyllion authors, especially the Latin ones, most willingly and most systematically exploit these forms and literary devices that add a particular 'emotional' coloring to their works. Therefore, the influence of the lyric and – what may be even more important – the tragic turns out so pervasive. The latter does often shape the overall structure of a poem. The division of the action into scenes, the limited number of characters who appear singly or in twos and speak individually rather than in a dialogue, finally, the motif of the tragic error as the factor determining the plot, all these features – as Richardson stressed[249] – result from the fact that the Latin poets compose their epyllia, indeed, with an eye to tragedy.

We can already say that many of the above-mentioned qualities are easily recognizable in Dracontius's miniature epic. As far as the number of personae is concerned, the Carthaginian author is consistent in limiting it to a necessary minimum. Therefore, in the *Hylas* Hercules is deprived of the company of the Argonauts. Similarly, Jason appears to be left completely alone in Colchis.[250] The protagonists, indeed, more often seem to speak one after another, like Helenus, Cassandra, and Apollo in the *De raptu Helenae* (episode I), rather than have a real, vivid dialogue. One is tempted to observe that the most lively conversation between Dracontius's characters is the one between Orestes and his mother. Not rare, conversely, is the situation when a personage is a true soloist addressing only the reader. Alone are Hercules weeping for Hylas and Paris as the shipwrecked sailor crying over his fate. Dorilas also appears singly in his remarkable performance of the lament over the miserable death of prince Orestes. In fact, our Carthaginian willingly confesses that he draws his inspiration from the tragic genre – most openly, as we know, in the *Medea* and in the (*nomen est omen*, I should add) *Orestis Tragoedia* – which does not mean of course that he himself would have any intention whatsoever to question the epic format of his poems.[251]

On the other hand – we can also state this at the very outset of the present chapter – what Dracontius's texts certainly lack for is the sentimental coloring, not less idiosyncratic of the epyllic genre. His portrayal of Medea, so much different from her Ovidian counter-

---

[248] See above in Ch. I.1.

[249] See above in Ch. I.1.

[250] If we do not take into consideration the illusory mention of the *sodales*, see above in Ch. I. 3. 3.

[251] See above in Chs. I. 2. 3 and I. 2. 4 and below in Chs. I. 4. 3 and I. 4. 4.

part (in the *Metamorphoses* 7), turns significant in this context: his Medea does not talk about love either with herself or with her nurse. In fact, as we surely remember, in *Romuleon* 10 the nurse is not the girl's confidante but, on the contrary, a horrifying guardian of her cruelty. The most beautiful sentimental passage that we have from Dracontius's pen is the courteous and truly subtle praise addressed by Paris to Helen in the moment of their encounter in Cyprus. The speech is so impressive that one can almost hardly blame the queen for her spontaneous reaction. Unfortunately, Paris's words are immersed in a wider context of a clearly satiric overtone: one finds out quite soon that the youngster, rhetorically skillful as he is, in fact, does not embody manly courage. Thus, the praise of Helen given by Dracontius's Paris remains merely a preview, an unfulfilled promise of a romantic love story that this epyllion could be, had our poet only wanted to compose it in such a convention.

Therefore, the observations made in previous chapters have already led us to certain conclusions about Dracontius's exploitation of diverse generic strategies. The aim of the present chapter is to discuss this question in a fuller and more systematic way. What I intend to concentrate on is above all the tragic, sometimes even dramatic *sensu stricto*, dimension of Dracontius's poems. It should not be less interesting though to pay attention also to other elements and other intertextual as well as 'intergeneric' aspects of his four epyllia, showing that the Carthaginian did draw upon both (high and ancient) literary tradition and, likewise, upon his contemporary culture.[252]

I. 4. 1. *HYLAS*

I have already noted that the *Hylas* with its overall structure and, what is even more relevant, with its 'message' is still rather far from tragic, which, along with the absence of the narrator-moralist, makes it notably different from Dracontius's other epyllia. In fact, the final lament of Hercules closes with quite 'optimistic' statement, fully concordant, to be exact, with the reading of the whole story announced by the poet in his short introduction (*Fata … versa … in melius*, ll. 1-2; *Exulta, genetrix, nimium laetare, beata / ante parens hominis, pulchri modo numinis auctor*, ll. 162-163). Apparently, Alcmena's son finds a convincing and satisfactory explanation of the event to give to Hylas's mother. Needless to say, he himself seems more than pleased with similar interpretation of the boy's disappearance. This very closure as well as the general tone of Hercules's lament – it is more than clear that what he weeps for is that there will be nobody to admire his deeds now[253] – make the passage much more parodistic than tragic, indeed.[254]

---

[252] As I have mentioned, this is what Bright emphasizes in his book. The point as such is not wholly wrong; indeed, it can be argued that what Dracontius exploits are also elements of the popular culture of his time (mime and pantomime can be certainly defined so). Yet some of Bright's conjectures, especially about the Vandal influences on Dracontius's poems, are quite hard to accept.

[253] See ll. 152-158: *O frustra nutrite, puer, spectator ubique / virtutis per cuncta meae (te teste pericla / saepe tuli, cum victus aper, cum fracta leonis / colla Cleonaei telo parcente necantur, / cum simul Antaeum rapui Telluris alumnum): / quis mihi sudorem lasso post proelia terget? / Quis comes alter erit cum dat fera bella noverca?*

[254] See Bright 1987: 41-42.

Let us focus now on other means of expression and literary conventions employed by Dracontius in his juvenile yet certainly not negligible poem. The lengthy first scene opens with a charming picture in which we see Cupid, the little winged boy, sitting on his mother's lap and demanding caresses:[255] *Fuderat Idalius gremio se forte parentis / pinniger et collum violentis cinxerat ulnis / oscula pura rogans* (ll. 4-6). After this short description, the narrator allows his protagonists to speak. As I have already mentioned, Cupid's speech, inserted into two speeches by Venus, is a mere enumeration of victims of the little divinity and as such quite a typical catalogue of themes to be elaborated in erotic poetry. Venus's words, however, are composed as a conventional prayer with the usual hymnic invocation at the outset:

O mundi domitor, caeli quoque, flamma Tonantis,
numen posco tuum cuius sub iure vaporo,
per tua tela, puer, fecundis illita flammis,
ut des effectum votis de more parentis.
Nil rude, nate, precor nec supplex improba posco (8-12)

The ostentatiously submissive tone of Venus's speech (*numen tuum*, *posco*, *precor*, *supplex*) sounds striking indeed, much exaggerated, as it seems, if one takes into consideration that the addressee is actually a somewhat spoilt and not too patient child. Still, a more careful reader should discover soon that Dracontius always employs this sort of language whenever he imitates the prayer form. Juno speaking to Venus, in the *Medea*, is similarly obsequious, and so is the latter approaching, again, her little son. Needless to say, in the *OT*, the petition directed to Diana by pious Agamemnon sounds also most humble. In fact, in prayers, no matter who the speaker and the addressee are, our poet never deviates from the dictates of the generic convention:[256] the introduction resembles a hymn of praise, and the very request a supplication. Undoubtedly, it could be interpreted as an example of compositional schematism, yet this sort of schematism is simply not less idiosyncratic of late antique verse than prose.

The second scene, describing the transformation of Cupid, is even more visual than the beginning of the first one. Indeed, one may have an impression that the author does his best to make his reader imagine this episode as a theatrical spectacle. Cupid, as Bright justly noted,[257] is shown here as a pantomimic actor wearing a costume: a robe, under which he tucks his wings, and a mask. Typical of a mime artist is also the very flexibility of his body and the grace with which he moves:

moxque dei vultus vestivit imago Naidis;
tendit membra puer, longos ut crescat in artus,
ut possit complere dolos ac iussa parentis;

---

[255] Since what we focus on now are especially the generic connotations of certain passages, it should be noted that the very scene of conversation between Venus and Amor is a regular part of late antique epithalamia, see already Morelli 1910: 405 ff.; Bright 1987: 29. In addition, worth reading are succinct remarks on the phenomenon of 'mixing of genres' in the *Hylas*, and in Dracontius's epyllia in general, by Weber 1995: 238-245.

[256] As Bright (1987: 51) notes commenting on Juno's address to Venus in the *Medea*.

[257] Bright 1987: 35-37.

<usque> pedes fluitans vestis laxatur ad imos,
candida diffusi ludunt per colla capilli
et vento crispante gradu coma fluctuat acta,
frons nudata decet diviso fulgida crine;
et velut invitos gressus pudibunda movebat
incedens fluxoque latent sub tegmine pinnae. (81-89)

Certainly, a god in disguise, in particular when he is disguised as a girl, looks funny enough, and not less hilarious than Hercules during his truly pitiful lament. Still, I do not think that the ironic portrayal of the god and the hero given by Dracontius in his poem should be seen as carrying a more profound anti-pagan message.[258] Our poet is here not more – and not less – malicious than Ovid telling us how Jove lays aside his glorious dignity and assumes the semblance of a bull (*Met.* 2.847-851).

Bright, following Gennaro D'Ippolito,[259] argues convincingly that this little episode seems to allude to a very popular, especially in the culture of the later Empire, subtype of pantomime, i.e. the aquatic mime. The association is all the more natural since the whole scene takes place *Penei sub fonte* (l. 54) and the female protagonists are the Naiads, the spring nymphs, who woken up by Cupid – as we remember, the divine boy has thrown a stone into the water – emerge, even jump out, of the water (*exiliunt cunctae*, l. 79), just like (nude, obviously enough) aquatic mime actresses. It seems one can accept the conjecture proposed by D'Ippolito that Dracontius describes here a scene actually exploited and performed in such spectacles,[260] so – in other words – he 'quotes' or 'paraphrases' a theatrical motif, just as if he quoted, or rather truly paraphrased, a literary theme *sensu stricto*. At the same time, however, it seems most reasonable to suppose that the poet's actual aim is not so much to describe or remember one specific spectacle – he himself and his readers must have seen hundreds of them – but rather, precisely, to convince his public that this whole scene could be imagined, visualized and hence 'seen' in a sense, having in mind, of course, images, colors, costumes, and actresses one could watch many times in real theatrical spectacles. In other words, here Dracontius, through his poetry, tries not just to imitate but indeed to emulate the aquatic mime.[261]

Allusions to the aquatic mime and, more widely speaking, to pantomime will become one of the most important – and most intriguing – components of Dracontius's epyllion

[258] As Bright (1987: 43-44) argues, see also above.

[259] D'Ippolito 1962: 4-5.

[260] D'Ippolito (1962: 4), analyzing the most significant in this context prologue to the *Medea* (to which I shall return below), asks logically: "Il poeta prosegue invocando Melpomene, la musa tragica, e ci addita così rappresentazioni mimiche come fonti per la prima parte del suo epillio, ove proprio si riscontrano le singolari innovazioni acquatiche nel mito, tragedie per la seconda, che invece segue sostanzialmente la versione mitica tradizionale. Perché negar fede alla dichiarazione dello stesso poeta?" D'Ippolito also supposes that aquatic mime could have inspired the first scene of the poem as well, i.e. the conversation between Venus and Cupid. It is possible in fact (though hardly provable of course), considering that a similar scene can be found also in the *Medea*, precisely in the first, pantomimic part of the poem.

[261] See more below in reference to the *Medea*. On the emulation of visual arts in late antique poetry, see the indispensable Roberts 1989a: 66-121.

poetics. Therefore, the juvenile *Hylas* once again turns out a text worthy of our attention, a prelude to later, more mature poems. But it should be stressed in this place that when exploiting, or rather truly creating, pantomimic scenes (and pantomimic images), the Carthaginian did not always and only aim to give to his work a somewhat frivolous coloring (which, on the other hand, would be fully concordant with the epyllic tradition). Such is the case in the *Hylas*: an imaginative reader should not find it too difficult to see the nude mimic actresses in the Naiads jumping out of the water. Still, as we shall soon discover, Dracontius is not less impressive, and certainly he is more moving, when using elements of the tragic pantomime.

I. 4. 2. *DE RAPTU HELENAE*

A peculiar quality of the *De raptu* is the fact that each of the five major scenes of the poem was composed in different literary conventions. In the previous chapter, I have already discussed the so-called Salaminian episode (or scene II), being indeed a sort of *controversia* and as such a good example of prose inspirations in Dracontius's poetry.[262] Now, we shall pay more attention to the remaining four segments, namely: Paris's arrival to Troy (scene I), the storm at sea (scene III), the encounter with Helen in Cyprus (scene IV), and finally, the unexpected and ostensibly happy return to Troy of the young prince with his bride (scene V).

I have noted above that the first episode consists of two parts. The more descriptive first part shows Paris, definitely bored with the rural life, approach Troy, among the worst possible omens,[263] and appear to his rather confused, if not embarrassed indeed, family (*ammissumque nefas generosa mente fatetur / fusus in ora rubor*, ll. 105-106; *convictusque pater veniam de prole negabat*, l. 108[264]). The main objective of this scene is, undoubtedly, to present the shepherd prince in an unfavorable light: what is emphasized is his certainly improper behavior – after all, he interrupts a religious ceremony (*Dum pergunt et templa petunt, prorumpit in agmen / pastor et attonitos elata voce salutat*, ll. 89-90) – and his vain boasts (*Nec pastor sit vile, Phryges: ego iurgia divum / compressi, nam lite caret me iudice caelum*, ll. 98-99). This whole sub-unit is, above all, ironic, even one could say somewhat comic, as far as the characterization of the protagonist is taken into account.

The subsequent episode is remarkably different. First and foremost, it is already full of a true dramatic tension, also in the formal sense as we can really have the impression of

---

[262] On interactions between prose and poetry in late antiquity and, more specifically, on a sort of fashion in late antique poetry to draw inspirations from prose, see especially Roberts 1989a: 11-12; more generally: 39-65.

[263] See ll. 71-77: *Vix viderat arcem / lassus, et intactae procumbunt culmina turris, / ingemit et tellus, muri pars certa repente / concidit et Scaeae iacuerunt limina portae; / tunc Simois siccavit aquas, crystallina Xanthi / fluminis unda rubet, sudat pastore propinquo / Palladium vel sponte cadunt simulacra Minervae.*

[264] Wolff (1996: 128-129 n. 67) proposes to understand *convictus* as "confondu;" he also maintains the *negabat*, as in the manuscript, following Vollmer's suggestion: "ut voluerit poeta dicere, Priamum se ipsum accusando negavisse dignum esse cui Paris ignosceret." I find it convincing.

'watching' a theatrical spectacle.[265] Its two personae, speaking one after another, as if they were indeed on stage (in a sort of Senecan drama), are the twin seers, Helenus and Cassandra. The narrator's role is now reduced to the one of a 'stage director': the comments he gives are more than brief and focus only on the question how the 'actors' should perform their parts: *Tunc Helenus vates templum dimisit et aram / et procul exclamat* (ll. 119-120); *Dum loquitur, Cassandra venit furibunda sacerdos / et matrem complexa canit* (ll. 134-135).

The speeches by the two characters are, obviously enough, full of affectation, which harmonizes not only with the topic itself but also with the tragic (and dramatic) convention, hence exclamations, oxymorons, rhetorical questions: [Helenus:] *quid pietas crudelis agit, quid perditis urbem?* (l. 121); *Sed quid fata veto, quid fixos arceo casus, cum nihil adversis prosit prudentia signis? / Me fortuna potens expectat Pyrrhus et ingens* (ll. 131-133); [Cassandra:] *Quid, mater iniqua, quid, pater infelix, quid funera nostra paratis? / Immemor heu pietas* (ll. 135-137); *Sed quid vana cano?* (l. 152). Both seers predict the events of the war to come, especially the most horrible ones: the killing of Hector, the death of little Astyanax thrown from the walls, the slaying of Priam at the altar, finally, their own fate. Still, Cassandra tries also to avert the disaster somehow: she appeals to Troilus and Hector, to her parents, and to all Trojan citizens (*surgite, cives*, l. 159; *hoc cives audite mei, laudate parentes*, l. 176) to kill Paris as a sacrificial victim for the angry goddesses, Juno and Minerva, and thus to save the city: *Pectore Cisseo rapiatur pignus acerbum / macteturque nefas et Pergama nostra pientur, / placetur Iuno, placetur virgo Minerva* (ll. 164-166).

With Cassandra's speech the action reaches its climax. What she says is so moving and so deeply logical (she stresses, above all, Paris's objective guilt: *Vrbibus in multis mos est donare Salutem / mortibus insontum, sed vos mactate nocentem, / ut liceat servare pios*, ll. 169-171) that the main character may already seem doomed; one is tempted to conclude that he could be saved now only by a miraculous event. This is precisely what happens. Suddenly, to the seers' as well as to the reader's surprise, Apollo appears on stage just like a model *deus ex machina*, making the associations with tragic drama of Euripidean provenance[266] even more evident. Needless to say, Apollo's intervention saves the ill-fated shepherd-prince since the warnings of the two prophets compared with his words and orders must sound unbelievable and insignificant.

Therefore, this 'mini tragedy' ends ostensibly with a true *laetus exitus* (just like Euripides's *Iphigenia in Tauris* or *Helen*, to quote two most classic examples). Nonetheless, some particulars do not allow us to be so optimistic. First of all, Apollo's intervention, just like the speeches of Helenus and Cassandra several verses before, is introduced by

---

[265] On the segment as reminiscent of tragic drama, see Bright 1987: 99. On dramatic (tragic) structure of the whole poem, without being more specific though, see already Morelli 1912: 114: "in carmine nostro, quod ex 655 versibus constat, 231 personarum verba tuentur. Atqui in tam panso orationum corpore actio minime languet; immo saepe tam sunt motae, tantis impletae furoribus, ut interdum non epicum opus sed tragoediam legere videamur."

[266] Which, still, does not have to be interpreted, in my view, as proof of Dracontius's direct knowledge of Euripides's plays. His skillfulness in exploiting Euripidean themes, as well as Euripidean literary devices and tools, could be a result of general erudition, especially of reading most varied rhetorical material. A similar point can be made in reference to the Euripidean 'flavor' of the *OT*, as argued by Schetter 1985: 53 and Santini 2006: 55.

the narrator. This time, it would still be a mistake to argue that the poetic *ego* is, again, a mere 'director' whose role is to inform the reader-spectator what character should appear on stage in a given moment. Quite the contrary, the narrator, fully exploiting his omniscience and even demonstrating it, clearly defines the true intentions of the god: *visus adest cunctis Phrygibus Thymbraeus Apollo, / qui mercede carens conclusit Pergama muro / et genus ingratum poenas persolvat avari / exoptat* (ll. 184-187). Thus, a careful reader must know from the very beginning that whatever Apollo will do shall be done to take revenge on the Trojans. Consequently, he/she should not be much surprised finding out that the god turns out a sophist, manipulating the truth and misleading his human audience. It is, in fact, very impressive how skillfully Dracontius combines in this scene two different conventions. On the one hand, he is quite consistent in shaping it as a tragedy with a *laetus exitus* and even encourages us, the readers, to feel like listeners-spectators. Therefore, he allows his protagonists to speak and hides himself behind the mask of a 'director', or – to put it differently – reduces his narratorial comments to mere 'stage directions'. Still, on the other hand, he intertwines when it is necessary a (discreet) epic element, the voice of an *omniscient* narrator, into this dramatic structure.

There is yet another interesting aspect. This scene, a mini-tragedy with an (ostensible) happy ending, opens the whole story. For a careful reader this should be another alarming signal. "If at the beginning things go well for the protagonist(s), at the end they must go badly" is one of the most obvious formulas quoted to describe the tragedy. A 'happy ending' at the very outset of the poem is thus a clear sign that the true final must be a catastrophe. Besides, the concept of a 'happy ending at the outset' sounds paradoxically enough and ironically enough to be interpreted as tragic irony.

The scenes III and IV, the storm at sea and the encounter of Paris and Helen in Cyprus, are two most 'epic' segments of the entire poem. What makes them epic is not only the narration but above all very interesting literary connotations they carry. A competent reader will immediately notice that they both evoke nothing more and nothing less than Virgil's *Aeneid*. That is also why the passage treating the storm at sea is placed right after the Salaminian episode.[267]

The storm was, in fact, a motif exploited in Paris's story.[268] But what makes Dracontius's version particular is firstly a clear reference to Virgil's *Aeneid* 1 (ll. 81-123)[269] and secondly – equally important – the change of the customary sequence of events. 'Normally' the storm occurs after Paris's elopement with Helen and is part of the adventure which brings them back to Troy. Dracontius, placing the scene before the very episode of

[267] Certainly, as Bright (1987: 117; 120) emphasizes, the storm at sea is an epic device par excellence, serving to move the hero from one adventure to the next, dating as early as from Homer's *Odyssey* Book 5. In Dracontius, the scene is also necessary as an entr'acte between the Salaminian episode and the very story of Paris and Helen since the storm makes a good explanation why Paris is not to be followed by his companions from now on.

[268] Bright (1987: 118) points to the *Cypria* as an interesting analogy.

[269] See the comment ad loc. in Wolff 1996: 152-153 n. 227; earlier Agudo Cubas 1978: 279. Bright (1987: 118) rightly points to Africus, the wind specified by Dracontius in the opening verse of the passage (l. 385) as a clear indication of the source. The Canadian scholar also notes a certain analogy between Paris meeting Helen in Dracontius and Aeneas meeting Dido in the *Aeneid*.

the couple's encounter, gives a legible indication that Virgil inspired not only his description of the *procella* but also (and especially) the image of the two leading protagonists: in his version of the story Paris meeting Helen is, indeed, a 'new embodiment' of Aeneas meeting Dido.

As a matter of fact, there is some further similarity between the two epic heroes, Odysseus and Aeneas, experiencing the storm at sea and Dracontius's Paris. The constitutive part of the theme appears to be the lament of the hero. It is already Homer's Odysseus who weeps the miserable form of his death and wishes he had perished at Troy and had had his funeral rites. The motif is, naturally, echoed by Virgil in the *Aeneid*: *o terque quaterque beati, / quis ante ora patrum Troiae sub moenibus altis / contigit oppetere* (*Aen.* 1.94-96).[270] Interestingly, also Paris cries over his fate, yet, as we remember, the language he employs is quite peculiar. The young Trojan exalts the carefree and safe life of the shepherd. To be exact, contrasting the two models of life, of the shepherd and of the sailor, is by no means unusual: an excellent example of the topos can be found in Horace's *Ode* 1.1.[271] It is significant, however, that the laudation is given here by the very same protagonist who earlier rejected his humble and boring lifestyle and set off for a journey to Greece precisely to wash away the stigma of once being a *pastor*.

In addition, the passage is stylistically interesting, providing one more of so many examples of Dracontius's technical mastery. It combines two Virgilian vocabularies, the pastoral and the epic: the shepherd's *carmen*, echoing the *Eclogues* and the *Georgics*,[272] is incorporated into an image modeled on the *Aeneid*. One should also note that the bucolic inclusion is, in fact, long (almost half of the whole episode: 23 verses out of 50: ll. 402-424 as inserted into ll. 385-434), besides its imagery is very pastoral indeed: the little pleasures of the shepherd's life are worth emphasizing here, such as milking the sheep, making cheese, especially if contrasted with – and named just a few lines later – hardships born by rulers:

Mulgere balantum depressis ubera mammis
decedente die noctis venientibus umbris
quantus amor, cum lacte novo iam caseus albens
formatur manibusque premit lac pastor ad orbem! (414-417)

Nam gravis est regnare labor, metus excutit ingens
corda ducum, ne bella ruant, ne tela minentur
exitium crudele: necis timor omnis ubique est. (420-422)

---

[270] Interestingly, the topos is also present in the *Tristia* 1, defined often (Rahn 1958) as 'Ovid's Odyssey', and indeed marked with clear epic coloring: *nec letum timeo; genus est miserabile leti* (*Tr.* 1.2.51); *est aliquid, fatove suo ferrove cadentem / in solida moriens ponere corpus humo, / et mandare suis aliqua et sperare sepulcrum / et non aequoreis piscibus esse cibum* (*Tr.* 1.2.53-56).

[271] See *Carm.* 1.1.15-18: *Luctantem Icariis fluctibus Africum / mercator metuens otium et oppidi / laudat rura sui; mox reficit rates / quassas, indocilis pauperiem pati.* It seems interesting to note that Ovid in the *ex Ponto* makes a similar point, and – like Dracontius's Paris here – employs the same bucolic vocabulary: *at, puto, sic urbis misero est erepta voluptas, / quolibet ut saltem rure frui liceat!* (*ex P.* 1.8.39-40); *ipse ego pendentis, liceat modo, rupe capellas, / ipse velim baculo pascere nixus oves; / ipse ego, ne solitis insistant pectora curis, / ducam ruricolas sub iuga curva boves* (*ibid.*, 51-54).

[272] See Agudo Cubaz 1978: 280-281; Bright 1987: 120.

The change of style seems an excellent sign of Paris's 'temperamental' instability: he is supposed to play the hero – as he himself wished – but he plays, even recites, the shepherd's part, as if he forgot the one of 'Aeneas'. It is hardly surprising that the narrator once again cannot avoid calling him a *pastor* (l. 432).

However insubordinate the protagonist may be, a competent reader should probably guess quite easily that the epic motif of the storm at sea is to be a prelude to a 'romantic' episode. Thus, further parallels with the *Aeneid* Book 1 and the scene of the encounter of Aeneas and Dido are just inevitable.[273] Firstly, it is the meeting in the temple: of Juno in the *Aeneid*, of Venus in the *De raptu*, and the invitation from an unknown queen to her residence.[274] Secondly, there are the bird omens with the 'obligatory' swans indicating Venus's presence. In the *Aeneid*, they are immediately given a positive interpretation by a mysterious archeress who only when turned back is recognized by Aeneas as his mother. The swans, pursued initially by the bird of Jove, now "skimming the ground, and seeking the quiet stream,"[275] betoken the happy return of the Trojan fleet. In the *De raptu*, apart from the swans, there are doves: an obvious sign of marriage; yet the whole message is less propitious: the kite and the hawk signify war and death, as an augur brought by chance to Cyprus immediately explains.[276] Thirdly, it is the extraordinary

[273] See Bright 1987: 122; 124 and much earlier Morelli 1912: 109. Yet the Italian scholar notes soundly: "Ad haec declaranda, a similitudine cum Vergilio incipiendum. In dearum templis inter se primum vident Paris et Helena, Aeneas et Dido; hi in Iunonis, illi in Veneris aede; ibique primas amoris flammas suscipiunt. Inde ad regiam pergunt ubi, Veneris iussu, cum Helena tum Dido Cupidinis spiculis feriuntur. Ne tamen huic similitudini nimium ponderis tribuamus monet magna pars quam apud omnes scriptores in Helenae Paridisque amoribus conciliandis habet Venus; quam magna exemplorum copia et picturae testantur, in quibus amantibus Aphrodite adsistit uno vel pluribus Amoribus comitata." As a matter of fact, the specific examples he gives later on, of Colluthus and Dares, are, as Bright (1987: 125-126) argues, not truly convincing. Nevertheless, it is right to point out that already in Virgil the 'romantic' setting was typical – and thus easily recognizable for the reader – rather than original. Jason met Medea in Hecate's shrine at least from Apollonius's times, Amor's interventions were ubiquitous in Medea's, Dido's, and Helen's stories.

[274] Still, in the *De raptu* the order is reversed: Paris, as shipwrecked sailor is offered accommodation in the queen's temporary residence. On the way there, in the temple, he meets Helen and, as we know, they do not hesitate too much to elope.

[275] I paraphrase John Dryden's translation (*Aen.* 1.449) accessible online at: http://andromeda.rutgers.edu/~jlynch/Texts/aeneis.html [May 18, 2010].

[276]

Namque tibi reduces socios classemque relatam
nuntio, et in tutum versis aquilonibus actam,
ni frustra augurium vani docuere parentes.
Aspice bis senos laetantis agmine cycnos,
aetheria quos lapsa plaga Iovis ales aperto
turbabat caelo nunc terras ordine longo
aut capere, aut captas iam despectare videntur
(*Aen.* 1.390-396)

Interea nivei volitant per litora cycni
flumine contempto, placidas hinc inde columbas
molliter intendunt omnes per inane vagari,
quas insanus agit rapidusque sequente volatu
miluus insontes cunctas clamore fatigat,
quas super accipiter volitans gravis imminet ales.
(*De raptu*, 453-58)
conubium spondent praefulgens ore decoro

appearance of the male protagonist, who naturally must attract the queen.[277] Nevertheless, at this very point, the differences are not less important than the similarities: in the *Aeneid* it is the mother Venus herself to make Aeneas beautiful, whereas Paris, obviously enough, once again changes his clothes, now wearing (needless to say) Tyrian purple and gold. In addition, what he will seduce with are also words, yet his words like all his beauty are simply perfidious.

Therefore, it could be argued once again that Paris playing (or trying to play) Aeneas is a model exemplification of the fact that what we read is a 'non-Homeric' epic. Just like the poet who dares not be a second Homer or Virgil but considers himself a fox eating the leavings despised by the two *numina*, his protagonist, Paris, is not able to become a true *heros*, even were he assigned such a role. Yet the difference between them two is quite obvious: the poet knows his place, Paris quite the contrary.

Last but not least, let us have a look at the final scene, probably the most significant of the entire poem. As I have already pointed out, what makes it unique is the complete lack of characters' speeches; all the events are recounted by the narrator. A careful reader will certainly not ignore this sudden change as in all previous segments the protagonists can speak at will, even though the poet – whenever he finds it necessary – comments on their words (in this very scene what he comments on are not words but the actual feelings of the protagonists).

One is tempted to suppose that this unexpected lapse into silence of all the actors may be a sign, a suggestion, given by the author to read this scene precisely as pantomimic, as a mute spectacle, which this time is a tragic pantomime of course. Certainly, once again – just like in the case of the aquatic mime evocations in the *Hylas* – it would be quite pointless to wonder if and how faithfully Dracontius 'quotes' here a single scene of a single show. It seems more relevant that the poet also now tries to induce us, his readers, to imagine that we are watching a play.

What is the sense of employing a similar literary strategy? The episode closes with a very alarming simile. Its immediate point of reference is Polites, Troilus's companion, but it should not be an over-interpretation to argue that it may also comprehend all heroes named in the poem. Polites, as we remember, is compared to a shadow which does not move on its own but only imitating someone else's movements, or even, to quote Bright, "in obligatory response to external acts."[278] Thus, it is quite natural we have the sensation that all we are watching thanks to the narrator's words may be, precisely, a sort

---

haud aliter puppesque tuae pubesque tuorum
aut portum tenet aut pleno subit ostia velo.
(*ibid.*, 399-400)

Idaliae volucres, de gente Tonantis olores
promittunt genitam, sed miluus horrida fata;
Ditis enim signatur avis … (*ibid.*, 463-466)

There are, in addition, some Silius Italicus's (*Pun.* 4.105-119) imitations in the above-quoted Dracontius's passage, see already Morelli 1912: 107 (who also points at an allusion to Statius), recently Simons 2005: 268.

[277] See *Aen.* 1.589-593.

[278] Bright 1987: 132. Bright makes a similar point interpreting the scene as taking place in the world of shades, yet he does not emphasize the possible pantomimic connotations it may have.

of shadow play, a pantomimic performance given (would it be so?) indeed by the shades in the Underworld. Those shades merely imitate, or evoke, with an empty gesture their past deeds;[279] they are already doomed, even reconciled to their fate and do not try to resist it. One can hardly imagine a more expressive, although mute, closure of the story of Paris and his crime, the crime that has determined his own future and the future of thousands of others.

I. 4. 3. *MEDEA*

Emphasizing aqua- and pantomimic inspirations in the *Hylas* and the *De raptu*, I have argued that they should be interpreted as a sort of *aemulatio* rather than as an imitation or 'quotation' *sensu stricto*. It is quite certain that composing his poem and enriching it with such (extra-literary) elements, Dracontius did have in mind some more or less specific performances or some most often repeated scenes or 'effects'. It is also probable that he presumed that his literary audience should have a similar, comparable to his own, 'theatrical erudition'. It seems, however, that what he aimed at most of all was, precisely, to *make* his readers *imagine* a given episode, to make them believe that through the verbal description they can see it not worse (possibly better) than in the theater.

A declaration that the poet intends to compete with pantomimic and tragic representations can be found in the narratorial prologue to the *Medea* and it is these words of the poet himself that make me quite convinced the above conclusion should be right. For Dracontius here, clearly indicating the epic character of his poem (*Te modo, Calliope, poscunt optantque sorores: / dulcior ut venias ... / ad sua castra petunt*, ll. 26-28), states nonetheless: *Nos illa canemus, / quae solet in lepido Polyhymnia docta theatro / muta loqui /.../ vel quod grande boat longis sublata cothurnis / pallida Melpomene, tragicis cum surgit iambis* (ll. 16-18 & 20-21). In other words, what has hitherto been 'reserved' for Polyhymnia and Melpomene, i.e. for pantomimic and tragic treatments, is now presented/represented in an epic version. A closer reading of the second part of the epyllion, which is, indeed, 'tragic' in its content and form (not stopping to be epic though), but at the same time is not a simple imitation of Seneca's *Medea* for instance (which should be the most obvious point of reference), makes me presume that also in the first part Dracontius used his 'sources' in the very same manner, i.e. alluding to the issue and not reproducing one single model.

The most natural aqua-mimic passage of the poem seems to be the scene showing Amor emerge out of the sea and move his wings to dry them:

At ille
fluctibus e mediis surgens rutilante capillo
excussit per inane caput, quatit impiger alas,
ut pinnas desiccet aquis: micat ignis ut astra
plausibus excussus pueri, per cuncta videres
scintillare diem, volitant super aequora flammae. (96-101)

[279] One need not add that Dracontius's main point of reference in shaping the scene so must have been Virgil's Book 6 of the *Aeneid*.

What makes this charming description even more visual is the juxtaposition of two opposites: water and fire. The supposition of D'Ippolito[280] seems plausible, namely that here Dracontius could have in mind – and probably hoped that his readers' associations would be quite similar – a (real) spectacle in which fireworks were used as a kind of 'special effect'.

The opening (mini) scene presenting Jason jump out of his boat and swim to the Colchic shore could be also inspired by the aquatic mime: *solus Iason adhuc vento currente carina / prosilit in fluctus et litora visa natatu / nudatus ceu nauta petit* (ll. 42-44).[281] In fact, even the subsequent passage still seems to have some 'theatrical' flavor, not any more aqua- but precisely pantomimic. It is quite impressive how many details are mentioned in just a few lines: the Colchians, astounded, watch the boat, notice the sailor, start chasing him, capture him. All this does look like a perfect theme for a pantomimic scene 'interpreted' by the narrator:

> *Sed Colchis*[282] *alumnus,*
> *nuntius ille redit secum comitante iuventa,*
> *ut nossent quid puppis erat, quid vela, quid arbor.*
> *Membra viri mox nuda vident fugientis ad undas;*
> *quem sequitur directa manus capiuntque paventem*
> *et manibus post terga ligant. ...* (44-48)

In the whole first part of the *Medea*, various protagonists speak several times. We have the lengthy Olympic scene, in which we can hear Juno and Venus 'converse', soon after we can hear what Venus says to Amor, Medea prays to her goddess, the nurse addresses the priestess, Jason lying on the altar talks to Amor who has come to save him, later on Jason answers Medea who has just proposed marriage to him, Bacchus apostrophizes Aeëtes. Thus, in this sense it could hardly be argued that the segment is mute, as is mute, indeed, the final scene of the *De raptu*. Nevertheless, the quickness of the action, the subsequence of new and new images, the adverb *ecce* used a few times by the narrator,[283] as if he really informed us, the readers: "look here, what is going on now is this, and now that" (*ecce trahebatur ceu taurus pulcher Iason*, l. 179; *videt ecce volantem / atque salutantem puerum*, ll. 199-200), and – what may be most important – the fact that all characters, in particular Medea, are presented 'from the outside', in action, whereas we learn nothing about their feelings (it is only from the outer symptoms described by the nurse that we find out that the heroine has fallen in love), all this provokes associations with a dramatic form, with a performance that appeals above all to our sense of vision.[284] In this respect, one could speak once again of the emulation with pantomime.

---

[280] D'Ippolito 1962: 3.

[281] D'Ippolito 1962: 3.

[282] I do not find it necessary to accept here Duhn's conjecture *Colchus*, as Wolff (1996: 54) does. Kaufmann (2006a: 70 & 143) maintains *Colchis*.

[283] Bright (1987: 53) notices this detail: "*Ecce* has something of the effect of a stage exclamation to draw attention to a character making his entrance."

[284] The cinematographic character of the first segment of the *Medea* was emphasized by S.P. Kyriakides in his study (which, unfortunately, I could not use myself) on the origins of the neo-Hellenic poetry, see D'Ippolito 1962: 4 n. 14.

In comparison with other scenes of the first segment, particularly long turn out the two episodes taking place atop Mount Olympus: the conversation of Juno and Venus and the one between the latter and Cupid. In both cases, the term 'conversation' seems much exaggerated as each time what we can hear is only the speech by the party formulating a request. The answer Venus gives to her mother-in-law's lengthy (ll. 52-80) petition is surprisingly brief (ll. 82-84) and as such – although the goddess of love underlines her submissiveness to Juno – may appear not quite polite.[285] Still, while Venus at least says something in response to Jove's wife, Cupid later on does not even open his mouth. Once more Richardson's observation that the epyllic characters speak singly rather than in a dialogue proves fully applicable.

Like in the analogous passage of the *Hylas*, also in these two scenes the allusion to the prayer convention is very clear, even ostentatious. It strikes both by the hymnic invocation to Venus 'sung' by Juno[286] (nevertheless, she does emphasize her position as *regina divum*) and by the words that Cypris addresses to her son, called the generative force of the world:

Juno to Venus:

Lasciva Venus, iucunda modesta
blanda potens mitis, fecunda venustas amoris,
pulchra voluptatum genitrix et numen amantum,
te divum regina precor, matrona Tonantis (52-55)

Quae[287] *corda parentis*
flectis et exutum telo candente Tonantem
despiciat me saepe iubes nec castus Olympum
destituat; sit ut imber olor, bacchetur adulter
vel quocumque meum placuit mutare maritum,
non queror. (71-76)

Venus to Amor:

Quem protinus illa volantem
occupat et crines componit mater Amori
ac puerum complexa fovet dans oscula nato.
Sic blandita iubet: <<Pyrois, mens ignea mundi
atque vapor fecunde poli, successio rerum,
affectus natura genus fons auctor origo,
tu vitae fecunda salus, tu blanda voluptas,
tu princeps pietatis, Amor, te praeduce mundo
alternant elementa vices et non perit orbis,
cum pereant quaecunque <creat>, nec sentit ademptum
successu redeunte novo. (124-134)

Sollicitus tamen ista para cautusque memento:
Medeam fixurus eris.>> ... (143-144)

At the same time, in both these prayers some lighter tones, or undertones, can be found and, more than probably, this is not a casual effect but a result of the – idiosyncratic

[285] Nonetheless, Dracontius's Venus is incomparably more polite than Ovid's Apollo addressing his mother, who similarly invokes her twin children in a quite lengthy prayer, in the episode of Niobe: <<*desine!*>> *Phoebus ait,* <<*poenae mora longa querella est!*>> (*Met.* 6.215). What is the main point here is that Dracontius should not be accused of 'compositional schematism' or any sort of 'ineffectiveness' because the speeches by the two divinities are so unproportional. Apparently, his gods behave and react just like Ovid's, which is not a wholly unserious comment on my part: they are, indeed, quite similar in their malignity and vengefulness (especially in the *Medea*).

[286] Completely different was, in fact, the language Juno employed in her speech to Venus in *Aen.* 4.94-104.

[287] Wolff (1996: 55) proposes here the conjecture *quod*, Kaufmann (2006a: 70 & 162) though argues, convincingly in my view, for the 'traditional' *quae*. I follow her edition in the above-quoted passage.

of our poet – willingness and ability to play with words and juxtapose contradictions. Juno, as we have said, is humble, but also confident of her position; she recognizes Venus's power even over her own husband, but in the very same phrase jokes at Jove's expense in a truly Ovidian manner indeed.[288] Invoking Venus, she calls her both *lasciva*[289] and *modesta*. Venus, addressing her son with most humble request, does not stop to treat him like a little child: she holds him against her bosom, gently caresses his hair, and gives him sweet kisses.[290] Closing her speech, she once again remembers him – as if he were, indeed, a little, impatient and forgetful, brat – what he is supposed to do.

Still, this gentleness, subtlety, and lightness of tone clashes with the content of the very request. Juno de facto encourages Venus to take revenge on Diana; the raging virgin (*furibunda virago*, l. 62) is to be an object, a mere pawn here: *discat amare furor, tandem sit blanda sacerdos, / templa pharetratae contemnat virgo Dianae, / despiciat delubra deae* (ll. 63-65). Venus, treating her son with tenderness and respect, frightens him, and also us, the readers, with an image of a priestess possessing power over gods, elements, heaven, and earth (ll. 136-140). As we can see, the two Olympic scenes provide further examples of the mixture of moods, so peculiar to this whole poem: the humbleness of the suppliant combines with her sense of advantage over the addressee, irony, lightness, and charm blend with horror. A similar amalgam of contradictory tones can be found in the epithalamic passage, worth mentioning here to complete the, as we can see quite long, list of generic strategies used by Dracontius in this epyllion. The wedding guests of Medea and Jason are, naturally enough, *Hymen*, *Lascivia*, *Libido*, *Affectus*, *Oscula*, *Concordia*, *Gratia*, *Lusus*, yet, unnaturally enough, *Ingratia* and *Oblivio* (ll. 263-271).[291]

We have already indicated the most general aspects of the second, 'tragic' segment of Dracontius's epyllion on the Colchian witch. In comparison with the 'pantomimic' one, it is much more static, its main element being the lengthy prayers of the heroine. Medea prays first, right after she hears about the wedding planned in Creon's palace,[292] to Luna

---

[288] Bright (1987: 51) only states that "Dracontius is merely following the dictates of generic convention," apparently neglecting the subtle irony in Juno's words.

[289] The way in which Dracontius himself connotes *lascivus* is best demonstrated by the fact that it is the main *epitheton ornans* to describe Aegisthus in the *OT*.

[290] Considering the poet's clear declaration that his aim in the first part of the *Medea* is to emulate pantomime, I believe that D'Ippolito's conjecture (see above) – that the scene between Juno and Amor, exploited earlier in the *Hylas*, is of such provenance – is all the more plausible.

[291] The scene finds its (at least a sort of) parallel in the second part, where Jason and Glauce's wedding is described (ll. 475-483). The poet does not exploit here the very epithalamic motif as such but mentions the Furies, Tisiphone, Megaera, and Allecto, as witnesses of signing of the matrimonial contract. For an excellent analysis of the passage and its legal connotations, see Santini 2006: 22-31.

[292] I need not repeat after Bright (1987: 75) that Dracontius is "perhaps unique in having the wedding actually take place." This interesting novelty of his is certainly related to his general intention to compose the two 'stories', Medea's and Glauce's, as parallel. As I have already stressed, in the second part it is Medea to turn into a 'new Diana', cursing and even punishing the sinners. Hence also a certain compositional schematism: Medea is not exiled like elsewhere, she is simply 'forgotten' by all other characters, Creon, Glauce, and most of all Jason (whose memory is generally like a sieve; some time earlier he similarly forgets about his companions).

(ll. 396-430) and Dis and the Furies (ll. 436-460). Next, having prepared the deadly gift for Glauce, the crown, she addresses the Sun (ll. 497-508). Finally, in the very moment of sacrifice, she once again invokes all those gods: *Sol testis avus Sol Persice Mithra, / Luna, decus noctis, Furiae, Proserpina, Pluton: / accipe, Sol radians, animas, tu corpora, Luna, / nutrimenta animae; fundit quem mucro cruorem / sumite vos, Furiae, noctis rex exigat umbras; / spiritus in ventos* (ll. 538-543). The narrator, especially showing the priestess pray to Luna and Dis with the Furies, is (like earlier in the *De raptu*) a mere 'stage director' pointing at some special effects accompanying the heroine's speeches and at her scenic movement:

> *Sic fata sacerdos*
> *suspexit non ire polos nec Luna videtur*
> *sic tauros urgere suos, sed cursibus astra*
> *ignitis responsa dabant. Gavisa sacerdos*
> *vertit ad infernum gemitus regemque barathri*
> *secura iam voce ciet Furiasque precatur* (430-435)

> *Dixerat et terra spatium tremibunda ciebat:*
> *quo steterat Medea loco, telluris hiatus*
> *finditur. Attonitas inclinat cautior aures*
> *et surgens … ait …* (461-464)

Soon after, however, he reassumes his usual role: it is he who informs us about the coming of the new day, the one of Jason and Glauce's wedding, it is he who describes the fatal gift, it is finally he who recounts the two crucial events, i.e. the fire in palace, which kills the king and the young couple (on Jason's death more below), and above all the filicide. As a result, the poem does not lose its epic character, the description can be as precise and as visual as possible, albeit the very scene of the filicide is also truly theatrical: Medea speaks again and the narrator again supplies information about her scenic movement. In fact, theatrical par excellence is her subsequent action, i.e. carrying the bodies to the citadel,[293] arousing – the poet-commentator adds – terror and pity in her 'spectators' (the Theban princes):

> *Tunc genitrix furibunda manum suspendit et ensem*
> *ac fatur ...* (537-538)

> <<*Miseros hoc ense necabo,*
> *quo genitor feriendus erat: nihil ipsa dolebo,*
> *si ingrata maneat nullus de gente superstes.*>>
> *Haec ait et geminos uno simul ense noverca*
> *transegit pueros, Quos sic portabat ad arcem*
> *(ut proceres videre nefas, timuere cruentam*
> *et doluere simul), ceu quondam baccha Lyaei*
> *saeva caput iuvenis mater gestabat Agaue.* (544-551)

Finally, her departure from the stage, also recounted by the poet, seems not less theatrical:

[293] For *arcem*, I follow Wolff's (1996: 73) translation. Certainly, as the commentator notes himself (p. 222 n. 264.), *arx* can be understood also as the royal residence, the royal palace.

Occupat illa gravem funesto corpore currum,
ire furore sidens taetros simul imperat angues.
Tolluntur celeres, mox se tellure levabant,
iam nutant per inane rotae hinc inde labantes,
aera saeva petit volitans quadriga venena[294] (562-566)

Dracontius's *Medea* is, still, also tragic in one more, very unique dimension. It is a poem in which the author in a very classic – I would say Sophoclean, not implying of course direct allusions – manner elaborates the motif of the tragic guilt and even, in a sense, of *pathei mathos*, the knowledge through suffering. As we know, Medea's fate has been fully determined by the gods. On the one hand, there are Juno, Venus, and Amor who plan and exact the revenge on the (too) powerful priestess, or rather on Diana whose obedient servant is Medea. On the other hand though, the catastrophe of the heroine is the result of Diana's curse: it is Diana, having learnt about Medea's betrayal, who predicts Jason's unfaithfulness, the death of children, and her eternal wandering:[295]

Sed iustius opto:
perfidus egregiam contemnat nauta iugalem,
dulcior affectus vel amara repudia mittat;
funera tot videat fuerint quot pignora mater,
orba parens natos plangat,viduata marito
lugeat et sterilem ducat per saecula noctem;
advena semper eat, se[296] *tanti causa doloris*
auctorem confessa gemat. ... (293-300).

Medea, in her key expiatory prayer addressed precisely to Diana, refers to the problem of betrayal. Having been betrayed herself, she asks the goddess to punish her own wrongdoers and pleads guilty acknowledging that she also must be punished:

da veniam, Medea precor. Cum clade suorum
non decet ira deos. Mereor pro crimine poenam,
te feriente tamen, non ut mendicus Iason
sit vindex, regina, tuus, qui criminis auctor
ipse fuit: miseram solus non puniat, oro,
qui mecum feriendus erat (416-421)

---

[294] Here I follow Wolff (1996: 74) who maintains *venena*, as in the tradition, see also his explanations on p. 222 n. 270. Kaufmann (2006a: 444) is not convinced. In l. 563, however, I am hesitant to accept Duhn's *furor residens*, as Wolff does.

[295] Simons (2005: 168-169) is right juxtaposing the passage with the one in Valerius Flaccus's *Argonautica* 6, where Hecate-Diana laments her worshipper's abduction: *deseris heu nostrum nemus aequalesque catervas, / a misera, ut Graias haud sponte vageris ad urbes. / non invisa tamen neque te, mea cura, relinquam. / magna fugae monumenta dabis, spernere nec usquam / mendaci captiva viro meque ille magistram / sentiet et raptu famulae doluisse pudendo.* (ll. 497-502). Certainly, the attitude of the goddess toward Medea is quite different in the two scenes.

[296] I do not change Wolff's text here, but I find it fair to mention that Kaufmann (2006a: 302) militates against the generally accepted Duhn's conjecture *se*, quite logically, indeed: "Der Eingriff ist nicht nötig, zumal er eine inhaltliche Wiederholung bedingt, denn *tanti ... doloris* bezöge sich gleichzeitig auf *causa* und *auctorem*."

Quinque dabo inferias (sat erunt pro crimine nostro
illustres animae): niveam cum Iasone Glaucem,
mortibus amborum regem superaddo Creonta
et natos miseranda duos, mea pignora, supplex
offero, sacrilegos nostro de corpore fructus,
ne prosit peccasse mihi. ... (425-430)

Thus, Medea becomes Diana's instrument of punishment, used against the unfaithful husband, the adulterous princess (therefore, it is personally she who gives Glauce the crown) and her immoral father, yet at the same time – in the act of expiation – apart from these three victims, she also offers to her goddess a unique sacrifice of the fruits of her own womb.[297] In other words, she turns into the instrument of punishment for her very self, too (like Sophoclean Oedipus indeed). She will give back to Diana all that once made her distant from her patroness, all that transformed her from the priestess into the mother and the wife. Instead of the once refused sacrifice of Jason, she offers now a (much) multiplied sacrifice, becoming again the original *xeinoktonos*. This way, as I have already mentioned, the whole poem forms a sort of *Ringkomposition* and the protagonist, taking off in a chariot driven by dragons, seems to return to where she has come from as she does not have to escape from Jason, like her literary archetypes. Still, will Diana want her back, Diana who has said: *lugeat et sterilem ducat per saecula noctem; / advena semper eat* (ll. 298-299)? Will a cruel pagan divinity accept so inhuman a sacrifice from her human worshipper?

I. 4. 4. *ORESTIS TRAGOEDIA*

It would be hardly original to observe that the *OT* is the poem in which Dracontius most willingly makes his protagonists speak in lengthy monologues, sometimes even in dialogue, and moreover, the dialogue in which – the reader can be quite certain – the two parties do not only hear but also listen to each other.[298] Bright, commenting upon the fact, concludes: "As Aricò notes, these [the speeches] are used, in addition to their obvious functions, for the moralizing comments of the poet, and above all to present the characters themselves directly. This is precisely because the poet conceives of the poem as essentially a drama, not as a narrative genre, and therefore, the speeches are the central material. The narrative merely sets the stage and moves us from one speech to the next."[299]

---

[297] It is possible that the inspiration for the late antique poet was a motif from Seneca: Seneca's Medea states that she has soothed her brother and father by sacrificing her sons *fratri patrique quod sat est, peperi duos* (*Medea*, l. 957). Van Zyl Smit (2003: 156) notes: "An additional reason she [Medea] adduces for including the children is that she does not want to have profited from her association with Jason. In this respect one is reminded of Seneca's Medea, who suffers the delusion that she has regained her virginity by destroying her children by Jason."

[298] For a list of dialogue scenes in the *OT*, see especially Aricò 1978: 88-91.

[299] Bright 1987: 202.

The observation would be very right, were the main point not so obviously wrong. In truth, the *OT*, exactly like the *Medea*, is the poem clearly defined by Dracontius himself as epic as the appeal addressed to Melpomene is unambiguous enough: *Te rogo, Melpomene, tragicis descende cothurnis / et pede dactylico resonante quiescat iambus* (ll. 13-14). What is tragic in this epic text is only (but also as much as) the theme.

Certainly, taking into consideration the conclusions already drawn, it seems quite plausible to read this narratorial declaration in the very same way as we have interpreted the parallel statement in the *Medea*, as a preview of the poet's intention to emulate through an epic poem the tragic versions of the story. Now, as it can be presumed, the author will also aim, at least at times, to make his literary audience believe that the sensation they have when reading is quite similar to the one to be experienced in the theater.

Nonetheless, it is an oversimplification to argue that "the narrative merely sets the stage and moves us from one speech to the next." In fact, in the *OT* one can find episodes in which the narrator indeed does play the mere 'stage director', still, there are also scenes in which it is only he, and not the protagonists, to speak, revealing for instance the true (= hidden) feelings of his characters. Let us focus on a few particularly informative examples.

The narrator fully dominates the scene showing the Mycenaeans await Agamemnon's return (ll. 108-132). The central figure of the episode is, needless to say, Clytemnestra. The poetic *ego*, with a precision guaranteed by his omniscience, describes the queen's real emotions:

> *constitit, insipiens ut adultera, regia coniux,*
> *publica planctigeris execrans gaudia votis*
> *(anxia sollicito quatiuntur corda pavore),*
> *supplicium expectans scelerum veniente marito,*
> *atque oculos per cuncta iacit mandante timore,*
> *et pallor premit ipse genas fervore recenti;*
> *attamen infelix animo versatur adulter.* (117-123)

The first strictly dramatic moment of the scene is only the appearance of Cassandra, who – as we know – arrives to Mycenae alone and before Agamemnon himself (the king being detained in Tauris). The prophetess's entrance on stage, and her exit several lines later, could be, indeed, compared to the one of a *deus ex machina*: *ipsa Clytaemnestrae sacro correpta furore / longius exclamat* (ll. 136-137); *dixit, et elisam retinent per transtra rudentes* (l. 152). She speaks with ironic affectation, greeting the queen of the Pelasgians and the 'good shepherd' Aegisthus, the avengers of Troy, and her appeal turns into a catalyst of the action and of the regicide itself: *quid dubitatis adhuc vestros relevare timores? /…/ tempus adest et fata iubent et culpa perurget!* (ll. 142-144). Next, the narrator's attention focuses again on Clytemnestra and her physiological reactions as well as on her emotions and plans:

> *provida terruerant reginam dicta nefandam.*
> *it pallor super ora redux, facinusque parare*
> *disponit sub corde truci: furor urget amoris*
> *sollicitusque timor grassatur mente paventi.*
> *maesta domo quasi laeta redit terrente pavore;*
> *ingrediens thalamos suspiria longa trahebat,*
> *corde premens gemitus et gaudia vultibus aptans.* (153-159)

Thus, it could hardly be said that what we find in the above-quoted passage are mere 'stage directions'; what the poet emphasizes is not only the movement but also the feelings of the heroine. On the other hand, what we are still given here is a very visual description, a true picture. It seems the reader can quite easily 'see' how the queen behaves and, later, 'hear' her voice in the very subsequent scene (ll. 160-231) being actually, as I have already stressed,[300] a Clytemnestra's solo, interrupted by Aegisthus's fully ignorable question:[301] "how shall we do it?" [*scil.* kill the king, of course]. So as not to lower the dramatic tension, the narrator closes this episode not only with a quite usual simile (the two conspirers are like a venomous snake) but also with a brief scene of 'affaire d'amour', initiated – as every action of the pair – by the woman. This picture too is very expressive and above all, as stressed earlier, deliberately disgusting.

The very moment of regicide (ll. 232-283) is for the most part presented by the narrator who only quotes, so to say, the words of the queen greeting the returning husband (ll. 250-253). This, again, makes the description precise, even minute, and deeply moving. One can have an impression that the poetic *ego* speaks now as if he were a tragic witness,[302] indeed, recounting events he has just seen. As such, this passage also appeals strongly to the reader's imagination, especially because of the juxtaposition of two extremely contrasting, but at the same time strikingly complementary, images.[303] The first one shows the returning king in his gore of battle and a shining crown on his head and the other Agamemnon's head cut in two and his royal diadem dashed by Aegisthus:

bellorum maculis rutilabat, sanguine pulcher,
grandis in aspectu, pugnarum horrore decorus;
qualis erat referens caelo, post bella gigantum,
Iuppiter astriferam, stellata fronte, coronam,
atque coruscales fundebat vertice flammas. (240-244)

---

[300] See above in Ch. I. 3. 4.

[301] As I have already noted, Aegisthus of the *OT* is as passive as other Dracontius's male protagonists and it is most clearly indicated by the fact that he practically does not speak (except for this short and banal question). The only 'solo' played by Aegisthus is the scene showing him chase the prince Orestes and the Trojan treasure (ll. 305-315). He does not speak, only acts and, needless to say, he is deplorable in his actions: we can see him in Tyrian purple of course, first looking for the prince, next for the treasure, finally raging as, in his view, he will not be able to rule without the means. The scene has some pantomimic flavor for me. Certainly, it is a pure conjecture, a personal impression even, and it is not my intention to force it. Still, if it was so indeed, it could also be interpreted as the (further) degradation of the protagonist: being so mean, he does not even deserve to play a tragic hero. Dracontius does apply different generic styles to different protagonists: Dorylas for instance, being a servant, is presented in a pantomimic, slightly comic, entourage (see more below).

[302] The poet's words describing the killing of Agamemnon find their parallel in Seneca's *Agamemnon*, in Cassandra's speech at the beginning of the fifth act. Dracontius, as it appears, modeled his description on Seneca's passage; he even exploited the same simile, comparing the killed king to a wild boar caught in nets (Sen. *Agam.* 892-896; Drac. *OT* 265-268).

[303] As justly emphasized by Bright 1987: 151-152.

> *erigit ille* [Egistus] *trucem dextra vibrante bipennem,*
> *et ferit incautum caput, impius, impete mortis,*
> *ac diademalem frangit, cum vertice, frontem*
> *in partes hinc inde duas. ...* (258-261)

This segment, undoubtedly one of the culminating points of the entire poem, ends with the above-mentioned unique song of lamentation sung by the poet himself.[304]

We should note then that the whole part dedicated to the arrival and murder of the king of Mycenae is not simply a drama but rather a well-planned combination of epic and dramatic, i.e. tragic, elements. On the one hand, we can find here typically epic devices, like descriptions and similes, on the other, indeed, passages in which even the narrator gets involved in the story to the extent that he really turns into its witness. Undoubtedly, every single time the dramatic component prevails the action reaches a certain turning point. Such is the case when Cassandra appears on stage precipitating the regicide with her prophecy, and such is the case in the closure of this segment when the poetic *ego* (almost) recites the part of the tragic chorus bewailing the death of the protagonist.

The next over two hundred lines of the poem is an amalgam of most varied themes and not less diverse literary strategies. These include the speeches by Clytemnestra, first to her frightened partner (ll. 321-334), next to her subjects (the peculiar 'coronation speech' of hers in ll. 384-411[305]), the narratorial descriptions of the young prince Orestes and his Athenian education (ll. 284-304) as well as of the wickedness of the new Mycenaean 'rulers' (worth remembering is especially the lengthy comment made by the poet of which a big part is addressed directly to Clytemnestra, ll. 412-452[306]), one more lament over the murdered king, this time sung by the citizens (ll. 342-349).

One scene is particularly interesting here, indeed original, since marked with some features, as we already know, quite willingly employed by Dracontius in his epyllia. This is precisely the unique show given by Dorylas (ll. 350-381), first of all for Clytemnestra and Aegisthus (who, in fact, will pay him lavishly for his convincing performance: *muneribus cumulatur opum, quod gaudia ferret / mentibus incestis*, ll. 380-381), but also for us, the readers. The episode has a certain aqua-mimic coloring as it depicts Dorylas immerge in the water up to his head and next, all wet, run to the city crying and lamenting. The scene is, again, aimed to appeal to our senses and make us visualize this little 'spectacle'. It is also worth noting that the performance by the *paidagogus* – although of fundamental importance for the action of the entire poem as the old man's testimony guarantees the prince's safety and, eventually, the punishment of the regicides – precisely because false, has a somewhat lighter overtone. After all, the literary audience knows that prince Orestes is alive and living well with his provident sister and his devoted friend in the intellectual center of their world. Thus, Dorylas's solo can be seen as a sort of interlude between more serious (also because not pretended but 'true', at least within the reality of the fiction) and much gloomier episodes. In fact, it is inserted between the citizens' lament and Clytemnestra's coronation speech. One more comment should be added here.

---

[304] See above in Ch. I. 2. 4.

[305] See above in Ch. I. 3. 4.

[306] See above in Ch. I. 2. 4.

As it appears, our Carthaginian poet follows quite strictly Horace's instructions: *si dicentis erunt fortunis absona dicta, / Romani tollent equites peditesque cachinnum, / intererit multum, Davosne loquatur an heros* (*AP*, ll. 112-114). In the *OT*, tragic parts and tragic masks are reserved for kings and princes (tragic characters can be, at least in certain moments, Agamemnon, Orestes, and Clytemnestra,[307] yet never the shepherd Aegisthus). The good (and quite cunning[308]) slave, Dorylas, is allowed to perform a monodrama written for his very self, yet not in the tragic convention.

The crucial segment of the poem, the "Orestes," to use Bright's label,[309] opens like a tragic drama, indeed (ll. 456-514). What we see first, in the full sense of the word, is the faithful band of Agamemnon's servants gather at night at Agamemnon's tomb to practice necromancy, if truth be told. The voice of the whole group, and a sort of coryphaeus, is again Dorylas.[310] It is he who in his fervent prayer invokes the dead king and the deities of vengeance, the Furies. It is he then – exactly like Cassandra in the first part – who becomes a catalyst of another crime, or rather of the act of justice this time. The narrator, as he usually does in similar moments, reduces his interventions to mere stage directions, separating Dorylas's speech and Agamemnon's response with the briefest possible comment: *dixit et ex imo gemuit vox missa sepulchro* (l. 500). Apparently, the poet once more, as many times before, tries to stimulate all our senses, not just the vision but also the hearing.

The next scene (ll. 515-625) shows the mutual dream of two friends, the gentle prince Orestes and his strong-minded companion Pylades, and their conversation when awake, which – as we know – has substantial consequences.[311] What follows (ll. 626-802) is already the culminating part of the whole poem: the story of the young men's return to Mycenae and of the revenge taken on the regicides. The beginning, as it should be emphasized, is depicted in fully epic colors. It is indicated even by certain intertextual connotations: the two youngsters stealing through the night are compared to Diomedes and Ulysses, the protagonists of the *Doloneia* in the *Iliad* Book 10 (ll. 635-638). On their way they meet Dorylas who recognizes his pupil and, full of joy, prepares a small group of faithful royal servants for Orestes's arrival. Bright notes rightly that Orestes, like Ulysses, "is the rightful ruler presumed lost at sea, who must return by stealth and kill the usurp-

---

[307] Clytemnestra especially turns tragic at the very moment of her death, when, as I have emphasized above (see in Ch. I. 3. 4), she regains her innocence.

[308] Therefore, Bouquet (see Bouquet – Wolff 1995: 30) is not fully mistaken to associate the figure of Dorylas with the romance convention; he has, indeed, some features of the cunning slave of the Plautine comedy. Yet Grillone (2008: 16) is right criticizing his statement that the figure of Dorylas and his whole show is dramatically useless. Quite the contrary, it is totally useful both dramatically (Dorylas, as Grillone justly stressed, guarantees the prince's safety) and stylistically. Dracontius deliberately composes his *OT* as a combination of the serious and the lighter, the tragic and (yes) the romance, therefore, as I have emphasized above, Dorylas's show is a necessary interlude between two very serious scenes.

[309] Bright 1987: 163.

[310] As Bright (1987: 165) rightly notes, even though I do not share his opinion that the scene is modeled directly on the *Choephori*.

[311] See above in Ch. I. 3. 4. about the metamorphosis of the sentimental gentle prince Orestes into a true *Orestes vindex*.

ers to regain his position (Dorylas is to that degree analogous to Eumaeus the faithful servant who facilitates the homecoming)."[312] It should also be added that the surprise with which Dorylas reacts on seeing the prince – *Vivis alumne?* (l. 645) – does have a somewhat romance flavor: the meeting of Orestes and his *paidagogus* looks, indeed, like a coincidental encounter in a faraway place, so typical of the romance plot.[313] Finally, Pylades starts the slaughter in the royal palace,[314] as if he were a truly Homeric hero, the new Ajax: *apparet, violentus atrox, Pylades in aula, / qualis in hoste fuit trux irrevocabilis Aiax, / Hectora cum peteret clipeo septemplice tectus* (ll. 710-712).

It is only the scene of the matricide (ll. 729-802) to reveal fully dramatic features. As I have already stressed, this scene provides also an example of the most vivid dialogue in the entire poem. Bright even speaks of "an effect equivalent to stichomythia,"[315] which might be a bit exaggerated, but undoubtedly the two antagonists fully dominate the stage, allowing the narrator to indicate solely which one of them speaks when and how they should act out their parts: *conturbata parens, nudis exerta papillis, / orabat natum* (ll. 739-740); *tum natus /…/ ait* (ll. 745-746); *dixit* (l. 755); *natus ait* (l. 762); *dixit, et ad patris veniens dat verba sepulchrum* (l. 767). The poet's role is only to close the whole episode (worth remembering is the fact that it is also the narrator who has recounted Agamemnon's death). It should be emphasized that the poet, trying to maintain an elementary sense of *decorum*, hides the very moment of matricide,[316] keeping it out of sight of both us, the readers, and of Orestes himself: *quod potuit pietas, vultus avertit Orestes* (l. 780). What he underlines is only the horror and the unnaturalness of the fact: the sun veils its face (ll. 781-783), what can be heard is the evil joy of the Erinyes (*laudat Enyo nefas, dextram capulabat Erinys*, l. 785), but what *can be seen* is the unusual tenderness and modesty of dying Clytemnestra regained at the moment of her death.[317] Finally, to appeal once more to our imagination, he ends with the words: *candida puniceo rutilantur membra cruore, / verbere corporeo pressas quatiebat harenas: / tandem iussa mori vitam cum sanguine fudit* (ll. 792-794).[318]

In comparison with earlier segments of the poem, the closing part seems strikingly different indeed, and especially the unit describing the events taking place after the killing of Clytemnestra and before the Athenian trial. What is (undeniably) changed is the very narrative technique, being now not just epic but even romance, with the typical multiplication of motifs, or (truly) imbroglios, in which the main character becomes involved. As I have already stressed, the section describing, or rather merely enumerating

---

[312] Bright 1987: 173.

[313] As also Bright (1987: 173) underlines.

[314] The killing of Aegisthus is depicted as vividly as possible (see above in Ch. I. 3. 4) to be comparable to the image of the murder of Agamemnon.

[315] Bright 1987: 176.

[316] The moment is noted also by Bright 1987: 181: "Dracontius tries his best not to describe the deed directly, and in fact does not ever say that Orestes struck the blow."

[317] See above (Ch. I. 3. 4.) on Clytemnestra drawing her garment down not to lie naked after death.

[318] The effect is stressed by the simile given right after in ll. 796-797: *sic duo terribiles fulva cervice leones, / caede iuvencarum satiati, lustra reposcunt.*

the rape of Hermione, the slaying of Pyrrhus, the appearance of Clytemnestra's ghost causing Orestes's fury, the arrival of Molossus, Pyrrhus's avenger, the reaction of Pylades who sends the young king (temporarily mad) to Tauris, the meeting with Iphigenia who recognizes and cures her poor brother to elope with him and with Diana's statue (ll. 803-886) is only 84 lines long (the trial scene is of comparable length, 76 lines). What is even more interesting and significant is the very accentuation: the passage devoted to Orestes's madness is the longest here (ll. 838-861), depicted – one should admit – quite convincingly, and the second in length is the one treating the encounter in Tauris (ll. 867-886). The slaying of Pyrrhus at the very altar, impious as it is, is given *two* lines: *repperit Aeacidem subientem templa deorum, / adgreditur iuvenem, securum obtruncat ad aram* (ll. 817-818). Much more space is dedicated to the reaction of Orestes on hearing about the abduction of his fiancée:

> *nuntius Hermione venit de virgine rapta,*
> *stirpis Achilleae Pyrrhi praedante rapina.*
> *mox furit Atrides, qui sic exorsus amico:*
> *<<Nos alius vocat ecce labor, novus ignis amoris.*
> *quid faciam? scelus est passim rapiatur adulta*
> *sponsa toris promissa meis. tu regna guberna;*
> *ibo ego per gladios, flammas et mille cohortes*
> *(nam decet ultorem patris sibi quippe mereri),*
> *dum tamen eripiam clamantem nomen Orestis>>.* (807-815)

It is worth noting that romance-like – and romantic par excellence – quality defines the very picture of the miserable girl crying out for her fiancé to come and save her as painted by the young and, as we can see, again very sentimental Mycenaean king. In this context, the killing of Pyrrhus, however brutal, seems an event which is maybe not wholly negligible but certainly less important, a *mere* act of justice, as Orestes himself argues in his brilliant defense speech: *Pyrrhus erat raptor, vindex post bella rapinae* (l. 934). In fact, the killing of Pyrrhus does not turn into a dramatic theme (as earlier Agamemnon's and Clytemnestra's); it is not even given a longer description. Apparently, it is the poet himself to absolve his main character of this sin, even before the very trial, by completely marginalizing it in his narrative and by employing so ostentatiously non-tragic poetics in the whole section.

Thus, we can see how even the style and literary strategies employed throughout the poem contribute to the achievement of the goal which is clearly defined at its outset, namely the purgation of Orestes. The poet-narrator seems to do all he can to facilitate this final verdict, even though – as I have noted above (Ch. I. 3. 4) – he does not discourage us, his readers, at all from asking questions, especially those concerning the limitations of human justice and the illimitableness of the *clementia caeli*. As such, the *OT* proves a text coherent in its compositional diversity but open and thought-provoking in its message.

I. 5. Dracontius's epyllia: final remarks

It may be usefully provocative to call the epyllion a "*Gattung ohne Geschichte*."[319] It is undoubtedly one of those genres of ancient literature that must be described with carefulness and prudence, without forcing too simple and too narrow definitions. This prudence is desirable precisely because it is a form which is experimental par excellence, not having one unquestionable archetype and, indeed, not developing in a linear and regular manner. Nonetheless, Allen's skepticism, however salubrious at the time, was much exaggerated, what has been already proven by several valuable studies discussing the epyllion – in particular the Latin one (the neoteric and the Augustan) – in a diachronic perspective. The miniature epic (especially Latin, again), diverse as it may be, reveals some 'constants' recognized and reused by authors for whom the very 'classical' phase of the Roman poetry, labeled often (still too often maybe) as its 'golden age', is a quasi-mythical past.

In my present study on the four poems by Dracontius, I have concentrated precisely upon this problem, namely how certain features, idiosyncratic of 'classical' Latin epyllia,[320] are echoed, interpreted, and reinterpreted by a poet who was so thoroughly educated and well-read, but also so creative as the Carthaginian lawyer of the times of Gunthamund and Thrasamund.

I have focused first on the very figure of the narrator, whose clear, even ostentatious presence within the text was defined by Perutelli as one of the determinants of the Latin epyllion. In Dracontius's poems this element also plays an essential role and it is so not only because the poet-narrator unequivocally judges, or simply classifies, his protagonists.[321] What seems most interesting and worthwhile is in fact the very form of these narratorial interventions, which are remarkably diverse, evoking the style of an *adlocutio sponsalis*, a prayer, a *kommós*, and sometimes, precisely, an 'objective' comment provided by a 'modern' man looking from a certain perspective (which means anachronistically) at a mythical story and a human situation that a given myth may represent. Indeed, Dracontius's poetic *ego*, being always emotionally involved in a story he tells, and not concealing his engagement at all, does not reveal himself merely in affected (too often quite banal) exclamations, as it happens even in the *Ciris*, occasionally in Ovid (notably in the Myrrha episode in *Met.* 10) or, as we shall soon see, in the *Aegritudo Perdicae*.

Similarly, Dracontius's narrative style appears to have quite a lot in common with the one that could be regarded as peculiar to 'classical' Latin epyllia.[322] Undoubtedly, a reader

---

[319] I quote here the title of the conference held at the University of Zurich in July 2009; for more information, see: http://www.klphs.uzh.ch/Veranstaltungen/epyllion_beschreibung.php [June 14, 2010].

[320] Certainly, since what I have emphasized throughout this study is the fact that there is *no* one single model of the Latin epyllion, I treat and use the expression 'classical Latin epyllia' as paradoxical, a helpful paradox though.

[321] Certainly, the labels Dracontius uses in reference to his protagonists are, simply, monotonous, as also Aricò (1978: 92) notes. Yet, as I stress above, his narrator speaks *not only* through such obvious epithets.

[322] At the same time, virtually all crucial aspects of Dracontius's narrative style, its episodicness, compositional parallelism, preference of juxtaposition and contrast to logical interrelation-

of four mythological poems by the Carthaginian, especially a contemporary one, may be utterly surprised by the novelty of treatment, the incompleteness and sketchiness of or, on the contrary, the (exaggerated, as one might say) emphasis put on certain scenes or motifs. Upon a more careful look, however, one can discover that these reinterpretations or changes do not happen to be introduced without a more distinctive purpose. Not wholly meaningless is the information about Medea and Jason's stay in Colchis for four years, nor the fact that in the final act of revenge-expiation the former priestess of Diana sacrifices also her unfaithful husband. Not without a reason does the poet depict the attitudes of the sides of the future war in the Salaminian scene in the *De raptu*. The episode showing the unexpected visit of Agamemnon in Tauris also turns out relevant, or even the mention of prince Orestes's diligence during his studies in Athens.

Portraying his protagonists (also the female ones), Dracontius certainly does not aim at constructing convincing *ethopoiae* of an Ovidian flavor. Thus, one could say that his characters are one-dimensional. Such is the ideal Agamemnon who, except for heroic, has at most a few 'bourgeois' traits. Such is the unsure of himself, falsely romantic, and pusillanimous Paris. Similarly, the characterization of Clytemnestra, probably the most intriguing of Dracontius's *dramatis personae*, is not the characterization of a 'sinner' who *videt meliora probatque deteriora sequitur*. Apparently, our poet is more interested in the social (rather than psychological) consequences of a moral transgression, or a crime committed by an individual. In addition, Dracontius, a lawyer well-aware of the power of a word, prefers to show his protagonists from the outside, in action and – what seems particularly worthwhile – by their speeches. His Apollo portrayed this way, having in fact quite typical features of an epyllic vengeful god, turns into an alarming example of skillful – and utterly dangerous – sophist juggling with words and with the very truth.

The most interesting quality of Dracontius's poetics may be the compositional diversity and the exploitation of many variegated styles and literary strategies. This tendency to a generic mixture is also an element belonging to the epyllion heritage, even though one could hardly disagree with an argument that the poetological multidimensionality of Dracontius's texts, especially of the *Orestis Tragoedia*, much surpasses all that is known from the tradition of the Roman miniature epic.[323]

Dracontius is particularly efficient in using certain dramatic devices (dialogues, monologues, a sort of songs of 'chorus', the appearance of a character as a '*deus ex machina*'). What may be more relevant though is the fact that he is also very skillful in playing with the tragic irony (notably in the *De raptu*) and even seems to understand and imitate the notion of knowledge through suffering. The presence of this motif turns his *Medea*, in its

ship between single scenes, as well as many other 'minor' features, like the use of catalogues or enumerations, are also typical of late antique poetry as such. Certainly, the fact can be hardly surprising if one takes into consideration that the true 'forerunners' of late antique poetics are Ovid, Lucan, and Statius, the poets whose style has much more in common with 'neoteric' or 'post-neoteric' experimentalism and mannerism than with classical or classicizing cult of opus *simplex dumtaxat et unum*. For the qualities of late antique poetry and poetics, see especially the fundamental chapter in Roberts 1989a: 38-65.

[323] In fact, I would say that Castagna's (1997b: 108) conclusion, "Insomma: una impressionante mescolanza di generi, di stili, di *loci* convenzionali di tradizione varia" that I shall also quote below in Ch. I. 6, is somewhat more applicable to Dracontius than to the *Aegritudo Perdicae*.

tragic segment, into a deeply moving poem (such is, at least, my very own impression). It is, in fact, quite tempting to say that with Dracontius the Latin epyllion regains its tragic dimension, which was completely lost in Ovid.[324]

Our Carthaginian shows a unique talent for imitating, even emulating, through his poetry the visual arts, in particular the pantomime, which was most probably the leading theatrical form of his times. The pantomimic 'effects' exploited by Dracontius can emphasize the tragic sense of a poem: such is their role in the final segment of the *De raptu Helenae*. They can, quite the reverse, add to single scenes some charm and lightness (like the aqua-mimic elements in the *Hylas*), they can also make the narration more dynamic and visual, almost cinematographic, like in the opening units of the *Medea*. Therefore, an intelligent and imaginative reader can, indeed, not merely read but also – at least at certain moments – 'see' and 'hear' Dracontius's poems, which does not mean at all that their belonging to the narrative genre should be questioned.

If we define the neoteric and the Augustan epyllion as the core, the main text so to speak, of a history of the genre, the history which indeed is incomplete and not fully reconstructible, the four poems by Dracontius must be considered (only) its postscript. Nevertheless, this is a postscript apparently worth reading not less than the very main text, also because the main text is so lacunose.

I. 6. The *Aegritudo Perdicae* and the epyllion tradition

A young man by the name of Perdica,[325] a student of the Athenian schools and a faithful worshipper of all gods, except Venus and Amor unfortunately, becomes an object of vengeance of the love divinities. When, on his way back home to his mother Castalia, whose face he cannot remember as he has left her in his early childhood, tired, he takes a nap in the grove of Amor, Cupid appears in his sleep disguised as Castalia. The youngster, naturally enough, falls passionately in love with the woman of his dreams, but to his utter dismay upon reaching home, he recognizes her in his mother. Distressed, he cannot sleep at night as he is well aware whose fate could become his own: *adgressum namque parentem / Oedipoden thalamos matris vult fama subisse / incestosque toros* (ll. 125-127). The mother, deeply worried with her son's sudden illness (even though, certainly, the

---

[324] Perutelli (1979: 109) shrewdly notes: "le *Metamorfosi* rispondono a un ordine universale … Tale ordine non può tollerare lotte traumatiche e allora interviene il meccanismo della metamorfosi ad annullare gli squilibri che si siano in qualche modo verificati: è un meccanismo che agisce nel racconto senza impulsi esterni, un movimento quasi automatico che si pone al di fuori del controllo e dell'intervento del narratore, giacché mediante la metamorfosi la struttura stessa del mito esclude il trascendere dei conflitti in una dimensione tragica. Così il tragico non diventa mai caratterizzante del poema di Ovidio." In fact, I myself pointed out this fundamental difference between Ovid's and Dracontius's treatment of the Medea story in my comparative analysis of *Met.* 7 and *Rom.* 10, see Wasyl 2007a.

[325] On the tradition of the story as exploited by the anonymous poet, see especially Bright 1987: 223-230.

modest boy has not shared with her his horrible secret), summons the leading physicians, but none of them is able to determine the etiology of Perdica's disease. It is only Hippocrates, who, by chance being in the neighborhood, gives the right diagnosis. The mere analysis of medical symptoms does not bring an immediate answer, yet once Castalia enters the boy's room, everything becomes clear: *ingreditur mater: tum quae fuit ante tenenti / mitis et in lentos motus aequaliter apta, / inprobiter digitos quatiens pulsatibus urguet, / sic mentis confessa nefas* (ll. 167-170). Hippocrates states, as enigmatically as he can: *causa subes, mater: medicinae munera cessent; / hic animi labor est: hebeo. iam †ceteri dicant†*! (l. 173-174)[326] and departs from the stage. Now the mother addresses her son asking of him to reveal the name of the woman he desires so much, apparently hoping for a classic happy ending: *si virgo est, hymenaeos iungere possum; / si vero matrona foret viduata marito, / ne dubites, <haec> cura mea est* (ll. 180-182). But Perdica is still silent and, alone, suffers through another night. He sees, at least in his mind's eye, Amor and Pudor fighting for his spirit. The heroic boy ultimately challenges Amor to a mortal duel (ll. 210-218). A new day rises; the mother, trying to save her son, summons to the palace all the fair ladies in town, maidens and matrons, to pass by Perdica's couch. All in vain. The next and last night falls. The youngster acknowledges Venus's victory and decides to die, but he tries to find the kind of death that would be most efficient and most perturbing for Amor. Finally, he chooses hanging and, seeing his antagonist's anxiety, feels almost happy presuming himself the winner of this unique combat: *quid turbaris, Amor? puto, vincimus!* (l. 282). Before dying, he still finds some time for composing a triumphant epitaph to be carved on his gravestone: *HIC PERDICA IACET SECVMQVE CVPIDO PEREMPTVS* (l. 290).

Such is the story told in a poem certainly not written by Dracontius himself[327] but most probably penned by someone belonging to the same, or at least similar, literary milieu.[328] The only doubt might be whether the *Aegritudo Perdicae* should be considered anterior or, on the contrary, posterior to Dracontius's texts.

At first sight, its composition as well as some aesthetic qualities could point to its anteriority. The *Aegritudo*, not being at all wholly unoriginal, is a poem clearly modeled on Ovid. Allusions to Ovid's history of Myrrha are quite obvious:[329] in fact, Anonym ap-

---

[326] See below for some notes on the *crux* and the conjectures proposed by editors.

[327] We can already speak of certainty in this respect, see now especially Zurli 1996; earlier Wolff 1988. For a general review of the problem of attribution and dating of the poem, see Galli 1996: 227-229. I shall mention in particular only Romano (1985: 379 n. 10) who after many years returned to the *AeP*, and – unlike in his earlier study (1958-59), where he argued that the poem was composed by an imitator of Dracontius – was more prone to believe that it could have been Dracontius himself to elaborate the theme he himself had earlier suggested.

[328] The problem has been amply discussed, but nowadays the Vandal African environment is considered the most probable. The new arguments adduced by Privitera (1996: 142-146) seem especially convincing. The Italian scholar concludes (p. 144-145): "opere, come l'*Orestis tragoedia* e l'*aegritudo Perdicae* sembrano essere entrambe dei *fallout* culturalmente e ambientalmente assai omogenei, in una cornice referenziale in cui scambi diretti tra i vari operatori culturali non potrebbero aprioristicamente escludersi."

[329] See already Ballaira 1968 and more below.

pears to shape his protagonist as a kind of anti-Myrrha, just like he shapes him also as an anti-Oedipus,[330] of which Perdica himself seems well aware. But in addition, the poet tries to imitate some other, more general aspects of Ovid's poetics. These include: elaborate descriptions, full of most varied details[331] (especially the, literary par excellence, description of the grove of Amor in ll. 25-40[332]), catalogues (like the catalogue of beauties in ll. 228-233), finally monologues of the miserable protagonist who has to choose between Amor and Pudor[333] as if he were, indeed, an Ovidian Medea whom Cupid persuades one way but the reason another. All this, undoubtedly, evokes the oeuvre and the *ars poetica* of the Sulmonian. Certainly, Dracontius is never so straightforward in his Ovidian inspirations. Can we, still, establish the dating on the basis of the attitude to the literary tradition?

Persuasive seem the arguments adduced to prove the opposite, i.e. the author's posteriority to Dracontius. Upon a closer look, one can discover in the *Aegritudo* some allusions to the poems by the Carthaginian lawyer. We have already mentioned that the very subject of the epyllion appears to be taken from Dracontius's *Hylas* where the little Cupid, enumerating his triumphs, states: *alter erit Perdica furens atque altera Myrrha* (*Hyl.*, l. 41). The juxtaposition of Perdica and Myrrha seems particularly interesting here, especially if one takes into consideration the fact that the anonymous poet, indeed, exploits the analogies between the two stories.

Naturally, in this case one could also suggest that it might have been Dracontius to have drawn upon our Anonym.[334] More convincing (not wholly conclusive though) could be another argument. The two texts, the *Hylas* and the *Aegritudo*, have one more detail in common, which is noticeable for a very sensitive reader. In the *AeP* Amor, executing his mother's will to punish the miserable youngster with fatal love, also disguises himself (as Castalia, needless to say): *mutatusque ore Cupido / Castaliam reddit Perdicae nomine matrem* (ll. 78-79). One – a sensitive reader, as I have admitted above – might be tempted to consider the phrase *mutatus ore* a subtle allusion to the impressive scene of Dracontius's *juvenilium* depicting Cupid wear the costume and *the mask* (of a Naiad).[335]

---

[330] See specifically Di Rienzo 1999a.

[331] Schetter (1991b: 108-109) points, among others, at the image of Amor preparing the arrow; its Ovidian inspiration may be found in *Met.* 5.379 ff. Schetter generally argues strongly for the priority of the *AeP*: he sees in the poem a typical example of the neoteric epyllion, in certain aspects comparable with Reposianus's *De concubitu Martis et Veneris.*

[332] Malamud (1993: 161) notes acutely: "The grove itself is even more of a literary cliché than Perdica is: in lines 25-39, the poet mentions the plants connected with the myths of Daphne, Venus and Adonis, Attis and Cybele, Narcissus, and Philomela – trees and flowers which clearly mark the grove as a literary landscape that signifies fatal love. Ironically Perdica, whose only personality trait in the text is his devotion to his studies, finds himself unable to read the signs around him."

[333] Mariotti (1969: 390) points at Virgil's *Aen.* Book 4 and the 'paradigmatic' Dido's dilemma. Romano (1985: 383) indicates an Ovidian flavor (in part. *Met.* 1.618 ff.), but he refers especially to Prudentius's *Psychomachia*. Schetter (1991b: 110-113) strongly opposes to the interpretation of the poem from a Christian perspective.

[334] See Zurli 1996: 260 and his comments on Romano 1985 and Schetter 1991b.

[335] Interestingly, Romano (1985: 381) proposes to consider the dependence of the *AeP* upon pantomime. What he points out is not this sole scene but the general structure of the poem, com-

Another point, however, related not to the *Hylas* but to the *Orestis Tragoedia* seems most important, and in fact most convincing. As Tiziana Privitera[336] demonstrated, the young Perdica has some traits of Dracontius's Orestes. He is similarly a boy born in a rich, indeed royal, family (*suae regalia limina matris*, l. 84) who has studied in the intellectual capital of his world,[337] Athens, since his early childhood, so early that he cannot remember his mother's face (Orestes apparently can, but his memories of his mother are, initially, surprisingly unrealistic). Besides, exactly like Orestes,[338] he has applied himself to his studies: *studiis animos praebebat et aures* (l. 20). What is most relevant though is the fact that whereas in the *OT* the Athenian education of the main character makes a logical part of the sequence of events, in the *AeP* the motif turns out completely irrelevant. In truth, the reader has no idea whatsoever where the story takes place and hence does not need such precise information at all. The detail, or to be exact the allusion, makes sense only if one recognizes in Perdica an *alter ego* of Dracontius's Orestes, another descendant of a noble family, but – apparently – raised by one parent (Perdica, even more than Orestes, seems just fatherless), impelled by fate or gods' revenge to commit a crime against his own mother.

Privitera notes another interesting point. In Dracontius's *Hylas*, as mentioned above, Perdica is described with a par excellence 'Oresteian' epithet: *Perdica furens*. It cannot be ruled out, as the Italian scholar argues, that this unique combination ("implicit assimilation," as she puts it) of the two literary figures, possibly a Dracontius's own invention, could have inspired the anonymous poet to compose a separate text, an epyllion, devoted exactly to 'another' Orestes.

If we accept this conjecture, the *AeP* can be seen, indeed, as proof of an interest, a respect maybe, on the part of its author for Dracontius and his poetry.[339] On the other hand, the poem can hardly be defined a Dracontian 'imitation' *sensu stricto* also because the protagonist himself seems to reveal a sort of 'anxiety of influence'. In fact, what he strives for is precisely not to turn into any of his literary archetypes: Oedipus, Myrrha, or Orestes, eventually choosing death rather than crime, and (interestingly) the kind of death that Myrrha has attempted.[340]

---

posed, as it seems, of subsequent images.

[336] Privitera 1996: 144.

[337] Thus, the bourgeois coloring of the poem is quite clear, exactly like in the *OT*. It would be much exaggerated though (as Zurli justly emphasized 1996: 236) to read the *AeP*, as Morelli (1920) once postulated, as a "novella in versi." Above all, the general tragic tenor of the poem as well as the presence of the divine element (first of all the very motif of the gods' revenge) do not allow its classification as a 'romance'.

[338] See above in Ch. I. 3. 4 about the lection *bene sollicitum* chosen by Grillone (*OT*, l. 288).

[339] As already argued by Romano 1958-59: 170 n. 2: "I richiami alla poesia di Draconzio sono innumerevoli e sono da attribuire ad imitazione cosciente da parte del poeta di P. che deve essersi proposto come modello da imitare il poeta ormai affermato."

[340] Logically (should logic be applied to interpreting literary stories), it is hardly explicable why Amor is so perturbed seeing that Perdica plans to hang himself. From the intertextual perspective, an explanation might be, indeed, that what the boy manages to achieve is precisely to avoid turning into a (male) Myrrha.

Toutes proportions gardées, the term 'emulation' might be more relevant here. The anonymous poet, initially, models his main character on Dracontius's Orestes only to make more visible (later on) the differences between the two figures. He also exploits in particular these literary devices that were usually marginalized or deeply reinterpreted by Dracontius in his epyllia, in the first place the sentimental coloring. It is much more palpable even in the narratorial comments. The author of the *AeP* certainly understands the narrator's presence within the text as one of the main compositional features of his miniature epic;[341] he also provides it with a suitable introduction.[342] What is most important though – and somewhat different from analogous speeches by Dracontius's poetic *ego*[343] – it is a clear, even ostentatious emotional involvement and sympathy of the poet for his protagonist, labeled – wherever possible – as *infelix* or *miser* (see ll. 19, 22, 82, 94, 114, 205, 262). In the *AeP* almost every new scene opens with narratorial intrusions, laments, and exclamations, determining the general mood and the inevitable *maestus exitus* of the story:

> *Heu, Perdica, gravis aestus radiosque micantes*
> *solis te fugisse putas lucosque petisse,*
> *ignoras: intus gravior tibi flamma paratur!* (72-74)

> *Heu quotiens iuvenis mutata est mente figura*
> *vel quotiens pulsante deo nova forma secuta est!*
> *quam miser ut vidit, suscepit vulneris iram;*
> *haesit et insano obstipuit deceptus amore.* (92-95)

> *sola tibi dulci numquam, Perdica, quieti*
> *tradidit assiduis ardentia lumina flammis.* (104-105)

> *at non te, Perdica, umquam puer ille Cupido*
> *vel partem minimam patitur decerpere* <*somni*> (191-192)

This unique identification of the speaking *ego* with his hero reaches its climax in a kind of 'proem in the middle',[344] or rather a brief invocation preceding the final section

---

[341] Schetter (1991b: 94-98), who argues strongly for the (neoteric) epyllic character of the poem, points out precisely the subjective narration and the poet's intrusions upon the narrative as the most typical, indeed classic, determinants of the genre.

[342] If we take into consideration the lacuna after l. 12, the narratorial introduction is 14 lines long, which is – as Castagna (1997b: 103) emphasized – more or less one twentieth of the whole poem. This is, roughly, the same proportion that we find in Dracontius's *De raptu* and *Medea* (in the *OT* the prologue – if we agree that it ends in l. 24 – is already proportionally briefer, but, as we remember, the narrator's interventions throughout the poem are much more frequent and variegated).

[343] In Dracontius, as we remember, the narrator sometimes sings a sort of 'song of lamentation' over his protagonists, such is the case in the *De raptu* with the sixfold repetition of *damnatur/damnantur*, such is the case in the *OT* in the narratorial speech after the scene depicting the murder of Agamemnon, yet these intrusions are (above all) never so banal.

[344] The very presence of the 'proem in the middle' could be seen, in fact, as another point in common between the *AeP* and the *OT*. Nevertheless, I would not consider this analogy particularly significant.

of the poem. Its addressee is the muse of epic poetry, Calliope. The poet, growing weaker just like Perdica himself,[345] exhausted with his struggle with the 'horrible' love, asks of the Muse courage and strength to be able to describe the emaciation of the youngster. Quite effective seems the juxtaposition of antonyms, *macies* and *vires*, albeit this proem in its whole sense sounds rather amusing, if not comic indeed:

> *Nunc, o Calliope, nostro succurre labori:*
> *non possum tantam maciem describere solus,*
> *nec nisi das animos viresque in carmina fundis,*
> *quae mihi mandasti iam possum expromere, Musa.* (246-249)

Besides, the very idea of invoking the muse of epic as a patroness of a theme that is par excellence 'elegiac' is effective, being it *macies*, treated with a medical precision much surpassing the one typically employed in love poetry.[346] In fact, if Perdica is a hero at all, the hero who might deserve Calliope's applause,[347] he is a true "hero of immobilism."[348]

The narrator's compassion for his protagonist is stressed also – and above all – as early as in the opening lines of the poem directed to Amor himself, invoked, so to speak, instead of the muse. In truth, the 'appeal': *Dic mihi, parve puer: numquam tua tela quiescant?* (l. 1) is, still, not a conventional apostrophe at all. Quite the contrary, it sounds much more like a reproach, emotionally marked[349] for certain (the poet does speak on behalf of his miserable main character), yet not wholly free from some lighter overtones. As Luigi Castagna justly comments: "il senso non è qui: <<cantami…>>, ma piuttosto, discorsivamente: <<dimmi un po', ragazzo>>. Sembra di vedere il poeta-maestro con una mano sul fianco e l'altra con l'indice alzato, come a rimproverare un discepolo."[350] Indeed, an imaginative reader should not find it too hard to see in the poet a strict teacher admonishing his disobedient pupil, Amor.

If we remember that in the proem in the middle, quoted right above, the speaker similarly plays with the form of the apostrophe, reducing *ad absurdum* the figure of a poet in-

[345] Malamud (1993: 169) underlines this unusual parallel between the poet and Perdica.

[346] As stressed also by Castagna 1997b: 106. In fact, the poet's technicality in this description is quite impressive: *Primus languentes pallor perfuderat artus, / tempora demersis intus cecidere latebris / et graciles cecidere modo per acumina nares, / concava luminibus macies circumdata sedit / longaque testantur ieiunia viscera victus, / arida nudati distendunt brachia nervi, / ordine digestae consumpto tegmine costae / produnt quidquid homo est et quod celare sepulchris / mors secreta solet: satis est tibi, saeve Cupido?* (ll. 250-258).

[347] To give a classic example of Calliope patronizing a heroic theme, we might quote Virgil's *Aen.* 9.525 ff. where Calliope is invoked to sing the advantages of Turnus. In point of fact, the *Aeneid* Book 9 is the principal point of reference here. *Nostro succurre labori* in l. 246 is a direct quotation of the incipit of Nisus's invocation to Luna: *tu, dea, tu praesens nostro succurre labori* (*Aen.* 9.404), see Grillo 2010[2]: 127.

[348] To use the stimulating definition of Di Rienzo 1999a: 546. As the Italian scholar emphasizes, this utter inactiveness of Perdica will not allow him to turn into a new Oedipus.

[349] The poet's 'invocation' to Amor is quite strongly emotionally marked: *hoc tibi restabat postremum, saeve Cupido! / at dirum in matris iuvenem conpellis amorem!* (ll. 5-6). As Zurli (1987: 1) explains in his apparatus: "At … particula apta exclamationi indignationem exprimenti retinenda."

[350] Castagna 1997b: 111.

spired by the muse Calliope, this clash of serious and unserious tones must be interpreted as a deliberate literary strategy. Apparently, the narrator intends that the reader should recognize his involvement in the story, also the involvement of a 'moralist', as a pose, comparable indeed to the one usually associated with the Ovidian oeuvre.[351] Therefore, a few subtle allusions to myths known from the *Metamorphoses* can be found as early as in the introduction.[352] It may be worth mentioning that the word *frondes* in line 2 (*non sat erant frondes*), however most naturally associable with the episode of Daphne, can also be seen as a discreet allusion to the 'epyllion' about Myrrha. The reference turns clear in the final part of the proem. The poet speaks now exactly like his Ovidian archetype. Just like Ovid, who before starting to tell the story of Myrrha, warns fathers and daughters,[353] the potential victims of his narrative, should they follow it too closely, the narrator of the *AeP* addresses mothers and, most probably, their sons,[354] forbidding them to read or – if they still decide to – imposing upon them the 'single right interpretation' of his text. Indeed, it seems that the words of the poet-moralist could hardly sound more ostentatious and at the same time – which is not at all unintentional – less convincing:

Ovid:	The poet of the *AeP*:
dira canam: procul hinc natae, procul este parentes, *aut, mea si vestras mulcebunt carmina mentes,* *desit in hac mihi parte fides, nec credite factum;* *vel, si credetis, facti quoque credite poenam.* (*Met.* 10.300-303)	*claudite nunc animos miserandaque pectora, matres,* *ne scelus hoc vestras iteratum polluat aures* *neu vos sollicitas temptet dolor iste nefandus* .... *viderit ac simili poena commissa †recussit†.*[355] (10-13)

The sentimental coloring, so typical of the *AeP*, is best revealed in the way in which the characters are portrayed, in particular the main one. Perdica, 'sentenced' to be a new Myrrha, does embody truly girlish emotions and girlish manner of behaving, choosing to suffer alone by night and in a complete silence.[356] He strives to remain silent especially when – which happens actually only once – the other *dramatis persona* par excellence,

[351] See already Morelli 1920: 91: "Non crediamo alle sue intenzioni moraleggianti: è un luogo comune ... come nel suo maestro Ovidio, che serve a creare una specie di contrasto drammatico fra la riluttanza del casto poeta e l'orrore dell'argomento."

[352] *non sat erant frondes, non undae nec fera nec fons, / non satyrus, non taurus amans, non ales et imber, / non tristes epulae, per quas petit aera Tereus?* (ll. 2-4). See in particular the minute comments by Castagna 1997b: 112-118.

[353] The parallels between Ovid's introduction to the Myrrha story and the proem to the *AeP* were emphasized by Ballaira 1968: 222-223, see also Schetter 1991b: 100.

[354] There is lacuna in l. 12, but it seems most logical to conjecture so, see also Castagna 1997b: 123-124.

[355] In l. 13, Grillo (2010: 14) opts for the conjecture *recuset*, proposed in fact already by Bährens 1883: 113.

[356] See *Met.* 10.368 ff.

his mother, tries to induce him to talk.[357] The Aesopic answer that the youngster gives to Castalia – who guesses that her son is suffering from love, not suspecting though, at least it appears so,[358] how ill that love might be – is addressed primarily to the readers:

> *<<nate, precor, miserere mei, miserere tuorum:*
> *lumina tu partus, tu me facis esse parentem.*
> *indica: si virgo est, hymenaeos iungere possum;*
> *si vero matrona foret viduata marito,*
> *ne dubites, <haec> cura mea est. hoc maesta verebar,*
> *inclitos ne forte toros temptare mariti*
> *cogeret acer amor matrisque gravaret honorem.>>* (178-184)
> *<<mater>>, ait <<discede, precor: plus uris amantem.>>* (188)

In fact, it is only the readers who remain the sole confidants and the sole witnesses of the boy's feelings. While Dracontius does not allow any of his protagonists, in particular Medea, to give a long, emotional monologue, the author of the *AeP* makes of this means of expression the key compositional element of his poem. In comparison with what Perdica says by night and without witnesses (unless we, the readers, are considered) the words of other protagonists are incomplete, ambiguous, and, as such, often tragic in their irony. We have just heard Castalia's part, but Hippocrates's speech is even more incomplete. Hippocrates – who appears and then departs from the stage as a *deus ex machina*, which strongly resembles similar 'special appearances' in Dracontius's epyllia (of Apollo in the *De raptu* or Cassandra in the *OT*) – actually speaks to his very self when examining the patient. His words, a true *sermo doctus* (l. 154), are aimed above all at defining his persona as a famous doctor; their additional goal being, needless to say, to underline the poet's competence in using such a learned language.[359] Yet when upon Castalia's entrance the true cause of the boy's illness becomes clear, Hippocrates says only: *causa subes, mater: medicinae munera cessent; / hic animi labor est: hebeo. iam †ceteri dicant†*! (ll. 173-174). This *†ceteri dicant†*, however problematic, shows sufficiently well how hard the renowned doctor strives to avoid naming the very cause of the youngster's *labor animi* (since, as Perdica himself warns us, *fari scelus est, admissi <sic> quoque crimen*, l. 99). Apparently, he would rather someone else did it, the miserable boy, his chaste mother,[360] or

[357] Ballaira (1968: 223) notes acutely that in the *AeP* it is directly the mother to play the traditional role of the nurse.

[358] The mother apparently has understood more than she says as she emphasizes in her speech that her son's ill passion must not be fulfilled, see Schetter 1991b: 111.

[359] *quid, medicina, taces? rationem redde petenti. / non isti calor est, pulsu nec vena minatur / (nam sacrae partes, quibus omnis vita tenetur, / discordare parent, ut mox elementa resolvant, / quae faciunt hominem, dum quattuor ista ligantur); / <non> stridens gremium vivaces inpedit auras; / non omenta suas per mollia viscera sedes / <   >, non corda vagi pulmonis anhelant / intercepta sero, non ilia concita costis / incutiunt saevos iaculata saepe dolores: / displicet os solum, quod sunt suspiria longa* (ll. 155-166). On Anonym's skillfulness in using, indeed intertwining, different languages, technical-scientific and more traditionally 'poetic', see Grillo 2010[2]: 92-96 & 98-99.

[360] *†ceteri dicant†!* transmitted in the fourteenth century *Harleianus* 3685 (H), being the *codex unicus* containing the *Aegritudo Perdicae*, is indeed hardly defensible both for metrical reasons (the last syllable is long in the *ceteri*, however similar abbreviations can be found elsewhere in the

eventually we, the readers. And, if we presume that a thing, once named, begins to exist and may begin to fascinate … One can hardly resist the impression that our poet-moralist tries to lead his protagonists, as well as us, his readers, into temptation, not less than his master Ovid loved doing.[361]

The focus on the personage, and even the psyche of the main character, the abovementioned sentimental coloring, together with other canonic elements, such as the overall 'tragic' composition, the motif of ill, incestuous love with which the gods punish an innocent – or at least unaware of his/her crime – human being, causing his/her catastrophe, all this defines the *Aegritudo Perdicae* as a text quite concordant with the conventions of the (neoteric) epyllion,[362] indeed more than so rich in their structure, styles, tones,

text of the *AeP*, see Grillo 2010²: 106) and for the logical ones. As Grillo (2010²: 61) emphasizes in his recent edition of the poem: "Personalmente escluderei senz'altro la possibilità di mantenere *ceteri dicant*; e ciò non tanto per le difficoltà metrico-prosodiche … quanto per il fatto che sarebbe assurdo che l'autore facesse dichiarare ad Ippocrate la propria impotenza di medico in presenza di un diagnosticato *morbus animi* e poi gli facesse consigliare di chiamare ad esprimere il proprio parere i suoi colleghi." Grillo himself proposes (or actually proposes *anew*, see Zurli 1987: 8 app.: "*-ra dicat* (iam Havet) Barbasz") the conjecture *cetera dicat*, indicating (pp. 61-62) that the line could be read comparatively with a passage from Maximianus's el. 3.48-70 (on the entire Maximianus's 'elegy' 3, see below in Part Two Ch. II. 3. 2), where Boethius orders the boy in love to speak, i.e. reveal his feelings and desires. To be exact, the analogy was emphasized already by Ratkowitsch (1986: 52) who argued that the *AeP* (ll. 152 ff.) was a model for Maximianus's passage (but see also Zurli 1991). Zurli (1987: 8) in his edition maintains †*ceteri dicant*†, but in the apparatus he states: "*-ra discas* puto" (see also his explanations in Zurli 1986: 195-196). The conjecture is interesting (as stressed also by Grillo 2010²: 107) as it fully concords with Castalia's behavior subsequent to Hippocrates's visit: the mother immediately starts to beg her son to tell her who the woman he is in love with is. *Cetera discas* seems also attractive because it additionally may imply the fact suggested in the hypotext, namely that Castalia probably quite soon realizes what the very issue is, only that she does not verbalize it as clearly as she could.

[361] In the Myrrha episode a model example of such 'leading the readers into temptation' may be the phrase *mea si vestras mulcebunt carmina mentes* (*Met.* 10.301) quoted above.

[362] So Schetter 1991b. Castagna (1997b: 107-108), however, stresses that the definition does not comprise all the compositional elements to be found within the poem: "i tempi, i luoghi, un paio dei personaggi principali (il protagonista Perdicca II, re di Macedonia e il medico Ippocrate) appartengono anche alla <<realtà>> ... della storia: come in quelle novelle inserite a modo di *excursus* nel corso di opere storiche. ... Le loro vicende però sono quelle dei personaggi della vita comune di ceto borghese ... e ciò rammenta piuttosto lo sfondo sociale ed i valori del romanzo greco o della commedia nuova. ... Insomma: una impressionante mescolanza di generi, di stili, di *loci* convenzionali di tradizione varia." Certainly, the *AeP* reveals an openness to the influences of various genres and styles, which is, on the one hand, a natural quality of the epyllion genre, on the other hand, undoubtedly, a feature of late antique poetics. The point is though that the whole 'historical flavor' of the poem, emphasized by Castagna, is practically imperceptible: within the text as such there is no suggestion whatsoever that Perdica has anything to do with Perdiccas II of Macedon. As Bright (1987: 241) justly notes, the protagonist "has but one characteristic: he is miserable." Thus, one can really have doubts if the anonymous author even took into consideration the 'historicity' of the figures he exploited in his poem. In fact, it should be noted that also in Dracontius's *Hylas* Perdica's name is evoked as if he were a fully mythical character, indeed comparable to (and

and overtones poems by Dracontius. Nonetheless, it should be remembered that – only except for the affected monologues – in Dracontius we can find all the most important features of the miniature epic, although the interpretation of some themes may turn out untypical and surprising. Therefore, it does not seem that comparing the *AeP* and the four texts by Dracontius one should really speak of a different understanding of the heritage of the genre or, all the more, of "two clearly differentiated traditions of the epyllion."[363] It appears that what we can see in this case is rather two quite different literary personalities and – what is most relevant – clearly two different intellectual personalities.

The author of the *AeP* is probably inferior to Dracontius also as far as the range of poetic talent is taken into account. Similarly, he does not represent a comparable depth of the moral reflection (at least, his only text known makes us assume so). The Carthaginian lawyer induces us, in his remarkable way, to pose ourselves the elementary questions about the measure of evil, the consequences of moral transgression, both individual and social, the responsibility of an individual for his/her crimes, even those unintentional ones. What makes the anonymous poet unique is a sort of a true literary skillfulness, and indeed intelligence, thanks to which he proposes an Ovidian ambiguity instead of the Draconian seriousness. One can hardly deny that as a result his poem, not being undoubtedly a masterpiece, can be read with certain pleasure.

---

not different from) Myrrha. Romano (1985: 381), who, as I have mentioned earlier, proposed the *Aegritudo*'s dependence upon pantomime, noted that among the pantomimic themes performed in African theaters there were Hippolytus, Iocasta, and Antiochus and Stratonice. This also shows that the ostensibly historical figures were treated just like other 'mythical' names and themes.

[363] Bright 1987: 247.

PART TWO

The Elegy without Love: Maximianus and His *Opus*

II. 1. The supposed *liber elegiarum* or how to make Maximianus readable as an elegiac poet?

It is remarkable that among the genres reactivated by the 'twilight poets' of Latin antiquity one can find the Augustan elegy, a form apparently fallen into disuse after the miserable death in exile of the youngest of the *elegicorum trias*, Ovid.[1] What is not less significant is the fact that the elegiac corpus of Maximianus, composed presumably, although not indisputably – as it is only the author to give us his own story – in the sixth century A.D.,[2] enjoyed considerable popularity in subsequent centuries being paraphrased,[3] quoted, and even recommended as a schoolbook.[4] Maximianus was, indeed, one of the *auctores* respected in the Middle Ages, yet it might be implied that his medieval copyists and, consequently, readers paid relatively less attention to the very 'elegiac' form of the oeuvre than to its ethical content.[5]

The modern history of the definition – or rather the redefinition – of Maximianus's work in its formal context starts, as W. Ch. Schneider rightly observes,[6] at the beginning of the sixteenth century. In 1501, a young Venetian humanist by the name of Pomponius Gauricus prepared an edition of the corpus, which was actually only the third edition al-

---

[1] On elegy, or rather on the use of elegiac verse in Latin poetry after Ovid and before Maximianus, see succinct comments by Pinotti 2002: 247-248. Pinotti entitles this short (pp. 247-252) final chapter of her book, treating both of the elegiac verse in the Imperial literature and of Maximianus, "L'elegia dopo gli elegiaci."

[2] On the dating of Maximianus's corpus, see now in particular: Mastandrea 2005; 2004 and Schneider 2003: 50-54; see also Schneider's notes on the personage of the author (pp. 45-50). The German scholar adduces arguments for considering the name 'Maximianus' as ficticious: the extension –ian– suggests that he intended to present himself as 'adopted' by a new family, precisely the family of 'the Great of Rome'. Earlier: Merone 1948; Shanzer 1983. The proposal of Ratkowitsch (1986) to postdate Maximianus's poetry to the Carolingian period has found, in effect, little support; a short summary of the arguments against the thesis of Ratkowitsch is given by Consolino 1997: 363-365.

[3] See especially Leotta (1985) and his analysis of the ninth century paraphrase of Maximianus's 'elegy' 1 (the text was published by various scholars, recently by Schneider 2003: 200-201).

[4] On which below. On the medieval reading of Maximianus, see Coffman 1934: 252-3, n. 2.

[5] Maximianus was copied with other late antique writings of mainly ethical character, the *Disticha Catonis* and the fables of Avianus, see Schetter 1970: 1. It is worth noting, however, that in one of the best manuscripts (*Etonensis, 150 Bl.* 6.5) Maximianus's work is included with Ovid's *Remedia Amoris*, which, as Coffman (1934: 251) notes, at least suggests their affinity to the Roman love poetry. Before Gauricus, several fourteenth century manuscripts attribute Maximianus's work to Cornelius Gallus, see Consolino (1997: 366) quoting Mariotti 1994^2: 215.

[6] Schneider 2001.

together.[7] It is apparent that Gauricus intended to focus on the formal, i.e. generic, aspect of the oeuvre, since he proposed to read it not just as 'a piece of poetry which happens to be composed in elegiacs' but precisely as 'erotic elegies'. The young editor divided the 686 verses into six separate poems. His division did not follow those made in the two earlier editions,[8] nor did it reflect the textual appearance of Maximianus's verses in the medieval manuscripts.[9] Pomponius Gauricus singled out four pieces treating four various women episodes (Lycoris, Aquilina, Candida, *Graia puella*) and two more 'poems' constituting the introduction and the conclusion of the oeuvre, respectively. The division of the text into six separate 'elegies', the center of which are those devoted to female protagonists, was undoubtedly inspired by the reading of the love poetry of Tibullus, Propertius, and Ovid. Gauricus, as it seems, aimed to format Maximianus's text as 'classical' collection of elegies, comparable with the books of the Augustan masters. What is more, the eager youngster announced that the edition he had prepared contained not just a work modeled on the Augustan elegists but actually a work *by* an Augustan elegist, namely by Cornelius Gallus, the ill-starred singer of Lycoris.

It is not improbable at all that Pomponius Gauricus was a clever forger rather than merely a naïve lover of the ancient literature. Nevertheless, what does strike in his approach to Maximianus's verses is not only certain reluctance to accept the mysterious name mentioned in l. 486 (el. 4.26) as the very name of the author but also a strong determination to make the edited text really look like 'classic' Roman elegy. The young Venetian did his best to adapt the late antique 'material' (which seemed elegy-like to him) to what he knew about the genre created by Gallus not simply because he was a forger, but much more because he was a 'humanist' (even though a forger, he still merits the title) and recognized the exemplary status of the Latin literature of the 'golden age'.[10] It is symptomatic that for Gauricus the fundamental marker of 'elegy' (= Augustan elegy), apart from the meter, was the erotic content and the book format: it must comprise (several) separate poems. Apparently, the young manuscript-hunter did not even take into consideration the elegiac *carmina continua*, sometimes also dedicated to love: *Ars Amatoria*, *Remedia Amoris*,[11] both by the matchless experimentalist, Ovid, not to speak of the

[7] The two previous ones were the Utrecht edition (*editio princeps*) of 1473 by N. Ketelaer and G. de Leempt (see Agozzino 1970: 213) and the Paris edition published around 1500 (as for the latter, I follow the information provided by Schetter 1970: 6).

[8] Cf. Schneider 2001: 446-447.

[9] The manuscripts present the text either continuously, or, in more cases, display within the continuous written text various initial and paragraph graphic signs which can be understood as segmentation indicators; yet, since there are enormous differences in the segmentation of the text from manuscript to manuscript, these signs can hardly serve as a basis for determining the inner structure of the work. On the question, see in the first place Schetter 1970 (on the problem of the division of Maximianus's text in part. pp. 158-162).

[10] Schneider (2001: 456-457) sounds very right saying that Gauricus connected Maximianus's poem with the name of Gallus "not simply to make money, but mainly because of the renaissance of classical antiquity, to which the classical poetry of the Augustan age should serve as the decisive guide."

[11] One might also think of the *Fasti* and, to some extent, of the *Tristia* 2, see more below.

late antique *De reditu suo* by Rutilius Namatianus (which he of course could not know[12]), which is in fact not so far from erotic tones, at least as love for the *Urbs* is concerned.[13]

Interestingly, even though the ascription to Gallus was eventually refuted, the arrangement of Maximianus's corpus made by Gauricus, and, which is actually the core of the problem, his very 'conclusion' that Maximianus is interpretable as an elegist precisely because his work consists of – or at least is divisible into – separate poems treating love or, more exactly, love memories of an old man, now not at all a lover, gained acceptance (or at least prevailed). Contemporary editors cannot simply do without Gauricus's text division even if they propose to read the poem as *carmen continuum*.[14] Critics, who would often label Maximianus as "the last Roman elegist," emphasize the poet's dependence on the great Augustan models for whom the 'standard' form was a collection of various (= independent) 'elegies'.[15]

Now, the point is that, on the one hand, the ecdotic tradition of the work, patronized, so to speak, by Gauricus, does aim to draw attention to two most important aspects of Maximianus's poetry. Firstly, that its poetic persona is a *senex decrepitus*, unfit for love and ready to die (as he presents himself in ll. 1-292 and 675-686, or, if we prefer Gauricus's pattern, the elegies 1 and 6), telling us his love stories in episodes (which might be entitled *Lycoris*, *Aquilina*, *Candida*, *Graia puella*, or 'elegies' 2, 3, 4, and 5, respectively); secondly, that Maximianus (the author) did intend his *opus* to be viewed against the Augustan elegy, and in particular – not exclusively though, as we shall see – against this subtype of the Augustan elegy that might be labeled as 'erotic'. On the other hand, it is hardly questionable that Maximianus's oeuvre read as *liber elegiarum* strikes with a complete lack of symmetry between the framing elements, namely the introductory 'elegy' 1 (292 verses long) and the final 'elegy' 6 (only 12 verses long). A confirmed 'classicist' (being both, as it still happens at times, a classical scholar and an advocate of classicism) could even suspect that most probably who we deal with must be, if truth be told, a rather mediocre poet who did not possess the 'right' sense of proportion. Yet what is much worse, a similar reading, especially if it led to an assumption that single elegies can be treated as self-contained units, could wholly blind us to the fact that the pieces *are* interrelated and even constitute, as Schneider emphasizes, a "*discursive continuity*."[16]

---

[12] The *editio princeps* of the *De reditu* being published only in 1520 in Bologna by JB Pius.

[13] Fo (1986: 14, n. 15), mentioning these works as examples of 'elegiac *carmina continua*', emphasizes the particular nature of each of them because of which none of these texts is to be interpreted as 'model' elegiac *carmen continuum*.

[14] In the two most recent editions, Schneider 2003 as well as Sandquist Öberg 1999 number the verses both continuously and according to the division by Gauricus. Guardalben 1993 maintains Gauricus's division.

[15] Pinotti 1989: 185. Similarly Fo (1986: 14, n. 15) who also notes: "Che la forma standard proposta dai più autorevoli modelli latini per questo aspetto del genere elegiaco sia quella della raccolta di vari brani indipendenti mi sembra difficilmente impugnabile." Interestingly, Fo himself in his next paper (1987: 349-350) on the problem presents the question as follows: "Ora, noi siamo di fronte ad un'opera che è una raccolta di elegie (o – meno probabilmente – una sola grande elegia) ... Massimiano scrive elegie (o una grande elegia a episodi)."

[16] Schneider 2001: 455, but also Fo 1986, 1986-1987.

The old man we meet in 'elegy' 1 shares with us his love experiences. His narration is exemplarily late antique in its 'episodicness' and 'non-linearity': the scene of which Lycoris is the heroine takes place certainly many years after the ones with Aquilina and Candida and maybe even not before the 'affair' with the *Graia puella.*[17] Nevertheless, the narration as such shows a vertical orientation[18] as its culminating point is the event happening in Greece: the protagonist's humiliating collapse into impotence, described in 'elegy' 5 and explaining why he opened his speech with a kind of *invocatio mortis.* The narrator's voice, the voice of the same old man, commenting and judging from his present perspective the facts that he is about to remember or has just remembered, can be heard in the 'prologues'[19] to 'elegies' 3, 4, and 5, as well as in the passage concluding 'elegy' 4. These comments clearly indicate that single episodes should not be read as detached from the lengthy introductory part as their role is, indeed, to illustrate what in more general way is said or suggested in 'elegy' 1.[20] On the other hand, the 'prologue' to 'elegy' 3 announces the story of juvenile love, the *Aquilina* episode, but could also be understood as an allusion to 'elegy' 5 (*Nunc operae pretium est quaedam memorare iuventae / atque senectutis pauca referre meae*, ll. 1-2).[21] In fact, 'elegies' 3-5, where the events happen almost in a chronological order, from the early youth to the very old age, could be considered a segment within a wider structure.

For all these reasons, it can hardly be surprising that some scholars, most recently Schneider[22] in particular, do find it is an attractive idea to interpret Maximianus's oeuvre as *carmen* or *opus continuum*, rather than as a cycle[23] or even a collection of elegies, especially as a collection of separate elegies. All the more so because the term elegy, should it have the 'Augustan' connotations of erotic elegy, can be applied only to the four texts describing love experiences of the main character. The brief coda, or 'elegy' 6, could be also seen as a Maximianean 'version' of Ovidian elegiac closures (*Am.* 1.15 and 3.15). Still, it

[17] I explain below why 'elegy' 2 cannot be wholly compared with 'elegies' 3-5.

[18] See Schneider 2001; 2003 and Fo 1986-1987. Agozzino (1970: 86) interprets 'elegy' 3 as the center of the *opus.*

[19] The term 'prologue' in reference to ll. 1-4 of 'elegy' 3 and ll. 1-6 of 'elegy' 4 was first used by Schetter 1970: 159. In addition, Schetter sees the verses 55-60 of 'elegy' 4, which he proposes to attach to 'elegy' 5, as a prologue to 'elegy' 5. Schetter's proposal is convincing, in fact, it is accepted by Fo 1986: 21 and Consolino 1997: 386. On the other hand, the 'prologue' verses to 'elegy' 5 could be also seen as a passage in between 'elegies' 4 and 5; undoubtedly, these lines also share some common points with the verses preceding them. Therefore, even Fo (1986-1987: 104-105), analyzing this whole context, considers here the possibility of treating Maximianus's text as *carmen continuum.*

[20] Schneider 2001: 452-453; 455.

[21] As Spaltenstein (1977: 93; 1983: 68 (C. 180)) argues. Fo (1986: 16) *contra.*

[22] Schneider 2003: 21-36 and 2001: 461-463; earlier Ehwald 1889 and Spaltenstein 1983.

[23] Schneider (2001: 455) notes acutely that the term 'cycle' should not be applied too loosely or too broadly, otherwise it will lose its hermeneutic potential. In fact, apart from relationships between the 'elegies' 1 and 6, there are certain common points between 'elegies' 2 and 5: both treat the man's old age, and between 'elegies' 3 and 4 – both seem to treat his youth (for certain 'elegy' 3, and presumably 'elegy' 4). Still, I too (like Schneider) would hesitate to see these analogies as indicators of the cyclic composition *sensu stricto.*

is absolutely impossible to find among the books by Tibullus and Propertius or in Ovid's *Amores* any parallel whatsoever to the huge 'elegy' 1.

In addition, the division of the *opus* into six separate poems does marginalize and deprive of their unique function the passages standing in between the single episodes which should be read both in the context they follow and the one they precede. This concerns first of all the lines 55-60 of 'elegy' 4,[24] but also the lines 279-292 of 'elegy' 1 which, indeed, within the introductory piece seem a kind of second ending, un "improvviso bis fuori programma,"[25] but can also be seen as a prelude to the story of Lycoris.

On the other hand, the *opus maximianeum* is not at all a homogeneous whole and will not become such if we label it as *carmen continuum*.[26] Quite the contrary, the variety of motifs, literary strategies, even forms is best exemplified by the lengthy 'overture'. The four love episodes are very different from one another. In fact, one may have an impression that they turn out almost contradictory in their content. For how is it possible to combine the lament of the old man stating in l. 511 ('elegy' 4.51): *Et nunc infelix tota est sine crimine vita* or the declarations of *pudicus* old bachelor given in 'elegy' 1 with what he says in 'elegy' 2 about his lifelong *connubium* with Lycoris?

Therefore, one really could, if not should, wonder whether the oeuvre in its final shape as we possess it now – the shape we have no reasons to consider 'incomplete' or 'unfinished' – is not an amalgam of elements, texts, indeed *poems*, of which, if not some, at least one was composed earlier than others and even functioned (circulated?) separately. This suggestion was made by Alessandro Fo, analyzing 'elegy' 2 (or ll. 293-366) and justly emphasizing its objectively different character. It is undoubtedly much more conventional: conventional par excellence is the very name of the heroine, conventional is the entire situation, i.e. the elegiac *foedus amoris* broken by the unfaithful female lover. To tell the truth, if we discuss here the possibility of the texts functioning separately – or at least of being read separately – it should be noted, despite what has been said above, that similar possibility exists also in the case of each of the remaining three love episodes, but especially if we wholly liberate them from their respective prologues and treat lines 371-460 ('elegy' 3.5-94) as *Aquilina* piece, lines 467-514 ('elegy' 4.7-54; if not 7-50, in

---

[24] The passage is worthy of quoting in its full context to demonstrate that it is, indeed, correlated both with the moral 'message' of the lines that precede it and with the episode it introduces: *Et nunc infelix tota est sine crimine vita / et peccare senem non potuisse pudet. / Deserimur vitiis, fugit indignata voluptas; / nec quod non possum, non voluisse meum est. / Hoc etiam meminisse licet, quod serior aetas / intulit, et gemitus, quos mihi laeta dedit, / si quis has possit naturae adtingere partes, / gnarus et ut sapiens noxia saepe velit. / Interdum rapimur vitiis trahimurque volentes, / et quod non capiunt pectora bruta volunt.* (511-520 / el. 4.51-60).

[25] Fo 1986: 20. This does not mean, however, that 'elegies' 1 and 2 are easily combinable into a unity, as Spaltenstein argued. The arguments against such a statement provided by Fo (pp. 18-20) are fully convincing.

[26] As Fo (1986: 14) notes rightly: "la drammaticità della questione è molto sminuita dal fatto che gli stessi sostenitori della prima ipotesi [that the *opus* is *carmen continuum*] non possono fare a meno di riconoscere che di fatto il *corpus* è appunto organizzato in una successione di momenti ben distinti."

fact[27]) as *Candida* piece, and lines 521-674 ('elegy' 5.1-154) as *Graia puella* piece. Nonetheless, if we do see them this way, as if naked, we immediately notice that they hardly make a coherent 'segment' on their own, without the narratorial announcements. The juxtaposition of 'elegies' 3 and 4 may seem logical. The first one presents a young man who – once he is allowed to love (and even to make love) – gets so bored and disappointed that he chooses the *vita pudica*. The other one depicts someone celebrated for his *sancta gravitas* who suddenly starts to dream about a beautiful cymbalist, Candida, and – however he sins only in his words – loses his reputation. Yet how can one connect with the two pictures the story of an elderly diplomat who is seduced by a sensual Greek girl and, even though the first night he fully satisfies her (as well as himself), the very next one he turns out shamefully weak?

The only guarantee that all these adventures, as well as the long *connubium* with Lycoris, happen to one and the same man is the statement made by the narrator: "it is all I, it is all my life." At the same time, it would be quite hard not to suspect that the poet plays with us, his readers, implying that it is possible to combine into one person a bashful and chaste bachelor, a faithful elegiac lover (a *coniunx* indeed), someone who has opted for the *vita pudica* and the *sancta severitas*, and, finally, the old man proving his manhood. Once again, we clearly see that in Maximianus's *opus* not less important than the episodes as such is the wider narrative context, created not only in the introduction and the final but also in all the narratorial interventions, especially those in between single stories.

For this reason, logical and convincing seems Schneider's proposal to read *opus maximianeum* as a "continuous poem with integrated [four] exempla,"[28] rather than as a 'collection'. As I have mentioned, the enormously long 'elegy' 1 hardly makes a good part of a 'cycle of elegies'. Not less important though is the question related to the placement and the function of the 'prologues' and the 'intermediary passages'. To be exact, the opinion that the poetry of Maximianus constitutes a "*discursive continuity*," a "*unity of action and argument*"[29] is shared also by Alessandro Fo, who emphasizes that we should "apprezzare l'intento di Massimiano di costruire una struttura unificatrice nell'aver egli racchiuso fra due poli a tema prevalente vecchiaia – morte quattro brani di soggetto erotico."[30] Nonetheless, this 'unifying structure', of which the Italian scholar speaks, is not only comprised of the two 'poles' ('elegies' 1 and 6 making a sort of a 'frame') but also of the narratorial interventions, the announcements and the comments within the work. Hence, as I have noticed, it is theoretically (and even practically) possible to single out each of the four

---

[27] In fact, Spaltenstein (1977: 89; 1983: 240-241 (CC. 2355; 2360)) argues that ll. 51-60 should all be seen as an introduction to the following episode. I do not share the opinion (similarly Fo 1986-1987: 103 and Schneider in his edition 2003: 185) as, in my view, it is hardly questionable that the phrase *Hoc etiam meminisse licet* in l. 55 makes an excellent 'new paragraph' mark. Still, if we were to read the *Candida* episode as a truly self-contained unit, just a love case, I believe that we could do without ll. 51-54.

[28] Schneider 2001: 461.

[29] Schneider 2001: 455, who admits that this conclusion was also reached by Fo.

[30] Fo 1986: 21.

erotic parts for separate reading; in such a case, however, it is much better to read each of them without its 'prologue' and, in the case of 'elegy' 4, also without its 'epilogue'.

Still, the interpretation of the *opus* as *carmen continuum* or even a 'continuous poem with integrated exempla' is problematic for one particular reason. If we accept it, Maximianus, an epigone, a late antique imitator of great 'classics' turns out an 'insubordinate student' who ignores the models of his masters and in particular the fact that what the Augustan elegists wrote were *libri elegiarum*. Therefore, his text must be formatted precisely like the books of the elegists to make him readable as, and indeed to consider him an elegiac poet. Such was the reasoning of Pomponius Gauricus (who besides wanted obviously to change Maximianus into Gallus), but this kind of approach has often been, and sometimes still is, typical of classical philologists.

Schneider is right arguing that Maximianus's work should be seen in the context of late antique poetics,[31] the poetics in which stiff divisions between styles and genres disappear, in which one can observe a tendency, if not a fashion, to mix genres. Undoubtedly, Maximianus's *opus* is an example of a very subtle play with generic devices, what is best shown in the famous hymnic passage of 'elegy' 5, as well as in the entire introduction. From this perspective, it could generally be stated that this oeuvre is an embodiment of generic mixture and as such it can easily deviate in its form from the Augustan canons. In other words, it can fully be a *carmen continuum* rather than a *liber elegiarum*. This at the same time does not mean of course that it is a work in which a competent reader, the contemporary or late antique one, would not recognize allusions to the Augustan elegy.

Nevertheless, it is also worth remembering that elegy and epic, or all the more elegy and narrative poetry, in ancient literature never were oceans apart. The examples from Greek poetry are quite obvious. But, what is much more relevant, elegy and epic met again thanks to Ovid, the most important and the most beloved among Maximianus's 'teachers'.[32]

Ovid, as we know and as I have already mentioned, generally tried to combine elegy, or at least the elegiac meter, with a bigger form and a rather surprising content, didactic (or quasi-didactic) or aitiological (it is not my intention now to provide a more precise definition of the *Fasti*). The same Ovid in his late, exilic poetry proposed a 'blend' of elegy and epic, giving in the *Tristia* 1 his unique 'Odyssey'.[33] Jo-Marie Claassen notes rightly: "Ovid's known predilection for generic mixture allows his ostensibly autobiographical exilic works to be interpreted as heroic narrative written in the elegiac metre, an <<elegiac epic>> of sorts."[34]

Certainly, I am quite far away here from arguing that the *Tristia* 1, the *Ars Amatoria*, or the *Remedia Amoris* should be seen as a paradigm, a generic model for Maximianus's elegiac 'narrative'. At most, I would rather suggest that our late antique poet learned from

---

[31] Schneider 2001: 460-461; 2003: 36-40.

[32] On Ovid in Maximianus, see recently Bellanova 2004; Schneider 2003: 70-74.

[33] See Rahn 1958: 116. I myself focused on epic elements in the *Tristia* in Wasyl 2004.

[34] Claassen 1999: 69. Within the *Tristia* 1, after the opening poem, a kind of introduction to the whole exilic oeuvre, elegies 2 and 4 (storm on the sea) are interconnected, framing the 'epic' el. 3 (the last night in Rome). It is true though that the dependence of individual elegies of the *Tristia* 1 on *Tr.* 1.1 is hardly comparable to what we find in Maximianus.

the Sulmonian to experiment with the literary form, to offer novel, not yet explored solutions. In this respect, he turns out to be a very gifted, and not insubordinate at all, student, the student who quickly finds his own path and walks it courageous and self-confident. The elegy he created, or indeed rediscovered, combines literary tradition (the tradition of the Augustan elegy), the potential of a genre (the narrative potential, which in fact the ancient elegy always had[35]), and – last but not least – the author's talent and wit.

II. 2. The polyphony of lament: themes and forms in 'Elegy' 1

The diversity of themes, moods, and forms is not *a* characteristic but *the* characteristic of Maximianus's poetics. The fact is made clear in the part of the work that must be interpreted as programmatic even if we hesitate to interpret it as separate 'elegy' 1, the long opening piece (ll. 1-292). 'Elegy' 1 is a bravura of the poet's skills in playing with various literary devices. As such, it merits a closer re-examination, focused not so much on its general subject(s) but precisely on the topoi, the vocabulary, and the forms it exploits. Therefore, what I provide below is not a summary, an expanded 'table of contents' but rather this kind of thematic (and formal) analysis.

The erotic language and themes, constantly present in 'elegies' 2-5, in 'elegy' 1 are only 'guest starring', precisely in ll. 59-100. It is in this passage that the poetic persona, now a *tremulus senex*, confesses that he was once a young gentleman (the antithesis *olim-hodie* is also often exploited in erotic elegy), handsome and pleasing everyone: *cunctis formosus ego gratusque videbar* (l. 71), a *sponsus generalis* (l. 72) on seeing whom every girl blushed and sought to hide herself but in such a way that she could give him at least a glimpse of some part of her:

erubuit vultus visa puella meos
et modo subridens latebras fugitiva petebat,
non tamen effugiens tota latere volens,
sed magis ex aliqua cupiebat parte videri,
laetior hoc potius quod male tecta fuit. (66-70)

The two adjectives used in l. 71, *gratus* and *formosus*, are easily recognizable as technical terms of erotic elegy.[36] Yet what is particular here is that both are used to describe a man. Especially *formosus* sounds unusual in this context as it was a commonplace to praise the elegiac *puella* for being *formosa*; in fact, also our author later speaks of *formosa Lycoris* (l. 293 / 'elegy' 2.1). It appears then that Maximianus portrays his protagonist as

[35] In other words, one could say that the conclusions I propose are not so distant from those once reached by Spaltenstein. True, but the difference is that I would never state, as he did, that Maximianus's oeuvre is similar "à ce qui est du genre narrative (épopée, roman, histoire) et non à l'élégie augustéenne," see Spaltenstein 1977: 99; 1983: 195 (C. 1997).

[36] Webster 1900: 69.

a dandy, a narcissist elegiac (self)lover. To be exact, the image is not so one-dimensional: some verses earlier the young man is shown as a brave hunter and sportsman, not at all effeminate (we shall return to this aspect later), and in the following distich he also turns out *castus*, which, considering the sixth century context, may not be completely free from Christian associations, but it should not be forgotten that the notion is not alien to the elegiac tradition, either (from Catullus's 16.5-6 to, particularly relevant here, Ovid's *vita verecunda ..., Musa iocosa, Tr.* 2.354[37]):

> *sed tantum sponsus, nam me natura pudicum*
> *fecerat, et casto pectore durus eram.* (73-74)

Nonetheless, the dominant tone of the old man's confession in this passage is one of egotistic self-appreciation. He preferred not to suffer "the bondage of wedlock, however pleasant"[38] (*nullaque coniugii vincula grata pati*, l. 62), remaining "cold bachelor upon a wifeless bed" (*viduo frigidus usque toro*, l. 76),[39] rather than to marry a girl who would not have been the very one. A well-trained reader will immediately notice the Ovidian connotation of Maximianus's words as the long list of 'ingredients' to make an ideally beautiful woman given in ll. 77-100 (*Quaerebam gracilem, sed quae non macra fuisset*, l. 85; *Candida contempsi, nisi quae suffusa rubore / vernarent propriis ora serena rosis*, ll. 89-90; *Aurea caesaries demissaque lactea cervix*,[40] l. 93; *Nigra supercilia, frons libera, lumina nigra*, l. 95; *Flammea dilexi modicumque tumentia labra*, l. 97) evokes – but at the same time counters – the catalogues known from Ovid's *Amores* 2.4[41] and *Ars Amatoria* 3.263-288.[42] Whereas the poet born in Sulmo declared: *centum sunt causae, cur ego semper amem* (*A.* 2.4.10) and assured that every woman could please a man (*AA.* 2.658-662; 3.263-288), the late antique elegist summarizes: *Omnis foeda mihi* (l. 77). Were the reading of Maximianus to be confined only to ll. 59-100, one might easily presume that the tenor of the work is rather even, nostalgic maybe, but not mournful and not without some lighter shades.

However, as I have mentioned above, the passage 59-100, marked with expressions and motifs known from erotic poetry, stands in sharp contrast to the general tone of 'el-

---

[37] Also *Amores*: *et nulli cessura fides, sine crimine mores / nudaque simplicitas purpureusque pudor. / non mihi mille placent, non sum desultor amoris: / tu mihi, siqua fides, cura perennis eris.* (*Am.* 1.3.13-16). We see Ovid speaking of his *pudor* and Maximianus emphasizing that he was *pudicus*. Like Ovid, Maximianus points out his *simplicitas* in el. 5.40 / l. 560: 'subcubui, Tusca *simplicitate* senex'.

[38] For the English translation of Maximianus I quote, unless I find the translation incorrect, Lind 1988; here Lind 1988: 321.

[39] *Vincula grata pati* (l. 62), as Webster (1900: 68) notes, an erotic paradox; the expressions *frigidus* and *viduo toro* also belong to the elegiac language, as Consolino (1997: 373) points out.

[40] Webster (1900: 71) notes: "aurea: the fashionable color in Augustan times, especially with filles de joie." It is tempting to conclude that Maximianus's ideal is but a sum of literary (= fictitious) women of the Roman poetry, a kind of his 'Corinna'.

[41] See Consolino 1997: 373.

[42] As Webster (1900: 69) notes, one might also point to *Ars* 2.658-662 (*Nigrior Illyrica cui pice sanguis erit*, l. 658) and, quite opposite in its sense and thus closer to our author, *Remedia Amoris* 325-330 (*Qua potes, in peius dotes deflecte puellae*, l. 325).

egy' 1 (or, if preferred, the introductory part of Maximianus's oeuvre). What seems worth noting is the fact that the poet himself emphasizes this contrast; he, somewhat abruptly, breaks up the description of his would-be wife, adding a bitter comment, as if he were disciplining his very self:

> *Singula turpe seni quondam quaesita referre;*
> *et quod tunc decuit, iam modo crimen habet.* (101-102)

'What was once proper for a youngster, is not so for an old man', the topos, deep-rooted in ancient poetry, brings back the theme with which the whole oeuvre opens: the grim old age, *miseranda senectus* (l. 55), as contrasted with youth, love (Webster is probably right juxtaposing Maximianus's *turpe seni* with Ovidian *turpe senex miles, turpe senilis amor, Am.* 1.9.4[43]), even life. It is symptomatic that a medieval author of the *Accessus ad auctores* notes when writing about Maximianus:

> *In hoc autem libro senectutem cum suis viciis vituperat iuventutemque cum suis deliciis exaltat. est enim sua materia tarde senectutis querimonia.*[44]

For the twelfth century commentator, the book can be epitomized as *querimonia tarde senectutis*, a lament of (over) the old age; interestingly, he does not even mention the love topic. The observation indicates quite well the fact that Maximianus is interpretable not only in the context of erotic elegy but also, if not mainly, from that perspective of the Roman elegy, or even elegy in general, to which the well-known term *flebilis elegia*[45] seems more appropriate, that is the elegy of sorrow and complaint,[46] the *tristis elegia* of the exiled Ovid, programmatically opposed to the writings of the Love's teacher (*non sum praeceptor amoris, Tr.* 1.1.67). Ovid is, in fact, a model particularly close to the late antique poet, which we have already noticed also in the 'erotic' part of 'elegy' 1. It is precisely Ovid's *Tristia* that we can read in the subtext of the phrase *Non sum qui fueram* (l. 5), one of the most famous, if not the most famous, Maximianus's lines, willingly reused by his admirers from the anonymous imitator of the ninth century until the Italian proto-Romantic poet, Ugo Foscolo.[47] The relevant Ovid's passage is *Tristia* 3.11.25 ff.[48] *Poeta-exul*, addressing an enemy who mocks at his misfortunes, begs:

---

[43] Webster 1900: 73.

[44] See Huygens 1954: 20.

[45] Ovid, *Amores* 3.9.3. Interestingly, the term *querimonia* as referred to elegy is used by Horace in *Ars Poetica* 75-76: *versibus impariter iunctis querimonia primum / post etiam inclusa est voti sententia compos*.

[46] See l. 370 (el. 3.4), where Maximianus himself calls his work *maestum opus*. It is worth mentioning that Schneider (2003: 44-45) proposes the *Nugae* as the original title of Maximianus's oeuvre, in the sense of 'lamentation' ('Klagereden'), not 'trifles'. Yet I find Butrica's (2005: 563) objections convincing.

[47] Leotta 1989.

[48] The allusion is noticed also by Spaltenstein 1983: 81 (C. 1016), Leotta 1989: 81, and Schneider 2003: 72. Webster (1900: 61) points to Hor. *Carm.* 4.1.3: *non sum qualis eram*, the poem exploiting the theme of old age and love, in which, however, having first declared: *me nec femina nec puer / iam nec spes animi credula mutui* (ll. 29-30), the poet eventually confesses his feelings for

non sum ego quod fueram. Quid inanem proteris umbram?
quid cinerem saxis bustaque nostra petis?
Hector erat tunc cum bello certabat; at idem
vinctus ad Haemonios non erat Hector equos.
me quoque, quem noras olim, non esse memento:
ex illo superant haec simulacra viro.
quid simulacra, ferox, dictis incessis amaris?
parce, precor, Manes sollicitare meos! (25-32)

We can speak here not only of verbal echoes. The very imagery employed in the two texts is also parallel. Both poets compare their present situation to the one of a 'living death'. Ovid calls himself but an empty shadow (*umbra inanis*, l. 25; *simulacra*, l. 30), the ashes and tomb (*cinis*, *busta*, l. 26) that the mysterious *improbus* should not profane. Maximianus announces that the best of him has perished (*periit pars maxima nostri*, l. 5) and expresses a moving wish to die as soon as possible:[49]

Solve precor miseram tali de carcere vitam,
mors est iam requies, vivere poena mihi. (3-4)

vivere cum nequeam, sit mihi posse mori.
O quam dura premit miseros condicio vitae,
nec mors humano subiacet arbitrio.
Dulce mori miseris, sed mors optata recedit;
at cum tristis erit, praecipitata venit.
Me vero heu tantis defunctum partibus olim
Tartareas vivum constat inire vias. (112-118)

Occasionally, similar confessions can be also found in Ovid who in *Tristia* 3.7.7, paraphrasing a typical epistolary formula, admits: *vivere me dices, sed sic, ut vivere nolim*. The most striking example is maybe a passage from *Tristia* 3.2. *Poeta-exul* directs a fervent prayer to gods asking that the door of his tomb be open:

ei mihi, quod totiens nostri pulsata sepulcri
ianua sub nullo tempore aperta fuit!
cur ego tot gladios fugi totiensque minata

---

the young Ligurinus. Maximianus, at least in this 'elegy' 1, keeps repeating that an old man is unfit for love. Leotta (1989: 81) mentions also Propertius's 1.12.11: *non sum ego qui fueram*. Consolino (1997: 367-368) rightly observes though that in this case (as in the case of Horace's *Carm*. 4.1), we may speak of some verbal echoes, but the contexts are still completely different. Therefore, she emphasizes associations with *Tr*. 3.11, arguing, however, that the situations of the two poets are similar, but not entirely the same: whereas Ovid actually asks for forgiveness, Maximianus does invoke death as such. Yet, what Ovid says in *Tr*. 3.11 is very much in tune with Maximianus, as I point out above.

[49] Consolino (1997: 368-369) points out similarities between Maximianus and Boethius who in the elegy opening his *De consolatione philosophiae* expresses the wish that death terminate the suffering of the old. What is common between the two authors is the motif of *deprecatio senectutis*, the observation that death delays to put an end to the life of the wretched, and a kind of *makarismos*: 'wishes' to die at the right time.

obruit infelix nulla procella caput?
di, quos experior nimium constanter iniquos,
participes irae quos deus unus habet,
exstimulate, precor, cessantia fata meique
interitus clausas esse vetate fores! (23-30)

In Maximianus we hear the pitiable *senex* pray Mother Earth to show mercy to her suffering child and take him back to restore dead limbs to their native soil:

suscipe me, genetrix, nati miserere laborum:
membra peto gremio fessa fovere tuo;
horrent me pueri, nequeo velut ante videri,
horrendos partus cur sinis esse tuos?
Nil mihi cum superis, explevi munera vitae,
redde, precor, patrio mortua membra solo.
Quid miseros variis prodest suspendere poenis?
Non est materni pectoris ista pati. (227-234)

This time we cannot speak of verbal repetitions but, instead, of an analogy of literary strategies adopted by the two poets. Ovid several times makes use of the prayer and the prayer-like elements, exploiting the emotional potential of this form. Prayers, in fact, mark his *elegia tristis* with a special flavor of 'sadness'.[50] Maximianus's prayer to Mother Earth is supposed to produce a similar effect on the reader, provoking a kind of tender sympathy. The rhetoric he employs is quite important, the expressions like *membra fovere gremio* (l. 228), *maternum pectus* (l. 234) evoke the sweetness associated with the concept of motherhood (as Webster observes,[51] there is also the tombstone reminiscence in *gremio tuo* if referred to the earth, an aspect to which I shall soon return), which, perforce, makes the reader think of the old man in terms of a helpless child. We should admit that the late antique elegist is a true master at playing with various, sometimes opposite, emotional undertones: his description of the *senex* is for the most part overtly ironic – in fact, the praying old man is shown "leaning on his cane" (*baculo incumbens*, l. 223), propping with *truncus* "his tottering legs"[52] (*trunco titubantes sustinet artus*, l. 235; the word used here, *truncus*, a log, is a humorous exaggeration if applied instead of *baculus*, a cane, earlier in l. 223[53]) – yet at times, like in ll. 227-234, not wholly unsympathetic.

Ovid in his exilic elegies, advertised as a kind of palinode of "the playful singer of tender love" (*tenerorum lusor amorum*, *Tr.* 4.10.1), often re-exploits motifs typical of erotic poetry. One of such reinterpretations can be found in the *Epistulae ex Ponto* 1.10. The letter is built upon the theme of *erotica pathemata*,[54] where symptoms of love are comparable to signs of other diseases: lassitude (*languor*, technical term in erotic elegy), aversion to food, insomnia, pallor, weak, emaciated limbs. These sorts of trouble – the *poeta-relegatus*

[50] We should think in the first place of the two interrelated elegies of the first book, 1.2 and 1.4 or of *Tr.* 3.8.

[51] Webster 1900: 85.

[52] Lind 1988: 324.

[53] Webster 1900: 86.

[54] Nagle 1980: 61-62.

adds – do not result from immoderate drinking or passion. Their cause is the exile. The poet is ill with homesickness (ll. 31 ff.):

> *longus enim curis vitiatum corpus amaris*
> *non patitur vires languor habere suas.* (3-4)
>
> *os hebes est positaeque movent fastidia mensae,*
> *et queror, invisi cum venit hora cibi.* (7-8)
>
> *is quoque, qui gracili cibus est in corpore, somnus,*
> *non alit officio corpus inane suo.* (21-22)
>
> *vix igitur possis visos agnoscere vultus,*
> *quoque ierit quaeras qui fuit ante color.*
> *parvus in exiles sucus mihi pervenit artus,*
> *membraque sunt cera pallidiora nova.* (25-28)

Maximianus once again follows in Ovid's footsteps. His *senex* suffers from the very *senectus*. The late antique elegist uses the technical term *languor*: (*hoc quoque quod superest languor et horror habet*, l. 6, and in the verbal form: [mens mea] *corpore languet / atque intenta suis obstupet illa malis*, ll. 125-126[55]) and, like his model, among the symptoms of the illness, mentions the unnatural, deathlike paleness,[56] loss of appetite related to indigestion (a pitiful paradox: *praestat ut abstineam – abstinuisse nocet*, l. 160), changed walk, growing smaller and weaker like a baby:

> *Ipsaque me species quondam dilecta reliquit,*
> *et videor formae mortuus esse meae.*
> *Pro niveo rutiloque prius nunc inficit ora*
> *pallor et exsanguis funereusque color.* (131-134)
>
> *Quae modo profuerat, contraria redditur esca,*
> *fastidita iacet, quae modo dulcis erat* (161-162)
>
> *Non habitus, non ipse color, non gressus euntis,*
> *non species eadem quae fuit ante manet.* (211-212)
>
> *Contrahimur miroque modo decrescimus, ipsa*
> *diminui nostri corporis ossa putes.* (215-216)
>
> *Fitque tripes, prorsus quadrupes, ut parvulus infans* (219)

Thus, both poets propose a very particular use of the motif of *erotica pathemata* as both declare to compose what might be called "elegy without love:"[57] in Ovid's case, because he was punished precisely for his two crimes (*duo crimina*, *Tr.* 2.207), *carmen*

---

[55] Webster (1900: 75) quotes Ovid's *Tr.* 4.1.4: *mens intenta suis ne foret usque malis.*

[56] Webster (1900: 76) juxtaposes Maximianus's l. 134 with Ovid's *Tristia* 3.1.55: *exsangui … colore.*

[57] I paraphrase Conte's approach to the *Remedia Amoris* as expressed in the title of his study, *L'amore senza elegia: i "Remedia Amoris" e la logica di un genere*, see Conte 1991 and 1994 (in English).

et error, in Maximianus's, because what once was proper, now is a *crimen* (l. 102). For both celebration of the *teneri amores* has the flavor of the forbidden fruit: Ovid tries to avoid the very theme[58] (though the more he does, the more intensely present it is in the hypotext) and Maximianus tells stories of which none ends well.[59] Both, instead of love, focus on what remains if the *teneri amores* are taken away: the sadness. For Ovid, it is the sadness of exile as public and spiritual death, for Maximianus, the sadness of the old age, *primitiae mortis* (l. 209). For both in their mournful state (Maximianus: *in luctu*, l. 7; Ovid: *luctibus*, *Tr.* 1.1.6), and in their mournful elegy, there is no room for *lusus* and joy as there is no room for poetic embellishment or charm: Ovid sends his book to Rome unadorned, with rough and disordered hair (*incultus*, *Tr.* 1.1.3; *hirsutus passis ut videare comis*, *ibid.* 12), he admits to finding no pleasure in joining words to meter (*parvaque, ne dicam scribendi nulla voluptas / est mihi nec numeris nectere verba iuvat*, *ex P.* 4.2.29-30[60]); Maximianus writes "no alluring poems" since "the greatest joy of song has fled"[61] (*Carmina nulla cano, cantandi summa voluptas / effugit et vocis gratia vera perit. / … non blanda poemata fingo*, ll. 127-129). It is worth noting that both poets advertise their works as ostentatiously autobiographic and as such opposed to *blanda poemata*.

In light of all these analogies we may conclude that the Ovidian *elegia tristis*, understood precisely as the one in which love is absent by definition, constitutes a kind of 'first inspiration' (the 'root cause', so to speak) for Maximianus's text: what the late antique poet adopts is the general tone of sadness as the mood of someone who cannot be what he was once (*non sum qui fueram*) and certain literary strategies (among which also the ostentatious autobiographism, as mentioned above). Still, the end-product can hardly be interpreted as an Ovidian imitation, even though the allusions to the poet born in Sulmo are ubiquitous throughout the oeuvre. Besides, in Maximianus's work, and especially in the long opening section, there are strains traceable back not only to Ovid's elegy, and even not just to elegy as such, but also to other literary forms and motifs.

Richard Webster in his commentary points out rightly the presence of sepulchral commonplaces in Maximianus's text.[62] The observation is all the more important because, as it should be emphasized, it refers not only to linguistic but also to structural aspects of the work, in particular of 'elegy' 1. The late antique poet makes quite an extensive use of words and phrases belonging to the tombstone vocabulary, which is very much in

---

58 As stated in the programmatic *ex P.* 1.1: *accipe, quodcumque est, dummodo non sit amor. / invenies, quamvis non est miserabilis index, / non minus hoc illo triste, quod ante dedi. / rebus idem, titulo differt* (14-17).

59 Lycoris's episode is summed up as follows: *His lacrimis longos, quantum fas, flevimus annos, / est grave quod doleat commemorare diu* (el. 2.73-74 / l. 365-6); Aquilina's case opens with the words: *Nunc operae pretium est quaedam memorare iuventae / atque senectutis pauca referre meae, / quis lector mentem rerum vertigine fractam / erigat et maestum noscere curet opus* (el. 3.1-4 / l. 367-370); Candida's story is commented in this manner: *et nunc infelix tota est sine crimine vita / et peccare senem non potuisse pudet* (el. 4.51-52 / l. 511-512), finally, the affair with *Graia puella* ends up with the shameful disability to perform the sex act.

60 See Webster 1900: 75.

61 Lind 1988: 322.

62 Webster 1900: 8, and later on throughout his commentary, especially to 'elegy' 1 (pp. 58-89).

tune with the general idea of the poem, namely that the present state of the protagonist, the *tarda senectus*, can be compared only to the one of the living death (*mortua membra*, l. 232; *vivamque iacendo*, l. 239;[63] *Quo postquam iacuit, misero quid funere differt?*, l. 237). Indeed, what Maximianus seems to imply is that as the old age is similar to death,[64] then the very body of an old man is similar to the grave in which he buries his own senses:

> *Morte mori melius, quam vitam ducere mortis*
> *et sensus membris sic sepelire suis.* (265-266)

One passage is particularly relevant, however, that is the one evoking not just epitaphic phraseology but the very composition of tombstone inscriptions, or epitaphs in general, regarded also as a literary form.[65] The description made in ll. 9-78, a kind of a self-portrait of the *senex* as a young man, is modeled on typical epitaphic presentations,[66] often written in the first person, as if the deceased spoke for themselves. As a matter of fact, the epitaphic inclusion can be also found in Ovid's exilic elegy (*Tristia* 3.3),[67] where it underlines the deeply emotional character of the letter addressed to the poet's wife. Maximianus's passage is too long, though, to be called just an 'inclusion'. Besides, it is closely interrelated both with the preceding and the following part of the text and hence cannot be interpreted as a self-contained unit (in fact, it 'naturally develops', so to speak, into the catalog of women given in ll. 79-100).

The section takes the usual eulogistic tone of epitaphs: the 'dead person' is presented as a renowned orator (*orator toto clarus in orbe fui*, l. 10),[68] possessing all of the required physical and moral qualities (*his ornatum meritis*, l. 59). Expressions like: *toto in orbe* (l. 10), *provincia tota* (l. 59), *cunctis* (l. 64), *omnibus* (l. 72) are typical hyperboles of the graveyard style.[69] Yet the whole picture is, again, a combination of tinges, serious and less serious. Among the merits of the young man, apart from his physical strength, stamina, patience, contentment with little,[70] there is also mentioned the eagerness in carousing (*cessit et ipse pater Bacchus stupuitque bibentem / et, qui cuncta solet vincere, victus abit*,

---

[63] Spaltenstein (1983: 156 (CC. 1680-1682)), Guardalben (1993: 56; 119), and Sandquist Öberg (1999: 108; 143) prefer here *vivatque iacendo* as given in codices B, F, G.

[64] Webster (1900: 68) notes that the paradox describing death (and love) is used by Maximianus to describe the old age: *Tu me sola tibi subdis, miseranda senectus, / cui cedit quicquid vincere cuncta potest*, ll. 55-56.

[65] Luxorius and especially Ennodius use the form in their epigrams; Venantius Fortunatus develops the form into a longer composition, like for example *Epitaphium Vilithutae*.

[66] Webster 1900: 62.

[67] See *Tr.* 3.3.71-76: *quosque legat versus oculo properante viator, / grandibus in tumuli marmore caede notis: / hic ego qui iaceo tenerorum lusor amorum / ingenio perii Naso poeta meo; / at tibi qui transis ne sit grave quisquis amasti / dicere Nasonis molliter ossa cubent*. We might also think here of Ovid's poetic autobiography in *Tristia* 4.10.

[68] Webster (1900: 62) observes that the verse closing is borrowed from the tombstones.

[69] Webster 1900: 69.

[70] *Pauperiem ... amavi*, l. 53, as Webster (1900: 67) observes, one of the commonplaces that became a tombstone cant.

ll. 43-44),[71] whereas his natural bashfulness is complemented by a distaste for *puella foeda et rustica*. Thus, the section does not even pretend to be a 'conventional' epitaph. Rather, it is an ostentatious play with the form. In fact, what the 'epitaph' seems to commemorate is not a person in general, once young and beautiful (the reader cannot ignore the detail that the 'deceased' is still alive, or at least *vivit iacendo*), but, more accurately, the very youth, the joy and 'true' life now buried in the decrepit body. Besides, if we take into consideration the fact that the poem opens with the words which cannot be understood otherwise than as a pathetic complaint, indeed a kind of *invocatio mortis* (*Aemula quid cessas finem properare senectus? / cur et in hoc fesso corpore tarda venis?*, ll. 1-2), the 'epitaphic' section assumes quite a particular connotation: it seems as if the 'epitaph' were written not to defeat death but to precisely invoke her, to beseech her to come:[72]

> *solve precor miseram tali de carcere vitam,*
> *mors est iam requies, vivere poena mihi.* (3-4)

A sensitive reader will certainly not remain totally indifferent to what Maximianus says about the *vitia senectutis*. His image of the wretched old man, tired with his own life and his very self, however ironic at times, is neither inexpressive nor banal. Nevertheless, what one must notice in the first place (provided that one is conversant with the Latin literary tradition) is the overt self-consciousness of this poetry: the late antique elegist enjoys playing with forms and themes, sometimes altering their original meaning or function (an 'epitaph' inserted into a kind of *invocatio mortis* is an example of such an alteration), and expects that his readership will discover this intertextual dimension of his work. Therefore, it seems to be quite a hard task to read Maximianus's poetry entirely as a 'serious' piece of literature, paying attention only to the 'sad' and 'realistic' content and not to the artful form.

We must not forget, however, that one of the reasons of the medieval popularity of our poet was precisely the fact that his text does also offer a possibility of such 'serious' reading. The author of the *Accessus ad auctores*, quoted earlier, gives the following summary of the oeuvre:

> *Maximianus civis esse romanus unus ex nobilioribus ex libri auctoritate narratur, forma quoque electus ac rethorice artis ceterarumque artium diversarum peritia instructus veraciter probatur. in hoc autem libro senectutem cum suis viciis vituperat iuventutemque cum suis deliciis exaltat. est enim sua materia tarde senectutis querimonia. intentio sua est quemlibet dehortari ne stulte optando senectutis vicia desideret. utilitas libri est cognitio stulti desiderii, senectutis evitatio. ethice subponitur quia de moribus tractat.*[73]

The medieval commentator tries to classify Maximianus's poetry on the basis of its content and aim. In his opinion, the general tendency of the text is apotreptic: it serves to

[71] Szövérffy (1967-68: 355-356), who proposes to interpret Maximianus's poetry as satiric (especially with anti-feminist tendency), notes this passage.

[72] Webster (1900: 60) notes that the verb *properare* used in l. 1 is typical of tombstone vocabulary. Yet, it is technical of premature death, whereas here the sense is quite the opposite: *senectus cessat properare finem*. *Mors–requies*, death as peace is a typically sepulchral motif.

[73] See Huygens 1954: 20.

dissuade the readers from longing for the old age (bearing in mind the *senectutis vicia*).[74] As regards the subject, the book treats 'morals' and thus can be labeled as 'ethical'. In fact, in many medieval manuscripts, Maximianus is categorized as *ethicus*.[75] Although the stamp does not seem particularly informative at first sight, we should remember that late antiquity and (especially) the Middle Ages often described the hexametric poetry of Horace (*Sermones*, *Epistulae*) and Juvenal (satires) using the term 'ethica'. Both satirists (it is *Orazio satiro* whom we meet in Dante's *bella scola*[76]) were read above all for the instructive *exempla* they gave.

A closer analysis of Maximianus's text reveals several Horatian and Juvenalian inspirations. It is of particular importance, however, that what we find in the Late Latin elegiac *opus* (again, mainly in the introductory part or 'elegy' 1) are not only allusions to specific passages but also similar themes and motifs. Their presence is too conspicuous not to invite the comparative reading along with analogous statements of Horace and Juvenal.

The description of the young man given in ll. 9-78 is undoubtedly (over)idealized,[77] which is related to its 'epitaphic' dimension, analyzed above. He is characterized by very 'Roman' qualities: *eloquentia* (*orator toto clarus in orbe fui*, l. 10; *saepe perorata percepi lite coronam, / et merui linguae praemia grata meae*, ll. 13-14), *virtutis opes*, *tollerantia rerum* (l. 33). *Tollerantia rerum* reveals itself in endurance, despite hunger, little rest, cold, heat, wind, rain (ll. 35-40). The resources of virtue are demonstrated in hunting, wrestling, and running:

> *Si libuit celeres arcu temptare sagittas,*
> *occubuit telis praeda petita meis;*
> *si placuit canibus densos circumdare saltus,*
> *prostravi multas non sine laude feras;*
> *dulce fuit madidam si fors versare palaestram,*
> *inplicui validis lubrica membra toris.*
> *Nunc agili cursu cunctos anteire solebam* (21-27)

Pointing out hunting as a preferable leisure activity for a young man, almost a synonym of manliness, is not casual. A careful reader of Horace will probably remember that the poet born in Venusa, addressing his young friend Lollius determined to cultivate a *potens amicus*, recommends hunting precisely as *Romanis sollemne viris opus* (*Epist.* 1.18.49), bringing good health and fame. Interestingly, Horace opposes hunting and fighting to staying home writing poetry; a young man, striving to move up high on

---

[74] Similarly Eberhard of Bethun (ca 1212): *Quae senium pulsant incommoda maxime scribit / Et se materiam Maximianus habet.* Coffman (1934: 253 n. 2), who quotes this distich, notes that "though the following passage … is vague and general, certainly the love poetry by implication is not the important element."

[75] See e.g. the manuscript kept by the British Museum, *Reg. 15 A VII*, presenting Maximianus in the context of Cato, Theodulus, and Avianus: *explicit primus liber de moribus .s. catho*; *explicit scds liber de moribus .s. theodulus*; *explicit tertius liber de moribus .s. avianus*; finally: *explicit IIII' liber ethicorum .s. maximianus*. See already Bährens 1883: 315-316.

[76] *Divina Commedia*, *Inf.* 4.89.

[77] Szövérffy 1967-1968: 356.

the social ladder (achieving the friendship of the powerful, *petere nobiles amicos*, is a condition sine qua non in this respect), is supposed to become *vir Romanus*, not a versifier devoted to the "peevishness of his unmannerly muse:"[78] *surge et inhumanae senium depone Camenae; adde, virilia quod speciosius arma / non est qui tractet; scis, quo clamore coronae / proelia sustineas campestria; quamvis nil extra numerum fecisse modumque / curas* (*Epist.* 1.18.47; 52-54; 59-60). Maximianus's youngster is more *kalokagathos* as he can intertwine hunting, wrestling, and running with composing 'alluring poems' and 'competing at tragic song'. Nor will he hesitate to defeat others in drinking capacity, however difficult it is "to make one mind bear two ways of living that clash:"[79]

> *Saepe poetarum mendacia dulcia finxi,*
> *et veros titulos res mihi ficta dabat* (11-12)
>
> *nunc tragici cantus exsuperare melos*[80] (28)
>
> *At si me subito vinosus repperit hospes*
> *aut fecit laetus sumere multa dies,*
> *cessit et ipse pater Bacchus stupuitque bibentem*
> *et, qui cuncta solet vincere, victus abit.*
> *Haut facile est animum tantis inflectere rebus,*
> *ut res oppositas mens ferat una duas.* (41-46)

The juxtaposition of being satisfied with little food and spending night and day carousing with some drunken friend does produce a comical effect, which is aimed at counterbalancing the tone of complaints about the old age made again in ll. 55-58. Nevertheless, one could hardly miss the fact that even in this passage Maximianus focuses on ethical aspects or, to be exact, on the ethos of an ideal young man (who, as he emphasizes some verses later, is supposed to be *laetus*[81]), the ethos based upon cultural and literary tradition. Maximianus's *iuvenis* looks very much like a young Roman aristocrat of Ho-

---

[78] I paraphrase the translation of Horace's *Epist.* 1.18 available online at: http://www.authorama.com/works-of-horace-8.html [May 27, 2010].

[79] Lind 1988: 320. What is interesting, in the following lines Maximianus alludes to Horace's *Carm.* 3.21.9-12. Webster (1900: 66) observes that "the juxtaposition of *Socratem* and *Catonem* here almost proves that Hor. *Carm.* 3.21.9-12, in *Socraticis madet / sermonibus* brings the same charge against Socrates as against Cato – hence the use of *madet*." I would say that what Maximianus proposes is a very literal, and therefore ironic, reading of Horace's expression.

Maximianus:	Horace:
Hoc quoque virtutum quondam certamine magnum	*non ille, quamquam Socraticis madet*
Socratem palmam promeruisse ferunt,	*sermonibus, te negleget horridus:*
hinc etiam rigidum memorant valuisse Catonem;	*narratur et prisci Catonis*
non res in vitium, sed male facta cadunt. (47-50)	*saepe mero caluisse virtus.* (*Carm.* 3.21.9-12)

[80] In l. 28 I follow Guardalben's (1993: 34) lection.

[81] See ll. 105-108: *Exultat levitate puer, gravitate senectus: / inter utrumque manens stat iuvenile decus. / Hunc tacitum tristemque decet, fit clarior ille / laetitia et linguae garrulitate suae.*

race's times, what is more, his philosophy of life is also very 'Horatian'. The contentment with little he is so proud of imposes the association with the *Venusinus*. It should suffice to place together the relevant passages:

> Horace: *amice pauperiem pati* (*Carm.* 3.2.1); *contentus parvo* (*Serm.* 2.2.110); *nil cupientium ... castra peto* (*Carm.* 3.16.22-23); *contemptae dominus ... rei* (*ibid.*, 25).
>
> Maximianus: *Pauperiem modico contentus semper amavi / et rerum dominus nil cupiendo fui* (ll. 53-54).

If Maximianus's picture of a model young man could be viewed against a parallel description by Horace, the analogy in portraying the old age is even closer, which does not mean, however, that the late antique elegist only repeats certain expressions or remarks. In fact, Horatian motifs in Maximianus's text are given a much more 'pessimistic' interpretation. Let us take into consideration ll. 181-190. Paraphrasing Horace's *Epist.* 1.5.12,[82] the poet asks: *Quo mihi fortunam, si non conceditur uti?*:

> *Quid mihi divitiae, quarum si dempseris usum,*
> *quamvis largus opum, semper egenus ero?*
> *Immo etiam poena est partis incumbere rebus,*
> *quas cum possideas est violare nefas.*
> *Non aliter sitiens vicinas Tantalus undas*
> *captat et appositis abstinet ora cibis.*
> *Efficior custos rerum magis ipse mearum*
> *conservans aliis, quae periere mihi;*
> *sicut in auricomis dependens plurimus hortis*
> *pervigil observat non sua poma draco.* (181-190)

For Horace, accumulating wealth was 'simply' pointless if one should not be allowed to use it. Such is the sense of the simile he gives in *Sat.* 1.1.62-72, a man who would say: *nil satis est* (l. 62), obsessed with the desire to have more and more, is ridiculous in his greed, comparable only to Tantalus, thirsty and hungry in the middle of foods and water which elude his grasp. Maximianus's picture is less black and white. For him an old man, poor in his richness, must not dissipate what he possesses because he is supposed to keep it: he has become a guardian of his own wealth,[83] even though he guards it not for himself but for others. Thus, he is not only similar to Tantalus or to the dragon in the garden of Hesperides,[84] in fact, he must be like Tantalus: it is just as much a crime (*nefas*) to squander one's wealth as it is a punishment (*poena*) to depend upon it, to care for it. Once again irony is intertwined with pathos. An old man is ridiculous because he cannot (even, he must not) avoid being so. Old age is pathetic by nature.

---

[82] The analogy is noticed by Ratkowitsch (1986: 45) who justly emphasizes the presence of two *ethici*, Horace and Ovid, in Maximianus's oeuvre.

[83] The very expression *custos rerum* is Horatian (*Carm.* 4.15.17), see Webster 1900: 80.

[84] The golden apples were symbolic of youth and love, which means everything that the old age is deprived of. An old man is 'sentenced' to guard goods of which only the young will be allowed to make use.

Similarly, 'more pessimistic' is Maximianus's version of the well-known passage from the *Ars Poetica* devoted to *aetatis cuiusque mores.*[85] Juxtaposing the two descriptions, one can notice that details pointed out by Horace are exaggerated in the late antique text. If Horace's *senex* manages all his affairs *timide gelideque*, delaying (*dilator*, l. 172), Maximianus's is doubtful and trembling, maybe also of fear (*dubius tremulusque*, l. 195), dreading foolishly his every act (*stultus quae facit ipse timet*, l. 196). If Horace's *senex* is afraid of the future (*<p>avidusque*[86] *futuri*, l. 172), Maximianus's is expectant of ill (*semperque malorum / credulus*, ll. 195-196). Finally, if Horace's *senex* glorifies the times when he was young (*laudator temporis acti / se puero*, ll. 173-174), Maximianus's not only praises the past but also despises the present years (*laudat praeteritos, praesentes despicit annos*, l. 197). Horace's *senex* is *censor minorum* (*castigator censorque minorum*, l. 174), probably too harsh a critic to be taken seriously, Maximianus's though lays himself open to ridicule believing to be the only wise and learned:[87] in fact, "he laughs with those who mock him," not fully aware, as it seems, that by doing this he "grows happier in his very shame:"[88]

Horace, *A.P.* 169-174:

Multa senem circumveniunt incommoda, vel quod
quaerit et inventis miser abstinet, ac timet uti,
vel quod res omnis timide gelideque ministrat,
dilator, †spe longus†, iners <p>avidusque futuri,
difficilis, querulus, laudator temporis acti
se puero, castigator censorque minorum.

Maximianus, 195-200:

Stat dubius tremulusque senex semperque malorum
credulus, et stultus quae facit ipse timet.
Laudat praeteritos, praesentes despicit annos,
hoc tantum rectum, quod sapit ipse, putat.
Se solum doctum, se iudicat esse peritum,
et quod sit sapiens, desipit inde magis.

Arridet de se ridentibus, ac sibi plaudens
incipit obprobrio laetior esse suo. (207-208)

The author of the *Accessus ad Auctores* is right arguing that Maximianus's poetry constitutes a kind of *vituperatio senectutis*. Indeed, the picture of the old age given in 'elegy' 1 is overtly 'satiric' both because of the very tone of particular comments and because of its intertextual dimension. The late antique elegist portrays the *senex* through observations made by two greatest Roman satirists, Horace and Juvenal. If Horace's *Ars Poetica* 169-

---

[85] A motif, as we know, originating from Aristotle, *Rhet.* 2.12.1388 b 31. Aristotle's description of an old man, *ibid.*, 2.13. Consolino (1997: 371) points at some similarities between Maximianus and Horace, *Epist.* 2.2.55 f.

[86] I follow Brink's (1971: 239-240) edition and his commentary on the passage, therefore I read *pavidus futuri*, 'afraid of the future', not *avidus futuri*. The whole line 172 is, in fact, far from easy to understand; on *†spe longus†*, see Brink 1971: 239.

[87] For l. 198 Webster (1900: 81) notes also Horace's *Epist.* 2.1.83: *vel quia nil rectum, nisi quod placuit sibi ducunt*; for l. 200: *Carm.* 1.34.2-3: *insanientis dum sapientiae / consultus erro.*

[88] Lind 1988: 324. In l. 207, Maximianus may, in fact, allude to Horace's *A.P* 101: *ut ridentibus adrident*. If so, the sense of the allusion may be quite sarcastic. Horace speaks of the reaction of the public watching comedy and applauding the play that suits their tastes. In this context, the old man might be considered at one time a spectator and an actor playing unconsciously his own comedy.

174 inspired Maximianus's sketch of the old man's *mores*, Juvenal's *Satura* 10.188-288[89] turned out an excellent source of information on physical symptoms of aging. In this case the 'Tuscan' poet does not quote or paraphrase specific phrases, nor does he follow Juvenal's technique as such: instead of catalogue of similes,[90] he provides a 'precise' list of the afflictions of old age, enumerating them one by one. Problems with hearing, sight, changed looks, dry, parched skin, bad health, weak digestion, being unfit for love are all treated more or less in detail by Juvenal.[91] What is interesting, we might presume that Juvenal's description is more minute and vivid (in many aspects it is), yet at one point it is Maximianus whose remark seems, in effect, more pungent. Juvenal depicts the old man's dementia, which characteristics are forgetting the name of one's slaves and not recognizing faces of old friends or even children,[92] while Maximianus summarizes bitterly: *nec credere possis / hunc hominem, humana qui ratione caret* (ll. 143-144). Such generalization can hardly be found even in Juvenal.

So far, I have shown that Maximianus is readable in the context of Latin 'ethical' poetry because of the subject he treats (*aetatis cuiusque mores*) and because of the authors he alludes to, in particular Horace and (additionally) Juvenal. It is not less interesting, however, that the very style of Maximianus's expressions is in some respects similar to that of 'ethical' (or satiric) poets. Hugo of Trimberg in his *Registrum* praises Maximianus for *multi notabiles versus*.[93] In other words, *Maximianus* is *sententiosus*; his poetry, particularly in the introductory part, abounds in units (aphorisms: *sententiae*, *proverbia*) easily detachable from their original context and reusable for new purposes, in *florilegia* offering moral precepts for schoolboys. It is worth quoting some most telling examples:

> *virtus fulvo pretiosior auro* (19)
>
> *maior enim mediis gratia rebus inest* (82)
>
> *Haut facile est animum tantis inflectere rebus,*
> *ut res oppositas mens ferat una duas.* (45-46)
>
> *Diversos diversa iuvant; non omnibus annis*
> *omnia conveniunt; res prius apta nocet.* (103-104)
>
> *Cuncta trahit secum vertitque volubile tempus*
> *nec patitur certa currere quaeque via.* (109-110)
>
> *Ortus cuncta suos repetunt matremque requirunt,*
> *et redit ad nihilum, quod fuit ante nihil.* (221-222)

---

[89] See Webster 1900: 73.

[90] See Juvenal, *Sat.* 10.219-226, where the poet enumerates all possible diseases an old man may suffer from.

[91] Juvenal: dry skin and changed looks, ll. 191-195; deafness, ll. 213-216; problems with sight, ll. 227-228; gastric problems, ll. 203-204; impotence, ll. 204-206; bad health in general, as mentioned above, 219-226. Maximianus: *tremulus senex*, l. 195; Juvenal: *cum voce trementia membra*, l. 198.

[92] *Sat.* 10.232-239.

[93] Curtius 1990: 58 n. 68 (in the Polish edition 1997: 64 n. 80).

quaecumque solent per se perpensa placere,
alterno potius iuncta decore placent. (31-32)

In fact, Maximianus's diction is aphoristic. His statements about old age, moral and physical condition of the *senex*, often compressed into one or two distichs, are almost 'naturally' convertible into separate proverbs or exclamations. One must admit that these remarks are for the most part not at all facile. Below, I list some of such maxims recomposed into a kind of short *deprecatio senectutis*, starting with an apostrophe to the personified Old Age and ending with a grim conclusion: "it is better to die rather than to live so wretched a life." This draft 'florilegium' intended as a sort of 'Maximianus minor' is aimed at showing that the reading of the work as a dissuasion from longing for the old age (*quemlibet dehortari ne stulte optando senectutis vicia desideret*) is, indeed, one of the interpretive possibilities suggested in the text:

Tu me sola tibi subdis, miseranda senectus,
cui cedit quicquid vincere cuncta potest;
in te corruimus, tua sunt quaecumque fatiscunt,
ultima teque tuo conficis ipsa malo. (55-58)

Singula turpe seni quondam quaesita referre,
et quod tunc decuit, iam modo crimen habet. (101-102)

Cogimur a gratis animum suspendere rebus,
atque ut vivamus vivere destitimus. (155-156)

Lux gravis in luctu, rebus gratissima laetis,
quodque omni peius funere, velle mori. (7-8)

O quam dura premit miseros condicio vitae,
nec mors humano subiacet arbitrio.
Dulce mori miseris, sed mors optata recedit;
at cum tristis erit, praecipitata venit. (113-116)

Iam pavor est vidisse senem, nec credere possis
hunc hominem, humana qui ratione caret. (143-144)

Talia quis demens homini persuaserit auctor
ut cupiat, voto turpior esse suo? (151-152)

Morte mori melius, quam vitam ducere mortis
et sensus membris sic sepelire suis. (265-266)

It would be an oversimplification, however, to argue that the ethical dimension of Maximianus's poetry, stressed by his medieval enthusiasts, objectively prevails over other aspects of the text.[94] As I have already emphasized – and the conclusion can be only re-

[94] As argued by Agozzino (1970: 47; 27) who, as it appears, follows the medieval interpretation of Maximianus quite strictly, concluding that Maximianus's poetry is a "raccolta sapienziale ... di lettura <<facile>>, agevole anche ai *pueri* delle scuole;" "il <<Massimiano>> è *ethicus* ... nella descrizione dei *mala senectutis* ... e quindi nell'insegnamento che ne deriva per chi non voglia adeguarsi al ciclo della vita: ciò comporta anche la vituperosa impotenza del vecchio osceno: al let-

peated after reading the entire work – one can hardly point at its one overall tendency, whether 'serious' or 'ironic', autobiographic or just the opposite. The lengthy introductory part ('elegy' 1) programmatically plays with several literary traditions, encouraging the reader to focus not less on the 'content' than on the very 'form' of the poem. In fact, it is through the form, and even through particular forms (like 'epitaph' or 'prayer'), recalled, reused, often reinterpreted, that the meaning of the oeuvre in all the variety of tones is generated. Undoubtedly, 'elegy' 1, constituting a kind of "*motivating context*"[95] for the whole *opus*, announces and determines its 'elegiac' dimension. As I have shown, what Maximianus proposes is a very peculiar, even inverted version of the Latin elegy: the elegy without love. In the 'erotic' passage of 'elegy' 1 (ll. 59-100) the ideal elegiac lover cannot enjoy the *teneri amores* because he has not found a girl worth to be his partner. For his miserable *alter ego*, the *senex decrepitus*, what was once proper now is a *crimen* (l. 102). It is tempting to translate this *crimen* as 'a sin'; indeed, what our poet seems to offer is the 'Augustan' elegy and the 'Augustan' *eros* rethought and rewritten in the Christian era. What is important, however, is the fact that Maximianus's *eros*, so different from the love cherished by the Augustan elegists, is not yet *eros Christianus* either, spiritual and not carnal. Even though our poet points at his *castitas* several times, his sensual description of an ideal *puella* (or of the two quite specific girls, the beautiful cymbalist Candida and the *Graia*, on which below) can hardly be epitomized with the phrase uttered some time later by Venantius Fortunatus: *non caro, sed hoc quod spiritus optat amo.*[96] The ethical discourse is tangible throughout the text, yet it cannot be said that Maximianus composed an elegy moralisée. The message of the work is neither simple nor univocal, just as its very structure is neither simple nor homogeneous (*simplex et unum*, as Horace would say). The opening piece ('elegy' 1) persuades the readers into activating their whole poetic memory and reading Maximianus not as a 'new' Augustan or quasi-Augustan elegist but as a bold, and so unfaithful, translator of the 'classical tradition' into the language spoken by quite a different culture.

---

tore (come quello tardoantico e quello medievale, abituato ad una lettura transletterale) la saggia deduzione ed il salutare ribrezzo."

[95] See Schneider 2001: 453.

[96] Venantius Fortunatus, *Carm.* 11.6.4, addressed to Agnes (written most probably after the death of Radegund, see Reydellet 2004: 188). In his poetic letters to the two nuns, Radegund and Agnes, the 'Merovingian *vates*', as Fortunatus can certainly be called, quite often makes use of the elegiac erotic vocabulary, creating a sort of new semantics for the portrayal of the male-female relationship. Instead of a corporeal union, he advertizes a spiritual union, instead of sensual and sexual love, familial affection, like between mother and son (with Radegund) or brother and sister (with Agnes). Nevertheless, it not always turns out wholly unproblematic; in fact, in this very letter quoted above, Fortunatus refers to gossip about his loving relationship with Agnes, declaring vehemently that he loves Agnes exactly like he loves his own sister Titiana, see in passing George 1992: 173; on Fortunatus's reuse of the elegiac language in his *carmina*, see in particular Consolino 1977. Fortunatus exploits besides the language of Ovid's *Heroides* in his (or in fact Radegund's) *De excidio Thuringiae* (*App. Carm.* 1), see in particular Consolino 1993a, and especially in his mystic epithalamium *De virginitate* (8.3) composed for Agnes, see in particular Campanale 1980. For comparative reading of several *loci* in Maximianus and Fortunatus, see Schneider 2003: 55-61.

II. 3. Love memories in episodes: 'Elegies' 2-5

II. 3. 1. 'ELEGY' 2: *LYCORIS*

'Elegy' 1 read in accordance with the ecdotic tradition seems to have a sort of double final. First, the poet sums up his laments with a sententious phrase: *poena minor certam subito perferre ruinam, / quod timeas gravius sustinuisse diu* (ll. 277-278). Right after, however, he adds seven more distichs being in fact, to use Fo's expression, a "bis fuori programma" as he once again stresses here the afflictions of old age. The aspects on which he focuses now are loneliness and, as it could be said, social exclusion of an old man (*nec quisquam ex tantis praebet amicus opem*, l. 282), the contempt shown to him even by his own slaves (*ipsi me pueri atque ipsae sine lite puellae / turpe putant dominum iam vocitare suum*, ll. 283-284). This short 'paragraph' is closed again with two sentences:

Felix qui meruit tranquillam ducere vitam
et laeto stabiles claudere fine dies.
Dura satis miseris memoratio prisca bonorum,
et gravius summo culmine mersa ruit. (289-292)

It is tempting to think that this (finally!) must be the end. But, if we resist the temptation and continue to read, we soon discover that the so-called 'elegy' 2 is indeed a development, even an amplification, of themes suggested a few lines before. In ll. 283-288, the narrator pointed at the sense of isolation and lack of respect that the *senex* suffers even in his own household; now, he is to demonstrate a much worse example of this experience. Now, it is not only slaves who disappoint him, but also the most beloved woman with whom he has spent so many years, being one mind and one life, the one and only Lycoris, rejects his embrace and seeks younger partners. What is more, on seeing him, she spits and covers up her face (ll. 293-304 / el. 2.1-12). The picture is so impressive and corresponds so well with the mood of the introductory part – besides, the familiar lamentative tone sounds again in ll. 309-316 (el. 2.17-24) – that the reader is quite ready to miss the inaccuracy mentioned above, namely that the old bachelor all of the sudden turns out to be a lovelorn 'husband'. Maximianus finds his way to make us pay no attention to the fact that his different speaking egos are hardly one and the same person.

From the literary point of view, the part devoted to Lycoris is, as we have already said, the most conventional one. Conventional par excellence is the very theme of the unfaithfulness of the female lover, even though it is worth noting that Maximianus's Lycoris, unlike her Augustan counterparts, does not seek a richer but 'only' a younger man. As it appears, she reveals certain characteristics of those insatiable women destroying their partners, well-known from the epigrammatic, but also the elegiac, tradition[97] (*me potius reddidit ipsa senem*, l. 300 / el. 2.8). The motif though is not stressed too strongly. Maximianus is quite turpistic in his description (*Nauseat et priscum vomitu ceu fundit amorem, / inponit capiti plurima dira meo*, ll. 307-308 / el. 2.15-16), nonetheless, one can hardly

[97] Consolino 1997: 391-392; in elegy, see in particular Propertius 3.19.1-2.

agree with Szövérffy that the text has a clearly satirical and antifeminist tendency.[98] Quite the reverse, since the subject as such is very peculiar (an old lecherous woman), the poet's approach could be, needless to say, very aggressive. Maximianus, however, is gentle, even delicate, in portraying this lady of the Balzac age. He does not ridicule her self-assuredness but rather speaks with true sympathy and tenderness:

Atque tamen nivei circumdant tempora cani
et iam caeruleus inficit ora color,
praestat adhuc nimiumque sibi speciosa videtur
atque annos mecum despicit illa suos.
Et, fateor, primae retinet monimenta figurae,
atque inter cineres condita flamma manet.
Ut video, pulchris etiam vos parcitis, anni,
nec veteris formae gratia tota perit. (317-324 / el. 2.25-32)

The very main topic of the episode is particularly worthy of attention, i.e. the elegiac *connubium*, the union based on mutual faithfulness and lifelong devotion. This kind of relationship, the foundation of which should not be passion any more but rather *honor*, *pietas*, and a kind of filial affection,[99] is what Maximianus offers to his Lycoris:

Dicere si fratrem seu dedignaris amicum,
dic patrem; affectum nomen utrumque tenet.
Vincat honor luxum, pietas succedat amori (361-363 / el. 2.69-71)

The motif, present in Catullus, as well as in other elegists, gains its unique significance in Ovid. It is already in the *Amores* 1.3 that one can hear a declaration: *tu mihi, siqua fides, cura perennis eris. / tecum, quos dederint annos mihi fila sororum, / vivere contingat teque dolente mori!* (ll. 16-18). Yet it is his exilic letters addressed to his wife that are most expressive in this respect, where she is portrayed as a faithful, almost heroic, companion with whom, unfortunately, he is not allowed to live the old age. The poet, being himself tired and aged,[100] can only guess how his beloved one might look like at the moment. Unlike Maximianus, noting a bit ironically: *sum grandaevus ego, nec tu minus alba capillis* (l. 347 / el. 2.55), he is never really to see his wife's white hair:

---

[98] Szövérffy 1967-68: 362-364. The scholar interprets the work as satirical, of strongly antifeminist tendency, arguing that what the 'elegy' 2 offers is a rather overdrawn picture of a lecherous, libidinous, selfish woman who abandons loyalty and faith. Maximianus portrays himself as her victim, defenseless and helpless in his loyalty. Thus, the result is a generic antifeminist satire, largely based on the motif of the *exclusus amator.*

[99] Consolino (1997: 392) points at a somewhat similar passage in Lygdamus, Tib. 3.1.23: *haec tibi vir quondam, nunc frater, casta Naeera.* As we can see, however, the difference is quite significant. Once again, Maximianus turns out to be sensitive and understanding toward his Lycoris, who apparently would not be ready to admit that she *is* of his age, and allows her to address him as 'father', rather than as 'brother'.

[100] See *ex P.* 1.4.1-6: *Iam mihi deterior canis aspergitur aetas, / iamque meos vultus ruga senilis arat: / iam vigor et quasso languent in corpore vires, / nec, iuveni lusus qui placuere, iuvant. / nec, si me subito videas, agnoscere possis, / aetatis facta est tanta ruina meae.*

te quoque, quam iuvenem discedens urbe reliqui,
credibile est nostris insenuisse malis.
o, ego di faciant talem te cernere possim,
caraque mutatis oscula ferre comis (*ex P.* 1.4.47-50)

Ovid's poems are often composed as the form of *adlocutio*, or even appeal: the exile reminds his wife that through his poetry she has turned into a model of *fides*, a new Penelope, and she is supposed to comply with this unique role of hers.[101] Certainly, Maximianus's 'address' to Lycoris can hardly be considered an allusion to Ovid's elegies in the literal sense of the word: the two situations are entirely different. A point in common is, however, precisely the very protreptic tone. In comparison with other love episodes (the *Aquilina*, the *Candida*, the *Graia puella*), the so-called 'elegy' 2 is completely non-narrative, it is actually not a story but, indeed, an *adlocutio*, a request, written only when love is already over (in this respect, the part devoted to Lycoris can also be defined as 'elegy *without* love').

A typical element of the persuasive style employed by Maximianus are similes: animals love places they know well (ll. 337 ff. / el. 2.45 ff.), soldiers respect veterans, peasants and riders weep for the animals that served them (ll. 351-354 / el. 2.59-62). It is only Lycoris who deserts what is familiar to choose what she is not acquainted with (ll. 343-344 / el. 2.51-52). Typically, the stress is placed on one's own advantages, those that belong to the past: *Si modo non possum, quondam potuisse memento* (l. 349 / el. 2.57 – the sexual overtone of the phrase is quite charming), but also those that can still be boasted: *en facio versus et mea dicta cano* (l. 356 / el. 2.64). Again, it would be hard to speak here of an allusion *sensu stricto*, but it is worth remembering that Ovid in the letters to his wife also mentions his poetry, the poetry that will make her immortal. Most typical of the protreptic style is, however, the *sententiositas*, also easily noticeable here. This turns out to be another quality for which 'elegy' 2 can be seen indeed as a continuation of the introductory part:

Omnia nemo pati, non omnes omnia possunt / efficere (333-334 / el. 2.41-42)

Nonne placet melius certis confidere rebus?
Eventus varios res nova semper habet. (345-346 / el. 2.53-54)

par aetas animos conciliare solet. (348 / el. 2.56)

Quis suam in alterius condemnet crimine vitam
et quo pertendit claudere certet iter? (359-360 / el. 2.67-68)

Vincat honor luxum, pietas succedat amori,
plus ratio quam vis caeca valere solet. (363-364 / el. 2.71-72)

---

[101] See *ex P.* 3.1.43-46: *magna tibi inposita est nostris persona libellis: / coniugis exemplum diceris esse bonae. / hanc cave degeneres. ut sint praeconia nostra / vera; vide famae quod tuearis opus.*

One can hardly disagree with A. Fo that the last phrase in particular does not really match the whole context,[102] whereas read on its own it makes a perfect motto.[103] But the very closure formulated in the following distich seems even more abrupt and incoherent, the closure in which a careful reader will hear an echo of the final words of 'elegy' 1:

His lacrimis longos, quantum fas, flevimus annos,
est grave quod doleat commemorare diu. (365-366 / el. 2.73-74)

dura satis miseris memoratio prisca bonorum,
et gravius summo culmine mersa ruit. (291-292)

As it appears, this is supposed to be (at last!) a true separation mark, suggesting a change both in themes and, above all, in literary strategies. The lament, as it can be guessed from the words *quantum fas, flevimus* and *est grave … commemorare diu*, is to be replaced now with different means of expression.

II. 3. 2. 'ELEGY' 3: *AQUILINA*

Indeed, the next episode of the *opus*, the 'elegy' 3 or *Aquilina*, preceded, as we know, by a short prologue, offers a different topic: not the present life of the old man but an event from his youth, and a different, now clearly narrative form. The story to be told here is also, like all Maximianus recounts in his poetry, ostentatiously 'autobiographic': the poet remembers his first erotic experience, his first, still very immature, even 'rustic'[104] love for a girl by a usual, and thus seemingly true, name of Aquilina:[105]

---

[102] Fo 1986-1987: 96. Fo (1987: 366) is most probably right pointing out Maximianus's carelessness in this very ending part of 'elegy' 2. What it may also possibly indicate is the fact that the poet was much more playful than serious in composing his 'protreptic' and as such he did not, indeed, pay too much attention to what maxims to mix together.

[103] To such an extent that it was proposed by Karol Estreicher Jr and ultimately accepted as the motto of the Jagiellonian University. On the case, see more information available online at:
http://www.ces.uj.edu.pl/european/krakow/plusratio.htm [May 18, 2010].

[104] Webster (1900: 95) rightly points at Ovid's *Ars Amatoria*, where the motif of a young man's *rusticitas* is exploited: *Quantum defuerat pleno post oscula voto? / Ei mihi, rusticitas, non pudor ille fuit. / Vim licet appelles: grata est vis ista puellis: / Quod iuvat, invitae saepe dedisse volunt* (1.671-684). Interestingly, similar point is made in 'elegy' 5, where the poet emphasizes his *simplicitas* with which he falls for the *Graia puella*, opposing it precisely to *ars* embodied, so to speak, by the woman, fully aware of how to use this particular (witch)craft: *Subcubui, fateor, Graiae tunc nescius artis, / subcubui, Tusca simplicitate senex* (ll. 559-560 / el. 5.39-40).

[105] Mastandrea (2005: 156) proposes to interpret this, ostensibly unfictitious, name as a speaking one, an antonym of Candida, thus 'a girl of dark skin'. Compare also Schneider's (2003: 101) "kleine dunkle Adlerin." I must admit though that I find not really convincing his reading of the female protagonists and the message their names might convey (see pp. 99-110), except for Lycoris's, which is a quite clear case. Ratkowitsch (1986: 50) sees in Aquilina almost an embodiment of devil, which is related to her quasi-allegorizing interpretation of Maximianus's oeuvre.

> *Captus amore tuo demens, Aquilina, ferebar*
> *pallidus et tristis, captus amore tuo.*
> *Nondum quid sit Amor vel quid Venus ignea noram,*
> *torquebar potius rusticitate mea.*
> *Nec minus illa meo percussa Cupidine flagrans*
> *errabat, tota non capienda domo.*
> *Carmina, pensa procul nimium dilecta iacebant,*
> *solus amor cordi curaque semper erat.* (371-378 / el. 3.5-12)

The emotions of the young protagonists are described through stereotypical expressions and motifs, in the first place the motif of *erotica pathemata*, the 'symptoms of love'. It is worth noting, however, that it is actually for the first time that the theme is used in its proper context in Maximianus's oeuvre. As we remember, in 'elegy' 1 certain terms, already clearly associable with erotic poetry, were employed in their (at least ostensibly) 'original' sense to indicate 'real' illness and weakness, i.e. the old age. In 'elegy' 3, we meet the young and inexperienced lover who is pale and sad as well as languishing (*His egomet stimulis angebar semper et ardens / languebam, nec spes ulla salutis erat*, ll. 409-410 / el. 3.43-44). His partner is "no less smitten by the same desire,"[106] neglecting all she would love doing before.

The love of the two youngsters is passionate, all the more because it is forbidden. Both, guarded by adults, could not express their real feelings[107] if not by trying to speak to each other at least with sighs and in secret, but even this, eventually, did not pass unnoticed.

> *Me pedagogus agit, illam tristissima mater*
> *servabat, tanti poena secunda mali.* (383-384 / el. 3.17-18)

> *mox captare locos et tempora coepimus ambo*
> *atque superciliis luminibusque loqui,*
> *fallere sollicitos, suspensos ponere gressus*
> *et tota nullo currere nocte sono.*
> *Nec longum: genetrix furtivum sensit amorem*
> *et medicare parans vulnera vulneribus*
> *increpitat caeditque: foventur caedibus ignes,*
> *ut solet adiecto crescere flamma rogo.* (391-398 / el. 3.25-32)[108]

In this very moment, a competent reader should notice that the whole situation, described here as ostensibly true, is totally 'literary':[109] the old man's *alter ego* and Aquilina are nothing more than a new embodiment of Ovid's Pyramus and Thisbe (*Met.*

[106] Lind 1988: 328.

[107] Certain analogies could be found in Tibullus 1.2.

[108] I follow the punctuation proposed by Sandquist Öberg 1999: 118.

[109] Consolino (1997: 378) speaks of the "tasso di letterarietà." The Italian scholar notes some other interesting associations: the female protagonist stands almost in between Dido and pseudo-Virgilian *Ciris*; the girl kept and guarded by her parents resembles the one presented in eclogue 2 by Nemesianus; the figure of *pedagogus* originates from comedy.

4.55 ff.).[110] This association can be seen as an additional hint allowing us to interpret the piece as a quasi-epic 'inclusion' inserted into a larger elegiac structure. What is more important though is the fact that the mythological evocation, once recognized, determines our perception of the text. Being aware of the tragic final of Ovid's epyllion – which, needless to say, inspired the plot of Shakespeare's *Romeo and Juliet* – we cannot follow the story told by the late antique elegist if not with a certain anxiety, asking ourselves what now will be the end of the two kids' love affair. Unlike Pyramus and Thisbe, Aquilina and her beloved are saved; Maximianus's episode closes with a sort of *laetus exitus* and as such could be seen as an inversion of the Ovidian model. In fact, however, the case is not so simple.

The problem, as it is well-known, seems to be resolved by Boethius, the *scrutator maximus rerum*,[111] whom the young man addresses in despair, begging for help. In Maximianus's text, Boethius appears just like Hippocrates in the *Aegritudo Perdicae*[112] and, just like the latter, he immediately gives the right diagnosis. What is more, he also proposes a specific, albeit quite surprising, therapy:

Mox ait: <<Occultae satis est res prodita causae,
pone metum, veniam vis tibi tanta dabit.>>
Prostratus pedibus verecunda silentia rupi,
cum lacrimis referens ordine cuncta suo.
<<Fac>> ait <<ut placitae potiaris munere formae.>>
Respondi: <<Pietas talia velle fugit.>>
Solvitur in risum exclamans: <<Pro mira voluntas!
Castus amor Veneris, dicito, quando fuit?

---

[110] See Fo (1986-1987: 98-99) who carefully enumerates the analogies: "Per quanto riguarda la prima parte del racconto, ... l'analogia della situazione generale risulta evidente e ... si riscontrano anche paralleli puntuali. Piramo e Tisbe vivono vicini e si innamorano. Come Massimiano e Aquilina sono ostacolati. ... *nutu signisque locuntur* (*Met.* IV 63), come Massimiano e Aquilina ... Infine entrambe le coppie ingannano i custodi e si incontrano nottetempo."

[111] Shanzer (1983: 190), who interprets Maximianus's portrayal of Boethius as ironic, emphasizes that the apostrophe: *Hic mihi, magnarum scrutator maxime rerum, / solus, Boethi, fers miseratus opem* (ll. 413-414 / el. 3.47-48) plays upon the juxtaposition of a very lofty expression: *magnarum … maxime rerum* and the, rather inappropriate in this sense, *scrutator* (used normally of poking, delving, or grubbing around for things). In sum, the apostrophe is too elevated in style for the erotic context: "Boethius's talents which had been used for examining *caeli plagas* are here deployed in rather low busy-body affairs." One should remember though that *scrutari* is a medical technical term denoting the examination of hidden things, see Zurli 1991: 314. Shanzer points at l. 418 / el. 3.52: *mitibus alloquiis pandere clausa iubes*, showing Boethius's readiness to perceive the causes of the young man's grief, which, in her opinion, is a parodying allusion to Philosophia's promise given in *Consolatio* 1.P.4: *Si operam medicantis exspectas, oportet vulnus detegas.* As for the relationship between Maximianus and Boethius, see especially the paper by Bertini 1981.

[112] As noted above in Part One Ch. I. 6, the analogy was noticed by Ratkowitsch 1986: 52, but Zurli's (1991) further comments should also be taken into consideration here. As he concludes (p. 318): "l'uso poetico della lingua medica in Massimiano passi *anche* (ma non solo …) per il tramite dell'epillio adespoto di ambiente draconziano." On the analogy, see also recently Grillo 2010^2: 61-62.

Parcere dilectae, iuvenis, desiste puellae,
impius huic fueris, si pius esse velis.
Unguibus et morsu teneri pascuntur amores,
vulnera non refugit res magis apta plagae.>>
Interea donis permulcet corda parentum
et pretio faciles in mea vota trahit. (425-438 / el. 3.59-72)[113]

As it appears, it can be often somewhat hard for a modern mind not to think of Boethius from the perspective of his martyr-like death, and – what is maybe even more difficult – not to think that the sixth century readership (at least not in the most pro-Gothic circles[114]) saw the author of the *Consolatio* only as a quasi-saintly figure not subject to any 'misrepresentation'. Therefore, Maximianus's portrayal of Boethius has been interpreted as hostile or ironic.[115] In fact, the philosopher does seem to be acting like a pander, not only advising his inexperienced friend to go ahead and violate the girl but even bribing her parents to make them favorable to their daughter's sin. On the other hand, there have also been fully positive readings, emphasizing that Maximianus's Boethius is, indeed, cast in the role of a true and very efficient therapist.[116]

Undoubtedly, the literary audience can find it somewhat surprising that the philosopher speaks – and with a fluency – the language of erotic elegy,[117] as if he were a true *praeceptor amoris*. Significant are especially his words on *pietas*, which he interprets with a provocativeness worthy of Ovid of the *Ars Amatoria*, quite differently from Maximianus himself in his appeal to Lycoris. As it appears, the reader would rather expect that, once Boethius the philosopher becomes a co-protagonist of a love story, the poetics and the mood of the piece should change. It should not be 'romantic' now but 'serious'. In fact,

---

[113] I follow the punctuation proposed by Sandquist Öberg 1999: 120, but in ll. 429 / el. 3.63 I maintain *fac*, as in Agozzino 1970: 196, Guardalben 1993: 80, and Schneider 2003: 181.

[114] Hence the political interpretation of Anastasi (1948: 1951) who in his two papers emphasizes the political overtone of the elegy (and Ennodius's epigram, *carm*. 2.132, on which below in Part Three Ch. III. 3. 2), overtly hostile to the philosopher and strongly pro-Gothic.

[115] Anastasi (1951) speaks of ironic, even sarcastic tone, aiming at denigrating the posthumous glory of the philosopher for political reasons. Szövérffy (1967-68: 361) also argues that the elegist attributes to Boetius a derogatory and insulting role. Alfonsi (1941-42) speaks of ironic cynicism. Shanzer (1983: 192) also interprets the picture as ironic, but in her opinion, it is precisely the tone that militates against the Anastasi's theory of political slur. The portrayal of the philosopher as given by the two poets is too parodic to be serious propaganda.

[116] Agozzino 1970: 88-89, Bertini 1981: 283, and recently Mastandrea (2005: 157) who, I must admit, gives a somewhat too short shrift to all 'non-positive' interpretations.

[117] Fo (1986-1987: 98; 100) notes rightly: "Da tutto ciò emerge fortissimo il sospetto che, qualunque cosa Boezio abbia in realtà detto, o Massimiano abbia inteso mettergli in bocca, questa cosa sia stata poi filtrata dalla dizione elegiaca e dalla 'poetica' massimianea al punto che è del tutto e interamente il poeta elegiaco a parlarci ... può darsi che l'episodio narrato in el. III rifletta un avvenimento realmente accaduto, ma certo v'è in esso molta letteralizzazione." Shanzer (1981: 192) goes much further as she proposes to see Maximianus's Boethius as a literary figure: "Magister Boethius is summoned up in an imaginary colloquy presented as fact – in much the same way that Vergil will be used by Dante, and had been used by Fulgentius the Mythographer." For Consolino (1997: 380), on the other hand, Boethius is here a "personaggio in carne ed ossa."

one could be almost sure that the philosopher should deliver a speech in a protreptic or apotreptic tone, like Maximianus himself loves doing. But what happens is quite the opposite: *cedit Philosophia Elegiae.*

The following scene, in which the philosopher 'seduces' Aquilina's parents, appears even more problematic. Now, as I believe, some of Maximianus's readers could start to suspect that the piece is about to assume some satirical flavor; after all, philosophers were quite often exposed to ridicule by the Roman authors. In this very moment, however, there is a sudden change in the course of events: the parents do begin to favor their daughter's sin as the blind love of gold conquers the natural love (*Auri caecus amor nativum vincit amorem*, l. 439 / el. 3.73[118]). It is clear now that the story is not to end like the one of Pyramus and Thisbe (so maybe, a reader might conjecture, it will end just well, like a 'true' romance). Unfortunately, the young man, once allowed to fulfill his dreams, no longer desires the girl, who leaves him intact. The would-be tragic lover lauds virginity: *<<Salve sancta>>, inquam, <<semperque intacta maneto, / virginitas, per me plena pudoris eris.>>* (ll. 449-450 / el. 3.83-84). Boethius, told about the event, congratulates the youngster. His role seems to be eventually explained: rather than a pander, he turns out a true healer, helping his young friend get rid of the incontrollable passion:[119]

> *<<Macte>>, inquit, <<iuvenis, proprii dominator amoris,*
> *et de contemptu sume trophaea tuo.*
> *Arma tibi Veneris cedantque Cupidinis arcus,*
> *cedat et armipotens ipsa Minerva tibi.>>* (453-456 / el. 3.87-90)

As I have emphasized, throughout 'elegy' 3, which – like most of Maximianus's oeuvre – could seem ostentatiously autobiographic, the poet proposes a very subtle play with the literary tradition: his protagonists, quite common at first sight as common the name of Aquilina may sound, find their counterparts in couples known from myth and 'fiction'. The role in which Boethius is cast is also associable with a persona well-known from love novel or romance. In fact, we might even add that the very narrative strategy adopted to tell Aquilina's story is to some extent comparable with the one of the romance genre. It would be exaggerated to speak of a true *peripateia* or – more properly in the romance context – *peripateiai* as the rule behind the episode recounted by Maximianus, neverthe-

---

[118] A well-trained reader would probably add Horace's *carm.* 3.16.9-11 *aurum per medios ire satellites / et perrumpere amat saxa potentius / ictu fulmineo.*

[119] Fo (1986-1987: 99-100) tries to shed at least some light upon the question 'why Boethius?', why this particular figure was chosen for the role of *praeceptor amoris*. The Italian scholar points at a very subtle network of intertextual links between Maximianus's work (in particular 'elegy' 3) and Boethius's *Consolatio*, arguing that the philosopher dedicates much of his attention to the problem of love as a passion that cannot be controlled, and thus should rather be avoided. Also Shanzer (1983: 194) gives a very intriguing, although, indeed, hard to prove, explanation of the appearance of Boethius's figure in Maximianus's elegy. In her opinion, the details of Boethius's life counterbalance those of the poet. "Boethius had a reputation for lasciviousness in youth (Ennodius), ... in his *senectus* he wrote an important philosophical and literary work which demonstrated a change of heart from the ways of his youth, and he came to a quasi-saintly end as a political martyr. As such he makes a fine complement to the *persona* Maximianus who was unrealistically chaste in youth, and is depicted as tortured by his desires and impotence in old age."

less, at least a few times, the reader can witness a sudden – and surprising – reversal of the plot: the appearance of Boethius, his reaction to the laments of the young man, the unexpected behavior of the parents, the rapidity with which the ardor dies, the final laudatory speech of the philosopher.

The story, which starts like the one of Pyramus and Thisbe, seems to end with a moralizing lesson that a reader might indeed expect, finding out that Boethius is supposed to intervene; and the forbidden love does not bring about the catastrophe of the young couple. Does it mean – to return to the main question I have posed above – that what Maximianus offers is a kind of 'romanzo a lieto fine', a happy ending, happy also because morally right?

The readers probably still remember the prologue declaration: *maestum noscere curet* [lector] *opus* (l. 370 / el. 3.4). Soon, will they hear the narrator say, commenting on the whole episode:

> *Sic mihi peccandi studium permissa potestas*
> *abstulit atque ipsum talia velle fugit.*
> *Ingrati, tristes pariter discessimus ambo:*
> *discidii ratio vita pudica fuit.* (ll. 457-460 / el. 3.91-94)

The passage is not a mere denouement. What is emphasized here is the disappointment, the sadness of the two protagonists.[120] A careful reader will certainly not miss the fact that several lines earlier Aquilina's departure, still as a virgin, was described in like manner: *illaeso corpore tristis abit* (l. 446 / el. 3.80). In addition, it is worth remembering that *tristis* is used in the opening section ('elegy' 1.107: *hunc tacitum tristemque decet*) as one of the main qualifiers of the old man: the *senex* is supposed to be *tristis* as the young man is *laetus*. Webster argues that the word appears in this context as the opposite of *iucundus* or *gratus* and so could be seen almost as a technical term meaning "unfit for love" and "without love's joys."[121] Webster's conclusion is probably somewhat hasty: the word could hardly be considered technical *sensu proprio*; it is true, however, as can be judged specifically from the above-quoted passage from 'elegy' 3, that the adjective does refer to a sort of 'sadness' resulting from the lack of sexual pleasure. As I have already mentioned, Maximianus's interpretation of the genre he 'reanimated' is quite unique, precisely for the fact that what he offers is a kind of (erotic) elegy without love. The *Aquilina* case seems to provide an explanation of this paradox: love (meaning: sex) was sacrificed to chastity.

---

[120] Most scholars (as I myself) presume that *ambo* refers to the young couple, not to the *puer* and Boethius. Such hypothesis was first proposed by Anastasi 1951: 76. More recently Shanzer (1981: 191) gave a very interesting interpretation. She presumes that Boethius's acting as a pander should be taken mostly at face value (as I have mentioned above, the American scholar thinks that Maximianus's approach to the philosopher is ironic). "<<We>> here must be Boethius and the poet who have split up, because Maximianus rejected his gift, and turned to virtue." What the American scholar finds overtly ironic in Boethius's speech to the youngster – and therefore suggesting that the philosopher is in fact not so enthusiastic about his conversion to chastity – is the statement that even Minerva should yield to him. Shanzer points at an allusion to Ovid's *Am.* 1.15, which in her opinion marks Boethius's words ironically.

[121] Webster 1900: 73.

Thus, it would be tempting to read this piece – if not the whole oeuvre[122] – as a form of protreptic for sexual renunciation. In such a context, Boethius could indeed be seen as *praeceptor castitatis*, proposing the most efficacious therapy to help his 'patient' dampen his passion (a kind of *remedium amoris* in fact) and, consequently, to choose the right and the safest way of life.

What blurs the image, however, is precisely the comment to the episode made by the narrator: *ingrati, tristes*, reinforcing the sound of the previous *tristis*, in l. 446 (el. 3.80), still ringing in the reader's ears. Sexual abstinence does not bring joy; it brings the opposite, sadness. Nor does it bring satisfaction instead; rather, it causes displeasure and the feeling of separation. 'Elegy' 3 does not offer an easy solution. What is more, it does not even provide a clear statement that 'all ended well'. On the contrary, a reader who would still expect a usual romance happy ending must be ultimately disillusioned. A reader convinced that the story must have a 'moral' – which might be, of course, more important than just a naïve happy ending – may well agree that the lesson to be learned here could be summarized as follows (to quote Fo): "la passione d'amore è peccaminosa (vv. 74 *crimen*; 77 *nefas*; 91 *peccare*) e va repressa in nome della virtù e della pudicizia (vv. 87 s. *macte ... iuvenis, proprii dominator amoris etc.*), anche se ciò porta a tristezza (v. 93): si tratta di un trionfo morale (v. 88), del resto è solo l'elemento della proibizione a rendere tanto fascinoso il tutto (anche per Piramo e Tisbe il divieto esasperò l'amore: *Met.* IV 64): una volta permesso, ecco che non ha più sapore."[123] Yet what could hardly pass unnoticed is precisely the fact that it is *not* Maximianus's text itself to verbalize such a 'positive' message.[124] This silence speaks.

II. 3. 3. 'ELEGY' 4: *CANDIDA*

'Elegy' 4, the second of the two most retrospective episodes, starts, like the previous one, with an autothematic introduction, situating this section in the larger narrative context. Once again, like in 'elegy' 3, we hear the clear voice of the narrator, pointing out his advanced age, even – as he has already done in the opening unit – ridiculing his present condition as *delira senecta* (*Conveniunt etenim delirae ignava senectae*, l. 463 / el. 4.3). Indeed, what he proposes is a kind of sentimental journey into the idyllic land of youth:

> *Sic vicibus variis alternos fallimus annos,*
> *et mutata magis tempora grata mihi.* (465-466 / el. 4.5-6)

I have already emphasized the literariness of Maximianus's portraits of his protagonists. Women in particular as depicted by our poet are distinctive for their convention-

[122] This is how some contemporary scholars, notably Szövérffy 1967-68, Agozzino 1970, and Ratkowitsch 1986, try to explain the medieval popularity of Maximianus's oeuvre. In Szövérffy's opinion for instance, for the Middle Ages, Aquilina's story might sound like a praise of virginity. Indeed, such a reading would be possible precisely if one removed the very final lines.

[123] Fo 1986-1987: 102.

[124] Consolino 1997: 382.

ality but at the same time for some exceptional charm: let us remember once again his Lycoris, a lady of the Balzac age. Candida, the heroine of the present episode, quite in accordance with her descriptive name,[125] has some usual attributes of a beauty, well-known from Latin erotic poetry:[126] candid appearance (thus Candida), perfect hairdo, white fingers, sweet voice. What is unique about Candida – although one should remember that the elegiac *puellae doctae* were supposed to be musically gifted – is her skillfulness in playing the cymbals. The poet's description allows us to almost visualize the girl with cymbals hanging all over her body dancing and singing:

Virgo fuit, species dederat cui candida nomen
Candida; diversis nam bene compta modis.[127]
Huic ego per totum vidi pendentia corpus
cymbala multiplices edere pulsa sonos;
nunc niveis digitis, nunc pulsas pectine cordas
arguto quicquam murmure dulce loqui. (467-472 / el. 4.7-12)[128]

Hanc ego saltantem subito correptus amavi (475 / el. 4.15)
cantabam dulces quos solet illa modos. (482 / el. 4.22)

Whereas 'elegy' 3 was the most 'dramatic' among Maximianus's stories, with three characters, dialogues, a quasi-romance plot, and a definite ending, the *Candida* episode is for the main part narrative: it is the poet (the narrator) to recount the whole story, making use of the direct speech only three times. Interestingly, it is in one of these few phrases, quoting a comment made by someone observing the man's reaction, that the name of our poet is mentioned for the first and last time in the entire oeuvre:

Atque aliquis, cui caeca foret bene nota voluptas:
<<cantat, cantantem Maximianus amat.>> (485-486 / el. 4.25-26)[129]

This anonymous viewer, who – knowing himself just too well the power of blinding desire – immediately names the phenomenon, is the only witness we have of Maximianus's identity. The passage, again, seems to give grounds for reading the work from an autobiographic perspective, although it must be remembered that apparently no other

[125] Webster (1900: 103) notes, not improperly in fact, it may be a hint that she belonged to the demi-monde, where names were usually eloquent. On the other hand, the name Candida may also evoke a somewhat similar name of Ovid's Corinna.

[126] Consolino (1997: 383) points to similarities with the pseudo-Virgilian *Copa* and *Carmen Priapeum* 27.

[127] I agree with Guardalben (1993: 122) that the lection *bene compta comis*, accepted by some editors, from Bährens to Schneider, "può forse apparire <<facile>>."

[128] In l. 471 / el. 4.11 I follow Guardalben (1993: 86) who accepts the conjecture *pulsas* proposed by Schetter 1970: 89-90 and Tandoi 1973: 143.

[129] In l. 486 / el. 4.26 similarly Webster 1900: 43 and Guardalben 1993: 88 (Guardalben omits the comma after *cantat*). Sandquist Öberg, on her part, proposes to insert the quotation mark after *cantat* (which in this reading is the predicate of *aliquis*), following Giardelli (see already Webster 1900: 104): *atque aliquis, cui caeca foret bene nota voluptas, / cantat: <<Cantantem Maximianus amat.>>*

source verifies what – if any – extratextual message such 'testimony' carries. For the posterity 'Maximianus' has become, indeed, a wholly literary character.

As a matter of fact, the statement made by the mysterious passerby, recognizing easily the reasons behind the unusual behavior, epitomizes quite well the actual subject of the whole unit, devoted not just to another particular love story, this time with a Candida, but rather to the very problem of love, or precisely: desire (*voluptas*, qualified as *caeca*), as a pathological condition – Maximianus seems to have no doubts about it (*O quotiens demens, quotiens sine mente putabar! / Nec, puto, fallebar: non bene sanus eram*, ll. 483-484 / el. 4.23-24) – the syndromes of which should be enumerated. The male protagonist of 'elegy' 4, like his previous 'incarnation' in 'elegy' 3, embodies all of the typical symptoms of love: he silently suffers his "pleasing wounds"[130] (*coepi tacitus vulnera grata pati*, l. 476 / el. 4.16), he sees his beloved one in his mind's eye even if she is away from him, he talks to himself, he sings her songs, insane, mad (ll. 483-484 / el. 4.23-24), as if the beautiful singer put a spell on him (in l. 486 / el. 4.26 our poet probably does play upon the double entendre of *cantat*):

Singula visa semel semper memorare libebat,
haerebant animo nocte dieque meo.
Saepe velut visae laetabar imagine formae
et procul absenti voce manuque fui;
saepe, velut praesens fuerit, mecum ipse loquebar,
cantabam dulces, quos solet illa, modos. (477-482 / el. 4.17-22)

The fury is too often revealed even if one's lips are sealed. What gives away the man's secret affliction is his pallor and blush, but especially his sleep:

Certe difficile est abscondere pectoris aestus,
panditur et clauso saepius ore furor.
Nam subito inficiens vultum pallorque ruborque
interdum clausae vocis habebat opus.
Nec minus ipsa meas prodebant somnia curas,
somnia secreto non bene fida meo. (487-492 / el. 4.27-32)

Maximianus's reader, well aware of the literariness and self-consciousness of his verse, easily recognizes the topoi of erotic poetry; this time the whole piece is, in fact, built upon the motif of *erotica pathemata*, in previous units used only to color certain passages. Therefore, the story of Candida, especially in its first part, seems also much more 'static' than the piece dedicated to Aquilina, the poet's attention being focused not so much on the two protagonists as on the very phenomenon of 'passion' (*pectoris aestus*; *furor*, ll. 487-488 / el. 4.27-28), the above-mentioned phenomenon of desire.

In fact, only the very final of the episode is dramatic. The man, crying out in deep sleep for his beloved to come, is overheard by her father. The latter jumps up, expecting to find there his daughter, but sees only the poor dreamer murmuring the girl's name. As Consolino justly observes,[131] the questions put by the father do resemble those of

[130] Lind 1988: 330. On *vulnera grata* as one of the most favorite Maximianus's expressions, see Webster 1900: 104.

[131] Consolino 1997: 385.

Macrobius, exploring the role and significance of dreams (<<*Vana putas an vera? sopor ludibria iactat / an te verus*>>, *ait,* <<*pectoris ardor agit? / Credo equidem assuetas animo remeare figuras, / et fallax studium ludit imago suum.*>>, ll. 503-506 / el. 4.43-46). Apparently, the late antique readership was particularly sensitive to such issues; in addition, the motif of a lover fulfilling his desire only in dreams belonged to the very canon of topics in erotic literature (the example of the *Aegritudo Perdicae* could be also cited here). Yet, if the readers supposed that after this sudden change of plot the story would be still continued toward a more typically 'romance' finale for example, once again they might feel slightly disappointed. Evidently, Maximianus loves playing upon his audience's expectations, promising to tell *turpes casus* and yet not verbalizing these moments of the story that would probably seem most intriguing. Like the *Aquilina* episode, this piece also ends surprisingly, at least if an abrupt conclusion could be considered a 'surprising ending'. Our narrator briefly summarizes: 'the father asks me to utter more words' (l. 508 / el. 4.48) and immediately adds:

> *Sic ego, qui cunctis sanctae gravitatis habebar,*
> *proditus indicio sum miser ipse meo,*
> *et nunc infelix tota est sine crimine vita,*[132]
> *et peccare senem non potuisse pudet.* (509-512 / el. 4.49-52)

The readers might be somewhat frustrated not only because once more a love story turns out to be a story without love, and consequently without sex, but also because what they might find particularly interesting in ll. 509-510 (el. 4.49-50) are those few hints regarding the 'I-speaker' of Maximianus's poetry. The hints are not followed, however, by more specific explanations but only by two mournful assertions: *et nunc infelix tota est sine crimine vita, / et peccare senem non potuisse pudet.*[133] The passage is captivating because what is said now exceeds just a declaration of choosing the chaste life, made in 'elegy' 3. We hear about the 'public opinion', the general esteem paid to our protagonist for his *sancta gravitas*, which esteem he presumably must have lost as a result of this miserable unmasking (*indicio meo*!) of his 'true' nature. In this context, it is tempting to

---

[132] In l. 511 / el. 4.51 Schneider (2003: 185) omits *tota*.

[133] The perfect infinitive used in l. 512 / el. 4.52 deserves some explanation. Fo (1986-1987: 104) proposes the following interpretation: "l'episodio gli ha fatto perdere la reputazione, di modo che ora, da vecchio, egli si trova a vergognarsi, ma non può vergognarsi di aver peccato, perché la sua vita è *sine crimine*; dice allora di trovarsi da vecchio a vergognarsi, ma, paradossalmente, di non aver potuto peccare (= pur non avendo potuto peccare); oppure: vergognarsi per aver solo voluto ma non potuto peccare. Il paradosso, in ogni caso, starebbe nel doversi vergognare a causa della perdita di reputazione di santità nell'opinione generale, pur non avendo peccato." Thus, Fo suggests that the ll. 511-512 / el. 4.51-52 should be understood as: "ed ora tutta la mia vita è infelice (pur) senza che io abbia commesso alcuna colpa / ed il vecchio si vergogna (ma) di non aver potuto peccare." Consolino (1997: 384, n. 74), however, objects to Fo's reading. She emphasizes that it can hardly be supported by the text syntax and proposes to return to Webster's understanding of *potuisse* as aorist with reference to the present ("il poeta si vergogna, ora, di non essere più in grado di peccare ... per raggiunti limiti di età"). Webster (1900: 105) notes that such a use of aorist was frequent in the Augustan poets.

speculate about his actual status;[134] still, it seems not less enticing to examine the question of the very intention of Maximianus's text. Why does our poet propose a kind of 'phenomenology of desire' (blind: *caeca voluptas*) exploiting the example of a man who, eventually, turns out to have been commonly respected for his *sancta gravitas*? And why does he, already for the second time but now even more emphatically that in 'elegy' 3, acknowledge that sexual abstinence brings unhappiness (*infelix ... est sine crimine vita*)? What is more, why does he claim that the old man is ashamed not to be able to sin any more (not to have been able to sin), indicating that he, in fact, still wants what he cannot do: *Deserimur vitiis, fugit indignata voluptas; / nec quod non possum non voluisse meum est* (ll. 513-514 / el. 4.53-54).

As it could be expected, the text itself does not provide a clear, immediate answer. Instead, the story of Candida develops[135] into the next and final episode, which for many reasons can be understood as climatic for the whole oeuvre, also because of the temporal plane on which it takes place. The reader's attention is redirected from the past to the present: once again we meet the protagonist as an old man and once again we hear his confession of guilt:

> *Hoc etiam meminisse licet, quod serior aetas*
> *intulit, et gemitus, quos mihi laeta dedit,*
> *si quis has possit naturae adtingere partes,*
> *gnarus et ut sapiens noxia saepe velit.*
> *Interdum rapimur vitiis trahimurque volentes,*
> *et quod non capiunt pectora bruta volunt.* (515-520 / el. 4.55-60)[136]

II. 3. 4. 'ELEGY' 5: *GRAIA PUELLA*

We have thus reached the final and, as it appears, the most important episode. The youngster is now presented again as an elderly man, a respected citizen and diplomat sent to the East on a mission. There, he meets a girl typically – and 'topically' – beautiful, as required by the canons of erotic poetry. In fact, she looks and acts as if she read advice given by the Augustan elegists:[137]

> *Haec erat egregiae formae vultusque modesti,*
> *grata, micans oculis nec minus arte placens,*
> *docta loqui digitis et carmina fingere docta*
> *et responsuram sollicitare lyram.* (535-538 / el. 5.15-18)

---

[134] The interpretation by Ratkowitsch (1986) is, in fact, oriented at this particular question. She concludes that the environment for which and by which Maximianus's oeuvre was produced was actually the monastery.

[135] On the division between 'elegy' 4 and 5, see above in Ch. II. 1 and especially in Fo 1986-1987: 104-105.

[136] In l. 517 / el. 4.57 I follow the majority of editors (Agozzino 1970: 238; Guardalben 1993: 92; Sandquist Öberg 1999: 126) and read *si*, not *set* as Schneider 2003: 185 and Webster 1900: 45.

[137] See Consolino 1997: 388; Spaltenstein 1983: 250 (CC. 2423-2425); Alfonsi 1941-42: 338.

The portrayal of the *Graia puella* is, undoubtedly, one of the most sensual descriptions of female beauty, at least in Maximianus's poetry:

> *Quis referat gressus certa sub lege moventes*
> *suspensosque novis plausibus ire pedes?*
> *Grande erat inflexos gradibus numerare capillos,*
> *grande erat in niveo pulla colore coma.*
> *Urebant oculos stantes duraeque papillae*
> *et quas astringens clauderet una manus.*
> *A, quantum mentem stomachi iunctura movebat*
> *atque sub exhausto pectore pingue femur!* (543-550 / el. 5.23-30)

The girl stands at the old man's windowsill all through the night and sings sweetly. She also cries, sighs, and turns pale. All these are, again, the topoi of erotic poetry: an upside down *paraklausythyron*, the *erotica pathemata*, and as such should not be taken at face value. Indeed – the narrator clearly states it (only *ex post*, though) – the girl, well aware of her sensuality and knowing how to use it, *pretends* she has fallen in love. She makes a kind of a 'show', apparently understanding love as if Ovid were her teacher: not as a 'truth', but as a 'fiction', a game having certain rules. These rules must be learned, otherwise one acts the fool, precisely like our protagonist, the Tuscan simpleton. Despite his age, he turns out to be still as inexperienced as he was when 'dating' Aquilina:

> *Nam cum se nostro captam simularet amore,*
> *me potius vero fecit amore capi.*
> *Pervigil ad nostras astabat nocte fenestras,*
> *nescio quid Graeco murmure dulce canens.*
> *Nunc aderant lacrimae, gemitus, suspiria, pallor*
> *et quicquid nullum fingere posse putes.*
> *Sic velut afflictam nimium miseratus amantem*
> *efficior potius tunc miserandus ego.* (527-534 / el. 5.7-14)

> *Subcubui, fateor, Graiae tunc nescius artis,*
> *subcubui, Tusca simplicitate senex.* (559-560 / el. 5.39-40)

As it is well known, the main part of the episode treats the narrator's embarrassing collapse into impotence. To be exact though, his love affair with the *Graia puella* lasted two nights, of which during the first one – should we believe the version he gives – his performance "was almost too strenuous for an old man"[138] (*set mihi prima quidem nox affuit ac sua solvit / munera, grandaevo vix subeunda viro*, ll. 567-568 / el. 5.47-48). Already the following night is a disaster:[139]

---

[138] Lind 1988: 333.

[139] In 'elegy' 5, editors propose different collocations, especially as regards ll. 31-50. The core of the problem concerns the placement of verses describing the old man's impotence during the second night, having in mind that the first one was more than successful. Fo's (1986-1987: 107-108) proposals are followed by Guardalben (1993: 98-100) in his edition: according to this view, the lines 39-46 and 47-50 should be placed right after l. 30, whereas lines 31-38 after l. 50. This way, we achieve the following arrangement: the protagonist admits his falling in love with the beautiful Greek girl (described in detail right before); next, he remembers the first, fully successful, night

proxima destituit vires, vacuusque recessit
ardor, et in Venerem segnis ut ante fui. (569-570 / el. 5.49-50)

The reader's poetic memory will immediately suggest that the piece should be read in the context of Ovid's *Amores* 3.7, also devoted to the very same problem. Still, the differences are blatant. The poet born in Sulmo, describing his completely unexpected indisposition, focuses mostly on the future: what frightens him is not so much this unfortunate episode but rather the thought that it may be a preview of what will happen on a regular basis in his old age:

Quae mihi ventura est, siquidem ventura, senectus,
cum desit numeris ipsa iuventa suis?
a, pudet annorum: quo me iuvenemque virumque?
nec iuvenem nec me sensit amica virum! (*Am.* 3.7.17-20)

In this context we might say that Maximianus's *senex* is a kind of Ovid's *alter ego*, a personification of the figure that the Augustan poet only predicted. In Ovid, the girl, disillusioned, suspects that the situation is either a result of some magic practices or simply proof that the partner has been unfaithful. Therefore, she gets jealous (*Am.* 3.7.77-80), just as Maximianus's *Graia puella*, which – considering the age of her lover – must sound rather pathetic:

<<Quae te crudelis rapuit mihi femina?>>, dixit,
<<cuius ab amplexu fessus ad arma redis?>>
Iurabam curis animum mordacibus uri
nec posse ad luxum tristia corda trahi.
Illa dolum credens: <<Non>>, inquit, <<fallis amantem,
plurima certus amor lumina semper habet.>> (581-586 / el. 5.61-66)

It is the unfortunate *senilis amator* to admit his unfitness in the most stereotypic way, we should say: *En longo confecta situ tibi tradimus arma, / arma ministeriis quippe dicata tuis* (ll. 597-598 / el. 5.77-78). The comment has some satirical flavor and as such might be interpreted as an allusion to Petronius's *Satyricon* 130.4: *paratus miles arma non habui* or possibly to *carmina Priapea* 83.[140] But a special point of reference could be, again, Juvenal's *Satire* 10.[141] If so, the episode described in 'elegy' 5 could be seen as an amplification of a comment made precisely in the opening section and, therefore, as a clear indication that the oeuvre does require the intratextual reading. It is worth noting, however, that the general tone of the piece cannot be simply labeled as satirical, although our poet makes use of the figure of hyperbole, which may sound ironic or rather parodic at first sight.

The above concerns firstly and mainly the style. A careful reader will notice that the poetic imagery and style employed here is more elevated than in the previous pieces. In

---

and confesses that the second was not so any more (ll. 39-50). Subsequently, he tries to give an explanation for this miserable fact, i.e. the girl's fragility and her cries frightened him: <<*Grandia*>>, *clamabat*, <<*tua nunc me brachia laedunt: / non tolerant pondus subdita membra tuum.*>> / *Derigui, quantusque fuit calor ille recessit* (ll. 33-35). Schneider maintains the traditional order.

[140] See Consolino 1997: 387; on associations with Petronius also Webster 1900: 106.

[141] See above in Ch. II. 2 on the allusions to Juvenal's *Sat.* 10 in the introductory piece.

fact, only in this episode does our poet make use of mythological similes, whereas in other elegies mythology is virtually absent, which is one of the main differences between Maximianus and his Augustan models.[142] The similes are, so to speak, quite obvious: Ulysses listening to the Sirens, Troy defeated because of the Greek tricks,[143] Jove more than often subject to flames of love:

Illam Sirenis, stupefactus cantibus, aequans
efficior demens alter Ulisses ego;
et quia non poteram tantas evadere moles,
nescius in scopulos et vada caeca feror. (539-542 / el. 5.19-22)[144]

Subcubui, fateor, Graiae tunc nescius artis,
subcubui, Tusca simplicitate senex.
Qua defensa suo superata est Hectore Troia,
unum non poterat fraus superare senem? (559-562 / el. 5.39-42)

Nec memorare pudet tali me vulnere victum,
subditus his flammis Iuppiter ipse fuit. (565-566 / el. 5.45-46)

The crowning of the 'elegy' is the famous – if not ill-famed – speech of the *Graia puella* (ll. 607-672 / el. 5.87-152). Actually, as the commentators have already rightly observed, one should distinguish here two strongly interrelated parts, of which only the first one (ll. 607-624 / el. 5.87-104) can be interpreted as overtly parodic: as shown by A. Ramirez De Verger in his minute analysis, it does mock the style and structure of a ritual lament.[145] This hiatus between the form and content is, in fact, emphasized by the poet himself:[146] the old man, hearing the girl deploring his languorous member, bursts into laughter (*irridens*, l. 626 / el. 5.106). Her second monologue though provokes no such reaction on the part of the *senex*.

It is worth emphasizing that the passage corresponds with similar complaints in Ovid's *Amores* 3.7 and Petronius's *Satyricon* 130. What makes the difference, however, apart from the length of the speech is the very speaker: in Ovid and in Petronius, it is the man to direct a severe *obiurgatio* to his disabled *mentula*. To be exact, Maximianus also does allow his male protagonist to express shortly his shame and disappointment (ll. 593-600 / el. 5.73-80) – once again the reader can hear the old man complaining about his

---

142 Recently, Consolino (1997: 388), who also emphasizes that through the comparisons to heroic mythological figures the poet can be both self-ironic and apologetic.

143 Fo (1986-1987: 109) notes justly that a careful reader can think here of Virgil's *Aen.* 2 and the image of the Greeks depicted there.

144 In l. 539 / el. 5.19 I follow the punctuation proposed by Guardalben 1993: 98.

145 Ramirez De Verger (1984: 150) objects to Kleinknecht's (1937: 195-199) classification of the whole piece (ll. 607-672 / el. 5.87-152) as a parodic hymn. In his opinion, the two sections should not be mixed: whereas ll. 607-624 / el. 5.87-104 are modeled on a ritual lament, ll. 631-672 / el. 5.111-152 are an eulogium.

146 This is also noted by Fo 1986-1987: 110.

condition of being unfit for love: <<*Cogimur heu segnes*[147] *crimen vitiumque fateri, / ne meus extinctus forte putetur amor*>> (ll. 593-594 / el. 5.73-74). But it is the unsatisfied *Graia puella* whom he casts in a tragic role, indeed, of a woman lamenting the passing of her life partner. Ramirez De Verger demonstrates that the unit (ll. 607-624 / el. 5.87-104) is built upon elements typical of a ritual *góos* with: (1) the apostrophe to the deceased and the expressions of sorrow (rhetorical questions), (2) the narrative part: praising the past and bemoaning the present fate of the 'widow', and (3) the epilogue, where the initial motif of suffering and sorrow recurs.[148] *Mentula* is, in fact, wholly personified: it is compared to a corpse, lying pale on the funeral pyre: *Nempe iaces nullo, ut quondam, perfusa rubore, / pallida demisso vertice nempe iaces* (ll. 619-620 / el. 5.99-100);[149] *Hinc velut exposito meritam te funere plango* (l. 623 / el. 5.103), and addressed as a 'companion of sadness and joy' and 'the most faithful confidant of secrets': *consors laetitiae tristitiaeque meae, / conscia secreti semper fidissima nostri* (ll. 614-615 / el. 5.94-95). The expressions used in the apostrophe are full of affection: *deliciae divitiaeque meae* (l. 608 / el. 5.88).[150] Hardly surprising is the employment of the military vocabulary, quite frequently exploited in such a context.[151] It is actually the *senex* to propose this rhetoric in his short address to the girl *En longo confecta situ tibi tradimus arma* (l. 597 / el. 5.77), and the latter to accept the challenge in her 'song'. She presents the *mentula* as an armored warrior – at least as far as the crested head is concerned – standing at guard and full of fervor:

> *astans internis pervigil obsequiis;*
> *quo tibi fervor abit, per quem feritura placebas,*
> *quo tibi cristatum vulnificumque caput?* (616-618 / el. 5.96-98)

Both the form and language adopted in the piece are undoubtedly too elevated if aimed simply to render the frustration of a girl finding her lover unable to perform the sex act. Therefore, the reader's first reaction is probably the same as the one of the *senex*, in particular one can note this specific moment in the text in which the protagonist becomes in fact a kind of *porte-parole* of the reader. One laughs considering the passage ostentatiously unserious, just a literary play, a parodic indeed, still for quite a few perhaps

---

[147] *heu segnes* also Sandquist Öberg 1999: 130. Webster 1900: 48: *heuque senes*. Guardalben 1993: 102: *hercle senes*. The adjective *segnis* is used by Ovid in his *Amores* 3.7.13-14: *membra … segnia*.

[148] Ramirez De Verger 1984: 153. As the scholar observes (p. 155), stylistically it also resembles the *góos*.

[149] In l. 619 / el. 5.99 I follow the punctuation as in the vast majority of editors, see Webster 1900: 49, Agozzino 1970: 268, Guardalben 1993: 106, and Sandquist Öberg 1999: 132.

[150] The affectionate language employed by Maximianus in the piece resembles the one used by Catullus in two *carmina* devoted to Lesbia's sparrow, see especially *carm.* 2: *Passer, deliciae meae puellae* (l. 1); *et solaciolum sui doloris* (l. 7). The relationship between the poems by Catullus and Maximianus's 'elegy' 5 is emphasized by Arcaz Pozo 1995.

[151] As a matter of fact, one could mention here the very motif of *militat omnis amans*, so deep-rooted in the elegiac tradition.

even indecorous,[152] paraphrase of a 'naturally' solemn theme.[153] What is more, it is quite likely that some readers would subscribe to the diagnosis given by the old man observing the woman's somewhat exaggerated behavior:

> *Hanc ego cum lacrimis deducta voce canentem*
> *irridens dictis talibus increpui:*
> *<<Dum defles nostri languorem, femina, membri,*
> *ostendis morbo te graviore premi.>>* (625-628 / el. 5.105-108)

As a matter of fact, it might be tempting to interpret the girl's lament as an indication of her libidinousness and, consequently, to suspect that the unit may have some satiric flavor aimed at portraying through this particular example the nature of women 'in general', bent on nothing more but momentary sexual pleasure.[154]

A more careful reader, however, will not ignore the fact that what the girl says, provocative as it is in form, cannot be judged as simply obscene, improper or/and 'twisted'. It is, actually, the very *Graia puella* to protest vigorously (*furens*) against such misreading of her words; it is fascinating, indeed, to observe how Maximianus uses his personae, first the *senex*, now the *puella*, to anticipate the possible reaction of his literary audience:

> *Illa furens: <<Nescis, ut cerno, perfide, nescis:*
> *non fleo privatum, set generale chaos!>>* (629-630 / el. 5.109-110)

The arguments put forward by the girl at the beginning of her second monologue to support the declaration that what she deplores is not a private but general chaos could hardly be considered shallow. She focuses precisely on the problem of sex, rejecting the

---

[152] Therefore, probably Spaltenstein's (1983: 267 (C. 2567)) note: "ce morceau est ahurissant," quoted also by Ramirez De Verger 1984: 152.

[153] In fact, Virgilian phrases are first used by Petronius in his *Satyricon* 130 to describe the lack of reaction on the part of *mentula*. Consolino (1997: 390) rightly observes that a similar technique can be found in Ausonius's *Cento*.

[154] It is especially Szövérffy (1967-1968: 363-364) who shows this approach. In his opinion, 'elegy' 5 is even more overt than the *Lycoris* piece in portraying the man as an innocent victim of the woman, especially if we compare it to its model, Ovid's *Amores* 3.7. "Maximianus not only devotes much more space to obscenities than Ovid does, but also accentuates the images with satirical elements. In Ovid, the girl's reproaches are brief; most of the complaints are uttered by the poet himself. Here the roles are reversed. When all fails, the *Graia* … sets out to recite what amounts to a phallic hymn addressed to the *mentula*. It is not a simple amplification of the Ovidian poem. Its purposeful amplification of the comic and satirical elements renders it a full-fledged satire of high rank. Its object, however, is not Maximianus but the young *Graia*, whose sensuous nature is perfectly characterized by this phallic hymn. … This turns the whole poem into a cleverly formulated invective against women, who are always bent on their own pleasure and who regard pleasure and sexual satisfaction as the center of not only their own life, but also of the whole universe. …The phallic hymn with its "cosmic imagery" is a pure mockery; it serves only to describe the twisted world of women in which sex prevails." In fact, according to Szövérffy, there are two probable reasons which may explain Maximianus's popularity in the Middle Ages. One (mentioned above) is the story of Aquilina which sounds like a praise of virginity, the other, probably major, the antifeminist tendency of two of his satires.

asexual or anti-sexual vision of the world. What she emphasizes is the creative power of *mentula* (the pronoun *haec* clearly refers to the apostrophe made in l. 607 / el. 5.87) and – which sounds particularly worthy of note – in human beings, the natural correlation between the body, epitomized, so to speak, by the phallus, and the mind. These two elements, the woman seems to warn, must be seen as complementary. This point, in fact, was already made in the first part of the *Graia*'s speech, where the *mentula* was described as solace providing peace of mind (even soul): *Tu mihi flagranti succurrere saepe solebas / atque aestus animi ludificare mei* (ll. 611-612 / el. 5.91-92). Now, the girl gives a special attention to *concordia diversi sexus* and the phenomenon of a corporeal union when two minds are transformed into one body:

Haec genus humanum, pecudum volucrumque, ferarum
et quidquid toto spirat in orbe, creat.
Hac sine diversi nulla est concordia sexus
hac sine coniugii gratia summa perit.
Haec geminas tanto constringit foedere mentes,
unius ut faciat corporis esse duo. (631-636 / el. 5.111-116)

When reading the previous passages, one could suspect that Maximianus's main goal was to amuse, if not to embarrass, his audience proposing a just too obvious mockery. Now, it seems quite clear that the matter behind the 'controversial' form is far from trivial. Our poet refers to questions widely discussed in his epoch, especially in philosophical and ecclesiastical circles, which often propagated the ideal of asceticism, self-restraint, and 'divine' control of the mind over the body.[155] The 'sexual creature' praised by the *Graia puella* in her song stands in sharp contrast to the model of the human being emancipated from the flesh, sometimes (though not always) recommended in the writings of the Church authorities of that age,[156] especially in the treatises and poems concerning marriage.[157] The latter seems particularly relevant here as Maximianus's girl points pre-

---

[155] Of the vast literature on the subject, I will mention only the indispensable Brown 1988.

[156] Schneider (2001: 463-464; 2003) makes the same point. He interprets the whole Maximianus's oeuvre as "a statement in late antique discourse on corporeality," arguing that "with her song, the sensual Greek woman responds directly to the denial of the corporeal world propagated in that time by the shepherds of the Christian community to their flock" in the epoch "which venerated experienced ascetics for their withdrawal from sexuality, their incorporeality and their emancipation from the flesh." Generally, I fully agree that Maximianus's poetry should be seen as a "discourse on corporeality," but I do not agree with the sharp divisions he makes (see the example below). I myself do not find Maximianus anti-Christian only because he is anti-ascetic (which he definitely is). In particular, I find it hard to accept Schneider's (2001: 464) conclusion that "Maximianus's joyful … memories … stand in opposition to St. Augustine's self-accusations in the *Confessiones* respecting his carnal obsessions in adolescence and early manhood." In fact, Augustine's attitude toward marriage, and even toward human sexuality, is "far from extremities," as justly emphasized by Nehring 2005: 197-199.

[157] Like the mystic epithalamia by Paulinus of Nola or Venantius Fortunatus. At the same time, however, we must be very careful not to draw too schematic divisions here. Only taking into consideration the case of the epithalamic genre as used by the Christian authors, on the one hand, we can indeed indicate poets promoting the idea of virginity, like the two mentioned above. Still, on the

cisely to *coniugii gratia*, which, as she emphasizes, depends on the sex act. It is sexuality – she adds in the following distich – that makes the human person attractive:

> *Pulchra licet pretium, si desit, femina perdit;*
> *et si defuerit, vir quoque turpis erit.* (637-638 / el. 5.117-118)

Stylistically, the second part of the *Graia*'s speech is not less encomiastic than the first,[158] yet the tone of the provocation is lighter, mainly because the very term *mentula* is consistently avoided, being present only in the hypotext through the above-mentioned pronoun *haec*. This 'terminological gap' justifies, if not enables, a more serious reading of the final part of 'elegy' 5 not just as a manifestation of obscenity but precisely as a 'poetic' voice in late antique debate about corporeality,[159] the voice emphasizing the role of *eros* as the generative force (*O vere nostrum fructiferumque bonum!*, l. 642 / el. 5.122)[160] and the source of the cosmic order (hence the *generale chaos* in l. 630 / el. 5.110).[161] Thus, the structure of the whole passage is built upon the motif of the mild dominance[162]

---

other hand, a devoted Christian, and later bishop, Ennodius, in his epithalamium complained that ascetism had become a kind of 'disease endemic in the culture of his times' (paraphrasing the expression of Dodds, quoted in a critical context by Markus 1990: 81). Ennodius did emphasize the value of love (and sexuality), encouraging his addressee, Maximus, to marry.

[158] Ramirez De Verger (1984: 150) shows that the passage follows the traditional norms of *encomium*. Consolino (1997: 390) points out that the second part of the *Graia*'s speech is structurally much closer to hymn than the first. She refers to Kleinknecht's (1937: 195-199) conclusions.

[159] See the above-mentioned interpretation of Schneider (2001: 464), which I find inspiring, even though, as I have said above, too unilateral.

[160] Thus, as it has been emphasized many times, the hymn to eros, if not Eros, sung by the *Graia puella* can be compared to Lucretius's invocation to Venus opening his *De rerum natura*. On the Epicurean accent in Maximianus's oeuvre, see recently especially Schneider (2003: 93-96) who even goes as far as to argue that Maximianus through his poetry is 'erecting' the altar of Venus to which the entire Universe bows, opposing Venus to *Virgo* celebrated by the Christians.

[161] Similarly, Fo (already 1986-1987: 109-110) opts for a wholly serious reading of the piece. In his final paper (Fo 1987: 350-352), devoted specifically to the question of the 'message' of Maximianus's *opus*, the Italian scholar proposes the following view: "Massimiano ritiene l'eros una componente particolarmente importante della vita stessa … insegnamenti filosofici gli hanno spiegato che l'eros è una forza cosmica centrale di coesione e rigenerazione. … l'eros [risulta] ... importante per l'individuo: in quanto forza che ne conturba la vita interiore esercitando una irresistibile attrazione e in quanto forza a cui sono legati non solo il piacere, ma anche la felicità. … è d'altra parte sicuramente avvertita [nelle elegie] la sua strettissima connessione con un pungente problema morale. … Discende da ciò la cotinua dualità di atteggiamenti che domina il *corpus*, in una ininterrotta oscillazione fra esaltazione del fascino dell'eros, illustrazione della sua importanza … e, dall'altro, coscienza della peccaminosità dell'eros, aspirazioni ascetiche all'astinenza, esaltazione di pudicizia e verginità, giustificazioni e riserve."

[162] Therefore, also in this passage military vocabulary is exploited in verbal structures like *cedunt tibi, vincere amas*, expressions: *virtus, fortia facta*, also *pervigiles labores*: *mixtaque sunt ludis fortia facta tuis* (656 / el. 5.136); *Nam tibi pervigiles impendunt saepe labores* (659 / el. 5.139); *Mira tibi virtus, mira est patientia: victos / diligis et vinci tu quoque saepe voles. / Cum superata iaces, vires animosque resumis / atque iterum* vinci, *vincere rursus amas* (667-670 / el. 5.147-150).

of *eros* over individuals (a virgin), worldly powers, tyrants, Mars and Jove, wild animals, even wisdom:

> *Cedunt cuncta tibi; quodque est sublimius, ultro*
> *cedunt imperiis maxima sceptra tuis.*
> *Nec substrata gemunt, sed se tibi subdita gaudent;*
> *vulnera sunt irae prosperiora tuae.*
> *Ipsa etiam totum moderans sapientia mundum*
> *porrigit invictas ad tua iussa manus.*
> *Sternitur icta tuo votivo vulnere virgo*
> *et perfusa novo laeta cruore iacet.*
> *Fert tacitum ridetque suum laniata dolorem*
> *et percussori plaudit amica suo.* (645-654 / el. 5.125-134)[163]

> *Tu mihi saepe feri commendas corda tyranni,*
> *sangineus per te Mars quoque mitis erit.*
> *Tu post extinctos debellatosque gigantes*
> *excutis irato tela trisulca Iovi.*
> *Tu cogis rabidas affectum discere tigres,*
> *per te blandus amans redditur ipse leo.* (661-666 / el. 5.141-146)

It is presumable that Maximianus's statement on sexuality and corporeality made in 'elegy' 5 is so ostentatiously 'literary' to captivate the readership; it would be hard indeed to remain indifferent to such peculiar rhetoric. Yet these purposely exaggerated lamentations and praises are also an excellent form of evasion on the part of the author who, apparently, does not intend to express views that being more 'neutral' or unequivocal might be understood as fully 'his own'. In fact, the whole speech is put into the mouth of the girl who – as we should remember – is well aware of her sensuality and wears it, just like a costume, playing a woman in love.[164] 'Elegy' 5, being undoubtedly the most important among Maximianus's love episodes, is at the same time the most overtly theatrical. And, as if he were, indeed, supposed only to give some stage directions and not his own comment that might legitimize the girl's words, the male protagonist limits himself to announcing, 'exit the *Graia puella*':

> *Conticuit tandem longo satiata dolore,*
> *me velut expletis deserit exequiis.* (673-674 / el. 5.153-154)

---

[163] Here I quote the text as edited by Webster 1900: 50 and Guardalben 1993: 108.

[164] Fo (1986-1987: 110) supposes that the fact that the speech is put into the mouth of the girl may be due to a kind of *pudor*, a certain reluctance to speak openly of the carnal love, if not with some sense of sin. As the Italian scholar concludes, it might have been this particular conviction that sexual love was in its nature somewhat sinful which made the poet emphasize that the reason of his falling in love with the cunning *Graia puella* was, as a matter of fact, her cheating (she pretends love and this way puts a spell on him) and not simply his own, 'deliberate' wish to experience an erotic affair.

II. 3. 5. AND YET *NON OMNIS MORIAR*: THE CODA (OR 'ELEGY' 6)

The 12-lines long epilogue ('elegy' 6) with its very shortness – especially if one measures it against the huge opening section – indicates that the most important things have already been told and what remains for the main character is to go off stage himself. Indeed:

Omnibus est eadem leti via, non tamen unus
est vitae cunctis exitiique modus,
Hac pueri atque senes pariter iuvenesque feruntur,
hac par divitibus pauper egenus erit.
Ergo quod attritum quodque est vitabile nulli,
festino gressu vincere praestat iter. (680-685 / el. 6.5-10)

It is not casual that the whole final section is clearly autothematic in tone. A careful reader has already realized that every detail confessed throughout Maximianus's *opus* has been purposely selected by the speaking *ego*. This 'speaking *ego*' – especially in the so-called 'Schetter's prologues' – not only introduces his audience to topics to be treated in single episodes, often adding a short yet meaningful comment, but also quite openly explains why a certain theme has been considered apt for his *opus*. It is worth noting, besides, how much these statements, and especially the *lector* mentioned in l. 369 (el. 3.3) or *carmina vana* mentioned in l. 464 (el. 4.4), unmask the ostentation of *nil scribens ipse* declared in 'elegy' 1:[165]

Nunc operae pretium est quaedam memorare iuventae
atque senectutis pauca referre meae,
quis lector mentem rerum vertigine fractam
erigat et maestum noscere curet opus. (367-370 / el. 3.1-4)

Restat adhuc alios turpesque revolvere casus
atque aliquo molli pascere corda ioco.
Conveniunt etenim delirae ignava senectae,
aptaque sunt operi carmina vana meo. (461-464 / el. 4.1-4)

In the epilogue one meets the same self-conscious author, as always totally in control of his verse and even predicting his own immortality through this poetic work.[166] A well-trained reader once again will notice how Maximianus evokes his favorite master, Ovid,

---

[165] *carmina nulla cano* in l. 127 and *non blanda poemata fingo* in l. 129. But in fact, right counter to this statement runs already what our *senex* emphasizes in 'elegy' 2: *non me adeo primis spoliavit floribus aetas: / en facio versus et mea dicta cano* (ll. 355-356 / el. 2.63-64).

[166] Surprising as it may seem, it was only Fo (1986-1987: 111-116) to actually verbalize that l. 12 with *hac parte vivere* refers to the poetic work owing to which the *senex* will live, even though his old body will be dead. The final phrase is, indeed, as Fo explains, based upon a paradox, quite well invented, it should be added; the *senex* arises (*surgo*) to walk his path to death, which brings about sadness, naturally enough (therefore, he is *infelix*). He has in fact just wept his own death, as if he were participating in the funeral rites (*defleto funere*). But precisely thanks to this death and his lament (which is his poetry of course), he will remain alive.

the young Ovid of the *Amores*, but also Ovid revealed in his last and most important oeuvre:

Ovid:	Maximianus:
ergo etiam cum me supremus adederit ignis, *vivam, parsque mei multa superstes erit.* (*Am.* 1.15.41-42)	*Infelix ceu iam defleto funere surgo,* *hac me defunctum vivere parte puto.* (ll. 687-688 / el. 6.11-12)
cum volet, illa dies, quae nil nisi corporis huius *ius habet, incerti spatium mihi finiat aevi:* *parte tamen meliore mei super alta perennis* *astra ferar ...* *siquid habent veri vatum praesagia, vivam.* (*Met.* 15.873-876; 879)	

II. 4. Maximianus's elegy: final remarks

At the very outset of the above-mentioned 'coda' (the so-called 'elegy' 6), Maximianus once again addresses the *aetas verbosa*, the Old Age, the invocation of which has opened his entire *opus*. Now, however, he asks her quite straightforwardly: "cut off ... your wretched complaints:"[167]

Claude, precor, miseras, aetas verbosa, querelas!
Numquid et hic vitium vis reserare tuum?
sit satis, indignum leviter tetigisse pudorem,
contractata diu crimina crimen habent. (675-678 / el. 6.1-4)

The two distichs, being indeed a kind of *captatio benevolentiae*,[168] give the reader an opportunity to recapitulate the most important points of Maximianus's oeuvre, i.e. (1) the sad and mournful tone (*querelae*), idiosyncratic of the introductory part but recurring later in narratorial comments, and (2) the content, the *crimina*, being probably both the afflictions of old age and love memories, all the more 'sinful' if cherished by a *senex*.[169] The poet, as it appears, suggests that we see his work as a whole the protagonist, the speaking *ego*, and (finally) the author of which is one person: the *defunctus* who will live (paradoxically) thanks to the lament sung at his funeral.

In fact, as I have argued in Chapter II. 1, there are (considerable, in my view) reasons to interpret Maximianus's *opus* as a continuity, which does not mean at all that it makes a homogeneous unity either stylistically or as far as certain 'biographic' details are concerned. As an *opus continuum*, the text has some quasi-epic qualities: it is a 'story', or

[167] Lind 1988: 335.

[168] Fo 1986-1987: 115.

[169] Fo 1986-1987: 114.

rather 'stories', told by a first-person narrator who looks at them from a certain perspective (one could even say that what we can observe here is a model distance between the time of narration and the time of *fabula*, unusual in elegy[170] but quite natural in epic). The epic coloring is perceptible in particular in the episode dedicated to Aquilina, being a sort of a 'new version' of Ovid's epyllion on Pyramus and Thisbe.

The stories are to constitute a kind of 'biography', an image of life experience, above all of love experience, of an individual who assures us that he is one and the same person. But we know only too well how many discrepancies can be found in this picture, how many facts seem to disagree: a bachelor, a *coniunx*, the choice of *vita casta*, yet interrupted by temptations in dreams as well as 'affairs' in the real world. Consequently, it turns out quite difficult to determine who our protagonist once was (who was he not? A renowned orator, a poet, a *poeta tragicus* even, a sportsman, a worshipper of Bacchus, finally a legate) and even who he is today. If truth be told, all we know is that he is a (miserable) old man who now, when his days are numbered, seems to recognize two principal forces: death and (yet) *eros*. This *eros* though cannot be properly described if one uses simply the language of the traditional love elegy (for example from Ovid's *Amores* or *Ars Amatoria*), charming as it may be; the *senex* himself likes speaking it at times (see ll. 59-100). The generative, indeed cosmic, power of *eros* can be rendered only if one employs a different poetics, the poetics of hymn, inspired by Lucretius rather than by the 'playful' Sulmonian. Still, it is not casual that this hymn to *eros* is not sung by the main character himself. The old man – one may have the impression – tries at times to wear the mask of a *sapiens*: hence his *sententiositas*, hence maybe also his words uttered when reflecting upon the episode with the *Graia puella*: *gnarus et ut s a p i e n s noxia saepe velit* (l. 518 / el. 4.58). As it appears though, he himself is well aware how unconvincing this disguise must be. In fact, the old age has brought him neither wisdom, nor peace of mind;[171] what it has brought him is only the sense of deep humiliation that can be expressed by the form of an elegiac complaint, or even better: through the language of satire.

In the passage quoted above, the poet uses a verb defining in a perfect way both his narrative technique and the very essence of his oeuvre: *tetigisse* (l. 677 / el. 6.3). Indeed, too many times have we noticed that our elegist merely touches upon certain themes, leaving always something untold or unexplained. The impression is probably strongest in 'elegy' 4, where the 'romance' ends well before it really begins and nonetheless, as we are informed, the reputation of the male protagonist is ruined. At the same time, however, we are not given any clues as to his status that has been diminished except for, rather enigmatic, *ego, qui cunctis sanctae gravitatis habebar* (l. 509 / el. 5.49). The preceding one 'elegy' 3, concluded in a much different manner than the reader would expect at its beginning, also points at the speaker's *vita pudica*: what is stated though is that choosing such a lifestyle brings sadness. And last, 'elegy' 5: here the male protagonist is no longer *castus*, he is impotent instead; and the absence of sexual love, so characteristic of Maximianus's elegy, is not an attitude, a choice – as it is promoted even in the address to Lycoris – it is a failure. This time everything seems put into words. If anything is missing, it is one detail: the man's

[170] As justly emphasized by Pinotti 1989: 185-186.

[171] Similarly, Fo 1987: 352.

final comment to the eulogium of *mentula* sung by the *Graia puella*. If this passage is to be considered the climax of the whole *opus*, and even its 'message' (which it most probably is, in fact), one should not forget that the poet does not speak here in the first person.

Therefore, the interpretation of Maximianus's oeuvre cannot be, as I have already emphasized, reduced to one (more or less) simple formula. This peculiar ambiguity or indefiniteness can disappoint, if not displease, some readers, although these are also features through which Maximianus can appeal to our modern, even post-modern sensitivity. The elegist himself – mysterious as he is – does not describe his desired audience, but it would be hard not to have an impression that he is a poet belonging to the Roman intellectuals of the post-Roman world. It is so not only because of the subtlety and diversity of the literary allusions he makes, expecting from his public to decipher them of course. Maximianus's most 'intellectual' quality may be his very attitude of bitter self-reflection and, precisely, his reluctance to propose too straightforward answers. Consequently, the elegy he composed is not merely a swan song of the genre practiced by the Augustans, but rather a voice, a polyphony of voices on the old age and love as felt and perceived between late antiquity and the early Middle Ages.

PART THREE

The Roman Epigram in the Romano-Barbaric World

III. 1. Martial and the definition of the Roman epigram

It is hard to determine which of his poems Catullus himself – had he ever been asked the question – would have considered his major achievement: the longer, learned texts, the epithalamia, the epyllion, the 'proto-elegies' (to use the label frequently proposed by contemporary criticism), or – on the contrary – the very *nugae*, only ostensibly simple and spontaneous. Doubtless though if we knew his writings solely from Martial's testimony, we would regard him as an epigrammatist par excellence.[1] Interestingly, also Pliny the Younger sees in the poet from Verona the true model of the Roman minor poetry.[2] Both Martial and Pliny recognize as a constitutive property of Catullus's poetics the freedom, or even somewhat brutal realism of speech, giving to his texts a unique taste, the *sal*. It is precisely the *sal*, in the opinion of the two authors, to determine the nature of the Roman epigrammatic writing.[3] Martial, who juxtaposes the two 'kinds' of epigram, the Greek and the Latin one, indicates their specific qualities as the *lepos Cecropius* and the *sal Romanae Minervae*,[4] respectively.

---

[1] Which, to be exact, is not confirmed by other ancient classifications. Apparently, Catullus is quite problematic to classify for the ancient theoreticians; he is quoted either as *lyricus* or as *iambicus*, see Citroni 2003a: 15 and in more detail (both sources cited by Citroni) Wiseman 1985: 246-262 and Scherf 1996: 93-97.

[2] See Citroni 2003a: 11-12, esp. n. 6 with the list of specific passages from Martial and Pliny. Citroni notes justly that Martial's and Pliny's attitude to Catullus can be interpreted as a result of the tendency already typical of the Roman literature of the Imperial era to search for models no more in Greek but in the Latin poetry of the 'golden age', the late Republican and the Augustan.

[3] Pliny is not as specific in this definition as Martial, but he apparently also differentiates between the Greek and the Latin epigram. Judging epigrams in Greek, he always emphasizes such qualities as *humanitas, venustas, dulcedo, amor, gratia*, whereas when speaking of the Latin ones, he points out their *amaritudo* usually coexisting with some erotic element, see Citroni 2003a: 13.

[4] See Martial, 4.23: *Dum tu lenta nimis diuque quaeris / quis primus tibi quisve sit secundus, / Graium quos epigramma comparavit, / palmam Callimachus, Thalia, de se / facundo dedit ipse Bruttiano. / qui si Cecropio satur lepore / Romanae sale luserit Minervae, / ille me facias precor secundum*. For Martial, a (Latin) epigram deprived of *sal* is inacceptable, see 7.25: *Dulcia cum tantum scribas epigrammata semper / et cerussata candidiora cute, / nullaque mica salis nec amari fellis in illis / gutta sit, o demens, vis tamen illa legi! / nec cibus ipse iuvat morsu fraudatus aceti, / nec grata est facies cui gelasinus abest. / infanti melimela dato fatuasque mariscas: / nam mihi, quae novit pungere, Chia sapit*. Interestingly, in the dedicatory poem 5.2, introducing a book addressed (at least ostensibly) to the ladies, Martial stresses: *Matronae puerique virginesque, / vobis pagina nostra dedicatur. / tu, quem nequitiae procaciores / delectant nimium salesque nudi, / lascivos lege quattuor libellos: / quintus cum domino liber iocatur; / quem Germanicus ore non rubenti / coram Cecropia legat puella*. On Martial's awareness of the differences between the Greek and the Latin epigram, see generally Swann 1994: 61. Citroni (2003a: 10) notes very justly that the specific character of

In truth, however, as Mario Citroni[5] demonstrated, Martial and Pliny do not really have in mind one and the same thing when – both quoting Catullus's authority – they try to define the sort of poetry they practice. A careful reader should notice that Pliny, describing the most varied *carmina minora*, his own as well as those by his friends (among which most probably also Martial's), finds their archetypes in the writings of Catullus and Calvus (he usually names the two authors together), which means: in the neoteric tradition. Apparently, such poetry, in Pliny's view, has no definite metrical profile: all meters used by the Neoterics seem acceptable.[6] A privileged position though is given to the Phalaecean, associable with the most famous poems by the Veronian, the dedication for Nepos (*carm.* 1), the *Sparrow* (*carm.* 2), the *Kisses* (*carm.* 5). Pliny would consider it a fully natural thing to compose a whole book of poems in the Phalaeceans (*Epist.* 7.48: *Postremo placuit exemplo multorum unum separatim hendecasyllaborum volumen absolvere, nec paenitet*).[7] The terminological questions are not less interesting. Pliny most willingly calls all these *carmina minora*, also those by Martial, simply *versiculi* or, even more vaguely, *ineptiae, lusus, ioci*,[8] while he does not pay too much attention to the word *epigramma*. A passage from his letter where the author ponders what title to choose for the collection of his texts is quite symptomatic. He mentions among the possible options: *epigrammata, idyllia, eclogae, poematia, hendecasyllabi* (he finally decides on the *Hendecasyllabi*). It is quite obvious that the epistolographer is rather far away from any sort of generic precision.[9]

---

the Roman epigram, always emphasized by Martial himself, has often been blurred by philologists who have tried just too hard to demonstrate its dependence upon the Greek model.

[5] In this chapter, I refer extensively to the conclusions reached by Citroni in his remarkable paper (2003a), see also the specific citations above and below.

[6] Citroni 2003a: 19.

[7] Besides, it is interesting that Pliny, as Citroni (2003a: 19-20) stresses, seems to place these *carmina minora* in the context of lyric poetry, which is completely irreconcilable with the epigrammatic tradition.

[8] All these 'terms' are known from Catullus, but the word *versiculi* is used by Catullus only in reference to his poems in the Phalaeceans, see Citroni 2003a: 16. Apparently, Pliny when employing these Catullan expressions understands them quite literally as referring to occasional poetry, indeed, the poetry composed merely for fun at one's leisure, and not, as it was in fact in Catullus, the poetry that is only ostensibly 'unserious' and 'negligible', whereas in truth constitutes a 'manifesto' of literary and ethical attitude of its author, see Styka 1994: 121-123; 1995: 188-190.

[9] See *epist.* 4.14.8-9: *Unum illud praedicendum videtur, cogitare me has meas nugas ita inscribere 'hendecasyllabi', qui titulus sola metri lege constringitur. Proinde, sive epigrammata sive idyllia sive eclogas sive, ut multi, poematia seu quod aliud vocare malueris, licebit voces; ego tantum hendecasyllabos praesto*. The passage is quoted by Citroni 2003a: 16 and by Mondin 2008: 465. What is interesting, as Mondin points out, a similar lack of precision will be later on shown by Ausonius, an epigrammatist himself and a professor of rhetoric. In reference to the erotic epigrams by Pliny, Apuleius, and Plato Ausonius will use interchangeably the terms *poematia, epigrammata, epyllia*. On late antique understanding of the term *epigramma*, see especially Mondin's thorough analyses (pp. 463-494). On the meaning of the word *epigramma* in Sidonius, see Di Rienzo 2005: 237. Di Rienzo notes rightly that Sidonius does not refer the term *epigramma* directly to the genre defined by Martial, or even to the 'epigrammatic spirit'; what he describes is simply a wide range of minor poetry, from *nenia funebris* to *nuga*.

Martial, who quotes the very same Catullus, places him in a completely different context. As it is well known, the poet from Bilbilis establishes a kind of 'canon' of the Latin epigrammatists, above all in his programmatic *praefatio* to Book 1:[10] Catullus, Domitius Marsus, Albinovanus Pedo, finally Lentulus Gaetulicus, all worth remembering for their *lasciva verborum veritas*. Repeating a few times the very same names,[11] Catullus seems to imply that this 'list' is generally accepted and recognized (which, in fact, is not exactly the case[12]). What is not less relevant, Martial, describing his own writings (and Catullus's, by the same token), employs terminology much different from the one to be found in Pliny. He quotes the typically Catullan expressions, like *lusus*, *ineptiae*, *ioci*, merely to connote and not to denote the literary genre he practices, and he generally avoids the noun *versiculi*, apparently quite liked by Pliny.[13] The term that for Martial has the quality of a true generic label is only the *epigramma*,[14] used not coincidentally as early as in the preface to Book 1 and appearing 31 times throughout his oeuvre.[15]

Still, another difference may be even more interesting and more important. As I have already mentioned, the *carmina minora* as defined by Pliny revealed a neoteric polymetrics, which in practice was equal to the lack of any specific rules whatsoever: all meters sanctioned by the Neoterics seemed acceptable and, above all, the Phalaecean (to the extent that Pliny's book was to be entitled the *Hendecasyllabi*). Martial, on the contrary, proposes – and he turns out to be very consistent in his approach – a truly well-organized and disciplined metrical variety. He chooses as his main meter the elegiac distich, which means the meter of the Greek epigram.[16] His 'second preference' is the Phalaecean, used much less frequently but relevant precisely as *the* meter to be naturally associated with Catullus; thus, it is not at all unintended that the Phalaecean is exploited in the programmatic[17] poem 1.1: *Hic est*

---

[10] Book 1 *praef.*, ll. 10-13: *lascivam verborum veritatem, id est epigrammaton linguam, excusarem, si meum esset exemplum: sic scribit Catullus, sic Marsus, sic Pedo, sic Gaetulicus, sic quicumque perlegitur.*

[11] Catullus, Marsus, and Pedo are mentioned together in 5.5.5-6: *sit locus et nostris aliqua tibi parte libellis, / qua Pedo, qua Marsus quaque Catullus erit*; Catullus and Marsus in 2.71.3: *protinus aut Marsi recitas aut scripta Catulli* and 7.99.7: *nec Marso nimium minor est doctoque Catullo*; Marsus and Pedo in 2.77.5: *disce quod ignoras: Marsi doctique Pedonis*; Gaetulicus appears only in the *praef.* to Book 1.

[12] Pliny, as Citroni (2003a: 23) notes, does not mention at all Domitius Marsus and Albinovanus Pedo.

[13] See Citroni 2003a: 15-16. In Martial, as the Italian scholar underlines, the term *versiculi* has an overtly negative connotation and is used only in reference to the writings of his enemies.

[14] Puelma (1997: 207-208) stresses that Martial actually turns (quite deliberately) the word *epigramma* into a generic label.

[15] Citroni 2003a: 15.

[16] The Greek epigram is virtually 'bound' to the elegiac distich. The only different meter used by the Greek epigrammatists with a certain regularity (but very rarely, in sum) is the iambic trimeter, see Citroni 2003a: 21.

[17] In fact, Martial uses the Phalaecean a few times in his programmatic opening poems, see 3.2, the dedication to Faustinus; 5.2, the dedication to the Ladies; 6.1; 11.1.

quem legis ille, quem requiris, / toto notus in orbe Martialis. Finally, his 'third preference' is the scazon.[18]

Martial's polymetrics is partially, but in fact *only* partially, comparable with Catullus's. Certainly, the poet from Bilbilis, just like Catullus, indicates as his meters the elegiac distich, the Phalaecean, and the scazon, the proportions, however, are quite different.[19] The unquestionably dominant position of the elegiac distich clearly defines his twelve *libelli* as books of *epigrams* and not as most varied *carmina minora* in Pliny's style. At the same time, the regular presence of some other meters, especially of the Catullan Phalaecean, differentiates these *Latin* epigrams by Martial from the Greek epigrammatic writing, in practice using only the elegiac distich. By employing the Phalaecean, especially in a few opening texts, the poet from Bilbilis underlines the specific quality of the *Roman epigram*, the epigram seeking inspiration in Catullus, the master of the Phalaecean. It is also Catullus, together with Marsus and Pedo – such at least is the view that Martial strives insistently to impose upon us – to provide the model of the *lasciva verborum veritas*, of the *sal*, similarly idiosyncratic of the Roman and not of the (charming) Greek epigram.

Thus, upon a closer look, we can reconstruct the manner in which Martial tries to describe the genre he practices, the *epigramma*, quoting, indeed somewhat instrumentally, Catullus's authority; instrumentally, because he does seem to force the idea that the poet from Verona is interpretable and should be interpreted as a 'full-fledged' epigrammatist. Still, this obviously purposeful misreading of Catullus turns out less relevant than Martial's poetological self-consciousness. Just like he is quite certain of the metrical profile and the character of the Roman epigram (or, at least, of what he labels as the Roman epigram), the author from Bilbilis is quite determined to defend some specific decisions he takes regarding the composition of epigrams in hexameter and constructing the so-called *epigrammata longa*.[20] The latter are, in fact, an important component of Martial's poetics, which should be pointed out as another difference between his epigrams and the epigrammatic tradition of the Greeks.[21]

Consequently, what the poet from Bilbilis leaves for his successors is a truly clear vision of what the Roman epigram is, what it should be, in what respect it should be different and in what parallel to its Greek counterpart, finally, what its 'national', Roman

---

[18] As Citroni (2003a: 19-20) calculated, in Martial the prevalence of the elegiac distich is indisputable (73.1% of all epigrams); the Phalaecean comprises 19.4% and the scazon – 6.4%. What is more, this proportion is quite regular in all of his 12 books.

[19] Among Catullus's minor poems, we find 48 elegiacs, 44 Phalaeceans, and 8 choliambics, see Citroni 2003a: 20.

[20] On writing epigrams in hexameter, see especially 6.65. Interestingly, Martial in this poem defends so strongly his right to compose epigrams in hexameter (although, paradoxically, within his books one can find only two hexametric poems, 1.53, 6.64, and two more hexametric monostichs, 2.73 and 7.98), while for Pliny the idea seems quite normal. The motif of *epigrammata longa* is more frequent; it appears, in fact, also in the same 6.65; see besides 1.110, 2.77, 3.83, 10.59. For more specific data, see Citroni 2003a: 24-25.

[21] See Citroni 2003a: 25. On *epigrammata longa* in Martial, see the celebrated paper by Szelest 1980; in addition Ciocci 1985; on *epigramma longum* as such, from Martial to late antiquity, see now the impressive two-volume publication by Morelli 2008.

connotations are. However, it seems significant that, just like in his own times Martial was not the only littérateur practicing the minor poetry and, most probably, not the only author trying to provide some framing of this tradition, varied as it was, also later, after Martial, there still coexisted different and often competing views of those poetic *lusus* and *ioci*.[22] Reading Claudian or Sidonius, one can indeed come to the conclusion that what they created is much closer to the 'multiform' *carmina minora* mentioned by Pliny than to Martial's *epigramma*. Ausonius's poems, today classified as epigrams, were not compiled together by the author himself.[23] As regards their nature, they are strongly influenced by the Greek epigram; in many cases, one could even speak of a 'translation' or a 'variation' based upon one single Greek model,[24] which is an attitude completely alien to Martial. In fact,[25] the first Latin poet who intentionally followed Martial's definition of the Roman epigram, and also Martial's conception of the *liber epigrammaton*, was only Luxorius,[26] an author active in Carthage during the last decade(s?)[27] of the Vandal occupation of the North Africa in the sixth century.

Luxorius, indeed, happens to be named the "Martial of the Vandals" or the "Carthaginian Martial,"[28] even though, as some scholars justly emphasize, the label may be very misleading as it could imply that he was a mere epigone, an imitator, whereas, in truth, the case is quite reverse.[29] Martialian inspirations in Luxorius are not at all unequivocal and they cannot be classified as repetitions of single motifs or points. In my own view, if the definition is to be used at all, it is only because of his allusions to the Martialian *model*

---

[22] Mondin (2008: 397), opening his thorough study on the length of the late antique epigram, notes acutely: "Anche dopo l'esperienza di Marziale, e nonostante la sua esemplare fortuna, l'epigramma rimaneva una forma poetica poco canonizzata."

[23] See Kay 2001: 11.

[24] See Kay 2001: 14-19 (and his further commentary on single poems); Benedetti 1980.

[25] Citroni (2003a: 29) himself closes his paper by saying that Martial's disciplined variety was re-employed only by Luxorius on the verge of the Middle Ages. Indeed, the analyses I provide (especially at the beginning of Ch. III. 2. 1 and in Ch. III. 2. 2) fully corroborate this general impression of the Italian scholar.

[26] In choosing the form of the name 'Luxorius', instead of 'Luxurius' as proposed and strongly defeated by Happ 1962; 1986 I: 142-158, I follow the approach of Dal Corobbo 2006: 37: "Tenendo conto … della quasi totalità degli editori di Lussorio, compresi Rosenblum e Shackleton Bailey, i due più recenti, se si eccettua Happ, nell'impossibilità di fornire altri elementi risolutori, è bene conservare la paradosi." Indeed, except for Happ, all other editors seem to subscribe to what already was said by Riese: "Nihil itaque ad pristinam formam restituendam hinc redundat lucri" (I quote after Rosenblum 1961: 37 n. 13).

[27] Luxorius's *floruit* is usually dated to the age of the king Hilderic (523-530). Probably the main part of the *libellus* was, indeed, composed during the times of Hilderic, still some poems, as emphasized by Dal Corobbo (2006: 38; 41; 239-240), were written later, during the reign of Gelimer (530-534). Fassina (2006: 144-145), on the other hand, argues that the literary activity of Luxorius can be dated not only to Hilderic's reign but starts earlier, still in the times of Thrasamund (496-523).

[28] Luxorius is called the "Carthaginian Martial" by Rosenblum 1961: 52. On Luxorius as "Vandalorum Martialis," see already Meyer 1835: XXXII, more recently Bertini 1974: 106 or Strzelczyk 2005: 284.

[29] See more below, especially in Ch. III. 2. 4.

of the epigram, and in particular to the above-mentioned 'disciplined variety', typical of each of the twelve books by the poet from Bilbilis.[30] Of major importance here is the unique metrical discipline through which Martial's *libelli* fully subscribe to the epigrammatic tradition (the tradition of the elegiac distich), yet at the same time to the Roman, Catullan heritage. Luxorius's own disciplined polymetrics is not identical (because he is *not* a mere imitator), but it is comparable.[31]

III. 2. "The Martial of the Vandals:" Luxorius, the follower and the innovator

III. 2. 1. THE DULL EPIGRAMMATIST AND HIS NOT TOO LEARNED PUBLIC: LUXORIUS'S SELF-PRESENTATION[32]

A characteristic peculiar to Martial's poetics is undoubtedly his self-consciousness. Martial can be seen both as a 'practician' and as a 'theoretician' of the genre he explores, the *epigramma* (the term, as we already know, should be emphasized). A few of his books open with *praefationes* in prose,[33] almost in all at the very outset one can find some kind of introductory poems: the poet's self-presentation, dedications, the address to the reader, the *adlocutiones ad libellum*. Due to the above the literary audience acknowledges that the

[30] The *Liber de spectaculis*, *Xenia*, and *Apophoreta* do not really count here; in fact, as it is well known, they represent a different kind of an epigrammatic collection; they do not comprise prose prefaces or *epigrammata longa* and almost all poems are written in the elegiac distich, see also Citroni 2003a: 27-28.

[31] *Si licet parvis componere magna* I should add because Luxorius's one *liber epigrammaton* is to be compared here with twelve books by Martial. On the other hand, Martial is hardly equal to Luxorius as far as the metrical variety is concerned, see below in Ch. III. 2. 2.

[32] In the present subchapter, I focus on Luxorius's introductory poems: 287-290 Riese^2 = IV, 441-444 Bährens = pp. 110-113 Rosenblum = 282-285 Shackleton Bailey = pp. 10-14 Happ = pp. 72-77 Dal Corobbo. I provide the numeration proposed in the most 'influential' editions of Luxorius's *liber epigrammaton*: Riese^2 Fasc. I (quoted simply as Riese 1894), Bährens IV (quoted simply as Bährens 1882), Rosenblum 1961, Shackleton Bailey 1982, Happ 1986 I. The most recent edition with the Italian translation and commentary by Dal Corobbo (2006) is for the most part concordant with the Latin text of Luxorius found in Happ (which is indeed, as Dal Corobbo states, the most important edition to date; see also Dal Corobbo's notes on the tradition of Luxorius's text, pp. 55-66). What is particularly valuable in Dal Corobbo's work, except for a very substantial presentation of the *status quaestionis*, is the accurate Italian translation, which makes a truly good complement to Happ's volumes and does corroborate many of his editorial choices. Interpreting Luxorius's poems, one must be aware, however, that the reading of many passages is still a matter of debate. The conjectures proposed by Shackleton Bailey are thought-provoking, even if at times difficult to accept without doubts. Indeed, sometimes Luxorius as read by Shackleton Bailey seems quite a different, though not less interesting, poet.

[33] For Martial's proems, see in particular the specific study by Borgo 2003.

writer is a truly mature author, confident of his goals and certain about the convention he has chosen.

A quality that makes Luxorius really comparable to his renowned predecessor is precisely the similar poetic self-consciousness. His *liber epigrammaton* is composed of only eighty nine texts,[34] among which, however, as many as the first four (that is 4.49% of the whole collection)[35] are of autothematic character. They also form a kind of an introductory series providing information about the poet himself and his literary goals and expectations.

The arrangement of these poems is very logical: at the beginning, a text addressed to the 'first critic', Faustus, next an epigram directed to the reader, subsequently a kind of *adlocutio ad libellum*, an address to the poet's book, and finally five distichs advertizing the *brevitas*, typical of the epigrammatic genre. It seems also significant that the four pieces are composed each in a different meter: the Phalaecean, the Senarius (Iambic Trimeter Acatalectic), the Lesser Asclepiad, and the elegiac couplets. Apparently, the series is to be a sample of the poet's technical mastery; indeed, it is worth noting that in his less than one hundred poems Luxorius employs thirteen different meters, which – if compared with Martial's use of eight meters in 1,561 epigrams – does prove his versatility and willingness to try various metrical forms.[36] At the same time, it is not irrelevant that within this opening section, one can find precisely the 'Catullan' Phalaecean, evoked by Martial in his own 1.1, and the elegiac distich, the very meter of the epigrammatic genre as practiced by the Greeks and, as I have emphasized above, the dominant meter in Martial, despite his (relative) polymetrics.[37] Actually, also in Luxorius the main meter is the elegiac distich and the other most frequently used – again like in Martial – the Phalaecean. Therefore, as Mario Citroni noted,[38] our sixth century Carthaginian should, indeed, be seen as the first true follower of Martial's 'disciplined variety'. Still, what Luxorius proposes is not a mere repetition[39] of the Martialian-Catullan 'triad': the elegiac distich, the Phalaecean, the scazon. His scheme is slightly different: the elegiac couplets, the Phalaecean, and the dactylic hexameter.[40]

---

[34] I do not include the poem *Luxori in Anclas* (203 Riese^2), edited both by Happ (1986 I: 9-10) and by Dal Corobbo (2006: 72) before *Metro Phalaecio ad Faustum*, the opening poem of the *liber epigrammaton*, and by Rosenblum afterwards (as No 90, on p. 164). On the authorship of the poem, see Rosenblum 1961: 49-51.

[35] For the statistics, see the useful table provided by Dal Corobbo 2006: 49. One should remember, however, that Dal Corobbo's data refer to 90 texts, the *In Anclas* included.

[36] Rosenblum 1961: 70-71. On Luxorius's well-organized polymetrics, see more below in Ch. III. 2. 2. In fact, the four introductory poems make part of a larger unit (the first 23 epigrams of the *liber*), the aim of which is to exhibit the poet's technical competence.

[37] See the data provided in Ch. III. 1.

[38] See the already quoted Citroni 2003a: 29.

[39] See also in Ch. III. 2. 2.

[40] In Luxorius, the percentage is of course different from the one found in Martial, yet the dominance of the elegiac distich is not less clear: 48 poems of 89 (it is also used in the *In Anclas*, see above). 10 poems are written in the Phalaecean and 9 in the dactylic hexameter. The choice of the hexameter should not be considered casual since Martial himself defended it in his 6.65 as a meter

In what follows, I shall give a few comments on each of the introductory texts, emphasizing in particular their autothematic character. Luxorius, as one soon discovers, is a very self-conscious (and quite self-assured) poet, yet – what can hardly seem surprising in an epigrammatist – he is rarely totally serious and rarely should be taken at face value. But this is definitely what makes reading him all the more interesting.

1. *Metro Phalaecio ad Faustum*

(287 Riese^2 = IV, 441 Bährens = pp. 110-111 Rosenblum = 282 Shackleton Bailey = pp. 10-11 Happ = pp. 72-75 Dal Corobbo)

The opening poem brings some information not only about the author and his *liber* but also about the person who is supposed to be the first reader and, apparently, the most competent critic of Luxorius's epigrammatic oeuvre, a certain Faustus.

The poet, as we soon learn, is – or at least wants to be known – as a gentleman,[41] already advanced in his years, who now compiles into one little book the verses he composed once as a young man (*puer*).[42] Yet, as it can be easily noticed, he strives quite hard not to be taken for someone just too openly preoccupied with himself and his own literary production. Rather, what strikes us in the opinion he gives about these juvenilia is a clear tone of self-irony, if not self-depreciation.[43] He defines himself as *poeta insulsus*, even as a poet of frozen wit (*ingenium frigens*), composing for sheer joy and without effort:

apt also for epigrams. Besides, the hexameter is employed in five or six (see Ch. III. 3. 1. 1) poems by the author of the *Unius poetae sylloge*; it is also quite willingly used by Ennodius (25.7% of all his epigrams), see more below in Ch. III. 3. 2. 1. Interestingly, Luxorius did not leave any poem composed in scazons (Rosenblum 1961: 71; Happ 1986 I: 93).

[41] The superscription of *liber epigrammaton* says: *Viri clarissimi Luxori et spectabilis*; similarly in the superscription of *epithalamium Fridi* we can read: *a Luxorio viro clarissimo <et> spectabili.* For the possible explanations for the attribution of such a title, see Rosenblum 1961: 39-43; Dal Corobbo 2006: 41-43.

[42] Rosenblum (1961: 174) notes justly: "In its strictest sense, *puer* means a boy up to the age of sixteen or seventeen but it was also used of young men older than that." Happ (1986 I: 194), apparently taking at face value the poet's statement, argued that the *liber epigrammaton* contained only Luxorius's juvenilia. Dal Corobbo (2006: 38; 41; 239) objects to this opinion, arguing that at least some poems must have been composed after 533, when the poet was probably in his forties: Dal Corobbo (following Schubert 1875) supposes that Luxorius was probably born in the times of Guntamund (484-496).

[43] Interestingly, as a very careful reader of the late antique poets may notice, a similar motif can be found in Sidonius Apollinaris's *Carm* 9 to Felix: Sidonius also asks his addressee why he insists upon the publication of his 'worthless' juvenilia: *quid nugas temerarias amici, / sparsit quas tenerae iocus iuventae, / in formam redigi iubes libelli, / ingentem simul et repente fascem / conflari invidiae et perire chartam?* (ll. 9-13). The similarity (noticed, to my knowledge, only by Tandoi 1970: 38) shows that Luxorius's *olim puer* should be, indeed, seen as a topos rather than as an exact age indication. But also, which is not less important, the same point is made by the anonymous author of the *Unius poetae sylloge*, most probably a contemporary of Luxorius and a close reader of his *epigrammaton liber*. The poet, apparently alluding to the passage in Luxorius, declares in his *Prae-*

quos olim puer in foro paravi
versus – ex variis locis[44] *deductos –*
(illos scilicet, unde me poetam
insulsum puto quam magis legendum),
nostri temporis ut amavit[45] *aetas,*
in parvum .... conditos libellum (5-10)

Nec me paeniteat iocos secutum
quos verbis epigrammaton facetis
diverso et[46] *facili pudore lusit*
frigens ingenium, laboris expers. (21-24)

A reader familiar with the epigrammatic vocabulary will immediately recognize the intertextual value of these statements. As it has already been suggested, the very meter, the Phalaecean, together with the diminutive *libellum* point ultimately at Catullus, the archetypic model of the Roman poetry of the *nugae*, the 'not serious' works, avoiding grand themes. At the same time, the direct reference for Luxorius's text is still not (only) Catullus but rather Martial who, employing the Phalaecean in his own opening poem of Book 1, declares himself a follower of Catullus.[47] An additional hint that *Ad Faustum* should be associated with Martial's 1.1 is given in line 21: the phrase *verbis epigrammaton facetis* echoes Martial's *argutis epigrammaton libellis* (1.1.3).[48] As a matter of fact, what is worthy of notice here is not only the allusion as such. Martial, as we know, defining his poetry, uses precisely the word *epigramma* and not the Catullan expressions like *lusus, ineptiae, ioci*. Indeed, he consciously turns the word *epigramma* into a generic label.[49] In this context, it seems quite significant that the African follower of Martial, when classifying his own poetry, repeats the very technical term of his predecessor.[50]

---

fatio (90 R): *Parvula quod lusit, sensit quod iunior aetas* (l. 1). It can hardly be argued that this is something else than a (mere) topos. On the *Sylloge* and its *Praefatio*, see more in Ch. III. 3. 1. 1.

[44] On the reason why I prefer the lection *locis* to *iocis*, see below.

[45] On the reason why I prefer *ut amavit* to *autumavit*, see below.

[46] The lection *diverso et*, transmitted in the A (the siglum assigned to the Codex Salmasianus by Riese, see 1894: XII), was emended by Bährens (1882: 387) to *diversos* (and earlier by Mähly in his recension to Riese[1]). Similarly *diversos* in the second edition by Riese 1894: 248, Rosenblum 1961: 110, and Shackleton Bailey 1982: 236. Happ (1986 I: 11) and after Happ Dal Corobbo (2006: 74) propose anew *diverso et*. I find the arguments given by Dal Corobbo (p. 175) for the lection worth considering.

[47] The use of the Phalaecean in Martial's 1.1 is a kind of a complement to what has been said right above in the prose preface to Book 1, where Martial *expressis verbis* names Catullus as one of his literary predecessors: *Lascivam verborum veritatem, id est epigrammaton linguam, excusarem, si meum esset exemplum: sic scribit Catullus, sic Marsus, sic Pedo, sic Gaetulicus, sic quicumque perlegitur*, see above in Ch. III. 1.

[48] See in particular Giovini 2004: 7, but the association was already noted by Happ 1986 II: 31.

[49] See above in Ch. III. 1.

[50] Certainly, Luxorius's single use of the word *epigramma* can be hardly compared to Martial's employment of the term up to 31 times, as noted above in Ch. III. 1 (see the already quoted Citroni 2003: 15). What is important, however, and what does make Luxorius's case different from what we

Equally important as the reuse of the 'official' denotation of the genre proposed by his model is the allusion to another concept that for Martial was essential to the Roman understanding of the epigram, namely the *sal*. It was precisely the *sal* that Martial pointed out as the fundamental marker of the Roman *epigramma*, opposing it to *lepos*, typical of the Greek counterpart of the genre. Yet, as we have seen, the very use of the word reveals Luxorius's contrariness: the opening text declares that the poet we are about to read is an antonym of what an epigrammatist should be as instead of being *salsus*, he is *insulsus*, i.e. insipid, dull.[51] In addition, the expression *ingenium frigens* is used a few lines below, and *frigidus* – if referred to qualities of style – is, indeed, employed as a synonym of *insulsus*.[52]

It is quite clear that this whole figure of self-depreciation should be interpreted as a kind of *captatio benevolentiae*:[53] a poet having doubts about his work, ready to joke at his own expense wins all the more easily the sympathy of his audience. What might be added though – and here particularly the very adjective *insulsus* turns out informative – is that a 'programmatic' statement of this sort can be seen as a reversal of the topos of emulation: the epigrammatist we read does not advertize himself as a 'new' Martial, willing to compete with the predecessor, but rather as a "bungler."[54] This epigrammatic jest is also an excellent example of *affektierte Bescheidenheit*, idiosyncratic of late antique style.

It is in this context that the opening lines (1-2) of the poem should be reconsidered. Rosenblum, Happ, and Dal Corobbo[55] read in the first verse *Ausus post veteres*,[56] emphasizing Luxorius's reference to the "poets of old,"[57] whereas Shackleton Bailey proposes a completely different conjecture, *Lusus hos veteres*:

---

find in Sidonius for example (Sidonius happens to use the word *epigramma* understanding it, as it seems, in a somewhat similar way to Pliny, see above in Ch. III. 1), is a combination of several elements: the metrical 'self-consciousness', the character (composition as well as topics) of the whole *liber*, and, finally, the presence of the term *epigramma* used in Martialian context.

[51] *Insulsus* of course derives from *salsus* (in + salsus) *OLD*: "unsalted;" (of actions, style etc.) "unattractive, dull, boring, stupid." Martial himself, as Giovini (2004: 16) also notes, uses the adjective commenting on the epigrams of Sabellus, yet in litotes. He praises the addressee for writing, indeed, not without a wit, *non insulse scribis*, the quatrains and distichs. However, as he adds, *facile est epigrammata belle / scribere, sed librum scribere difficile est* (Book 7.85).

[52] *OLD*: *frigeo* (of words): "to have no effect, fall flat;" *frigidus* (of arguments etc.): "failing to produce the effect intended, making no appeal, feeble, flat, lame, frigid;" (of subjects, tasks): "unimportant, dull, tedious." The best example is provided by Quintilian quoting Cicero's critics, 12.10.12: *in salibus frigidum*. Giovini (2004: 22 n. 22) focuses on another interesting passage in Cicero's *De oratore* 2.260, where *frigidus* seems to be used indeed as an antonym of *salsus*: Cicero, analyzing a kind of a linguistic joke, when one pretends to understand an expression literally and not in the intended sense, states that: *haec aut frigida sunt, aut tum salsa, cum aliud est exspectatum.*

[53] Dal Corobbo 2006: 174; Giovini 2004: 10.

[54] I quote the word proposed by Rosenblum (1961: 111) in his translation.

[55] Riese (1894: 247) and Bährens (1882: 386) read similarly: *Ausus post veteres tuis, amice, / Etsi iam temere est, placere iussis.*

[56] As transmitted in the A.

[57] As translated by Rosenblum 1961: 111. *Post veteres* can be interpreted in this context as *post veterum praeclara carmina* (Dal Corobbo 2006: 174). Rosenblum provides examples from Martial

Happp and Dal Corobbo:	Rosenblum:	Shackleton Bailey:
Ausus post veteres tuis, amice, *etsi tam temere est, placere iussis,*	*Ausus post veteres, tuis, amice,* *Etsi iam temere est, placere iussis,*	*Lusus hos veteres, tuis, amice,* *etsi iam temere est, placere iussis,*

Shackleton Bailey's proposal is based on a notion which occupies an important place in Luxorius's poetics: the "Carthaginian Martial" does stress the unserious, 'ludic' character of his writings (in the very *Ad Faustum*, we can observe: *iocos* in l. 21, *verbis facetis* in l. 22, *lusit* in l. 23, finally *ridiculum*[58] in l. 26).[59] But the prevailing lection *Ausus post veteres*, especially if read – and translated – carefully,[60] makes a good complement to the figure of affected modesty. What we obtain is a quite typical pose of the late antique *literatus* who, only too willingly, acknowledges his inferiority to the masters of old and – even if he follows the examples they set – has no emulative pretensions whatsoever.[61] It might

referring to the poets of old as *veteres* (8.69.1-2; 10.78.14; 11.90.7). Giovini (2004: 13), however, being himself enthusiastic about Shackleton Bailey's conjecture, emphasizes that in all these passages the adjective is never substantivated but always concords with *poeta*. Still, Luxorius's substantivated *veteres* could be taken as an example of the brachylogic style, which he sometimes likes using (see Dal Corobbo 2006: 175).

[58] Shackleton Bailey proposes for the final lines (25-26): *causam, carminis unde sit voluptas / edit ridiculi sequens poema*, which makes *ridiculi* concord with *carminis*, all the other editors leave *ridiculum*, which thus concords with *poema*.

[59] Giovini (2004: 13), as said above, wholly accepts the conjecture. Hunt (1988: 334), similarly positive about the proposal, draws attention to an interesting point: "*Lusus hos* ... augurs well for the editing, brilliant in the fulfillment of this collection, Not only, in its place, does it remove the supremely unsatisfactory *Ausus post*: it obviates the transposition, mooted by Riese ("fort. recte" Bährens), of lines 5 and 6 below, obviates making lines 7-8 a parenthesis (Riese, Bährens), and allows, in a poem characterized by verbal echoes, ring composition (~23 *lusit*, 25-26 *carminis ... ridiculi*)."

[60] Rosenblum in his main text proposes a rather 'linear' translation, which indeed – as he himself acknowledges in the commentary – "offers some difficulty:" "Daring, after the poets of old, to obey your orders, even if it is now a rash act ..." (1961: 111 & 173, the commentary). It could have been better, if the editor had decided for the version he suggested in the commentary (p. 174), rendering *post veteres* as "inferior to:" "though inferior to." But the problem is also due to the punctuation. Rosenblum (unlike Riese (!) he follows for the most part) puts a comma after *veteres*, which shows that he does read *Ausus post veteres* as a separate unit. Riese, Bährens, Happ, and Dal Corobbo do not; therefore, Dal Corobbo's (2006: 73) translation, based on a better punctuation, sounds clearer, indeed. The Italian translator begins from *etsi* and emphasizes that *post veteres* should be read in this context: "Anche se il farlo dopo i poeti antichi è cosa da pazzi, osando obbedire ai tuoi commandi ..." Another reason why Dal Corobbo's understanding of the text seems more complete may be acceptance of the lection *tam temere est* (as proposed by Happ, see above), instead of *iam* (present already in Riese and Bährens): *iam* may imply the sense 'now' and be seen as opposed to *post* (see in fact Rosenblum 1961: 173).

[61] As such the passage can be compared to Dracontius's self-definition as *vilis vates* in the narratorial prologue of his *De raptu Helenae* (see above in Part One Ch. I. 2. 2). An important, and in my view indeed decisive, argument for the lection *Ausus post veteres* is the one adduced by Zurli (2005a: 38-42) in his edition of Coronatus. Zurli emphasizes the fact, noted in passing in previous

be in fact because of this lack of 'emulative pretensions' – or, if one prefers, a reluctance to put them forward openly – that Luxorius eventually does not name any specific models (even though his Martialian inspirations are recognizable for a well-trained reader).

While in the opening verses the old poets are alluded to, Luxorius's contemporary literary culture is mentioned in line 9. Our epigrammatist states that he once wrote verses *nostri temporis ut amavit*[62] *aetas*. Rosenblum renders the whole passage as follows: "They [the poems] appealed to the tastes of our generation, but actually they are such as to make me think of myself as a bungler rather than as a poet worth being read."[63] The translation, however slightly imprecise, is not unacceptable, yet it highlights all the more Luxorius's contrariness: he is presented as someone who, on the one hand, expresses his low opinion on his own writings and, on the other hand, does not shrink from noting that he was so popular an author. Much simpler would be just to leave the phrase as it is and conclude that Luxorius says 'only' that he once composed verses 'as his generation loved'. This in fact, I think, opens up a possibility of two interpretations. We may understand *olim ... paravi versus ... nostri temporis ut amavit aetas* as "I once ... composed verses ... *suiting the tastes* of our generation,"[64] but also as "I once ... composed verses ... as our generation *loved (doing)*." If so, it could be inferred that Luxorius intends to define himself, indeed, in the context of the literary preferences of his time but also as a representative of a certain milieu.

---

studies, that Coronatus in the prefatory letter to his *De ultimis syllabis* (the letter is directed precisely to Luxorius) alludes to the opening words of *Ad Faustum*. Indeed, Coronatus's *temerarium, qui audeat aliquid post veterum librorum doctrinam (minuere vel aliquid superaddere)* can hardly be a casual echo of Luxorius's *Ausus post veteres tuis, amice, / etsi tam temere est.*

[62] Here Shackleton Bailey proposes another major conjecture: *autumavit* instead of *ut amavit* (see the collation of the passage in the four editions below), which indeed (as emphasized by Hunt 1988: 334), together with the initial *Lusus hos veteres*, obviates making lines 7-8 a parenthesis, but it also changes completely the sense of the whole statement. In this version, it is his generation who judged Luxorius as *poeta insulsus* (maybe preferring the old poets). Such a reading, however, interesting and even amusing as it is, seems less convincing if we take into consideration the intratextual perspective: in the very next poem Luxorius asks his (contemporary, as it appears) reader why he reads him having at his disposal the books by the old poets.

Happ and Dal Corobbo:	Rosenblum:	Shackleton Bailey:
quos olim puer in foro paravi	*Quos olim puer in foro paravi*	*quos olim puer in foro pa<ra>vi,*
versus – ex variis locis deductos –	*Versus ex variis locis deductos*	*versus ex variis iocis deductos,*
(illos scilicet, unde me poetam	*(Illos scilicet unde me poetam*	*illos scilicet unde me poetam*
insulsum puto quam magis	*Insulsum puto quam magis*	*insulsum, puto, quam magis*
legendum),	*legendum),*	*legendum*
nostri temporis ut amavit aetas,	*Nostri temporis ut amavit aetas,*	*nostri temporis <a>utumavit aetas,*

[63] See Rosenblum 1961: 111. *Nostri temporis ... aetas* in the sense of 'our generation' can be compared to Ausonius's *aetas recentis temporis*, *Com. prof. Burd.* 2.6, as noted by Rosenblum 1961: 175 and Giovini 2004: 16.

[64] As proposed by Dal Corobbo 2006: 73: "i versi che un tempo – quand'ero giovane – ho scritto in mezzo alla gente, ricavandoli da occasioni diverse e *adeguandomi ai gusti* della nostra generazione."

Two more important qualities of Luxorius's epigrams are emphasized in the passages of *Ad Faustum* quoted above. As we remember, our poet reveals that he wrote his verses *in foro* (l. 5). A literal translation, like the one by Rosenblum: *in the Forum*,[65] secure as it often may be, might also turn out rather misleading[66] in this context as the word *forum* used here seems to point not just at the place but also at the people that can be met in it,[67] or even more generally, at the everyday life of the Carthaginian *forum*. Luxorius's *in foro*, as Giovini[68] argues convincingly, stresses a particular aspect of his poetics, in fact, the aspect indicated also by Martial as essential to the poetics of *epigramma*, namely the realism:[69] the realism in portraying a mad teacher, an angry dice player, a drunken woman, and so many others.[70] Therefore, I would say that in the following line (6), the lection *locis*, transmitted in the A, sounds more logical than *iocis*, proposed by Bährens[71] and accepted only by Shackleton Bailey:

Happ and Dal Corobbo:	Rosenblum:	Shackleton Bailey:
quos olim puer in foro paravi	*Quos olim puer in foro paravi*	*quos olim puer in foro pa<ra>vi,*
versus – ex variis locis deductos –	*Versus ex variis locis deductos*	*versus ex variis iocis deductos,*

As it has been noted before, the jocular tone of Luxorius's poetry is hardly questionable (which might be an argument for *iocis*). On the other hand, the phrase *versus ex variis locis deductos*, understood as 'taken from various occasions', 'inspired by various occasions',[72] seems to emphasize the above-mentioned sense of *in foro*.

---

[65] Rosenblum 1961: 111. The American editor explains in the prefatory part of his edition (p. 44): "At first glance, the mention of the Forum would seem to indicate that Luxorius engaged in public life when young, ... but [he] nowhere hints about his public career. *In foro* ... refers only to his activities as a student and teacher." It should be remembered though that in classical Latin *forum* and *schola* are often opposed, as *ThLL* VI 1, 1205, 22 ff. shows: Sen. *Contr.* 13: *scholam quasi ludum esse, forum harenam*; *ibid.* 9 *praef.* 5 *e scholis in forum transeuntes*, etc.

[66] See the ironic remarks in Giovini 2004: 11.

[67] *OLD* gives the sense: "the people in the street." *Il dizionario della lingua latina* provides an interesting example explaining the expression *in foro* as *in pubblico*: Cic., *fin.* 3.4: *arripere verba de foro*, "cogliere parole dalla folla." Cicero, describing the language of philosophy, argues: *ars est enim philosophia vitae, de qua disserens arripere verba de foro non potest.*

[68] See Giovini 2004: 11-12, but also his further remarks on Luxorius's realism and its limits (esp. pp. 161-164 and 338-340) with which I generally agree.

[69] Martial, as it is well known, openly declares: *non hic Centauros, non Gorgonas Harpyiasque / invenies*: *hominem pagina nostra sapit* (10.4.9-10), opposing the epigram treating everyday life to grand poetry, exploiting mythological themes.

[70] See 294 R; 333 R; 363 R. In the following subchapters, wherever I focus more on general aspects of Luxorius's epigrammatic writings and less on the analysis of particular lections, I provide only the numeration in Riese^2, quoted simply as R (similarly in Ch. III. 3. 1, devoted to *Unius poetae sylloge*, in which, as for the text, I follow the recent edition by Zurli 2007).

[71] Bährens 1882: 386.

[72] As proposed by Dal Corobbo (2006: 73) in his translation: "i versi che un tempo – quand' ero giovane – ho scritto in mezzo alla gente, ricavandoli *da occasioni diverse*." Happ (1986 I: 105; II 20-21), on the contrary, interprets *loci* here in the rhetorical sense as *themata*.

Finally, as the closing part of the poem announces, Luxorius's verses are also to be marked by *facilis pudor* (l. 23), the light morality.[73] And indeed, a reader who seeks this kind of amusement should not be disappointed. An effeminate lawyer, a royal eunuch who put on a *mitella*, an aged virgin getting married, an impotent doctor marrying a woman thrice a widow, a husband who made his wife prostitute herself for the sake of having sons, or a blind man who knew beautiful women by touch are just a few figures to be found in the unusual world of Luxorius's epigram.[74]

It is time now to focus on the other protagonist of the poem, its addressee Faustus. His task, as it has already been mentioned, is quite unique. Faustus – if we should believe the testimony of his 'compeer'– a great teacher of *ars grammatica*, is not only a 'mere' dedicatee of the *liber epigrammaton*. Cast in the role of a literary *patronus* – as clearly indicated by the double use of the word *iussa* (l. 2: *placere iussis*; l. 19: *duriora iussa*), so well-known from the *recusationes* composed by the Augustan poets – he is, indeed, made corresponsible for the book to be published. Not only – as a distinguished specialist[75] – is he supposed to be the first reader and critic of Luxorius's juvenilia, he is also expected to choose a certain number of other readers among whom individual poems[76] should be circulated:[77]

Ausus post veteres tuis, amice,
etsi tam temere est, placere iussis,
nostro Fauste animo probate conpar,
tantus grammaticae magister artis, (1-4)
[versus]
in parvum tibi conditos libellum
transmisi memori tuo probandos
primum pectore; deinde, si libebit,
discretos titulis, quibus tenentur,
per nostri similes dato sodales. (10-14)

---

[73] On the nexus *facilis pudor*, see in particular Giovini 2004: 21-22. On Faustus, see generally Kaster 1997: 283-284.

[74] 295 R; 298 R; 301 R; 309 R; 322 R; 357 R.

[75] See the thorough analysis of the nexus *memor pectus* by Giovini 2004: 17-19.

[76] As it can be inferred from *discretos titulis, quibus tenentur* (l. 9). On the question of the authenticity of the titles of Luxorius's poems, see in particular Rosenblum 1961: 65-69 and recently Dal Corobbo 2006: 159-161. It is generally acknowledged that the authenticity of Luxorius's titles is doubtful. But, on the other hand, the problem still merits a much closer analysis, modeled on the one provided by Zurli in his thorough study (2007: 35-43) on the *Unius poetae sylloge*. Zurli dedicated some of his attention to the question of the authenticity of Luxorius's titles showing that in certain cases the title must indeed be taken into consideration (and as such it can hardly be attributed to a mere 'copyist'), otherwise we risk a complete misunderstanding of a poem, see in particular Zurli 2002a: 58-60, but also 1993. One might be tempted to wonder whether the author of the titles could not be Faustus: in such a case, his responsibility for the *liber* would be even stronger. Yet it cannot really be conjectured from the statement made by the poet in l. 9.

[77] An interesting parallel can be found in Statius's prose preface to *Silvae* 2: Statius finishes the letter to his friend Melior with a request regarding his poems: *Haec qualiacumque sunt, Melior carissime, si tibi non displicuerint, a te publicum accipiant; si minus, ad me revertantur.*

As we can see, the 'next readers', selected by Faustus, are to be friends, or even *sodales*, similar to the poet and his addressee. In classical Latin poetry, the word *sodalis*, belonging to the so-called 'language of *amicitia*', was often exploited by authors wanting to emphasize their relationship with a particular literary – and social – circle.[78] This exclusiveness, as we can see, is also stressed in Luxorius's text: the *sodales* he thinks of are presumably other *grammatici*, like himself and Faustus.[79] Most probably another common denominator would be the age: as it seems, Luxorius, Faustus, and their *sodales* are all representatives of the above-mentioned 'our generation' who shared similar pastimes, in the first place verse writing, and/or had similar literary tastes.

At the same time, one interesting reservation is made: the readers to whom Faustus will present Luxorius's epigrams should not be *doctiloqui nimisque magni*. The addressee is in fact blackmailed by our poet: since the *index*[80] of the little book will contain both names, of its author and of the dedicatee and the 'first critic',[81] Faustus might be equally derided, should he recommend it to the 'speaking learnedly' and the eminent:

> *Nam si doctiloquis nimisque magnis*
> *haec tu credideris viris legenda,*
> *culpae nos socios notabit index:*
> *tam te, talia qui bonis*[82] *recenses,*
> *quam me, qui tua duriora iussa*
> *feci nescius, inmemor futuri.* (15-20)

---

[78] Therefore, the word can be found in Catullus, always in reference to persons he defines as his 'closest friends'. Interestingly, the term *sodalis/sodales* is used quite often by the exiled Ovid who is very systematic in emphasizing that, despite his physical absence, he is still bound by the ties of friendship with many representatives of the socio-cultural elite of Augustus's Rome. In Martial, the presence of the word is also noticeable. For precise statistics (for Catullus, Ovid, and Martial), see e.g. the resources accessible online at: http://www.intratext.com/LATINA/ [May 19, 2010].

[79] Kaster (1997: 415-417) in his prosopography lists Luxorius in the category of "Dubii, Falsi, Varii." As he argues, we have no decisive proof whatsoever to be sure that Luxorius was really a professional *grammaticus* and the expressions *conpar* and *nostri similes … sodales* indicate only that he and Faustus were friends and not co-professionals. I do not find Kaster's arguments wholly convincing, especially those concerning Coronatus's letter addressed to Luxorius, which, as it seems, does give certain clues that Luxorius may have been not just a *grammaticus* but even a *sophista* (see also Happ 1986 I: 85; Dal Corobbo 2006: 42). In particular, however, I would not find it problematic that the 'conventional' understanding of *nostri similes … sodales* in *Ad Faustum* would "imply that Luxorius had requested his poems be circulated among his fellow grammarians." Rather, as Zurli (2002b: 229) emphasizes, "questo liber – si rammenti sempre – è opera di un <<grammatico>> (Luxorius, appunto), pubblicato a cura di un grammatico (l'amico Fausto), concepito per una cerchia di amici letterati." Indeed, it seems that at least some late antique poets, especially those cultivating the classical forms and themes, were 'professorial' poets, composing mainly for their fellows (I think of Ausonius in the first place). But, 'professorial' poetry need not always mean 'mediocre'.

[80] On the playful use of the legal vocabulary in l. 17 (*index* means 'the title' but also 'a witness', which is complemented by *culpae socios*, 'accomplices'), see Rosenblum 1961: 175.

[81] Happ (1986 II: 27) reconstructs the 'title' of the book as follows: "Luxuri viri clarissimi et spectabilis ad Faustum liber epigrammaton."

[82] Bährens (1882: 387) and after him Shackleton Bailey propose *bonus*, which, instead of qualifying the poems as good, emphasizes a rather favorable approach of the addressee.

A reader as contrary as Luxorius loves being could comment here that it is, indeed, hardly surprising that a dull epigrammatist does not even aspire to please too learned a public. More seriously speaking (if it is fair to speak seriously about jokes), the "Carthaginian Martial" is obviously joking again; in fact, in the very next poem, announced as the one revealing the source of pleasure to be found in his verses, he may be saying quite antithetically (also here the interpretations vary) that the *docti* do not wholly dislike his *nugae*. Besides, addressing the audience of not too refined taste is commonplace of the epigrammatic genre. Luxorius's concern about the reaction of the *doctiloqui* can be juxtaposed with what Martial states about the *malignus interpres* and the *ambitiose tristis*, always ready to criticize someone else's work.[83] What differs him from Martial – at least from what Martial declares in the very opening lines of his epigrammatic oeuvre, where he presents himself directly to the anonymous *lector* as *toto notus in orbe Martialis* (1.1)[84] – is rather the whole concept of addressing the general public by means of the figure of the first reader and critic, Faustus. In this respect, Luxorius's approach is indeed more 'Catullan' than 'Martialian'.

2. *Iambici ad lectorem operis sui*
(288 Riese^2 = IV, 442 Bährens = pp. 112-113 Rosenblum =
283 Shackleton Bailey = p. 12 Happ = pp. 74-75 Dal Corobbo)

It is only in the subsequent poem that our late antique epigrammatist refers to his own unnamed *lector*. As it has been specified in the final two lines of *Ad Faustum* (ll. 25-26), the main subject of *Iambics to the reader* is to be the source of pleasure which can be found in Luxorius's poetry: *Causam, carminis unde sit voluptas, / Edit ridiculum sequens poema.* Yet before this topic is taken up, the poet – developing the motif already suggested in the previous text, where imitating the masters of old has been called a 'rash act' – asks his reader quite openly: "why do you turn the pages[85] of my book, if you could find enjoyment in reading old authors?" Furthermore, Luxorius stresses what makes the difference so sharp: whereas the works by the *prisci* were admirable for their excellent harmonies, his little book contains only trifles composed by a 'novice', a boy indeed (as stated in *Ad Faustum*: *olim puer*, l. 9).[86] As we can see, the reader is treated here almost as Faustus was before, as an accomplice of the author (in *Ad Faustum*, it is said explicitly: *culpae nos socios notabit index*, l. 17), corresponsible for the fact that such frivolities are publicly known:

---

[83] See the prose preface to Book 1 (ll. 7-17): *Absit a iocorum nostrorum simplicitate malignus interpres nec epigrammata mea inscribat: improbe facit qui in alieno libro ingeniosus est. ... si quis tamen tam ambitiose tristis est ut apud illum in nulla pagina latine loqui fas sit, potest epistula vel potius titulo contentus esse. epigrammata illis scribuntur qui solent spectare Florales.*

[84] See also 6.60.2: *me manus omnis habet.*

[85] On the sense of *retexis* as used here, see Rosenblum 1961: 177; Happ II 1986: 35.

[86] Giovini (2004: 26) notes justly that a good parallel can be found in Martial's 1.113, where the poet also addresses a reader willing to waste his time reading his juvenilia. Interestingly, also these trifles – as we learn – are to be saved thanks to the poet's friend and editor: *Quaecumque lusi iuvenis et puer quodam / apinasque nostras, quas nec ipse iam novi, / male collocare si bonas voles horas / et invidebis otio tuo, lector, / a Valeriano Pollio petes Quinto, / per quem perire non licet meis nugis.*

Priscos cum haberes, quos probares, indices,
lector, placere qui bonis possent modis
nostri libelli cur retexis paginam
nugis refertam frivolisque sensibus
et quam tenello tiro lusi viscere? (1-5)

The second part of the epigram provides the answer to this, provocative of course, question. Besides – as most editors agree reading in line 6: *et forte doctis si illa*[87] *cara est versibus* – like the previous text, it also treats of Luxorius's relationship with the sophisticated audience. Since the interpretations of lines 6-8 proposed by different editors vary quite significantly, it is best to collate the main variants:

Happ and Dal Corobbo:	Rosenblum:	Shackleton Bailey
et forte doctis si illa cara est	*An forte doctis illa cara est*	*Et forte doctis [si] illa cara est*
versibus,	*versibus,*	*versibus*
sonat pusilli quae laboris	*Sonat pusillo quae laboris*	*sona<nt> pusilli qui laboris*
schemate,	*schemate,*	*<s>commata,*
nulla decoris, ambitus sententia –	*Nullo decoris, ambitus, sententiae?*	*nulli decoris, ambitus, sententiae?*

According to Rosenblum, Luxorius's poetry (*pagina* to be exact) is characterized by a small form (*pusillo ... laboris schemate*).[88] Happ (followed by Dal Corobbo) and Shackleton Bailey correct *pusillo* to *pusilli*,[89] but that is where the similarities between the German and the American philologist end. Let us examine Happ's reading first. In his opinion, what is defined here is not the structure, the form of the poems, but rather their stylistic, or even rhetorical quality[90] (and once again, like in the previous text, we hear about the 'little effort': *pusilli laboris* evokes *laboris expers*). In such a context, it

[87] The A transmits *si illa* and it is followed by Bährens 1882: 387, Happ 1986 I: 12, Dal Corobbo 2006: 74. *Si* is deleted by Riese in both his editions (see 1894: 248) and Rosenblum 1961: 112, which consequently changes the sense: *doctis* is treated now as an adjective of *versibus*. Besides, Riese, followed by Rosenblum, proposes *an* against *et* transmitted in the A, which stresses the interrogatory sense. Giovini (2004: 32) finds the reading *doctis versibus* inacceptable as it strongly discords with the figure of *captatio benevolentiae* employed throughout the poem. It is true, but on the other hand, the adjective *doctus* if referred to *versus* could be understood as ironic (Dal Corobbo 2006: 176) and, as we already have seen quite many times, Luxorius loves being contrary. Shackleton Bailey (1982: 236) obviates *si* but emphasizes in the apparatus: "doctis dativus est."

[88] As in Rosenblum 1961: 113: "book ... whose structure is limited", see also his comments on p. 177. Riese (1894: 248) renders l. 7 as *Sonat pusillo quae laboris †schemate*, Rosenblum only removes the *crux*.

[89] Already in Bährens 1882: 387: *Sonat pusillique e ...*

[90] *Schema* in rhetoric is used as an equivalent of 'a figure of speech'. Giovini (2004: 33-34) takes this lection into consideration, but he also notes: "Può darsi pure che Lussorio abbia inteso affermare ... che i suoi *versus* (o la sua *libelli ... pagina*) risuonino di *sententiarum orationisque formae* ... frutto di scarsa fatica oppure d'una scrittura figurata e per metafore di modesto impegno e di nessuna eleganza, ma non mi sembra che questa sia una peculiarità stilistica distintiva del *dicendi genus* del poeta africano: Lussorio sminuisce i propri meriti ma non si attribuisce caratteristiche di demerito che gli sono estranee."

seems logical indeed to emend *nullo*, transmitted in the Codex Salmasianus, as Happ does. What he proposes is *nulla … sententia* with two genitives of quality used in place of adjectives. In Happ's version, Luxorius actually acknowledges that his epigrams appeal to the readers, also to the learned ones (as the dash[91] instead of the question mark clearly indicates), because of their 'simplicity', and in particular due to lack of (exaggerated) poetic embellishment and 'ostentation'.[92]

Shackleton Bailey highlights a different aspect. First of all, he is convinced that the poet once again, as in *Ad Faustum*, does not address the *docti* as his potential public but rather those of plainer taste. Besides, he conjectures *comute* of the Codex Salmasianus not to *schemate* (as Riese) but to *scommata*.[93] In the following line, he proposes genitive qualifiers of the noun *versus*. As a result, the peculiarities of Luxorius's poetry are, in his version, 'teasing, taunting expressions' (that cost no effort), lack of *decor* and *ambitus*, and lack of *sententia*, i.e. a (moral) judgment.[94] The last, as we remember, has been already mentioned in *Ad Faustum*, where the poet emphasizes his *facilis pudor*. All these features are indeed markers of the epigrammatic genre, stressed also by Martial.[95]

The poem closes with another important remark concerning the nature of Luxorius's epigrams (ll. 9-10). They do attract the readers – here presumably the average public is taken into consideration[96] – for their similarity to 'funny' theatrical spectacles. The allusion to the poet's contemporary culture is quite obvious: the theatrical, especially mimic

---

[91] Dal Corobbo, who reads the passage exactly like Happ, places a comma here, like Bährens 1882: 387. The question mark is used by Riese 1894: 248.

[92] See Happ 1986 II: 42-44; Dal Corobbo 2006: 176. *Ambitus*: 'pompousness', 'ostentation' (the translation proposed by Rosenblum 1961: 113).

[93] Bährens (1882: 387) already proposed *scommate*, which actually seemed acceptable to Happ (1986 II: 41, as he put it: "Baehrens' *scommate* ist hübsch"), only that, as he emphasized, the word probably did not exist in Latin in Luxorius's times. Giovini (2004: 35-36) is inclined to believe that Luxorius might use the term *scomma* in the sense close to the one proposed by Macrobius in his *Saturnalia* 7.3.2-3: *scomma enim paene dixerim morsum figuratum, quia saepe fraude vel urbanitate tegitur et aliud sonet, aliud intellegas*.

[94] Rosenblum (1961: 113) interprets somewhat similarly: "with not a whit of elegance, ostentation or serious thought."

[95] As emphasized by Giovini (2004: 25-29), who concludes justly: "il carme, che può apparire una sorta di mea culpa autoreferenziale dell'autore, consapevole dei limiti tecnici, delle mende strutturali, dell'atrofia stilistica, nonché della generale frivolezza della sua *libelli pagina*, costituisce invece, sulla base dei nessi intertestuali con i modelli ripresi e contraffatti, in testa Marziale, una dissimulata e abile rivendicazione di consapevole appartenenza a una tradizione e a una scuola di poesia che risale appunto al grande poeta spagnolo e nel cui solco fecondo Lussorio vuole inserirsi con orgoglio, seppure quale tardo epigono."

[96] The interpretation of the whole passage depends on the reading of the previous three lines. If we agree with Shackleton Bailey that the poet ironizes the approach of the *docti* to his verses, what he says sounds as: "my poems are despised by the learned, but you, <<normal>> reader, do love them." If we accept Happ's interpretation, it can be paraphrased as Dal Corobbo (2006: 176) did: "se i critici … apprezzano questa silloge poetica per il suo carattere non problematico, allora – e nel dirlo Lussorio mostra un certo autocompiacimento – anche il lettore normale può accostarla con animo sereno."

and pantomimic, performances were extremely popular in Vandal Carthage and had their impact on authors practicing more 'literary' genres as Dracontius's example clearly indicates. The comparison with *iocosa theatra* is, besides, a one more hint what an important factor in Luxorius's epigrams is the realistic, often parodistic, imitation of life. And only a competent reader will notice that speaking of epigrams as theatrical performances is a literary topos itself:[97]

Dal Corobbo:	Happ:	Rosenblum and Shackleton Bailey:
hanc iure quaeris et libenter inchoas, *velut iocosa si theatra pervoles!*	*hanc iure quaeris et libenter inchoas,* *velut iocosa si theatra pernotes!*[98]	*Hanc tu requiris et libenter inchoas,* *Velut iocosa si theatra pervoles.*

3. *Asclepiadei ad librum suum*
(289 Riese² = IV, 443 Bährens = pp. 112-113 Rosenblum = 284 Shackleton Bailey = p. 13 Happ = pp. 74-75 Dal Corobbo)

In the third of his introductory poems, Luxorius addresses his very book. The associations with earlier *adlocutiones ad libellum* by Horace (*Epist.* 1.20) and Martial (1.3) are immediate and are indeed what the poet expects from us. Luxorius's *Ad librum* must be read together with Martial's 1.3, and it is so not just because the African epigrammatist reuses the motif already exploited by his predecessor, but rather because the way in which he does it defines his attitude to the model. Luxorius, reversing the situation described by Martial, speaks in a tone that we know so well from his previous poems, of an ostentatious irony, or even depreciation of his literary productions. At the same time, his reinterpretation of the theme can be seen as a kind of playful and light, but quite clear, acknowledgement of his inferiority to the predecessor: the Carthaginian author in a certain sense implies that his own book and his own versifying do not deserve as much attention as Martial's.

In Martial, the *parvus liber* prefers to go away and dwell in the bookshops of the quarter named *Argiletum*, although the poet's bookcase stands empty for it; similarly, in Horace's *Epist.* 1.20, the poet tells his book-slave: *paucis ostendi gemis et communia laudas, / n o n i t a n u t r i t u s* (ll. 4-5). In Luxorius, the little book hurries to reach homes of the great and the bookshelves of the stately Forum, escaping the poverty of his master at whose place it lay in a tiny nook covered with dust and almost completely devoured by bookworms. In Martial, the *liber* flees as it cannot stand the author's constant erasures (also in Horace's *Epist.* 1.20, the book is *pumice mundus*, l. 2). In Luxorius, there is not

[97] See again Martial's prose preface to Book 1, ll. 16 ff. (quoted also by Giovini 2004: 29-30): *epigrammata illis scribuntur qui solent spectare Florales. non intret Cato theatrum meum, aut si intraverit, spectet. videor mihi meo iure facturus si epistolam versibus clusero: Nosses iocosae dulce cum sacrum Florae / festosque lusus et licentiam vulgi, / cur in theatrum, Cato severe, venisti? / an ideo tantum veneras, ut exires?* On "Martial's theater," see succinct remarks in Skwara 1997.

[98] Happ maintains the lection *pernotes* of the Codex Salmasianus.

even a mention of this, which concords with the pose of negligence he assumes throughout his work:

Martial, 1.3	Luxorius
Argiletanas mavis habitare tabernas,	*Parvus nobilium cum liber ad domos*
cum tibi, parve liber, scrinia nostra vacent. (1-2)	*pomposique fori scrinia publica*
sed tu, ne totiens domini patiare lituras	*cinctus multifido veneris agmine*
neve notet lusus tristis harundo tuos,	*nostri diffugiens pauperiem laris,*
aetherias, lascive, cupis volitare per auras (9-11)	*quo dudum modico sordidus angulo*
	squalebas, tineis iam prope deditus (1-6)

Luxorius's book at his master's home lies covered with dust and falls prey to worms. A careful reader will recall now precisely Horace's *adlocutio ad libellum* in *Epist.* 1.20. Horace, addressing his *liber* disguised as a rebel slave, prophesies:

carus eris Romae donec te deserat aetas:
contrectatus ubi manibus sordescere volgi
coeperis, aut tineas pasces taciturnus inertis
aut fugies Vticam aut vinctus mitteris Ilerdam. (Hor., *Epist.* 1.20.10-14)

It is worth noting that Luxorius in his epigram also speaks of a multitude of readers who may look down upon the runaway: *si te dispiciet*[99] *turba legentium* (l. 7); in addition, he uses the adjective *sordidus* (in Horace, *sordescere*). Nevertheless, as it is the case with motifs taken from Martial, also here the late antique poet generates a sense practically opposed to the one that can be found in Horace. Horace warns the book about the miserable fate of one who chooses a public life, despising the safe refuge offered by the master. In Luxorius, the book suffers poverty staying at home where it is exposed to dirt and worms. It could be argued that what we can observe in Luxorius is a kind of ironic reinterpretation of the Horatian-Martialian topos. The late antique epigrammatist derides the attitude of a poet-admirer of his own work whose *amor proprius* is inextricably intertwined with certain mistrust, if not a sense of superiority toward the wider public. Horace, in addition to what has been cited above, portrays the 'prospective' reader of his book as a sated and languid lover (*cum plenus languet amator*, l. 8) or as a stammering, old elementary school teacher in the city's outskirts (*hoc quoque te manet, ut pueros elementa docentem / occupet extremis in vicis balba senectus*, ll. 17-18). Martial, on the other hand, emphasizes the squeamishness of the Roman literary audience (*nescis dominae fastidia Romae*, l. 3).[100] Luxorius, who before expresses his doubts about the *doctiloqui*, now acknowledges also

[99] Happ (1986 II: 50-51) and Dal Corobbo (2006: 177) propose to maintain the traditional *dispiciet* transmitted in the A.

[100] It is not less symptomatic what Martial says in the following lines (4-8) of his poem: *crede mihi, nimium Martia turba sapit. / maiores nusquam rhonchi: iuvenesque senesque / et pueri nasum rhinocerotis habent. / audieris cum grande sophos, dum basia iactas, / ibis ab excusso missus in astra sago.*

the possibility that his book may be simply disdained or at least disregarded,[101] yet he does not really ironize (at least not overtly) about its readers, diverse as they may be inter *Romulidas et Tyrias manus* (l. 8).[102]

The whole poem closes with a distich which is to be the book's epitaph in case it fails to please the audience and 'ends its days'. Almost all editors accept in line 11 *facile est*, as transmitted in the Codex Salmasianus, yet, as the incorrect translation by Rosenblum exemplifies, the passage can be quite easily misunderstood. The motto does not concern those "who easily endure their envy of fame,"[103] or those "who do not mind being grudged their fame."[104] The point is that, as Vincenzo Tandoi emphasizes, *facile est* should be interpreted here as 'it is probable (that ...)'.[105] Therefore – as literally as possible – the two lines could be rendered as: "content to stay at home should be the one for whom it is probable to suffer the envy of (his) fame." What is essential is the fact that the distich must be seen as a moral, a warning indeed, given by one who has tried hard and experienced failure. In other words, in Luxorius, it is the book to say *expressis verbis* what in Martial or in Horace the author only implies with his *non ita nutritus* (Hor., *Epist.* 1.20.5) or *sed poteras tutior esse domi* (Mart. 1.3.12). Is it too pessimistic (or too seriously pessimistic) to make a good motto?[106] Pessimistic as it is, it should not probably be given more credence than the statement that what we read are juvenile trifles of a dull epigrammatist:

---

[101] Happ (1986 II: 51) emphasizes that *dispiciet* should be understood here not so much as 'despised' than as 'disregarded', 'ignored', even 'missed'.

[102] Giovini (2004: 45) argues that Luxorius's somewhat pompous *Romulidae* may have a slightly negative connotation, especially if read as an allusion to Persius's *sat.* 1, an ironic picture of the Roman 'golden youth' ready to listen to poetry when sated: *ecce inter pocula quaerunt / Romulidae saturi quid dia poemata narrent* (ll. 30-31). I wonder, however, if we can really speak of an intentional allusion here. On the other hand, the very description of Luxorius's literary audience is interesting here: the homes of the great but also the public bookshelves of the Forum, the Romans, the Carthaginians, multicultural Romano-Barbaric Carthage, indeed. On *Romulidae* as Carthaginians of Roman descent, see Rosenblum 1961: 179.

[103] Rosenblum 1961: 113 & 179-180 (commentary). Interestingly, Rosenblum in his commentary notices the association with Phaedrus's 1.3.13, emphasized also by Tandoi (1970: 38) as essential for understanding Luxorius's concept.

[104] The correction proposed by R. Browning (I quote after Tandoi 1970: 39).

[105] Tandoi 1970: 39. The *Latin dictionary* by Lewis and Short gives an example of Terence's *Andr.* 720 (see online: http://www.perseus.tufts.edu/hopper/morph?l=facile&la=la#lexicon [May 19, 2010]), quoted also by Tandoi, and suggesting the sense: 'certainly', 'unquestionably'. Hence, the translation could also sound somewhat stronger: 'content to stay at home should be one for whom it is *certain* to suffer the envy of (his) fame'. This, I believe, is the general idea behind Dal Corobbo's (2006: 75) version (this time much more an interpretation than a translation): "È necessario che si contenti di stare a casa propria chi sa già in partenza che non avrà successo." Tandoi, on his part, proposes the following translation: "Deve sapersi contentare del proprio stato chi acquistando fama può facilmente esporsi all'invidia altrui."

[106] Giovini (2004: 47), himself an enthusiast of Shackleton Bailey's proposals, seems to think so.

isto pro exequiis claudere disticho:
contentos propriis esse debet locis,[107]
quos laudis facile est invidiam pati. (9-11)

Nevertheless, Shackleton Bailey, evidently too disappointed with the lection to leave it as it is, proposes here one of his most controversial conjectures:

Contentos propriis esse decet focis
quos laudis pigitum est invidiam pati.

What we obtain is a beautiful moral, a *sententia* that can be easily detached from its original context and used separately as true 'winged words', an excellent closure of the whole poem and, indeed, the author's words of approval addressed to the 'bold' book: "content to stay at home should be (only) the one whom troubles being exposed to the envy of fame." Were it only more acceptable paleographically ...

4. *De quod epigrammata parva in hoc libro scripserit*
(290 Riese^2 = IV, 444 Bährens = pp. 112-113 Rosenblum = 285 Shackleton Bailey = pp. 13-14 Happ = pp. 76-77 Dal Corobbo)

The last of Luxorius's introductory poems, if compared with the previous three, may seem somewhat plainer. However, also here our poet does not really give up his ostentatious contrariness. The whole text is built upon a canonical motif of the epigrammatic genre: the defense of *brevitas.*[108] A well-trained reader will soon notice echoes of Martial's 2.1,[109] yet of all merits of a concise book named by the predecessor, Luxorius keeps only the third and last one: the shorter it is, the less boring it turns out for its audience. Quite logically, the fewer faults it also contains:

Martial, 2.1	Luxorius
tertia res haec est, quod si cui forte legeris, *sis licet usque malus, non odiosus eris.* (7-8)	*Hic mea concinno si pagina displicet actu,* *finito citius carmine clausa silet.* *Nam si constaret libris longissima multis,* *fastidita forent plurima †vel vitio†.* (7-10)[110]

[107] On *debet*, preferred by Happ against *decet*, see Dal Corobbo 2006: 177. Instead of *locis*, Riese (1894: 249) proposed *iocis*, which, however, is rarely used in figurative sense. Besides, *locus* can also mean 'social rank' and the sense seems also applicable to the Luxorian phrase, as Dal Corobbo admits (similarly, earlier Tandoi 1970: 39).

[108] Lausberg (1982: 60-61) is right emphasizing that the piece is not an apology of *epigramma brevis* as such but rather of epigram as a *Kleinform*, as opposed to the 'grand' poetry; similarly Mondin 2008: 400.

[109] See also Giovini's (2004: 49-51) observations.

[110] I quote the text as edited by Happ 1986 I: 13-14 and Dal Corobbo 2006: 76 and the comments on pp. 178-179. Happ leaves *†vel vitio†* as *nondum sanatum*. Rosenblum and Shackleton Bailey propose *vel vitia* and remove the *cruces*.

Throughout his poem, Martial presents similar 'advantages' of a *liber exiguus*: he speaks also of wasting less paper and saving the copyist's time and effort (ll. 3-6). Strangely enough, the African author is more 'serious'. As if responding those who would be ready to belittle his talent, he points out brevity as a positive quality per se. As he argues, the year is composed of short months, brief are the days of both winter and spring, great use is found in small things. The conclusion sounds even more straightforward: "no pleasure is given beyond measure:"

***
si quis hoc nostro detrahit ingenio,
attendat modicis condi <de> mensibus annum,
et faciles hiemis, veris et esse dies;
noverit <in> brevibus magnum deprendier usum.
Ultra mensuram gratia nulla datur. (2-6)[111]

A reader who is used to Luxorius's pose of 'affected modesty' might be surprised indeed, first because what is expressed quite clearly is that the poet's talent should not be 'belittled' (in *Ad Faustum*, the *ingenium frigens* has been emphasized) and, second, because our epigrammatist seems to challenge the value of all the 'grand' literature as such, which Martial actually never did.[112] Certainly, there were poets before Luxorius stating without hesitation, 'a big book is a big nuisance', yet who could expect Callimachean bravery from an author defining himself first as *poeta insulsus quam magis legendus*?

III. 2. 2. THE *LIBER EPIGRAMMATON* AND ITS CHARACTERISTICS

The disciplined polymetrics constitutes, as we already know, one of the most important qualities of Luxorius's *liber epigrammaton*. It is well exemplified by the introductory poems but even better by the first 23 epigrams of the collection[113] (metrically, the four opening texts are, in fact, a part of this larger unit). Within this quite huge segment, constituting roughly one fourth of the whole *liber*, one can find all the thirteen meters used by the poet: elegiac distich, Phalaecean, hexameter, Lesser Asclepiad, Lesser Sapphic, Iambic Trimeter (Senarius) Acatalectic, Anapestic, Anacreontic (Dimeter Ionic a minore with Anaclasis), Anacreontic (Iambic Dimeter Catalectic or Dimeter Catalectic Ionic a minore), Glyconic, Trochaic Tetrameter Catalectic, Elegiambic (Archilochian), and Iambelegiac.[114] What is more, one can even notice that within these 23 poems, it is still Luxorius's two main meters, the elegiac distich and the Phalaecean, which hold the privileged

[111] Also here, I quote Happ's edition. On Shackleton Bailey's conjectures, see Giovini 2004: 54-58.

[112] See also Giovini 2004: 51-53.

[113] As noticed justly by Dal Corobbo 2006: 161. In fact, after the poem 309 R, *Anacreonticum in medicum inpotentem*, the dominant meter is the elegiac distich.

[114] See Rosenblum 1961: 70-85. For some further information, see Dal Corobbo 2006: 161-165, Happ 1986 I: 93 and his thorough study on Luxorius's metrics and prosody on pp. 199-280.

position: the elegiac couplets are employed seven times and the Phalaecean five times.[115] Interestingly, the hexameter, almost as important for our poet as the Phalaecean, is used now only once; eight more poems composed in the hexameter are placed in the second part of the book, in which one can find more epigrams of epideictic and ecphrastic character and fewer scoptic texts.[116] In other words, without becoming too schematic of course, one could also point at a certain difference between the first and the second half of the *liber*, the first being more 'satirical' and the second somewhat more 'serious'.

Since the elegiac distich is indisputably the main meter of the collection, it is axiomatic that the series of poems composed in the same meter (we can find a few such series within the book) will be texts written in the distich. Nonetheless, there are two cases when two epigrams in the Phalaecean and two poems in the hexameter are juxtaposed. The first refers to two scoptic texts, *In vetulam virginem nubentem* (301 R) and *In medicolenonem* (302 R), the second concerns two epigrams, a laudation and an epitaph (353 and 354 R), dedicated to one and the same person, a beautiful Egyptian hunter by the name of Olympius. What is also worth mentioning, within the *liber*, there are generally seven pairs of epigrams treating the same topic or the same protagonist, of scoptic, ecphrastic, and laudatory character. Twice, two poems making such a pair are metrically different. In as many as in four cases, the two epigrams have different number of verses.[117] It seems quite natural to conclude that the author aims to achieve the effect of *variatio*: the texts dedicated to the same subjects are to make the collection more coherent but, on the other hand, they should not appear as mere repetitions of identical motifs, identical meters, and identical number of verses.

Speaking of general qualities of Luxorius's *epigrammaton liber*, one can note a considerable number of the so-called *epigrammata longa*.[118] There are, in sum, twelve such

---

[115] Hence, we shall find 41 more poems in the distich within the remaining 66 texts of the *liber* (I do not include *In Anclas*, see above in Ch. III. 2. 1) and 5 more in the Phalaecean.

[116] The only text in the hexameter within the first 23 poems is a scoptic piece 300 R. The next one will be only 325 R. Interestingly, apart from 300 R and 327 R, all other poems in the hexameter are non-scoptic. Some of these hexametric texts treat subjects with 'epic' connotations, so to speak (325 R, 367 R), two are epitaphs (345R, 354 R), two are *laudationes* (353 R, 373 R), however jocular in its overtones the other one may be. This, I think, cannot really challenge Happ's (1986 I: 93) general statement that there seems to be no correlation between meter and genre in Luxorius, but it may show that at least the hexameter appears to display a somewhat 'serious' tenor for our poet. I would add that it may not seem totally coincidental that the hexameter is used in the two epitaphs, see below in Ch. III. 2. 3. 3.

[117] Pairs: 307-308 R, 312-313 R, 334-335 R, 341-342 R, 343-344 R, 353-354 R, 361-362 R; pairs differing in meters: 307-308 R, 361-362 R; pairs differing in the number of verses: 307-308 R, 334-335 R, 341-342 R, 343-344 R.

[118] I presume, following in fact Mondin (2008: 425-426; 428-429), that texts having 14 and more verses should be regarded as such. Mondin calculates the average length of Luxorius's epigrams as 8.2 lines, which is, in fact, more than in the *Sylloge* (5.8) and in Ennodius (5.7). It is worth noting, besides, that Luxorius does not write one-verse epigrams at all and he composes monodistichs quite rarely, indeed, which also differentiates him from the poet of the *Sylloge* and Ennodius (as well as from Martial, in fact, as Happ (1986 I: 93) already noticed). Certainly, one can wonder what number of *epigrammata longa* should be defined as considerable (and whether 13% is the

poems, which constitutes over 13% of the entire collection.[119] They are composed in different meters. We have four texts in the Phalaecean, four in the hexameter, and 'only' three in the elegiac distich. One is written in the Anacreontic. These epigrams are, which is not wholly irrelevant, not only of epideictic, ecphrastic or laudatory (in other words 'serious') but also of scoptic character.[120] Besides, what seems pertinent is the very fact that a long epigram par excellence is the opening text, *Ad Faustum*. Luxorius in many aspects appears a very precise and very self-conscious poet, fully aware of his literary choices, therefore, in my view, the above composition should not be considered coincidental. The Carthaginian, I believe, quite clearly indicates that he recognizes a specific kind of epigram, the *epigramma longum*.[121] This way Luxorius, in a sense, acknowledges his affinity with Martial in another 'field' since Martial does not only practice writing long epigrams but above all several times speaks in defense of such poems. His 6.65 may seem particularly interesting here, where the poet from Bilbilis explains that it is usual and allowable to compose both long epigrams and epigrams in hexameters.[122] Thus, it might not be merely casual that as many as four of Luxorius's *epigrammata longa* are composed in the hexameter; just as not merely casual seems also the very fact that the Carthaginian chose the hexameter, advertized by his predecessor,[123] as his third measure. A competent reader should discover that

---

sufficient number), however, I would not agree with Bertini (2008: 495) that "L'*epigramma longum* in Lussorio è in realtà assai raro;" as a matter of fact, it turns out more frequent than among his contemporary epigrammatists. As for Martial and his approach to the *epigramma longum*, I think that the poet's declarations are really more important here than mere statistics (which account for 7.6%), just as they were, in my view, for Luxorius as his quite conscious (however not obsequious) follower. And declaratively, as I have already emphasized, Martial is very much a supporter of the *epigramma longum*.

[119] If we define as Luxorius's *epigrammata longa* poems which are 14 and more verses long, we can list as such: 287 R (26 ll., Phalaecean), 301 R (14 ll., Phalaecean), 302 R (14 ll., Phalaecean), 304 R (22 ll., distich), 309 R (18 ll., Anacreontic), 320 R (16 ll., distich), 332 R (14 ll., Phalaecean), 333 R (14 ll., distich), 345 R (18 ll., hexameter), 351 R (14 ll., hexameter), 353 R (14 ll., hexameter), 354 R (14 ll., hexameter). It would be disputable to include here also 350 R because of the state in which this text is preserved: ll. 9-10 and 13-14 are interpolations from Claudian. Thus, I presume that it is safer to calculate the percentage of Luxorius's *epigrammata longa* as 13.48% (including only 12 texts listed above, of which we can be certain); Mondin (2008: 426) proposes 14.6%, apparently (I believe so because he does not specify it) including also 350 R. Nonetheless, the data he provides (especially the tables on pp. 427-431) are truly invaluable.

[120] Scoptic are: 301 R, 302 R, 309 R, 333 R.

[121] Which is also stressed by the very placement of such texts within the book: they are sometimes juxtaposed, like 301 R and 302 R, and sometimes, on the contrary, preceded and followed by very short texts, see Mondin 2008: 436.

[122] Mart. 6.65: *<<Hexametris epigramma facis>>* scio dicere *Tuccam. / Tucca, solet fieri, denique, Tucca, licet. / <<sed tamen hoc longum est.>> solet hoc quoque, Tucca, licetque: / si breviora probas, disticha sola legas. / conveniat nobis ut fas epigrammata longa / sit transire tibi, scribere, Tucca, mihi*. The poem might be read as very 'wayward' as it is neither particularly long, nor hexametric. The point is though that it follows a truly long text (32 lines long), precisely in the hexameter.

[123] Even though, as we remember, Martial himself turns out much more an 'advocate' of hexametric epigrams than a 'practician' of such a form.

this is at the same time a change and, indeed, a continuation: a change because Martial's third meter was the scazon (which Luxorius completely ignores), and a continuation because it was the poet from Bilbilis who argued for hexametric epigrams.

It is true that Luxorius never quotes Martial, but he does follow (not servilely though, which can hardly be seen as a flaw) the general character of the genre the latter defined. As we already know, the Carthaginian – certainly, with some contrariness yet clearly enough – underlines the realistic and satirical coloring of his epigrams, recognizing the heritage of the *sal Romanae Minervae*, so important for Martial. Indeed, *scoptic* pieces account for almost an exact half of his *liber*.[124] Significantly, what constitutes the second half is *non-scoptic*: ecphrastic or epideictic texts, *laudationes*, epitaphs, and autothematic poems.[125] These sub-types of *epigrammata* also belong to the Martialian canon.[126] Besides, it should be emphasized that a part of Luxorius's *liber* (at least 13 pieces) is dedicated to themes related to the circus and, broadly speaking, to sports: description of the amphitheater, descriptions of paintings to be seen on a circus stable or of paintings or mosaics showing hunters, and, above all, texts presenting sportsmen themselves, charioteers and hunters. As concerns the last-named texts, some of them are laudatory and some scoptic. This whole group of poems can be interpreted as another allusion to the predecessor, this time to Martial's *liber de spectaculis*, which again does not mean that the Carthaginian adopts single motifs or stresses the same details and aspects that his model found particularly worthwhile.[127]

---

[124] As emphasized by Dal Corobbo 2006: 49-50. The Italian scholar is right that one should distinguish from other scoptic texts the two political satires by Luxorius (341-342 R) attacking the king's official who took the property of others by force. The name of the official, Eutychus, is probably the transliteration of Bonifatius: Boniface was entrusted the treasure of Gelimer during the war with Belisarius. He eventually came to terms with Belisarius and kept a great part of Gelimer's wealth for himself. He was notorious for his rapacity as the two epigrams show. The question is to what extent they can also be seen as proof of Luxorius's civil courage. Happ (1986 II, 326-327) argues strongly for the poet's *Zivilcourage*, emphasizing that it should be taken into consideration when giving a general judgment on his personality. The poems are, indeed, very bitter and, in point of fact, especially the first one accuses of greed not just the official but also the king: *Quid gravius hostis, fur aut latrunculus implet, / talia si dominus atque minister agit?* (ll. 5-6). Dal Corobbo (2006: 239-241), however, notes soundly that these verses were in truth composed only in the twilight of the Vandal ruling in Carthage. At the same time, the Italian scholar, very justly in my view, defends Luxorius (see pp. 47-48) against the accusations of servilism once formulated by Bouchier.

[125] See useful typologies and statistics provided by Dal Corobbo 2006: 49; 153.

[126] On Martial as an epigrammatist who must not be seen only as a brilliant 'point-maker' with rapierlike wit, see the already canonical paper by Citroni 1969. What we shall not find in Luxorius as regards this unique heritage of non-scoptic Martial are sympotic, erotic, and 'reflective' epigrams. On the other hand, however unsentimental Luxorius might appear at first sight, it is, in my own opinion, very superficial to accuse him of emotional indifference or utter coarseness. His sense of humor is sharp and malicious, but he does show a tendency to maintain some elementary *decorum* (also in poems treating sex and especially peculiar sexual preferences, see Ch. III. 2. 3. 1) and he can be tender, see 345 R, the epitaph for Oageis's little daughter.

[127] On sport in Luxorius's epigrams, see Laville 1974 and now especially Dal Corobbo (2006: 266-268) who provides a succinct but very informative (and simply well-done) overview of the subject.

We have already made a few comments about the arrangement of the book, noting the juxtaposition of pieces devoted to the same themes or the same personages (there are, as mentioned above, seven such pairs, yet we do not find in Luxorius longer sequences). Also poems composed in the same measure are sometimes placed side by side and, just to repeat, this refers not only to epigrams written in the elegiac distich but also to two texts in the Phalaecean and two texts in the hexameter. In addition, pieces not making a strict pair may be grouped together too, but they have a motif in common. There is a cycle of epigrams dedicated to water: two poems about fountains (347-348 R) followed by a piece about a well dug in a dry mountain (349 R) and, finally, a text about the hot springs of Cirne (350 R). Most probably it is not wholly coincidental that after this cycle, we can find two poems treating rather schoolish themes (351 R, *De sententiis septem philosophorum*; 352 R, *De Ianuario mense*) and, right after, a 'true' pair of epigrams devoted to the hunter Olympius (353-354 R). The above examples are, in fact, the most evident ones; such interrelations though can be also much subtler and they are certainly worthwhile to be still searched for.[128]

On the other hand, our author aims at diversity and change. It is best shown in the unique display of polymetrics within the first 23 poems of the collection. Sometimes longer 'segments' composed of epigrams written in the elegiac distich are divided by a text or texts in a different measure. For instance, within epigrams 328-344 R, we can find two poems in the Phalaecean, 332 R and 336 R; all others are in couplets. Within pieces 362-371 R, after five epigrams in the distich, there is one in the hexameter and, later, again four in the distich. A block of texts 345-354 R (interestingly, these are the two epitaphs, 345 R for Oageis's little daughter and 354 R for Olympius) is a sort of a mixture: hexameter, five poems in the distich, hexameter, distich, two poems in the hexameter). The Asclepiad and the Senarius are juxtaposed twice: 314-316 R are arranged as Asclepiad-Senarius-Asclepiad, 360-361 R as Senarius and Asclepiad. It is more than certain that further examples could be adduced.

Similar conclusions could be proposed in reference to the thematic arrangement of the book. I have already mentioned that one can speak of a certain difference between the first more 'satirical' half and the other, more 'serious' one. Pieces of like character are also grouped into 'units', sometimes separated by one or two different texts. Thus, we can distinguish a block of scoptic epigrams 294-311 R (interestingly, the first and the last text are written in Lesser Sapphic) separated by two poems of laudatory character dedicated to Fridamal. Within a sequence of satirical[129] pieces 336-344 R, we can find one exception: 339 R is epideictic but actually more grotesque than serious in its content (to quote the title: *De duobus qui se conpedibus, quibus vincti erant, ceciderunt*).

---

[128] An excellent example of such extremely subtle but quite fascinating interrelations between two juxtaposed epigrams may be the one proposed by Zurli (1993: 35) in his interpretation of the true (yet veiled, needless to say) sense of 364 R, *In mulierem pulcram castitati studentem*. He reads it in the (zoophilic) context of the following poem, 365 R, *De eo qui cum Burdo diceretur filiae suae Pasiphae nomen inposuit*. Zurli's reading, bold as it is, is very alluring in my own view as I find it fully concordant with what I perceive as Luxorius's sense of humor and (sic!) Luxorius's ambiguity and subtlety in treating such 'controversial' themes.

[129] One should remember that, as mentioned above, 341-342 R are political satires and not solely scoptic pieces.

All this points to carefulness with which Luxorius composed his *liber*, doing his best to make it varied, multi-colored, simply interesting to read and appealing to the literary audience also with its inner architecture, which is logical but without exaggeration and not at all banally schematic. One can interpret as a certain disproportion only the fact that there seems to be no clear closure, comparable to the quite lengthy introductory part. To be precise though, it is worth noting that the last four poems, 372-375 R, are composed in three main meters of the collection, the Phalaecean (372 R), the hexameter (373 R), and the elegiac distich (374-375 R). Besides, the charming, however tragic in its message, piece about a cat who died after devouring a too big mouse makes not a bad final to Luxorius's little oeuvre. What is more, Martial himself appears to pay relatively less attention to closures, at least in some of his books.[130] Once more, one could conclude that the associations with the poet from Bilbilis are, in Luxorius's case, not so much inevitable as rather justifiable.

III. 2. 3. THE POEMS: AN OVERVIEW

III. 2. 3. 1. Scoptic epigrams

Statistically, scoptic epigrams make no more than half of Luxorius's *epigrammaton liber*. One could hardly deny, though, that it is precisely because of these poems that the Carthaginian can be remembered by his readers. Undoubtedly, the world he depicts seems extremely strange and turned upside down, abounding in unusual, abnormal individuals rather than in types personifying ordinary human faults or weaknesses.[131] This choice of themes determines, in fact, his originality as the protagonists he introduces, unique as they are (although too frequently most of them eventually prove to be just sexual deviants ...), never appear to be mere copies of their Martialian predecessors. Therefore, even the personages representing jobs traditionally derided by epigrammatists, when portrayed by Luxorius, are funny not only and not so much because of their lack of professionalism but rather because of their weirdness and, indeed, deviation, even though quite often they also turn out incompetent.[132]

What makes Luxorius's teacher (294 R) peculiar is not merely his savage roaring and thwacks (like it is in Martial) but much more his dreadful fury that should, in fact, exclude him from the ranks of *grammatici*.[133] Similarly, the lawyer (295 R) is not really unskilled and still loses his cases. Quite the contrary, he does have all the potential to be successful. Nevertheless, more than on professional ambitions, he seems to be focused on satisfying his (homo)sexual desires.[134] The preferences of the charioteer Vico (336 R)

---

[130] See generally Sullivan 1991: 218 and, more specifically, Fowler 1995.

[131] As noted also by Dal Corobbo 2006: 152.

[132] Thus, Dal Corobbo (2006: 184-185) is right correcting Giovini's statement about 295 R, a piece dedicated to an effeminate lawyer. See similarly Happ (1986 II: 322) about 340 R.

[133] See below in Ch. III. 3. 1. 2 for the comparative reading with Anonym's 96 R.

[134] Another lawyer among Luxorius's protagonists (340 R) is, indeed, incompetent and the only field in which he seems to achieve something is his relationship with his concubine Charis.

are not different, which must be somewhat surprising in someone who should embody manly strength and hardness.[135]

The epigram quite representative in this context is the one devoted to a doctor Marinus (302 R). Doctors, among professions, are one of Martial's most favorite targets, but the jokes he makes about them are not too hard to guess, though (undeniably) everlasting. What he likes emphasizing is their incompetence, needless to say fatal to their patients, to quote only 1.30: *Chirurgus fuerat, nunc est vispillo Diaulus: / coepit quo poterat clinicus esse modo.*[136]

Luxorius's doctor[137] is unusual in a different way. Ostensibly, he seems to be fully dedicated to his 'mission'; that is, at least, what the poet-narrator would think judging by his paleness and the esteem with which everybody greets him after a many days' absence.[138] The truth, however, turns out quite the opposite. In fact, Marinus has been acting as a procurer in a brothel but, what is more, he has some particular reasons to do this 'extra' job. He is a voyeur,[139] yet what he loves observing are not nude girls but men excited with desire. That is not the end; the medical procurer hopes that his clients will finally also pay some attention to what he wishes to offer them. Hence his love paleness, elegiac so to speak,[140] and hence, most probably, his popularity in town.[141] When reading the poem, one can indeed come to a conclusion that it is not a satire on doctors en bloc but rather a very accurate and very specific portrait of an individual, a pseudo-professional, a cheater in truth as he neglects his duty, and a deviant at the same time. So

---

The poem, as most of Luxorius's texts, is very difficult to interpret, see Dal Corobbo 2006: 237-239 and, especially, Zurli 1993: 43-46.

135 There are more poems deriding bad, losing charioteers and most of them can probably be interpreted as quite typical 'fan-style' jokes; which seems to be confirmed only by the kind of joke our poet makes here. Dal Corobbo (2006: 222) may be right implying that some of such texts could have been 'ordered' by single factions. For a thorough analysis of the poem, in particular of its point, see Zurli 1993: 36-38.

136 See also 5.9 (where some erotic undertones can be found); 6.53; 8.74; 9.96.

137 Another doctor to be found among Luxorius's characters is the protagonist of 309 R; still, he appears there only as an impotent marrying a woman thrice a widow and not as a representative of his profession. For specific analysis of the poem, see Giovini 2004: 167-183.

138 Shackleton Bailey (1982: 244-245), as usual so to speak, proposes a different lection for ll. 4-5. Since I do not analyze the passage in detail, I shall not focus on the problem. I shall only note that I find particularly successful the translation by Dal Corobbo (2006: 87), especially of *manum pudicam* in l. 4: [te] *credebam medicum velut peritum / curam febribus et manum pudicam / de factis logicae parare sectae / aut de methodicis probare libris* (ll. 3-6) – "ti stimano medico esperto nel curare la febbre e *onesto nella professione*, secondo la prassi della scuola logica, o abile a far diagnosi sulla base dei testi della scuola metodica." Giovini (2004: 140-141) follows the lection proposed by Shackleton-Bailey: [te] *credebam medicum velut peritum / curam febribus et malae podag<r>ae / logicae placitis parare sectae / aut de methodicis probare libris.*

139 Giovini (2004: 137-139) compares Luxorius's 302 R with some Martial's texts, especially 11.71, in which doctors are also presented as (heterosexual) erotomaniacs, concluding (justly) that "Lussorio riesce davvero a superare il maestro in fatto di turpitudine."

140 Giovini 2004: 139-140.

141 Dal Corobbo 2006: 195.

exact a characterization might imply that the protagonist of the epigram is a real person. On the other hand, if we take into consideration that Marinus turns into an embodiment, even an 'accumulation', of so extra-ordinary – but also (and this is most intriguing) quite frequent among Luxorius's 'heroes' – features, we can begin to question his authenticity. Undoubtedly, what the poet intends here is to shock us, presumably even more than just to make us laugh. Thus, he cannot be content with what would be average, even with regard to its faults. He chooses or creates (probably both) personages almost out of this world, but also such to whom nothing human is alien.

Among Luxorius's pseudo-professionalists, one can find an alleged poet (316 R) who finds enough satisfaction and confirmation of his merit in popularity in rather 'suspicious' circles.[142] One can also find artists, in particular female ones, who completely differ from the skilled citharode or pantomimus described by the author of the *Unius poetae sylloge*. The ugly cymbalist Gattula (361 R) frightens her spectators not only with her awkward dancing. She also – as the subsequent poem specifies (362 R) – tries to offer a price to be loved. All in vain though; the epigram is closed with one of the most macabre Luxorius's points: *Sed si forte aliquis moechus surrexit ab umbris, / cui talis placeas, huic tua dona dato!* (362 R, ll. 7-8).[143] The pantomimist Macedonia (310 R), however a dwarf, loves acting tall beauties like Andromache or Helen.[144] A competent reader will not miss intertextual connotations of the poem, especially the allusions to Juvenal's *Sat.* 6 (ll. 504-507),[145] which does not mean of course that Luxorius's target is not a real person. When reading this epigram, again, like in many other cases, one can easily accuse our poet of lack of subtlety, or even of cruelty toward his protagonists. Nonetheless, one should pay attention to the fact that the point, or – to be exact – the message, however straightforward, is serious and almost gnomic. Macedonia plays the part of a tall and beautiful woman because she believes that this way she will turn out (or at least seem) to be someone else. Therefore, she tries to cheat not only her public but also, if not above all, herself.

---

[142] The point is, unfortunately, corrupted and cannot be satisfactorily reconstructed. The poem is in Lesser Asclepiad, like Anonym's 131 R. In this case, however, we can hardly speak of specific connections between the two texts (in some other cases, they are quite clear, see below in Ch. III. 3. 1. 2). I think, what both poets do (independently, as I would argue) is alluding to the Horatian lyric meter par excellence, the one of *Carm.* 1.1 and 3.30.

[143] For more detailed analysis of the poem, see Giovini 2004: 72-83. The Italian scholar notes that Gattula seems to be the reverse of the protagonist of *Carm. Priap.* 27, Quintia.

[144] Quite interesting seems, indeed, this change of tastes, emphasized by Giovini 2004: 293-294. For Ovid, it was rather a drawback for a woman to be (too) tall. In Dracontius's *De raptu* (*sic longior artus / et procera regens in poplite membra venusto*, ll. 520-521) it is already quite the reverse. Speaking of Dracontius's *De raptu* (certainly, this observation has nothing to do with Helen's being tall), I am pretty sure that Giovini is right (pp. 296-297) arguing that in l. 5: *motibus et falsis crescere membra cupit* Luxorius alludes to, in fact quotes Dracontius's *De raptu*, 636: *motibus et falsis veras imitata figuras*, the effective simile of Polites to a specter. This only shows what renowned author Dracontius must have been among his 'compatriot' poets. Dracontius is, in fact, alluded to also by the anonymous poet of the *Sylloge* in his epigram on Medea (obviously enough), 102 R, see Zurli 2007: 77. Similarly, Dracontian influences can be found in *Anonymi versus serpentini*, see Zurli's notes in Zurli – Scivoletto – Paolucci 2008: 33-35.

[145] See Giovini 2004: 292-293; Dal Corobbo 2006: 206-207.

The poet's words are thus aimed at provoking a salutary disillusionment: *Hac spe, crede, tuos incassum decipis artus: / Thersiten potius finge, quod esse soles!* (ll. 7-8). Put differently, "accept what you *truly* are, not what you *pretend* to be." If we often, or too often, see Luxorius as a provocative, sometimes obscene, and sometimes superficial poet (though the latter is simply unjust and results mainly from the difficulties one may come across interpreting and even trying to understand his texts), we should remember that his points and the lessons he gives can also be so bitterly wise as this one.

It may appeal to a contemporary reader that among Luxorius's pseudo-professionalists one can find a false necromancer (299 R). Fascination with magic in the culture of late antiquity, especially in 'Apuleian' Africa, even in the Christian period, can be hardly surprising.[146] What may attract our attention is rather the extreme rationalism with which the Carthaginian treats the topic. His protagonist strives to earn a living from practicing the art of magic because he is hungry and because he, apparently, has no better idea of how to make ends meet. In addition, he is ignorant of the art he practices. This seems enough to provoke our laughter and pity. But even more worth remembering may be the bitter comment of the poet-narrator: *aliquid credis / dare quod possit superis Pluton / pauperibusque?* (ll. 7-9) – "do you (really) believe that Pluto could give something to the poor of the world?"[147] Indeed, Luxorius speaks here as a "razionalista illuminato"[148] who does not believe in ancient gods, or at least in their interest in human matters; he does not appear to believe in the afterlife as such, either.[149] And besides – which may be most relevant – he does not seem to believe in any possible change of social relations on earth. The destitute will not find help even in magic …

A lawyer who gives priority to perverse pleasure over his professional career, a doctor performing, in truth, a quite different 'job' and for very particular reasons … One can hardly deny that Luxorius, most probably not less than his public, is fascinated by sex, especially sex of irregular varieties[150] as well as by bizarre phenomena of all kind. Hence

[146] On Luxorius's interest in magic, see Courtois 1955: 128-130.

[147] For ll. 7-9 I follow the lection and the punctuation (which also turns out quite important here) proposed by Happ 1986 I: 20 and 1986 II: 128; Dal Corobbo (2006: 84 & 191) also follows Happ. *Superi* in the sense of 'humans', 'people on earth' is used by Luxorius also in 319 R, hence my paraphrase above. Rosenblum (1961: 119) translates: "in your belief that Pluto can give something to the destitute in the upper world," specifying in his commentary (p. 186): "*superi* means <<the gods above,>> but here it refers to human beings." On *superi*, see also Dal Corobbo 2006: 216.

[148] Dal Corobbo 2006: 190.

[149] As for the point of the poem: *Puto quod peius / egeas totum semper in orbem, / mage, si poscis membra perempta* (ll. 9-11) (in l. 9 *posces* in Rosenblum 1961: 118), Dal Corobbo (2006: 85) translates "se insisti a voler avere qualcosa da queste membra morte," apparently following the proposal of Romano (1968-69: 174, n. 39): "se alle membra morte chiedi qualcosa." Rosenblum (1961: 119) interprets more macabrely: "if you demand the limbs of corpses," adding, unambiguously enough, in his commentary (p. 186): "The beggar does not confine himself to filching food but also takes away parts of the corpse." Even more provocative is Shackleton Bailey (1982: 243) in his, as usual controversial, conjecture of three final verses: *quin, peto, quo peius / egeas, totum semper in aevum / mage, depascis membra perempta?*

[150] See already Garson 1977-78: 12.

his interest in sexual experiences of a hermaphroditic girl (317 R). Hence also the attention he pays to the fact that a royal eunuch has placed a *mitella* on his head (298 R). Why? Because the *mitella*, worn by ladies of pleasure and the (effeminate) people of the East,[151] perfectly underlines the identity of the beautiful youngster? Or rather because it is a "cappellino con pendagli," the pompons being precisely the attributes the eunuch lacks?[152]

The list of Luxorius's adulterers and (wretched) deviants is long and very varied. A *moechus* (297 R) who may stop making love only when he is drunk or, ultimately, when he drinks a poison. An old man (307-308 R) who keeps at home many girls, even though he cannot use them any more; what he practices thus is a sort of *mentis adulterium* (308 R, l. 6). Interestingly, the very same *Incurvus* tries hard to imitate the youth and goes hunting despite his gout. An old husband (322 R) who makes a prostitute out of his chaste wife herself only to have sons.[153] Finally, a catamite (321 R) buying interest of his partners – the casual ones but also of the one he cares for most – with his property, the heritage of his ancestors.[154] It seems worthwhile focusing on the point: *Nescioquid miserum est, quod celas, Becca: talento / vendere debueras, si bona membra dares!* (ll. 5-6). In fact, we, the readers, shall not learn what makes Becca pay so stiff a price for love. This is not the only example of a similarly incomplete (and as such quite thought-provoking) point.

In truth, the epigrams which protagonists are not, ostensibly, sexually active seem particularly interesting. A hairy, slovenly Stoic philosopher (358 R) who by day appears a model of virtue and continence and by night changes into an *incubus* (l. 9) is not so untypical of the epigrammatic tradition,[155] although the poem as such is well-written, indeed.[156] The figure who may really astound us though is the heroine of 364 R, *In mulierem pulcram castitati studentem*. The text has attracted scholarly attention because of its topic and unusual point. The protagonist is an embodiment of contradictions: a beauty of snow-white body observing all the rules of chastity, a Pallas in her way of life, a Cypris in terms of her body. She resigns without regret from the solace (*levamen*, l. 5) that a husband[157] might give her, preferring not even to see males: *Te neque coniugii libet excepisse*

[151] See Juv. *Sat.* 3.66, but also *Aen.* 4.215-216, where Iarbas depicts Aeneas (engaged obviously in the relationship with Dido) as Paris wearing *mitra*.

[152] See Giovini (2004: 106, esp. n. 9) quoting Ferruccio Bertini's interpretive proposal. See below in Chs. III. 3. 1. 2 and III. 3. 2. 2 for the poems on eunuchs by the author of the *Sylloge* and by Ennodius.

[153] For the reading of the poem, see Giovini 2004: 153-161.

[154] For the reading of the poem, see Giovini 2004: 320-327.

[155] As argued justly also by Dal Corobbo 2006: 276. A Martialian example may be, indeed, 1.24.

[156] On the poem, see specifically Zurli 2002b. See also Dal Corobbo 2006: 276-278, especially his notes on the point (Dal Corobbo follows Happ's lection in l. 10). For the interpretation of the poem, see in addition Giovini (2004: 63-72), who follows Shackleton Bailey in understanding the *fulmen*, especially his observations on Christian elements in the epigram on pp. 71-72, and in Giovini 2008: 513-515.

[157] *Coniugium* pointing at a legitimate (= normal) husband, see below for Zurli's (1993: 30-36) explanation.

levamen, / saepius exoptans nolle videre mares (ll. 5-6).[158] Nevertheless, she has a fancy for this desire/pleasure, however hateful:[159] *Haec tamen est animo, quamvis exosa, voluptas!* (l. 7). Therefore, the poet asks her in his point: *Numquid non mulier conparis esse potes?* A genially ambiguous *fulmen* matches perfectly well so tastefully malicious a poem, the poem almost teasing senses. 'Someone like you'.[160] Who is meant then? Another asexual? A male as virtuous as she is[161] or maybe not heterosexual? Or, considering her misandry, maybe rather a female partner? In such a case, the epigram would be an excellent counterpart of Martial's 6.64.5.[162]

Loriano Zurli (justly) admonishes critics pointing out the ambiguity of the word *conpar* in the last verse. In his view, what is ambiguous in 364 R is the whole second part of the poem, from the expression *coniugii levamen* in l. 5, through (especially) the *nolle videre mares* in l. 6, until *conpar* in l. 8. The Italian scholar indicates that Luxorius, as artfully as only he can, implies that the chaste beauty, in truth, finds pleasure in … *eros bestialis*.[163] The interpretation is, needless to say, bold and certainly not given *expressis verbis* by the poet (who aims precisely at being as unequivocal as possible), but we must admit that the arguments adduced by Zurli turn out quite persuasive, firstly, the fact that the subsequent poem (365 R) in a sense at least also refers to zoophilia,[164] and secondly, the probable allusion to Luxorius's *In mulierem pulcram* in the epigram *De electione coniugis* attributed to Coronatus (224 R). A woman is mentioned in line 6 of this text who *cogetur*

[158] For preferring *exoptans* in l. 6 (as an example of quite typical *Appositionsnominativ*), see Zurli 1993: 32, followed by Dal Corobbo 2006: 287.

[159] Rosenblum (1961: 159) translates: "Nevertheless, you have a fancy for this pleasure, hateful though it may be to you!" In my paraphrase above I have omitted especially "to you" he proposed. In fact, *quamvis exosa* does not really specify to whom the desire nurtured by the lady might be hateful. In effect, it may well involve the (possible) observers.

[160] In fact, the lection proposed in the Codex Bellovacensis is also worth mentioning: *cum paris*, giving a not less intriguing point, see Dal Corobbo 2006: 288.

[161] See Rosenblum 1961: 239.

[162] Such interpretation is preferred by Giovini 2004: 83-90, earlier Shackleton Bailey 1979: 54, and, most probably, already Petschening 1877: 491; most probably, because he argues that the point of this poem is worthy of Martial. In fact, one might say that in its ambiguity and hidden sense(s), it is much beyond Martial.

[163] See Zurli 1993: 33. Zurli focuses first on the word *mares* which, in his view, does not refer to men, but precisely to males; thus, what she does not want to see is the muzzle of her unique 'lover'.

[164] 365 R is entitled *De eo qui cum Burdo diceretur filiae suae Pasiphae nomen inposuit* and the very point of the epigram is not less genial than frightening: *Surrexit duplex nostro sub tempore monstrum, / quod pater est burdo Pasiphaëque redit* (ll. 5-6), so in fact the actual problem described here is not bestiality but, as we can see, incest. Zurli (1993: 35), in my opinion, is also right arguing for the authenticity of the title of 365 R. In fact, first of all the, peculiar par excellence, sense of the poem can be fully grasped only if we read both the title and the point, secondly (this refers also to the arrangement of Luxorius's *liber*), 365 R matches quite well the poem on the chaste lady, especially if we accept Zurli's interpretive proposal. One more point worth emphasizing here is precisely what I have mentioned above, namely Luxorius's unique 'subtlety' in treating controversial matters. As we can see especially in 364 R (but to some extent also in 365 R), Luxorius may focus on utterly perverse cases, but (in effect) he is as unstraightforward as possible.

fervens clunem submittere asello.[165] Anyhow, the brilliant piece 364 R perfectly demonstrates how fascinating but at the same time singularly difficult to read the poet Luxorius is and, most probably, will still remain.[166]

Many other protagonists of the *epigrammaton liber* by the Carthaginian could also be classified as 'clinical cases' or 'marvels of nature', even though they do not reveal sexual perversions. In some of these texts, the poet exploits themes known from the epigrammatic tradition, though always adding a new, unexpected detail, like for instance, in pieces treating drunkards. Luxorius's *ebriosus* (311 R) not only drinks constantly but also – and this makes him 'original' – does not eat at all. His female counterpart (363 R) should, in the narrator's view, have her face where her thigh is, then Bacchus would be properly placed.[167]

A hunchback (315 R) boasts about his noble birth, but he does it inefficiently, mentioning most varied gentes: *nunc Iuliorum prole te satum tumens, / nunc Memmiorum Martiique Romuli* (ll. 2-3). This poem, too, could be interpreted as an amplification of already elaborated motifs as Luxorius's protagonist is not merely a mythomaniac, like his Martialian predecessors,[168] but also a cripple. The point, just like the one in the epigram about the actress Macedonia, sounds cruel: *natura nobis, unde sis natus, doces* (l. 7).[169] Apparently, the poet fully subscribes to the opinion, quite typical of the ancients, that physical beauty and aristocratic origins must come together.[170]

A dwarf (296 R), just like a cricket, surprises with the strength of his voice, especially when he bursts out into fury, exciting a true admiration of his 'public': *Miramur, tantum capiant quae membra furorem, / ut sit forma levis, clamor et ira gravis* (ll. 5-6).[171] Finally,

---

[165] See Zurli 1993: 36.

[166] Zurli (2007: 123, n. 38) is (unfortunately) most probably right in his, quite pessimistic, statement: "che la 'equivocità' lussoriana quale procedimento artistico vada spesso a scapito dell'immediata *perspicuitas*, è fatto noto ai suoi lettori ... da cui discende la mia convinzione che Luxorius ... resti ... il poeta peggio compreso di tutta la letteratura latina." Nonetheless (especially for those who, like myself, are convinced that the Carthaginian is, indeed, one of the most intriguing Latin poets), the best way out is simply to read him and to propose his texts for reading. A good example may be the initiative of Prof. Bertini who read and commented Luxorius with his PhD students in 1998/1999. The publications subsequent to that seminar: Bertini 2002 and (later) Giovini 2004 provide many truly helpful insights into Luxorius's poetics.

[167] The epigram is certainly obscene and not easy to interpret, as Boatti (2002: 155-158) stresses. If we accept Bruère's comments to Rosenblum's translation, as Dal Corobbo (2006: 285-286) does, we may read the poem as alluding to the myth about Bacchus's being born from Jupiter's thigh. As such, it will turn out to be not simply obscene but also quite elaborate.

[168] See especially Martial's 4.11, 5.17, as well as Juvenal's *Sat.* 8 and Ausonius's *epigr.* 26 (Green/Kay), pointed out by Giovini 2004: 310-311.

[169] Giovini (2004: 313) notes interestingly that the point can have an extra-meaning. The boasting hunchback is puffed up with pride, but he also quite literarily puffs up his humpback, making it even bigger.

[170] Similarly Dal Corobbo 2006: 210. However, see below for a much more straightforward expression of the conviction in Ennodius's 2.112.

[171] As for *ut* in l. 6, see Happ 1986 II: 113 and Dal Corobbo 2006: 186. Giovini (2004: 283-291) points at possible Lucretian inspirations (especially Lucretius's theory of voice emission) in the poem.

a dice player (333 R) is strange and pitiable not only because of his ruinous passion but rather due to his behavior which is utterly difficult to comprehend. Vatanans, too, flies into fury both when he loses and – which happens rarely and by mistake not by skill – when he wins. The point of the poem is corrupted, yet the text is worth reading precisely for the convincing and very visual indeed description of madness, the madness that almost deprives Vatanans of human qualities.[172]

Vatanans, the 'inhuman' madman, quite similar in fact to the *grammaticus furiosus* mentioned at the outset of the present subchapter, concludes this brief overview of Luxorius's (anti)heroes: pseudo-professionalists, deviants, abnormal types, deformed beings, false moralists. It is up to the readers to decide whether and, if so, to what extent they should see in those almost surrealistic figures real citizens of the sixth century Carthage or – what may be even more important – a picture of the life in *Felix Karthago* ruled by the Vandals as given by a Roman intellectual. We shall return to this question later. Now, in the final part of this subchapter, to once again justify the label of the "Martial of the Vandals" I have still decided to use in reference to our poet, I would like to look at the scoptic Luxorius in the context of his predecessor and model. A brief comparative reading of a few parallel motifs as elaborated by the Carthaginian and, earlier, by the author from Bilbilis should help us notice and emphasize differences, proving Luxorius's creativeness and independence, as well as some intriguing convergences. Hopefully, it may also help demonstrate that even if one considers Martial the greatest Roman epigrammatist (whom he certainly was), it is still quite worthwhile paying some attention to his late antique 'fellow'.

1. A lover of ugly women:

Martial 1.10

Petit Gemellus nuptias Maronillae
et cupit et instat et precatur et donat.
adeone pulchra est? immo foedius nil est.
quid ergo in illa petitur et placet? tussit.

3.76

Arrigis ad vetulas, fastidis, Basse, puellas,
nec formosa tibi sed moritura placet.
hic, rogo, non furor est, non haec est mentula demens?
cum possis Hecaben, non potes Andromachen.

Luxorius 329 R, *In eum qui foedas amabat*

Diligit informes et foedas Myrro puellas;
quas aliter pulcro viderit ore, timet.
Iudicium hoc quale est oculorum (Myrro, fatere)
ut tibi non placeat Pontica, sed Garamas?
Iam tamen agnosco, cur tales quaeris amicas:
pulcra tibi numquam, sed dare foeda potest.[173]

[172] Firstly and mainly because what he loses is the mind, the reason, therefore the point (I quote the extant part): *Non iam huic ludum sapientum calculus aptet*. For the specific reading of the poem, see Giovini 2004: 194-210.

[173] I follow Dal Corobbo's text. Giovini (2004: 218 & 225), as usual, quotes Shackleton Bailey's edition, but in l. 2 he also proposes his own conjecture, instead of *quas <medio> aut pulchro – quas <niveo> aut pulchro*, which is to emphasize the contrast between *Pontica* (*Poenica* in ShB, who follows Petschening's conjecture) and *Garamas* in l. 4.

Loving an ugly woman can be interpreted – as it happens in the Greek epigram[174] – as proof that the feeling is really true and strong. Martial though treats the topic differently, with the bitterness typical of the Roman *epigramma*. The poet from Bilbilis exploits it twice. In 1.10, he presents a certain Gemellus who is eager to marry Maronilla, even though, at least physically, she does not seem too attractive. Nonetheless, the motive behind his determination turns out quite rational. The (model) point of the poem shows that what attracts him most is her cough. The reader guesses instantly that what is the actual focus is the inheritance the bereft husband may come into. In 3.76, Bassus's gerontophilia proves, in Martial's view, nothing else but his madness (*furor*, *mentula demens*, l. 3).[175]

Luxorius's Myrro, at least at first sight, seems to reveal both some of Bassus's *furor* and a bit of Gemellus's self-interestedness as he seeks solely ugly partners. In the final of the poem, we learn, however, that his attitude can be easily explained: it is only such women that might treat him favorably. It is worth noting that what we find in the *In eum qui foedas amabat* is the kind of point Luxorius likes making at times (we have seen it before in 321 R). Ostensibly, the closure may seem fairly unsurprising and as such not exactly witty. Yet what is most interesting is to be found 'outside' the very text, in the reader's guesses. Why are Myrron's preferences so strange? Is it not because he himself tries to hide a horrible deformation or a defect? A reader already familiar with Luxorius's protagonists must think precisely this way. If so, Myrro in his approach turns out to be not merely rational and logical but even (!) praiseworthy. Seeking a woman of his kind, Myrro appears to know well his own measure, as if he were a Stoic *sapiens*, indeed.[176] It seems worth stressing above all that the poem can appeal to quite different readers. A subtle intellectual, like Luxorius himself, might regard as really amusing the unusual paradox that a hideous deviant may be, in point of fact, a model of self-knowledge. Someone of simpler, if not more vulgar, taste can find pleasure in the very sexual overtone.

2. An old man trying to hide his age:

Martial 3.43	Luxorius 343 R, *In eum qui, ut senior dici nollet, multas sibi concubas faciebat †et horrebat senex vocari†*[177]
Mentiris iuvenem tinctis, Laetine, capillis, *tam subito corvus, qui modo cycnus eras.*	*Accusas proprios cur longo ex tempore canos,* *cum sis Phoenicis grandior a senio,*

[174] The motif of loving an ugly woman, frequently exploited in European Baroque poetry, appears in the Greek epigram of Marcus Argentarius (*AP* 5.89) precisely as an unusual aesthetic concept: such love is a sort of challenge and thus proof of a true involvement. In Ausonius's *epigr.* 88 (Green/Kay), the motif gains some elegiac connotations as an allusion to Tibullus's 3.19.5-6: the protagonist loves ugly Crispa because of jealousy: to all she may seem ugly, to his very self beautiful. See Giovini (2004: 213 & 217) who lists the two examples.

[175] Both examples are noted by Giovini 2004: 215-216.

[176] The conclusion, bold as it may be, but in my view truly thought-provoking, was proposed by Giovini 2004: 220.

[177] The title is corrupted, see recently Dal Corobbo 2006: 243-244.

non omnes fallis; scit te Proserpina canum:
personam capiti detrahet illa tuo.

6.57

Mentiris fictos unguento, Phoebe, capillos
et tegitur pictis sordida calva comis.
tonsorem capiti non est adhibere necesse:
radere te melius spongea, Phoebe, potest.

et, quotiens tardam quaeris celare senectam,
paelicibus multis te facis esse virum?
Incassum reparare putas hac fraude iuventam;
harum luxus agit, sis gravis ut senior.

A man who cannot accept the fact that 'everything flows' and strives hard to hide his age seems a charming topic for comedy and satire. Thus, it should not be surprising that an epigrammatist could also find it worthwhile focusing on such a protagonist.[178] The two old men portrayed by Martial try to look better choosing quite 'innocent' solutions, so to speak. Laetinus simulates youth by dying his hair, Phoebus fabricates false hair with ointment.[179] They both behave rather comically also in this sense that they could, indeed, pass for (stage) comic characters; quite significant is the noun *persona*, the mask, used in the final of 3.43 or a, very theatrical indeed, sight gag implied in the point of 6.57, namely: wiping off Phoebus's false hair from his head with a sponge.

Luxorius's *senex decrepitus* applies a less naïve method, at least as it might seem. He pretends to be young playing the part of Casanova. What he achieves, however, is quite the reverse: all his obviously vain efforts to turn into a vigorous lover must reveal that he is but a *gravis senex.*[180] One can hardly deny that the protagonist depicted by Luxorius is also to some extent tragic, which is a quality that his Martialian counterparts do not have at all. He seems besides much less stereotypic; in fact, he looks much less like an 'ordinary' comic character, even though his behavior most probably was not – as it is not today, either – so unusual. One could even say that it is Luxorius's *senex*, precisely because he is not just one-dimensional but rather tragic in his comicalness, who appeals more to a modern reader.[181]

---

[178] The topic does appear in the epigrammatic tradition, as Dal Corobbo (2006: 243) stresses correcting Happ.

[179] Both examples are noted by Giovini 2004: 246-247.

[180] Certainly, Luxorius here plays quite efficiently with the connotations of the adjective *gravis* which, in reference to the old age and to an old man, can have both positive ('serious') and negative ('fastidious') connotations, see Giovini 2004: 253.

[181] Giovini (2004: 255-256) does not point at the tragicalness of Luxorius's old man but instead at certain sympathy that the poet seems to have for his protagonist. I am not sure if I would call it 'sympathy', but indeed what I also perceive in this text is a kind of emotional overtone, which is virtually absent in Martial's 3.43 and 6.57.

3. An aged woman and sex:

Martial 10.67

Pyrrhae filia, Nestoris noverca,
quam vidit Niobe puella canam,
Laertes aviam senex vocavit,
nutricem Priamus, socrum Thyestes,
iam cornicibus omnibus superstes,
hoc tandem sita prurit in sepulchro
calvo Plutia cum Melanthione.

Luxorius 301 R, *In vetulam virginem nubentem*

Virgo, quam Phlegethon vocat sororem,
Saturni potior parens senecta,
quam Nox atque Erebus tulit Chaosque,
cui rugae totidem graves, quot anni,
cui vultus elefans[182] *dedit cutemque,*
mater simia quam creavit arvis
grandaeva in Libycis novo sub orbe,
olim quae decuit marita Diti
pro nata Cereris dari per umbras:
quis te tam petulans suburit ardor,
nunc cum iam exitium tibi supersit?
An hoc pro titulo cupis sepulcri,
ut te cognita fama sit loquatur,
quod <<stuprata viro est anus nocenti>>?

A lady still having fancy for sexual pleasure despite her old age is a figure not less attractive for an epigrammatist than her male counterpart. Luxorius portrays his heroine following (quite straightforwardly) Martial. The poem *In vetulam virginem nubentem* is, in point of fact, one of a very few texts in which the Carthaginian so openly and so clearly alludes to a specific piece by his predecessor (10.67),[183] maintaining the meter, the Phalaecean, the topic, the stereotypic, mythological descriptions of the old age listed apostrophically, and even the form, the epitaph (only in Martial the whole poem imitates the epitaphic structure, whereas in Luxorius, it is only the final verse to evoke the grave inscription). It is beyond doubt this time the African intends to emulate his master and, as we shall see, he turns out quite successful.

Martial's Plutia even in grave has not changed her 'lifestyle', so to speak: she still "itches with lust alongside Melanthio."[184] The point is amusing, albeit the concept as such can hardly be considered fully original: a few epitaphs of the *Anthologia Palatina* are built upon the motif that the deceased still feel what they used to, thus an old female drunkard is thirsty even after her death.[185]

[182] Dal Corobbo (2006: 193), following Happ (1986 I: 21) – but similarly already Riese 1894: 254 – argues that the lection *elefans* should be maintained (Bährens 1882: 393 and Shackleton Bailey 1982: 244 correct it to *ele**ph**ans*) as this spelling, occurring in codices and inscriptions, is transmitted in all the three passages in which the word appears in Luxorius. But note that in the case of *Anth. Lat.* 195 and 196 Riese^{2} = 375 and 376 Bährens = 186 and 187 Shackleton Bailey = 108 and 109 Zurli all editors write *ele**ph**anto* / *ele**ph**ans* even though Riese himself (similarly Bährens and Zurli) notes in the apparatus (1894: 160): "195. De elefanto *A*;" "196 De e(ae *V*)lefanto *BV*;" "elefans *ABV*."

[183] Giovini (2004: 113-116) also juxtaposes the two texts.

[184] I quote the translation by Shackleton Bailey 1993 II: 387.

[185] See Dal Corobbo (2006: 192) who adduces some interesting examples of the epigrams of the *Anthologia Palatina* and, in particular, the most relevant here *AP* 7.353.

What Luxorius proposes in his text is quite different. His heroine is a *virgo longaeva* who now suddenly, when her days are almost over, decides to get married. Paradoxically, a person of this sort could make a much easier target than Plutia since what she reveals is a pitiable inconsistency, indeed. Directing the shafts of satire against the lustful *anus* would be, however, a mere repetition or at most an amplification of the Martialian concept. What the Carthaginian proposes instead is a completely dissimilar, totally surprising final. He implies that in this case the main villain is not the miserable *vetula pruriens* but rather her 'admirer', if so gentle a word can be used in reference to someone who has committed the crime described in the peculiar epitaph: *stuprata viro est anus nocenti* (l. 14). Thus, the true (anti)hero of the poem turns out this deviant, still apparently almost absent in the text.[186] What his motives are and how 'horrible' he must be: these are, again, questions that the readers must answer for themselves.

4. A blind man quite pleased with his handicap:

Martial 8.51	Luxorius 357 R, *In caecum qui pulcras mulieres tactu noscebat*
Formosam sane, sed caecus diligit Asper. *plus ergo, ut res est, quam videt Asper amat.*	*Lucis egenus, viduae frontis,* *iter amittens, caecus amator* *corpora tactu mollia palpat* *et muliebres iudicat artus,* *nivei cui sit forma decoris.* *Credo quod ille nolit habere* *oculos, per quos cernere posset,* *cui dedit plures docta libido.*

In the seventh book of his *Saturnalia*, Macrobius notes that human defects can quite frequently be derided but with certain moderation and delicacy. For if it may be acceptable to scoff at someone's baldness or irregular nose, nevertheless *contra oculorum orbitas non sine excitatione commotionis obicitur* (*Sat.* 7.3.12).[187] The reading of Martial's distich about a blind man, and a blind man in love, makes us believe that this unique principle of *decorum* is recognized also in epigrammatic writing. Asper seems handicapped in comparison with other people not only because he cannot see but also because of the fact that his disability does not allow him to admire the beauty of his own beloved. Nevertheless, the charming epigram turns into a true compliment for its addressee. Firstly, despite his problems, he has a lovely and praiseworthy girlfriend. Secondly, his affection for her is most probably much deeper and gentler since it is not based on the lust of the eyes. Thirdly – yet this message is hidden quite well between the lines – Asper cannot see how gorgeous his lover is, but what he can do is to contemplate her charm in a different and much *fuller*

[186] Which makes the poem original but also shows precisely the aspect I have already stressed above, i.e. Luxorius's subtlety. In fact, *In vetulam virginem* turns out (at least this is my impression) not at all as much misogynic, or at least not as easily misogynic as it might have been.

[187] Giovini (2004: 327-328) quotes the passage.

manner (*plus ... quam videt ... amat*)[188] than those who admire the girl looking at her only from a certain distance. Naturally enough, the blind perceive everything through touch ... And, needless to say, their sense of touch is particularly well developed ...

Luxorius, as it can be easily guessed, does not find it difficult to emphasize the erotic overtone of the theme. But, considering the nature of his wit, one could ask whether he is able to show a comparable tact. The blind man he depicts personifies a unique sort of sensory compensation. Just like Martial's Aper, he uses his touch to counterbalance his vision defect. This does not prevent him from losing his way, but nonetheless, miraculously enough, allows him to judge the limbs of women he meets and even to recognize the one whose body is of particularly striking snow-white beauty.[189] Undoubtedly, the poem can be considered an amplification: Luxorius in his portrayal of the blind man points out all the details that his predecessor, Martial, did not want to define too clearly. It is worth noting, however, that even though the protagonist of *In caecum* is a blind lecher, the epigram never turns obscene and, what is relevant, it never derides the handicap itself. Quite the contrary, the poet makes us admire his hero in a sense. For although he is a blind lover, a *caecus amator*, he differs significantly from his counterparts in satire or comedy. When in Horace (*Sat.* 1.3) the *caecus amator*, literally not blind at all, provokes laughter as he misses most varied faults of his beloved,[190] Luxorius's protagonist, despite his ostensible defect, sees much more than those who are fully fit and healthy; and such is precisely the point of the poem.[191] It is true that he also happens to be a lecher – and this is the detail that the epigrammatist stresses and makes fun of – but at the same time, he is a true craftsman. One can hardly miss the expression *docta libido* placed purposefully at the very end of the text. It is a joke, full of typically Luxorian contrariness, but it also underlines with a certain recognition the man's cleverness; the connotations of the adjective *doctus* are, obviously enough, more than positive. Thus, the protagonist as conjured up by the Carthaginian is not merely an 'ordinary' deviant, he is rather a fine artist of eroticism. And the whole epigram is similarly a little masterpiece, in addition composed in the Anapestic.

---

[188] As suggested by Giovini 2004: 329. I fully agree with his interpretation of the sense of Martial's *plus ... amat*, also because it matches perfectly well what Luxorius proposes in his elaboration of the theme of *caecus amator*.

[189] Certainly, for Luxorius, a Carthaginian, the snow-white beauty, apart from being just a literary topos, must have had some additional real meaning (hence also the opposition *Pontica*/ *Garamas* in 329 R, l. 4). The conjecture proposed by Bährens (1882: 417) in l. 5, *coloris* instead of *decoris* is, however, unnecessary. Boatti (2002: 152) finds it an 'interesting embellishment', but I would agree with Giovini (2008: 536) that it is rather banalizing.

[190] See *Sat.* 1.3.38-40: *illuc praevertamur, amatorem quod amicae / turpia decipiunt caecum vitia aut etiam ipsa haec / delectant, veluti Balbinum polypus Hagnae*, see also Giovini 2004: 335.

[191] Boatti (2002: 154), quoting her colleague L. Radif, notes that the adjective *plures* used in the last line has, indeed, an additional sexual overtone. In the first place, it refers to *oculos*, but it could also imply *plures* (*mulieres*) since we have *muliebres artus* in l. 4.

II. 2. 3. 2. Epideictic and ecphrastic epigrams

Flowers, gardens, animals, buildings, mosaics, little objects of everyday life making it nicer and more beautiful epitomize Luxorius's poetic world not less than dwarfs and erotomaniacs. A hundred-leafed rose (366 R) of fragrance and hue[192] worthy of heavenly honor; a colocasia[193] (372 R) growing better under the poet's roof than in the garden (*plus tecto ut vigeat, solet quam horto*, l. 6);[194] the heavenly garden of Oageis (369 R) containing a collection of all existing herbs healing all the diseases, even possibly death itself;[195] a boar fed in the palace *triclinium* (292 R); a fountain in the shape of Neptune, the god of salty water, pouring forth sweet water now (348 R); a well dug in a dry mountain (349 R); an amphitheater built on a country estate (346 R); an unbelievably fit young acrobat (373 R): all these phenomena represent the beauty and unusualness of the place and time, of the *Felix Karthago* (and yet happy), once again conquered and destroyed and once again resurrected.

If in the previous subchapter describing Luxorius's scoptic epigrams we have spoken of "the world turned upside down," now we should only reuse this Curtius's term.[196] The colocasia flower apparently reverses the laws of nature growing in an environment that should be quite strange for it. A boar, the animal of Mars, is so tame that it does not even tear down the Parian marble and taking food from the hand of its master seems more likely dedicated to Venus than to the god of war.[197] It is precisely the epigrams treating of animals – from which, interestingly, the main part of the *liber* starts – that exemplify best Luxorius's surprise with his contemporary times.

---

[192] Interestingly enough, as Dal Corobbo (2006: 290) justly notes, Luxorius, as usual, is far from unambiguous in his description of the rose; we can hardly be sure whether it is yellow (as could be implied from the first line: *Hanc puto de proprio tinxit sol aureus horto*) or red (since: *fluxit in hac omni sanguine tota Venus*, l. 4). On the 'botanical' aspects of the poem, see Di Salvo 2005: 216. On the 'triumph of rose' in the poetry of late antiquity, see the edition by Cupaiuolo 1984.

[193] Happ (1986 II: 434), followed by Di Salvo (2005: 219-220), conjectures that Luxorius has in mind *nymphaea nelumbo*, the sacred lotus (today it is more often called *nelumbo nucifera*). Dal Corobbo (2006: 301-302) suggests that it might rather be *arum colocasia* or *colocasia antiquorum*.

[194] Actually, it is far from unequivocal where actually the plant grows, whether it is on the roof, as Dal Corobbo (2006: 145) implies, or rather inside the house, of which already Rosenblum (1961: 247) is quite certain. I actually follow his view also because I find quite convincing the observations adduced by Razzetti (2002: 188) that the whole poem is built upon the figure of contrast between what is inside and what is outside. However, much more important than this detail seems the very paradox stressed in the poem: a garden plant grows better in an unnatural environment.

[195] On the poem, see specifically Zurli 1994b; Razzetti 2002: 169-176. Di Salvo (2005: 218) remembers justly that the Vandals were, indeed, very interested in medicine. There is another poem by Luxorius praising the garden, this time of Eugetus (332 R). In fact, as Courtois (1955: 339) argues, with some hesitation though, Oageis and Eugetus may have been one and the same person; compare also Happ's (1986 I: 325) arguments on the impossibility of such identification on glottological grounds. Dal Corobbo (2006: 56 & 230) fully accepts Courtois's conjecture.

[196] See the classic chapter in Curtius 1990: 94-98 (in the Polish edition 1997: 103-107).

[197] Radif (2002: 7-8) justly emphasizes the antithesis Mars-Venus in the first and the last line of the poem.

A homebred fish, kept for pleasure in the royal pool[198] – which for it is the entire sea it would never change for true freedom (291 R, ll. 4-6) – does not fear to take food from the hand of its feeder (just like the boar described in the very subsequent text), taught to come when summoned (ll. 2-3).[199] The epigram, given its privileged position within the collection (it follows the autothematic opening), can be probably interpreted, at least superficially, as a praise of elegance of the royal court of the Vandal rulers, where the old Roman 'fashions', sophisticated and unusual as they may have been, are still cultivated.[200] A competent reader should also notice a certain parallel with Martial's 4.30,[201] similarly dedicated to Domitian's fish, of which all have names and each comes summoned at its master's voice. The sacred fish reveal a unique ability to recognize their lord's *numen*: *qui norunt dominum manumque lambunt / illam qua nihil est in orbe maius* (ll. 4-5). Luxorius himself mentions such spontaneous, however unnatural, attachment of animals (sea birds) to their feeder only in the poem written for Fridamal (305 R), a youngster whom he treated with particular respect and maybe even affection.[202] In *De piscibus*, the point is quite different and, if truth be told, rather intriguing. The fish, by being docile to its master, appeases its hunger; it learns that it is profitable for it to be obedient and to express it with a proper gesture, "a gentle movement of its head," a bow in other words: *sic famem gestu loquaci et †mitiori vertice† / discit ille quam sit aptum ventris arte vincere* (ll. 7-8).[203] Thus, on the one hand, Luxorius apparently 'only' rationalizes the Martialian motif: a domestic fish is but an animal fawning to get some food (though, it would seem more natural were it a dog or a cat). But on the other hand, the clear anthropomorphization of the fish, especially in the two final lines of the poem (*gestu loquaci, mitiori vertice*, even *discit*) may induce a suspicious reader (maybe not only a modern one) to look for some additional, hidden tones and overtones. The unnatural behavior of the fish might, indeed, resemble the behavior of well-trained courtiers.[204] Could it be even the attitude of the Roman subjects, the intellectual elite for instance, to their barbarian rulers? Certainly,

---

[198] Quite probably its royal 'cultivator' might have been Hilderic, known for his gentleness, see Di Salvo 2005: 202.

[199] In l. 3 Dal Corobbo (2006: 76 & 179) follows Happ (1986 I: 15) and maintains *nec pavescit regia<m>* instead of *nec pavescit retia*, preferred by Riese, Rosenblum, and Shackleton Bailey. Certainly, *retia* might imply a macabre overtone, even though it might also, as suggested by Radif (2002: 7), stress the paradoxicalness of the situation: the fish is not afraid of the nets as it knows that they will not bring any harm to it.

[200] As Rosenblum (1961: 181) notes in his commentary: "In the last years of the Republic the cultivation of fishponds was somewhat of a craze among the nobles." Apparently, the Vandal kings imitated the 'antique' noble fashion of the Romans.

[201] See already Rosenblum 1961: 181; Dal Corobbo 2006: 179-180.

[202] See more below. On the relationship between Luxorius and Fridamal, see now particuarly Fassina 2006: 143. 305 R is, in truth, laudatory in its tone, as justly noticed by Radif 2002: 9, see also Dal Corobbo 2006: 179.

[203] Dal Corobbo (2006: 181), having explained the problems with the exact sense of the *mitiori vertice*, finally agrees with Rosenblum's (1961: 115) interpretation: "gentle movement of its head."

[204] As suspected already by Rosenblum 1961: 181.

the Aesopic language of our poet never reveals it. Besides, Luxorius himself could have been one of such court poets ...[205]

If the poem *De piscibus* echoes Martial, such allusions are not less clear in 360 R, *De pardis mansuetis*. A reader familiar with Martial's texts is well aware how fascinated the poet of Domitian was with strange behavior of wild beasts in the circus. A hare is spared by a lion which suppresses its normal wildness because it belongs to the emperor (1.14).[206] A leopard carries a yoke, tigers vouchsafe patience to the whip, stags champ golden bits, Libyan bears are cowed with reins, a boar obeys a purple halter, bisons draw chariots, an elephant performs an agile dance as its black master orders, lions go after hares but let them escape or love them when caught[207] (1.104). All this is possible only because the beasts know whom they serve: *haec clementia non paratur arte, / sed norunt cui serviant leones* (ll. 21-22).

Luxorius describes a similarly marvelous sight of his time (*mira nostri forma ... saeculi*, l. 6): tame fierce leopards[208] together with trained dogs hunt their prey and later, submissively, bring what they have caught. However, also in this epigram the point reveals most interesting. Martial only implies that the beasts instinctively feel what it would mean for them to disobey the emperor's will and ruin 'his' spectacle. The Carthaginian expresses this hidden thought of his predecessor even too clearly: *O qui magister terror est mortalium, / diros ferarum qui retundit impetus, / morsum repertis ut cibis non audeant!* (ll. 11-13). Fear is this unusual teacher capable of changing the nature of wild animals. The fear of human beings, *terror mortalium*, makes leopards obey. But it will suffice to change the order of words to hear a different moral: *o qui magister mortalium est terror*. Fear changes nature of animals and of humans.[209] Yet the fear of whom? We should not expect that Luxorius will elaborate on such topics.

The Carthaginian stresses a quite different aspect. Let us focus on the opening lines of the poem. *Cessit Lyaei sacra fama numinis, / lynces ab oris qui subegit Indicis* (ll. 1-2).

---

[205] On Luxorius and other poets of the *Anthologia Latina* as court poets serving the "conquerors of Romans," see already Rosenblum 1961: 25 ff.; but compare George's (2004) corrections of his utterly traditional view of the relationships between the Roman littérateurs and the Vandal overlords. Similarly Strzelczyk (2005: 278-285) speaks of "Kamaryla dworska, Luksoriusz i *Antologia łacińska*." Miles (2005) adds some interesting remarks on the poets of the *Latin Anthology* as encouraged by the Vandal kings to participate in the "creation of a secular space in Vandal Africa" in an era of strong religious tensions between the Vandals, being Arians of course, and the African Catholic church.

[206] For the list of Martial's poems treating the theme of wild animals that have become tame, see Rosenblum 1961: 181. It is worth noting that at times Martial plays with the motif: 2.75 refers to a situation when an apparently tame lion has eaten two boys.

[207] I paraphrase, however freely, Shackleton Bailey's (1993 I: 119-120) translation.

[208] What kind of animals the *pardi* described by Luxorius might have been, see Rosenblum 1961: 236-237; Radif 2002: 21. The analogies between Luxorius's 360 R and Martial's 1.104 are noted by Radif 2002: 22-23 and Dal Corobbo 2006: 280.

[209] Radif (2002: 22) apparently notices this additional sense of Luxorius's point. She proposes the following translation of the passage (p. 21): "O quale maestro è per gli uomini il terrore;" Dal Corobbo (2006: 135): "Che razza di maestra è per gli uomini la paura;" Rosenblum (1961: 157) quite differently: "Oh, what a master is the fear of human beings!"

What we experience today exceeds all we have heard in mythological stories. Bacchus, as they say, yoked to his chariot wild beasts, the lynxes. It was possible though only because they were overcome by wine. We, the contemporary Carthaginians, can do great things, greater than the ancient heroes or even gods ever did. It is we who are to construct the brave new world. This motif appears frequently in our poet's epigrams. We learn from 369 R, *De horto domni Oageis*, that the heavenly garden contains all that has been discovered by the science of Apollo and Asclepius and, presumably, it can even provide the elixir of immortality. In another epigram describing unusual behavior of animals (330 R) – this time a monkey sits on the back of a dog – we hear the praise of happy times and a happy kingdom given as openly as possible: *Quanto magna parant felici tempora regno, / discant ut legem pacis habere ferae!* (ll. 3-4).

The topos sounds in poems treating of components of everyday life. The poet is pleased to see a well dug in a dry mountain (349 R) epitomizing, so to say, old literary adynata: *Quis hunc non credat ipsis dare Syrtibus amnes, / qui dedit ignotas viscere montis aquas?* He enjoys the thermae of Cirne (350 R) erected in an area that used to be inaccessible and sterile.[210] With admiration does he look at an amphitheater built on a country estate near the sea (346 R).[211] It is quite predictable that the whole text is composed of Luxorius's most favorite figure of speech, the paradox:

Amphitheatrales mirantur rura triumphos
et nemus ignotas cernit adesse feras.
Spectat arando novos agrestis turba labores
nautaque de pelago gaudia mixta videt.
Fecundus nil perdit ager, plus germina crescunt
dum metuunt omnes hic sua fata ferae.

As we can see, the erection of the amphitheater has not caused the destruction of the land that could be used for agriculture; on the contrary, the camps can now be even more

[210] As I have mentioned above, the text is unfortunately corrupted. The very theme of water, as well as of thermae and baths, is quite popular in late antique African poetry; Ottria (2002: 52) rightly speaks of a "celebrazione dell'acqua." One can point at the ecphrases by Felix (210-214 R), *Versus balnearum* (377 R), the poems from *Unius poetae sylloge* (especially 119-125 R). For the Polish translation of Felix (by A. Pawlaczyk), see Strzelczyk 2005: 355-357. The theme of human culture changing the nature is of course one of the leitmotifs of the Roman literature. Particularly relevant may be here a passage from Statius's *Silvae* 2.2, *Villa Surrentina Pollii Felicis*, a poem Luxorius alludes to, especially in 304 R (see more below): *his favit natura locis, hic victa colenti / cessit et ignotos docilis mansuevit in usus. / mons erat hic ubi plana vides; et lustra fuerunt, / quae nunc tecta subis; ubi nunc nemora ardua cernis, / hic nec terra fuit: domuit possessor, et illum / formantem rupes expugnantemque secuta / gaudet humus. nunc cerne iugum discentia saxa / intrantesque domos iussumque recedere montem* (ll. 52-59).

[211] However, as Dal Corobbo (2006: 253) notes acutely, the description, focused only on the reaction of the spectators looking at the construction of the building, gives us no information whatsoever about where the amphitheater really is or what it really looks like. This, in my view, may also point at the fact that what Luxorius describes (if not constructs) is a mythical reality, a new mythology in which 'real' details do not matter that much.

productive as there will be no danger of crop damage by wildlife.[212] A true miracle, one could say: the city lifestyle and the city leisure activities have been translated to the countryside and open to the rustics, and still there are people to plow and to harvest. The effort, the rest, the village, the city, the nature, the culture: everything is mixed to form the new, resurrected, and prosperous kingdom of Carthage.

Yet, in Luxorius's poetic world not only animals and buildings can be unusual. Now, it is time to meet an extraordinarily skilled young sportsman whose deftness seems to stand in sharp contrast to the lack of professionalism of the inefficient charioteers and the ugly performers. An acrobat leaped above the balcony of the amphitheater (373 R). We are obliged to believe it as the witness of the fact was the poet himself who, being at first also quite skeptical, bet the youngster that he would repeat his 'unearthly' achievement. He did, but if we read the text closely enough, we may turn fairly certain that the young athlete, having won (and drunk) the Greek wine, might have lost his unique abilities. Thus, one can really wonder whether the spectacle of this sort can ever be seen again.[213] And was it true at all? – a suspicious reader might ask. Well, it is only Luxorius to know … Anyhow, this poem also closes with a point that openly proposes a juxtaposition, or even a contraposition, of the contemporary times and the mythical past. The Carthaginian athlete surpasses Daedalus also because he does not pretend to be a bird against his nature but uses his human body, his human muscles, to 'rise into the air' (at least for a while): *Non iam mirabar sumtis te, Daedale, pinnis / isse per aetherios natura errante meatus: / hunc magis obstipui, coram qui plebe videnti / corpore, non pinnis, fastigia summa volavit* (ll. 8-11). Thus, the young acrobat turns into a new hero, he becomes a part and a protagonist of the new mythology in which miracles seen and performed by the contemporaries, the contemporary Carthaginians, replace those known from ancient legends. "Poetry and propaganda at the court of Hilderic?"[214] Most probably, yes. But we should also remember how diverse, beautiful, yet at the same time ugly is the everyday life as described by our "Martial of the Vandals."

---

[212] It is quite interesting to compare two quite different interepretations of the point, Rosenblum's and Dal Corobbo's. For Rosenblum (1961: 223), "so many wild beasts will be removed from their haunts for use in the arena that the land from which they have been cleared will be used for cultivation." For Dal Corobbo (2006: 253), "gli animali selvatici che di solito devastano le colture, ora temono il destino che il circo riserverebbe loro."

[213] Line 7: *atque meo gravior levis extitit ille periclo* turns out quite difficult to understand as Rosenblum's (1961: 163) incorrect translation shows ("though weighed down by my wager he turned out to be light enough"). The point is – as Tandoi (1970: 62) and later Happ (1986 II: 439), followed by Dal Corobbo (2006: 305), emphasized – that *periculum* must be interpreted as *damnum*, in a legal sense, "ne rispondo io," as Dal Corobbo specifies. So the poet (unintentionally) has turned responsible for the fact that the youngster might have lost his skills. And there is more. In fact, the poet as the eye witness of the event (it is quite interesting that the poem is written in such personal tone and perspective) risks that, if the acrobat does not repeat his performance – which is quite probable, considering that he has drunk so much –, he will lose his credibility.

[214] As it can be easily guessed, I paraphrase the title of the book by Cameron 1970.

Some of Luxorius's epigrams can be classified as ecphrastic. These are descriptions of pieces of art: paintings, mosaics, sculptures, and reliefs.[215] The poet's interest in this field and these themes can be also interpreted as another common point between him and his 'classical' model, although – needless to say – the tradition of ecphrastic epigram starts long before Martial. Such poems, although frequently exploiting motifs of scarce originality (which can be hardly surprising, in fact), reveal the same unique sense of observation that we have already seen in Luxorius's scoptic pieces; they also allow us to learn about his concept of aesthetics.

Paradoxically, I propose to begin this brief overview from a text of which one cannot be certain whether or not it should be considered a description of art, a painting or a sculpture, whereas thematically it, once again, concerns wildlife. One of the finest, in my view, Luxorius's epigrams depicts a she-bear's parturition (331 R).[216] The poet starts from quoting a belief, indeed very popular throughout antiquity, that bears are born wholly shapeless and it is only their mothers who lick them into shape.[217] For Luxorius, this objective fact (as the ancients thought) turns into the epitomization of the creative process. The she-bear becomes an artist, a craftsman (*faber*, l. 6; see the expert terms used in the text: *expolit*, *creat*, *formatur*, *lingua magistra*, i.e. the tongue as a chisel, *sculpendo facit crescere membra*) who – by sculpting in an unformed, lifeless block of stone and changing it into a desired, finished shape – in a sense gives life to her (or his, *mutatis mutandis*) work. Thus, creating is almost generating; indeed, the mother bear seems to

---

[215] Certainly, as ecphrastic can be defined also the poems I have already mentioned, describing buildings, like *De amphitheatro* (346 R) or *De thermis* (350 R). Now, I shall concentrate specifically on epigrams treating sculptures, reliefs, mosaics, paintings as my main aim is to point out some aspects related to Luxorius's attitude to art (and its objectives) as such.

[216] It is worth quoting the poem in Art Beck's English translation, published in *Artful Dodge* 28/29, available online at: http://www3.wooster.edu/artfuldodge/introductions/2829/beck.htm [May 20, 2010]

Lambere nascentis fertur primordia prolis
ursa ferox, placido cum facit ore genus.
Expolit informes labris parientibus artus
et pietas subolem rursus amore creat.
Attrito truncum formatur corpore pignus,
dum sculpendo facit crescere membra faber.
Officium natura suum permisit amanti:
formam post uterum lingua magistra parit.

They say, that when the fierce bear gives birth, she gently
forms her baby with her mouth,
shines and polishes its pliant, shapeless body
with her lips and, with pious devotion,
once more, tenderly, creates another generation.

The way a master craftsman sculpts
a soft clay limb into life, she molds the flesh
of her exhausted, battered whelp
into something promising.

Nature has surrendered its good duty
to a loving creature--who licks things into shape
first with her uterus, and then
with her wise tongue.

[217] For the general explanation of the phenomenon, see already Rosenblum 1961: 210; Radif 2002: 12 n. 12; Dal Corobbo 2006: 228, who also points at ancient texts exploiting the belief.

give birth twice: *formam post uterum lingua magistra parit* (l. 8). Creation is an act of love comparable only to maternal affection (*Officium natura suum permisit amanti*, l. 7; *et pietas subolem rursus amore creat*, l. 4). The wildlife, Luxorius appears to be saying, gives the best, the model example of what the art is and what it should be. At the same time, this unusual image also shows how interrelated art and nature are in our poet's view. The two worlds, the two orders do (and should) overlap.[218]

In fact, for Luxorius good art should imitate nature. Describing a relief on the bottom of a cup or a plate (a *discus*) – an example of applied art par excellence, in which a *rustica*[219] removes a thorn from Satyr's foot (371 R)[220] – the author emphasizes first of all the realism of the scene: *Nil falsum credas artem lusisse figuris: / viva minus speciem reddere membra solent* (ll. 5-6). Rosenblum is quite right commenting that what we find here is "the Luxorian paradox: the copies are more lifelike than life itself,"[221] but it is worth remembering that a very similar version of this topos of realism in art[222] can be found already in Martial. The picture of Issa, Publius's favorite lapdog, is so realistic that it resembles her much better than she does herself.[223] In a sculpture of Hector that sweats on seeing Achilles (367 R) – the two figures apparently face each other[224] – Luxorius admires precisely the 'true' sweat and the 'true' fear: (*verus sudor*, l. 3; *testaturque suam viva formidine mortem*, l. 9). Wondrous art seems to reverse the laws of the underworld (*ars mira potest legem mutare barathri*, l. 7). Signs of life infused by the goddess herself (*Cypris candidulo reddita marmore / veram se exanimis corpore praebuit*, ll. 1-2) can be found also in the sculpture of Venus (356 R) with flowers growing on it.[225]

---

[218] Radif (2002: 13) notes acutely: "In una visione platonica dell'arte come imitazione della natura avremmo pertanto, nel caso dell'orsa di Lussorio, una natura che chiede aiuto all'imitazione di se stessa per portare a compimento il proprio lavoro."

[219] I have maintained the original word as what has been discussed about the epigram is, in fact, the very age of the female protagonist, to the extent that whereas Ziehen (1898: 51) first saw in her an old country woman, Rosenblum (1961: 161) translated *rustica* as a "country girl." What is really important though is that the adjective has clearly Ovidian connotations: *rustica* – "quae amoris vim non sentit," which adds to the scene as pictured by our poet (his favorite) allusively obscene overtone, see Zurli 1994a.

[220] On the poem, see specifically Tandoi 1964; Zurli 1994a; Razzetti 2002: 182-187.

[221] Rosenblum 1961: 246.

[222] It is, in fact, a topos as literary as others and Dal Corobbo (2006: 299) is right to call it this way.

[223] See Mart. 1.109.18-23: *picta Publius exprimit tabella, / in qua tam similem videbis Issam, / ut sit tam similis sibi nec ipsa. / Issam denique pone cum tabella: / aut utramque putabis esse veram, / aut utramque putabis esse pictam.*

[224] In fact, as Dal Corobbo (2006: 292) notes, the poet, as usual, is not at all specific in his description. We cannot be sure if the statue is placed in Troy or rather presents Hector in Troy, whether it makes part of a group or not.

[225] On the poem, see specifically Zurli 1993: 38-43; Ottria 2002: 66-72. Dal Corobbo (2006: 274) is not wrong in his observations, but I find his judgment of this poem definitely too harsh.

A peculiar quality of art stressed by our poet is the ability to express the essence of a certain thing or notion. What strikes in the image of Fame (313 R)[226] to be seen on a circus stable are her actual features: *Verum, Fama, tibi vultum pictura notavit, / dum vivos oculos iuncea forma gerit. / Tu, quamvis totum velox rapiaris in orbem, / pulcrior hoc uno limine clausa sedes*. An artist depicting a hunter has done well stressing the man's skill by painting eyes on his hands (334-335 R).[227]

What is sometimes possible in art is a surprising convergence between the subject of a certain work, a sculpture for instance, and the way in which it has been made. A bronze Chimera "has endured the flames that she formerly spewed forth"[228] (355 R). At the same time, this 'artificial' Chimera, thanks to the flames, has been improved: she is not dangerous any more like the 'real' or rather mythical one: *facta est melior Chimaera flammis* (l. 3). Contemporary culture once again excels ancient legends. On the other hand, art can also change and reverse some conventional associations or topoi. Neptune as a fountain figure (348 R) now reigns over sweet waters (*Post pelagus dulces hic tibi dantur aquae!*, l. 2).[229] Cupid turned into a little statue (347 R), through art, pours forth water now instead of burning his victims with fire as he used to do (*pro facibus proprias arte ministrat aquas*, l. 2).[230]

Unique among Luxorius's ecphrases, even because of its very length (22 lines, a true *epigramma longum*), is the poem dedicated to Fridamal (304 R), a text of both ecphrastic and laudatory character. It can be easily divided into two, almost equal parts. The first one describes a huge tower situated in the garden, a place of relaxation for its owner. A careful reader should certainly discover in this true *locus amoenus* some echoes of Statius's ecphrases of the villas of Manilius Vopiscus at Tibur (*Sil.* 1.3) or of Pollius Felix at Surrentum (*Sil.* 2.2).[231] The beauty of nature neighbors the beauty of culture: a grove, fountains, a statue of Diana, beautiful rooms full of masterpieces. One mosaic seems of

---

[226] The preceding poem (312 R) is a sort of praise of Fame in which, interestingly, Fame is syncretized with Fortune.

[227] Rosenblum (1961: 215) is most probably right complaining that what our poet praises is a "remarkably primitive style of painting." Indeed, we are not obliged to believe that what Luxorius classifies as a 'masterpiece' was such in truth. The motif of eyes on hands sounds undoubtedly much more original in the poem on the blind 'artist of eroticism' as I have labeled the protagonist of 357 R. On the other hand, George (2004: 142) seems right noting that Luxorius, in the two pieces, "reflects the well-attested interest in magic."

[228] Rosenblum 1961: 153.

[229] The text, however two verses long, is not free from interpretive problems, especially the first line (*Quam melior, Neptune, tuo sors ista tridenti est*) in which one has to decide whether to maintain the lection of the A *tridenti*, as Shackleton Bailey (1982: 271) and Dal Corobbo (2006: 124 & 257) do, or to follow the Bellovacensis with the lection *tridente*, as Rosenblum (1961: 149) and Happ (1986 I: 52) propose.

[230] Quaglia (2002: 34-35) notes that what may be implied here may be hot water and if so, the poem could be seen as a subtle allusion to Martial's 5.1.6: *sive salutiferis candidus Anxur aquis*. It may be worth adding that this contrast between fire and water, both treated here as emblems of Amor, can recall the charming scene of Dracontius's *Medea* showing Amor emerge from the water.

[231] See already Rosenblum 1961: 190; Fassina 2006: 139.

special value; to be found inside of the building, it depicts the addressee, Fridamal, slaying a wild boar. The second part of the poem is focused on this 'piece of work'. What is interesting is the fact that the whole description is directed at the very addressee of the epigram: it is he to be cast in a double or even triple role: he is the dedicatee of the text, the theme of the mosaic, and the ideal spectator to whom it is presented (= described): *admiranda tuae tamen est virtutis imago, / Fridamal, et stratae gloria magna ferae* (ll. 13-14). Of all pictures described by Luxorius this very mosaic probably will not be remembered particularly well by us, his contemporary readers (unless we believe our poet that it was, indeed, a masterpiece[232]). What we may find most relevant about it is rather the fact that its main aim seems to be to show the courage and the strength of the youngster. The boar as depicted on the mosaic is laid low by sudden death even before the blow (of Fridamal's spear) penetrated its body.[233] *De turre in viridiario* is, as mentioned above, not less an ecphrasis than a clear-cut *laudatio*. Fridamal in the scene of hunting is portrayed – what a careful (and well-educated) reader will also easily notice – as a typical Roman brave young man, indeed like the one we know from Horace's letter to Lollius (*Epist.* 1.18.44-52).[234] Besides, the braveness of his hero (apparently, in the full sense of the word) and addressee is emphasized by the poet himself: *qui solitae accendens mentem virtutis amore* (l. 15). In fact, as I have already noticed, Fridamal seems to be one of very few protagonists of the *epigrammaton liber* treated by Luxorius with such authentic respect that may, indeed, induce us to suppose that in this case the person is particularly important, even dear in a sense, to our poet[235] and, at the same time, this is someone truly outstanding, maybe preparing himself to assume the leading role in the state one day. If we accept Alessia Fassina's conjecture that Fridamal might have been Thrasamund and Amalafrida's son, who died too early to be noticed and mentioned by the historians, we can certainly read the epigram 304 R as propagandistic.[236] Undoubtedly, *De turre in viridiario* emphasizes all that should be emphasized in a text of this sort: the richness, the excellent taste,

---

[232] Or unless we take into consideration the data provided by archaeology. As noted by Clover (1978: 15), the famous hunting mosaic found at Bordj-Djedid in the nineteenth century offers a striking parallel to Luxorius's description. See also Strzelczyk 2005: 289-290.

[233] I paraphrase Rosenblum's (1961: 123) translation. The American scholar proposes the following interpretation of the passage (p. 191): "The paradox in this poem is that instead of having the boar take the charge on his speed and letting it bleed to death, Fridamal hit the animal so hard that he concussed it to death. The boar dropped before the spear penetrated its body (*ante ictum*)." Bertini (2008: 495 & 500-501) suggests that what Luxorius actually criticizes in the poem is lack of realism of the scene. I am not sure, however, if this is the case. We should note that in 335 R, the poem about the hunter, a very similar motif can be found: *signatum veluti contulit exitium* (l. 4). In *De turre in viridiario*, this motif is only amplified.

[234] As noticed also by Fassina 2006: 140. Both in Horace and in Luxorius, the youngsters hunt for boars, which clearly symbolizes virtue. See above in Part Two Ch. II. 2 for parallel motif in Maximianus's 'elegy' 1.

[235] In Fassina's (2006: 143-145) view, Fridamal could have been Luxorius's patron. She also proposes an interesting interpretation of Luxorius's cento *Epithalamium Fridi* as written precisely for Fridamal.

[236] See Fassina 2006: 140 & 142.

the courage, and the truly 'princelike' leisure activities of the youngster, who, in addition, resembles Roman aristocrats and even Roman emperors.[237] If so, the epigram portraying Fridamal seems to encode one more message: our resurrected *Karthago* is Roman again. The Vandals themselves turned Romans.

III. 2. 3. 3. Laudationes *and* epitaphia

In comparison with scoptic pieces in the *epigrammaton liber*, the laudatory ones are definitely less frequent. They can be found, though. A unique addressee of Luxorius's praises is Fridamal, as mentioned right above. Laudatory in their overall sense are the poems about the hundred-leafed rose or the gardens. A charming praise of the poet's dog – indeed comparable to Martial's 1.109 – is the text 359 R.[238]

Artists, circus performers, charioteers are much more often reproached than complimented by the Carthaginian. We may probably still remember the short Macedonia (310 R), the ugly Cattula (361-362 R), the charioteer Pascasius who often falls (327 R) or the anonymous Egyptian charioteer of the Greens (324 R) who does the same thing as if he were Icarus and Phaethon, Cyriacus, the old charioteer, cursing the unwilling public (306 R), or, finally, Vico (336 R) who could win if only *corruptor* ei *sit recto ponendus* (l. 5).[239] Nevertheless, one can also find true heroes among Luxorius's protagonists. One of them is the impressively skillful youngster who leaped above the balcony of the amphitheater (373 R). Besides, there are charioteers meriting praise. The Egyptian Memnon (293 R), black like his mythical namesake, will never share the latter's fate: there will be no Achilles to conquer him.[240] Praiseworthy is also Iectofian (328 R), the charioteer of the Greens, similarly compared, or even contraposed, to another mythical figure, Pelops. Pelops won only one praise, Hippodamia, the addressee of the present text won many. Once again, the present surpasses the past and turns more mythical than myth itself.[241]

The longest of Luxorius's *laudationes* is dedicated to the circus hunter, the Egyptian Olympius (353 R). Actually, our poet focuses on this protagonist in two texts, first in the *laudatio* and right after in the epitaph. The typicality of topoi and expressions exploited in the two poems should not blind us to their quality and originality. Olympius is praised for his truly mythical Heraclean strength (*Alcides collo scapulis cervice lacertis*, 353 R, l. 4) but also for his black skin (*Nil tibi forma nocet nigro fuscata colore*, 353 R, l. 6). The similes employed here are obviously regular,[242] but at the same time they make the description

[237] Fassina (2006: 141-142) justly stresses that the picture of Diocletian hunting for a wild boar given in the *Historia Augusta* 15.26 has a clearly ideological-propagandistic overtone.

[238] For the interpretation of this, quite lovely, piece, see Radif 2002: 14-19.

[239] In original: *corruptor tibi.*

[240] Interestingly, the epigram is placed in the book right after the two poems about unusual animals, the fish and the boar, and before the first scoptic piece. As it appears, Luxorius does not intend to start his book right from satiric texts.

[241] On the other hand, it is certainly not coincidental that the poem is preceded by the epigram about Pacasius (327 R), the charioteer who often falls.

[242] As noted by Copello (2002: 84-85), but, in my view, her judgment of the poem is too harsh.

sensual and aestheticizing.[243] Yet what is stressed above all is the popularity, even love, that Olympius has won among his fans. It is this very love that has made him uniquely beautiful in their eyes (*Grata voluptatis species et causa favoris*; *Postremum tanto populi pulcrescis amore, / foedior est quantum pulcher sine viribus alter*, 353 R, ll. 1 & 13-14). Thus, Luxorius indeed looks at the sportsman from the perspective of the public,[244] the crowd that admires and loves him.

In the epicedium (354 R) – I find the term appropriate due to the measure used by the author, the hexameter, and because of the structure of the poem, dominated by the laudatory part – Luxorius emphasizes again the charm and popularity of the hero, the popularity owed not only to his skill but also to moral qualities[245] (*saepe placens, agilis, gratus, fortissimus, audax*; *qui, licet ex propria populis bene laude placeres, / praestabas aliis ut tecum vincere possent*, 354 R, ll. 2 & 5-6). The epigram – which is quite natural in this context – exploits the motif of *puer senex* (*qui puer ad iuvenes dum non advixeris annos, / omnia maturo conplebas facta labore*, 354 R, ll. 3-4).

In the second, lamentative, part of the text one can find typical exclamations (*Heu! Nunc tam subito mortis livore peremptum / iste capit tumulus*, 354 R, ll. 9-10). More stress is, however, given to another aspect, Olympius's immortality resulting from fame: *Sed nihil ad Manes hoc funere perdis acerbo: / vivet fama tui post te longaeva decoris / atque tuum nomen semper Carthago loquetur* (354 R, ll. 12-14).

It is hard not to have an impression that the epigrams dedicated especially to Olympius, as well as to some other skillful sportsmen from circus arenas, do express the poet's admiration for those individuals but also (and above all) for the entire Carthaginian culture, in particular the one of circus and sport in general, the culture that, eventually, took captive her rude (Vandal) conqueror and resurrected in the new, somewhat changed context: there are now Vandal rulers sitting on the balconies of amphitheatres, the very same Vandal rulers erect splendid buildings and whom they (as well as we all) admire are black-skinned athletes.

Epitaphion de filia Oageis infantula (345 R), if compared with the one for Olympius, however similarly composed in hexameters, is more 'lyrical' in its general tone. It opens with a lamentative part; worth noting is besides its very regular structure: *lamentatio*, *laudatio*, and *consolatio* have six verses each. The *lamentatio* abounds in exclamations and emotionally marked expressions, the very first words of the poem being *Heu dolor!* (see also l. 5: *Quam facile offuscant iucundum tristia lumen!*). The *laudatio* exploits the motif of *puella anus* and does it in a very charming manner, adapting it to the person of the protagonist. The little Damira, a three-year-old girl, delighted with her beauty and bashfulness – which is, in fact, a traditional, stereotypic so to speak, virtue of women, especially the young ones, but also objectively a quite typical (= real) feature of children this age – as well as with her sweet, bird-like voice[246] and speaking skills. Luxorius once

---

[243] As noted justly by Laville 1974: 277.

[244] See Laville 1974: 283.

[245] On the *kalokagathia* of Olympius as stressed by Luxorius, see also Laville 1974: 277; Dal Corobbo 2006: 271.

[246] See Copello (2002: 78-79) for a very good analysis of the passage.

again brilliantly combines a conventional compliment with an acute observation. It is just normal, and indeed very true, that a three-year-old child speaking fluently excites admiration of all adults. A laudatory topos as elaborated by the Carthaginian changes into a lovely, but realistic, portrait of the sweet little girl:

grata nimis specie, verecundo garrula vultu,
naturae ingenio modicos superaverat annos.
Dulce loquebatur, quidquid praesumpserat ore,
linguaque diversum fundebat mellea murmur,
tamquam avium vernare solet per tempea cantus. (8-12)

The *consolatio* presents the gentle little soul among the just. At the same time, it is also a subtle praise of the victorious general Oageis, who heard about his daughter's death while he was defending Libya. The poem closes with the phrase: *ipsaque sub tali flevit Victoria casu* (l. 18). Probably, it is already now when we really learn about the actual reasons behind the composition of the epitaph that, certainly, could have been written as a gift for Oageis. Still, it is quite hard, at least in my view, to agree with Giuliana Laville that "la circostanza del carme sembra essere per Lussorio più la vittoria del padre che la morte della figlia."[247] The praise of Oageis is woven into this whole mournful context with a remarkable tact and the charm with which the little protagonist is depicted makes the poem worth reading and remembering not merely as a conventional *munus* for a powerful friend.

III. 2. 4. LUXORIUS'S EPIGRAMS: FINAL REMARKS

Presumably, the labels "the Martial of the Vandals" or "the Carthaginian Martial" were applied to Luxorius almost automatically. It seemed quite obvious that a late, 'twilight' author must have been an epigone who strove as hard as possible to imitate his grand ancestor, even though he would have never – he simply could not have – been successful in such emulation. A copy, in principle, cannot be better than the original.[248]

Already Rosenblum, reapplying the label, added with some reservation: "Luxorius may be called the Carthaginian Martial, but his canvas is exceedingly small. As a word painter of life in Carthage he does not reveal to us a detailed view of his city comparable to the Roman scenes illustrated by the epigrams of Martial. We learn little about the everyday doings of the Carthaginians and even less about the poet's activities. We miss Martial's personal touch; we are not invited by Luxorius to accompany him on his daily rounds."[249] Nowadays, scholars are even more hesitant to use the epithet, stressing that

[247] Laville 1974: 277.

[248] As expressed clearly even by Courcelle in his review to Rosenblum's edition, quoted justly by Dal Corobbo 2006: 50: "supporte mal la comparaison même avec un Martial." The expression "Vandalorum Martialis" dates back to Meyer (1835) and as such it does epitomize the approach of the nineteenth century philology.

[249] Rosenblum 1961: 52.

the Martialian influences in Luxorius are, in point of fact, not as ubiquitous and as obvious as we would expect.[250]

Indeed, even a comparative reading of a few texts devoted to parallel subjects shows that it is very rare that we can speak of an emulation *sensu stricto*, i.e. a situation when the Carthaginian in his single poem evokes one single poem by his predecessor, employing the same meter, the same topoi, and, finally, the same theme. What is more frequent is, for instance, a tendency to surpass Martial in a selected aspect, especially in realism or even turpism of treatment. It is best exemplified by the epigram on the medical procurer Marinus, who undoubtedly can hardly find a true counterpart among Martialian doctors. Luxorius, which is quite certain on the other hand, does read the poet from Bilbilis thoroughly, but elaborating single motifs, he quickly walks his own way, at times developing or completing Martial's 'hints' or observations. Consequently, a Martialian blind man who *plus amat quam videt* turns into the brilliant erotomaniac characterized by a *docta libido*. Hence also the conclusion that the unnatural meekness, of beasts and of humans, results just from fear is expressed more clearly than it is in Martial.

As I have already explained, I have decided to quote the term "Martial of the Vandals" not to point out Luxorius's epigonism or Luxorius's close resemblance to Martial in every single poem of his (which is simply not true), but – on the contrary – to emphasize his poetological self-consciousness, indeed comparable to the one of his predecessor, *si parva licet componere magnis*, one book against twelve. The poet from Bilbilis proposed his very clear vision of the epigrammatic genre, which should have a well-defined origin (as we remember, Catullus was cast, somewhat forcefully, as the *archegetes* of the genre), a well-defined metrical profile (similarly Catullan, but much more distich-oriented), a well-defined taste (the *sal Romanae Minervae* as opposed to the *lepos Cecropius*), and, finally, a well-defined name, the *epigramma* (which of course situated the genus also in the context of Greek epigrammatic writing and not in the context of lyric forms, as Pliny would see the *carmina minora*). Martial's contemporaries, as well as authors composing minor poetry in subsequent centuries, did not have a comparably 'clear vision' of the genre they practiced.

Only Luxorius can be juxtaposed with Martial in this respect. Like Martial, he seems more precise than his fellow littérateurs[251] in describing the genre he develops and, as it appears, he defines it with an eye to Martial's *epigramma*. It is true that the very term *epigramma* appears in Luxorius only once, but it appears in the programmatic piece, *Ad*

[250] See especially Zurli 2007: 123-124.

[251] Thus, I must say that I both agree and disagree with Loriano Zurli, cited above, who emphasizes that it is quite shallow to see in Luxorius the Carthaginian Martial since Luxorius never actually quotes Martial whereas the author of the *Sylloge* does. Certainly, it is not quotations or even very clear-cut allusions that make Luxorius the follower of Martial (and from this standpoint, I can only agree with Zurli). If he is comparable with (and even *to*) Martial, it is only because of some *systematic* qualities of his book that I have pointed out throughout this chapter. On the other hand, the poet of the *Sylloge* does quote Martial and he certainly reads him very closely, but he reads him somewhat differently from Luxorius. He certainly appears to be less 'theoretic' in his approach to the genre: he does not use the keyword *epigramma*, he pays much less attention to the measures and as such he is less comparable with Martial than Luxorius.

Faustum, and – which may be even more relevant – it appears *only* in Luxorius. Neither the author of the *Sylloge* nor Ennodius – presumably two most important epigrammatists among Luxorius's contemporaries – *ever* used it.[252]

Following the poet from Bilbilis, the Carthaginian also composes a book (*liber*) of deliberate structure in which *iuxtapositio* is intertwined with *variatio*, the book preceded by a lengthy (longer than in Martial) introductory part. It should be added that a similar collection is also the epigrammatic oeuvre by an anonymous author, most probably a Luxorius's compatriot, the so-called *Unius poetae sylloge*. Yet the poet of the *Sylloge* cannot be really compared to Luxorius if the polymetrics is taken into account. In fact, even Martial cannot.

At the same time, as we know, Luxorius's metrical triad is not a mere repetition of the Martialian one; it is similar but not identical (distich, Phalaecean, hexameter instead of distich, Phalaecean, scazon). Besides, the proportions are different, even though the dominant position of the elegiac distich is evidently maintained. This is so precisely because of a larger metrical diversity. The same could be said about the content of Luxorius's poems. It is also relevant to mention, as pointed out above, the general convergence between the Carthaginian and the author from Bilbilis. Both define the satiric (scoptic) coloring as essential and distinctive quality of their epigram; both, however, focus also on more serious themes. Both are capable of noticing the beauty of nature, art, architecture, and sport.

Nevertheless, as Rosenblum pointed out, Luxorius's canvas is, indeed, exceedingly small. On the one hand, the poet tries to be – and is – realistic, even veristic in his descriptions. Therefore, he does not give us types embodying, for example, usual drawbacks of certain professions and professionalists, but instead individuals who have a few more personal traits than only the lack of professionalism. On the other hand, the individuals he chooses are so extra-ordinary in their misfortune, physical defects, deviations, bad habits that they seem almost unearthly. They are not less unnatural than the trained fish, the panthers changed into hound dogs, the colocasia growing in a house or the well dug in a dry mountain. In fact, Luxorius's *liber* does not offer us a panorama of everyday life in Carthage in the first three decades of the sixth century, although it does provide some – fragmentary (!) – information. What we can learn is that in that Carthage there were schools (maybe it was not only *grammatici furiosi* to teach there), courts (since there were lawyers, whatever they might be like), there were spectacles in theaters (at least pantomimic), games, amphitheaters (erected even on country estates), there were rulers and aristocrats who loved to be surrounded by beautiful things, stayed in beautiful environment, and cultivated Roman (!) traditions. All these are a kind of mosaic cubes of which the reader can try to compose *a* picture. In this picture, we must place somewhere the noisy and raging dwarf, the hundred-leafed rose, the old charioteer cursing his public, and the young acrobat who leaps above the balcony in the amphitheater.

Martial, most probably, intended to describe in his twelve books of *epigrammata* and the *Liber de spectaculis* the whole truth about his Rome, her splendor, filth, usual citizens met in the Via Flaminia, and her 'celebrities'. Luxorius – which, in my view, shows his

[252] And, as mentioned above, Sidonius Apollinaris uses it in a completely different and much less precise sense.

originality and not his inferiority to the predecessor – laid emphasis precisely on the extremes. In fact, his *liber* is not a mirror that should reflect the Carthaginian daily life but rather a synthesis and, indeed, a metaphor. Therefore, his collection – again *unlike* the ones by Martial – is not dedicated to an average reader but only to the one proficient in decoding hidden meanings.

As I have said, Luxorius's ugly individuals are not less symbolic in their 'realism' than the superb buildings and the new heroes. What is represented – not literally but in a figurative sense – by those strange people, unnatural animals, wonders of architecture is the new (old) Carthage. It is the *Karthago* whose ruins, a few generations before, were "the mere byplay of barbarians." But it is also the *Karthago* whose current citizens – including Luxorius and his public, the Roman intellectual elite born after the 'end of the world' in 439 A.D. – enjoyed again a period of certain stabilization, however fragile and marked with bloodshed at the courts of the Vandal rulers. Finally, this is the *Karthago* where – thanks to those barbarian rulers – culture, popular as well as high, the eternal pride of the African metropolis, started to regain its former splendor. Hence, the Carthage of paradoxes. And it is paradoxes – a figure loved by Luxorius and ideal, indeed, in its conciseness and symbolicalness – that are used to describe that truly unusual moment in history.

III. 3. Luxorius and his contemporary epigrammatic writing

III. 3. 1. *UNIUS POETAE SYLLOGE*

III. 3. 1. 1. The sylloge *and its characteristics*

In the poem *Ad Faustum* opening his *liber epigrammaton*, Luxorius asks the addressee to distribute his juvenile 'trifles' among friends, encouraging them to review these texts. We shall never know it for certain (it is obvious), but it is not at all impossible that the anonymous author of the *Sylloge* might be one of those Luxorius's *sodales*.[253] Anyhow, it seems more than probable that whoever wrote the epigrams published by Riese as cc. 90-197, it was not only a Luxorius's contemporary but also a close reader and sometimes an imitator of his poetry.[254]

It is now generally accepted that 90-197 R should be attributed to one author.[255] What is even more relevant though, is the fact that the poems can – and should – be

[253] It is, indeed, tempting to see it this way, even though it cannot be proven of course. Nevertheless, it is logical to conclude that the author of the *Sylloge* is an African poet of Luxorius's milieu, see Zurli 2007: 125-126. Another of Luxorius's *sodales* might have been Coronatus (see Zurli 2005a: 41-42) and still another the anonymous author of *versus serpentini* (see esp. Zurli's and Paolucci's notes in Zurli – Scivoletto – Paolucci 2008: 33-36 & 87-96).

[254] See the arguments gathered by Zurli 2007: 15-19; 115-126; quite similarly (and independently from Zurli) Kay 2006: 1-7.

[255] See especially Zurli's (2007: 45-68) analysis of the poet's metrics and prosody.

seen as belonging to a sylloge (I have fully accepted Zurli's 'title'), a collection, a mixture of epigrammatic texts of various character: epideictic, descriptive, mythological, finally scoptic;[256] in addition, a collection showing some inner order. It is determined above all by the presence of pairs and – unlike in Luxorius – cycles of pieces dedicated to the same topic. Upon a closer look, one can even conclude that this may be the most important, certainly the easiest to notice,[257] factor behind the arrangement of the *Sylloge*. Apparently, to put it as simply as possible, the anonymous poet did like elaborating and re-elaborating the same subjects.[258]

There are, in sum, 22[259] pairs and cycles, in which one series is composed of *five* texts (*De balneis*, 119-123 R), two of four (*De iudicio Paridis*, 163-166 R; *De tabula*, 192-194 R[260]), five of three (*De malis Matianis*, 133-135 R; *De Narcisso*, 145-147 R; *De Galatea in vase*, 152-154 R;[261] *De citro* 169-171 R; *De capris* 186-188 R), and fourteen of two.[262] What is more, we can find a few sequences of such cycles: *De Europa* (143-144 R)–*De Narcisso* (145-147 R)–*De equa Filagri...* (148-149 R); *De iudicio Paridis* (163-166 R)–*De Hyacintho* (167-168 R)–*De citro* (169-171 R); *De Bumbulo* (190-191 R)–*De tabula* (192-194 R)–*De elephanto* (195-196 R). Interestingly, we can even speak here of a certain arrangement within the sequence: in the 143-149 R we have a pair–a triad–a pair, in the 190-196 R a pair–a tetrad–a pair, in the 163-171 R a tetrad–a pair–a triad.

The compositional order of the *Sylloge* is determined also by other more general analogies. Within the collection, one can find true segments, some of which quite large, of poems treating similar themes. The first one is placed right after the *Praefatio* and before

---

256 See below for more specific information. What I shall emphasize now is only the fact that this diversity makes Anonym's poems comparable with Luxorius's *liber* and different from at least two more collections of minor poetry (epigrammatic in a sense, but quite alien to the Martialian tradition) found in the *Anthologia Latina*, the above-mentioned *Anonymi versus serpentini*, and the *Aenigmata Symphosi*.

257 As Zurli (2007: 27) emphasizes. In fact, there are also other, subtler interrelations between the poems of the collection. For a thorough insight into the aspect, see Zurli's observations on pp. 21-34.

258 Already Riese (1894: XXI) notes shrewdly: "a *Praefatione* ... incipiens ... saepe plura easdem res *Aliter* rursusque *Aliter* ... quasi e certamine poetico orta describunt." In fact, if I am not mistaken in my calculations, out of 108 poems of the collection 56 (which is over a half) make part of a pair or a cycle. To be even more precise, 28 poems make part of a pair and 28 of a larger series.

259 Two poems though are lost and what is still extant are only titles: *De termis* (124-125 R, but the second piece is lost) and *De Iove in pluteo* (139-140, here similarly the second piece is not extant). Kay (2006: 191; 193; 239) sees it differently. In his view, the superscription *aliter* can be interpreted not only (as it usually is) as implying that what has been lost is an epigram treating the theme of the previous one but also, on the contrary, a piece dedicated to the theme of the subsequent one.

260 The piece labeled by Riese as 193 was divided into two poems by Shackleton Bailey and by Zurli; thus, 183 SB / 105 Z is the first six lines of Riese's 193, 184 SB / 106 Z is lines 7-14 of Riese's 193.

261 In fact, the cycle dedicated to Galatea could be interpreted even as a tetrad, only that the first of these poems (151 R) treats the very mythological heroine, the other three (152-154 R) Galatea as pictured on a salver.

262 See the list in Zurli 2007: 24. See also other Zurli's notes on the cycles and their characteristics (pp. 24-27).

the first scoptic piece and comprises texts having some Christian overtone (91-95 R), an epitaph (the only one we have from Anonym's pen) for a little Christian boy and a few shorter (and rather diverse) poems.[263] The cycle of epigrams on baths is also worthy of attention (119-123 R), preceded (not coincidentally, for certain) by a quatrain on Thetis and followed by two[264] pieces on hot rooms. One may find even more interesting – especially a reader somewhat disappointed by the performances of Luxorius's Macedonia and Gattula – a block of texts dedicated to various arts and artists (111-115 R). There is a sequence of scoptic pieces (127-131 R). Most often though mythological poems are juxtaposed. These may be typical cycles, like *De Narcisso* (145-147 R) and *De Hyacintho* (167-168 R), or a series of epigrams having a motif in common, for instance the unit on Jove and his love conquests (*<De Iove et Leda>–De ovo Ledae–De Europa–Aliter*, 141-144 R), the one on Galatea and her picture on a salver (151-154 R), or three texts describing sculptures of mythological protagonists (*De Daphne–<De Marsya>–De Philocteta*, 172-174 R). It is hardly coincidental that a distich on Bellerophon is followed by the one on the Chimera (97-98 R). However, the combination of pieces on the Trojan theme is particularly remarkable, composed of a cycle devoted to the judgment of Paris (163-166), preceded by a two-verse piece on Achilles (unfortunately corrupted, 161 R) and a hexametric distich *De Troia* (162 R).

The observations gathered above already allow us to conclude that the *Sylloge* is, indeed, an *opus epigrammaticum* comparable with Luxorius's *liber*. Still, comparable does not mean identical of course. The very epigrammatic tradition in its richness invites diversity and the anonymous author has his own, quite well-defined literary preferences. Luxorius's sense of humor is not at all alien to him; in fact, some texts by the two '*sodales*' merit a comparative reading, which will reveal their interrelations. But, in general, he composes much fewer satirical pieces (17 out of 108) and more epideictic[265] and descriptive. His true 'field of expertise' is mythology and the above-mentioned erudite mythological poems, quite rare in Luxorius.[266] In some cases, it is beyond doubt that these are ecphrastic texts (like the unit *De Daphne–<De Marsya>–De Philocteta*, 172-174 R). In others, it is less certain but not at all improbable.[267]

---

[263] *De velo ecclesiae* (91-91ᵃ R); *De christiano infante mortuo* (92 R); *De iudicio Salomonis* (93 R); *De cereo* (94 R); *Aliter* (95 R). As we can see, these texts are rather far from homogeneous if the content is taken into consideration. Nonetheless, their very presence is a certain difference in comparison with Luxorius. Especially the epitaph, much more Christian in tone than Luxorius's epitaph for the little Damira (345 R), shows that the anonymous author was, indeed, "prossimo alla spiritualità (e all'ortodossia) cristiana" (Zurli 2007: 118). It may not be wholly irrelevant that he placed these poems right after the *Praefatio*, which is a privileged position, needless to say.

[264] The second one missing though, see above.

[265] As emphasized already by Riese 1894: XXI.

[266] Which does not mean of course that Luxorius's pieces are easier to read, quite the contrary. Luxorius's mythological epigrams, or rather those in which he only evokes a mythological protagonist, are always ecphrastic: 312-313 R; 325 R; 347-348 R; 355-356 R; 367 R.

[267] Kay (2006: 86; 101; 171; 240; 242; 243; 246; 262; 291; 313; 319) supposes that ecphrastic could be also the poems on Bellerophon (97 R), Medea (102 R), Thetis (118 R), *<De Iove et Leda>* (141 R), *De ovo Ledae* (142 R), *De Europa* (143-144 R), *De Narcisso* (145-147 R), the very poem on

Generally speaking, Anonym's epigrams are also shorter than Luxorius's.[268] Like the latter, he avoids monostichs, but what he does write quite often are two-verse pieces.[269] On the other hand, he seems much less interested than his fellow in composing *epigrammata longa*; in fact, we have only three such texts from his pen.[270] Yet interestingly, it is precisely the lengthy 20-line poem *De circensibus* (197 R), an allegorical interpretation of the circus as an image of the universe, that concludes the collection, at least in the form in which we possess it now.

Finally the difference concerning metrics is significant, if not crucial. As I have stressed, the impressive – and impressively well-organized – polymetrics determines the structure of Luxorius's *liber epigrammaton* and constitutes an important factor of the poetics of the "Martial of the Vandals." The anonymous author, writing very 'classical' epigrams, certainly modeled on those by the poet from Bilbilis, as the quotation in *De lenone uxoris suae* (127 R) best exemplifies,[271] apparently does not pay attention to this aspect. His metrical portfolio, if juxtaposed with Luxorius's, is exceedingly limited: the elegiac distich prevails (98 texts), the second measure is the hexameter (presumably 6 poems[272]), the third the Phalaecean (3 texts); there is also one piece in the Lesser Asclepiad. These are, needless to say, very 'epigrammatic' meters and even those 'sanctioned' by Luxorius. Nonetheless, the fact that the *Praefatio* (besides remarkably short) is composed in the elegiac couplet indicates that the anonymous poet does not recognize – or does not intend to recognize – the unique, 'Catullan' value of the Phalaecean as used by Martial in his 1.1 and 'reconfirmed' by Luxorius in his *Ad Faustum*.

Similarly, Anonym can be hardly compared to the author of the *epigrammaton liber* if poetic self-consciousness is taken into account. At least, he does not turn his very self and his oeuvre into a theme on its own as his fellow does. The *Praefatio* is impressive, precisely, in its conciseness, reflecting an objective quality of Anonym's poetics: he prefers quatrains, indeed.[273] What is even more interesting though, the *Praefatio*, ostentatiously brief as it is, clearly alludes to Luxorius's introduction (I mean *Ad Faustum* but also *Ad lectorem*). This does prove the hypothesis that the author of the *Sylloge* is – and wants to be seen as – a close reader of Luxorius.

Galatea (151 R), not only those on Galatea on a salver (152-154 R), *De Hyacintho* (167-168 R), *De Pyrrho* (177 R), *De Sphinga* (180 R).

[268] Anonym's average is 5.8; Luxorius's – 8.2, see Mondin 2008: 428-429.

[269] Twenty in sum; in Luxorius we have only 3 such texts.

[270] 117 R, *Laus omnium mensuum* (24 ll.); 149 R, *Aliter* (14 ll.) a scoptic piece on the lawyer Filager; 197 R, *De circensibus* (20 ll.).

[271] The epigram closes with a line from Martial's 3.24.14, a poem on a Tuscan soothsayer who wanted to sacrifice a goat to Bacchus and, eventually, had his hernia cut by a bumpkin who thought that an ancient ritual so required: *dum iugulas hircum, factus es ipse caper*.

[272] The second line of the piece on Achilles (161 R) is corrupted and thus we cannot be sure whether it should be seen as hexametric or elegiac (as Shackleton Bailey proposes in his apparatus filling the lacuna). I find it more plausible that it was a two-verse poem in hexameters, considering the subject and (what seems even more important) the fact that the subsequent text, *De Troia*, is a hexametric distich.

[273] See Mondin 2008: 428.

90 R^2 / 78 ShB / 1 Z, *Praefatio*:

Parvula quod lusit, sensit quod iunior aetas,
quod sale Pierio garrula lingua sonat,
hoc opus inclusit. Tu, lector, corde perito
omnia perpendens delige quod placeat.

The first line evidently evokes Luxorius's quos *olim puer ... paravi* (*Ad Faust.*, 6; and in l. 23: *diverso et facili pudore lusit*) but also – what is not less worthy of notice – *nugis refertam frivolisque sensibus / et quam tenello tiro lusi viscere* (*Ad lect.*, 4-5). It should be added that the *parvula aetas*[274] in a sense amplifies Luxorius's *puer* and *tenellum tirum*.

The second line is even more interesting and richer in subtle allusions. We cannot certainly miss the word *sal* with its epigrammatic par excellence (Martialian) connotations. The topos of affected modesty is, however, equally important, the same that we recognize from *Ad Faustum* and *Ad lectorem*.[275] *Garrula lingua*, as N.M. Kay explained,[276] evokes the Ovidian version of the myth of the Pierides who tried to compete with the Muses but lost and were turned into *picae*. Thus, the anonymous author compares himself to a bird noted for garrulity and imitative faculties. On the one hand, this seems to be an excellent concept of epigrammatic poetry: epigrammatic, which means satirical (salty) and as such imitating and mocking human weaknesses. On the other hand, this is indeed an expression of the *affektierte Bescheidenheit*, so desirable in an epigrammatist and, all the more, in a late antique poet.

Finally, the *adlocutio ad lectorem* in lines 3-4 is also an element typical of the epigrammatic genre, in particular practiced by Martial.[277] It is worth emphasizing that an expert reader is given here, in point of fact, the rights of a critic who can judge and choose what he/she likes most. The decisive criterion is thus the pleasure, again, exactly like in Luxorius (*libenter inchoas*, *Ad lect.*, 9). At the same time, the very same reader – in a very subtle way – is 'obliged' to read first the whole work (*omnia*). In truth, one can hardly find better proof that what follows the *Praefatio* are not only poems penned by a single author but also a coherent unity.

---

[274] Kay (2006: 66) is right, indeed, that the *parvula* and the *iunior aetas* are hardly fully synonymic.

[275] See the passages emphasized above, *Ad Faust.*, 8: *insulsum puto quam magis legendum*; *Ad lect.*, 7: *sonat pusilli quae laboris schemate*. Interestingly, Kay (2006: 67) commenting Anonym's *sonat* in l. 2 notes that "the present tense of the verb contrasts with the past tense of the other verbs in the sentence (*lusit ... sensit ... inclusit*)." This is precisely what we have in Luxorius's *Ad lectorem*: *et quam tenello tiro lusi viscere? / Et forse doctis si illa cara est versibus, / sonat pusilli quae laboris schemate* (ll. 5-7).

[276] See Kay 2006: 66-67.

[277] Interestingly, the anonymous author who immediately addresses his *lector* is, in this aspect, closer to Martial than Luxorius who, as I have noticed above, first maintains the 'Catullan' convention and addresses a single, personalized reader (and critic), Faustus, and only later speaks *ad lectorem*.

III. 3. 1. 2. The poems: an overview

A careful reader will easily notice in the *Sylloge* several echoes of Luxorius's poetry; as we have seen, some can be found already in the *Praefatio*. There is, however, a poem constituting a true 'climax' of all these allusions and a clear example of an emulation *sensu stricto*. This is the epigram 181 R, *De catto qui comedens picam mortuus est*, modeled on the last text of the *epigrammaton liber*, 375 R, *De catto, qui cum soricem maiorem devorasset, apoplexiam passus occubuit*.[278] The choice can hardly be considered casual, firstly, because 375 R, being (most probably) the closure of Luxorius's collection and a very good piece indeed, must have been well remembered by his readers, secondly, because it was also remarkably brief (4 lines). The very 'event' was described as concisely as possible: *Immensi soricis cattus dum membra vorasset, / deliciis periit crudior ille suis* (ll. 1-2) and what was stressed in the remaining two verses was (as usual in Luxorius) the paradoxicalness of the whole situation: *Pertulit adsuetae damnum per viscera praedae; / per vitam moriens concipit ore necem*. Thus, there remains enough 'empty space': elements to be added or better developed. This is precisely what the anonymous poet does. He turns the Luxorian theme into a ten lines long true 'story' (which is quite a lot for his epigrams). We learn exactly what happens and why: a cat,[279] accustomed to consume mice, seizes a magpie in mistake for a mouse in the dark and voraciously swallows its whole head,[280] unfortunately the horny beak included. The description of the causes of the poor creature's agony is not less precise: *claudunt rabidam cornea labra gulam. / Faucibus obsessis vitalis semita cessit / et satur escali vulnere raptor obit* (ll. 6-8). Therefore, Anonym's version fully deserves to be called an amplification in which what is more elaborated, in comparison with the model, is the 'plot' as such (now we are given much more details than when reading Luxorius), but also its fabular,[281] or quasi-parabolic value, which in Luxorius is very discreet. Now, the cat is clearly labeled greedy (*vorax*, l. 4; *edax*, l. 5), which means 'guilty', and so punishable: *Poena ... praesens praedonem plectit edacem*. The very point highlights in a hyperbolic tone (this is precisely what makes it amusing) not just a punishment but even an unprecedented vengeance of the already dead magpie upon its killer: *Non habet exemplum volucris vindicta peremptae: / hostem pica suum mortua discruciat* (ll. 9-10).

De catto is certainly a unique case of literary emulation par excellence, proving that the anonymous Carthaginian poet did draw on his compatriot and (possibly) *sodalis*. In some other texts of the *Sylloge*, the Luxorian inspirations are less 'systematic' and obvious but not really hard to discover. This concerns above all scoptic epigrams. They are, as I have already noted, considerably less frequent in the *Sylloge* than in the *epigrammaton*

---

[278] 375 R was pointed out as an emulation of Luxorius's 181 R already by Schetter 1986: 304 = 1994: 465.

[279] It is interesting to note the alliteration imitating cat's purring, especially in the opening line of the poem: ***Mordaces morsu** solitus consumere mures*. There is something similar in Luxorius's 375 R, where in particular **r** but, in fact, also **m** are repeated throughout the poem (see the text above). Apparently, also in this respect Anonym imitates the author of the *epigrammaton liber*.

[280] I paraphrase Kay's (2006: 322) translation.

[281] This connotation seems quite palpable, yet interestingly, as Kay (2006: 322) observes, "there is nothing strikingly similar in the ancient fabular corpus."

liber; consequently, the list of Anonym's 'anti-heroes' is also much shorter but, nonetheless, quite varied.

Faults derided by the anonymous author are, in fact, quite varied. Interestingly, what he mocks at is even the black skin (182-183 R), which he finds almost inhuman, proper rather to a demon from hell: *Dira †atramentatum† rapiant sibi Tartara monstrum; / custodem hunc Ditis debet habere domus* (183 R, ll. 5-6). Most probably, the poet of the *Sylloge* was not more hostile to the black-skinned than many of his readers, the Carthaginian (white) Romans, but it is worth noting that in Luxorius we never find similarly adverse comment on color. Quite the contrary, let us recall the praises of Memnon, the son of Night (293 R),[282] or, especially, Olympius: *Nil tibi forma nocet nigro fuscata colore* (353 R, l. 6). Would it be that our Anonym, a racist apparently,[283] wanted to be also a bit anti-Luxorian, at least in this poem?

What he laughs at may be some quite 'ordinary' (for Luxorius probably too ordinary) physical ailments, like hernia.[284] The author of the *Sylloge* sees in it an amphora subject to potters' tax (137 R) or an extra head (thus the point of 138 R: *Nam te si addictum mittat sententia campo, / vispillo ignoret quod secet ense caput*, ll. 3-4). The situations he also finds amusing are paradoxical scenes of everyday life, like the fact that a husband, claiming descent from the line of Barbatus and the ferocious Varitinna, lets his wife beat him with her slipper and pull out his beard (156 R).[285] It is rather she to reveal some heroic[286] ancestry: *Illa Salautensi magis est de stirpe creata, / audet quae proprium sternere calce virum* (ll. 7-8). The scene as such is effective enough to elicit laughter, but – as we can see – part of the wit here are also the exemplary (at least to our poet) proper names: *Barbatus, Varitinna, Salautensis stirps*.[287] This shows that the anonymous author enjoys, at least at

[282] The analogies between Luxorius's 293 R and Anonym's 182-183 R are pointed out by Kay 2006: 325-326 and Zurli 2007: 120 n. 28. Interestingly, the poems on *Aegyptius* follow the one on the cat: apparently the poet deliberately juxtaposes the two texts alluding to Luxorius.

[283] In fact, he turns out racist also in the piece on Memnon, where he states clearly in the point: *Iam tunc monstratur maneat qui Pergama casus, / cum nigrum Priamus suscipit auxilium* (189 R, ll. 5-6).

[284] Martial pokes fun at men with hernias in 3.24 and 12.83, but these poems have nothing to do with Anonym's 137-138 R. Interestingly, as I have already mentioned, the poet of the *Sylloge* quotes the final of Martial's 3.24, a poem on a priest castrated by mistake by a rustic, in his text on a man who pimps his own wife (127 R). The quotation: *dum iugulas hircum, factus es ipse caper*, makes a good point for the piece describing a cunning Greek, a *leno uxoris suae*, who, unexpectedly, was deprived of his wife and home by the client he planned to cheat. Yet Kay (2006: 200) notes justly: "It is an interesting point whether the *AL* poet and his readers were aware of or concerned about the context of the quotation, or whether it had become proverbial for <<the biter bit>>."

[285] In point of fact, the situation described here is based on two quite common topics: claiming of false ancestry and husband-beating wives, see also Kay 2006: 273-274. Thus, one can really have doubts whether the protagonist is a 'real' person or whether he is rather a combination of comical motifs.

[286] Hence the use of typically epic verb *sternere* in the point, l. 8, see also Kay 2006: 275.

[287] The significance of these names is now lost, but some conjectures can be proposed, see Kay 2006: 273-275.

times, a sort of 'intellectual' humor, requiring certain erudition from his public.[288] Hence the mythological allusions, like in the point of the epigram mocking a mean miller who does not even hire an ass to turn his millstone but does the job himself (103 R): *Per te namque terens Cererem patiere labores, / quos quaerens natam pertulit ipsa Ceres* (ll. 7-8). Hence also the pun closing the piece on a doctor's student who has been ordered by his master to lead a saddled horse through public places (159 R): *Artis prolixae breviavit tempora doctor: / incepto puerum reddidit Hippocraten* (ll. 5-6). To understand the joke, one must possess an elementary knowledge of Greek. The poet's philological interests may be best exemplified by the final phrase of the text on a eunuch (109 R): *Omnem grammaticam castrator sustulit artem, / qui docuit neutri esse hominem generis* (ll. 5-6).[289]

A somewhat similar individual of unknown gender (*ignoti fabula sexus*, 129 R, l. 5) is the passive homosexual Martinus who has neither a female name, which would match more his preferences, nor 'martial' limbs. This is finally a protagonist of Luxorius's style. But a certain Bumbulus turns out even more Luxorian (190-191 R). He is a dwarf who loves the company of (most probably) a troupe of spear-carrying entertainers.[290] Interestingly enough, he does it for quite logical reasons: he can feel safe among them: *Sed ratio est: mixtus longis Pygmaeus in armis, / ne te deprensum grus peregrina voret* (190 R, ll. 3-4). Thus, Bumbulus seems to resemble a bit the short actress Macedonia and Myrro, fully understandable (if not praiseworthy) in his strange decisions. This is not the end though. Bumbulus, having adopted the name of a depraved charioteer – in which he has delighted his father, a sports fan[291] – surpasses his namesake in moral perversion. The charioteer was the pimp of young girls he kept at the circus, this Bumbulus procures old lecherous women. In other words, we have all we need here: physical deformation, pretending to be someone else, a sort of cunningness, panderism, sexual desires of old women, and even an attack on a circus charioteer, i.e. a true florilegium of Luxorius's characters.

---

[288] For similar reasons, I believe, he likes so much mythological themes, a preference he shares with another *poeta-grammaticus* (most probably) of the same Carthaginian milieu, the (similarly) anonymous author of *versus serpentini*, see the recent edition by Zurli – Scivoletto – Paolucci 2008. The point is though that (this is at least my impression) this sort of themes and this sort of humor give some flavor of 'professorialism', or even 'easy professorialism' I would say, to Anonym's epigrams, which is wholly absent in Luxorius. On the other hand, Luxorius is certainly more demanding and more intriguing to read.

[289] Zurli (2007: 122-123) points at some analogies between this poem and Luxorius's piece on a eunuch wearing a *mitella* (298 R). D'Angelo (1993) notes that grammatical metaphors of this kind were often exploited in poems treating of sexual deviations.

[290] I find Kay's (2006: 342-343) interpretation of the somewhat mysterious *conventus nostros* in l. 1 convincing.

[291] Lines 5-6: *Nec frustra ostendis proprio placuisse parenti / quod turpis nomen sumpseris heniochi* are understandable only if one reads the second piece dedicated to Bumbulus (191 R). There, the poet mentions his father's sports preferences: he supported the Greens. As it appears, Bumbulus's father was not at all aware of why his son adopted the name of the charioteer. As a matter of fact, after his father's death, having inherited his estate, Bumbulus has also turned out unfaithful: *Discordat multum contra suscepta voluntas: / dilexit genitor prasinum, te russeus intrat* (191 R, ll. 4-5). The sexual overtone of the phrase is quite clear.

Luxorian flavor is palpable especially in Anonym's epigrams treating of bestiality. It is worth noting, however, that Luxorius himself is paradoxically quite far from straightforward when elaborating on this theme. He is more than indirect when alluding at (possible) zoophilic preferences of the chaste beauty (364 R). He is similarly not at all literal speaking of Burdo (365 R). His Burdo, in point of fact, is not a mule, although the *scelus* he commits truly turns him into an animal:[292] *Surrexit duplex nostro sub tempore monstrum, / quod pater est burdo Pasiphaëque redit* (ll. 5-6).[293]

The author of the *Sylloge*, focusing on bestiality *sensu stricto*, does not hesitate to call it by its right name. The motif appears first in 130 R, *De Caballina meretrice*, describing a sporting lady who kicks during sex. Thus – the poet comments with an intriguing sensibleness – despite her shining beauty, she should be coupled with hairy mules: *hirsutis tamen est petenda mulis, / qui possint pariles citare iunctas* (ll. 5-6).[294] The pair of epigrams 148-149 R depicts the opposite situation, the protagonists of which include a male human, a lawyer Filager, and a female animal: his mare.

The two poems, quite long (12 and 14 verses, respectively), differ in meter and form. The first one, composed in the elegiac distich, is, indeed, a mini-story, revealing the same narrative skill of the anonymous poet that we have seen in his version of Luxorius's piece on the ill-fated cat.[295] We are provided with a quite exact characterization of the hero, a poor and hardworking lawyer (*Causidicus pauper media sub nocte lucubrans*, l. 1), who in addition (yet this is specified in the second piece) is very successful (*cuius voce sacrum tonat tribunal / et palmas capiunt lares Vitenses*, 149 R, ll. 2-3) and, above all, upright (*Defensor probe tristium reorum*, 149 R, l. 1) – which is truly laudable, considering his profession. A certain event is described with similar precision, and the scene may presumably be not less surprising for us, the readers, than for Filager himself:

Causidicus pauper media sub nocte lucubrans
cornipedis voluit terga fricare suae.
Sed cum corpus equae dextra famulante titillat,
invasit iuvenem prodigiosa Venus.

[292] To quote Ovid's Myrrha, *Met.* 10.324-328: *coeunt animalia nullo / cetera dilectu, nec habetur turpe iuvencae / ferre patrem tergo, fit equo sua filia coniunx, / quasque creavit init pecudes caper, ipsaque, cuius / semine concepta est, ex illo concipit ales.*

[293] Therefore, I must admit that I am myself not less surprised than Zurli (1993: 35) that Shackleton Bailey, a distinguished philologist as he was, did not understand the joke and labeled the title as unauthentic.

[294] The point of the poem, more than in other epigrams by Anonym, turns out quite difficult to understand (and as such somewhat Luxorian). Kay (2006: 207) follows Courtney's exposition: "[Caballina] should be coupled with mules able to urge on their yoke-partners whilst keeping them in step, whereas in her excitement she ignores Ovid's precept *ad metam properate simul* (*Ars* 2.727)." Zurli (2007: 92-93) specifies: "Durante l'accoppiamento, *Caballina* – a significant name – kicks; ad onta delle sue belle forme (vv. 3-4) essa è così *petenda* da *muli* insipidi e ruvidi, coi quali (paradossalmente, essendo questi quadrupedi sterili) s'adempie appunto, nel suo caso, al precetto ovidiano: sanno infatti tirare *iunctas* (scil. *calces*), e cioè <<coppiole>>, come fa lei."

[295] In fact, Luxorius himself does not compose epigrams being such 'mini-narratives', whereas Anonym does it quite willingly, also in his mythological poems.

Nam qua longa solet †quadrupia† carpere sessor,
subducens durae pendula crura viae,
hanc fovet, amplexum molitur dumque caballae
adterit adsiduo pene fututor hebes. (148 R, 1-8)

One must admit that Luxorius, in comparison with what we find here, is remarkably subtle. Thus, it seems more than probable that Anonym's intent is, indeed, to excel his fellow in the obscenity of treatment.

The piece closes with a point evoking – which also appears purposeful – the one made by Luxorius, precisely, in his text on Burdo:

Luxorius, 365 R:	Anonym, 148 R:
Surrexit duplex nostro sub tempore monstrum, *quod pater est burdo Pasiphaëque redit.* (5-6)	*Par crimen flammae nostris fors intulit annis:* *Pasiphae tauro, Filager arsit equa.* (11-12)

The second epigram on Filager (149 R) assumes the form of an 'appeal', a fervent 'petition' (see *rogamus* in l. 10) addressed to the "upright defender of the wretched accused:"[296]

Expellas animo nimis, rogamus,
mores inlicite libidinantes.
Horrendum vitium est in advocato
orando solito movere caulas
subantis pecudis tenere gambas. (10-14)

The whole text, even more than the previous one, is built upon the figure of contrast. The solemn style and the content are primarily contrasting (see especially the above quotation). A living contrast is, however, above all the very protagonist who combines the best personality traits: professionalism, dedication, and, to repeat, righteousness, with terrible deviation. Therefore, naturally enough, a reader conversant with Luxorius's poems must juxtapose him with some characters of the *epigrammaton liber*, and in particular with Marinus (302 R), seemingly a devoted doctor. Therefore, it may be not casual that the meter used here is the Phalaecean,[297] the measure of Luxorius's *In medicolenonem*. But, if Marinus only appears to be dedicated to his mission (the one of a doctor, yet he is undeniably much more involved in his other 'job'), Filager really *is* both good and terrible. This is a true paradox of the human nature, quite willingly described by our contemporary psychology. This paradox is (paradoxically) not taken into consideration by Luxorius, the suspicious rationalist. Once again, one may conjecture that portraying the lawyer who has gone astray, the anonymous author tries to compete with his '*sodalis*'.

This brief overview of scoptic epigrams by the poet of the *Sylloge*, focused in particular on texts somehow comparable with those by Luxorius, can be concluded with a juxtaposition of two, apparently, quite significant pieces. They are significant because presumably they are autothematic in a sense, even though – needless to say – our two poets would have never acknowledged that the protagonists they portrayed could represent

[296] Kay 2006: 254.

[297] Certainly, one can also point at the fact that the Phalaecean is used by the anonymous poet in the piece on Caballina (130 R), a (prospective) female zoophile.

themselves. It can hardly be considered a coincidence that both Luxorius and his anonymous fellow dedicated the first scoptic piece of their collections to the figure of a teacher (in this context, the position of *De magistro ludi neglegenti*, 96 R, in the *Sylloge* must be interpreted as another allusion to the *epigrammaton liber*[298]). School was, most probably, the natural environment of the two epigrammatists, a milieu that shaped their identity as Roman 'intellectuals' and maybe even their professional field (quite certainly so in the case of Luxorius, the *sophista*). Undoubtedly, school was the place and reality they looked at intently and critically.

Luxorius, 294 R, *Sapphicum in grammaticum furiosum*

Carminum interpres meritique vatum,
cum leves artem pueros docere
diceris vel te iuvenes magistrum
audiunt verbis veluti disertum,
cur in horrendam furiam recedis
et manu et telo raperis cruentus?
Non es, in quantum furor hic probatur,
dignus inter grammaticos vocari,
sed malos inter sociari Orestas.

Anonym, 96 R *De magistro ludi neglegenti*

Indoctus teneram suscepit cauculo pubem,
quam cogat primas discere litterulas.
Sed cum discipulos nullo terrore coercet
et ferulis culpas tollere cessat iners,
proiectis pueri tabulis Floralia ludunt.
Iam nomen ludi rite magister habet.

The two epigrams, *Sapphicum in grammaticum furiosum* and *De magistro ludi neglegenti*, are, in point of fact, utterly different. The piece by Luxorius may even seem quite astounding because of its ostentatious seriousness, emphasized by the use of epic vocabulary (*cur in horrendam furiam recedis / et manu et telo raperis cruentus*?, ll. 5-6).[299] Interestingly, the teacher depicted here might be either a *magister artis grammaticae* (as implied in line 2, where tender boys are mentioned) or a *sophista* since he is listened by young men following a course in rhetoric (ll. 3-4). This deliberate imprecision – one can hardly suspect that our poet, a professor himself, could not distinguish between various 'academic' ranks – is presumably aimed at stressing that similar 'mad teachers' (unfortunately) can be found everywhere. Luxorius's protagonist is not merely a Martialian *magister sceleratus*[300] but a madman *sensu stricto*, engulfed by an Orestean *furor* unbecoming in someone who is supposed to be learned and who is responsible for the education of the youth. Thus, the point concluding this poem cannot simply be a (mere) ironic remark or a joke. Giovini notes acutely that with his *dignus inter grammaticos vocari*, Luxorius evokes in a negative context Ausonius's expression used in *Commemoratio professorum Burdigalensium*.[301] In other words, what Luxorius offers to the mad teacher is not a *commemoratio* but – on the contrary – a sort of *damnatio memoriae*: *non es* ...

[298] 96 R is the seventh piece of the *Sylloge*, following the mini-cycle on Christian topics and preceding the first mythological poem; Luxorius's 294 R is the eighth text of the *liber*, opening the longer unit of scoptic epigrams.

[299] See Giovini 2004: 280-281.

[300] Martial 9.68; see also 10.62.

[301] *Et, Citari dilecte, mihi memorabere, dignus / grammaticos inter qui celebrere bonos* (Aus., *Com.* 13.1-2), see Giovini 2004: 281-282.

dignus inter grammaticos vocari. A reader who discovers this subtle allusion should not consider this piece shallow,[302] but it certainly is not only amusing; apparently, this was not the poet's intention. Rather, it was to be serious, indeed (with a pinch of sarcasm, surely), just as serious – in Luxorius's view – was the problem he described. Psychopaths – he seems to be warning his audience – must not teach in schools.

In comparison with *Sapphicum in grammaticum furiosum*, the epigram composed by the author of the *Sylloge* appears to be much lighter and, in fact, more humorous. Its main character is a negligent elementary teacher (that is a *magister ludi*) who is unable to keep order among his pupils. The only way to discipline the riotous boys is to terrorize them, otherwise they throw around their writing tablets, celebrating a sort of *Floralia*. Therefore, his name of *magister ludi*, games teacher, turns out quite proper. The pun is certainly not ineffective.

The teacher depicted here is – the poet stresses it in the very first word of his text – *indoctus*. This is actually the main reason why he cannot manage his class. One may wonder, however, if the situation described by our Anonym is not a reply, an antithesis in a sense, given to Luxorius who – like Martial earlier – criticized cruel teachers and the school terror as such. It may seem amusing, even touching, to view the image of misbehaving, ostensibly innocent, children. But in the hypotext, one can quite easily hear the poet's question: should children be allowed to misbehave? What he says in line 4 is hardly ignorable, namely that the *magister* turns out *iners*, indolent, incompetent, when he ceases from eliminating the boys' errors with the cane. In other words, through his light scoptic piece, the author of the *Sylloge* seems to ask somewhat provocatively, "Can (even should) school be <<non-oppressive>>? Is it possible at all to educate <<without stress>>?"

This peculiar dialogue, or at least juxtaposition of opinions, of the two Carthaginian littérateurs on school and teachers concludes the part of my analysis in which I put more emphasis on the similarities between the *Sylloge* and Luxorius's *epigrammaton liber*. In fact, one may have an impression that, as far as the scoptic epigram is concerned, the anonymous poet does treat Luxorius as his point of reference, sometimes even a model with whom he tries to compete. If ecphrastic and epideictic pieces are taken into consideration, apart from certain similarities, one can easily notice relevant and quite profound differences. An obvious one is the fact that our Anonym so willingly exploits mythological themes. As I have already mentioned, many of these texts are most probably ecphrases. It seems so especially if they offer a description of a single, particularly significant scene of a mythical story, the scene we can really imagine as painted or carved. A good example may be the piece on Bellerophon (97 R), remarkably visual in its conciseness: *Bellerophon superans incendia dira Chimaerae / victor Gorgoneo nubila tangit equo*.[303] In some other mythological poems, the author reveals his ability to treat within a couple of lines almost the entire story as known from the literary tradition. Such is the case in the text *De Sphinga* (180 R) evoking, in point of fact, the whole Theban theme, from the appearance of the Sphinx to the death of Oedipus's sons: *Ales virgo lea crevit de sanguine*

[302] Thus, I cannot agree with the negative judgment by Dal Corobbo 2006: 184.

[303] At least a few other examples could be given here. The most interesting one may be, similarly very visual and quite moving, epigram on Medea (102 R), on which see now especially Zurli 2007: 73-78.

Lai, / Thebano nascens et peritura malo. / Haec fecit thalamos Idipum conscendere matris, / ut prolem incestam mutua dextra necet. Sometimes, a mythical character or event is given an additional comment by the narrator-poet, usually a comment on the variability of fortune or inevitability of fate,[304] as in the poems on Hecuba (105 R), Thetis (118 R), or Telephus (184 R). These observations are not necessarily serious or moralizing. In *De Lauconte* (99 R), one can easily hear a clearly burlesque overtone: the priest, so they say, is punished so harshly for having done violence only to the back of a wooden nag.[305] Let us also listen to the 'appeal' with which the anonymous author concludes the second piece on Europa (144 R): *Humano tandem veniam donemus amori, / si tibi, summe deum, dulcia furta placent* (ll. 3-4). A careful reader of Martial could possibly think here of an even more malicious remark directed by the poet from Bilbilis to the most excellent Father of the Gods in one of his *Apophoreta* (180 *Europe picta*): *Mutari melius tauro, pater optime divum, / tunc poteras Io cum tibi vacca fuit.* In fact, if one tried to search for some parallels for our Anonym's mythological epigrams among Martial's poems, they could be found exactly in the *Apophoreta*, among several ecphrases describing most varied *sigilla*, sculptures or paintings.[306] But, obviously, the author of the *Sylloge* is incomparably more fond of mythological themes and more versatile in elaborating them than Martial ever was.

Speaking of Martialian *Xenia* and *Apophoreta*, it is worth emphasizing though that their poetics appears much more attractive to our nameless Carthaginian epigrammatist than to Luxorius. Luxorius, practically, does not pay attention to objects of everyday use (the sole exception seems to be his 371 R, *De rustica in disco facta*) and he utterly ignores such details as fruit or dishes, simple or sophisticated. His fellow looks at similar little things with pleasure and interest. He composes a trio on Matian apples (133-135 R, *De malis Matianis–Aliter. Laus–Aliter. Vituperatio*), comparing them, both in the 'eulogy' and in the 'attack', to apples known from mythology. Martial does the same in his *Xenia*.[307] In another trio, he praises citrons[308] for being healthful and delicious in their three different flavors (169-171 R). He seems most delighted describing a luxurious – even extravagant – dish, the stuffed goose, modeled, as it appears, on the so-called *porcus Troianus*, one of the specialties of the Roman cuisine,[309] *De ansere, qui intra se capit*

---

[304] The *varietas Fortunae* is a classic theme typical of school rhetorical exercises and as such it is exploited also by the author of the *versus serpentini* in his distichs similarly treating of mythological subjects, see the comments by Paolucci in Zurli – Scivoletto – Paolucci 2008: 87-96.

[305] The piece is worth quoting in full: *Laucontem gemini distendunt nexibus angues / cumque suis genitis sors habet una patrem. / Quod tantum iligni violarit terga caballi, / hinc tolerasse ferunt saeva venena virum. / Quid sperare datur superum iam numine laeso, / cum sic irasci ligneus audit ecus?* For the conjecture *audit* in l. 6, see Zurli's (2007: 70-73) comments.

[306] See especially *Apoph.* 170-181.

[307] Martial 13.37. See also Kay 2006: 220.

[308] Shackleton Bailey (1982: 115 n. 158) was astoundingly certain that the title of the cycle, *De citro*, must have been unauthentic; in his view, the poem treated apples. Yet, as was pointed out already by Courtney (1989: 200), the very first line *septa micant spinis* shows clearly enough that the fruit cannot absolutely be an apple. Kay (2006: 294) provides lucid arguments for identifying it as a citron, *citrus medica*.

[309] The term *porcus Troianus* was used since at least the time of the orator C. Titius, see Zurli 2007: 24. Kay (2006: 308) is right stressing that "Roman cuisine was fond of stuffed meat ... But

copiam prandii (176-176, 9-18 R / 165-166 SB / 87-88 Z). Naturally enough, the two texts abound in mythological similes: *Quis non credat ecum Graiam celasse phalangem, / si parvus tantas anser habet latebras?* (176 R, ll. 7-8); *Cedat Cecropii lascivans bucula fabri, / qua consuerat amor claudere Passiphaen; / cedat et ille, dolo sollers quem struxit Epeos, / qui gravidus bellis Pergama solvit ecus* (176, 9-18 R / 166 SB / 88 Z, ll. 5-8). No wonder that the poet who, as we can see, does not intend to present himself as abstemious wrote also a hedonistic praise of a day of wine, women, and song (157 R). The theme as such is far from original but apparently not so trite to be avoided by epigrammatists; even Martial exploited it occasionally.[310]

Just like fruits and dishes, also animals inspire the anonymous author. Nevertheless, in the *Sylloge* we shall not find a homebred fish, a boar fed in the palace *triclinium*, or well-trained leopards. Our poet likes animals that are ostensibly quite normal, yet he is always able to discover in them something intriguing. Describing a glamorous, at least in his view, white-red bird (132 R), a pheasant or (more likely) a cockerel, he nearly turns into an elegist cataloguing the admired parts of the body of his love-object:[311] *Alae colla comae pectus femur inguina cauda / Paestanis lucent floridiora rosis* (ll. 3-4). Still, he is also ready to 'acknowledge' a black ant carrying grains that, in his view, resembles Pluto abducting Proserpina: *Namque ut Plutonis rapta est Proserpina curru, / sic formicarum verritur ore Ceres* (104 R, ll. 7-8). He notices a goose, not yet stuffed this time (106 R), that is – as he puts it – an "edible burglar alarm:"[312] *nam fercula mensae / conplet et adservat nocte silente domum* (ll. 3-4). Finally, he praises the cuttlefish (107 R), indicating that it provides both food and writing ink: *Praestat carne cibos, apicum dat felle figuras* (l. 5). This piece, exploiting mythological similes even better than those quoted above, reveals our poet's literary interests (and skillfulness) as what is stressed in the point is the fact that the benefits of sepia, meat and bile, should be used only by the *docti*, the experts in two types of arts, culinary and poetic: *Hanc potius doctos adsumere convenit escam, / quae sapit in morsu et probat articulos* (ll. 7-8).[313] As for the latter, a competent reader should easily guess that the author points at peculiar qualities of the genre he practices, i.e. the bitter epigram.

Some echoes of typically Luxorian admiration for the world in which a human being is capable of dominating a fierce beast can be found in the *Sylloge* only in the pair of poems on the elephant (195-196 R). Here, we do indeed hear that the monstrous animal,

---

these epigrams take the practice to the extreme, with the stuffed animal concealing a regression of other cooked animals and stuffings inside it, like a set of Chinese boxes." For other poems dedicated to various kinds of stuffing, see *AL* 225-230 R, of which 226 R and 228 R are by Coronatus.

310 See e.g. Mart. 11.52.

311 As noted justly by Kay 2006: 216-217. Fully anthropomorphic is also the description of the bird's face: *Candida Phoebeo praefulgunt ora rubore* (l. 1). I find Kay's arguments that the bird as described here seems a cockerel rather than a pheasant convincing.

312 To quote Kay's (2006: 116) brilliant expression.

313 What makes the point truly effective is the fact that it actually operates on both levels, literal (emphasizing that cuttlefish is delicious to eat) and metaphorical (alluding not at all to food but to literature, and in particular to satirical poetry), see Kay's (2006: 121-122) comments on *escam* and *sapit in morsu*.

once tamed, carries out the orders of its master: *fert tamen et domitus residentis iussa magistri* (195 R, l. 5). From the second piece, we learn even more clearly that so savage and terrifying a creature when dead, eventually turns into mere material (however precious) that humans can use. It is from its tusks that we produce the scepter for consuls, ornaments for tables, and even all the paraphernalia for playing the *tabula lusoria*. As for the last-named, there is no need to remind that, although extremely popular at the time, it was also – in the opinion of the ancients themselves – the least recommendable of leisure activities. The point is quite significant: *Haec est humanae semper mutatio sortis: / fit moriens ludus, qui fuit ante pavor* (196 R, ll. 9-10). The expression *mutatio sortis humanae* may seem a bit surprising as it does not really suit its context: one could hardly disagree that "elephants do not provide an example of *humana sors*."[314] On the other hand, what the poet aimed at could have been, precisely, to make us reflect for a while on the changeability of fate,[315] but also on certain paradox, namely that a terror and a plaything are not oceans apart. A sensitive (too sensitive maybe) reader could – like in the case of some of Luxorius's poems – wonder again what additional (= hidden) meaning these words might convey. But an epigrammatist, better than anyone else, always knows how to avoid saying too much.

Alongside fruit, food, and animals, also objects change into themes elaborated by the author of the *Sylloge*. These may be truly little things, like wax candles used in churches (94-95 R) or an oil-fueled lamp (185 R). Such texts (being only two or four verses long) must be, quite naturally, juxtaposed with Martial's cycle of *Apophoreta*, describing artificial light of various kinds.[316] There is a poem on a *gillo* (136 R), a vessel for cooling water.[317] There is a piece advertizing a sedan chair (101 R) as a vehicle for modest married ladies.[318] There is, last but not least, a unit of epigrams dedicated to the game of *tabula* (192 194 R),[319] an element of everyday life that Martial himself did not wholly ignore as the little group of *Apophoreta* 14-18 indicates. Our anonymous poet does not forget to add to these, rather general in fact, descriptions an appropriate moralizing comment calling this hobby a *damnosa voluptas* (193, 7-14 R / 184 SB / 106 Z, l. 5) and emphasizing that it is a sort of war, however pleasant (*Indica materies blandum certamen amicis / offert, sed belli fert simulacra tamen*, 194 R, ll. 1-2). Nonetheless, he is quite far from the tone of indignation we shall soon hear in Ennodius's words.[320]

---

[314] Kay 2006: 364.

[315] The motif appears also in a few mythological epigrams, see the ones mentioned above, on Hecuba (105 R), on Thetis (118 R), on Telephus (184 R).

[316] Mart. 14.39-44, see Kay 2006: 79.

[317] See similarly Martial's *Apoph.* for a somewhat similar theme, the *lagona nivaria*, 14.116-118, Kay 2006: 228.

[318] Kay (2006: 97) may be quite right noting that "it could stand as a reasonable piece of advertising for the manufacturer or retailer."

[319] As mentioned above, 193 R is now divided into two separate pieces, the first one being Riese's 193 ll. 1-6, the second ll. 7-14. Interestingly, the cycle is followed by a pair of epigrams on the elephant, which is certainly not coincidental, considering the mention of *tabula lusoria* in 196 R.

[320] See below (in Ch. III. 3. 2. 2) Ennodius's *Carm.* 2.133.

The epigrams of the *Sylloge* reflect, besides, their author's interests in art and culture. This is well exemplified by the already mentioned texts treating mythology, yet even better by poems of ecphrastic character, which is clear, even declared *expressis verbis*. In addition, it should be stressed that the anonymous poet devotes one of his pieces to theorical aspects of art, painting in particular. *De tabula picta* (150 R) focuses on the moment when, thanks to the artist who skillfully chooses appropriate colors, the outline drawing of a panel painting gains life in a sense and turns into reality: [hunc vultum] *formavit similem, probante vero / ludentem propriis fidem figuris / ut, quoscumque manu repingat artus, / credas corporeos habere sensus* (ll. 5-8). This is the same topos of realism in art that we know quite well from Luxorius who, as we may still remember, in his ingenious epigram on the she-bear, compares creating to generating, or even giving birth. Anonym has a quite similar view on the creative process, which is why in every piece of art, whether applied or not, what attracts him is the illusion of life. In the cycle of texts treating Galatea on a salver (152-154 R)[321] what he highlights, with a remarkable charm indeed, is the sensuality of the whole scene: the nude nymph, however only fictitious, truly allures and arouses desire that apparently can fully dampen another (more primordial, as it might seem) craving, the hunger:

pulcherrima Nais,
prandentum inflammans ora decore suo. (152 R, 1-2)

Comtas nolo dapes; vacuum mihi pone boletar:
quod placet aspiciam, renuo quod saturat. (153 R, 3-4)

In medio generata salo nunc arte magistra
perveni ad mensam: hic quoque nuda nato.
Si prandere cupis, differ spectare figuram,
ne tibi ieiunus lumina tendat amor. (154 R, 1-4)

In three poems describing marble sculptures of Daphne, Marsyas, and Philoctetes (172-174 R), he stresses the extraordinary talent of the sculptor who managed to exploit the natural qualities of his material, the variegated marble, achieving – by carving only – the appropriate color.[322] As a result, the marble statue makes an impression of being alive and feeling the pain:

Frondibus et membris servavit dextera sollers
congruus ut sculptis posset inesse color.
Dant mirum iunctae ars et pictura decorem,
ostendit varius cum duo signa lapis. (172 R)

Aërio victus dependet Marsya ramo
nativusque probat pectora tensa rubor.
Docta manus varios lapidem limavit in artus;
arboris atque hominis fulget ab arte fides. (173 R)

---

[321] It can hardly be considered coincidental that the cycle on Galatea (151-154 R), first as a mythological figure, then on her picture on a salver (*De Galatea in vase*), follows directly the poem *De tabula picta*.

[322] See Kay's (2006: 299) notes on a similar kind of sculpting.

Docta manus vivos duxit de marmore sensus;
sentit [Philocteta] *adhuc poenam, tristis et in lapide.* (174 R, ll. 3-4)

Indeed, reading the *Sylloge*, one can perceive the charm of little things, the beauty of pieces of art, the skillfulness of artists: painters or sculptors, but also, as we shall see, representatives of performing arts. Our nameless Carthaginian is delighted listening to a citharode (113-114 R) whose voice and lyre sound as one: *Ars laudanda nimis, cuius moderamine sacro / unum ex diversis vox digitique canunt!* (114 R, ll. 9-10). He willingly watches men and women performing together a weapon dance *pyrricha* (115 R), in which they fight but do not hurt one another in the peace bringing contests (*Lusus habet pugnam, sed dant certamina pacem; / nam remeare iubent organa blanda pares*, ll. 9-10). He acknowledges the expressiveness of a mime (111 R) who, crossing the boundaries of gender (*Mascula femineo derivans pectora flexu / atque aptans lentum sexum ad utrumque latus*, ll. 1-2), speaks with his gesture: *Tot linguae quot membra viro. Mirabilis ars est / quae facit articulos ore silente loqui* (ll. 9-10). Finally, he admires the superhuman deftness of a funambulist (112 R) who "rushes along a path scarcely easy for birds,"[323] proving that the fictitious story of Daedalus was true: *Daedalus adstruitur terras mutasse volatu / et medium pinnis persecuisse diem; / praesenti exemplo firmatur fabula mendax: / ecce hominis cursus funis et aula ferunt* (ll. 7-10). It is easy to notice that the four epigrams – quite accomplished, although built upon well-known motifs – make a certain unity, which is even better stressed by the fact that almost all have the same length (ten verses; only the first piece on a citharode is eight lines long). What they all point at is the human skillfulness thanks to which seemingly disparate or even opposite elements, like fight and agreement, silence and speech, walking and flying, the human voice and the sound of a lyre, can unite in perfect harmony.[324] In addition, especially in the piece on the funambulist, some echoes of Luxorius's praise of contemporary heroes can be heard. In fact, when reading the *Sylloge*, not less than when reading Luxorius, one is tempted to believe that the poet's epoch must have been a time of peace and welfare, a time spent at the table, in theaters, in baths.

The last-named are quite willingly described by our anonymous epigrammatist, in which he turns out, indeed, not so different from his African fellow littérateurs.[325] The poems *De balneis* 110 R and 120 R (the latter makes part of the longest cycle of the collection, 119-123 R) give the names of persons who developed the baths. In the first case, it was Bellator, the landowner (ll. 5-6), in the second case – as it can be implied from the acrostich and telestich – the constructor was Filocalus and Melania the person who contracted for erection of the buildings.[326] This as well as other details, especially the very style employed

[323] Kay 2006: 141.

[324] Similarly, Kay 2006: 146.

[325] For Luxorius, see esp. 350 R, *De aquis calidis Cirnensibus*. Nonetheless, the five poems by Felix are particularly relevant here, *De thermis Alianarum* (210-214 R). It is quite certain that the author of the *Sylloge* imitated Felix, especially his first text, 210 R, to which he alluded in 110 R, *De balneis*. The similarities were noticed already by Courtney 1980: 37 ff., see also Kay 2006: 129-130.

[326] I follow Zurli's (2007: 82-85) interpretive proposal. For a somewhat different reading as well as for the history of recognition of the acrostich and telestich (the latter denied by some), see Kay 2006: 177-185.

to describe the baths (in particular the extensive use of deictic words: 110 R: *hic ubi*, l. 1; *Haec nunc*, l. 5; 119 R: *hic lavet; hic corpus reparans*, l. 7; 120 R: *huc properare*, l. 2; 121 R: *hic lavet*, l. 3) could suggest that the pieces were indeed composed as – at least potential – inscriptions.[327] Still, even had it been so, this does not deprive them of their 'literary' character; especially since eventually they became part of the collection of *poems*. On the other hand, the very fact that they could have been (planned as) 'true' inscriptions evokes the original, the primordial so to speak, function of the epigrammatic genre.

A place for relaxation, for body and mind, decorated with beautiful paintings, giving greater pleasure than the Cumaean coast and Baiae, baths with clear water, heated only by the solar power: that is how the complex erected by Melania and Filocalus is advertized. In 110 R, a more ostentatiously literary poetics is employed as an intelligent reader should easily recognize the topoi used earlier by Felix in his *De thermis Alianarum* (210 R).[328] A splendid edifice rose up on barren uncultivatable land. A human project "improves on nature's gifts, now that the salty shore abounds with salubrious water."[329] Once again, an ancient myth comes true: *Alpheum fama est dulcem per Tethyos arva / currere nec laedi gurgitibus pelagi. / Dant simile exemplum nostri miracula fontis: / vicinum patitur nec sapit unda salum* (ll. 9-12).

It may appear even more interesting to read two epigrams praising the resourcefulness of an ordinary man (the title calls him even poor, *De balneis cuiusdam pauperis*), certain Vita (178-179 R) who, thanks to his hard work and invention, has created for himself a true paradise on earth: baths together with a little garden, guaranteeing him food and good health. Our anonymous poet, thanks to his singular ability to pay attention to little, ostensibly usual things, managed to save from sinking into oblivion this lovely piece of everyday life in the sixth century Carthage.

If it seems to us that Luxorius, the "Carthaginian Martial," does not tell us enough about the real life in the North Africa of the last decades of the Vandal occupation, the author of the *Sylloge* tells us even incomparably less, in point of fact. His epigrams, unless they are satirical and concern individuals (and there are, in truth, very few such pieces: on Filager, Bumbulus, Martius, Caballina (?)), take place outside any specific context, in the world of culture, welfare, and elegance. In a world where ordinary things have extraordinary aesthetic quality, where an ant resembles Pluto and an apple the fruit from the garden of the Hesperides, where even the circus is not a place of popular entertainment but an allegory of the universe.[330]

---

327 As argued by Kay 2006: 129.

328 Reused also by Luxorius in his 350 R, *De aquis calidis Cirnensibus* and, to some extent, also in his 346 R, *De amphitheatro in villa vicina mari fabricato*.

329 Kay 2006: 128.

330 It is quite interesting that the motif, popular in the literature of late antiquity, was turned into an epigrammatic theme by our poet in his final piece 197 R (for the comments on the poem, see Kay 2006: 364-375). One might have an impression that the anonymous author intended once again to point at the non-literalness of the world as presented throughout his oeuvre and to stress his erudition.

Nonetheless, a careful reader should not ignore one particular poem, maybe the most essential in the entire collection:

De templo Veneris, quod ad muros <...> (100 R)

Caeduntur rastris veteris miracula templi
inque usum belli tecta sacrata ruunt.
Nam quae deiectis volvuntur saxa catervis,
haec sunt murorum mox relocanda minis.
Dilati Mavors conpendia cepit amoris:
per muros quaerit iam sua templa Venus!

As a matter of fact, even here the epigrammatist tries not to use too many words and avoids going into details. But the picture of the temple, the wondrous work of art, demolished only to reuse the stone in fortification walls, possibly around the time of Belisarius's invasion in 533-534,[331] is moving enough and clear enough to demonstrate how fragile and vulnerable the tradition and the beauty are. For the rulers, or the invaders, they may even be utterly ignorable. For the poet they make an autarchic world.

III. 3. 2. ENNODIUS AND HIS EPIGRAMS

III. 3. 2. 1. Jacques Sirmond's edition or was Ennodius a self-conscious epigrammatist?

The epigrammatic output of the "gentleman of the church," as Ennodius was brilliantly called by Stefanie Kennell,[332] is quite considerable (151 pieces in Hartel edition)[333] and truly interesting for a student of the history of the genre in late antique/proto-medieval (?) poetry; certainly not less interesting than the writings of the two Carthaginians, Luxorius and the author of the *Sylloge*, both presumably several years younger than our

---

[331] As conjectured by Kay 2006: 94. Interestingly, however, one cannot be really sure whether the information provided in the epigram refers to the Vandals or rather to the Byzantines carrying out the repairs of the city walls. As we know from Procopius, Vandals destroyed existing Roman town defences, but they allowed the walls of Carthage to remain, though they eventually fell into decay (thus it is possible that it was Gelimer who ordered the repair of the walls right before Belisarius's invasion). On the other hand, Procopius emphasizes that the town defences were immediately rebuilt under Belisarius. This makes Anonym's epigram all the more ambiguous as it is not necessarily 'anti-Vandal' in its message; it may well be directed against the Byzantine 'liberators'. On the disillusionment with the new rulers among the people of North Africa, see e.g. Strzelczyk 2005: 183-187.

[332] Kennell 2000b.

[333] Actually, we could speak here of 152 pieces as the cycle 2.125-126-127a-127b, *De asino et equa*, could (should) be read as four texts. On the other hand, within the book two poems by Ennodius's friends, Faustus and his son Messala, can be found (2.143-144). In addition, 2.150 is actually a verse *praefatio* to prose *Dictio* 13, whereas 2.90 a verse conclusion to *Dictio* 24. Therefore, in my view, Mondin (2008: 421 n. 34) is right concluding that in statistics, we should consider fully 'Ennodian' 148 pieces only.

future bishop of Pavia. Nevertheless, in this very case, one point must be stressed at the very outset. All these little poems, composed in the elegiac distich and occasionally in the hexameter, were never gathered into one, coherent collection (or book) by Ennodius himself. By the same token, the label *epigrammata* used to describe his minor (indeed, epigrammatic, as we are pretty sure) poetry is not Ennodian, either.[334]

Ennodius most probably planned a separate edition of his poetic oeuvre, but what interrupted these plans was, first, his elevation to the see of Pavia after 513 and, then, his sudden death in 521. It does not seem, however, that this was to be a collection limited to one single genre. On the other hand, it is similarly quite uncertain whether such *liber* would have comprised all the poems that are still-extant, Christian as well as those inspired by the 'pagan' tradition, or only the latter. What we possess – hence our conjectures concerning the literary projects of the future bishop[335] – is a very interesting text entitled *Praefatio totius operis poetici quod fecit* (*carm.* 2.66 = 187 Vogel). The title, as it can be implied from the use of the third person, is not authorial; nonetheless, it does epitomize the content of the piece built upon the motif of poetry as a *solacium*, a comfort in distress and sorrow:[336]

Dum mea multiplices mens anxia sustinet aestus
et reddor vitrei mancipium pelagi,
cumque procellosus refluentis portitor undae
Africus ut captas me rotat exuvias:
Pierius menti calor incidit, indiga serti
tempora mox cinxit laurus Apollinea,
tunc hederae viridis rubuerunt fronte corymbi,
Castalii mellis murmura blanda bibi.
Continuo ponens marcentes pectore curas
conplector laudem carmina laetitiam.

Luca Mondin[337] argues that a text exploiting so traditional, even paganizing imagery (the symbolics of poetic inspiration is above all 'paganizing' here) could not have been an adequate *praefatio* to a collection a part of which would have been also sacred hymns after the manner of Ambrose and a cycle of inscriptions, little panegyrics indeed, dedicated to twelve bishops of Milan (*carm.* 2.77-89 = 195-207 Vogel). The argument is sound as Ennodius himself in one of his *carmina* declares (*carm.* 1.9 = 43 Vogel, ll. 17-20): *Nunc linguam citharae, quae cantat pollicis ore, / sperne, fides: magis, ille, veni nunc, spiritus, oro, / cuius inexhausto reviviscit semper in anno / quicquid terra creat, gignit mare, parturit*

---

[334] The very term *epigrammata* appears only in the titles of two texts, 2.3, *De epigrammatis per armaria domni Fausti factis* (but here it refers actually not to Ennodius's poem but to the one by Faustus on which Ennodius writes) and 2.36, *Epigramma in subscriptione*. We can be hardly sure, however, if the titles are authorial and which of them are so, see Di Rienzo's (2005: 219-231) comments on the question.

[335] See recently Di Rienzo 2008: 540-541.

[336] For a thorough analysis of the poem, exploiting – as one can easily see – Catullus's (*mens anxia*, *carm.* 68.8) and Statius's (*Pierius menti calor incidit*, *Theb.* 1.3) phraseology, see Di Rienzo 2005: 20-23.

[337] Mondin 2008: 421.

aether.[338] Certainly, as a sort of counterargument, one could remember here that right after his *praefatio* emphasizing the salty taste of his *opus*, the poet of the *Sylloge* places a mini segment of epigrams, quite varied but all having a serious – and *Christian* – tenor. But, in point of fact, Ennodius's *carm*. 2.66 can hardly be compared to Anonym's 90 R. By no means could it be defined as a preface to an epigrammatic oeuvre.[339] If truth be told, however not at all displeasing to read, it is so vague, at least if metatextuality is taken into account, that it cannot be interpreted as an introduction to any specific kind of poetry, either. Consequently, all we might conjecture about Ennodius's understanding of literary genres, and in particular of the epigram, must be based not upon the poet's explicit declarations but only upon the analysis of the *carmina* themselves.

Such a method of interpretation was applied first by the Jesuit Jacques Sirmond who in 1611 published in Paris *opera omnia* by Magus Felix Ennodius,[340] divided – according to a clearly generic criterion – into *Epistulae, Opuscula miscella, Dictiones, Carmina*. The last-named comprised two books: the first one containing *itineraria*, epithalamium, verse letters, verse *dictiones*, poems treating various arguments, and twelve hymns; the second one precisely the *epigrammata* or the above-mentioned 151 minor *carmina*. Sirmond's scheme was imitated by Wilhelm Hartel in his edition for the *CSEL* and this scheme (= this division), in fact, is still effective, influencing our perception of the oeuvre by the bishop of Pavia. In other words, what we now define as Ennodius's epigrams are texts classified so by Jacques Sirmond. Ergo, it should be added that we see Ennodius as an epigrammatist and – what is more – we try to describe his concept of the epigrammatic genre (only) on the basis of Sirmond's interpretation. Therefore, it seems fundamental to determine whether the Sirmondian conclusions can be indeed considered acceptable.

---

[338] Thus, one could hardly disagree with the diagnosis once given by Polara 1987: 49-50: "è ancora irrisolto, in Ennodio, il conflitto fra cristianesimo e tradizione classica, e l'appassionato rimpianto per quest'ultima ... porta ad affermazioni e a descrizioni che stupiscono e scandalizzano alcuni commentatori moderni. ... quest'impegno tecnico costituisce una caratteristica di rilievo ... e contribuisce ad illuminare un aspetto non secondario della personalità di Ennodio, il gusto per un rapporto col patrimonio tradizionale del letterato rivolto prevalentemente agli aspetti formali e quindi la consapevolezza della loro importanza del significato che poteva avere, in un momento di forti tensioni fra mondo germanico e mondo romano, e, all'interno di quest'ultimo, fra tradizione classica e rigorismo cristiano, un tentativo di spostare l'attenzione su settori almeno apparentemente più neutri, meno compromessi con il passato, e perciò più facilmente recuperabili anche all'intervento di modernizzazione e ad un riuso che impedisce la totale decadenza e l'obblio."

[339] Which Anonym's 90 R certainly is, despite its briefness and despite the fact that the poet does not actually use the word *epigramma*, see my comments in Ch. III. 3. 1. 1.

[340] For the history of editions of Ennodius's texts, see Di Rienzo 2005: 9-19 and the paper by Kennell (2000a) he quotes. I fully agree with what Di Rienzo (2008: 542) notes comparing the two editions, by Hartel (1882) and by Vogel (1885): "Tuttavia, se per il testo ci si rivolge di norma al Vogel, la portata delle scelte fatte da Sirmond rimane ancora oggi intatta." In fact, for one who studies the poetics of Ennodius's writings the edition by Hartel, modeled on Sirmond (see above), is certainly much more useful than the one by Vogel. And, the other way around: if one is more focused on discovering "what Ennodius wrote in its material context, textually and archaeologically" (Kennell 2000b: 2), one must find Sirmond's (and Hartel's) reading tendentious.

The problem has been amply discussed by Daniele di Rienzo in his recent monograph (actually, the first monograph on Ennodius's epigrams). The Italian scholar emphasizes that Sirmond's reading of Ennodius was highly influenced by the climate of his epoch. The sixteenth century was a period of a true 'cult' of the short form, which must be interpreted, on the one hand, (still) as a heritage of Petrarchism, on the other hand, as a result of a fascination with the *Anthologia Palatina* as well as with the Roman 'minor' poetry by Martial and Catullus, the latter read precisely as Martial would have wished. The short form was not only admired and praised but also vastly practiced: the sixteenth (and seventeenth) century littérateurs willingly composed ecphrases, even entire books of *emblemata*,[341] and they loved writing epigrams on various subjects, secular as well as religious. Therefore, Sirmond, whose literary sensitivity was shaped in such an epoch, was fully capable of recognizing with precision and certain 'naturalness' the generic paradigm of Ennodius's *carmina minora*, discovering in them a clearly Martialian flavor.[342] At the same time – which is particularly relevant considering the fact that the bishop of Pavia was not less a devoted Christian than an ardent follower of the classical tradition – the French Jesuit did not propose an artificial, indeed false, division into Ennodius's *poemata sacra* and *poemata profana*. He justly concluded that the label *epigramma* should be applied *also* to epitaphs commemorating pious Christians, men and women, and to epigraphs of various kind: remarkably short, planned as inscriptions to be carved on marble plates attached in front of different rooms of the *Episcopium* (in which a competent reader could see some traces of Martial's *Apophoreta*[343]), but also longer ones, like the 'biographs' of the Milanese bishops. In point of fact, one could hardly disagree that epigrams originated precisely from inscriptions. Thus, in my view, we can fully subscribe to what Di Rienzo states in the closure of his book: "la variegata gamma di atteggiamenti, di temi e di interessi della seconda raccolta di *carmina* ennodiani è in linea con esperienze poetiche precedenti, e la posizione che occupa all'interno delle logiche del genere ... ci consente di confermare che l'etichetta *Epigrammata* data da Sirmond a questo *corpus* virtuale regge di fronte all'evoluzione del genere epigrammatico ... non regge però il confronto con la storia del testo e soprattutto con un presunto, ma forse mai realizzato, progetto editoriale di Ennodio delle sue opere in versi."[344]

The epigrams by Ennodius – as far as we can define them analyzing the above-mentioned virtual *corpus* – constitute indeed an unusual synthesis of rich and dynamic tradition of the genre, i.e. the Roman, Martialian tradition, but also the original one, the tradition of epigraphs and epitaphs (not at all alien to Martial himself), reactivated, so to speak, in Latin Christian poetry by pope Damasus. These include epitaphs commemo-

---

[341] Like those by Andrea Alciato (justly mentioned by Di Rienzo 2008: 544), which gave rise to the entire genre, the emblem book.

[342] As Di Rienzo (2008: 552 n. 25) stresses, Martial together with Virgil and Ovid are the most frequently echoed poets in Ennodius's minor poetry, see also the Index he provides in his book, Di Rienzo 2005: 257-263.

[343] In fact, one of such pieces, a distich *Ante horreum* (2.39 = 162b Vogel), evokes Martial's 14.208, see Di Rienzo 2005: 105-106.

[344] Di Rienzo 2005: 242, but the brief notes he makes in Di Rienzo 2008: 541-542 are also worth reading.

rating representatives of different statuses: a youngster, an adult man, a bishop, women: virgins, wives, and widows; eulogies of twelve bishops of Milan, from Ambrose to Theodorus: a clear compositional unity concluded by one-verse wishes of good life for the present bishop, Laurentius. Some of the little poems are epigraphs to be carved on sacral edifices: churches, baptisteries, sculptures, the *Episcopium* with its single parts; some are descriptive epigrams dedicated to little objects, like jewelry, tableware, but also a whip, as well as to the garden of Theoderic or to various animals, in particular horses and mules. There are also poems treating of literary matters. Finally, one can find quite frequent (making roughly one third of the entire *corpus*) satirical pieces.[345] This simple enumeration should suffice to prove that Ennodius's epigram, multidimensional as it is, is also totally accordant with the potential of the genre.

What the poet and the clergyman proposes within the group of satirical poems as such is, in fact, not less multidimensional. Some of them happen to be quite different from the scoptic epigrams by Luxorius or the author of the *Sylloge* as they may be charming and utterly innocent jokes, like the one addressed to a close friend: *Iure colis proprium natalem, pulcer Arator, / qui si non coleres, numquid arator eras?* (2.105 = 237 Vogel). On the other hand, Ennodius also wrote vehement invectives. In one of them, he attacks a citizen of Veneto who dared offend the Gauls, the poet's compatriots (2.35 = 148 Vogel), in another, even more intriguing and somewhat 'iambic' in its tone, he assaults an anonymous critic of his *opus*, called a *glutto* in the superscription[346] (2.68 = 189 Vogel). There are, among these satirical texts, poems treating Ennodius's very personal experiences. In one of them, he complains that a certain personage tempts his friends, as if he were, indeed, the Serpent in Paradise, inviting them to lavish banquets (2.64 = 185 Vogel). In another, he directs a venomous response, similarly exploiting the imagery of the Book of Genesis, to someone who sent him a basket of figs as an unwelcome gift (2.50 = 169 Vogel).

The last-named piece could be certainly classified as a sort of verse letter.[347] In fact, such a label seems applicable to at least a few of Ennodius's minor poems, in the first place to the texts written for Agnellus, a friend with whom our future bishop discusses the possible divulgation of some of his writings, presumably the *carmina* (2.108 = 257

[345] I list the types of Ennodius's epigrams as given by Di Rienzo (2005; 2008: 543), whose divisions are clear and quite satisfactory. Certainly, in some points one could propose different classifications, for instance two pieces labeled by Di Rienzo as 'literary' are clearly scoptic (2.68 = 189 Vogel; 2.96 = 216 Vogel). One might wonder besides whether within the epigraphs some more precise divisions should not be made to differentiate between very short texts (indeed, similar to the *Apophoreta*) and the longer ones.

[346] The whole poem exploits the metaphorics of food, see the analysis by Di Rienzo 2005: 204. Interestingly, this inept critic attacks, as the poet puts it, his *sanctus labor*: *Nescio cur sancto non parcas, stulte, labori* (l. 1). Vogel conjectures that what Ennodius may have in mind may be his *Libellus pro synodo*. If so, the piece could be seen as an element of Ennodius's religious-political involvement, not only an instance of a mere play with a literary form.

[347] Less serious, but incomparably more malicious, is Ausonius in his verse letter to Theon, *Epist.* 14 and 16, in which he comments presents Theon has sent him, oysters and apples, see my notes in Wasyl 2002: 105-106.

Vogel), whom he tries to ask for a horse as a gift (2.109 = 257 Vogel),[348] whom he finally beseeches not to break the promises once given (most probably, again, concerning the above-mentioned horse, 2.107 = 256 Vogel). *Carm.* 2.107 appears quite interesting also because it combines elements of verse *epistula postulatoria* with a sort of *dirae*, a curse thrown upon the perjurer. This is, besides, the only piece composed in a unique metrical format: one Sapphic strophe followed by four lines in the trochaic tetrameter. The poems directed to Faustus and his son, Messala, are not so emotional but similarly quite epistolary in their form. Messala, who himself sent before to Ennodius a verse 'card' asking him to return a book once borrowed, is accused of having made some prosodic mistakes (2.145-146 = 372-373 Vogel, see also *Versus Messalae*, 2.144 = 371 Vogel). Faustus, in a long letter (2.3 = 70 Vogel), is praised for his erudition the proof and source of which is his library collection. At the same time, with true benevolence and tact, he is encouraged to use his talent more fully and courageously. As it appears, *carm.* 2.3 may be a reply to a kind of '*apophoreta*' by Faustus, describing various segments of his library.

The epistolary character of some of Ennodius's epigrams can hardly surprise a reader who remembers several similar compositions by Martial.[349] Of Martialian provenance is, besides, also the above-mentioned iambic tone,[350] exploited in the poem aimed at a *glutto* criticizing our poet's *sanctus labor*. Once again, it seems logical to conclude that the more accurately the epigrammatic tradition – and even the *epigrammata* by Martial himself – is analyzed, the more natural, indeed appropriate, turns out the label used by Sirmond in reference to Ennodius's *carmina minora*.

If purely technical aspects are taken into account, such as metrics or the length of individual texts, Ennodius's minor poetry also fully qualifies as epigrammatic. The elegiac distich and the hexameter, the latter employed quite frequently because in as many as 38 pieces,[351] in addition two 'experiments': *carm.* 2.107 (= 256 Vogel), a Sapphic strophe plus four verses in trochaic tetrameter, and *carm.* 2.123 (= 327 Vogel) in five trochaic tetrameters, such a metrical profile makes of the future bishop of Pavia a poet not really similar of course but to some extent comparable with the author of the *Sylloge*. Apparently, both of them, willingly imitating Martial, do not notice the disciplined metrical variety of his books on which Luxorius focused his attention. As for the length of single texts, it is also Anonym rather than Luxorius to be juxtaposed with Ennodius.[352] Finally, one more

---

[348] The poem is composed in a charming convention of an appeal to the Muse whom the poet asks for the gift of Pegasus. The metaphor is so subtle and coherent that it, apparently, completely mislead Sirmond who entitled the piece *De versibus suis*. In fact, also Kennell (2000b: 118-119), as it seems, does not associate the piece with letters in which Ennodius makes inquiries about the horse; on p. 64 n. 95, she mentions the two poems addressed to Agnellus as "two epigrams on love and poetic inspiration."

[349] Di Rienzo (2008: 552 n. 26) points at the famous letter by Martial, 3.58, but some other examples could be given here: the invitations to a banquet: 5.78, 10.48, 11.52, 11.57, letters to friends performing military service: 6.25, 6.58, 9.45, 9.56 or staying away on their mission in provinces: 12.98.

[350] See especially Martial's 6.64. The analogies are pointed out by Di Rienzo 2005: 204.

[351] See Mondin 2008: 428. 38 pieces out of 148 is roughly 25.7%.

[352] The average length of a single epigram by Ennodius is 5.7, by the poet of the *Sylloge* – 5.8. It should be added that Ennodius, the only one among our three epigrammatists treated here,

characteristic that could allow us to place them side by side is their liking for composing cycles of poems on the same topic,[353] which, as we remember, Luxorius never does: what he 'confines' himself to are pairs. In Ennodius, we can find, in sum, twelve cycles: seven scoptic and five ecphrastic. The longest, satirical one, consists of five pieces (2.118-122 = 326-326d Vogel, *De quodam stulto qui Virgilius dicebatur*).

Within his cycles, our 'gentleman of the church' – once again one could say: like the poet of the *Sylloge* – tries to maintain symmetry and regularity, but also to propose a certain *variatio*. Thus, we can find very even sequences, like the above-mentioned segment dedicated to a fool who was called Virgil (*carm.* 2.118-122): five single distichs, or a block of pieces describing a bearded Goth wearing Roman cloths (*carm.* 2.57-59 = 182-182b Vogel): three two-verse texts in the hexameter. On the other hand, we can also find irregular combinations: the cycle on the eunuch Tribunus consists of four poems in the elegiac couplets: ten, two, four, and six verses long (*carm.* 2.69-72 = 190-190c Vogel). What is most interesting, however, Ennodius willingly uses the measure to provide some additional *variatio* within a cycle. To enumerate some examples: *carm.* 2.26-28 (= 134-134b Vogel): hexameter-hexameter-distich; *carm.* 2.52-55 (= 180-180c Vogel): hexameter-distich-hexameter-hexameter; *carm.* 2.46-49 (= 165-165c Vogel): hexameter-distich-distich-hexameter; *carm.* 2.29-31 (= 136-136b Vogel):[354] distich-hexameter-hexameter; *carm.* 2.125-127b (= 329-329c Vogel): hexameter-distich-hexameter-hexameter. As we can see, even having only two measures at one's disposal, it is possible to create quite variegated combinations.

Therefore, for objective reasons – such as forms, topic, meters, allusions to Martial, some echoes of other Roman epigrammatists, pope Damasus and his epitaphs as well as Ausonius with whom the future bishop shares certain fondness for writing cycles – the answer to the question posed in the title of the present subchapter, namely: "Was Ennodius a self-conscious epigrammatist?" should be positive. Subjectively, however, and the fact should not be ignored, Ennodius never defined himself as an epigrammatist; he never used the key-words *sal, lusus, ineptiae, ioci* (*epigrammata* would be just too much), he never addressed his reader, in particular, he never adopted the typical pose of affected modesty, and, last but not least, it appears he never had intention to compose

composes monostichs (there are four such pieces). As for the *epigrammata longa*, we can point out five texts: the epigraph treating Ambrose (2.77 = 195 Vogel, 14 ll.), an epitaph (2.1 = 46 Vogel, 16 ll.), the 'letter' to Faustus (2.3 = 70 Vogel, 20 ll.) and two ecphrases of gardens, 2.45 = 164 Vogel (16 ll.) and 2.111 = 264 Vogel (22 ll.), the praise of Theoderic's garden. For further information on the length of Ennodius's epigrams, see Mondin 2008: 428.

[353] This tendency is in fact, as Di Rienzo (2001: 109) rightly notices in his paper devoted specifically to Ennodius's cycles, quite typical of Ausonius, who, like Ennodius and unlike the anonymous poet of the *Sylloge*, writes also cycles of satirical pieces; in addition, there are some more examples of cycles within the *Anthologia Latina*. For some notes on cycles in the Roman epigrammatic poetry, see Mantke 1997; worth reading are also brief but acute remarks on Ennodius as an epigrammatist by Cytowska 1997.

[354] In fact, *carm.* 2.25 is devoted to the same topic as *carm.* 2.29-31, Pasiphae and the bull. Thus, the four pieces could be read at least as potential material for a four-texts cycle, in such a case arranged as hexameter-distich-hexameter-hexameter.

a selected *liber epigrammaton*. Thus, it seems plausible to argue that his approach to the epigrammatic genre was more intuitive than intellectual. If so, in this case it might be, indeed, fairer to speak not of a self-conscious (epigrammatic) poet but rather of the self-consciousness of his (epigrammatic) poetry.

III. 3. 2. 2. Notes on selected poems

A quasi-epic, indeed hexametric, thirteen verses long literary 'exercise' describing a horse excursion the poet made one night, seeking some relief from everyday problems (*carm.* 2.128 = 330 Vogel). A joke at the expense of Boethius, known – especially among the future generations – for his moral integrity of a *sapiens*, portrayed as an elegiac lover in whose hand sword turns into distaff and javelin into *thyrsus* (*carm.* 2.132 = 339 Vogel).[355] A clearly panegyrical in its tone ecphrasis of the garden of Theoderic (*carm.* 2.111 = 264 Vogel), an *epigramma longum* par excellence (22 verses),[356] being – especially in its first part – a true invocation to the hand of the divine king, the *dextera bellipotens*, horrible for its enemies, mild and tender, even life-giving for the plants it cultivates. A cycle of scoptic pieces describing a Goth Iovinianus wearing the Roman travelling-cloak, the *lacerna*, despite the beard and extraordinary height which betrays his barbarian origin (*carm.* 2.57-59 = 182-182b Vogel). Epitaphs for Melissa and Dalmatia (*carm.* 2.6 = 465 Vogel; 2.148 = 375 Vogel), virgins for whom worldly living was a continuous dying and it was only death to open for them the door to the true life. Five ecphrases dedicated to a *caucus* showing Pasiphae and the bull (*carm.* 2.25, 29-31, and 103 = 133, 136-136b, and 233 Vogel). An invective against a glutton (and apparently a usurer) who devours the life-blood of the poor (*carm.* 2.61-63 = 184-184b Vogel). An example of charming self-irony in a poem describing a Gaul who avenges his ancient loss by eating a goose, the savior of Rome (*carm.* 2.73 = 191 Vogel). A cycle of epitaphs commemorating Saint Ambrose and his eleven successors, embodying the virtues of an ideal bishop defined by Saint Paul (*carm.* 2.77-88 = 195-206 Vogel). Malicious in its elegance lampoon upon inconstancy of the clergy (*carm.* 2.74 = 192 Vogel).[357] Diversity – disparateness, one could say – of forms, styles, moods, themes, in particular this unique tendency to elaborate, not rarely

---

[355] Shanzer (1983), in the paper mentioned above in Part Two, in subchapter dedicated to Maximianus's 'elegy' 3 (II. 3. 2), interprets the similarities in the portrayal of Boethius in the *Aquilina* piece and here in *carm.* 2.132 as not coincidental. Di Rienzo (2005: 195), however, is right urging prudence here; in fact, considering that Ennodius's writings were kept after his death in the archive in Pavia and we can be hardly certain who had had access to them before they were discovered by Paul the Deacon, we cannot really determine whether Maximianus could have been acquainted with *De Boethio spada cincto* or not.

[356] If the text is to be interpreted still as an *epigramma*. As Polara (1993: 234) notes, it is "un'abile anche se un po' scontata mossa retorica che sposta il genere letterario dalla *loci descriptio* al panegirico." In codices following the chronology of Ennodius's writings, on which Vogel bases his edition, the poem immediately follows the *Panegyric* of Theoderic. On the poem, see now especially Gasti 2006.

[357] Interestingly, in codices the piece precedes, precisely, the circle dedicated to the bishops of Milan and the *Hymns*, see Di Rienzo 2005: 183.

within one poem, Christian and 'pagan' topoi[358] – for all those reasons it is utterly difficult, if not impossible indeed, to provide one synthetic overview of Ennodius's (virtual) epigrammatic *corpus*, the overview that would not be oversimplified. Therefore, in the present subchapter, I prefer to give some notes on selected texts and motifs, particularly interesting if read comparatively with certain poems by Luxorius and the author of the *Sylloge*, rather than to provide too general a definition.

Undoubtedly, Ennodius's *epigrammata* must not be interpreted only as an example of an *otium litteratum*, a sort of escape from the real world with its political problems or moral dilemmas.[359] Such a tendency is of course not wholly alien to him, which is best exemplified by the tone of the cited above *praefatio*. However, his minor poetry is indeed a mixture – unorganized, unselected and as such in a sense 'trustworthy' (which is not always the quality of a poetic work) – of literary culture, life experience, acquaintances, friendships or (sometimes) antipathies, faith and attachment to the classical tradition of a man of the church, sometimes even a politician, an intellectual, a worshipper of Evangelical Virtues, and a subtle aesthete. As such, apart from its poetic value,[360] it can be also seen as a precious document in history and civilization of the Theoderican era.

Ennodius's epigrams, if read in the context of almost contemporary poems by Luxorius or the author of the *Sylloge*, capture attention above all due to their dissimilarity. It is determined especially by the clear presence of the Christian element influencing both the content and form of many texts. At the same time, as I have already mentioned, in the *carmina epigrammatica* by the future bishop of Pavia, one can also easily recognize Martialian influences and some distinctive traits of late antique minor poetry as such, among which precisely the fondness for writing and rewriting the same themes (hence the cycles) or – most generally speaking – an ability to notice the beauty of little things, little objects, examples of applied art. Therefore, at least in some aspects, Ennodius's epigrams, in particular scoptic and ecphrastic ones, can be juxtaposed with those by Luxorius and the poet of the *Sylloge*.

Satirical pieces by Ennodius are, indeed, quite many and quite diverse. Some reveal above all their author's personal antipathies or grudges. Others focus on unusual events or unusual human cases.[361] Ennodius at times chooses protagonists whom Martial or even Luxorius could have found interesting: a drunkard and his wife not much different from her husband (2.137-141 = 364-364abc-365 Vogel and 2.147 = 374 Vogel),[362] a fool,

[358] Certainly, the problem merits further examination, for some interesting notes, see especially Di Rienzo 2003.

[359] As justly stressed also by D'Angelo 2001: 106-107.

[360] Ennodius as a littérateur is being understood better and better, if not discovered, now. Hence 'systematic' publications, like the series of *Giornate Ennodiane* or a very useful website entitled "Magnus Felix Ennodius goes internet" at: http://www.sbg.ac.at/ges/people/rohr/ennodius/ennodste.htm [May 21, 2010].

[361] Sometimes so unusual that they do resemble more themes of *dictiones* than a true life, see similarly Di Rienzo 2001: 112. The best example may be indeed a piece built upon a topic of declamation, *Versus de eo qui ut filium matri reconciliaret furtum fecit*, 2.23, see Di Rienzo 2005: 157-158.

[362] *Carm.* 2.137-141 lampoon the Praetorian prefect Honoratus as drinking to excess. *Carm.* 2.147, dedicated to his wife, attracts attention because of its form: *Uxor flasconis cupis dotata Falerni, / semper inexhausto pectus repleta Lyaeo, / quae Bacchum madidis colui venerata labellis* (ll. 1-3).

surprisingly called Virgil (2.118-122 = 326-326d Vogel). The advice the poet gives him sounds very 'Martialian', indeed: *Externo quotiens vocitaris nomine, demens, / si tibi sunt sensus, prospice ne venias* (2.121 = 326c Vogel). An *ignoramus* who dares be a teacher (*carm.* 2.96 = 216 Vogel): *Numquam discipulus, valeas dic unde magister?* (l. 3).

The bitter taste idiosyncratic of the *Roman* epigram can be easily felt – which is obvious – in poems about eunuchs. Ennodius, like the two Carthaginian epigrammatists, is fascinated by certain indefiniteness, even transgenderness, of such an individual, thus the simile of a hare used in *carm.* 2.52 (= 180 Vogel): *Vir facie, mulier gestu, sed crure quod ambo, / iurgia naturae nullo discrimine solvens, / es lepus, et tanti conculcas colla leonis!* Thus also the concept, similar to the one employed some time later by the author of the *Sylloge*:[363] *Respice portentum permixto iure creatum, / communis generis, satius sed dicitur, omnis* (2.54 = 180b Vogel). But, speaking of eunuchs, the future bishop can be even as literal as Martial:[364] *Ludit in ancipiti constans fallacia sexu: / femina cum patitur, peragit cum turpia, mas est* (2.55 = 180c Vogel).

Very interesting analogies with Luxorius can be found in the cycle of other epigrams dedicated to a eunuch, this time named Tribunus (*carm.* 2.69-72). The main theme of the first three texts is the instability of the protagonist, which makes him continuously wander but also 'err', even 'lie'[365] (see especially the second piece, 2.70): *Tu, quem lustratis transmisit gentibus* e r r o r (2.69 = 190 Vogel, l. 3); *Tutus falsa loqui poteris sine teste, Tribune: / ventus habet linquam ponderibus vacui* (2.70 = 190a Vogel); *Instabilem faciunt naturae damna Tribunum* (2.71 = 190b Vogel, l. 1). The term *error* used here has, obviously enough, additional Christian connotations, which is the sole, very subtle in fact, hint that the anomaly described here could be interpreted also in moral categories.[366] It is only in the final poem that the main character is clearly defined as *eunuchus* (the opening word) who *semina telluri non habet unde ferat* (2.72 = 190c Vogel, l. 2). The metaphor is not less elegant than easy to understand. In this context, the double entendre of the expressions used earlier in the first three pieces of the cycle can be fully grasped: *Testibus adseritur gens census vita, Tribune* (2.69 = 190 Vogel, l. 1); *Tutus falsa loqui poteris sine teste, Tribune* (2.70 = 190a Vogel, l. 1).[367] As such, the epigrams about Tribunus make also a very good example of the way in which Ennodius composes his cyclic units: their global sense

---

Bernt (1968: 12) interprets it as a jocular epitaph. For Di Rienzo (2005: 189), it is rather a 'label' of an amphora.

[363] D'Angelo (1993: 650 n. 15) notes this analogy between the poem by Ennodius and the one by the author of the *Sylloge*.

[364] Similarly Di Rienzo 2005: 164.

[365] Kennell (2000b: 122) notes justly that Ennodius had "essentially grammatical views on the mingling of incompatible things," hence his approach to the phenomenon of transgenderness as embodied by a eunuch, hence also, as D'Angelo (1993: 652-654) emphasizes, his amazement when describing the phenomenon of a mule (*carm.* 2.124: a rewriting of Claudian's *carm. min.* 18; *carm.* 2.125-127b). See especially 2.125 (= 329 Vogel): *Visceribus propriis externos fundere partus / Cogitur et generis subolem lactare ferini. / Iurgia naturae magno distantia calle!*

[366] But it should be stressed that Ennodius does not discuss the problem of homosexualism in religious categories, see D'Angelo's (1993) remarks on homosexualism as perceived in the sixth century.

[367] In point of fact, a similar pun is given also by the poet of the *Sylloge* in his epigram *De eunucho* (108 R): *fidus enim est custos, qui sine teste datur* (l. 7).

is revealed only once *all* elements are read. At the same time, two extreme poems are of particular relevance, the last one that finally resolves the 'puzzle' concerning the identity of the protagonist and the first one, being not coincidentally the longest of all. The key-word is the ambiguous noun *testibus*, opening the first text. If we read *testis, -is* as a 'witness', what is stated at the outset is, quite logically, that witnesses are necessary to testify to somebody's family, status, conduct, especially if the person is away from his birthplace (*antiquum quotiens linquimus hospitium*, l. 2), which is precisely what has happened to Tribunus: he leads a wandering life (*Tu, quem lustratis transmisit gentibus error*, l. 3). If we interpret *testis, -is* as a 'testicle', what is implied in the first line is not less significant: it is the manhood, being male, that guarantees all the above-mentioned values, namely family, status, and conduct, i.e. the values to which a eunuch is (actually) not entitled, even though – as the two subsequent verses explain – it is on these very values that he would like to build his identity: *vis dici locuples sublimis pulcher amicus* (l. 5); *Inrita dicta volant, adsertor non venit ullus, / nulla fides sexum detegit aut patriam* (ll. 7-8). In such a context, the main theme of the poem is the problem of self-perception and, consequently, of self-acceptance. Therefore, as I have noticed earlier, the cycle – and especially this opening piece – can be juxtaposed with some epigrams by Luxorius. The point of Ennodius's *carm.* 2.69, in its issue, sounds almost like the one in the text on the short Macedonia:[368]

Ennodius, *carm.* 2.69	Luxorius, 310 R
Mendicus vetulus timidus confusus anhelus, *his, verum perdens, utere nominibus.* (9-10)	*Hac spe, crede, tuos incassum decipis artus:* *Thersiten potius finge, quod esse soles!* (7-8)

In *carm.* 2.75 (= 193 Vogel), one can find the motif exploited, if not overexploited, by Luxorius's '*sodalis*', the poet of the *Sylloge*.[369] Its protagonist is a hippophile who, because of his peculiar fancy (actually) inherited from his ancestors,[370] attaches human names to the croups of his beloved animals: *Gaudet equis recti dissuasor, <et> prodigus aequi, / nomina qui digna studio superante caballis / subtrahit, opponens ad sancta vocabula clunem. / Sed procul est pecudes quod censet mentis iniquae: / propositum perstat generis quod stemmata fundunt.* As we can see, the bestiality (which is the core of the problem here) is only hinted at and in a very subtle manner. It is merely the word *clunis* that points at it and the pun in the first line: *equis/aequi*.[371]

One should not conclude, however, that subtlety and allusiveness is a constant quality of Ennodius's poems treating of sex. *Carm.* 2.97 (= 217 Vogel) developing the epigram-

---

368 Associations with the poem on a eunuch (298 R) are also natural. In fact, in his *In spadonem regium* Luxorius also treats, with his usual contrariness, the question of self-perception. Di Rienzo (2005: 167) speaks of some analogies with 315 R, *In gibberosum*.

369 The analogy is noticed by Di Rienzo 2005: 170.

370 This accent on traits inherited from parents is a motif for which the poem can, again, be juxtaposed with Luxorius's hunchback (315 R) or Anonym's Bumbulus (190-191 R).

371 Di Rienzo (2005: 170) notes rightly that the opening phrase echoes Horace's *Serm.* 2.1.26: *Castor gaudet equis* and *AP* 161-162: *imberbus iuvenis tandem custode remoto / gaudet equis canibusque*. As a matter of fact, it is quite amusing to think how a reader who recognizes this allusion may interpret, in the light of Ennodius's text, the – utterly 'innocent' – description of the young man by the *Horatius ethicus*.

matic par excellence topic of *vetula pruriens* is the best proof that this is not the case. It is at the same time an example of exercise in the grotesque style, as noted acutely by Di Rienzo:[372]

Algidus in vivo moritur dum corpore sanguis,
annorum glacies cum siccat pabula vulvae,
seminis et custos refugit cruor utilis inguen,
marcida cur iuveni sociaris, Galla, marito?
Pignoris in thalamis periet fiducia iuncto.
Nam subolem laxis mendacem vivere rugis
insimulans, epulis das prolem feta cloacae.
Adtulit hoc venter, quod coniunx iungat ad ora!

It could be argued that the piece as such 'evolves' from Martial's 2.34, as the very name of the 'heroine' indicates. But its aesthetic, its indeed ostentatious obscenity, resembles more the climate of Horace's *Epode* 8 than the above-mentioned text by the poet from Bilbilis or, truly elegant, even delicate, *In vetulam virginem nubentem* (301 R) by Luxorius. If any comment can be added to the epigram being, in point of fact, so self-explanatory as this one, it seems worth emphasizing that Ennodius here actually defines procreation as the principal objective of marriage. The opinion is purely Roman and purely traditional, but what matters is that we can hear it here from a deacon and a future bishop who, having taken a vow of celibacy himself, does not condemn sex as such, marital sex, needless to say.[373]

Carm. 2.97, in comparison with Luxorius's *In vetulam virginem* and Martial's 2.34, strikes with its obscenity. Ennodius's epigram on a blind man, *carm.* 2.112 (= 265 Vogel) is hyperrealistic and macabre, especially if placed side by side with the enchanting text by the "Carthaginian Martial:"[374]

Orbe pereffosso fluvidum de lumine vulnus
pestifer ostentans ora sepulta geris.
Caeca per innumeros facies portatur amicos;
qui te conspiciunt, iure dolent oculis.
Ebria marcenti locupletas flumine menta,
circumfers crasso sordida labra fimo.
Oscula nulla petas, madidam suspende mefitem:
te propter cupiam perdere quod video.
Quis putet ex oculis flammas coalescere turpes?
Nil videt, et rectum servat iter scelerum.

What is particularly noticeable in the poem is a clear conviction that an impairment, a physical deformation, must imply moral debasement. It is underlined in the point, be-

---

[372] Di Rienzo 2005: 171.

[373] Which is also well exemplified by his epitaphs for married women, see *Epith. Domnae Mellesae* (*carm.* 2.117 = 325 Vogel): *Hoc tantum mundi quod lex est corpore gessi, / exornans casta prole pudicitiam* (ll. 3-4) but also by his *Epithalamium Maximo* (*carm.* 1.4), strikingly different from Paulinus's *carm.* 25.

[374] For some comparative notes on the two poems, Luxorius's 357 R and Ennodius's 2.112, see Giovini 2004: 331-333.

ing in fact the only amusing moment in the text. The opinion as such was quite typical of the mentality of the ancients, but rarely was it expressed with similar emphasis.

Speaking of analogies or common themes in the epigrammatic writing of Ennodius and the two Carthaginians, Luxorius and the poet of the *Sylloge*, it is worth stressing another detail. Both Luxorius and his anonymous fellow pay some attention to dice playing. Luxorius does not analyze the general problem but – with his usual vigor – selects and describes individual players, a deviant and a madman (323 R; 333 R).[375] The author of the *Sylloge* concentrates on the very phenomenon of gambling and its moral implications: he is far from dramatizing, yet he states clearly enough that this is a ruinous passion nurtured by many and a kind of war, however bloodless (193, 7-14 R / 184 SB / 106 Z).

Ennodius, like the Carthaginian Anonym, focuses on the disastrous consequences of a similar hobby. What he depicts in *carm.* 2.133 (= 340 Vogel) is the *ostomachion*, a sort of puzzle played – should we believe the poet – especially by women. They, unlike men, are allowed to practice it, even though this useless, indeed demoralizing pastime (demoralizing as women learn to laugh at death) stirs up their natural frailty, deceitfulness, and secretiveness:

> *Sollicitata levi marcescunt corda virorum*
> *tormento: fas est ludere virginibus.*
> *Frangunt Marmaricis elefans quod misit ab arvis,*
> *per micas sparsum mox solidatur opus.*
> *De poena tenerae discunt cum fraude iocari:*
> *nam ridere necis munere femineum est.*
> *Angusta norunt res mille includere capsa,*
> *omne ebur haec, mulier, pectoris arca tui est.*

It is worth noting that both Ennodius and the author of the *Sylloge* emphasize the fact that the pieces, *cauculi*, *micae*, are made of ivory. Apparently, both are fascinated by the paradox that so enormous a beast must be killed to provide material for such a 'trifle' (see 196 R: *Monstrorum princeps ... arma tablistis, / discolor et tabulae cauculus inde datur*, ll. 1 & 7-8). *Carm.* 2.133, a truly subtle yet undoubtedly somewhat misogynic[376] poem, can be seen as a spectacular example of the moralizing attitude that the future bishop of Pavia adopts at times in his epigrams.

This moralism, (indeed: at times) noticeable in Ennodius's satirical pieces, does not always determine his view of the art. Generally, it could be said that, as a Christian of deep spirituality, he was convinced that art in its beauty and wonder, which a human being can (even should) admire, should only reflect, maybe complete, his/her inner beauty.[377] In this context, the text describing the exceptional ring of Firmina (*carm.* 2.98 = 229 Vogel) seems particularly worthy of notice. The scenes it shows are incredible and yet true, not only be-

---

[375] Presumably, in the subtext a careful reader will find the message that this peculiar hobby attracts, in particular, 'odd types', fanning their ill passions.

[376] As stressed by Di Rienzo 2005: 185. In fact, one may have the impression that a woman is depicted here as biblical Eve, the embodiment of sin.

[377] See *carm.* 2.10 (= 99 Vogel): *aurum culmen ebur tabulas laquearia gemmas / non datur humanis plus rutilare bonis* (ll. 9-10).

cause of the artist's skill. Above all, they exemplify the virtues of its owner: the (artificial) lion loses its natural wildness as it is Firmina to tame the beasts[378] and feed the poor:

Nil fallit simulans: quod finxit dextera, verum est.
Inmobilis stantem fugitat lepus arte molossum,
insertus rabidis ridet furor aureus ursis,
gestandus manibus saevit leo blandior ira.
Cognoscit dominam genius famulante metallo.
Mitigat illa feras, dum plebem pascit egentum.

But interestingly, even surprisingly, Ennodius, the subtle aesthete which he also is, does not condemn eroticism in art. At times, he sees in it an excellent means of expression through which a moral message can be conveyed. An artist depicting the innumerable *crimina* of Jove makes them commonly known and judged as they should be: *Argenti pretium est facinus retinere vetustum, / ne purum superet, quod furtis Iuppiter egit* (*carm.* 2.101 = 232 Vogel, ll. 3-4).[379] At times, however, our fervent Christian and deacon composes epigrams that could have been penned by the poet of the *Sylloge*, describing sensual Galatea. Five finely interrelated texts treat the love story of Pasiphae and the bull as presented on a silver *caucus* belonging to an unnamed person (*carm.* 2.25, 2.29-31, and 2.103[380] = 133, 136-136b, and 233 Vogel). What strikes in the first place is a very personal tone (the address in the second person opening *carm.* 2.25) and tenderness with which Ennodius speaks of his heroine. In his view, she is a gentle woman, demanding caresses and even a *misera puella* (2.31.3, see below), especially if compared to her 'lover', a completely animal-like, indeed brutal, bull:

Pasiphae, niveum linquis nec in arte iuvencum,
diffusis collo manibus petis oscula supplex,
pulcrior et certis inludis ficta puellis.
Candidus argentum superat bos luce coloris.
Vivit amor taurus mulier sine corpore vero. (2.25)

Et fictus rigidam servat, Venus inproba, mentem
taurus, ut admotis suspendat rostra labellis. (2.30)

What is more, Ennodius eventually 'allows' a true sex act between his two protagonists, rewriting in a sense the version of the myth known from Ovid: now it is not

[378] Di Rienzo (2005: 128) points at some analogies between this image and a similar scene in Dracontius's *Rom.* 1; in his view, it is not excluded that the two poets used a common source. One might also think here of Martial's epigrams on 'Domitian's' lions.

[379] The poet of the *Sylloge* in his epigrams on Europe also emphasizes Jupiter's trickery: *Fraude suos Genitor celat vel conplet amores* (143 R, l. 3). But eventually, the point he gives turns out quite contrary to what a reader, especially an upright one, might expect: *Humano tandem veniam donemus amori, / si tibi, summe deum, dulcia furta placent* (144 R, ll. 3-4).

[380] To be exact, *carm.* 2.103 does not belong to the very cycle describing the *caucus* mentioned in the title of 2.25 and 2.29, but it seems logical to read it together with other texts on Pasiphae, as Di Rienzo (2001: 112-116; 2005: 130-134) also does.

Pasiphae to turn into a (false) cow, but the bull to turn human.[381] Thus, the laws of nature are not broken. It may seem quite interesting indeed that the love between a woman and an animal is described most fully and with most sympathy (if not acceptance) not by Luxorius or by the author of the *Sylloge*, but by a Milanese deacon who never admits to having had anything personally to do with sex:

Laesa Venus non est, naturae vincula constant:
bucula Dedalei cessat mentita laboris.
Ingenio vivens nil mugit vacca biformis,
fictaque nec verum coitum dant ligna iuvencae.
Ecce iterum tauro mulier summittitur uxor,
humanas pecudum suspirant pectora flammas.
Vasta iugum cervix, cur suscipit area colli,
qualiter adstricto sudavit marcida loro! (2.103)

The group of poems dedicated to Pasiphae is worth reading for one more reason. Ennodius exploits here a topos used also by the Carthaginian epigrammatists, namely one of realism in art. Not only does he stress that the personages represented in a piece of art are lifelike, but he also and above all concentrates on their real feelings, even though neither the girl, nor the bull has the body (*Vivit amor taurus mulier sine corpore vero*, 2.25.5). In fact, the poet seems almost to identify with his protagonists, asking the painter, their 'creator':

Si tibi sunt animae, pictor, quibus inseris artem,
mollior in tauro claudatur spiritus, oro,
fortia si miserae non dantur corda puellae. (2.31)

For Luxorius, a sculptor is a mother (a mother bear) bearing her child, the *opus*. The poet of the *Sylloge* looks with admiration at a painter who gives body and senses to mere figures. For Ennodius, an artist may be even more: he is the owner and the giver of souls. In other words, he seems to be God the Creator:

Blanditur mulier, sentit bos, membra moventur.
Attulit ars formas: quis dedit hic animas? (2.29)[382]

In the present subchapter, I have focused only on a fragment of Ennodius's *corpus epigrammaticum*, the corpus – as we know – merely virtual and as such all the more not constituting a coherent unity. Thus, the examples I have chosen are not fully 'representative' in the exact sense of the word. Nonetheless, they are – as I believe – worth analyzing, especially if read in the context of epigrams by other authors, almost contemporary with the future bishop of Pavia. While Luxorius captures our attention with his boldness, at times obscenity, and at times lack of empathy or even cruelty toward his protagonists, if the anonymous poet of the *Sylloge* may seem a lover of beauty and elegance contained in little things – although he can be as malicious and hoarse as Luxorius sometimes is subtle and sensitive – it is worth remembering that both these extremes can be found in the epigrammatic writing by Ennodius.

---

[381] See Di Rienzo's (2001: 114-115; 2005: 132-134) notes on Ennodius's use of the nouns describing his two protagonists, the woman and the bull.

[382] As we can see, the cycle is composed as a sort of a puzzle: the answer to the question posed in 2.29 is given in 2.31.

CONCLUSION

A 'postscript': it is with this term that I have defined the four epyllia by Dracontius and their relationship with the 'main text' of Latin miniature epic as introduced into the Roman literature by the Neoterics and later practiced by some Augustan poets, whether as an independent poem or as a part of a larger structure. But the word 'postscript' could be, in point of fact, applied to all works described in the present book as they all seem to represent merely an appendix to a history of some genres of the Roman poetry. By the same token, each of the poets mentioned here could be labeled as an 'epigone'. Dracontius, recounting well-known mythological stories, and (all the more) the anonymous author of the *Aegritudo Perdicae*, so strongly influenced by Ovid, may appear epigones. The word 'epigone' may well refer to Maximianus, composing the "elegy after the elegists." Luxorius was also seen as an epigone and as such he was once named "the Carthaginian Martial."

Upon a closer look, however, none of the authors discussed in the present book seems classifiable as a mere second-rate imitator, even the author of the *AeP*, as I have put it, a skillful versifier rather than a 'serious' poet. They all exploit forms that are 'traditional', well-trodden, one might say, even though the latter adjective seems, at least, exaggerated; indeed, it is hardly applicable to miniature epic, which was by nature experimental, or to the Roman epigram that was still far from standardized as a genre even after Martial. But they all, making use of undeniably conventional means of expression and addressing certainly competent, elitist literary audience, do not appear to be solely 'prisoners of the past'. Their form, or forms, their topoi and vocabulary may be traditional, old or old-fashioned, if one wishes, but their comments, observations, and emotions refer to their contemporary times.

Therefore, I have decided to employ in the title of my book the expression *genres rediscovered*. I have found it fair to emphasize that the poets whose works have been studied here merit appreciation for their creativity, and indeed courage, in reusing and reinterpreting the classical – and truly classic – literary heritage. In addition, I have found it similarly fair to stress that for the students of Latin literature the borderline between the 'classical' and the 'post-classical' is, and should be, flexible. It is not my intention of course to imply that aesthetic and poetological differences should be ignored or blurred. Quite the reverse, these differences are profound and multidimensional and as such must be properly understood and explained. The main issue is the fact that studies of Latin literature – or rather of literature in general – and especially generic studies require a proper, i.e. diachronic, perspective. A description of a certain genre based merely on its most important or generally known representative/representatives will always risk becoming incomplete and limited. In genology, one must be utterly prudent in defining the 'main' and the 'marginal', the 'relevant' and the 'negligible'. In this sense, an insight into a few genres practiced by some 'classical' – and classic – Roman poets from the perspective of their 'post-classical' followers may be, also for a genologist, an intriguing rediscovery.

I have concluded each part of the book with respective final remarks (see Chapters I. 5; II. 4; III. 2. 4) where I discuss and summarize the most relevant questions. Thus, it should suffice now to recapitulate a few essential points only.

The epyllion, despite its 'exotic', Greek flavor (it treats solely of Greek mythology) is transplanted into the Latin poetry by the Neoterics who, via this 'new' Alexandrian narrative style – or indeed genre, however not defined as such by the ancient genology – try to describe the crisis of values in their own culture. Thus, already in Catullus the epyllic narrator does not speak as a Callimachean *poeta doctus* but as a poet-moralist instead. This unique quality of the Roman miniature epic is perfectly recognized by Dracontius. In his poems, the voice of the speaking *ego* sounds clear, too clear maybe, at least for some critics. Nevertheless, it is worthwhile listening carefully to what he says and analyzing what questions he poses to his mythological protagonists and, through them, to his readers. It is also worth the effort to note how multidimensional, stylistically and compositionally, and thus how far from banal his speeches are. Compositional diversity, skillfulness in using most varied literary techniques and in imitating most varied styles and genres, is besides a 'fixed value' of Dracontius's poetics, the value through which his epyllia fully subscribe to the tradition of the genre and even enrich it. What seems particularly worthy of attention is, however, Dracontius's sense of the tragic, a quality which similarly belongs to the heritage of the Roman miniature epic. As it appears, this is also the quality through which his epyllia could truly appeal to his literary audience. The cruelty of the ancient myth evoked by the Carthaginian lawyer, whose own life was not less dramatic, represented quite well the experiences of an epoch that "witnessed tragedies demanding the power of the tragic language of an Aeschylus or a Sophocles."

Maximianus's elegy results above all from a thorough, global, so to speak, reading of Ovid's elegies, the juvenile ones as well as those composed already in exile. This combination of both the erotic and querulous tone turns his *opus* into a synthesis of the elegiac genre. This synthesis involves a true polyphony of themes and forms. In Maximianus's elegy, there is room for epitaphic 'inclusions', hymnic passages, satirical coloring, or *sententiae*. His elegy fully exploits its narrative potential, especially when it presents an episode from the protagonist's youth as a new version of the history of Pyramus and Thisbe, this time with an ostensibly happy ending. But, much more than a coherent erotic autobiography, his elegy is a collage of diverse stories not fully corresponding with one another. What they all point to is a bitter self-reflection of a *senex* whom the passing time deprived of a chance to love, not bringing him any wisdom or peace of mind instead. It is hard not to interpret Maximianus's oeuvre as a reflection on the dilemmas of the late antique culture, in particular those on corporeality and sexuality of the human being.

By comparing Luxorius's *epigrammaton liber* with the epigrammatic writing of his two contemporaries, the anonymous author of the *Sylloge* (most probably also a Carthaginian and a close reader of the poems by his compatriot) and Ennodius (active in a completely different environment, in Theoderic's Italy), one can most fully comprehend why it is indeed fair to see in the Carthaginian *sophista* a follower, if not the follower, of the poet from Bilbilis. All of the features, so clearly indicated and stressed by Martial, like disciplined metrical variety, terminological precision, and especially the purposeful application of the term *epigramma*, the emphasis placed on the scoptic element (the *sal*), and autothematism, are recognized and methodically reapplied only by Luxorius. Luxorius is undoubtedly the only, comparable to Martial, theoretician of the genre he practices; he is, besides, an extraordinarily intelligent (and as such too often not easy to grasp), finely malicious, but at times also exceptionally subtle poet. Nonetheless, his two contemporaries are similarly worth remembering. The author of the *Sylloge*, a lover of mythology and mythological associations (yet sometimes even more obscene than Luxorius), should be recognized especially for his unique talent for paying attention to the charm of little things and Ennodius for his versatility, for the fact that in his epigrams he describes with equal ease the love between Pasiphae and the bull and the pious deeds and lives of the Milanese bishops. Luxorius then does merit the title of "the Martial of the Vandals," even though his poetic world is not at all identical with the Martialian one. While it is possibly the whole Rome of the Flavian era that is reflected in Martial's epigrams, Luxorius's epigrams focus only on the extremes, the extremes of the life in Vandal Carthage. In fact, Luxorius's epigrammatic world, weird as it is, is a world of paradoxes just as paradoxical may (must?) have seemed the revival of the Roman culture in Carthage ruled, or occupied as some would say, by the Vandals. In this respect, also Luxorius's epigram, like Maximianus's elegy and Dracontius's epyllion, the genres of 'classical' Roman poetry rediscovered in the Romano-Barbaric age, fully justifies the conviction that the culture of late antiquity is a culture which must be described simultaneously with two words: 'continuity' and 'change'.

BIBLIOGRAPHY

Abbreviations of journals etc. are based on those used in the annual bibliographical publication *L'Année philologique.*

EDITIONS AND TRANSLATIONS

DRACONTIUS AND *AEGRITUDO PERDICAE*

Dracontius

Opera omnia

BOUQUET 1995. Dracontius, *Œuvres*, t. III: *La Tragédie d'Oreste, Poèmes Profanes* I-V. Introduction par Jean Bouquet et Étienne Wolff. Paris: Les Belles Lettres, 1995 [I quote the Introduction as BOUQUET – WOLFF 1995, the Text and the Commentary as BOUQUET 1995].

MOUSSY – CAMUS 1985. Dracontius, *Œuvres*, t. I: *Louanges de Dieu*, Livres I et II. Texte établi, traduit et commenté par Claude Moussy et Colette Camus. Paris: Les Belles Lettres, 1985.

MOUSSY 1988. Dracontius, *Œuvres*, t. II: *Louanges de Dieu*, Livre III. *Réparation*. Texte établi et traduit par Claude Moussy. Paris: Les Belles Lettres, 1988.

VOLLMER 1905. *Blossii Aemilii Dracontii carmina*. Edidit Fridericus Vollmer. *MGH AA* 14. Berolini, 1905.

VOLLMER 1914. Dracontii *De laudibus Dei, Satisfactio, Romulea, Orestis tragoedia, Fragmenta*. Iterum recensuit Fridericus Vollmer. In *Poetae Latini minores*[2], vol. V, pp. 1-237. Lipsiae, 1914.

WOLFF 1996. Dracontius, *Œuvres*, t. IV: *Poèmes Profanes* VI-X, *Fragments*. Texte établi et traduit par Étienne Wolff. Paris: Les Belles Lettres, 1996.

Orestis Tragoedia

BÄHRENS 1883. *Orestis tragoedia*. Recensuit et emendavit Aemilius Baehrens. In *Poetae Latini minores*, vol. V, pp. 218-261. Lipsiae, 1883.

GIARRATANO 1902. Blossii Aemilii Dracontii *Orestes*. Recognovit Cesare Giarratano. Mediolani-Panormi-Neapoli, 1902.

GRILLONE 2008. Blossi Aem. Draconti *Orestis Tragoedia*. Introduzione, testo critico e commento a cura di Antonino Grillone, pp. 51-95. Bari: Edipuglia, 2008 /*InvLuc* 33/.

MÄHLY 1866. Anonymi *Orestis tragoedia* emendatiorem edidit Jacobus Maehly. Lipsiae, 1866.

MÜLLER (C.G.) 1858. Carmen epicum inscriptum *Orestis Tragoedia* quod ex codicibus Bongarsiano et Ambrosiano primum edidit C.G. Müller. Rudolstadt, 1858.

PEIPER 1875. Dracontii *Orestis tragoedia*. Recensuit Rudolf Peiper. Wratislaviae, 1875.

RAPISARDA 1964. *La tragedia di Oreste*. Testo con introduzione, traduzione, commento e indici di Emanuele Rapisarda, pp. 1-35. Catania: Centro di Studi sull'antico cristianesimo, 1964.

SCHENKL 1867. *Orestis Tragoedia*, carmen epicum saeculo post Christum natum sexto compositum emendatius edidit Karl Schenkl. Pragae, 1867.

Romulea

BÄHRENS 1883. Dracontii *carmina profana*. Recensuit et emendavit Aemilius Baehrens. In *Poetae Latini minores*, vol. V, pp. 126-217. Lipsiae, 1883.

DÍAZ DE BUSTAMANTE 1978. José Manuel Díaz de Bustamante. *Draconcio y sus carmina profana. Estudio biográfico, introducción y edición crítica*, pp. 267-384. Santiago de Compostela: Monograf. de la Univ. de Santiago de Compostela 44, 1978.

DUHN 1873. Dracontii *Carmina minora* plurima inedita ex codice Neapolitano edidit Fridericus de Duhn. Lipsiae, 1873.

KAUFMANN 2006a. Helen Kaufmann. Dracontius, *Romul.* 10 (*Medea*), Einleitung, Text, Übersetzung und Kommentar, pp. 65-103. Heidelberg: Winter, 2006.

LUCERI 2007. *Gli epitalami di Blossio Emilio Draconzio* (*Rom.* 6 e 7) a cura di Angelo Luceri. Roma: Herder, 2007.

WEBER 1995. *Der Hylas des Dracontius: Romulea 2* von Brigitte Weber, pp. 128-139. Stuttgart: B.G. Teubner, 1995 /Beiträge zur Altertumskunde; Bd. 47/.

Aegritudo Perdicae

BÄHRENS 1883. *Aegritudo Perdicae*. Recensuit et emendavit Aemilius Baehrens. In *Poetae Latini minores*, vol. V, pp. 112-125. Lipsiae, 1883.

GRILLO 2010. Antonino Grillo. *La* Aegritudo Perdicae *rivisitata. Testo criticamente riveduto, traduzione, commento e appendice esegetico-testuale. 2ª edizione rivista e accresciuta*, pp. 14-45. Messina: EDAS, 2010.

HUNT 1970. John Mortimer Hunt. *The Aegritudo Perdicae*. Edited with Translation and Commentary, pp. 1-35. Diss. Bryn Mawr Coll., PA, 1970.

RIESE 1906. *Aegritudo Perdicae*. Recensuit Alexander Riese. In Fr. Buecheler – A. Riese. *Anthologia Latina* I^2 2, pp. 285-296. Lipsiae, 1906.

ROMANO 1958-59. Domenico Romano. "Interpretazione della *Aegritudo Perdicae*." *AAPal* 19 (1958-59): 194-209.

VOLLMER 1914. *Aegritudo Perdicae*. Iterum recensuit Fridericus Vollmer. In *Poetae Latini minores*[2], vol. V, pp. 238-250. Lipsiae, 1914.

ZURLI 1987. *Aegritudo Perdicae*. Recognovit Laurianus Zurli. Leipzig: B.G. Teubner, 1987.

MAXIMIANUS

AGOZZINO 1970. Massimiano: *Elegie* a cura di Tullio Agozzino. Bologna: Biblioteca Silva di Filologia – Serie Testi, 1970.

BÄHRENS 1883. *Maximiani elegiae*. Recensuit et emendavit Aemilius Baehrens. In *Poetae Latini minores*, vol. V, pp. 313-348. Lipsiae, 1883.

FO 1984-85. Alessandro Fo. "L'*Appendix Maximiani* (= *Carmina* Garrod-Schetter): edizione critica, problemi, osservazioni." *RomBarb* 8 (1984-85): 151-230.

GUARDALBEN 1993. Massimiano: *Elegie della vecchiaia* a cura di Dario Guardalben. Firenze: Ponte alle Grazie, 1993.

LIND 1988. Gabriele Zerbi, *Gerontocomia:* On the Care of the Aged and Maximianus, *Elegies on Old Age and Love*. Edited and translated by L.R. Lind, pp. 319-336. Philadelphia, PA: Amer. Philosophical Soc., 1988.

PETSCHENING 1890. *Maximiani elegiae* ad fidem codicis Etonensis recensuit et emendavit M. Petschening. Berlin, 1890 /*Berliner Studien für Klass. Philol. und Archeol.* 11(2)/.

PRADA 1920. Giuseppe Prada. *Lamenti e guai di un vecchio: versione metrica delle elegie di Massimiano*. Abbiategrasso, 1920.

SANDQUIST ÖBERG 1999. *Versus Maximiani*: Der Elegienzyklus textkritisch herausgegeben übersetzt und neu interpretiert von Christina Sandquist Öberg, pp. 92-137. Stockholm: Almqvist och Wiksell, 1999 /Acta Universitatis Stockholmiensis. Studia Latina Stockholmiensia; 43/.

SCHNEIDER 2003. Wolfgang Christian Schneider. *Die elegischen Verse von Maximian: Eine letze Widerrede gegen die neue christliche Zeit*, pp. 162-193. Stuttgart: Franz Steiner Verlag, 2003.

WEBSTER 1900. *The Elegies of Maximianus*. Edited by Richard Webster, pp. 25-57. Princeton, 1900.

THE EPIGRAMMATISTS: ENNODIUS, LUXORIUS, CC. 90-197 RIESE (*UNIUS POETAE SYLLOGE*)

Ennodius

HARTEL 1882. Magni Felicis Ennodii *opera omnia*. Recensuit et commentario critico instruxit Guilelmus Hartel. *CSEL* 6. Vindobonae, 1882.

VOGEL 1885. Magni Felicis Ennodi *opera*. Recensuit Fridericus Vogel. *MGH AA* 7. Berolini, 1885.

Luxorius

BÄHRENS 1882. Luxorii *epigrammaton liber*. Recensuit et emendavit Aemilius Baehrens. In *Poetae Latini minores*, vol. IV, pp. 386-425. Lipsiae, 1882.

DAL COROBBO 2006. Fabio Dal Corobbo. *Per la lettura di Lussorio. Status quaestionis, testi e commento*, pp. 72-147. Bologna: Pàtron, 2006.

HAPP 1986 I. Heinz Happ. Luxurius. Text, Untersuchungen, Kommentar. Band I: Text, Untersuchungen, pp. 5-70. Stuttgart: B.G. Teubner, 1986.

HORVÁTH, KURUCZ 1963. Ferenc Kurucz ed. *Luxorius költeményei latinul és magyarul*. Gondotza és ellenöritze I.K. Horváth. Szeged, 1963 /Acta Universitatis de Attila József nominatae. Acta antiqua et archaeologica, t. VI/.

MEYER 1835. *Anthologia veterum Latinorum epigrammatum et poematum*. Editionem Burmannianam digessit et auxit Henricus Meyerus, t. I, pp. 125-151. Lipsiae, 1835.

O'CONNELL 1984. *The Epigrams of Luxorius*. Translated by R. O'Connell. Philadelphia, PA: Atlantis, 1984.

RIESE 1894. Luxorii *liber epigrammaton*. Recensuit Alexander Riese. In Fr. Buecheler and A. Riese. *Anthologia Latina* I^2 1, pp. 247-288. Lipsiae, 1894.

ROSENBLUM 1961. Morris Rosenblum. *Luxorius. A Latin Poet among the Vandals*, pp. 110-169. New York: Columbia Univ. Press, 1961.

SHACKLETON BAILEY 1982. Luxorii *liber epigrammaton*. Recensuit D.R. Shackleton Bailey. In *Anthologia Latina* I 1, pp. 235-286. Stutgardiae: B.G. Teubner, 1982.

cc. 90-197 Riese (*Unius poetae sylloge*)

BÄHRENS 1882. Incerti cc. 278-377. Recensuit et emendavit Aemilius Baehrens. In *Poetae Latini minores*, vol. IV, pp. 281-321. Lipsiae, 1882.

KAY 2006. *Epigrams from the Anthologia Latina*: Text, Translation and Commentary by N.M. Kay, pp. 39-64. London: Duckworth, 2006.

RIESE 1894. cc. 90-197. Recensuit Alexander Riese. In Fr. Buecheler and A. Riese. *Anthologia Latina* I^2 1, pp. 122-162. Lipsiae, 1894.

SHACKLETON BAILEY 1982. cc. 78-188. Recensuit D.R. Shackleton Bailey. In *Anthologia Latina* I 1, pp. 79-130. Stutgardiae: B.G. Teubner, 1982.

ZURLI 2007. *Unius poetae sylloge. Anthologia Latina* cc. 90-197, Riese = 78-188, Shackleton Bailey. Recognovit Loriano Zurli (traduzione di Nino Scivoletto), pp. 133-194. Hildesheim-Zürich-New York: G. Olms, 2007 /Bibliotheca Weidmanniana 11/.

OTHER ANCIENT AND MEDIEVAL AUTHORS AND WORKS

Accessus ad auctores

HUYGENS 1954. *Accessus ad auctores*. Édition critique par R.B.C. Huygens. Bruxelles: *Collection Latomus* 15, 1954.

HUYGENS 1970. *Accessus ad auctores. Bernard d'Utrecht. Conrad d'Hirsau. Dialogus super auctores*. Edition critique entièrement revue et augmentée par R.B.C. Huygens. Leiden: E.J. Brill, 1970.

Anonymi versus serpentini

ZURLI – SCIVOLETTO – PAOLUCCI 2008. Loriano Zurli – Nino Scivoletto (trad.) – Paola Paolucci (comm.). *Anonymi versus serpentini*. Hildesheim: Weidmann, 2008.

Ausonius

GREEN 1991. *The Works of Ausonius*: Edited with Introduction and Commentary by R.P.H. Green. Oxford, 1991.

KAY 2001. Ausonius, *Epigrams*: Text with Introduction and Commentary by N.M. Kay. London: Duckworth, 2001.

Catullus

GOOLD 1995. Catullus, Tibullus and *Pervigilium Veneris*. Second Edition Revised by G.P. Goold. Loeb Classical Library. Cambridge & London: Harvard Univ. Press, 1995.

Ciris

LYNE 1978. *Ciris*: A Poem Attributed to Vergil. Edited with an Introduction and Commentary by R.O.A.M. Lyne. Cambridge: Cambridge Univ. Press, 1978.

Claudian

RICCI 2001. Claudii Claudiani *Carmina minora*. Introduzione, traduzione e commento a cura di M.L. Ricci. Bari, 2001.

Coronatus

ZURLI 2005a. Loriano Zurli. Coronatus (traduzione di Nino Scivoletto). Roma: Herder, 2005 / *Anthologiarum Latinarum II Anthologia Salmasiana 3*/.

De rosis nascentibus

CUPAIUOLO 1984. Il *De rosis nascentibus*. Introduzione, testo critico, traduzione e commento di Giovanni Cupaiuolo. Roma: Ed. dell'Ateneo, 1984.

Horace

BRINK 1971. C.O. Brink. *Horace on Poetry: The Ars Poetica*. Cambridge: Cambridge Univ. Press, 1971.

JUREWICZ 2000 I. Kwintus Horacjusz Flakkus. *Dzieła wszystkie* / Quinti Horati Flacci *Opera omnia*, vol. I. Curavit Oktawiusz Jurewicz. Warszawa: PWN, 2000.

JUREWICZ 2000 II. Kwintus Horacjusz Flakkus. *Dzieła wszystkie* / Quinti Horati Flacci *Opera omnia*, vol. II. Curavit Oktawiusz Jurewicz. Warszawa: PWN, 2000.

Martial

SHACKLETON BAILEY 1993 I. Martial. *Epigrams*, vol. I. Edited and Translated by D.R. Shackleton Bailey. Loeb Classical Library. Cambridge & London: Harvard Univ. Press, 1993.

SHACKLETON BAILEY 1993 II. Martial. *Epigrams*, vol. II. Edited and Translated by D.R. Shackleton Bailey. Loeb Classical Library. Cambridge & London: Harvard Univ. Press, 1993.

SHACKLETON BAILEY 1993 III. Martial. *Epigrams*, vol. III. Edited and Translated by D.R. Shackleton Bailey. Loeb Classical Library. Cambridge & London: Harvard Univ. Press, 1993.

Ovid

ANDERSON 1991. P. Ovidii Nasonis *Metamorphoses*. Edidit William S. Anderson. Stutgardiae et Lipsiae: B.G. Teubner, 1991.

KENNEY 1994. P. Ovidi Nasonis *Amores*; *Medicamina faciei femineae*; *Ars amatoria*; *Remedia amoris* iteratis curis edidit E.J. Kenney. Oxonii: e Typographeo Clarendoniano, 1994.

WHEELER 1996. Ovid. *Tristia, Ex Ponto*. Translated by Arthur Leslie Wheeler. Loeb Classical Library. Cambridge & London: Harvard Univ. Press, 1996.

Statius

SHACKLETON BAILEY 2003 I. Statius. *Silvae*. Edited and Translated by D.R. Shackleton Bailey. Loeb Classical Library. Cambridge & London: Harvard Univ. Press, 2003.

SHACKLETON BAILEY 2003 II. Statius. *Thebaid*, Books 1-7. Edited and Translated by D.R. Shackleton Bailey. Loeb Classical Library. Cambridge & London: Harvard Univ. Press, 2003.

SHACKLETON BAILEY 2003 III. Statius. *Thebaid*, Books 8-12. *Achilleid*. Edited and Translated by D.R. Shackleton Bailey. Loeb Classical Library. Cambridge & London: Harvard Univ. Press, 2003.

Valerius Flaccus

MOZLEY 1972. Valerius Flaccus. *Argonautica*. Translated by J.H. Mozley. Loeb Classical Library. Cambridge & London: Harvard Univ. Press, 1972.

Venantius Fortunatus

REYDELLET 2004. Venance Fortunat. *Poèmes*, t. I: Livres IX-XI. Texte établi et traduit par Marc Reydellet. Paris: Les Belles Lettres, 2004.

SANTORELLI 1994. Venanzio Fortunato: *Epitaphium Vilithutae* (IV 26). Introduzione, traduzione e commento a cura di Paola Santorelli. Napoli: Liguori Ed., 1994.

Virgil

CONTE 2009. P. Vergilius Maro. *Aeneis*. Recensuit Gian Biagio Conte. (Bibliotheca Teubneriana) Berolini et Novi Eboraci: Walter de Gruyter, 2009.

FAIRCLOUGH 1999. Virgil. *Eclogues*, *Georgics*, *Aeneid*: Books 1-6. Translated by H. Rushton Fairclough. Loeb Classical Library. Cambridge & London: Harvard Univ. Press, 1999.

FAIRCLOUGH 2000. Virgil. *Aeneid*: Books 7-12, *Appendix Vergiliana*. Translated by H. Rushton Fairclough. Loeb Classical Library. Cambridge & London: Harvard Univ. Press, 2000.

DICTIONARIES OF THE LATIN LANGUAGE

IL DIZIONARIO DELLA LINGUA LATINA. Gian Biagio Conte, Emilio Pianezzola, Giuliano Ranucci eds. *Il Dizionario della lingua latina*. Firenze: Le Monnier, 2000.

OLD. P.G.W. Glare ed. *Oxford Latin Dictionary*, Oxford: Clarendon Press, 1996.

LEWIS and SHORT. Charlton T. Lewis and Charles Short eds. *A Latin Dictionary*. Online at: http://www.perseus.tufts.edu/cgi-bin/morphindex?lang=la [May 19, 2010].

ThLL. *Thesaurus linguae latinae*. Lepzig: Teubner, 1900-<2010 >.

SECONDARY SOURCES

1. STUDIES ON SPECIFIC POETIC GENRES

Epyllion

ALLEN 1940. Walter Allen Jr. "The Epyllion: A Chapter in the History of Literary Criticism." *TAPhA* 71 (1940): 1-27.

ALLEN 1958. Walter Allen Jr. "The Non-Existent Classical Epyllion." *SPh* 55 (1958): 515-518.

BARTELS 2004. Annette Bartels. *Vergleichende Studien zur Erzählkunst des römischen Epyllion*. Göttingen: Duehrkohp & Radicke, 2004.

BRIGHT 1987. David F. Bright. *The Miniature Epic in Vandal Africa*. Norman and London: Norman Oklahoma Univ. Press, 1987.

CRUMP 1931. Marjorie M. Crump. *The Epyllion from Theocritus to Ovid*. Oxford: Blackwell, 1931.

FUCECCHI 2002. Marco Fucecchi. "In cerca di una forma: vicende dell'epillio (e di alcuni suoi personaggi) in età augustea: appunti su Teseo e Orfeo nelle *Metamorfosi*." *MD* 49 (2002): 85-116.

HEUMANN 1904. Johannes Heumann. *De epyllio Alexandrino*. Koenigsee, 1904.

JACKSON 1913. Carl Newell Jackson. "The Latin Epyllion." *HSPh* 24 (1913): 37-50.

KIRKWOOD 1942. P. Kirkwood. *The Greek and Latin Epyllion*. Diss. Johns Hopkins, 1942.

MAY 1910. Gerhardus May. *De stilo epylliorum Romanorum*. Kiel, 1910.

MOST 1982. Glenn Most. "Neues zur Geschichte des Terminus <<Epyllion>>." *Philologus* 126 (1982): 153-156.

PERROTTA 1923. G. Perrotta. "Arte e tecnica nell'epillio alessandrino." *A&R* 1923: 213-229.

PERUTELLI 1979. Alessandro Perutelli. *La narrazione commentata: studi sull'epillio latino*. Pisa: Giardini, 1979.

REILLY 1953-54. J.F. Reilly. "Origins of the Word <<Epyllion>>." *CJ* 49 (1953-54): 111-114.

RICHARDSON 1944. Lawrence Richardson Jr. *Poetical Theory in Republican Rome*. New Haven: Yale Univ. Press; London: H. Milford, Oxford Univ. Press, 1944.

STYKA 1995. Jerzy Styka. *Fas et antiqua castitudo. Die Ästhetik der römischen Dichtung der republikanischen Epoche*. Trier: Wissenschaftlicher Verlag Trier, 1995 /Bochumer Altertumswissenschaftliches Colloquium Bd 19/ [on epyllion, pp. 220-230].

TOOHEY 1992. Peter Toohey. *Reading Epic: An Introduction to the Ancient Narratives*. Abingdon-New York: Routledge, 1992 [see pp. 100-120 & 211-223].

VESSEY 1970. D.W.T.C. Vessey. "Thoughts on the Epyllion." *CJ* 66 (1970): 38-43.

WOLFF 1988. Étienne Wolff. "Quelques precisions sur le mot <<epyllion>>." *RPh* 62(2) (1988): 299-303.

Elegy

BARTOL 1993. Krystyna Bartol. *Greek Elegy and Iambus. Studies in Ancient Literary Sources*. Poznań: Wydawnictwo Naukowe UAM, 1993 [on terminology concerning elegy, pp. 18-30; on Latin generic terminology, pp. 41-43].

DAY 1938. Archibald A. Day. *The Origins of Latin Love-Elegy*. Oxford: Blackwell, 1938.

JACOBY 1905. Felix Jacoby. "Zur Entstehung der römischen Elegie." *RhM* 60 (1905): 38-105.

LEO 1900. Friedrich Leo. "Elegie und Komödie." *RhM* 55 (1900): 604-611.

LEWANDOWSKI 1995. Ignacy Lewandowski ed. *Elegia poprzez wieki*. Konferencja naukowa. 8-9 XI 1994. Poznań: VIS Wydawnictwo, 1995.

LUCK 1959. Georg Luck. *The Latin Love Elegy*. London: Methuen, 1959.

MILLER 2002. Paul Allen Miller ed. *Latin Erotic Elegy. An Anthology and Reader*. London-New York: Routledge, 2002.

PINOTTI 1978. Paola Pinotti. "Sui rapporti tra epillio ed elegia narrativa nella letteratura latina del I secolo a. C." *GIF* 30 (1978): 1-26.

PINOTTI 2002. Paola Pinotti. *L'elegia latina: storia di una forma poetica*. Roma: Carocci, 2002.

URBAN-GODZIEK 2005. Grażyna Urban-Godziek. *Elegia renesansowa. Przemiany gatunku w Polsce i w Europie*. Kraków: Universitas, 2005.

Epigram

BENEDETTI 1980. Fabrizio Benedetti. *La tecnica del vertere negli epigrammi di Ausonio*. Firenze. Olschki Ed., 1980.

BERNT 1968. Günter Bernt. *Das lateinische Epigramm im Übergang von der Spätantike zum frühen Mittelalter*. München: Arbeo-Gesellschaft, 1968.

CIOCCI 1985. Rita Ciocci. "La durata dell'epigramma in Marziale e nella tradizione. Lettura di Mart. III 58." *AFLM* 18 (1985): 185-200.

CITRONI 1969. Mario Citroni. "La teoria lessinghiana dell'epigramma e le interpretazioni moderne di Marziale." *Maia* 21 (1969): 215-243.

CITRONI 1991. Mario Citroni. "L'epigramma." In F. Montanari ed. *La poesia latina. Forme, autori, problemi*, pp. 171-189 & 203-207. Roma: NIS, 1991.

CITRONI 2003a. Mario Citroni. "Marziale, Plinio il Giovane, e il problema dell'identità di genere dell'epigramma latino." In Ferruccio Bertini ed. *Giornate Filologiche Francesco della Corte* III, pp. 7-29. Genova: Istituto di Filologia classica e medievale, 2003.

DANIELEWICZ – BARTOL 1997. Jerzy Danielewicz and Krystyna Bartol eds. *Epigram grecki i łaciński w kulturze Europy*. Poznań: Wydawnictwo Naukowe UAM, 1997.

LAURENS 1989. Pierre Laurens. *L'abeille dans l'ambre. Célébration de l'épigramme de l'époque alexandrine à la fin de la Renaissance*. Paris: Les Belles Lettres, 1989.

LAUSBERG 1982. Marion Lausberg. *Das Einzeldistichon. Studien zum antiken Epigramm*. München: Fink, 1982.

LUISELLI 1973. Bruno Luiselli. "Sul significato socio-culturale dell'epigramma latino." *Studi Romani* 21 (1973): 441-450.

MAAZ 1992. Wolfgang Maaz. *Lateinische Epigrammatik in hohen Mittelalter. Literarhistorische Untersuchungen zur Martial-Rezeption*. Hildesheim-München-Zürich: Weidmann, 1992.

MONDIN 2008. Luca Mondin. "La misura epigrammatica nella tarda antichità." In Alfredo M. Morelli ed. *Epigramma longum. Da Marziale alla tarda antichità* (Cassino, 29-31 mag. 2006), pp. 397-494. Cassino: Edizioni dell'Università degli Studi di Cassino, 2008.

MORELLI 2008. Alfredo Mario Morelli ed. *Epigramma longum. Da Marziale alla tarda antichità* (Cassino, 29-31 mag. 2006). Cassino: Edizioni dell'Università degli Studi di Cassino, 2008.

MUNARI 1958. Franco Munari. "Die spätlateinische Epigrammatik." *Philologus* 102 (1958): 127-139.

PFOHL 1969. Gerhard Pfohl ed. *Das Epigramm. Zur Geschichte einer inschriftlichen und literarischen Gattung*. Darmstadt: Wissenschaftliche Buchgesellschaft, 1969.

PUELMA 1997. Mario Puelma. "Epigramma: osservazioni sulla storia di un termine greco-latino." *Maia* 49 (1997): 189-213.

SZELEST 1980. Hanna Szelest. "*Ut faciam breviora mones epigrammata, Corde*... Eine Martial-Studie." *Philologus* 124 (1980): 99-108.

2. STUDIES ON SPECIFIC AUTHORS AND WORKS

Dracontius and the *Aegritudo Perdicae*

Dracontius

Commentaries

Opera omnia

BOUQUET 1995. Dracontius, *Œuvres*, t. III: *La Tragédie d'Oreste, Poèmes Profanes* I-V. Introduction par Jean Bouquet et Étienne Wolff. Paris: Les Belles Lettres, 1995.

WOLFF 1996. Dracontius, *Œuvres*, t. IV: *Poèmes Profanes* VI-X, *Fragments*. Texte établi et traduit par Étienne Wolff. Paris: Les Belles Lettres, 1996.

Orestis tragoedia

GRILLONE 2008. Blossi Aem. Draconti *Orestis Tragoedia*. Introduzione, testo critico e commento a cura di Antonino Grillone, pp. 99-161 [see also Prefazione, pp. 7-47]. Bari: Edipuglia, 2008 /*InvLuc* 33/.

JARCHO 2000. Виктор Ярхо (Viktor Jarcho). "Эмилий Блоссий Драконций. *Трагедия Ореста*. Вступительная статья, перевод с древнегреческого и комментарии." In *Вестник древней истории* (*Journal of Ancient History*) 3/2000: 208 ff. /online at: http://ancientrome.ru/antlitr/dracontius/orest-f.htm [Sept. 27, 2010]/.

RAPISARDA 1964. *La tragedia di Oreste*. Testo con introduzione, traduzione, commento e indici di Emanuele Rapisarda, pp. 37-250. Catania: Centro di Studi sull'antico cristianesimo, 1964.

Romulea

DÍAZ DE BUSTAMANTE 1978. José Manuel Díaz de Bustamante. *Draconcio y sus carmina profana. Estudio biográfico, introducción y edición critica*, pp. 385-393 [see also pp. 33-242]. Santiago de Compostela: Monograf. de la Univ. de Santiago de Compostela 44, 1978.

KAUFMANN 2006a. Helen Kaufmann. Dracontius, *Romul*. 10 (*Medea*), Einleitung, Text, Übersetzung und Kommentar, pp. 105-466 [see also Einleitung, pp. 9-64]. Heidelberg: Winter, 2006.

WEBER 1995. *Der Hylas des Dracontius: Romulea 2* von Brigitte Weber, pp. 140-214 [see also pp. 21-127 & 215-256]. Stuttgart: B.G. Teubner, 1995 /Beiträge zur Altertumskunde; Bd. 47/.

Concordances

MARINO 1981. Rosanna Marino. *Concordanze della* Orestis tragoedia *di Draconzio*. Pisa: Giardini, 1981.

MARINO 1990. Rosanna Marino. *Concordanze degli epilli minori di Draconzio (*Romulea *I, II, VIII, X) con addendum alle concordanze dell'*Orestis tragoedia. Pisa: Giardini, 1990.

WOLFF 1989. Étienne Wolff. *Index nominum et verborum profani Dracontii praeter* Orestis tragoediam. Hildesheim-New York: Olms-Weidmann, 1989.

Studies

AGUDO CUBAS 1978. Rosa Maria Agudo Cubas. "Dos epilios de Draconcio *De raptu Helenae* y *Hylas*." *CFC* 14 (1978): 263-328.

ALFONSI 1964. L. Alfonsi. "Dracontiana. Su un momento cristiano dell'*Orestis tragoedia*." In *Oikoumene. Studi paleocristiani in onore del Concilio Ecumenico Vaticano* II, pp. 11-14. Centro di studi sull'antico cristianesimo Università di Catania, 1964.

ARDUINI 1987. Paolo Arduini. "Alcuni esempi di tecnica allusiva nel proemio dell'*Orestis tragoedia* di Draconzio." *Orpheus* 8 (1987): 366-380.

ARENA 1951. C. Arena. "Rapporti fra Reposiano e Draconzio." *Miscellanea di Studi di Letteratura Cristiana Antica* 3 (1951): 110-123.

ARICÒ 1978. Giuseppe Aricò. *Mito e tecnica narrativa nell'*Orestis tragoedia. Palermo, 1978 /*AAPal* 37 (1977-78): 5-104/.

BARWINSKI 1887. B. Barwinski. *Quaestiones ad Dracontium et* Orestis tragoediam *pertinentes. Quaestio I. De genere dicendi.* Diss. Gottingae, 1887.

BARWINSKI 1888a. B. Barwinski. "De Dracontio Catulli imitatore." *RhM* 43 (1888): 310-311.

BARWINSKI 1888b. B. Barwinski. "Quaestiones ad Dracontium et *Orestis tragoediam* pertinentes. Quaestio II. De rerum mythicarum tractatione." *Jahresbericht über das Königliche Katholische Gymnasium in Deutsch-Krone in dem Schuljahre 1887-1888* 33 (1888): 3-15.

BARWINSKI 1890. B. Barwinski. "Quaestiones ad Dracontium et *Orestis tragoediam* pertinentes. Pars III. De rationibus prosodiacis et metricis." *Jahresbericht über das Königliche Katholische Gymnasium in Deutsch-Krone in dem Schuljahre 1889-1890* 35 (1890): 3-10.

BELTRÁN NOGUER – SÁNCHEZ-LAFUENTE ANDRÉS 1998. María Teresa Beltrán Noguer and Ángela Sánchez-Lafuente Andrés. "Es la figura de Medea de Draconzio la Medea de Séneca?" In Luis Gil, Marcelo Martínez Pastor, Rosa María Aguilar eds. *Homenaje a J.S. Lasso de la Vega contexta*, pp. 295-302. Madrid: Ed. de la Universidad Complutense, 1998.

BISANTI 1983. Armando Bisanti. *Rassegna di studi su Draconzio* (1959-1982). Palermo, 1983.

BLOMGREN 1966. Sven Blomgren. "In Dracontii carmina adnotationes criticae." *Eranos* 64 (1966): 46–66.

BODELÓN GARCÍA 2000. Serafín Bodelón García. "Épica y lírica vándala." *Entemu* 12 (2000): 163-202 /online at: http://www.uned.es/ca-gijon/web/activida/publica/entemu00/a7.PDF [May 18, 2010]/.

BODELÓN GARCÍA 2001. Serafín Bodelón García. "Draconcio y el reino vándalo." *Epos* 17 (2001): 29-53 /online at: http://e-spacio.uned.es/fez/eserv.php?pid=bibliuned:Epos-68460B66-EC44-F562-C507-28F69858600B&dsID=PDF [May 18, 2010]/.

BOUQUET 1982. Jean Bouquet. "L'imitation d'Ovide chez Dracontius." *Caesarodunum* 17 bis (1982): 177-187.

BOUQUET 1989. Jean Bouquet. "L'*Orestis Tragoedia* de Dracontius et l'*Agamemnon* de Sénèque." *ALMArv* 16 (1989): 43-59.

BOUQUET 1996. Jean Bouquet. "L'influence de la déclamation chez Dracontius." In Jacqueline Dangel and Claude Moussy eds. *Les structures de l'oralité en latin*: colloque du Centre Alfred Ernout, Université de Paris IV, 2, 3, 4 juin 1994, pp. 245-255. Paris: Pr de l'Université de Paris-Sorbonne, 1996.

BOUQUET 2008. Jean Bouquet. "Le songe d'Oreste et de Pylade dans l'*Orestis tragoedia* de Dracontius." In Fabrice Galtier and Yves Perrin eds. *Ars Pictoris, Ars Scriptoris. Peinture, Littérature, Histoire.* Mélanges offerts à Jean-Michel Croisille, pp. 173-184. Clermont-Ferrand: Presses Universitaires Blaise Pascal, 2008 /Collection ERGA. Littératures et représentations de l' Antiquité et du Moyen Age 11/.

BRIGHT 1999. David F. Bright. "The Chronology of the Poems of Dracontius." *C&M* 50 (1999): 193-206.

BROŻEK 1980. Mieczysław Brożek. "Drakoncjusz – poeta w więzieniu." *Meander* 35 12 (1980): 553-562.

BRUGNOLI 2001. Giorgio Brugnoli. "L'*Ilias Latina* nei *Romulea* di Draconzio." In Franco Montanari e Stefano Pittaluga eds. *Posthomerica III*: Atti del seminario tenutosi a Genova il 27 aprile 1999, pp. 71-85. Genova: D.AR.FI.CL.ET. "F. Della Corte", 2001.

CASTAGNA 1997a. Luigi Castagna. *Studi draconziani*: 1912-1996. Napoli: Loffredo, 1997.

CASTAGNA – GALIMBERTI BIFFINO – GALLI 1995. Luigi Castagna – Giovanna Galimberti Biffino – Lavinia Galli. "Sul proemio (vv. 1-40) dell'*Orestis tragoedia* di Draconzio." In Luigi Belloni, Guido Milanese, Antonietta Porro eds. *Studia classica Johanni Tarditi oblata*, vol. 2, pp. 781-809. Milano: Vita e Pensiero, 1995.

CAZZANIGA 1950. Ignazio Cazzaniga. "Osservazioni intorno alla composizione dell'*Hylas* di Draconzio." Appendix to *Id. La saga di Itis nella tradizione letteraria e mitografica Greco-romana*, pp. 97-103. Milano-Varese, 1950.

CHATILLON 1952. F. Chatillon. "Dracontiana." *Revue du moyen âge latin* 8 (1952): 177-212.

CLERICI 1973. Ergisto Clerici. "Due poeti, Emilio Blossio Draconzio e Venanzio Fortunato." *RIL* 107 (1973): 108-150.

CORSARO 1961. Francesco Corsaro. "Problemi storico-letterari del cristianesimo africano nel V° secolo. Studi su Draconzio." *Miscellanea di Studi di Letteratura Cristiana Antica* 11 (1961): 5-32.

CORSARO 1979. Francesco Corsaro. "La presenza di Seneca tragico nella Spätantike; l'*Agamemnon* di Seneca e l'*Orestis tragoedia* di Draconzio." *SicGymn* 32 (1979): 321-349.

COURTNEY 1980. E. Courtney. "Observations on the Latin Anthology." *Hermathena* 129 (1980): 37-50.

COURTNEY 1984. E. Courtney. "Some Poems of the Latin Anthology." *CPh* 79 (1984): 309-313.

CRISTÓBAL 1988. V. Cristóbal. "Tempestades epicas." *CIF* 14 (1988): 125-148 [on Dracontius, pp. 125-135].

DE GAETANO 2009. Miryam De Gaetano. *Scuola e potere in Draconzio*. Alessandria: Ed. dell'Orso, 2009.

DE PRISCO 1977. Antonio De Prisco. "Osservazioni su Draconzio *Romul.* VIII 11-23." *Vichiana* 6 (1977): 290-300.

DE PRISCO 1992. Antonio De Prisco. "Due note al *De raptu Helenae* di Draconzio (*carm.* 8, 36 e 244)." In E. Flores, A. V. Nazzaro, L. Nicastri, G. Polara eds. *Miscellanea di studi in onore di Armando Salvatore*, pp. 221-231. Napoli, 1992 /Pubblicazioni del Dipartimento di Filologia Classica "F. Arnaldi" dell'Università degli Studi di Napoli Federico II; 7/.

DÍAZ DE BUSTAMANTE 2002. José Manuel Díaz de Bustamante. "El epilio *Medea* de Draconcio." In Aurora López and Andres Pociña eds. *Medeas: versiones de un mito desde Grecia hasta hoy*, pp. 697-718. Granada: Universidad de Granada, 2002.

EDWARDS 2004. M.J. Edwards. "Dracontius the African and the Fate of Rome." *Latomus* 63 (2004): 151-160.

ELLIS 1874. R. Ellis. "On the Newly Edited Poems of Dracontius." *JPh* 5 (1874): 252-262.

FRIEDRICH 1966. Wolf Harmut Friedrich. "Medea in Kolchis." *A&A* 12 (1966): 3-28.

FRIEDRICH 1967. Wolf Harmut Friedrich. *Vorbild und Neugestaltung. Sechs Kapitel zur Geschichte der Tragödie*. Göttingen: Vandenhoeck und Ruprecht, 1967.

GÄRTNER 2001. Thomas Gärtner. "Das Vogelprodigium im Helena-Epyllion des Dracontius: antike Vorbilder und mittelalterliches Nachleben." *Mnemosyne* 54 (2001): 345-349.

GIARRATANO 1906. Cesare Giarratano. *Commentationes Dracontianae*. Napoli, 1906.

GIL 1984. Juan Gil. "Dracontiana." In *Navicula Tubingensis. Studia in honorem Antonii Tovar*, pp. 161-166. Tübingen, 1984.

GRILLO 1988. Antonino Grillo. "Critica del testo ed esegesi. Su alcuni tormentati versi proemiali del *De raptu Helenae di Draconzio*." In Antonino Grillo. *Tra Filologia e Narratologia: dai pro-*

emi omerici ad Apollonio Rodio: Ilias Latina, Ditti-Settimio, Darete Frigio, Draconzio, pp. 115-127. Roma: Ed. dell'Ateneo, 1988.

GRILLO 2000. Antonino Grillo. "Linguaggio tecnico-scientifico in carmi draconziani: per l'esegesi e la sistemazione di versi problematici." In Paola Radici Colace and Antonio Zumbo eds. *Letteratura scientifica e tecnica greca e latina*: atti del Seminario internazionale di studi, Messina 29-31 ottobre 1997, pp. 193-207. Messina: EDAS, 2000 (= GRILLO 2010, pp. 84-96).

GRILLONE 1987. Antonino Grillone. "*Purgandus Orestes*. Bravura avvocatizia e cammino spirituale di Draconzio nell'*Orestis tragoedia*." *QC* 9 (1987): 77-102.

GRILLONE 1999a. Antonino Grillone. "Contributi al testo dell'*Orestis tragoedia* di Draconzio: in margine ad una recente edizione." *RomBarb* 16 (1999): 209-239.

GRILLONE 1999b. Antonino Grillone. "Note esegetiche all'*Orestis tragoedia* di Draconzio." *Maia* 51(3) (1999): 457-469.

GRILLONE 2000-2002. Antonino Grillone. "Sul testo dell'*Orestis tragoedia* di Draconzio." *RomBarb* 17 (2000-2002): 183-192.

GRILLONE 2004. Antonino Grillone. "L'*Orestis tragoedia* di Draconzio: mito e critica testuale." *RCCM* 46(2) (2004): 319-335.

GRILLONE 2005. Antonino Grillone. "Il divino nell'*Orestis tragoedia* di Draconzio." In *Aspetti e forme del mito: la sacralità*: atti del convegno internazionale di studi sul mito, Erice 3-5 aprile 2005, pp. 147-160. Palermo: Anteprima, 2005.

GRILLONE 2006. Antonino Grillone. "Osservazioni testuali ed esegetiche su due epilli draconziani (*Rom.* 8 e 10)." In L. Castagna ed. *Quesiti, temi, testi di poesia tardolatina Claudiano, Prudenzio, Ilario de Poitiers, Sidonio Apollinare, Draconzio,* Aegritudo Perdicae, *Venanzio Fortunato, corpus dei* Ritmi Latini, pp. 87-104. Frankfurt am Main: Peter Lang, 2006.

GUALANDRI 1974. Isabella Gualandri. "Problemi draconziani." *RIL* 108 (1974): 872-890.

HOUSMAN 1910. A.E. Housman. "Astrology in Dracontius." *CQ* 4 (1910): 191-195.

HUDSON-WILLIAMS 1939. A. Hudson-Williams. "Notes on Dracontius." *CQ* 1939: 157-162.

HUDSON-WILLIAMS 1946. A. Hudson-Williams. "Notes on Dracontius." *CQ* 1946: 92-100.

D'IPPOLITO 1962. Gennaro D'Ippolito. "Draconzio, Nonno e gli idromimi." *A&R* 7 (1962): 1-14.

KAUFMANN 2006b. Helen Kaufmann. "Intertextualität in Dracontius' *Medea (Romul.* 10*)*." *MH* 63 (2006): 104-114.

KLEIN 2001. Richard Klein. "Medea am Ausgang der Antike: Bemerkungen zum Epyllion *Medea* des christlichen Dichters Dracontius." *WJA* 25 (2001): 229-238.

KUIJPER 1958. Dirk Kuijper. *Varia Dracontiana*. Diss. Amsterdam, 1958.

LANGLOIS 1959. P. Langlois. "Dracontius." *RLAC* IV. Stuttgart, 1959: 250-269.

LAURÀ 1996. Mariella Laurà. "Strutture verbali e cesure nell'esametro della *Medea* di Draconzio." *BStudLat* 26(2) (1996): 568-9.

MAILFAIT 1902. Hubertus Mailfait. *De Dracontii poetae lingua*. Diss. Poitiers. Paris, 1902.

MARINO 1984-85. Rosanna Marino. "Sull'*Hylas* di Draconzio." *QCTC* 2-3 (1984-85): 111-122.

MARTIN PUENTE 1997. Cristina Martin Puente. "Las *Georgicas* de Virgilio, fuente del *Hilas* de Draconcio." *Emerita* 65(1) (1997): 77-84.

MAUERHOFER 2004. Kenneth Mauerhofer. *Der Hylas-Mythos in der Antiken Literatur*. München: K.G. Saur, 2004 [on Dracontius's *Hylas* pp. 311-380].

MORELLI 1912. Camillo Morelli. "Studia in seros Latinos poetas. II. De compositione carminis Dracontii quod est *De raptu Helenae*." *SIFC* 19 (1912): 93-120.

MOUSSY 1989. Claude Moussy. "L'imitation de Stace chez Dracontius." *ICS* 14 (1989): 425-433.

MÜLLER (L.) 1866. L. Müller. "Anonymi *Orestis tragoedia*." *RhM* 21 (1866): 455-467.

MURGATROYD 1992. Paul Murgatroyd. "Setting in Six Versions of the Hylas Myth." In Carl Deroux ed. *Studies in Latin Literature and Roman History* VI, pp. 84-93. Bruxelles: *Collection Latomus* 217, 1992 [some notes on Dracontius's *Hylas*].

NOSARTI 2009. Lorenzo Nosarti. "Tessere lucanee in Draconzio e Corippo." In Christine Walde ed. *Lucans* Bellum Civile. *Studien zum Spektrum seiner Rezeption von der Antike bis ins 19. Jahrhundert*, pp. 49-66. Trier: Wissenschaftlicher Verlag Trier, 2009 /Bochumer Altertumswissenschaftliches Colloquium. Band 78/.

POLARA 1974. Giovanni Polara. "Ricerche sul proemio nella poesia latina." *RAAN* 49 (1974): 135-153.

PRIVITERA 1996. Tiziana Privitera. "Oreste <<scholasticus>>: una nota a Draconzio." *Euphrosyne* 24 (1996): 127-146.

PROCACCI 1913. Giuseppe Procacci. "Intorno alla composizione e alle fonti di un carme di Draconzio." *SIFC* 20 (1913): 438-449.

PROVANA 1911. Ettore Provana. "Blossio Emilio Draconzio. Studio biografico e letterario." *MAT* 62 (1911): 23-100.

QUARTIROLI 1946. Anna Maria Quartiroli. "Gli epilli di Draconzio." *Athenaeum* 24 (1946): 160-187.

QUARTIROLI 1947. Anna Maria Quartiroli. "Gli epilli di Draconzio." *Athenaeum* 25 (1947): 17-34.

RAPISARDA 1955. Emanuele Rapisarda. "Il poeta della misericordia divina, I: L'unità del mondo religioso di Draconzio." *Orpheus* 2 (1955): 1-9.

RAPISARDA 1958. Emanuele Rapisarda. "Fato, divinità e libero arbitrio nella *Tragedia di Oreste* di Draconzio." *HJ* 77 (1958): 444-450.

ROMANO 1959. Domenico Romano. *Studi Draconziani*. Palermo: Manfredi, 1959.

ROSSBERG 1878. K. Rossberg. *In Dracontii carmina minora et Orestis quae vocatur tragoediam observationes criticae*. Stade, 1878.

ROSSBERG 1880. K. Rossberg. *De Dracontio et Orestis quae vocatur tragoediae auctore eorundem poetarum Vergilii Ovidii Lucani Statii Claudiani imitatoribus*. Diss. Nordae, 1880.

ROSSBERG 1883. K. Rossberg. "Zur *Orestis Tragoedia*." *Jahrbücher für classische Philologie* 29 (1883): 569-75.

ROSSBERG 1886. K. Rossberg. "Gedichte des Dracontius in der lateinischen Anthologie." *Jahrbücher für classische Philologie* 32 (1886): 721-728.

ROSSBERG 1887. K. Rossberg. "Neue studien zu Dracontius und der *Orestis tragoedia*." *Jahrbücher für classische Philologie* 33 (1887): 833-860.

ROSSBERG 1888-89. K. Rossberg. *Materialien zu einem Commentar über die* Orestis Tragoedia *des Dracontius*, I-II. Hildesheim, 1888-89.

SANTINI 2002. Giovanni Santini. "Aspetti del lessico giuridico in Draconzio, *De raptu Helenae* (*Romul.* 8)." In I. Gualandri ed. *Tra IV e V secolo. Studi sulla cultura latina tardoantica. Quaderni di Acme* 50 (2002): 253-296.

SANTINI 2006. Giovanni Santini. *Inter iura poeta. Ricerche sul lessico giuridico in Draconzio*. Roma: Herder, 2006.

SCAFFAI 1995. Marco Scaffai. "Il corpo disintegrato di Ettore in Draconzio, *Rom.* 9." *Orpheus* 16(2) (1995): 293-329.

SCHETTER 1980 (1994). Willy Schetter. "Medea in Theben." *WJA* N.F. 6a (1980): 209-221 (= W. Schetter. *Kaiserzeit und Spätantike. Kleine Schriften* 1957-1992 hrsg. v. O. Zwierlein, pp. 317-327. Stuttgart: Franz Steiner Verlag, 1994).

SCHETTER 1985. Willy Schetter. "Über Erfindung und Komposition des *Orestes* des Dracontius. Zur spätantiken Neugestaltung eines klassischen Mythos." *FMS* 19 (1985): 48-74.

SCHETTER 1987. Willy Schetter. "Dares und Dracontius: über die Vorgeschichte des Trojanischen Krieges." *Hermes* 115 (1987): 211-231.

SCHETTER 1989. Willy Schetter. "Dracontius togatus." *Hermes* 117 (1989): 342-350.

SCHETTER 1991a. Willy Schetter. "Rezension zu: Bright, D.F., *Miniature Epic*." *Gnomon* 63 (1991): 213-223.

SCHMIDT 1984 (2000). P. L. Schmidt. "*Habent sua fata libelli*. Archetyp und literarische Struktur der *Romulea* des Dracontius." In *Vestigia*. Studi in onore di Giuseppe Billanovich, pp. 681-697. Roma, 1984 (= P. L. Schmidt. *Traditio Latinitatis. Studien zur Rezeption und Überlieferung der lateinischen Literatur* hrsg. v. J. Fugmann, pp. 73-83. Stuttgart: Franz Steiner Verlag, 2000).

SIMONS 2005. Roswitha Simons. *Dracontius und der Mythos: christliche Weltsicht und pagane Kultur in der ausgehenden Spätantike*. München: K.G. Saur, 2005.

TRILLITZSCH 1981. Winfried Trillitzsch. "Der Agamemnonstoff bei Aischylos, Seneca und in der *Orestis Tragoedia* des Dracontius." In E.G. Schmidt ed. *Aischylos und Pindar. Studien zu Werk und Nachwirkung*, pp. 268-274. Berlin, 1981.

VAN ZYL SMIT 2003. Betine Van Zyl Smit. "A Christian Medea in Vandal Africa? Some Aspects of the *Medea* of Blossius Aemilius Dracontius." In A.F. Basson and W.J. Dominik eds. *Literature, Art, History: Studies on Classical Antiquity and Tradition*, pp. 151-60. Frankfurt am Main: Peter Lang, 2003.

WASYL 2007a. Anna Maria Wasyl. "Le metamorfosi di Medea in Ovidio, *Metamorphoses* VII, e Draconzio, *Romulea* X." *Eos* 94 (2007): 81-99.

WOLFF 1993. Étienne Wolff. "Quelques remarques sur l'élision dans la poésie de Dracontius." *RPh* 67 (1993): 95-101.

ZURLI 1998. Loriano Zurli. "A proposito di collazioni novecentesche. il caso della *Medea* di Draconzio." *RFIC* 26(3) (1998): 364-377.

ZURLI 2001. Loriano Zurli. "Dracontiana." *GIF* 53 (2001): 299-307.

Aegritudo Perdicae

Commentaries

GRILLO 2010. Antonino Grillo. *La* Aegritudo Perdicae *rivisitata. Testo criticamente riveduto, traduzione, commento e appendice esegetico-testuale. 2ª edizione rivista e accresciuta*, pp. 47-67 [see also pp. 69-139]. Messina: EDAS, 2010.

HUNT 1970. John Mortimer Hunt. *The Aegritudo Perdicae*. Edited with Translation and Commentary, pp. 36-107. Diss. Bryn Mawr Coll., PA, 1970 (1971).

Concordances

CHRISTIANSEN – DOMINIK – HOLLAND 2002. P.G. Christiansen – W.J. Dominik – J.E. Holland. *Anthologiae Latinae Concordantia*. Hildesheim-Zürich-New York: G. Olms, 2002.

RIZZO 1968. Silvia Rizzo. *Index verborum* Aegritudinis Perdicae *(Anth. Lat. 808)*. Ric. di Storia della lingua lat. II, Roma: Ed. dell'Ateneo, 1968.

Studies

ALTAMURA 1979. Dionysius Altamura. "De sermone eiusque vitiis in epyllio q. i. *Aegritudo Perdicae*." *Latomus* 38 (1979): 675-694.

BALLAIRA 1968. Guglielmo Ballaira. "Perdica e Mirra." *RCCM* 10 (1968): 219-240.

BARBASZ 1924. Guilielmus Barbasz. "In *Aegritudinem Perdicae* animadversiones." *Eos* 27 (1924): 29-39.

BARBASZ 1927. Guilielmus Barbasz. "De *Aegritudinis Perdicae* fontibus, arte, compositionis tempore." *Eos* 30 (1927): 151-169.

CASTAGNA 1997b. Luigi Castagna. "Su un proemio poetico tardolatino (*A.P.* 1-4)." *BStudLat* 27(1) (1997): 102-125.

CHAMOUX 1962. F. Chamoux. "Perdiccas." *Hommages à A. Grenier*, t. 1, pp. 386-396. Bruxelles: *Collection Latomus* 58, 1962.

DI RIENZO 1999a. Daniele Di Rienzo. "Edipo negato: la mediazione del desiderio in *A.P.*" *BStudLat* 29(2) (1999): 541-549.

GALLI 1996. Lavinia Galli. "Studi sull'*Aegritudo Perdicae*. Dall'*editio princeps* del 1877 al 1994." *BStudLat* 26 (1996): 219-234.

HUDSON-WILLIAMS 1939. A. Hudson-Williams. "Notes on *Aegritudo Perdicae*." *CQ* 33 (1939): 162.

HUNT 1990. J.M. Hunt. "*Aegritudo Perdicae* revisited." *CPh* 85(2) (1990): 132-147.

LAVILLE 1975. Giuliana Laville. "Retorica e ambiguità nell'*Aegritudo Perdicae*." *RAAN* 50 (1975): 153-167.

MALAMUD 1993. Martha Malamud. "Vandalising Epic." *Ramus* 22 (1993): 155-173.

MARIOTTI 1969. Scevola Mariotti. "Imitazione e critica del testo. Qualche esempio dall'*Aegritudo Perdicae*." *RFIC* 97 (1969): 385-392.

MATTIACCI 2004. Silvia Mattiacci. "Da Apuleio all'*Aegritudo Perdicae*: nuove metamorfosi del tema di Fedra." In *Concordia discors*. Miscellanea di studi in onore di A. Setaioli, pp. 417-436. Univ. di Perugia, 2004.

MESK 1939. J. Mesk. "*Aegritudo Perdicae*." *WS* 57 (1939): 166-172.

MORELLI 1920. Camillo Morelli. "Sulle tracce del romanzo e della novella. II. L'*Aegritudo Perdicae*." *SIFC* 1 (1920): 75-95.

ROMANI 2007. Silvia Romani. "Quando la virtù nuoce alla salute. Divagazioni sull'incesto." Online at http://www.turindamsreview.unito.it/link/Perdica.pdf [July 06, 2010].

ROMANO 1958-59. Domenico Romano. "Interpretazione della *Aegritudo Perdicae*." *AAPal* 19 (1958-59): 169-216.

ROMANO 1985. Domenico Romano. "Tradizione e novità nella *Aegritudo Perdicae*." In *Le trasformazioni della cultura nella tarda antichità*: Atti del Convegno tenuto a Catania, Università degli Studi, 27 sett.-2 ott. 1982: Coll. Storia XIX, pp. 375-384. Roma: Jouvence, 1985.

SCHETTER 1991b. Willy Schetter. "Vier Adnoten zur *A.P.*" *Hermes* 119 (1991): 94-113.

STUCCHI 2006a. Silvia Stucchi. "Aspetti dell'attenuazione della tematica incestuosa nell'*Aegritudo Perdicae*." In L. Castagna ed. *Quesiti, temi, testi di poesia tardolatina Claudiano, Prudenzio, Ilario de Poitiers, Sidonio Apollinare, Draconzio,* Aegritudo Perdicae, *Venanzio Fortunato, corpus dei* Ritmi Latini, pp. 105-122. Frankfurt am Main: Peter Lang, 2006.

STUCCHI 2006b. Silvia Stucchi. "Alcune note di lettura all'*Aegritudo Perdicae*." In *Quesiti...*, pp. 123-136.

WOLFF 1988. Étienne Wolff. "L' *A.P.*, un poème de Dracontius?" *RPh* 62 (1988): 79-89.

ZURLI 1986. Loriano Zurli. "Prolegomeni ad una nuova edizione della *Aegritudo Perdicae*." *GIF* 38 (1986): 161-219.

ZURLI 1996. Loriano Zurli. "L'*Aegritudo Perdicae* non è di Draconzio." In C. Santini and L. Zurli eds. *Ars narrandi: scritti di narrativa antica in memoria di Luigi Pepe*, pp. 233-261. Napoli: Edizioni scientifiche italiane, 1996.

Maximianus

Commentaries

AGOZZINO 1970. Massimiano: *Elegie* a cura di Tullio Agozzino. Bologna: Biblioteca Silva di Filologia – Serie Testi, 1970.

SANDQUIST ÖBERG 1999. Versus Maximiani: der Elegienzyklus textkritisch herausgegeben übersetzt und neu interpretiert von Christina Sandquist Öberg, pp. 138-152 [see also Einleitung, pp. 9-86]. Stockholm: Almqvist och Wiksell, 1999 /Acta Universitatis Stockholmiensis. Studia Latina Stockholmiensia; 43/.

SCHNEIDER 2003. Wolfgang Christian Schneider. *Die elegischen Verse von Maximian: Eine letze Widerrede gegen die neue christliche Zeit*, pp. 203-228 [see also pp. 11-132 & 147-159]. Stuttgart: Franz Steiner Verlag, 2003.

SPALTENSTEIN 1983. François Spaltenstein. *Commentaire des* Élégies *de Maximien*. Bibl. Helv. Rom. XX Rome: Institute Suisse, 1983.

WEBSTER 1900. *The Elegies of Maximianus*. Edited by Richard Webster, pp. 58-113. Princeton, 1900.

Concordances

MASTANDREA 1995. Paolo Mastandrea. *Concordantia in Maximianum = Concordanza ad* Elegiae *e* Appendix Maximiani (con app. bibliogr. a c. di Chiara Segui). Hildesheim: Olms-Weidmann, 1995.

Studies

ALFONSI 1941-42. Luigi Alfonsi. "Sulle elegie di Massimiano." *AIV* 101 (1941 42): 333 349.

ALFONSI 1942. Aloisius Alfonsi. "De quibusdam locis quos ex antiquis poetis Boethius et Maximianus repetiisse videntur." *Aevum* 1942: 86-92.

ALTAMURA 1982. Dionysius Altamura. "De Maximiani poetae sermone." *Latinitas* 30 (1982): 90-103 /*Latomus* 40 (1981): 818-827/.

ANASTASI 1948. R. Anastasi. "Boezio e Massimiano." *Miscellanea di Studi di Letteratura Cristiana Antica* 2 (1948): 1-20.

ANASTASI 1951. R. Anastasi. "La III elegia di Massimiano." *Miscellanea di Studi di Letteratura Cristiana Antica* 3 (1951): 45-92.

ARCAZ POZO 1995. Juan Luis Arcaz Pozo. "*Passer mortuus est*: Catulo (*carm.* 3) Ovidio (*am.* 3.7); Maximiano (*el.* 5. 87-104)." *CFC(L)* 8 (1995): 79-88.

BARNISH 1990. S.J.B. Barnish. "Maximianus, Cassiodorus, Boethius, Theodahad: Literature, Philosophy, and Politics in Ostrogothic Italy." *NMS* 34 (1990): 16-32.

BELLANOVA 2004. Addolorata Bellanova. "La lezione nostalgica di Ovidio negli amori senili di Massimiano." *AFLS* 25 (2004): 99-124.

BERTINI 1981. Ferruccio Bertini. "Boezio e Massimiano." In L. Obertello ed. *Atti del Congresso internazionale di Studi Boeziani*, Pavia 5-8 ott. 1980, pp. 273-283. Roma: Herder, 1981.

BOANO 1949. Giovanni Boano. "Su Massimiano e le sue elegie." *RFIC* N. S. 27 (1949): 198-216.

BRÖRING 1893. J. Bröring. *Quaestiones Maximianeae*. Diss. Monasterii, 1893.

BUTRICA 2005. J.L. Butrica. "Maximian" (rev. of W.C. Schneider. *Die elegischen Verse*). *The Classical Review* 55(2) (2005): 562-564.

CARRAI 1988. Stefano Carrai. "Echi massimianei nella *Sylva in scabiem* di Poliziano." *Interpres* 8 (1988): 276-282.

CAWSEY 1982. F. Cawsey. "A Note on Maximianus 5.66." *LCM* 7 (1982): 154.

COFFMAN 1934. George R. Coffman. "Old Age from Horace to Chaucer. Some Literary Affinities and Adventures of an Idea." *Speculum* 11 (1934): 249-277.

CONSOLINO 1997. Franca Ela Consolino. "Massimiano e le sorti dell'elegia latina." In Maria Luisa Silvestre and Marisa Squillante eds. *Mutatio rerum: letteratura, filosofia, scienza tra tardo antico e altomedioevo*: atti del convegno di studi (Napoli, 25-26 nov. 1996), pp. 363-400. Napoli: La città del Sole, 1997.

CUPAIUOLO 1997. Giovanni Cupaiuolo. "A proposito dell'esametro di Massimiano: un approccio al problema dell'ordine di composizione delle elegie." In Paolo D'Alessandro ed. *Scritti in onore di Giuseppe Morelli*, pp. 381-391. Bologna: Pàtron 1997.

DAPUNT 1949. Alois Dapunt. *Der Elegiker Maximianus und sein Verhältnis zu seinen Vorgängern, besonders Ovid*. Diss. Innsbruck, 1949.

DEL BARRIO 1985. Felisa Del Barrio. "Innovaciones de Maximiano Etrusco en el género elegíaco." In *Los géneros literarios (*Actes del VIIe Simposi d'Estudis Clàssics, 21-24 de març de 1983), pp. 247-253. Bellaterra (Barcelona), Secció Catalana de la Societat Espanyola d'Estudis Clàssics – Servei de Publicacions de la Universitat Autònoma de Barcelona, 1985.

EHWALD 1889. Rudolf Ehwald. *Ad historiam carminum Ovidianorum recensionemque symbolae*. Gothae, 1889.

ELLIS 1884. R. Ellis. "On the Elegies of Maximianus." I, *AJPh* 5(1) (1884): 1-15; II, *ibid.* 5(2): 145-163.

FO 1986. Alessandro Fo. "Il problema della struttura della raccolta elegiaca di Massimiano." *BStudLat* 16 (1986): 9-21.

FO 1986-87. Alessandro Fo. "Una lettura del corpus massimianeo." *AMArc* 8 (1986-87): 91-128.

FO 1987. Alessandro Fo. "Significato, tecniche e valore della raccolta elegiaca di Massimiano." *Hermes* 115 (1987): 348-371.

FRANZOI 2003-2005. A. Franzoi. "Note massimianee." *Sandalion* 26-28 (2003-2005): 205-213.

FRANZOI 2009. A. Franzoi. "Repertori elettronici, critica del testo, esegesi: una verifica su Massimiano elegiaco." In Loriano Zurli and Paolo Mastandrea eds. *Poesia latina, nuova e-filologia. Opportunità per l'editore e per l'interprete*: atti del Convegno internazionale (Perugia, 13-15 settembre 2007), pp. 401-408. Roma: Herder, 2009.

GAGLIARDI 1988. Donato Gagliardi. "Sull'elegia I di Massimiano." *Koinonia* 12 (1988): 27-37.

GÄRTNER 2004. Thomas Gärtner. "Der letzte klassische Elegiker? Zur Deutung der erotischen Dichtung Maximians." *Göttinger Forum für Altertumswissenschaft* 7 (2004): 119-161.

GUARDALBEN 1978. Dario Guardalben. *Studi su Massimiano*. Tesi di laurea dell'Università di Roma Fac. di Magistero, 1978.

HARTUNG 1967. Albert E. Hartung "The Non-Comic *Merchant's tale*, Maximianus and the Sources." *MS* 29 (1967): 1-25.

HUNT 1978. Iohannes Hunt. "Adnotatiuncula in Maximianum." *PP* 33 (1978): 59-60.

JAITNER-HAHNER 1988. Ursula Jaitner-Hahner. "Maximian und der *Fucus Italicus*. Ein unbekannter Textzeuge." In M. Borgolte and H. Spilling eds. *Litterae medii aevi*. Festschrift für Johanne Autenrieth zu ihrem 65. Geburtstag, pp. 277-292. Sigmaringen: Thorbecke, 1988.

KLEINKNECHT 1937. Hermann Kleinknecht. *Die Gebetsparodie un der Antike*. Stuttgart-Berlin 1937 [esp. pp. 195-199].

LEKUSCH 1896. V. Lekusch. "Zur Verstechnik des Elegikers Maximianus." In *Serta Harteliana*, pp. 257-262. Wien, 1896.

LEOTTA 1985. Rosario Leotta. "Un anonimo imitatore di Massimiano." *GIF* 37 (1985): 91-106.

LEOTTA 1989. Rosario Leotta. "Uno stilema massimianeo." *GIF* 41 (1989): 81-84.

LUTZ 1974. C.E. Lutz. "A medieval textbook." *YLG* 49 (1974): 212-216.

MARIOTTI 1974. Scevola Mariotti. "Cornelii Galli Hendecasyllabi." In *Tra latino e volgare. Per Carlo Dionisotti*, pp. 545-568. Padova: Antenore, 1974.

MARIOTTI 1994. Scevola Mariotti (a cura di Silvia Rizzo). *Scritti medievali e umanistici*, Roma: Edizioni di storia e letteratura, 1994[2].

MASTANDREA 2004. Paolo Mastandrea. "Aratore, Partenio, Vigilio, coetanei (e amici?) di Massimiano elegiaco." In Lucio Cristante and Andrea Tessier eds. *Incontri triestini di filologia classica* 3, 2003-2004, pp. 327-342. Trieste: ed. Università di Trieste, 2004.

MASTANDREA 2005. Paolo Mastandrea. "Per la cronologia di Massimiano elegiaco: elementi interni ed esterni al testo." In Manuel C. Díaz and José M. Díaz de Bustamante eds. *Poesia latina medieval (siglos V-XV)*: actas del IV Congreso del "Internationales Mittelateinerkomitee" (Santiago de Compostela 12-15 de septiembre de 2002), pp. 151-179. Firenze: SISMEL-Edizioni del Galluzzo, 2005.

MAUGER-PLICHON 1999. Brigitte Mauger-Plichon. "Maximianus: un mystérieux poète." *BAGB* 1999 (4): 369-387.

MERONE 1948. Emilio Merone. "Per la biografia di Massimiano." *GIF* 1 (1948): 337-352.

MERONE 1950. Emilio Merone. "Maximianea." *GIF* 3 (1950): 322-336.

MEYERS 2003. Jean Meyers. "La figure du vieillard dans les *Elégies* de Maximien: autobiographie ou fiction?" In Béatrice Bakhouche ed. *L'Ancienneté chez les Anciens*, vol. II. *Mythologie et Religion*, pp. 697-715. Université Montpellier III, 2003.

PINOTTI 1989. Paola Pinotti. "Massimiano elegiaco." In Giuseppe Catanzaro and Francesco Santucci eds. *Tredici secoli di elegia latina*: atti del convegno internazionale (Assisi, 22-24 apr. 1988), pp. 183-203. Assisi, 1989.

PINOTTI 1991. Paola Pinotti. "Da Massimiano a Shakespeare: rappresentazioni del tempo." *Vichiana* 28 (1991): 186-216.

POLARA 1989. Giovanni Polara. "Due note massimiane (v. 99-100; 119-120)." *Sileno* 15 (1989): 197-205.

RAMIREZ DE VERGER 1984. Antonio Ramirez De Verger. "Parodía de un lamento ritual en Maximiano (el. V 87-104)." *Habis* 15 (1984): 149-156.

RAMIREZ DE VERGER 1986. Antonio Ramirez De Verger. "Las Elegías de Maximiano. Tradición y originalidad en un poeta de última ora." *Habis* 17 (1986): 185-193.

RATKOWITSCH 1986. Christine Ratkowitsch. *Maximianus amat. Zur Datierung und Interpretation des Elegikers Maximian*. Wien: Verlag der Österreichischen Akademie der Wissenschaften, 1986.

RATKOWITSCH 1987. Christine Ratkowitsch. "Die Wirkung Maximians auf die *Comoediae elegiacae* des Vitalis und Wilhelm von Blois." *WS* 100 (1987): 227-246.

RATKOWITSCH 1990. Christine Ratkowitsch. "Weitere Argumente zur Datierung und Interpretation Maximians." *WS* 103 (1990): 207-239.

ROMANO 1970. Domenico Romano. "Il primo Massimiano." *AAPal* 4/29 (1970): 307-335.

RUIZ SÁNCHEZ – SÁNCHEZ MACANÁS 1985. M. Ruiz Sánchez and O. Sánchez Macanás. "Tibulo y Maximiano." In *Simposio Tibuliano. Conmemoración del bimilenario de la muerte de Tibulo*. Univ. de Murcia Sección de Filologia Clásica Simposio II, Depart. de Latin y Griego, pp. 391-397. Murcia, 1985.

SCHETTER 1970. Willy Schetter. *Studien zur Überlieferung und Kritik des Elegikers Maximian*. Wiesbaden, 1970.

SCHNEIDER 2000. Wolfgang Christian Schneider. "Das Ende der antiken Leiblichkeit. Begehren und Enthaltsamkeit bei Ambrosius, Augustin und Maximian." In Thomas Späth and Beate Wagner-Hasel eds. *Frauenwelten in der Antike. Geschlechterordnung und weibliche Lebenspraxis*, pp. 412-426. Stuttgart-Weimar: Metzler, 2000.

SCHNEIDER 2001. Wolfgang Christian Schneider. "Definition of Genre by Falsification. The False Attribution of the Maximianus Verses to Cornelius Gallus by Pomponius Gauricus and the <<Definition>> of their Genre and Structure." *RFIC* 129(4) (2001): 445-464.

SEQUI 1994. Chiara Sequi. "Massimiano elegiaco e *Appendix Maximiani*: rassegna di studi 1970-93." *BStudLat* 24(2) (1994): 617-645.

SHANZER 1983. Danuta Shanzer. "Ennodius, Boethius, and the Date and Interpretation of Maximianus's Elegia III." *RFIC* 111 (1983): 183-195.

SILVESTRE 1979. H. Silvestre. "La prison de l'âme (*Phédon*, 62 b). Nouveaux témoignages du Moyen Âge latin." *Latomus* 38 (1979): 982-986.

SPALTENSTEIN 1977. François Spaltenstein. "Structure et intentions du recueil poétique de Maximien." *EL* 10(2) (1977): 81-101.

STIENE 1986. H.E. Stiene. "Zu den beiden erotischen Gedichten der Maximian – Appendix." *RhM* 129 (1986): 184-192.

STRAZZULLA 1893. V. Strazzulla. *Massimiano Etrusco elegiografo*. Catania, 1893.

SZÖVÉRFFY 1967-68. Joseph Szövérffy. "Maximianus a satirist?" *HSPh* 72 (1967-68): 351-367.

TANDOI 1973. Vincenzo Tandoi. "La tradizione manoscritta di Massimiano." *Maia* 25 (1973): 140-149.

THIEL 1970. E.J. Thiel. "Beiträge zu den Ovid – Nachdichtungen Pseudo – *Ars Amatoria* und Pseudo – *Remedia Amoris*." *MLatJb* 7 (1970): 132-148.

TRAINA 1987. Alfonso Traina. "Le busse di Aquilina (Massimiano 3.37)." *RFIC* 115 (1987): 54-57.

TRAINA 1988. Alfonso Traina. "Postille." *RFIC* 116 (1988): 122-123.

WASYL 2007b. Anna Maria Wasyl. "Maximianus and the Late Antique Reading of Classical Literary Genres." *Classica Cracoviensia* 11 (2007): 349-377.

WATT 1995. William S. Watt. "Notes on Maximianus." *Eikasmos* 6 (1995): 243-248.

WEDECK 1952. Harry E. Wedeck. "An Analysis of the Techniques of Maximianus Etruscus." *Latomus* 2 (1952): 487-495.

WILHELM 1907. F. Wilhelm. "Maximianus und Boethius." *RhM* 62 (1907): 601-614.

ZURLI 1991. Loriano Zurli. "L'*Aegritudo Perdicae* e Maxim. 3." *BStudLat* 21 (1991): 313-318.

The epigrammatists: Ennodius, Luxorius, cc. 90-197 Riese (*Unius poetae sylloge*)

Ennodius

Studies

GIORNATA ENNODIANA I. Fabio Gasti ed. *Atti della prima Giornata Ennodiana*, Pavia, 29-30 marzo 2000. Pisa: Edizioni ETS, 2001 /Pubblicazioni della Facoltà di Lettere e Filosofia dell'Università di Pavia/.

GIORNATA ENNODIANA II. Edoardo d'Angelo ed. *Atti della seconda Giornata Ennodiana*. Napoli, 2003 /Pubblicazioni del Dipartimento di Filologia Classica "F. Arnaldi" dell'Università degli Studi di Napoli Federico II; 22/.

GIORNATA ENNODIANA III. Fabio Gasti ed. *Atti della terza Giornata Ennodiana*, Pavia, 10-11 novembre 2004. Pisa: ETS, 2006.

CARINI 1987. Mario Carini. "Recenti contributi alla critica Ennodiana (1960-1983)." *QC* 9 (1987): 327-342.

CARINI 1989. Mario Carini. *Due città per un poeta. Saggi su Magno Felice Ennodio*. Catania, 1989.

CONIO 1994. Silvia Conio. *Il libro II degli Epigrammi di Ennodio* (unprinted M.A. thesis / tesi di laurea). Napoli, 1994.

CYTOWSKA 1997. Maria Cytowska. "Magnus Felix Ennodius jako epigramatyk." In Jerzy Danielewicz and Krystyna Bartol eds. *Epigram grecki i łaciński w kulturze Europy*, pp. 199-206. Poznań: Wydawnictwo Naukowe UAM, 1997.

D'ANGELO 1993. Edoardo D'Angelo. "Tematiche omosessuali nella letteratura di età teodericiana. Il caso Ennodio." In *Teoderico il Grande e i Goti d'Italia*. Atti del XIII Congresso internazionale di studi sull'Alto Medioevo, Milano 2-6 novembre 1992, 2 vol., pp. 645-454. Spoleto, 1993.

D'ANGELO 2001. Edoardo D'Angelo. "Enigmistica ennodiana: il carme 2,51 (= 179 Vogel)." In *Atti della prima Giornata Ennodiana...*, pp. 101-108.

DI RIENZO 1999b. Daniele Di Rienzo. "Uomo buono o Omobono? (su Ennod. *carm*. 2, 1 = 46 Vogel)." *Vichiana* 4. Serie 1 (1999): 171-179.

DI RIENZO 2001. Daniele Di Rienzo. "Tema e variazioni in Ennodio: il ciclo di Pasifae e il toro (carm. 2, 25; 29-31; 103)." In *Atti della prima Giornata Ennodiana...*, pp. 109-118.

DI RIENZO 2003. Daniele Di Rienzo. "Intertestualità biblica nel II libro dei *carmina* di Ennodio." In *Atti della seconda Giornata Ennodiana...*, pp. 91-107.

DI RIENZO 2005. Daniele Di Rienzo. *Gli epigrammi di Magno Felice Ennodio* (con una prefazione di Antonio V. Nazzaro). Napoli, 2005 /Pubblicazioni del Dipartimento di Filologia Classica "F. Arnaldi" dell'Università degli Studi di Napoli Federico II; 27/.

DI RIENZO 2008. Daniele Di Rienzo. "Epigramma longum tra tardoantico e altomedioevo: il caso di Ennodio di Pavia." In Alfredo M. Morelli ed. *Epigramma longum. Da Marziale alla tarda an-*

tichità (Cassino, 29-31 mag. 2006), pp. 539-555. Cassino: Edizioni dell'Università degli Studi di Cassino, 2008.

GASTALDELLI 1973. Ferruccio Gastaldelli. *Ennodio di Pavia. Profilo letterario*. Roma, 1973.

GASTI 2006. Fabio Gasti. "Il giardino del re (Ennodio, *carm.* 2,111 H.)." In *Atti della terza Giornata Ennodiana...*, pp. 169-188.

KENNELL 1992. Stefanie Kennell. "Ennodius and the Pagan Gods." *Athenaeum* 80 (1992): 236-252.

KENNELL 2000a. Stefanie Kennell. "Ennodius and His Editors." *C&M* 51 (2000): 251-270.

KENNELL 2000b. Stefanie Kennell. *Magnus Felix Ennodius: A Gentleman of the Church*. Ann Arbor MI: Univ. of Michigan Press, 2000.

MORABITO 1947. S.P. Morabito. *Paganesimo e cristianesimo nella poesia di Ennodio*. Catania, 1947.

NAVARRA 1974. Leandro Navarra. *Ennodio e la <<facies>> storico-culturale del suo tempo*. Cassino: Editrice Garigliano, 1974.

POLARA 1993. Giovanni Polara. "I distici di Ennodio." In G. Catanzaro and F. Santucci eds. *La poesia cristiana latina in distici elegiaci*. Atti del Convegno Internazionale, Assisi, 20-22 marzo 1992, pp. 217-239. Assisi, 1993.

RALLO FRENI 1978. Rosalba A. Rallo Freni. "Atteggiamenti topici nel programma poetico di Magno Felice Ennodio." In *Scritti in onore di Salvatore Pugliatti*, vol. 5: *Scritti vari*, pp. 831-858. Pubblicazioni dell'Istituto di scienze giuridiche, economiche, politiche e sociali della Università di Messina 111, Milano: Giuffrè, 1978.

SCHETTER 1986. Willy Schetter. "Zu Ennodius carm. 2,1 Hartel." *Hermes* 114 (1986): 500-502.

Luxorius

Commentaries

DAL COROBBO 2006. Fabio Dal Corobbo. *Per la lettura di Lussorio. Status quaestionis, testi e commento*, pp. 149-308 [see also Status quaestionis, pp. 27-66]. Bologna: Pàtron, 2006.

HAPP 1986 II. Heinz Happ. Luxurius. Text, Untersuchungen, Kommentar. Band II: Kommentar. Stuttgart: B.G. Teubner, 1986.

ROSENBLUM 1961. Morris Rosenblum. *Luxorius. A Latin Poet among the Vandals*, pp. 173-254 [see also Part One: The Poet, pp. 1-108]. New York: Columbia Univ. Press, 1961.

Concordances

CHRISTIANSEN – DOMINIK – HOLLAND 2002. P.G. Christiansen – W.J. Dominik – J.E. Holland. *Anthologiae Latinae Concordantia*. Hildesheim-Zürich-New York: G. Olms, 2002.

Studies

BÄHRENS 1875. Emil Bährens. "Zur Luxorius der Anthologie." *RhM* 30 (1875): 477.

BÄHRENS 1876. Emil Bährens. "Zur lateinischen Anthologie." *RhM* 31 (1876): 89-104; 254-272; 602-613.

BALDWIN 1981. B. Baldwin. "Aquatic sex." *LCM* 6 (1981): 25.

BERTINI 2002. Ferruccio Bertini ed. *Luxoriana*. Genova: D.AR.FI.CL.ET. "F. Della Corte", 2002.

BERTINI 2006. Ferruccio Bertini. "Riuso e adattamento di testi classici negli epigrammi di Lussorio." In Lucio Cristante ed. *Il calamo della memoria. Riuso di testi e mestiere letterario nella tarda antichità*. Trieste, 27-28 Aprile 2006. Atti del II convegno (*Incontri Triestini di filologia classica* 5, 2005-2006), pp. 225-233. Trieste: Ed. Università di Trieste, 2006.

BERTINI 2008. Ferruccio Bertini. "Lussorio e l'epigramma latino tardoantico." In Alfredo M. Morelli ed. *Epigramma longum. Da Marziale alla tarda antichità* (Cassino, 29-31 mag. 2006), pp. 495-508. Cassino: Edizioni dell'Università degli Studi di Cassino, 2008.

BOATTI 2002. Anna Boatti. "Gli epigrammi 352, 358, 362, 363, 369 Shackleton Bailey." In F. Bertini ed. *Luxoriana...*, pp. 151-168.

COPELLO 2002. Silvia Copello. "*Anthologia latina* 340, 348, 350 Shackleton Bailey." In F. Bertini ed. *Luxoriana...*, pp. 73-86.

DIETZ 1987. K. Dietz. "Der Buckelige bei Luxurius (*Anth. Lat.* 315 R = 310 ShB). Ein Beitrag zum senatorischen Ahnenstolz." *RhM* 13 (1987): 175-185.

FASSINA 2006. Alessia Fassina. "Un mecenate alla corte vandalica: gli epigrammi lussoriani per Fridamal (AL 304-305 R^2)." *GIF* 58 (2006): 137-145.

FUSI 2002. Daniele Fusi. "Appunti sulla prosodia del Lussorio di Shackleton Bailey: alcune questioni di metodo." In F. Bertini ed. *Luxoriana...*, pp. 193-313.

GARSON 1977-78. R.W. Garson. "Observations on the Epigrams of Luxorius." *MusAfr* 6 (1977-78): 9-14.

GIOVINI 2004. Marco Giovini. *Studi su Lussorio*. Genova: D.AR.FI.CL.ET. "F. Della Corte", 2004.

GIOVINI 2008. Marco Giovini. "Lussorio fra modello epigrammatico ed echi cristiani." In Alfredo M. Morelli ed. *Epigramma longum. Da Marziale alla tarda antichità* (Cassino, 29-31 mag. 2006), pp. 509-538. Cassino: Edizioni dell'Università degli Studi di Cassino, 2008.

HAPP 1962. Heinz Happ. "Luxurius oder Luxorius? Ein Beitrag zur Lautgeschichte des spätlateinischen u." *Beiträge zur Namenforschung* 13 (1962): 243-257.

HUNT 1988. J.M. Hunt. "From the Classical to the Postclassical." *CPh* 83 (1988): 328-341.

LAVILLE 1974. Giuliana Laville. "La vita del circo ed altri spunti di realtà quotidiana negli epigrammi di Lussorio." *AAP* 23 (1974): 274-286.

LEVY 1927. F.W. Levy. "Luxorius." *RE* XIII 2 (1927): 2102-2109.

LÖFSTEDT 1980. B. Löfstedt. "Bemerkungen zu Luxurius." *AClass* 23 (1980): 97-105.

MARIOTTI 1964. Scevola Mariotti. "Luxorius e Lisorius." *RFIC* 92 (1964): 163-172.

OTTRIA 2002. Daniela Ottria. "L'acqua, gli dei di pietra e la chimera bronzea negli epigrammi di Lussorio 343, 344, 345, 350, 351 Shackleton Bailey." In F. Bertini ed. *Luxoriana...*, pp. 47-72.

PETSCHENING 1877. M. Petschening. "Beiträge zur Kritik lateinischer Schriftsteller." *Zeitschrift f. d. österr. Gymn.* 28 (1877): 481-492.

PETSCHENING 1889. M. Petschening. "Bemerkungen zu den *Poetae Latini Minores*." *Philologus* 48 (1889): 562-564.

QUAGLIA 2002. Riccardo Quaglia. "Traduzione e breve commento ad *Anth. Lat.* 341, 342, 346, 347 Shackleton Bailey." In F. Bertini ed. *Luxoriana...*, pp. 29-46.

RADIF 2002. Ludovica Radif. "Anomalie animali." In F. Bertini ed. *Luxoriana...*, pp. 5-28.

RAMMINGER 1988. J. Ramminger. "Zur Interpretation von Luxorius *Anth. Lat.* 305 R." *Philologus* 132 (1988): 297-307.

RAZZETTI 2002. Francesca Razzetti. "Per l'esegesi di alcuni epigrammi di Lussorio (364, 365, 366, 367 Shackleton Bailey)." In F. Bertini ed. *Luxoriana...*, pp. 169-191.

ROMANO 1968-69. Domenico Romano. "Ritratto di Lussorio." *AAPal* 29 (1968-69): 157-186.

SALANITRO 1991. G. Salanitro. "Lussorio nell'Enciclopedia Virgiliana." *Sileno* 17 (1991): 307-308.

SCHNEIDER (W.J.) 1999. W.J. Schneider. "*Beccas Talente*. Luxurius *Anth. Lat.* 316 ShB = 321 R." *Arctos* 33 (1999): 155-160.

SCHOLZ 1987. B. Scholz. "Archäologische Bemerkungen zu Luxorius AL 315 SB (320 R)." *Hermes* 115 (1987): 231-240.

SCHUBERT 1875. O. Schubert. *Quaestionum de anthologia codicis Salmasiani pars I. De Luxorio*. Leipzig, 1875.

SEAGER 1981. R.J. Seager. "Luxorius 82." *LCM* 6 (1981): 187.

STRZELCZYK 1990. Jerzy Strzelczyk. "Z dziejów życia umysłowego Afryki Północnej w dobie wandalskiej." *Vox Patrum* 19 (1990): 749-759.

TANDOI 1964. Vincenzo Tandoi. "Un'ecfrasi di Lussorio: *Anth. Lat.* 371 Riese." *RFIC* 92 (1964): 397-421.

TANDOI 1970. Vincenzo Tandoi "Luxoriana." *RFIC* 98 (1970): 37-63.

UGGERI 1966. G. Uggeri. "Lussorio, Sidonio Apollinare e un'iconografia di Diogene e Laide." *SIFC* 38 (1966): 246-255.

UGGERI 1968. G. Uggeri. "Per l'iconografia della Cavaspina di Lussorio." *AFMP* 1 (1968): 301-308.

WASYL 2008. Anna Maria Wasyl. "The Dull Epigrammatist and His Not Too Learned Public. Some Notes on Luxorius's Introductory Poems." *Classica Cracoviensia* 12 (2008): 197-220.

ZIEHEN 1898. J. Ziehen. "Archäologische Bemerkungen zur latein. Anthol." In *Festschrift O. Benndorf*, pp. 49-58. Wien, 1898.

ZIEHEN 1909. J. Ziehen. *Neue Studien zur latein. Anthol.* Frankfurt a. M.-Berlin, 1909.

ZURLI 1993. Loriano Zurli. "Esegesi e critica del testo. Qualche esempio da Luxorius." *GIF* 45 (1993): 29-46.

ZURLI 1994a. Loriano Zurli. "Codici referenziali, intertesto e ricadute testuali. Un esempio da Luxor. 371 R." *BStudLat* 24 (1994): 129-139.

ZURLI 1994b. Loriano Zurli. "Luxorius e la fitoterapia." *GIF* 46 (1994): 189-195.

ZURLI 2002a. Loriano Zurli. "Diadema Luxorii." *GIF* 54(1) (2002): 53-60.

ZURLI 2002b. Loriano Zurli. "Un <<Witz>> lussoriano (358 Riese^2 [= 535 Shackleton B.], 10)." *GIF* 54(2) (2002): 229-231.

cc. 90-197 Riese (*Unius poetae sylloge*)

Commentaries

KAY 2006. *Epigrams from the Anthologia Latina*: Text, Translation and Commentary by N.M. Kay, pp. 65-375 [see also Introduction, pp. 1-37]. London: Duckworth, 2006.

OPSOMER 2004. Th. Opsomer. *Companion to the* Latin Anthology, *with a Commentary on the Peiper-libellus (AL 90-197 R).* Diss. K. U. Leuven (Faculty of Arts, Dept. of Class. St.), 2004.

Concordances

CHRISTIANSEN – DOMINIK – HOLLAND 2002. P.G. Christiansen – W.J. Dominik – J.E. Holland. *Anthologiae Latinae Concordantia*. Hildesheim-Zürich-New York: G. Olms, 2002.

Studies

ADIEGO 1993. I.-X. Adiego. "Un maldestre epígon de Marcial (*Anth. Lat.* 138 R = 127 ShB)." *AFB* 16 (1993): 9-15.

BÄHRENS 1876. Emil Bährens. "Zur lateinischen Anthologie." *RhM* 31 (1876): 89-104; 254-272; 602-613.

BAUMGARTNER 1981. A.J. Baumgartner. *Untersuchungen zur Anthologie des Codex Salmasianus*, pp. 95 ff. Baden, 1981.

CAMERON 1992. Alan Cameron. "Filocalus and Melania." *CPh* 87 (1992): 140-144.

COURTNEY 1980. E. Courtney. "Observations on the *Latin Anthology*." *Hermathena* 129 (1980): 37-50.

COURTNEY 1984. E. Courtney. "Some Poems of the *Latin Anthology*." *CPh* 79 (1984): 309-313.

COURTNEY 1988. E. Courtney. "The Roman Months in Art and Literature." *MH* 45 (1988): 33-57.

COURTNEY 1989. E. Courtney. "Supplementary Notes on the *Latin Anthology*." *C&M* 40 (1989): 197-211.

COURTNEY 2005. E. Courtney. "*Anthologia Latina* 128 Riese." *MD* 55 (2005): 229-231.

DINGEL 1985. J. Dingel. "Über ein Akrostichon und ein Telestichon in der *Anthologia Latina* (394 u. 109 S.B.)." *WS* 19 (1985): 173-178.

OHL 1948-49. R.T. Ohl. "Some Remarks on the *Latin Anthology*." *CW* 42(10) (1948-49): 147-153.
PAOLUCCI 2002. Paola Paolucci. "Il ciclo di Galatea (*AL* 140-143 SB = 151-154 R)." *BStudLat* 32(1) (2002): 111-127.
PAOLUCCI 2003. Paola Paolucci. "Il ciclo di cedro nell'*Anthologia Latina* (169-171 R^2 = 158-160 SB)." *GIF* 55 (2003): 111-120.
PETSCHENING 1877. M. Petschening. "Beiträge zur Kritik lateinischer Schriftsteller." *Zeitschrift f. d. österr. Gymn.* 28 (1877): 481-492.
PETSCHENING 1889. M. Petschening. "Bemerkungen zu den *Poetae Latini Minores*." *Philologus* 48 (1889): 562-564.
SCHETTER 1986. Willy Schetter. "Rev. Baumgartner Untersuchungen zur Anthologie des Codex Salmasianus." *Gnomon* 58 (1986): 300-304.
ZIEHEN 1898. J. Ziehen. "Archäologische Bemerkungen zur latein. Anthol." In *Festschrift O. Benndorf*, pp. 49-58. Wien, 1898.
ZIEHEN 1909. J. Ziehen. *Neue Studien zur latein. Anthol.* Frankfurt a. M.-Berlin, 1909.
ZIEHEN 1919. J. Ziehen. "Ein kunsttheoretisches Epigramm der Salmasianus-Anthologie." *PhW* 39 (1919): 1051-1053.
ZURLI 2003. Loriano Zurli. "Sul ciclo del cedro in *Anthologia Latina*. Con un emendamento a c. 158 Shackleton B. (= 139 $Riese^2$)." *GIF* 55 (2003): 121-123.
ZURLI 2004. Loriano Zurli. *Apographa Salmasiana. Sulla trasmissione di Anthologia Salmasiana tra Sei e Settecento.* Hildesheim-Zürich-New York: G. Olms, 2004.
ZURLI 2005b. Loriano Zurli. *Unius poetae sylloge. Verso un'edizione di Anthologia Latina* cc. 90-97 Riese = 78-188 Shackleton Bailey. Hildesheim-Zürich-New York: G. Olms, 2005.
ZURLI 2007. *Unius poetae sylloge. Anthologia Latina* cc. 90-197, Riese = 78-188, Shackleton Bailey. Recognovit Loriano Zurli (trad. di Nino Scivoletto), pp. 3-126. Hildesheim-Zürich-New York: G. Olms, 2007 /Bibliotheca Weidmanniana 11/.

3. STUDIES ON ANCIENT AND MEDIEVAL LITERATURE, LITERARY THEORY, LANGUAGE, CULTURE, AND ART

ADAM – MAYER 1999. James Noel Adam and Roland G. Mayer eds. *Aspects of the Language of Latin Poetry*. Oxford: Oxford Univ. Press, 1999.
ALVAR EZQUERDA 1992. Antonio Alvar Ezquerda. "Relidad y illusion en la poesia latina tardoantigua, notas a propósito de estética literaria." *Emerita* 60 (1992): 1-20.
AMAT 1985. J. Amat. *Songes et visions. L'au-delà dans la littérature latine tardive*. Paris: Et. Augustiniennes, 1985.
ARRIGHETTI 2000. Graziano Arrighetti ed. *Letteratura e riflessione sulla letteratura nella cultura classica: tradizione, erudizione, critica letteraria, filologia e riflessione filosofica nella produzione letteraria antica:* atti del convegno, Pisa, 7-9 giugno 1999. Pisa: Giardini, 2000.
ARRIGHETTI – MONTANARI 1993. Graziano Arrighetti and Franco Montanari eds. *La componente autobiografica nella poesia greca e latina fra realtà e artificio letterario*: atti del convegno, Pisa, 16-17 maggio 1991. Pisa: Giardini, 1993 /Biblioteca di studi antichi № 51/.
AUERBACH 1965. Eric Auerbach. *Literary Language and Its Public in Late Antiquity and in the Middle Ages*. Translated by Ralph Mannheim. Princeton: Princeton Univ. Press, 1965.
BAEZA ANGULO 1995. Eulogio F. Baeza Angulo. "Pervivencia de los *Tristia* de Ovidio en la Antiguedad (ss. I-VII)." *CFC(L)* 9 (1995): 103-115.
BATTAGLIA 1959. Salvatore Battaglia. "La tradizione di Ovidio nel medioevo." *Filologia romanza* 6 (1959): 185-224.

BAŽIL 2002. Martin Bažil. "*De alieno nostrum*: les centons de l'Antiquité tardive et la théorie de l'intertextualité." *Listy filologické* 125(1-2) (2002): 1-32.

BÉCARES 2000. Vincente Bécares (et al. eds.). *Intertextualidad en las literaturas griega y latina*. Madrid: Ed. Clásicas, 2000.

BERLAN-BAJARD 2006. Anne Berlan-Bajard. *Les spectacles aquatiques romains*. Rome: École française de Rome, 2006.

BERTINI 1974. Ferruccio Bertini. *Autori latini in Africa sotto la dominazione vandalica*. Genova, 1974.

BEZZOLA 1944. Reto Bezzola. *Les origines et la formation de la littérature courtoise en Occident (500-1200)* Paris: Champion, 1944.

BISANTI 2007-2008. A. Bisanti. *La letteratura latina in Africa durante la dominazione vandalica* / online at: http://www.lettere.unipa.it/?scheda_doc=1852 [July 06, 2010]/.

BLOOMER 1997. W. Martin Bloomer. *Latinity and Literary Society at Rome*. Philadelphia: Univ. of Pennsylvania Press, 1997.

BONANNO 1990. Maria Grazia Bonanno. *L'allusione necessaria: ricerche intertestuali sulla poesia greca e latina*. Roma: Ed. dell'Ateneo, 1990 /Filologia e critica № 63/.

BORGO 2003. Antonella Borgo. *Retorica e poetica nei proemi di Marziale*. Napoli: Loffredo Editore, 2003.

BOWERSOCK – BROWN – GRABAR 1999. G.W. Bowersock – P.R.L. Brown – O. Grabar. *Late Antiquity: A Guide to the Postclassical World*. Cambridge, MA & London: Belknap Press of Harvard Univ. Press, 1999.

BRENNAN 1996. Brian Brennan. "Deathless Marriage and Spiritual Fecundity in Venantius Fortunatus's *De virginitate*." *Traditio* 51 (1996): 73-97.

BROWN 1978. Peter Brown. *The Making of Late Antiquity*. Cambridge, MA: Harvard Univ. Press, 1978.

BROWN 1988. Peter Brown. *The Body and Society. Men, Women, and Sexual Renunciation in Early Christianity*. New York: Columbia Univ. Press, 1988.

BRUGNOLI 1992. Giorgio Brugnoli. "Qualche riflessione sull'allusione intenzionale di antichi e moderni." *GIF* 44 (1992): 79-94.

BRUNS 1980. Gerald L. Bruns "The Originality of Texts in a Manuscript Culture." *Comparative Literature* 1980(2): 113-129.

BUTRICA 1984. James L. Butrica. *The Manuscript Tradition of Propertius*. Toronto: Univ. of Toronto Press, 1984.

CAIRNS 1972. Francis Cairns. *Generic Composition in Greek and Roman Poetry*. Edinburgh: Edinburgh Univ. Press, 1972.

CAMERON 1970. Alan Cameron. *Claudian: Poetry and Propaganda at the Court of Honorius*. Oxford: Clarendon, 1970.

CAMERON 1995. Alan Cameron. *Callimachus and His Critics*. Princeton, NJ: Princeton Univ. Press, 1995.

CAMERON (Av.) 1993. Averil Cameron. *The Mediterranean World in Late Antiquity. AD 396-600*. London-NewYork: Routledge, 1993.

CAMPANALE 1980. Maria I. Campanale. "*De virginitate* di Venanzio Fortunato (*carm*. 8, 3 Leo) un epitalamio mistico." *InvLuc* 2 (1980): 75-128.

CARRUTHERS 1990. Mary J. Carruthers. *The Book of Memory: A Study of Memory in Medieval Culture*. Cambridge: Cambridge Univ. Press, 1990.

CAVALLO – FEDELI – GIARDINA 1993². G. Cavallo – P. Fedeli – A. Giardina. *Lo spazio letterario di Roma antica*. Roma 1993² (5 vols.).

CHALON – DEVALLET – FORCE – GRIFFE – LASSÈRE – MICHAUD 1985. M. Chalon – G. Devallet – P. Force – M. Griffe – J.-M. Lassère – J.-N. Michaud. "*Memorabile factum*: une célebration de l'évergétisme des rois vandales dans l'anthologie latine." *AntAfr* 21 (1985): 207-262.

CHARLET 1988. J.-L Charlet. "Aesthetic Trends in Late Latin Poetry (325-410)." *Philologus* 132(1) (1988): 74-85.

CHIRI 1954. Guiseppe Chiri. *Poesia cortese latina. Profilo storico dal V al XII secolo.* Roma, 1954.

CHRISTIANISME... 1977. *Christianisme et formes littéraires de l'antiquité tardive en Occident.* Genève: Fondation Hardt, 1977.

CITRONI 1986. Mario Citroni. "Le raccomandazioni del poeta." *Maia* 38 (1986): 111-146.

CITRONI 1992. Mario Citroni. "Letteratura per i Saturnali e poetica dell'intrattenimento." *SIFC* 10 (1992): 425-447.

CITRONI 1995. Mario Citroni. *Poesia e lettori in Roma antica. Forme della comunicazione letteraria.* Bari: Laterza, 1995.

CITRONI 2003b. Mario Citroni. "I canoni di autori antichi: alle origini del concetto di classico." In *Culture europee e tradizione latina.* Atti del Conv. Internaz. di Studi, Cividale del Friuli, Fondaz. Niccolò Canussio, 16-17 nov. 2001, pp. 1-22. Trieste, 2003.

CLAASSEN 1999. Jo-Marie Claassen. *Displaced Persons. The Literature of Exile from Cicero to Boethius.* Madison: Univ. of Wisconsin Press, 1999.

CLOVER 1978. Frank M. Clover. "Carthage and the Vandals." In J.H. Humphrey ed. *Excavations at Carthage 1978 Conducted by the University of Michigan,* vol. VII, pp. 1-22. Ann Arbor, 1978 /online at: http://ftp.kermit-project.org/itc/history/conant/clover_carthage.pdf [May 18, 2010]/.

CLOVER 1986. Frank M. Clover. "Felix Karthago." *DOP* 40 (1986): 1-16.

CLOVER 1993. Frank M. Clover. *The Late Roman West and the Vandals.* Aldershot-Brookfield, 1993.

CLOVER – HUMPHREYS 1989. Frank M. Clover and R. Stephen Humphreys eds. *Tradition and Innovation in Late Antiquity.* Madison, WI: Univ. of Wisconsin Press, 1989.

COLTON 1995. R.E. Colton. *Studies of Imitation in Some Latin Authors.* Amsterdam: Hakkert, 1995.

CONSOLINO 1976. Franca Ela Consolino. "L'appello al lettore nell'epitaffio della tarda antichità." *Maia* 28 (1976): 129-143.

CONSOLINO 1977. Franca Ela Consolino. "*Amor spiritualis* e linguaggio elegiaco nei *Carmina* di Venanzio Fortunato." *ASNP* 7 (1977): 1351-1368.

CONSOLINO 1993a. Franca Ela Consolino. "L'elegia amorosa nel *De excidio Thoringiae* di Venanzio Fortunato." In G. Catanzaro and F. Santucci eds. *La poesia cristiana latina in distici elegiaci.* Atti del Convegno Internazionale, Assisi, 20-22 marzo 1992, pp. 241-254. Assisi, 1993.

CONSOLINO 1993b. Franca Ela Consolino. "Il discorso autobiografico nella poesia latina tarda." In *La componente autobiografica nella poesia greca e latina...,* pp. 209-228.

CONSOLINO 1999. Franca Ela Consolino. "L'eredità dei classici nella poesia del VI secolo." In Giancarlo Mazzoli and Fabio Gasti eds. *Prospettive sul tardoantico*: Atti del Convegno di Pavia (27-28 nov. 1997), pp. 69-90. Como: New Press, 1999 /Bibliotheca di *Athenaeum,* 41/.

CONSOLINO 2003. Franca Ela Consolino ed. *Forme letterarie nella produzione latina di IV-V secolo (con uno sguardo a Bisanzio).* Roma: Herder, 2003.

CONTE 1974. Gian Biagio Conte. *Memoria dei poeti e sistema letterario. Catullo, Virgilio, Ovidio, Lucano.* Torino: Einaudi, 1974.

CONTE 1984. Gian Biagio Conte. *Il genere e i suoi confini: Cinque studi sulla poesia di Virgilio.* Torino: Garzanti, 1984.

CONTE 1986. Gian Biagio Conte. *The Rhetoric of Imitation: Genre and Poetic Memory in Virgil and Other Latin Poets.* Edited and with a Foreword by Charles Segal. Ithaca-London: Cornell Univ. Press, 1986.

CONTE 1991. Gian Biagio Conte. *Generi e Lettori: saggi su Lucrezio, l'elegia d'amore, l'enciclopedia di Plinio*. Milano: Mondadori, 1991.

CONTE 1992a. Gian Biagio Conte. "Empirical and Theoretical Approaches to Literary Genre." In Karl Galinsky ed. *The Interpretation of Roman Poetry: Empiricism or Hermeneutics?*, pp. 104-123. Frankfurt am Main: Peter Lang, 1992 /Studien zur Klassischen Philologie № 67/.

CONTE 1992b. Gian Biagio Conte. "La retorica dell'imitazione come retorica della cultura: qualche ripensamento." *FAM* 1992(2): 41-52.

CONTE 1994. Gian Biagio Conte. *Genres and Readers: Lucretius, Love Elegy, Pliny's Encyclopedia*. Translated by Glenn W. Most; with a Foreword by Charles Segal. Baltimore: Johns Hopkins Univ. Press, 1994.

CONTE 2007. Gian Biagio Conte. *The Poetry of Pathos: Studies in Virgilian Epic*. Edited by S.J. Harrison. Oxford: Oxford Univ. Press, 2007.

COURCELLE 1964. Pierre Courcelle. *Histoire littéraire des grandes invasions germaniques*. Paris, 1964[3].

COURTOIS 1955. Christian Courtois. *Les Vandales et l'Afrique*. Paris, 1955.

CRISTANTE 2003. Lucio Cristante. "Grammatica di poeti e poesia di grammatici: Coronato." In F. Gasti ed. *Grammatica e grammatici latini: teoria ed esegesi* (Atti delle I Giornate ghisleriane di filologia classica. Pavia, 5-6 Aprile 2001), pp. 75-92. Como-Pavia: Ibis, 2003.

CULTURA ... CHRISTIANA 2001. *Cultura latina cristiana: fra terzo e quinto secolo*: atti del Convegno, Mantova, 5-7 novembre 1998. Firenze: Olschki, 2001.

CULTURA ... PAGANA 1998. *Cultura latina pagana fra terzo e quinto secolo dopo Cristo*: atti del Convegno, Mantova, 9-11 ottobre 1995. Firenze: Olschki, 1998.

CURTIUS 1990. Ernst Robert Curtius. *European Literature and the Latin Middle Ages*. Princeton, NJ: Princeton Univ. Press, 1990.

CURTIUS 1997. Ernst Robert Curtius. *Literatura europejska i łacińskie średniowiecze*. Kraków: Universitas, 1997.

CYTOWSKA 1973. Maria Cytowska. "Ostatni poeta starożytności – Wenancjusz Fortunatus." *Meander* 28 (1973): 307-320.

CYTOWSKA – SZELEST 1990. Maria Cytowska and Hanna Szelest. *Literatura rzymska. Okres augustowski*. Warszawa: PWN, 1990.

CYTOWSKA – SZELEST 1992. Maria Cytowska and Hanna Szelest. *Literatura rzymska. Okres cesarstwa*. Warszawa: PWN, 1992.

CYTOWSKA – SZELEST 1994. Maria Cytowska and Hanna Szelest. *Literatura rzymska. Okres cesarstwa. Autorzy chrześcijańscy*. Warszawa: PWN, 1994.

CYTOWSKA – SZELEST – RYCHLEWSKA 1996. Maria Cytowska – Hanna Szelest – Ludwika Rychlewska. *Literatura rzymska. Okres archaiczny*. Warszawa: PWN, 1996.

DANIELEWICZ 1971. Jerzy Danielewicz. *Technika opisów w* Metamorfozach *Owidiusza*. Poznań: UAM, 1971 /Prace Wydziału Filologicznego Seria: Filologia Klasyczna Nr 5/.

DANIELEWICZ 1983. Jerzy Danielewicz. "Semantyczne funkcje form metrycznych w poezji antycznej." *Pamiętnik Literacki* 74(1) (1983): 123-135.

DAVIS 1967. G. Davis. "Ad sidera notus. Strategies of Lament and Consolation in Fortunatus' *De Gelesuintha*." *Agon* 1 (1967): 118-134.

DE JONG – SULLIVAN 1994. Irene J.F. De Jong and John Patrick Sullivan eds. *Modern Critical Theory and Classical Literature*. Leiden: Brill, 1994.

DE LIBÉRA 1988. Alain de Libéra. "Od lektury do parafrazy. Uwagi o cytacie w średniowieczu." (przeł. W. Maczkowski) *Pamiętnik Literacki* 79(2) 1988: 331-344.

DE LUBAC 1959-1964. Henri de Lubac. *Exégèse médiévale. Les quatre sens de l'Ecriture*. 4 vols. Paris, 1959-1964.

DESBORDES 1979. Françoise Desbordes. *Argonautica. Trois études sur l'imitation dans la littérature antique*. Bruxelles: *Collection Latomus* 159, 1979.

DI SALVO 2005. Lucia Di Salvo. *Felicis munera mali. Momenti di vita quotidiana nella poesia di età romanobarbarica*. Roma: Carocci, 2005.

DISKIN 1998. Clay Diskin. "The Theory of the Literary Persona in Antiquity." *MD* 40 (1998).

DRINKWATER – ELTON 1992. John Drinkwater and Hugh Elton eds. *Fifth-Century Gaul: A Crisis of Identity?* Cambridge: Cambridge Univ. Press, 1992.

DRONKE 1969. Peter Dronke. *Medieval Latin and the Rise of European Love-lyric*. vols. 1-2. Oxford: Clarendon Press, 1969.

DRONKE 1984a. Peter Dronke. *The Medieval Poet and His World*. Roma: Storia e Letteratura, 1984.

DRONKE 1984b. Peter Dronke. *Women Writers of the Middle Ages: A Critical Study of Texts from Perpetua (+203) to Marguerite Porete (+1310)*. Cambridge: Cambridge Univ. Press, 1984.

DUTSCH 2008. Dorota Dutsch. "*Nenia*: Gender, Genre, and Lament in Ancient Rome." In Ann Suter. *Lament. Studies in the Ancient Mediterranean and Beyond*, pp. 258-280. Oxford: Oxford Univ. Press, 2008.

EASTERLING – MILES 1999. Pat Easterling and Richard Miles. "Dramatic Identities. Tragedy in Late Antiquity." In Richard Miles ed. *Constructing Identities in Late Antiquity*, pp. 95-111. London-New York: Routledge, 1999.

EDMUNDS 2001. Lowell Edmunds. *Intertextuality and the Reading of Roman Poetry*. Baltimore, MD: Johns Hopkins Univ. Press, 2001.

ELM 1994. Susanna Elm. *Virgins of God: The Making of Ascetism in Late Antiquity*. Oxford: Clarendon Press, 1994.

FANTHAM 1996. Elaine Fantham. *Roman Literary Culture: from Cicero to Apuleius*. Baltimore, MD: Johns Hopkins Univ. Press, 1996.

FONTAINE 1977. Jacques Fontaine. "Unité et diversité du mélange des genres et des tons chez quelques écrivains latins de la fin du IVe siècle: Ausone, Ambroise, Ammien." In *Christianisme…*, pp. 425-482.

FONTAINE 1980. Jacques Fontaine. *Études sur la poésie latine tardive d'Ausone à Prudence*. Paris: Les Belles Lettres, 1980.

FONTAINE 1981. Jacques Fontaine. *Naissance de la poésie dans l'Occident chrétien. Esquisse d'une histoire de la poésie chrétienne du IIe au VIe siècle*. Paris: Et. Augustiniennes, 1981.

FONTAINE 1998. Jacques Fontaine. *Letteratura tardoantica: figure e percorsi*. Brescia: Marcelliana, 1998.

FOWLER 1995. Don P. Fowler. "Martial and the Book." *Ramus* 24 (1995): 31-58.

FOWLER 1997. Don P. Fowler. "On the Shoulders of Giants: Intertextuality and Classical Studies." *MD* 39 (1997): 12-34 (= S. Hinds and D. Fowler eds. *Memoria, arte allusiva…*).

GAGLIARDI 1972. Donato Gagliardi. *Aspetti della poesia latina tardoantica: Linee evolutive e culturali dell'ultima poesia pagana dai novelli a R. Namaziano*. Palermo, 1972.

GAGLIARDI 1984. Donato Gagliardi. "Linee di sviluppo della poesia latina tardoantica." In *La poesia tardoantica: tra retorica, teologia e politica*. Atti del V corso della Scuola Superiore di archeologia e civiltà medievali, Erice 6-12 Dicembre 1981, pp. 51-73. Messina, 1984.

GAGLIARDI 1998. Donato Gagliardi. *Percorsi e problemi di letteratura latina imperiale*. Napoli: D'Auria, 1998.

GALINSKY 1992. Karl Galinsky ed. *The Interpretation of Roman Poetry: Empiricism or Hermeneutics?* Frankfurt am Main: Peter Lang, 1992.

GALLO – NICASTRI 1995. Italo Gallo and Luciano Nicastri eds. *Aetates Ovidianae: lettori di Ovidio dall'Antichità al Rinascimento*. Napoli: Edizioni Scientifiche Italiane, 1995 (Pubbl. Dell'Univ. degli Studi di Salerno. Sez. Atti Conv. Misc. 43).

GARZYA 1984. Antonio Garzya. "Retorica e realtà nella poesia tardoantica." In *La poesia tardoantica: tra retorica, teologia e politica.* Atti del V corso della Scuola Superiore di archeologia e civiltà medievali, Erice 6-12 Dicembre 1981, pp. 11-49. Messina, 1984.

GARZYA 1987-88. Antonio Garzya. "Gli antichi generi poetici nella tarda antichità." *AFLN* 18 (1987-88): 239-260.

GARZYA 1997. Antonio Garzya. *Percorsi e tramiti di cultura: saggi sulla civiltà letteraria tardoantica e bizantina con una giunta sulla tradizione degli studi classici.* Napoli: D'Auria, 1997.

GEORGE 1992. Judith W. George. *Venantius Fortunatus: A Latin Poet in Merovingian Gaul.* Oxford: Clarendon Press, 1992.

GEORGE 2004. Judith W. George. "Vandal Poets in their Context." In A.H. Merrills ed. *Vandals, Romans and Berbers. New Perspectives on Late Antique North Africa*, pp. 133-145. Burlington, VT: Ashgate, 2004.

GODMAN – MURRAY 1990. P. Godman and O. Murray eds. *Latin Poetry and the Classical Tradition. Essays in Medieval and Renaissance Literature.* Oxford: Clarendon Press, 1990.

GUALANDRI 1999. Isabella Gualandri. "Gli dèi duri a morire: temi mitologici nella poesia latina del quinto secolo." In Giancarlo Mazzoli and Fabio Gasti eds. *Prospettive sul tardoantico*: Atti del Convegno di Pavia (27-28 nov. 1997), pp. 49-68. Como: New Pr. 1999 /Bibliotheca di *Athenaeum*, 41/.

GUALANDRI – CONCA – PASSARELLA 2005. I. Gualandri – F. Conca – R. Passarella eds. *Nuovo e antico nella cultura greco-latina di IV-VI secolo.* Milano: Cisalpino, 2005 /*Quaderni di Acme* 73, Università degli Studi di Milano, Facoltà di Lettere e Filosofia/.

HALLETT – SKINNER 1997. Judith P. Hallett and Marilyn B. Skinner eds. *Roman Sexualities.* Princeton, NJ: Princeton Univ. Press, 1997.

HEXTER 1996. Ralph J. Hexter. *Ovid and Medieval Schooling; Studies in Medieval School Commentaries on Ovid's* Ars Amatoria, Epistulae ex Ponto, *and* Epistulae Heroidum. München: Arbeo-Gesellschaft, 1986.

HINDS 1997. Stephen Hinds. "<<Proemio al mezzo>>: Allusion and the Limits of Interpretability." *MD* 39 (1997): 113-122 /S. Hinds and D. Fowler eds. *Memoria, arte allusiva…*/.

HINDS 1998. Stephen Hinds. *Allusion and Intertext: Dynamics of Appropriation in Roman Poetry.* Cambridge: Cambridge Univ. Press, 1998.

HINDS – FOWLER 1997. Stephen Hinds and Don Fowler eds. *Memoria, arte allusiva, intertestualità / Memory, Allusion, Intertextuality.* Pisa, 1997 (*Materiali e Discussioni* 39).

HOLTZ – FREDOUILLE 1992. L. Holtz and J.-C. Fredouille eds. *De Tertullien aux Mozarabes.* Vol. I *Antiquité tardive et Christianisme ancien (IIIe-VIe siècles)*, Mélanges offerts à Jacques Fontaine Membre de l'Institut à l'occasion de *son* 70e anniversaire, par les élèves, amis et collègues. Paris, 1992.

HOLZBERG 2002. N. Holzberg. *Martial und das antike Epigramm.* Darmstadt, 2002.

HORSTMANN 2004. Sabine Horstmann. *Das Epithalamium in der lateinischen Literatur der Spätantike.* München: K.G. Saur, 2004.

*INTERTESTUALITÀ…*1995. *Intertestualità: il dialogo fra testi nelle letterature classiche*: atti del convegno internazionale (Cagliari, 24-26 novembre 1994). Amsterdam: Hakkert, 1995 /*Lexis* 13 (1995)/.

IRVINE 1994. Martin Irvine. *The Making of Textual Culture: <<Grammatica>> and Literary Theory, 350-1100.* Cambridge: Cambridge Univ. Press, 1994.

JAUSS 1982. Hans Robert Jauss. *Toward an Aesthetic of Reception.* Translated by Timothy Bahti. Minneapolis: Univ. of Minnesota Press, 1982.

KASSEL 1958. Rudolf Kassel. *Untersuchungen zur griechischen und römischen Konsolationsliteratur.* München: Beck, 1958.

KASTER 1997. Robert A. Kaster. *Guardians of Language. The Grammarian and Society in Late Antiquity*. Berkeley-Los Angeles-London: Univ. of California Press, 1997.

KELLY 1979. Henry Ansgar Kelly. "Tragedy and the Performance of Tragedy in Late Roman Antiquity." *Traditio* 35 (1979): 21-44.

KELLY 1993. Henry Ansgar Kelly. *Ideas and Forms of Tragedy from Aristotle to the Middle Ages*. Cambridge Univ. Press, 1993.

KITZINGER 1983. Ernst Kitzinger. *Early Medieval Art* (rev. ed.). Bloomington, IN, 1983.

KONSTAN 1977. David Konstan. *Catullus' Indictment of Rome: The Meaning of Catullus 64*. Amsterdam: Hakkert, 1977.

KUMANIECKI 1977. Kazimierz Kumaniecki. *Literatura rzymska epoki cycerońskiej*. Warszawa: PWN, 1977.

LAAKSONEN 1990. Hannu Laaksonen. "L'educazione e la trasformazione della cultura nel regno dei Vandali." In A. Mastino ed. *L'Africa romana*: atti del VII convegno di studio (Sassari, 15-17 dicembre 1990), pp. 357-361. Sassari: Ed. Gallizzi, 1990.

LA POESIA TARDOANTICA... 1984. *La poesia tardoantica: tra retorica, teologia e politica*. Atti del V corso della Scuola Superiore di archeologia e civiltà medievali, Erice, Trapani 6-12 Dicembre 1981. Messina, 1984.

LANA – MALTESE 1998a. Italo Lana and Enrico Valdo Maltese eds. *Storia della civiltà letteraria greca e latina, 2, Dall'ellenismo all'età di Traiano*. Torino: UTET, 1998.

LANA – MALTESE 1998b. Italo Lana and Enrico Valdo Maltese eds. *Storia della civiltà letteraria greca e latina, 3, Dall'età degli Antonini alla fine del mondo antico*. Torino: UTET, 1998.

LANGLANDS 2006. Rebecca Langlands. *Sexual Morality in Ancient Rome*. Cambridge: Cambridge Univ. Press, 2006.

LATTIMORE 1942. R. Lattimore. *Themes in Greek and Roman Epitaphs*. Urbana: Illinois Studies in Language and Literature 28, 1942.

LUISELLI 1992. Bruno Luiselli. *Storia culturale dei rapporti tra mondo romano e mondo germanico*. Roma: Herder, 1992.

LYNE 1971. R.O.A.M. Lyne. "The Dating of the *Ciris*." *CQ* 21 (1971): 233-253.

MALASPINA 1992-93. Elena Malaspina. "Il separatismo etnico a Cartagine e il suo archetipo didoniano." *RomBarb* 12 (1992-93): 1-22.

MANITIUS 1891. Max Manitius. *Geschichte der christlich-lateinischen Poesie bis zur Mitte des 8. Jahrhunderts*. Stuttgart, 1891.

MANITIUS 1911-1931. Max Manitius. *Geschichte der lateinischen Literatur des Mittelalters*. 3 vols. München, 1911-1931.

MANTELLO – RIGG 1996. F.A.C. Mantello and A.G. Rigg eds. *Medieval Latin: An Introduction and Bibliographical Guide*. Washington D.C.: Catholic University of America Press, 1996.

MANTKE 1997. Józef Mantke. "Cykle epigramów u poetów rzymskich." In Jerzy Danielewicz and Krystyna Bartol eds. *Epigram grecki i łaciński w kulturze Europy*, pp. 149-168. Poznań: Wydawnictwo Naukowe UAM, 1997.

MARCHETTA 1994. Antonio Marchetta. "La semantica di *formosus*." In *Id. Due studi sulle "Bucoliche" di Virgilio*. Roma: Gruppo editoriale internazionale, 1994.

MARCONE 2008. Arnaldo Marcone. "A Long Late Antiquity?: Considerations on a Controversial Periodization." *Journal of Late Antiquity* 1 (2008): 4-19.

MARENBON 2001. John Marenbon ed. *Poetry and Philosophy in the Middle Ages: A Festschrift for Peter Dronke*. Leiden-Boston-Köln: Brill, 2001.

MARKUS 1990. Robert Austin Markus. *The End of Ancient Christianity*. Cambridge: Cambridge Univ. Press, 1990.

MARROU 1938. H.-I. Marrou. *Saint Augustin et la fin de la culture antique*. Paris, 1938.

MARROU 1949. H.-I. Marrou. *Saint Augustin et la fin de la culture antique* (*"retractatio"*). Paris: Boccard, 1949.

MATHISEN – SIVAN 1996. Ralph Mathisen and H. Sivan eds. *Shifting Frontiers in Late Antiquity*. Aldershot, 1996.

MATTIOLI 1995. Umberto Mattioli ed. *Senectus: la vecchiaia nel mondo classico*, Vol. 2. Bologna: Pàtron, 1995.

MAZZOLI – GASTI 1999. Giancarlo Mazzoli and Fabio Gasti eds. *Prospettive sul tardoantico:* atti del Convegno di Pavia (27-28 Nov. 1997). Como: New Press, 1999 /Biblioteca di *Athenaeum*/.

McGILL 2005. Scott McGill. *Virgil Recomposed. The Mythological and Secular Centos in Antiquity*. Oxford: Oxford Univ. Press, 2005.

McKITTERICK 1990. R. McKitterick ed. *The Uses of Literacy in Early Mediaeval Europe*. Cambridge: Cambridge Univ. Press, 1990.

MERRILLS 2004. A.H. Merrills ed. *Vandals, Romans and Berbers. New Perspectives on Late Antique North Africa*. Burlington, VT: Ashgate, 2004.

MERRILLS – MILES 2010. Andy Merrills and Richard Miles. *The Vandals*. Chichester-Malden: Wiley-Blackwell, 2010.

MILES 1999. Richard Miles ed. *Constructing Identities in Late Antiquity*. London-New York: Routledge, 1999.

MILES 2005. Richard Miles. "The *Anthologia Latina* and the Creation of a Secular Space in Vandal Africa." *AntTard* 13 (2005): 305-320.

MITCHELL 2007. Stephen Mitchell. *A History of the Later Roman Empire. AD 284-641*. Malden: Blackwell Publishing, 2007.

MORELLI 1910. Camillo Morelli. "L'epitalamio nella tarda poesia latina." *SIFC* 18 (1910): 319-432.

MÜLLER (L.) 1894[2]. L. Müller. *De re metrica poetarum Latinorum praeter Plautum et Terentium libri septem*. Petropoli et Lipsiae, 1894[2].

NAGLE 1980. B.R. Nagle. *The Poetics of Exile. Program and Polemic in the Tristia and Epistulae ex Ponto of Ovid*. Bruxelles: *Collection Latomus* 170, 1980.

NEHRING 2005. Przemysław Nehring. *Dlaczego dziewictwo jest lepsze niż małżeństwo? Spór o ideał w chrześcijaństwie zachodnim końca IV wieku w relacji Ambrożego, Hieronima i Augustyna*. Toruń: Wydawnictwo UMK, 2005.

NEMETZ 1959. Anthony Nemetz. "Literalness and the Sensus Litteralis." *Speculum* 34 (1959): 76-89.

NUGENT 1990. S. Georgia Nugent. "Ausonius' <<Late-antique>> Poetics and <<Post-modern>> Literary Theory." *Ramus* 19 (1990): 25-50.

ONIANS 1980. John Onians. "Abstraction and Imagination in Late Antiquity." *Art History* 3 (1980): 1-23.

PARKIN 2003. Tim G. Parkin. *Old Age in the Roman World. A Cultural and Social History*. Baltimore-London: The Johns Hopkins Univ. Press, 2003.

PASQUALI 1942. Giorgio Pasquali. "Arte allusiva." *L'Italia che scrive* 25 (1942): 185-187.

PAVLOVSKIS 1965. Zoja Pavlovskis. "Statius and the Late Latin Epithalamia." *CPh* 60 (1965): 164-177.

PAVLOVSKIS 1973. Zoja Pavlovskis. *Man in an Artificial Landscape: The Marvels of Civilization in Imperial Roman Literature*. Leiden: *Mnemosyne* Suppl. 25, 1973.

PECERE – STRAMAGLIA 1996. Oronzo Pecere and Antonio Stramaglia eds. *La letteratura del consumo nel mondo greco-latino*: atti del convegno internazionale, Cassino, 14-17 set. 1994. Cassino: Univ. degli Studi di Cassino, 1996.

PIREDDA 1997. Anna Maria Piredda. "La figura femminile nella poesia di Venanzio Fortunato." *Sandalion* 20 (1997): 141-153.

POLARA 1987. Giovanni Polara. *Letteratura latina tardoantica e altomedievale*. Roma: Jouvence, 1987.

POLARA 2001. Giovanni Polara. *Ricerche sulla tarda antichità*, Napoli: Loffredo, 2001.

PUCCI 1998. Joseph Pucci. *The Full-knowing Reader: Allusion and the Power of the Reader in the Western Literary Tradition*. New Haven: Yale Univ. Press, 1998.

RABY 1953². Frederic James Edward Raby. *A History of Christian Latin Poetry*. Oxford², 1953.

RABY 1957². Frederic James Edward Raby. *A History of Secular Latin Poetry in the Middle Ages*, vol. 1. Oxford², 1957.

RAHN 1958. Helmut Rahn. "Ovids elegische Epistel." *A&A* 7 (1958): 105-120.

REIFF 1959. A. Reiff. *Interpretatio, imitatio, aemulatio. Begriff und Vorstellung literarischer Abhängigkeit bei der Römern*. Diss. Köln, 1959.

RENÉ 1994. Martin René. *Approche de la littérature tardive et protomédiévale: de Tertullien à Raban Maure*. Paris: Nathan, 1994.

REYNOLDS 1983. L.D. Reynolds ed. *Texts and Transmission*. Oxford: Clarendon Press, 1983.

REYNOLDS – WILSON 1991. L.D. Reynolds and N.G. Wilson. *Scribes and Scholars: A Guide to the Transmission of Greek and Latin Literature*. Oxford: Clarendon Press, 1991.

RICHÉ 1976. Pierre Riché. *Education and Culture in the Barbarian West*. Columbia: Univ. of South Carolina Press, 1976.

RICHÉ 1995. Pierre Riché. *Edukacja i kultura w Europie Zachodniej (VI-VIII w.)*. Warszawa: Volumen & Pax, 1995.

RICHLIN 1992. Amy Richlin. *The Garden of Priapus. Sexuality and Aggression in Roman Humor*. Oxford: Oxford Univ. Press, 1992.

ROBERTS 1989a. Michael Roberts. *The Jeweled Style. Poetry and Poetics in Late Antiquity*. Ithaca: Cornell Univ. Press, 1989.

ROBERTS 1989b. Michael Roberts. "The Use of Myth in Latin Epithalamia from Statius to Venantius Fortunatus." *TAPhA* 119 (1989): 321-348.

ROBERTS 1992. Michael Roberts. "Barbarians in Gaul: The Response of the Poets." In J. Drinkwater and H. Elton eds. *Fifth-Century Gaul: A Crisis of Identity?*, pp. 97-106. Cambridge: Cambridge Univ. Press, 1992.

ROBERTS 1994. Michael Roberts. "The Description of Landscape in the Poetry of Venantius Fortunatus: The Moselle Poems." *Traditio* 49 (1994): 1-22.

ROBERTS 1996. Michael Roberts. "The Latin Literature of Late Antiquity." In F.A.C. Mantello and A.G. Rigg eds. *Medieval Latin: An Introduction and Bibliographical Guide*, pp. 537-46. Washington D.C.: Catholic University of America Press, 1996.

ROBERTS 2001. Michael Roberts. "Venantius Fortunatus' Elegy on the Death of Galswintha (*Carm*. 6.5)." In Ralph Mathisen and Danuta Shanzer eds. *Society and Culture in Late Antique Gaul. Revisiting the Sources*, pp. 298-312. Aldershot: Ashgate, 2001.

ROBERTS 2002. Michael Roberts. "Creation in Ovid's *Metamorphoses* and the Latin Poets of Late Antiquity." *Arethusa* 35(3) (2002): 403-415.

RONCONI 1984. Alessandro Ronconi. "Fortuna di Ovidio." *A&R* 29 (1984): 1-16.

ROSSI 1971. L.E. Rossi. "I generi letterari e le loro leggi scritte e non scritte nelle letterature classiche." *BICS* 18 (1971): 69-94.

ROTOLO 1957. V. Rotolo. *Il Pantomimo. Studi e testi*. Palermo: Presso l'Accademia, 1957.

RUSSELL 1988. J. Stephen Russell ed. *Allegoresis: The Craft of Allegory in Medieval Literature*. New York-London: Garland, 1988.

SALVADORE 2001. Marcello Salvadore ed. (conclus. di Isola Antonino). *La poesia tardoantica e medievale:* atti del I Convegno Internazionale di Studi: Macerata 4-5 maggio 1998. Alessandria: Ed. dell'Orso, 2001.

SCHERF 1996. Johannes Scherf. *Untersuchungen zur antiken Veröffentlichung der Catullgedichte*. Hildesheim-Zürich-New York: Olms,1996.

SCHRÖDER B.-J. 1999. B.-J. Schröder. *Titel und Text*. Berlin-New York: De Gruyter, 1999.

SENDYKA 2006. Roma Sendyka. "W stronę kulturowej teorii gatunku." In Michał Paweł Markowski and Ryszard Nycz eds. *Kulturowa teoria literatury*. Kraków: Universitas, 2006.

SHANZER 1986. Danuta Shanzer. *A Philosophical and Literary Commentary on Martianus Capella's <<De nuptiis Philologiae et Mercurii>>, Book 1*. Berkeley: Univ. of California Press, 1986.

SILVESTRE – SQUILLANTE 1997. Maria Luisa Silvestre and Marisa Squillante eds. *Mutatio rerum: letteratura, filosofia, scienza tra tardo antico e altomedioevo:* atti del convegno di studi (Napoli, 25-26 nov. 1996). Napoli: La città del Sole, 1997.

SIMONETTI 2006. Manlio Simonetti (a cura di G.M. Vian). *Romani e barbari. Le lettere latine alle origini dell'Europa (secoli V-VIII)*. Roma: Carocci, 2006.

SKINNER 2005. Marilyn B. Skinner. *Sexuality in Greek and Roman Culture*. London: Blackwell, 2005.

SKWARA 1997. Ewa Skwara. "Teatr Marcjalisa." In Jerzy Danielewicz and Krystyna Bartol eds. *Epigram grecki i łaciński w kulturze Europy*, pp. 189-197. Poznań: Wydawnictwo Naukowe UAM, 1997.

SMITH 2005. Julia M.H. Smith. *Europe after Rome: A New Cultural History 500-1000*. Oxford Univ. Press, 2005.

SPITZMULLER 1971. Henry Spitzmuller. *Poésie latine chrétienne du moyen âge. IIIe-XVe siècle*. Paris, 1971.

STABRYŁA 1974. Stanisław Stabryła. *Funkcja noweli w strukturze gatunków literatury rzymskiej*. Wrocław: Ossolineum, 1974 /Polska Akademia Nauk – Oddz. w Krakowie. Prace Komisji Filologii Klasycznej Nr 14/.

STABRYŁA 1982. Stanisław Stabryła. *Problemy genologii antycznej*. Kraków, 1982 /Zeszyty Naukowe Uniwersytetu Jagiellońskiego DCXXXV/.

STARR 2001. Raymond J. Starr. "The Flexibility of Literary Meaning and the Role of the Reader in Roman Antiquity." *Latomus* 60 (2) (2001): 433-445.

STEHLÍKOVÁ 1990. Eva Stehlíková. "The Metamorphoses of the Roman Epithalamium." *Eirene* 27 (1990): 35-45.

STEVENS 1988. Susan T. Stevens. "The Circus Poems in the *Latin Anthology*." In John H. Humphrey ed. *The Circus and a Byzantine Cemetery at Carthage*, vol. 1, pp. 153-178. Ann Arbor, 1988.

STRZELCZYK 2005. Jerzy Strzelczyk. *Wandalowie i ich afrykańskie państwo*. Warszawa: PIW, 2005.

STRZELCZYK 2007. Jerzy Strzelczyk. *Pióro w wątłych dłoniach. O twórczości kobiet w wiekach dawnych*. Warszawa: DiG, 2007.

STYKA 1994. Jerzy Styka. *Studia nad literaturą rzymską epoki republikańskiej. Estetyka satyry republikańskiej, Estetyka neoteryków*. Kraków, 1994 /Uniwersytet Jagielloński. Rozprawy habilitacyjne Nr 274/.

STYKA 1995. Jerzy Styka. *Fas et antiqua castitudo. Die Ästhetik der römischen Dichtung der republikanischen Epoche*. Trier: Wissenschaftlicher Verlag Trier, 1995 /Bochumer Altertumswissenschaftliches Colloquium Bd 19/.

STYKA 2008. Jerzy Styka. *Sydoniusz Apollinaris i kultura literacka w Galii V wieku*. Kraków, 2008 /Polska Akademia Umiejętności. Prace Komisji Filologii Klasycznej Nr 38/.

SULLIVAN 1991. J.P. Sullivan. *Martial the Unexpected Classic. A Literary and Historical Study*. Cambridge: Cambridge Univ. Press, 1991.

SWANN 1994. Bruce W. Swann. *Martial's Catullus: The Reception of an Epigrammatic Rival*. Hildesheim: Zurich-New York-Olms, 1994 (*Spoudasmata* Bd. 54).

SZÖVÉRFFY 1971. Joseph Szövérffy. "A la source de l'humanisme chrétien medieval. *Romanus* et *Barbarus* chez Vénance Fortunat." *Aevum* 45 (1971): 77-86.

TARDI 1927. D. Tardi. *Fortunat: étude sur un dernier représentant de la poésie latine dans la Gaule Mérovingienne*. Paris: Boivin, 1927.

TRAVERSARI 1960. Gustavo Traversari. *Gli spettacoli in acqua nel teatro tardo-antico*. Roma, 1960.

VENANZIO FORTUNATO... 1993. *Venanzio Fortunato tra Italia e Francia*. Atti del convegno internazionale di studi, Valdobbiadene 17 maggio 1990, Treviso 18-19 maggio 1990. Dosson, 1993.

VERSTRAETE 1983. B.C. Verstraete. "Originality and Mannerism in Statius' Use of Myth in the *Silvae*." *AC* 52 (1983): 197-199.

VÖSSING 1993. K. Vössing. "Die *Anthologia Salmasiana*, das vandalische Karthago und die Grenzen der Stilanalyse." In K. Zimmermann. *Der Stilbegriff in den Altertumswissenschaften*, pp. 149-155. Rostock, 1993.

VÖSSING 1997. K. Vössing. *Schule und Bildung im Nordafrika der Römischen Kaiserzeit*. Bruxelles: *Collection Latomus* 238, 1997.

WAQUET 2001. Françoise Waquet. *Latin, or, the Empire of a Sign: from the Sixteenth to the Twentieth Century*. Translated by John Howe. London-New York: Verso, 2001.

WASYL 2002. Anna Maria Wasyl. *Rzymski list poetycki. Próba opisania gatunku*. Kraków: Księgarnia Akademicka, 2002.

WASYL 2004. Anna Maria Wasyl. "*Ovidius Heros*. Epic Elements in Ovid's *Tristia*." *Classica Cracoviensia* 8 (2004): 105-127.

WEDECK 1960. H.E. Wedeck. "The Catalogue in Late and Medieval Latin Poetry." *M&H* 13 (1960): 3-16.

WESOŁOWSKA 1991. Elżbieta Wesołowska. *Postaci w* Medei *i* Fedrze *Seneki w perspektywie akcji oraz interakcji scenicznej*. Poznań: Wydawnictwo Naukowe UAM, 1991.

WESOŁOWSKA 1998. Elżbieta Wesołowska. *Prologi tragedii Seneki w świetle komunikacji literackiej*. Poznań: Wydawnictwo Naukowe UAM, 1998.

WILLS 1996. Jeffrey Wills. *Repetition in Latin Poetry: Figures of Allusion*. Oxford: Oxford Univ. Press, 1996.

WILSON 1948. E. Faye Wilson. "Pastoral and Epithalamium in Latin Literature." *Speculum* 23 (1948): 35-57.

WISEMAN 1985. T.P. Wiseman. *Catullus and His World: A Reappraisal*. Cambridge: Cambridge Univ. Press, 1985.

WITKE 1971. Charles Witke. *Numen litterarum. The Old and the New in Latin Poetry from Constantine to Gregory the Great*. Leiden-Köln: Brill, 1971.

WRIGHT 1995. Neil Wright. *History and Literature in Late Antiquity and the Early Medieval West. Studies in Intertextuality*. Hampshire: Variorum, 1995.

WYPUSTEK 1993. Andrzej Wypustek. "The Problem of Human Sacrifices in Roman North Africa." *Eos* 81 (1993): 263-280.

ZABŁOCKI 1965. Stefan Zabłocki. *Antyczne epicedium i elegia żałobna. Geneza i rozwój*. Wrocław, 1965.

ZABŁOCKI 1968. Stefan Zabłocki. "Rozkład form antycznego epicedium i elegii żałobnej." In *Idem*, *Polsko-łacińskie epicedium renesansowe na tle europejskim*, pp. 7-34. Wrocław, 1968 / Studia staropolskie XXII/.

ZANKER 1987. G. Zanker. *Realism in Alexandrian Poetry: A Literature and Its Audience*. London: Croom Helm, 1987.

Index of Ancient and Medieval Authors and Works

Entries in the Index refer both to the main text and to the notes

TECHNICAL EDITOR
Mirosław Ruszkiewicz

PROOFREADING
Ewa Dedo
Anna Sorówka-Łach

TYPESETTING
Katarzyna Mróz-Jaskuła

Jagiellonian University Press
ul. Michałowskiego 9/2, 31-126 Kraków
phone: 12-631-18-81, 12-631-18-82, fax 12-631-18-83